East An

CW00324336

The principal sights:

Lift flap for map

Peter Sager

East Anglia

ESSEX, SUFFOLK and NORFOLK

Translated by
David Henry Wilson

PALLAS GUIDES

Front cover: Blickling Hall, Norfolk (Tony Stone Images/Tony Page)

Inside front cover: Angel roof, South Creake, Norfolk (Neil Holmes)

Back cover: Greene King sign, Bury St Edmunds, Suffolk (Peter Sager)

Inside back cover: Winter landscape Norfolk (Tony Stone Images/Tom Mackie)

SPECIAL THANKS TO OUR SPONSORS, NORWICH UNION AND GREENE KING

This book is part of the Pallas Guides series, published by Pallas Athene.
If you would like further information about the series, please write to:
Dept. EA., Pallas Athene, 59 Linden Gardens, London W2 4HJ

Series editor: Alexander Fyjis-Walker
Series assistant: Tara Ely

German edition first published by DuMont Buchverlag GmbH & Co., Köln 1990.
English edition published by Pallas Athene, 59 Linden Gardens, London W2 4HJ

© 1990 DuMont Buchverlag GmbH, Köln
All rights for all countries reserved by DuMont Buchverlag GmbH & Co., Limited Partnership, Cologne, Germany. The title of the German original is: *Ostengland*, by Peter Sager

Translation, adaptation, corrections and all additional material © Pallas Athene 1994
All rights reserved

ISBN 1-873429-07-X

Typeset by Nene Phototypesetters, Northampton
Printed by World Print, Hong Kong

Contents

Some Practical Hints

For Elle and Laura

Foreword

Let me begin with a confession: this book on East Anglia covers Essex, Suffolk and Norfolk but, to my regret, bypasses Cambridgeshire. This is partly for reasons of space, but mainly to avoid overlapping with my forthcoming book on Oxford and Cambridge.

In my account of this region, I have tried to follow the principle laid down by that most versatile of writers, Daniel Defoe, in his introduction to the second part of his *Tour through the Whole Island of Great Britain* (1724–6): 'We keep close to the first design of giving, as near as possible, such an account of things, as may entertain the reader, and give him a view of our country, such as may tempt him to travel over it himself ...'

I have a lot of people to thank. First, my many hosts in East Anglia, who so readily gave me access to their homes – in particular, H. and G. Heygate in Suffolk, of whose hospitality I made such frequent use. I received generous support from Catherine Althaus, the British Tourist Authority in London, and Scandinavian Seaways, whose captains Kullack and Schiller made my crossings on 'MS Hamburg' a continual pleasure that no Channel Tunnel could ever replace. Once again I am indebted to the staff of DuMont Verlag, and for this English edition to Barbara and Alexander Fyjis Walker, Tara Ely and George McHardy for their editing and research, and to David Henry Wilson for giving an English shape to my German thoughts.

This book is dedicated to my wife Else Maria and our daughter Laura Mareike, who shared and indeed enhanced my delight in the pleasures of East Anglia.

If there are gaps, then may I echo the appeal of *The Good Food Guide* to its readers: 'More reports, please.'

Hamburg, Winter 1993   Peter Sager

EAST ANGLIA

*Here is everything to delight the eye, and
to make the people proud of their country*
(William Cobbett: *Rural Rides*, 1830)

'Go East Young Man' urged the *Sunday Times Magazine* at the end of 1986, in an attempt to stir its readers out of their weekend lethargy. This was no mysterious orient, however, though it was a gold-rush of sorts. The advice did not concern sightseeing, but economics: 'Business in East Anglia is booming'. A boom in the land of wheat and beet? Had grain prices shot up, or Common Market quotas shot down? Had someone discovered oil beneath the gentle slopes of Suffolk? Well, no, it was nothing quite so spectacular. The boom had as much to do with the quality of life and landscape as with business and the balance-sheet.

This rural revolution, if such it can be called, was a long time coming, but when it did come, its effects were dramatic: small electronics firms sprang up along the M11 from Epping Forest to the Science Park in Cambridge; more new companies lined the extended A45 linking the Midlands – via Ipswich – with Felixstowe, the East Coast's expanding container port; there were new roads, new houses, villages with delicatessens, gourmet restaurants, and Chelsea fashions. The enterprise culture of the eighties had indeed gone east. Since the electrification of the London–Norwich railway line in 1987, a new generation of commuters had found its way to East Anglia: computer specialists, brokers, company lawyers, journalists, insurance agents, and entrepreneurs of all kinds. The country to the northeast of London seemed to be reflecting the explosive dynamism of the City itself.

The proof of the eighties' boom lay in the statistics. The 1989 edition of *Regional Trends* revealed that East Anglia had the fastest growing population in Britain (an increase of half a million since 1961), one of the highest rates of house-building (and price rises), and the highest gross productivity per household outside the counties south-east of London. It had the lowest rate of unemployment and the lowest crime rate in England and Wales, the lowest mortality rate (the highest being in Scotland), the lowest number of heart attacks (Northern Ireland had the highest), the smallest number of AIDS victims, and – in true Puritan tradition – the lowest expenditure per head on alcohol and tobacco. It was a region of records. Not for nothing was *New East Anglia* proclaimed as a region where economic opportunity went hand in hand with unspoilt countryside, outstanding architecture, a pleasant pace of life, and rural tranquillity. With no apparent difficulty, the traditional agricultural image of these counties blended together with the technological advances and requirements of a new society. It was a revolution which not even the recession of the early nineties could reverse.

What exactly *is* East Anglia? Different people have different ideas. Suffolk and Norfolk have always been its core, joined in more recent times by Essex. But some organizations spread their definition much further afield: BBC East Anglia, for instance, also covers Cambridgeshire, Hertfordshire and Northamptonshire; the Eastern Arts Board includes Bedfordshire, Hertfordshire, Cambridgeshire and Lincolnshire; the Countryside Commission embraces Bedfordshire and Lincolnshire, but excludes Essex; the Anglian Water Authority reaches out to Cambridgeshire, Lincolnshire, and parts of Buckinghamshire and Northamptonshire. And yet as long ago as 1086, William the Conqueror's Domesday Book put Essex, Suffolk and Norfolk together in one volume, and the rest of England's counties in another.

Perhaps it is an historical rather than a geographical unit. When the Romans left Britain, the Angles came from what is now Denmark and established the kingdom of East Anglia in the 6th century. Before King Egbert united England into a single kingdom in 829, East Anglia consisted only of the present-day Suffolk and Norfolk – the land of the Southfolk and the Northfolk. The region was bounded by the River Stour to the south and the Cam to the west – in other words, minus Essex, the land of the East Saxons, but including just a tiny piece of present-day Cambridgeshire. Since then the purists have maintained that East Anglia means Suffolk and Norfolk and nothing else. Even the south of Lincolnshire, which is also fen country, doesn't count as East Anglia, and there is an unmistakable language barrier between King's Lynn in Norfolk and neighbouring Sutton Bridge, where the hard Lincolnshire accent is closer to that of the Midlands (whereas Essex folk speak East Anglian).

Geologically speaking, East Anglia is comparatively young. It rests on Jurassic limestone, which bulges out in the northwest of Norfolk in the shape of Hunstanton's cliffs. Layers of clay and sand from the different ice ages have covered this flat limestone basin, which for a long time lay under water. The water remains a characteristic feature of East Anglia even now: the marshlands on the coast, the tidal estuaries of the rivers, whose silty arms reach deep into the land, the peaty lakes of the Broads, and the old swamps of the Fens. But just as typical of this varied landscape are the remains of the great forests of Essex and the conifer plantations over the former heaths of Breckland. It's a landscape whose beauty never asserts itself; its charm is more that of the gentle understatement.

The Scottish Highlands, the Lake District of the Romantics, the dramatic rocky coasts and fortresses of Wales – these would have been far more alluring to the 18th-century seeker of the picturesque than the flat slopes of East Anglia. It took Constable and Gainsborough – Suffolk's heavenly twins – John Sell Cotman and the watercolourists of the Norwich School to open early 19th-century eyes to the beauty of these lands. They painted everyday life in East Anglia, pastoral scenes and poverty, the fields and hovels of the farmworkers, the boats of the fishermen, the clouds, the light. It's as if these pictures had no frame, so boundless are the landscapes with their lofty skies and broad horizons.

11

'Nothing can exceed the beauty of the country,' wrote Constable in July 1831. And even today we can wander happily through this landscape as if it were a Constable painting virtually unchanged through the years.

On the map, East Anglia appears as a kind of hump pushing out in to the North Sea. In three of the four directions, it's a cul-de-sac, and before the Fens were drained and Essex forests cleared, the region was largely cut off from the rest of England. It lay, and still lies, remote from the central north-south routes. Intrepid explorers from my own country – Schinkel, Fontane, Johanna Schopenhauer, the philosopher's mother, Prince Pückler the great gardener – actually by-passed East Anglia: why make diversions when the journey was difficult enough as it was? It's true that Daniel Defoe described the journey from London to Ipswich in 1724 as an 'easy passage', but all the same the coach needed a full day. And in the middle of the 19th century, before the railway went as far as Lowestoft (1859), the coach took over twelve hours to get from London to Yarmouth.

The centuries of isolation have left their mark on the East Anglian character. The seamen display it best: 'they are an independent breed, obstinate as well, cantankerous even, but to those they like they display a warmth and friendliness that is hard to match, and the quality of fearlessness is always there,' writes the novelist Hammond Innes, who has lived in Suffolk for many years. 'The East Anglian is, of course, a solid man,' said J. B. Priestley of the archetypal farmer and sailor. 'Lots of beef and beer, tempered with east wind, have gone to the making of him.' It was from such men that Cromwell recruited his Ironsides – tough, reliable fighters, who could hold their drink as well as their Bible, not all of them as Puritanical as their reputation, but many as fanatical as William Dowsing's iconoclasts. East Anglia provided the backbone of the parliamentary army during the Civil War, whereas today – God Save the Queen in Sandringham – it is a mecca for Royalists.

Some of Britain's greatest admirals have come from this eastern coast – the most notable being Lord Nelson. The shoreline itself was always unprotected, falling victim to devastating floods, invasions by the Vikings, and the influences of Scandinavian,[1] Anglo-Saxon and Norman immigrants bringing new goods and new ideas from the Continent. It's a cosmopolitan coast with a dyed-in-the-wool Conservative hinterland – a mixture of extrovert European-ness and introvert insularity, Tory present and Nonconformist past. The last great rebellion against the Roman occupying forces, the last resistance to the Norman invasion, and the last peasants' uprising – all these took place in East Anglia, and it was from here that their respective leaders came: Queen Boadicea, Hereward the Wake, and William Kett.

Political radicals, religious dissenters, and hosts of freethinkers came from East Anglia, but they did not remain there. The most famous East Anglian Jacobin was Thomas Paine

---

1 From 1016 till 1066, under King Canute and his successors, England was part of a Scandinavian kingdom that stretched from Norway to Scotland. One relic of this in East Anglia is the many place-names with Scandinavian endings, such as -thorpe, -toft, or -by, e.g. north of Great Yarmouth: Filby, Hemsby, Mautby, Ormesby, Thrigby, etc.

from Norfolk, author of *The Rights of Man* and one of the prime inspirations for American independence. A Suffolk man, Bartholomew Gosnold from Otley Hall, organized the voyage of 'Goodspeed' and two other ships in 1607 to establish England's first successful colony, in Virginia, no less than thirteen years before the Pilgrim Fathers set out on the 'Mayflower' (whose captain, incidentally, came from Harwich). Many Puritans emigrated from here: they built a second Norfolk in Virginia, and a second Suffolk in Massachusetts.

More than three hundred years later, their descendants returned to these shores as bomber pilots. During the Second World War, the Allies built some 750 airfields on the flat surfaces of East Anglia. This was Churchill's unsinkable aircraft carrier. In the American military cemetery at Madingley, near Cambridge, there are long rows of stone crosses commemorating the deaths of 3,811 American servicemen. One John T. Appleby from Arkansas was stationed here, and left his mark in the form of the rose garden in the ruined abbey at Bury St Edmunds. Many of the runways have long since turned back into turnip fields, the airbase at Attlebridge is now a turkey farm, and the runway at Hethel is a testing-ground for Lotus racing cars. But the Americans have taken fifty years to leave: until recently East Anglia's rural idyll housed America's biggest military presence in Europe complete with a panoply of nuclear weapons. And with three nuclear power stations, East Anglia adds its own fuel to the flames of ecological controversy.

Over the centuries, the coast has changed continuously through erosion, storm and flood. The last great flood, on the night of 31 January 1953, claimed over 300 lives and made more than 30,000 people homeless. Rivers have changed their course, ports have come and gone, houses and whole villages have disappeared beneath the sea. 'The endless mutation of the British coast wonderfully symbolized the state of the nation,' wrote Paul Theroux in 1983, when at the end of his coastal journey around *The Kingdom by the Sea*, he was standing on the beach at Southend: 'The British seemed to me to be people forever standing on a crumbling coast and scanning the horizon.' Prospects are not encouraging: according to an *Anglian Coastal Study*, 1989, commissioned by the government, the sea level around the British Isles is expected to rise by about five feet during the next century as a result of global warming. Especially vulnerable: the coast of East Anglia.

The Countryside: Myth beneath the Plough

East Anglia has no large cities, no heavy industry, and no natural resources other than its bulbs and tubers. England's Industrial Revolution passed East Anglia by. It remained what it had always been: landscape. It's a landscape of farms and manor houses, villages and small market towns, with opulent rose gardens, and fields full of beet and cattle. There are no relics of an antiquated steel industry or of uneconomic coalpits, or run-down estates or hangdog dole queues, decaying inner cities, race riots, football hooligans, or incessant rain. Lucky East Anglia.

It does, of course, have an industrial history, but the relics are to be viewed with unadulterated pleasure: timber-framed houses, resplendent guildhalls, Gothic churches – all witnesses to a time of relatively dense population and flourishing industry. In the Middle Ages Suffolk and Norfolk were centres of sheep-breeding, with an attendant cottage industry of weavers (wool and worsted). Together with Somerset, and long before the rest of England, East Anglia spawned a prosperous rural middle class of cloth-makers and merchants. These clothiers, contemporaries of Chaucer, employed different workers in different places, organizing all the many processes – spinning, weaving, fulling, dyeing, bleaching – investing their capital, producing, and exporting. According to G. M. Trevelyan, these were undoubtedly England's first capitalist entrepreneurs.

It all began very modestly, with a few sheep-rearing monks. The high quality of this English wool soon led to demand from Europe. It was exported to and processed in Flanders, Burgundy, and Italy. In order to promote this native industry, King Edward III forbade the import of foreign textiles and clothing. Shortly afterwards, in 1334, he allowed Flemish weavers into the country, and the majority of them settled in East Anglia.[1] Their know-how was a prime factor in making English cloth a best-seller on the European market. Not for nothing is the official seat of the Lord Chancellor in the House of Lords called the Woolsack, for it is filled with wool from all corners of the British Empire, symbolizing the foundations of Britain's former wealth. East Anglia's grandiose wool churches stand on proverbial woolsacks too. The 17th century saw the end of the great age of East Anglian cloth-making, as echoed by the names of such pubs as 'The Golden Fleece' and 'The Woolsack' in Norwich. Mechanical looms destroyed the cottage industry, and the workers had no choice but to seek employment in the new factories or to emigrate. (Abraham Lincoln, for instance, was descended from a weaver who emigrated to America from Hingham in Norfolk.) The Industrial Revolution transferred the cloth industry from the villages to the towns, from south to north, and from wool to cotton.

East Anglia was only able to maintain a degree of prosperity through its agriculture. The east of England was London's granary, as well as supplying a large proportion of other foods for the ever expanding and insatiable metropolis. Today East Anglia and Lincoln-shire supply 40 per cent of Britain's wheat, 73 per cent of its sugar beet, and over 60 per cent of all its vegetables. This productivity is the result of industrialized agriculture on a grand scale. It began with the agricultural revolution of the 18th century, and East Anglia was in the very forefront.

Thomas Coke and Lord Townshend, known as 'Turnip Townshend', were gentlemen farmers from Norfolk, and pioneers of the agricultural revolution. On their estates at Holkham and Raynham Hall, they brought in new methods to improve cultivation, cattle-breeding, and the fertility of the soil. One of the most vital preconditions for this progress – and at the same time the cause of most bitterness – was enclosure. This reparcelling of agricultural land did not take place overnight. It was a long-drawn-out

---

1 The first Flemish weavers had already come to England in the early 12th century, under Henry I, and they settled in Worstead, a village near Norwich which gave its name to the cloth now known as worsted.

Henry Moore: Suffolk woolly, 1972

process that began in the late 16th century and ended in the early 19th. The concept of enclosure meant several things: fencing in common land, reclaiming waste land, exchanging and combining separate fields. Fallow land had to be developed, and good land had to be more profitably exploited, to provide more food for a growing population. (In 1500 England and Wales had fewer than 3 million inhabitants; in 1700 there were 5.5 million; in 1801, the year of the first official census, 9 million, and ten years later 10 million.) Enclosures gave an immense boost not only to the large landowners, but also to the economy as a whole; but for the many thousands of small farmers and labourers, they were a disaster. In Cobbett's words: 'when the farmers became *gentlemen*, their labourers became *slaves*'.

What the lords of the manor and the large farmers fenced in for their own exclusive use was generally land that actually belonged to them, but until then it had always been used by villagers and agricultural workers as common land, for grazing their cattle, collecting wood and cutting peat. These were traditional village rights and customs that had evolved over the centuries. Enclosures brought a radical end to this system of open, communal farming. The poorer villagers literally had the ground taken away from under their feet. At the climax of the process, in 1816, a farmworker from Norfolk wrote an anonymous letter to the 'Gentlemen of Ashill': 'You do as you like, you rob the poor of their Commons right, plough up the Grass that God sent to grow, that a poor man may feed a Cow, Pig, Horse, nor Ass; lay muck and stones on the road to prevent the grass growing ... There is 5 or 6 of you have gotten all the whole of the Land in this parish in your own hands and you would wish to be rich and starve all the other part of the poor ... We have counted up that we have gotten about 60 of us to 1 of you: therefore should you govern so many to 1?'

Even today, most of the English countryside still belongs to a relatively small number of people – fewer than 50,000 landowners – and in many places they still seem able to lay down the law.

Land Reform, economically motivated and imposed by a plethora of enclosure laws, especially during the reign of George III, did not entail dispossession *de jure* but *de facto*; it meant that tenants and leaseholders were driven off the common land. In his famous study, *The Making of the English Working Class*, E. P. Thompson writes: 'enclosure (when all the sophistications are allowed for) was a plain enough case of class robbery, played according to fair rules of property and law laid down by a parliament of property-owners and lawyers.'

Between 1792 and 1815 over one million acres of English land were enclosed, and the landowners grew richer while the farm labourers became poorer. And thus the enclosures created a huge source of cheap labour to man the factories of the Industrial Revolution. John Clare, son of a Cambridgeshire day labourer, wrote a number of poems describing the consequences of the enclosure laws; the Chartist leader Feargus O'Connor satirized their executors: those who put them into effect, Lawyer Grind and Lawyer Squeeze, and their masters, Mr Twist and Mr Grab and Mr Screw. Issuing pamphlets, raising fires, and tearing down fences, those affected made their violent and totally futile protests against the enclosures and in favour of the commons. In Suffolk an anonymous rhyme went the rounds: 'They hang the man and flog the woman / Who steals the goose from off the Common; / But let the greater criminal loose / Who steals the Common from the goose.'

In England and Wales today there remain barely 1.4 million acres of common land. One third of the 8,600 commons are designated Sites of Special Scientific Interest, and represent areas of countryside largely unchanged since the Middle Ages. But today scarcely anyone claims common rights in order to let the sheep graze or, like the women of Greenham, to protest against American rocket bases, and so these ecological oases threaten to run wild. Indeed eight per cent of all commons are inaccessible to the public, and the Open Spaces Society (England's oldest conservation group, begun in 1876 as the Commons Preservation Society, which at the end of the 19th century prevented the fencing-in of Epping Forest), together with various hiking associations, has been campaigning for decades for the restoration of these ancient rights.

*Protest against destruction of hedges in Necton, Norfolk: a row of crosses with plant-names marks
a field whose hedges have been destroyed by a farmer*

With the enclosures began the massive expansion and rationalization of agriculture that
have shaped the English countryside right up to the present. After the Second World
War diesel tractors, computerised combine harvesters, and ever more sophisticated
machinery transformed the face of East Anglia more rapidly than at any other time,
the fields becoming bigger and bigger, and the number of farmworkers constantly
dwindling. In 1811 one third of all employed people were at work on the land; in 1851
it was one fifth; today the figure is one fortieth – less than anywhere else in Europe.
And yet with an average area of some 25 acres, British farms are bigger than those
in the rest of western Europe. The flat fields of East Anglia stretch for miles and miles,
now often treeless and hedgeless. This is prairie farming, to use the emotive term of the
conservationists.

In spring 1985, a striking photograph appeared in *The Times*: like a Flanders trench,
a long row of white wooden crosses marked out the perimeter of a field in Norfolk. Here
a farmer had cut down a 300-year-old hedge in order to increase his acreage. Indignant
neighbours wrote on each of these crosses the name of a plant that had grown there. This

Thomas Gainsborough: The Suffolk Plough, c.1753–4

was, however, by no means an isolated case. Twenty-two per cent of all hedges in England and Wales have been cut down since 1947, some 186,000 miles – enough to encompass the Earth seven times. For many years farmers were even paid to destroy the hedges and drain ditches and ponds: state-subsidized vandalism for the sake of increased productivity all linked to the monstrous appetite of the Common Agricultural Policy. Not until late in the Thatcher era was the government suddenly stricken by a green conscience. And yet even then, despite official encouragement to grow new hedges as protection against wind and erosion, and as a valuable habitat for birds, butterflies and small animals, the eighties saw the destruction of more hedgerows than any previous decade – over 6,400 miles a year.[1]

It was not only the hedges that disappeared. Since 1945 England has lost 90 per cent of its ponds, 95 per cent of its hayfields – as seen in the paintings of Constable – half of its old

1   Some of England's hedges are the result of enclosures that took place 200 years ago. Others are many centuries old, and still show the boundaries between communities as they were in the Middle Ages or even earlier.

deciduous forests, and almost all its heathland. Riverside meadows and marshes and more and more grazing land have come under the plough. Nationwide, some 150,000 acres of wetlands are drained every year for questionable economic benefits. According to Oliver Rackham's *History of the Countryside*, the forty years following the Second World War saw more of the English countryside destroyed than the previous thousand years. And what destruction and drainage could not achieve on this triumphal march of agriculture was left to the underground movements of pesticides and nitrates.

East Anglia is an extreme and melancholy example of all these trends: a battleground for conservationists. The good clean countryside? While travelling around Suffolk, I saw scarcely a single field of cornflowers or poppies. In Essex, days passed before I saw a single butterfly. Half of the 55 different species of British butterfly are in decline, ten of them threatened with extinction. In this century 19 species of wild flowers have died out, 50 others are endangered. Only 200 curlews are now nesting in Britain, about 25 pairs of bitterns, and just one pair of red-backed shrike. Thanks to the indiscriminate use of pesticides and chemical fertilizers, England's land use is more productive than that of any other European country. But equally the groundwater (and hence the drinking water) contains considerably more nitrates than that of most other countries in Europe. In order to conform with EC water regulations, more than half the most productive, most nitrate-ridden fields in East Anglia would have to be taken out of production and restored to pastureland or some other use.

Utopian? On the contrary, it's a realistic possibility – and not only for reasons of conservation. For years now England's highly mechanized, monocultural approach to agriculture has resulted in overproduction of food – too much grain and milk powder, unusable surpluses in the face of drastic EC quotas. Since 1987 a new, more ecologically orientated agricultural policy has meant that farmers in certain areas are being paid to use traditional methods in order to preserve landscape, plants and animals. There are subsidies for those who plant trees instead of cereals or use their farms for recreational facilities. Forestry is in fact England's most heavily subsidized industry, though 90 per cent of Britain's wood still has to be imported. The EEC is also having a powerful reverse effect on British agriculture. Experts believe that, as a consequence of overproduction, up to 20 per cent of Britain's farmland (between 2½ and 5 million acres) will cease to be cultivated before the turn of the century. The large estates will survive, but the thousands of smallholders will go bankrupt. It is the biggest crisis the industry has known since the great depression of the 1870's, when cheap food from abroad and low wages depopulated whole villages and regions, and some 700,000 farmworkers and their families emigrated.

Today the total number of farmworkers in Britain is less than 117,000. Every day about 25 of these lose their jobs. A quarter of the rural population live below the poverty line – victims of low wages, poor job prospects, bad transport and living conditions. Even prosperous East Anglia was not exempt from this alarming trend, but rural poverty is not something one sees immediately. In contrast to the squalor of the cities, it hides itself in greenery, in remote cottages, behind the well-loved image of the good clean countryside.

The countryside is the nation's sacred cow. If a newspaper wants to increase its circulation, nothing, bar Royal and ministerial scandals, is more effective than a campaign to Save Our Countryside. And the worse England's reputation becomes as the industrial dirty man of Europe, the more proudly the nation clings to its illusion of greenness and pleasantness. At the end of the eighties there was a veritable boom in new country magazines. A good hotel could afford to be without a TV set, but not without its *Country Life*. Countless conservation groups gallop to the defence of wetlands, threatened butterflies, and public footpaths. And meanwhile the pressure on the countryside increases, especially where it is still more or less unspoilt, offering all the more scope to investors. One such region is East Anglia.

The home counties are already full to overflowing, and so East Anglia has become a second-home belt, a dormitory for the metropolis. Because of high rents in the City, many offices have moved to Colchester, Ipswich or Norwich. And of course, all the townsfolk yearn for a cottage in the country. The late eighties saw 40,000 new houses go up in Suffolk alone, before the slump of the early nineties put a temporary stop to the process. Five million acres of Britain's land are officially designated as green belt, but in Essex these came under increasing threat, as the speculators rubbed their hands at the thought of linking up the great conurbations. New roads, new commercial and leisure centres, large-scale tourist projects all ripped their way through to the heart of the country. According to Paul Edwards, director of the Suffolk Preservation Society, this is the main threat; preservation of the countryside takes precedence even over preservation of historic buildings. If agriculture continues to decline, what will happen to the fallow land, which by the turn of the century will cover an area as great as Devon and Cornwall put together? The crisis of English agriculture is also the crisis of the countryside. 'If farming goes, that will change dramatically,' fears the writer Michael Hamburger. 'The land will be sold, it will be like any other part of England.' But East Anglia's countryside remains, and one hopes will always remain, quite different from anywhere else.

Villages: Akenfield Revisited

Kersey and Cavendish, Fressingfield and Finchingfield, Little Easton, Great Snoring, Debenham, Lavenham, Long Melford ... what could be more enjoyable than travelling from one village to the next, from the unprepossessing, the forgotten, the remote, to the spick and span best-kept prize-winners of East Anglia? In Kersey, they have ducks swimming in the middle of the road (which fords the village stream); in Long Melford the main street seems like one long antique shop; in Lavenham I saw the finest medieval timbering; in the Old Rectory in Great Snoring I ate like a king; and on the village green in Cavendish I just stretched myself out in the grass to dream.

The countryside is not just nature, it's an inhabited, cultivated, historically evolved landscape. Villages are integral to the countryside, just as the pub is integral to the village and pickled onions are integral to a Ploughman's Lunch. There are about 130,000 villages in England, many if not most of them dating from the feudal estates that sprang up in Anglo-Saxon England. They already existed, then, before the Norman Conquest of 1066. Of course others have long since disappeared, their population decimated by the plague and by migration to the cities during the Middle Ages, with nothing remaining but a solitary church in the fields, like the one at Longham in Norfolk. East Anglia has one of the richest and most varied village landscapes in England.

'Even more than Big Ben or Westminster Abbey the English village is the visual symbol of our way of life.' This is how John Hadfield begins his anthology of English villages. The Suffolk writer Ronald Blythe even talks of a national village cult – 'the almost religious intensity of the regard for rural life in this country.' In 1969 his *Akenfield* was published – the classic portrait of an English village. 'Akenfield, on the face of it, is the kind of place in which an Englishman has always felt it his right and duty to live. It is patently the real country, untouched and genuine. A holy place, when you have spent half your life abroad in the services. Its very sounds are formal, hieratic; larks, clocks, bees, tractor hummings. Rarely the sound of the human voice.'

Akenfield is everywhere, a part of England's spiritual landscape, a myth based on a very real model: Grundisburgh, a village in east Suffolk which at the time had just 300 inhabitants, but has now swollen to 3,500. By faithfully reporting their words, Blythe recorded just how they live and how they think: farm labourers, fruit-pickers, village teacher, roofer, smith, saddler, shepherd, pig farmer, vet, vicar and gravedigger. *Akenfield* is the biography of an English village in the sixties … and now, twenty-five years later, it has gone.

What do you expect to find in a typical English village? A parish church, a rectory with a cedar tree in front of it; village green, village school, a pond or a clear running stream; one or two shops, at least one pub, and local beer served in the pub; not too far away, perhaps the Tudor manor house of the great landowner. A really good village also has a cricket team, a team of bell-ringers, and an amateur dramatic society. But what do you actually find today? The church is redundant, the Old Rectory is a restaurant, the village school is a crafts studio, the pond has been filled in, there are no cricketers on the green, and the little village shop is now a supermarket. The village is still there, as neat and tidy as ever, but somehow things are not the same any more.

Many villages in East Anglia are now the homes of commuters and pensioners, eager to live out their dream of country life, even if it's only at weekends. Today there are two types of people in the village: the prosperous folk from the town, and the poor locals. 'Two-nation countryside' is the term used by Howard Newby, a sociologist at the University of Essex. Most country dwellers are no longer employed in agriculture, and they are all the more determined to preserve the ideal of the village and to stave off all change. The country idyll, however, has thus turned into a kind of pastiche suburbia, for the village is now a dormitory or an old people's home. For young people it has become more and more difficult to find work and a home of their own in their parents' village. Before the recession of the early nineties, house prices soared, poorer people moved to estates outside the villages, and young people went away into the towns. An organization called the National Agricultural Centre Rural Trust (NACRT) under the patronage of Princess Anne set out to create affordable homes for people in the country, but the village school closed, the village shop had no customers, the vicar had no congregation, and the football club had no players. In many villages today, the only locals left are the old people. Village halls, symbols of communal life, are silent and slowly falling apart. During the eighties, it was the decay of the inner cities that hit the headlines: 'It will be inner village decay that dominates the nineties,' warned the *Sunday Times*.

The portents are not good, but all is not yet lost. The church is still standing, and the village green glories in an impressive sign. East Anglia is particularly rich in fine village signs – some of wrought iron, most of carved wood with brightly coloured scenes and figures. Quite a lot of them have been made by one man – Harry Carter, a teacher from Swaffham. He became famous in the fifties, when, to commemorate the Queen's coronation, he presented some of the villages on the royal estate at Sandringham with specially made signs. Then other villages decided they wanted to commemorate different events or characters, and so Harry carved the signs they wanted: the Cistercians in Sibton (colour plate 37), the Pedlar in Swaffham, the beam above the High Street in East Dereham depicting the legend of St Withburga. My personal favourite is in the lavender village of Heacham: the portrait of a woman in a feather hat and lace collar. Her name is Pocahontas, and she was the daughter of a 17th-century Native American chief. Pocahontas rescued a sea captain from King's Lynn who was about to be murdered; she sailed to England with him, and married a merchant's son named John Rolfe in Heacham. Three years later, at the age of twenty-two, the beautiful Pocahontas died on her way home to Virginia.

Pocahontas,
on Heacham village sign

Churches: Concerts with the Angels

Some years ago I stayed overnight at Maison Talbooth in Dedham, a small but comfortable country hotel, and in my room I found a letter of welcome, not from the owner but from the vicar of Stratford St Mary: 'You will see before you a typically English scene. It is a lovely view over the Stour Valley.' On the other side of the river, continued the letter, one could see a church which John Constable had often painted – the Perpendicular church of St Mary. 'You would be very welcome to join us at any time. Sincerely yours, M. H. Sharp.' The mixture of landscape, art and church was as English as the view itself.

England's village churches are as much a part of the landscape as English oak. Quite apart from their religious role, they are fixed points both geographically and socially, as is clear from the sporting term 'steeplechase'. Originally this denoted a horse race from one steeple to the next – an obstacle race over hedges, streams and ditches, such as could only take place in a land of hills and fields and, of course, churches. Thus did England's village churches provide the framework for this most earthly of pleasures. They stand as symbols of piety and patriotism, everyday rural life as well as that of the nation.

Go through the lych gate – a roofed gate where in former times the coffin would be set down while the mourners waited for the priest. Walk past the gravestones to the church itself, following the same path that has been trodden for hundreds of years by generation after generation, heading towards prayers and hymns, sermons, weddings, baptisms, funerals. You cross the worn-down threshold into the cool, darkened space. There is an Anglican smell of wax polish, damp walls and fresh daffodils. You are probably the only visitor. You can hear the ticking of the church clock, the creaking of the rafters, and the buzzing of flies skating on Victorian windows. 'Lovely church, isn't it?' says one of those indefatigable middle-aged ladies always to be found polishing the brass, arranging the flowers, or cleaning the pews, ever ready to look the visitor in the eye and give a homely touch of chit-chat to the House of the Lord. Worth their weight in gold, these ladies, for without them the vicar might just as well close his doors. Indeed, more and more of these churches are being made redundant. 'Recently,' complained the vicar of Stebbing, 'someone stole a Botticelli copy from us, just because of the frame. Gold frames are in, you see.' Then without more ado he let me have the key to St Mary's. In Loddon, a village between Norwich and Beccles, the vicar sent me to the post office to collect the gigantic church key; to get it, I had to leave my passport. 'Sorry,' they said, 'but we've had so much vandalism in our church, after-lunch vandalism, all sorts of things.' Once, the vicar told me, a gang of youths had used prayerbooks to set fire to a coffin that was lying in Holy Trinity. He had just got there in time to put it out.

'Halloa! Here's a church! ... Let's go in!' cries Mr Wemmick in Dickens' *Great Expectations*. The appeal is irresistible. And when you leave one church, there's always another one (or more) on the horizon to keep you steeplechasing. Church-crawling is an obsession which has claimed some famous victims: John Piper and his friend Benjamin Britten, who composed three church parables specially for the wonderful village churches around Aldeburgh; P. D. James 'I saw the prayerbooks, smelt the incense, and had a vision of two dead bodies. My God, I thought, I'm going to write about this church.' And that is what she did. Her thriller *A Taste For Death* begins with Miss Emily Wharton finding two dead bodies in the vestry of her parish church – a well-known politician and a tramp, both with their throats cut. Church-crawlers beware.

'What would you be, you wide East Anglian sky / Without a church tower to recognize you by?' wrote Sir John Betjeman. Between them Suffolk and Norfolk have well over a thousand churches dating from before the Reformation, not to mention those that came later. There are the great wool churches built by the clothiers of Suffolk, the flint churches of the marshes and coastal villages of Norfolk, and the timber-framed, shingled towers of Essex; outside East Anglia such a wealth of Norman and Gothic churches is only to be found in Somerset. And if you're interested in the few remaining vestiges of Anglo-Saxon architecture, East Anglia contains more examples than anywhere else in England.

In Suffolk I met a retired butcher who was an expert on round tower churches. In Sculthorpe, deep in the heart of Norfolk, the gravedigger opened the church for me ('That's funny, two Germans in one week') – a very ordinary-looking one that turned out to have a magnificent Norman font and stained glass windows by Burne-Jones and Morris. Equally surprising was the 'doom' in Wenhaston, Suffolk: a Last Judgement, painted on wood in about 1480, originally situated on the chancel arch, where the faithful would see before their very eyes what would happen to them when Christ would be their judge, seated on the rainbow, and St Michael would weigh their souls, and Hell in the shape of a giant fish's mouth would remorselessly swallow up the damned. More shockingly colourful than artistically subtle, it is a striking example of religious poster art in the Middle Ages.

Far beyond the standard you'd expect in the country are the angel roofs of East Anglia: trusses with hammer beams and ribs decorated with carved wooden angels whose backs and outstretched wings seem effortlessly to bear the full weight of the roof. These angel roofs are images of the vault of heaven, and the crowning glory of England's medieval timber technicians. Their finest works are to be found in Suffolk and Norfolk (not Essex), in the churches at Blythburgh, Bury St Edmunds, Mildenhall, Earl Stonham and Needham Market, Cawston and Knapton, Swaffham and Wymondham. The most triumphal of all these roofs is that of March, in Cambridgeshire. But even when there are no angels hovering over the nave, East Anglian churches can still offer the most dazzling hammer beam roofs. Ronald Blythe says that wood is the natural material for the English, in order to combine practicality with worthiness of form. Thus the misericords[1] offer sympathetic support to tired monks, while the carved scenes and figures are perfect examples of how comfort and devotion, the holy and the down-to-earth, may be brought together as the art of the practical.

All churches have a font, but very few in England have such a spectacular wooden

---

1 In the choir stalls of Norwich Cathedral, for example, there are more than 60 misericords, dating from between 1420 and 1515.

Waxwork of Sarah Hare, 1744, in Stow Bardolph church, Norfolk

The Grim Reaper, 1640, wooden figure in Little Barningham church, Norfolk

canopy as the village church in Lower Ufford, Suffolk. It is richly ornate, over sixteen feet high, a miniature Gothic spire from the middle of the 15th century. During the late Middle Ages, East Anglia developed its own type of font: at the foot of the column are four seated lions, between which are four wild men with clubs; around the rim of the basin are the four Evangelists together with more lions or angels. From this pattern evolved the so-called Seven Sacraments font: an octagonal basin with reliefs of the seven sacraments, the eighth side generally depicting the Crucifixion or another scene from the life of Jesus. This late Gothic type of font is almost exclusive to East Anglia, and of the forty remaining examples, only three are to be found outside Norfolk and Suffolk. There are particularly fine specimens in the churches of Cratfield, Sloley and Binham Priory. Sometimes these fonts stand on a stepped base, often in the form of a Maltese cross – for instance, in East Dereham, Little Walsingham and Walsoken.

Two of my favourite churches stand remote in the fields of Norfolk: Cawston and Salle. The church of St Agnes in Cawston has a magnificent hammerbeam roof with tracery spandrels, angels and saints, a late Gothic rood screen with twenty figured panels, and the

Medieval figures on bench-ends in Southwold ▷
and Blythburgh

The Pedlar, figure on a bench-end in Swaffham

Plough Gallery. In cosy proximity to each other beneath this gallery are the old inn sign from the Plough Inn (which, alas, closed in 1950), a funeral cart, and an iron plough which carries memories of an old country custom. On Plough Monday, the Monday after Epiphany, a plough would be brought to the church and blessed, while prayers would be offered up for a good harvest.

Not far away, in the shadows of some tall trees, is Salle, and just outside the village stands its Perpendicular church. This too has a symbolic plough, a seven-sacraments font with a Gothic canopy, misericords in the choir stalls, and monumental brasses. This wool church was built in the early 15th century, and even at that time was far too big for a community of barely 200 souls. Now there are just 50. In the summer of 1989, this magnificent, lofty edifice saw the inauguration of a series of concerts under the patronage of Prince Charles: 'Music in Country Churches'. Another music festival was started, some years ago, by the Reverend Mr Copley, vicar of Wangford in Suffolk, to take place in his own church and others in the area. He was inspired by the success of the popular church concerts that form part of the Aldeburgh Festival. It all marks a new musical culture for the east of England, with local ensembles as well as guest appearances by well-known orchestras and soloists. They have brought new sounds and new life to

these beautiful old churches, which neither God nor His organists have for so long been able to fill.

Less than two per cent of all English people now go to church. The decline of the traditional village community and of the parish congregation are two verses in the same requiem. Just as the village teacher disappeared with the closure of the village school, so too did the country parson leave his oversized Rectory, take on a small bungalow on the outskirts of the village, and then finally depart from the scene, having taken early retirement while the Church of England combined his little flock with those of various other out-of-the-way places. Here ended the lesson.

In the last 30 years the Church of England has closed 2,000 of its 17,000 churches, a quarter of them being demolished, legally even though some of them were listed buildings. (Not until 1986 did Church and State reach a binding agreement concerning consultation before demolition.) Holy stones have become millstones around the neck of dwindling communities. Nowadays the appeal for restoration and the temperature gauge of donations are as much a part of the church as its altar and its pulpit. The roof is caving in, the steeple is falling to pieces, the foundations are crumbling ... please save our church. In 1986 a trainer from Newmarket put a racehorse called St Wendred (plus all its prize money) at the disposal of the vicar of Exning for one year, as his contribution to the restoration fund of the local church. It may well have been the very first English church to have its own racehorse.

Some 250 churches are looked after by the Redundant Churches Fund, including such gems as All Saints in Icklingham and the remote coastal church of Covehithe. Some of these buildings are still occasionally used for worship, and others are the settings for concerts or exhibitions. They have a strangely moving atmosphere of their own, half familiar yet half alien, a mixture of sad desolation and comforting security. They are a natural and seemingly permanent part of the landscape, but they are lighthouses without a crew, still sending out their message of faith, but fading.

Even more elegiac than country churches, though more in use, are village graveyards. They may be scenes of melancholy, but they are also gardens of rest, local history written in stone, full of faded names and country news. On my travels, I always sought out the village cemeteries when I wanted to gauge the individuality of a place or simply to rest. 'There is nothing half so green that I know anywhere, as the grass of that churchyard; nothing half so shady as its trees; nothing half so quiet as its tombstones,' wrote Dickens, describing the cemetery at Blunderstone, birthplace of David Copperfield. The model for this fictional village was Blundeston, near Lowestoft in Suffolk.

An English graveyard, according to the countryside historian Oliver Rackham, contains on an average at least 10,000 bodies. The phosphate is particularly good for stinging nettles and chervil. Old village graveyards are full of cowslips and maidenhair, orchids and lady's bedstraw, up to a hundred different species of wild flower, herb and fern, and on the gravestones and the walls you'll find as many of moss and lichen. Some of them have long since disappeared from all other habitats. These overgrown havens attract birds, beetles, insects and butterflies. The place of the dead is alive and flourishing – a natural oasis in the midst of a threatened countryside. But some villages are ambitious. They covet the title of 'Best Kept Churchyard', and so what do they do? They cut down the plants, dispose of the old stones, line things up, straighten things out, plant rectangular flowerbeds, spray weedkiller everywhere, and cut the lawn till it's bowling-green flat. The Churchyards Handbook, issued by the Church of England, has condemned such activity as 'the cult of the lawn'. A graveyard, they say, is not a suburban garden. I found the perfect ecological cemetery in St James South Elmham, Suffolk, one of nine parishes sharing the name of South Elmham. The vicar of St James devotes as much care to describing in his leaflet the flora and fauna of his graveyard as he does to describing the details of his church: 'In an area of highly intensive agriculture, the churchyard is an island of safety for wild life.' Not everyone appreciates his viewpoint. The visitors' book contains the laconic comment: 'Churchyard needs grass cutting.'

In these old village graveyards one can see pretty clearly the pecking order of the community. The finest, most expensive tombstones are mainly to be found in the southern half, while the further north you go, the more melancholic it all becomes. These are the graves of the poor, of thieves, beggars, bastards and sometimes their mothers too. Those in the northern half were buried 'on the dog', as the East Anglians say. James Lees-Milne,

Sir J. Harsick and his wife, 1384,
brass in Southacre church,
Norfolk

29

a National Trust expert on country houses, once told me that if I wanted to know the history of the landowners, I should visit the parish church before I went to the manor house, so closely do village churches and churchyards reflect the rural hierarchy. Once you've caught the church-crawling bug, you will soon succumb to that of grave-hunting as well. England's churches and graveyards are great public collections of monumental art: some of it grandiose, some witty, some made by great sculptors, others by humble craftsmen serving the Great Leveller. In Palgrave, Suffolk, for instance, I saw the grave of a coachman called John Catchpole, who died in 1787. His tombstone was a sculpted six-in-hand coach. The church in Acton, near Sudbury, has one of the oldest and finest brasses in the whole of England (c.1320): Sir Robert de Bures, a knight armed cap-a-pie in chain mail. East Anglia is particularly rich in brasses, reflecting the wealth of wool and the ambitions of its soldiers and merchants alike. Their successors preferred pompous marble tombs, some of which are very fine, but we must not overlook the crumbling sandstone epitaphs of the ordinary folk, the sad and comic, trivial and poetic collection of last words. In Walcott, Norfolk, is the grave of the evidently none too popular William Wiseman, who died in 1847. He went to eternity, celebrated by the following couplets: 'Here lies the body of W.W. / He comes no more to trouble U, trouble U / Where he's gone and how he fares / Nobody knows and nobody cares.' In Homersfield, Suffolk, is a brief and stoic farewell to a child that died two weeks after birth: 'Came in / Looked about / Didn't like it / Went out.' In Walsoken, in northwest Norfolk, there is a late Norman church with many 17th and 18th century gravestones, and there I found the most succinct epitaph of them all, to one Charles Knight: 'Good Knight'.

Murder in the Belfry: The Art of Change-Ringing

In the old days, English churches announced a death with nine tolls of the bell, which were known as Nine Tailors, and the death knell was called Tailor Paul. And so *The Nine Tailors* has nothing to do with clothes at all, but concerns a sophisticated bellringing murder discovered by Lord Peter Wimsey. One New Year's Eve, Dorothy L. Sayers sends her aristocratic detective through driving snow to a godforsaken village in the Fens: 'Out over the flat, white wastes of fen, over the spear-straight, steel-dark dykes and the wind-bent, groaning poplar trees, bursting from the snow-choked louvres of the belfry, whirled away southward and westward in gusty blasts of clamour to the sleeping counties went the music of the bells of Fenchurch St Paul.' In this fictitious Fenland village[1] a man meets his death through the nine bells; imprisoned in the belfry, he is exposed to the chimes for nine long hours, while the bellringing team from the village – including the aptly named

---

1 The model for this village was Upwell. In the church at Terrington St Clement, another Fenland village, the Dorothy L. Sayers Society celebrated Lord Peter Wimsey's 100th birthday on 13 January 1990, by having *Kent Treble Bob Major* rung in a shortened version of 5,376 changes.

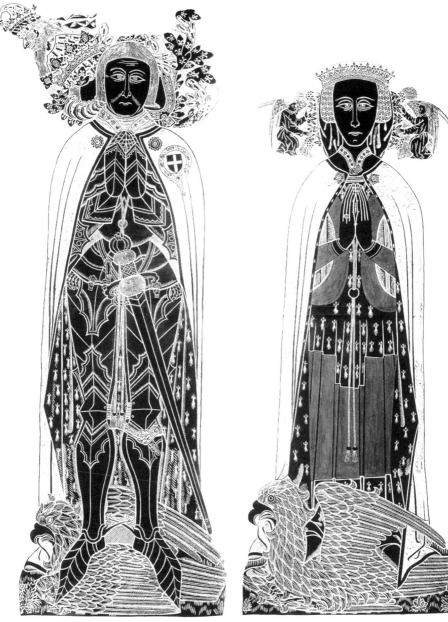

Henry Bourchier, KG, Earl of Essex and his wife, 1483, brass in Little Easton church, Essex

gravedigger Harry Gotobed – attempt to break the record for change-ringing: they ring a cycle called *Kent Treble Bob Major* with 15,840 changes, and no pause and no mistake. The fact that the fine art of bellringing is misused for a murder has less to do with the nature of bellringing than with the nature of human beings and of course the nature of the thriller-writer's work. Dorothy L. Sayers carefully constructed her novel and its under-lying psychology in accordance with the movements and cycles of change-ringing: 'the art of change-ringing is peculiar to the English, and, like most English peculiarities, unintelli-gible to the rest of the world.'

What drives English campanologists to play and enthuse over the sequent fifths of the Tittum system, or the cascading thirds of the Queen's change is a mystery which we are told ordinary mortals will never be able to solve.

As I travelled around Suffolk and Norfolk, where there are more steeples than in any other county, I kept hearing – often at unusual times – these extraordinary, totally unmelodic chimes in endlessly monotonous sequences, stubbornly refusing ever to form themselves into a tune, and then suddenly coming to an abrupt, if merciful, end. One day when the bells of Blythburgh were particularly nerve-racking, I went into the belltower. There I found six men and women in a circle, their bodies straining, their faces rapt, each one with a rope and sally (the soft handle towards the end of the rope) which he or she was pulling with both hands; they never let go of the ropes, but had them shooting up and down in a particular sequence known only to the initiated, and they stayed in rhythm to the invisible bells, happily swinging to and fro high above us within the belfry. If it hadn't been for the noise of the bells, you would have been able to hear a pin drop in that ringing chamber, so totally absorbed were the bellringers in their work. The youngest, Jamie, was eleven, and the oldest, John, was a retired oil company manager. There were two ladies and a young maths teacher named Stephen, who was tower captain. 'I'm utterly unmusical,' he informed me. I can't say I was surprised.

Change-ringing, you see, is a different sort of music. It's a matter of mathematical sound structures and permutations – nothing to do with tunes and all that sentimental stuff we ring out on the Continent. The English art of change-ringing corresponds to the cool, geometrical spirit of the Perpendicular builders and their cool, geometrical churches. The pleasure is one of construction, not of harmony. Stephen explained that bellringing entails getting a number of bells to ring in a particular combination that never repeats itself. Three bells, for instance, can ring in six different sequences: 123 – 132 – 231 – 213 – 312 – 321. With four bells, there are 120 different combinations possible; with five bells, the permuta-tions rise to 720. 'After that,' laughs the bell captain of Blythburgh, 'you can really get going.' If you haven't guessed it already, this is the origin of the expression 'ringing the changes'.

In a peal of eight, there are no less than 40,320 possible combinations and this so-called 'Major' was rung without a pause or a mistake by a team from Loughborough in 17 hours, 58 minutes and 30 seconds. Ten bells constitute a 'Royal', comprising 3,628,800 variations, and this would take 105 days to ring – heaven preserve us. St Peter Mancroft in Norwich has no less than twelve bells, a 'Maximus', which would yield a total of 479,001,600 different ding-dongs, and would take 12 bellringers a total of 38 years to ring. Not even the sports-crazy English have attempted that one. Yet. Bellringing must, however, rank pretty high on the list of eccentric hobbies. You might call it the ideal team game for individualists: each ringer pulls on his or her very own rope, but then together, like mountaineers, they climb to the peak of campanological ecstasy. Perhaps, then, Handel meant it as a compliment when he said that the bell was England's national instrument.

Stephen showed me *Diagrams*, a book full of numerical systems and figures by which the bellringers learn the individual methods. These scores have such resonant names as Plain Hunt on Six, Cambridge Surprise, Grandsire Doubles, Bob Major, and Tittum Bob Royal. Stedman Fivers is named after the father of English campanology, Fabian Stedman of Cambridge. In his *Tintinnalogia* of 1668, he set forth the art of change-ringing as it is still practised today. While the Blythburgh ringers were explaining all this to me, a stranger came in. 'Are you a ringer?' asked Stephen. 'Aye, from Yorkshire,' replied the man. He was on holiday in Suffolk, and without further ado, he was accepted into the band. Bellringers are always welcome among bellringers, and indeed some travel around deliberately just so that they can have a ring on every bell they can lay their hands on. Much sought after peals of bells are the twelve at Saffron Walden, the ten at Beccles, and one of the eight at Lavenham – the tenor bell of 1625, 'the sweetest bell in England'. Stephen is also one of those who collect bells: he has pulled the rope and its sally in over 1,300 churches. Since there are some 5,500 churches altogether in Britain with a peal of between five and twelve bells, his holidays are booked for the foreseeable future.

It is a sad fact that one third of all English steeples remain silent on a Sunday. This is not because the vicars have sold the bells ('Foolish people / Sold their bells to build a steeple.') One reason is that many bells and belfries are in an appalling condition. One of the great patrons of the bellringing art, the former Tory MP and multimillionaire Sir John Smith, has financed the restoration of bells in some 80 English churches. But there is also another reason: the lack of new bellringing blood. Only about 48,000 campanologists are left in England to practise the art of change-ringing.[1]

Before the war it was very different. 'Bell-mad, we were,' says one bellringer in Ronald Blythe's *Akenfield*, and his colleague Robert Palgrave tells how 'All the ringers were great walkers and you would meet them in bands strolling across Suffolk from tower to tower.' And then there are the subtleties of architecture and materials: 'The old bricks soak up the sound and sweeten it. The taller the tower, the quieter the bells in the village itself. The shorter, the louder.' In the old days everyone loved those bells, 'because they have spoken for the village so long and are its angel voices.' Many of the best ringers are deaf. 'It is all figures to them,' and they know the combinations off by heart. The names of bellringers are inscribed in the towers of Suffolk, and when you read them, says Robert Palgrave, 'you will be reading the names of many happy men.'

1 England's bellringers are organized at county level in a total of more than 160 clubs. The heart of this organization is the Central Council of Church Bell Ringers, who publish a newspaper called *The Ringing World*.

I saw these 'peal boards' for myself in many East Anglian churches. One of the icons of campanology hangs in the tower gallery of St Peter Mancroft. There, on 2 May 1715, the Norwich scholars, as they proudly called themselves, rang a Gransir Bob Triples – 5,040 variations in 3 hours and 18 minutes, 'and not one Bell misplaced or out of Course'. This is generally acknowledged by the experts to be the first historically documented example of change-ringing in the world. One year later, the Norwich scholars formed an association which they called Purse. When the members of this club were not using their strong arms for pulling ropes, they were using them for raising liquid refreshment, as evinced by the Ringers' Jug, an earthenware container for no less than 30 pints of ale. In the parish church at Hadleigh I saw a similar jug dating from the 18th century. Its inspiring inscription read: 'If ye love me due not lend me / Use me often keep me clenly / Fill me full or not at all / And that with strong and not with small.' Even in the 19th century, the community used to give the bellringers beer money for their services.

In his *Campanologia* William Shipway, in 1816, praised the bells of St Peter Mancroft in Norwich as 'the best peal of twelve in the kingdom'. The largest of these, the tenor, weighs two tons. (In 1909 a thirteenth bell was added - campanologists are presumably not superstitious.) For centuries they have rung out in celebration of the great events of the age, the city, and the nation – from the Armada of 1588 to the Queen's Jubilee. Tuneless they may be, but they have gone on stoically greeting all the changes of history in precisely the same way, and long may they continue to do so.

Manor Houses: Reservations for the Last Aristocrats

What the church is to the village, the country house is to the countryside. Whoever has land has power, and the most impressive outer sign of that power is the house of the landowner: state apartments for royal guests, Great Halls and Long Galleries for high society and Old Masters, refuges with endless panoramas over gardens, fields and forests. Age is the guarantee of quality, as the English never tire of telling the Americans: 'Actually, this house was built before your country was discovered.' The American has an uncomfortable feeling that he must still have been living in the trees. Henry James was an American who stood in awe and admiration: 'Of all the great things that the English have invented and made a part of the credit of the national character, the most perfect, the most characteristic, the one they have mastered most completely in all its details, so that it has become a compendious illustration of their social genius and their manners, is the well-appointed, well-administered, well-filled country house.'

What James was admiring, however, was an ideal such as Jane Austen described in *Mansfield Park*, and such as continued right through to the finale of Evelyn Waugh's *Brideshead Revisited*: the stately home as guarantor of order and morality, microcosm of a fixed social hierarchy.

The economic reality was harsher. The great families were as vulnerable as their tenants and farmworkers in the agricultural crisis of the late 19th century, which had been accelerated by cheap grain imported from America. The introduction of estate duties and death duties threatened the very existence of the landed gentry after 1894. Between 1870 and 1975 some 1,500 country houses were demolished, more than half of them after 1945. At the time, not many tears were shed. The housing shortage after the war made these rich mansions seem like a provocation, and their owners were like fossils from another world, survivors of a privileged caste who deserved to be bled dry by a state that cared for *all* its people. By the middle of the 20th century, the fate of the English country house was apparently sealed. In 1955 alone, 76 historic houses were torn down. But in the same year, the Duke of Devonshire, ignoring the advice of his 'Uncle Harold' (Macmillan, then Prime Minister), decided to return to Chatsworth, where his family had not lived since 1938. It was a turning-point.

The other turning point, back in 1949, was the decision by the 6th Marquess of Bath to open up his family estate, at Longleat, on a commercial basis. In 1966 he set up a safari park, and while some of his peers looked on with derision, others became envious as the Lions of Longleat rapidly became symbols of a new stately homes industry. The landed gentry had become businessmen and increasingly sophisticated ones.

Some lords of the manor, like Lord Coke of Holkham Hall in Norfolk, have turned their estates into multipurpose centres for education, leisure activities, art exhibitions, nature trails, fishing and hunting, camping, golf courses, picnic areas, marathon races, balloon and teddybear competitions, horseshows, and fun days for all the family. Another has turned his park into a riding school, a third runs a hi-tech Business Park. Others rent out their state apartments for balls, banquets, congresses, weddings and receptions. A particular favourite is the annual Stately Homes Music Festival. Chamber music has a long tradition in these houses, and from the 15th to the 18th century the landowners even used to entertain their guests with their own resident musicians. Now they're happy to collect the ticket money.

Today's aristocrats will do anything and everything to keep their family homes. It's not the lions in the safari park, but the owners themselves that are the really exotic creatures – they are the species threatened with extinction, and so they must parade themselves and their way of life before a paying public. And yet opening up the house, the garden, the art collection to the public is not a new phenomenon. In 1724, Daniel Defoe, impressed by the number and quality of East Anglian country houses (of which there are still nearly 1,000), wrote: 'Any traveller from abroad, who would desire to see how the English gentry live, and what pleasures they enjoy, should come into Suffolk and Cambridgeshire, and take but a light circuit among the country seats of the gentlemen on this side only, and they would be soon convinced, that not France, no not Italy itself, can out-do them, in proportion to the climate they live in.' With William Gilpin and Horace Walpole, pioneers of the picturesque, there came into being a new type of culture tourist: the *aficionado*, who journeyed from one stately home to another, making comparisons. In the mid-18th century, 'stately-homing' was as common as complaints about servants pestering for tips. When, at the end of the 18th century, East Anglia became a fashionable place to visit, Houghton and Holkham, Blickling and Raynham were among the houses that were open to the public at specific times. Even the legendary speed with which your modern coach party 'does' the sights is nothing new. In a letter dated 25 March 1761, Horace Walpole informs his friend George Montagu of his first visit in sixteen years to his parents' house, Houghton Hall in Norfolk: 'a party arrived at the same time as myself to see the house, a man and three women in riding-dresses, and they rode post through the apartments – I could not hurry before them fast enough – they were not so long in *seeing* for the first time, as I could have been in one room to examine what I knew by heart.'

Today he would have sold them souvenirs and directed them to the tearoom. Criticism of the trippers' mentality is now more ideological. Robert Hewison, in his book *The Heritage Industry*, describes the huge market in England's past as a monstrous, arch-conservative, spiritually middle-class view of England. A writer such as Neal Ascherson will regard the whole movement as vulgar English nationalism, a disastrous commercialization and glorification of the culture of the owning class. In this veneration of the past, the critics see the implication of some immortal and unchanging national order, to hide the fragmentation and destruction of the present.

It's a not very original, opium-for-the-people theory, and in my view it overlooks two vital factors: without organizations like the National Trust and the Historic Houses Association (which consists of some 400 house-owners), far more historic homes would have been lost for ever, together with all the real beauty of their parks and gardens, art and furniture. Furthermore, the life that these houses represent was not solely the preserve of the aristocracy. Under the roofs of the stately homes lived all levels and shades of English society: servants, craftsmen, gardeners, tenants, gamekeepers, farm and forest workers. These houses tell the history not merely of their owners, but also of their servants. As late as the Second World War, the 11th Duke of Bedford employed 50 servants and 200 workers on the park and estates of Woburn Abbey – one last, strange flowering of feudal splendour. Since the sixties, nearly all the stately homes have had a rapidly dwindling staff. One of the exceptions, though, is Chatsworth, where the Duke of Devonshire still employs some 18 gardeners and 70 domestic staff, including three night-watchmen, a clock-winder, and a man for the silver. By comparison Lady Cholmondeley runs Houghton Hall with a modest staff of seven, plus 15 others for the park and stables. Her neighbours, the Townshends of Raynham Hall, engage a butler only for special occasions. When I visited various country houses in East Anglia, I was usually served by the owner, occasionally by the daily help, and never by a butler. And if someone like the Duke of Grafton preferred not to answer questions about his staffing level, this was certainly because it was embarrassingly low rather than extravagantly high.

'Historic houses have a very important educational role to play,' explained the Duke of Grafton. 'At Euston Hall we hold a lot of charitable functions, for instance on behalf of threatened churches.' Lord Walpole regards the main role of the stately homes as being conservation of the countryside, by sensible forestry, planting hedges, and controlling the natural environment. He also holds literary readings and art exhibitions at Mannington Hall – a substantial contribution to the cultural life of the area. On the manor estate at Heydon Hall, Captain Bulwer Long personally supervises bonfire night on the fifth of November, among many other community tasks which he undertakes. Today it is the landed gentry more than the country parsons who tend the soul of the countryside. Even if the gentry have no power, they still have prestige and influence, and sometimes a title such as Lord Lieutenant, or High Sheriff (responsible for exercising royal jurisdiction in the counties – the oldest secular office in England, going back to the Anglo-Saxon kings). They survive, not as royal masters of ceremony, nor as recipients of state subsidies, but as managers of their own estates, and as intelligent, pragmatic heirs to the countryside.

The renewed self-confidence of the landed gentry has led to one of the most extraordinary phenomena in postwar British architecture: the renaissance of the country house. Since 1945 more than 200 have been built, with a particular boom in the fifties and sixties. 'The country house tradition in Britain is far from dead,' concludes John Martin Robinson in his book *The Latest Country Houses*. Of course not everyone knows about them, and there are in fact good reasons why they have never emerged from the shadows of the many hundreds of historic houses which have been demolished (and which in some cases they were built to replace): for one thing, very few of them are open to the public; for another, they are stylistically just about as exciting as Prince Charles's new suits. The majority of them conform very much to the upper-class taste of the last sixty years: Neo-Georgian, which is as popular now as the so-called Tudorbethan was with the Victorians. Indeed, Robinson believes that this style is essential for an English country house in an English park. He sees it as a traditional architectural form created for a traditional way of life, and so it is scarcely surprising that most people prefer a traditional architectural language. But even he is forced to admit that some of them are little more than 'grandiose bungalows'.

Does this mean that a great tradition of British architecture is now fizzling out in anachronisms? In East Anglia at any rate I did not see one convincing example of contemporary country house architecture. Each of my three counties did offer some splendid work by Norman Foster: his airport at Stansted, his insurance building in Ipswich, and his arts centre in Norwich (plate 60). But so far nobody has come up with a hi-tech manor house. Not even Norman Foster.

Brick Gables and Tulip Bulbs: The Dutch Connection

Anyone travelling through East Anglia will keep finding links with Holland. There is a Dutch quarter in Colchester, there are Dutch cottages in Southwold, and Dutch gables are everywhere. Holland is East Anglia's nearest neighbour on the Continent. First there was the Roman occupation (which left behind a nostalgia for Italy that has never quite disappeared), then came the Anglo-Saxon and Scandinavian links, and after that the turbulent liaison with Norman France, but since the Middle Ages it has been above all the Dutch connection that has eased England's long journey towards Europe. There has been a constant exchange of ideas and goods, of artists, engineers and scholars, puritans and Calvinists, refugees and tourists, traders and smugglers.

England and Holland were close trading partners, and as sometimes happens between partners, they also fell out; witness three bitter trade wars. They were allies in the war against Catholic Spain, and they were rivals in the quest for colonies in the Far East. In a declaration of 1585, Queen Elizabeth I called the Dutch England's 'most ancient and familiar neighbours'. When the Duke of Alba's forces occupied the Netherlands, Elizabeth I defended her fellow Protestants (and her maritime interests) against Philip II. Englishmen served in the Dutch army, and Dutch religious refugees emigrated in their thousands to England, and particularly to East Anglia. There is a Dutch Church in Norwich, which had the highest proportion of these refugees (one third of the population), and right through to the 20th century services here were held in Dutch. There was a similar movement in reverse, with East Anglian Puritans at the time of Archbishop Laud seeking refuge in Calvinist Holland. The philosopher John Locke, when he found himself in political trouble over his association with Lord Shaftesbury, went to Holland in 1682 and lived there for five years. It was actually in Holland that he published his first essays.

In the 14th century the English exported their wool to the Flemish weavers in Bruges, Ghent and Ypres, whereas in the 16th century the Dutch immigrants in Norwich and Colchester brought in new draperies that lifted the East Anglian cloth industry to ever greater heights. The Netherlands was England's main trading partner in the Middle Ages, first through Catholic Antwerp, and later through Protestant Amsterdam. Dutch fishermen sold their herring in the ports of East Anglia until draconian trade restrictions suppressed such competition. What could not be suppressed, however, was the flourishing industry of smuggling. The distilleries at Schiedam, the biggest in Europe during the 18th century, produced almost four million gallons of gin a year at that time, and most of it was smuggled to England in well-armed 200-ton cutters.

The sea that divided the two countries also bound them together in many different ways. The flatness of East Anglia created the same problems of coastal defence and drainage as beset the Dutch. For their channels, dikes and land reclamation, the English used Dutch drainage experts and Dutch methods of finance, and there were joint ventures such as Canvey Island in Essex and, shortly afterwards in 1634, the large-scale drainage of the Fens under the direction of Cornelius Vermuyden from Zeeland. It was a Dutchman, Joas Johnson, who in 1568 was commissioned to supervise the construction of the new port of Yarmouth. And if we go back still further, we will find in the village church of Haddiscoe in Norfolk an epitaph of 1525 to the Dutch 'dyke-reeve' Peter Peterson.

They traded and they quarrelled, they competed and they co-operated; what could be more natural than that they also intermarried? Anglo-Dutch marriages were at all levels,

---

1   The builder of Heveningham Hall in Suffolk, for instance, was of Dutch origin, Sir Gerard Vanneck.

George Vincent: Dutch Fair on Yarmouth Beach, 1812

from merchant to aristocrat.[1] In 1613, Prince Frederick William of Orange married a daughter of King James I, Elizabeth Stuart, the Winter Queen (their son was the dashing Prince Rupert), but undoubtedly the high point of the dynastic unions between the two countries came with the marriage in 1677 between William III of Orange, himself half-Stuart, and his first cousin Mary, a daughter of King James II, who was only fifteen years old and was four inches taller than her husband. After the Glorious Revolution of 1688, Parliament summoned King Billy and his wife together to the British throne. Unfortunately, the imported king, who was not particularly popular, met a relatively early death after a riding accident at Newmarket, but the era of William and Mary left England with a constitutional monarchy, Dutch gardens, and innumerable Delft vases for their tulips. Never again would the flower motifs on the pictures, chair-covers and bed curtains of the kingdom burst into such luxuriant bloom as in the days of William and Mary. As for the first gardening associations, these were not established by English enthusiasts, but by Huguenot immigrants from Holland. The cultivation of turnips and rape was also introduced by the Dutch after the drainage of the Fens in the 17th century. And who built

England's first sugar refinery, in 1912? A Dutchman named van Rossum, in Cantley on the Norfolk Broads.[1]

The Dutch connection is apparent in many spheres, and none more so than that of architecture and the fine arts. The red and orange pantiles characteristic of villages in Essex, Suffolk and, in particular, Norfolk, first entered East Anglian ports as ballast on Dutch ships during the 17th century. Later they were also manufactured in England. Charles I issued a patent for the production of 'Pantiles or Flanders Tyles' in 1636, but generally the year 1701 is regarded as marking the beginning of English production, by a firm in Tilbury, Essex, in which Daniel Defoe had shares. Another 17th-century Dutch influence to be seen everywhere in East Anglia is the brick houses with their dramatically curved gables. Country houses like Raynham Hall in Norfolk and Beaumont Hall in Essex (c.1650) have these Dutch gables, and so do many simple cottages, and the barn at Manor Farm in Kirby Bedon. One of the earliest examples of this Dutch Mannerism in East Anglia is Bourne Mill in Colchester (1591), and a later one is the Water Gate at Tilbury Fort (1670–84), designed by Charles II's military engineer, the Dutchman Sir Bernard de Gomme.

The 17th century was also the Golden Age of Dutch art, and Holland was a major centre of European culture, science and trade. In the wake of the close trade links, many Dutch artists came to England, and they were much sought after for their portraits, their pictures of horses and ships, and also for their chimney-pieces. In 1632 Anthony van Dyck settled in London, at the invitation of Charles I, and was swamped with commissions from the aristocracy. Next to that of the Queen, the most important Van Dyck collection in private hands is that of the Duke of Grafton in Euston Hall, Suffolk. This collection was built up by one of his ancestors, the 1st Earl of Arlington, who in 1667 married Isabella van Beverwaert from the House of Orange. The extent to which the landed gentry favoured Dutch and Flemish art can be seen from the collections in many of East Anglia's manor houses. Indeed the biggest exhibition of 17th-century Dutch painting ever held in England (Birmingham Museum, 1989) had no need to import any exhibits, since there was a choice from over 2,000 in British museums and private collections. In Holkham Hall, for instance, apart from one Rubens masterpiece, there are a number of great bird paintings by Melchior de Hondecoeter and hunting scenes by the Flemish artist Frans Snyders – both great favourites among the landed gentry. The showpiece of the 3rd Earl of Orford's collection in Wolterton Hall was Rubens' 'Landscape with Rainbow', which J. S. Cotman came specially to see in 1841. Today it hangs in the Wallace Collection in London. Another fine collection of Dutch and Flemish paintings was that of Sir Jacob Astley, which he put together in the early 19th century at Melton Constable Hall in Norfolk, but which no longer exists. Sir Robert Walpole in Houghton and Sir Andrew Fountaine in Narford Hall were also great East Anglian collectors, as was William Windham in Felbrigg Hall. The

---

1   The disease that has killed around ten million elm trees in England is known as Dutch Elm Disease because it was first diagnosed in Holland.

Willem van de Velde: Battle of Sole Bay, 1672

marine paintings of the van der Veldes are still to be seen there; he acquired these in the middle of the 18th century, including the monumental Battle of the Texel (*c*.1674), a naval battle that took place during the last of the three Anglo-Dutch wars. Willem van de Velde and son (also Willem), came from Leiden and died in London, having founded the English school of marine painting.

It was not just the landed gentry of East Anglia that collected these Dutch and Flemish masters in the 18th and early 19th centuries; merchants and upper middle-class people did so, too, including the banker Francis Gibson from Saffron Walden, whose Vermeer now hangs in New York's Frick Collection; the pharmacist Thomas Penrice from Great Yarmouth owned several paintings by the popular artist David Teniers the Younger, but the pride of his collection was Rubens' 'Judgement of Paris', now in the National Gallery in London; another was the Suffolk archaeologist Cox Macro, lifelong friend and patron of the Antwerp painter Peter Tillemans, who died at Macro's Little Haugh Hall, near Norton, in 1734. Macro, incidentally, had studied medicine in Leiden, as did the Norwich doctor and author Sir Thomas Browne. The leading English sculptor of the early 17th century, Nicholas Stone, had a Dutch education, and the landscape gardener Humphry Repton from Norfolk was apprenticed for four years to a banker in Rotterdam. And to complete the picture, Erasmus of Rotterdam taught at Cambridge.

Native artists also profited from these private collections.[1] Thanks to his patron in Great Yarmouth, the banker Dawson Turner, John Sell Cotman was able to study the works of Hobbema, Cuyp, Rubens and Teniers in the original. Jan Steen's 'The Christening Feast' (1664), which is now in the Wallace Collection, was also once Dawson Turner's. John Crome's patron, Thomas Harvey from Catton near Norwich, married to the daughter of an English merchant in Rotterdam, was not only a collector but also an art dealer, who specialized in Dutch and Flemish paintings. The earliest known Flemish work to have been commissioned by a Norfolk family is the Ashwellthorpe Triptych in the Castle Museum in Norwich: this was 'The Seven Sorrows of the Virgin' by the Master of the Magdalene Legend, painted c.1512–20 for an altar at Christopher Knyvett's home at Ashwellthorpe, a village southwest of Norwich.

Like Holland, East Anglia has a flat, broad coastal landscape with marshes, windmills[2] and often dramatic skies. It was therefore no coincidence that 17th-century Dutch landscape painting was of especial interest to the Norwich painters of the early 19th century. This Anglo-Dutch affinity was pointed out by John Constable in his third lecture to the Royal Academy in 1836, when he was discussing Jacob van Ruysdael's landscapes: 'Ruysdael ... delighted in, and has made delightful to our eyes, those solemn days, peculiar to his country and to ours, when without storm, large rolling clouds scarcely permit a ray of sunlight to break the shades of the forest. By these effects he enveloped the most ordinary scenes in grandeur ...'

In the 19th century, England tended to look towards America rather than to Europe, and so East Anglia lay on the wrong side of the country. Liverpool and Southampton, and the great international ports to the south and west were the ones that flourished, while those of East Anglia wasted away. Not until present times has the cry once again been 'Go east', but now once more the ports of Ipswich, Felixstowe and Great Yarmouth are becoming increasingly important for trade. Above all it is Dutch agricultural concerns that are expanding in East Anglia, and between Norwich and Amsterdam there are no less than four flights a day. Ipswich even planned a European Visual Arts Centre. 'It all shows how European we're becoming, and the role East Anglia has to play in this,' said Malcolm Bradbury, author and university professor in Norwich. Ian Chance, founder and director of the Wingfield Art and Music festival, also sees East Anglia in a European light: 'We look to Europe and not so much to London.' Perhaps like the sails of its old windmills, East Anglia's history is now turning full circle.

---

1 In the opinion of such experts as the London art dealer Sir Hugh Leggatt, many of the vicarages in Suffolk and Norfolk still contain a large number of unidentified 17th-century Dutch masters.

2 No other region in England has as many windmills as East Anglia. At the end of the 19th century there were about 1,500 corn and drainage mills in operation. Today there are about 60 in good working order.

Thomas Gainsborough (1727–88): Self-Portrait, c.1759

John Sell Cotman (1782–1842): etching by J. P. Davis based on drawing by Miss Dawson Turner, 1818

John Constable (1776–1837): Self-Portrait

Benjamin Britten (1913–76)

Horatio, Viscount Nelson, 1758–1805, by William Beechey 1801

William Morris (1834–96): photograph by Abel Lewis, 1880

P. D. James (b.1920)

Dorothy L. Sayers (1893–1957)

Malcolm Bradbury (b.1932)

ESSEX

I come not from Heaven, but from Essex
(William Morris)

For a long time I never bothered about Essex. Suffolk, Norfolk – the very names had a sort of rural poetry about them, whereas Essex seemed like pure prose. Most of my fellow travellers had the same idea, and were heading either for London or for Cambridge. Essex was not a destination – it was a transit county, a buffer zone between London and the 'real' East Anglia, between town and country. Essex was East Anglia's London suburb, an uneasy hybrid neatly encapsulated by the advertising slogan: 'Welcome to Essex, the best thing next to London'.

To the south is the Thames Estuary, to the north the Stour, and to the west the River Lea: a county with liquid borders. 'Essex begins somewhere among back streets in London's eastern suburbs,' wrote J. B. Priestley in his *English Journey*. The East End image has always persisted for this, the poor relation among the home counties. When people retired from the big city, they preferred to settle in the more southern counties. Genuine East Anglians didn't count Essex as home territory: 'too cockneyfied for the Londoners and too London for the real countryman.' But now things are beginning to change. 'Classy people used to move to Kent or Surrey,' explained Mr Collins, a farmer in High Laver, 'because south of London was chic, and east was middle class. But now Essex is becoming fashionable.' The people of Essex view their new-found status with mixed feelings of pride and regret, for being fashionable means more houses, less greenery, and more traffic. This 'new' trend, however, is not new at all.

When Daniel Defoe began his East Anglian tour in April 1722, he noted the housing boom in the Essex countryside: 'all the villages which may be called the neighbourhood of the city of London are increased in buildings to a strange degree.' Villages like Stratford (long since swallowed up by the East End) had more than doubled in size, while rents and house prices had shot up. As for traffic, Defoe had counted not less than 200 coaches travelling through some villages. But they were not tourists. They were 18th-century commuters, retired people from the City, merchants, dealers, and Londoners with second homes in the country. Wanstead, Walthamstow, Woodford and other villages then in Essex, though now part of Greater London, were popular not because of country life, but 'for good company' and 'excellent conversation' without the vices and excesses of the metropolis.

In Wanstead, where the M11 now meets the A12, Defoe visited one of the many newly built country houses, Wanstead House. Colen Campbell designed this early Palladian masterpiece (1715–20), having been commissioned by Viscount Castlemain, son of the head of the East India Company, Sir Josiah Child – 'a suddenly monied man' (John Evelyn). Sir Josiah's baroque monument, incidentally, in St Mary's, Wanstead, was made by the Flemish sculptor John van Nost in 1699, and depicts him as a gentleman in a Roman toga. Defoe was especially taken with the park and garden of Wanstead House. These had existed before the house was built, and were already so popular that the owners would only open them to the public on one or two days in the week, because 'the crowds grew too great'. Today the park is a golf course, and Wanstead House was one of the first country houses to fall to the demolition ball, in 1824.

Essex was where English kings had their country palaces and London cockneys their hovels. During the unplanned boom of the 19th century, the metropolis swallowed up more and more villages. Dickens called it 'London-over-the-border'. The Second World War increased the capital's pressure on the surrounding countryside, as Essex became London's reception centre and home for the bombed-out dockworkers of the East End. Harlow, Basildon, and other new towns sprang up on the drawing-boards and then on the beet fields. Today the Council for the Protection of Rural England and other environmental bodies fight to prevent the green belt from being further enveloped by the tentacles of the capital. But even they have not been able to prevent two-thirds of the toxic waste imported from the Continent from being dumped in Essex. And this in the county that gave birth to the founding father of greenery, William Morris.

In spite of such impositions, however, a good deal of Essex has remained clear of suburban dust. There is still plenty of unspoilt countryside, with idyllic villages and charming market and coastal resorts. Even its largest town, Southend, has no more than some 160,000 inhabitants and Colchester still retains the Roman lay-out of its streets. Essex, land of the East Saxons, was one of the most Roman, and later the most Norman regions of England. Village names like Layer Marney and Layer-de-la-Haye still recall the Norman conquerors. At the time of Domesday Book (1086), the first record of land ownership and taxable values, Essex had about 70,000 inhabitants (compared to over 1.5 million today), 250 watermills, and fishing and salting industries. Half the county was farmland, a fifth was forest, and the rest was pasture, heath and marsh. Exactly 500 years later, in 1586, the historian William Camden, in his *Britannia*, described Essex as being very fertile, with an abundance of saffron and wood, and extraordinarily rich. Of the saffron, all that remains is the name Saffron Walden; the wood was turned into ships and timber-framed houses; and the great wealth of the medieval cloth industry has long since faded from memory. The good clay soil, however, has kept Essex farming in pole position. Maldon houses England's largest fruit and vegetable canning factory, and it may well be that the strawberry jam on your hot buttered toast comes from Tiptree.

Essex is a county of two faces, one looking towards London, and the other towards East Anglia. The urbanized, industrialized south, with its oil refineries and electronics factories, makes a stark contrast to the countryside of the north and the marshlands of the coast. For

Harwich, view of town and port, c.1713

me, Essex is at its finest when it emulates Suffolk, in the green hills of the northwest and on the banks of its northern boundary, the Stour.

From Harwich to St Osyth: Roses and Peacocks

Harwich is the poor man's Dover. There are no white cliffs, no ruined castles, and no-one ever composed a nostalgic song about Harwich. But for me there is always a special feeling as I stand on the deck of the 'Hamburg', hear the first cries of the seagulls (I'll swear they have an English accent), see the gentle green hills and the little town with its two lighthouses – one smaller than the other – watch the launch bringing the Trinity pilot aboard (a traditional and totally unnecessary ritual), see the long row of red fireships at the entrance to the port, and the armada of white sailing boats going out of the

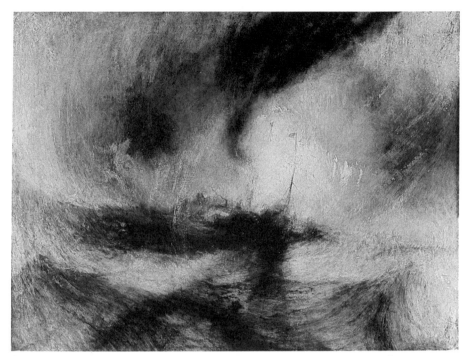

J. M. W. Turner: Snow storm – steamboat off a harbour's mouth (Harwich), 1842

broad river mouth towards the sea. Dover may be spectacular, but Harwich feels more like home.

Of course, Harwich – like any port in a storm – *can* be spectacular. In London's Tate Gallery hangs a painting (1842) with an unusually long title: 'Snow Storm – Steamboat off a Harbour's Mouth making Signals in Shallow Water and going by the Lead. The Author was in this Storm on the Night the Ariel left Harwich.' It's a detailed, documentary title that gives authenticity to the wild atmosphere and colours of this painting. It's by Turner, and he painted it because 'I wished to show what such a scene was like; I got the sailors to lash me to the mast to observe it; I was lashed for four hours and I did not expect to escape, but I felt bound to record it if I did. But no one had any business to like the picture.' A critic of the 1842 Royal Academy Exhibition complained that it was painted with 'soapsuds and whitewash'.

Harwich lies on a narrow peninsula at the end of the ten-mile long tidal mouth of the Stour, where it joins the River Orwell. It is protected by the tongue of land that lies opposite, and is a natural harbour. On the northern, Suffolk side of this double estuary lies the container port of Felixstowe, and on the southern, Essex side is the passenger port of

47

Harwich, with ferries to Esbjerg, Gothenburg and Oslo, Hamburg and Hoek van Holland. The Harwich Europort existed long before the Eurotunnel. When England's Postmaster-General signed an agreement with the town of Amsterdam in 1661, setting up regular postal communications, Harwich was the port they chose. Twice a week English mail-boats left here for the Continent. From here, too, the royals from the House of Hanover would sail to their German homes. In November 1734 Princess Anne, daughter of George II, waited 17 days in Harwich for a favourable wind that would enable her to join her husband, the Prince of Orange. Finally, the King lost patience and sent her to Dover. It was at Harwich that Princess Charlotte of Mecklenburg-Strelitz landed in September 1761 for her marriage to George III, and it was from Harwich that the body of Caroline, the estranged wife of George IV, made its last sad journey home to Brunswick in 1821.

Like all ports, Harwich has seen its share of kings and commoners, traders and tourists, the meek and the mighty, hellos and goodbyes, cheers and tears. In the last few months before the outbreak of World War II, some 10,000 German children landed here – the children of Jewish parents, evacuated after the November pogroms of 1938. The yellow and white chalets of Dovercourt, then as now a holiday camp, were their first English homes as they tried to adjust to life without parents, without money, but with hope.

'A pretty place and wants for nothing,' was Elizabeth I's comment when she came here in August 1561. The Tourist Office is grateful for any quotes, no matter how ancient, and sends us to places which not even the world's greatest advertising agency could turn into sights. Daniel Defoe was not exactly overwhelmed: 'Harwich is a town of hurry and business, not much of gaiety and pleasure.' Samuel Pepys – never one to forego life's pleasures – only came to Harwich when his work as Secretary to the Navy Board made it necessary (for Harwich was then a military shipyard).

Boats today land at Parkeston Quay, three miles from the old quay, near Half Penny Pier. If you should happen to miss your ferry, and thus be condemned to a night in Harwich, go along to the Electric Palace, an Edwardian cinema, one of the oldest in the country, restored and now a listed building. It opened in 1911 with the silent film *The Battle of Trafalgar*: Nelson's death, with piano accompaniment.

On the peninsula between Harwich and Colchester lie three coastal towns which developed into seaside resorts during the late 19th century. *Clacton* was the destination of the working class, *Walton* was for the middle class, and *Frinton* coddled the upper class, which in the twenties included the Prince of Wales, Douglas Fairbanks, and Winston Churchill. Today Frinton-on-Sea still relishes its high repute: you won't find any trippers' buses on the prom, or chips on the beach, or bingo on the front. Frinton preserves its aura of bored and boring refinement. In 1850 it was a village of 30 inhabitants, and today it has

1 HOUGHTON HALL   Entrance hall with statue of Hermes by Locatelli ▷

2 AUDLEY END Jacobean mansion, 1603–16

3 HOUGHTON HALL Country home of Sir Robert Walpole, 1722–35

4   HELMINGHAM HALL   Tollemache family's moated mansion, 16th–18th century

                              6   HOUGHTON HALL   Saloon by William Kent, *c.*1727 ▷

5   ICKWORTH   Country mansion of Earls of Bristol, 1795–1829

8 HOLKHAM HALL Palladian mansion of Earls of Leicester, 1734–9, by William Kent
◁ 7 HOLKHAM HALL Lord Coke and his spaniel Shrimp in the Marble Hall
9 LONG MELFORD Kentwell Hall

10   OXBURGH HALL   Tudor moated mansion, begun in 1482

11   David Cargill in park at ELSING HALL
               13   EUSTON HALL   11th Duke of Grafton with ancestor: Van Dyck's portrait of Charles I ▷
12   HEYDON HALL   William and Sarah Bulwer Long with lurchers Poppy and Lambton

15   HENGRAVE HALL   Tudor gatehouse, 1525–38

◁ 14   Tudor Festival at KENTWELL HALL, Moat House, *c*.1475

17   ST OSYTH'S PRIORY   Lord D'Arcy's Tower, 1553–8

16   WEST STOW HALL   Home of Mary Tudor's Master of the Horse, *c*.1520

18   HADLEIGH   Deanery Tower, gatehouse, 1495

22 SANDRINGHAM HOUSE   The Queen's country home in Norfolk, 1870

24   CASTLE RISING   Norman fortress, c.1150 ▷

23   AUDLEY END   Palladian Tea House Bridge by Robert Adam, 1782

6,500, half of whom have retired, and the other half of whom are about to retire. It has broad green fields on its steep shores, and it is blessed with one notable house: The Homestead, designed in 1905 by Charles F. A. Voysey, and standing in Second Avenue on the corner of Holland Road. It is a villa with an L-shaped groundplan and a slate roof, well proportioned, homely, and every detail (right down to the heart-shaped keyholes) the invention of Voysey himself. There is one other sight to see in Frinton: the east window of Old St Mary's, designed by Edward Burne-Jones and executed by William Morris – an Annunciation in aubergine and dark green.

The beach-huts of Walton promenade lie in neat echelons on the hillside. They bear such names as 'Sans Souci' and 'Monte Carlo', 'Jennifer' and 'Sheila' – faded beauties creaking in the sea-breeze. Women carry their white poodles along the promenade, young men flash their golden earrings, and middle-aged men roll their trousers up and paddle in the water on legs as spindly as those of the pier. The latter had to stretch out for half a mile before it could get to water six feet deep. Only then could the pleasure boats – which used to come every day from London – have enough water for mooring. But of course the pier, like most British piers, is less concerned with mooring than with entertainment: here you can play bingo, ride on the ghost train, lose your money on a fruit machine, or bounce on a Humpty-Dumpty. And in the midst of this cacophony, the anglers snore – until they get a bite.

Clacton-on-Sea also has a pleasure pier, built in 1873 and extended during the thirties (colour plate 33). 'Slots of Fun' they call it, and the pub on the pier is 'Cockney Pride'. Clacton, at the end of the eighties, had the highest rate of unemployment in East Anglia (22 per cent). For London's cockneys and East End dockers it has long been a popular weekend destination. Back in 1872, very few could afford a room in the Royal Hotel, whose stucco façade and wrought-iron balcony are typical of the seaside architecture of the period. The East Enders built their own holiday quarters west of Clacton, beyond the three Martello Towers[1] and the golf course and the former Butlin's Holiday Camp, and far out on Jaywick Sands.

Jaywick lies behind a long wall built as protection against flood in what used to be marshland. In 1928 an estate agent offered cheap plots of this barren land on which people could build whatever they liked. It was a parcel of fresh air and freedom for five pounds, covering an area of some 16 by 110 feet. In their hundreds, the East Enders put up their new dwellings – made of crates and old railway carriages, later stone, half garden shed, half bungalow, individualistic, anarchic, weird and wonderful, England's working-class ancestors of the hippy homes of California. The little streets of this Shangri-La are called Austin Avenue, Rover Avenue, Daimler Avenue, Bentley Avenue – every one a four-wheeled dream for the workers who bought their share of paradise for a fiver.

---

1 Clacton's Martello Towers (1810–12) are part of the coastal defences erected against the feared Napoleonic invasion. They were named after a *Torre della Mortella* on Corsica, which greatly impressed the English during the campaign of 1794.

'Why Worry' they called their houses, 'Happy Returns', or 'Finnegan's Rainbow'. With its Neo-Tudor verandahs and flaking paint, and its dilapidated beach cafés, Jaywick's charms were Clacton's headache - a holiday slum which the elders of the tribe would dearly have torn down. For years the shanty-town dwellers refused to be linked to the main drainage system. Even Pevsner, that most reliable of architectural guides, makes no mention of Clacton's architectural black sheep, although he gives telephone booths and public conveniences the full treatment. Of course, no-one would call Jaywick a beauty spot, but this anonymous architectural mess reveals more about little people's dreams than many a sociological study. There were other plots sold elsewhere along the coast of Essex, but most of those dwllings have long since been demolished. For the East Enders, they were a haven from the depressing council flats and suburban estates of the clinically planned new towns. 'Jaywick was anarchic, since it represented freedom,' wrote the English architectural historian Gavin Stamp, 'the freedom of the generation that had been through the trauma of the Great War to get out of the crowded grime of London, to escape, to be proud and independent.'

When I visited *St Osyth's Priory*, a few miles inland, the garden was a luxuriant mass of roses, and the great flint gate shone in the sunlight – an unforgettable sight. Osyth was the daughter of the first Christian king of the East Angles, and was probably executed by the Vikings because of her beliefs. After she had been beheaded, she walked for three miles with her head under her arm, clearly some kind of a world record. Shortly after 1100, Augustinian canons built a monastery on the site of her martyrdom. In the late 15th century, the prior had a residence built especially for himself and his guests a little way from the main buildings – a two-storey gatehouse with two massive side towers, complete-ly covered with a severe net of Perpendicular decoration, the battlements decorated with lozenge and chequerwork patterns of stone and flint – flushwork at its most brilliant, surpassing even the more or less contemporary gatehouse at St John's Abbey in Colchester, and similarly offering a far more resplendent façade to the outside world than to the monastery within. There are three narrow niches with figures and Gothic canopies next to and above the portal, reliefs of St George and the Dragon in the spandrels, and keystones with the heads of saints in the fan vault of the entrance: thus we are greeted by the great gate of St Osyth's, one of the finest monastery gatehouses in Europe (plate 17).

After this opening flourish, a wide sweep of lawn, Tudor walls of red brick, grey towers, evergreen topiaries, the scent of roses and the cry of peacocks – seldom did the Reforma-tion bring forth a more picturesque combination of monastery and manor house than that of St Osyth's Priory. In architectonic terms, the transition works effortlessly. In 1527, the last Prior, John Vintoner, built a residence opposite the gatehouse, and it was almost like that of a nobleman, complete with an impressive oriel window. When the 1st Lord D'Arcy, head of Edward VI's bodyguard, took over the secularized priory in 1553, he continued the flushwork of the gatehouse in two towers covered with an equally magnificent chequerwork pattern of limestone and septaria. One of his successors crowned the octagonal clocktower with a Georgian lantern (colour plate 20).

Since 1954 St Osyth's Priory has belonged to the writer and former Conservative MP Somerset de Chair. A few rooms in the Georgian wing are open to the public, one of them being the Whistlejacket Room. This is named after the most famous painting in the house – the portrait of a stallion rearing in fury, painted in 1762 by George Stubbs. The owner of the horse had his portrait painted by Reynolds, wearing the Order of the Garter. He was the 2nd Marquess of Rockingham, England's Prime Minister when the American colonies gained their independence, and together with his father he built the family seat of Wentworth Woodhouse in Yorkshire. After the death of the 10th Earl Fitzwilliam, part of the house's art collection passed to Lady Juliet de Chair. These pictures include four more of George Stubbs' paintings of horses and dogs. Next to these masterpieces, one is surprised to find some of the owner's own pictures – badly painted and horribly out of place. Equally vain is the display of letters from famous people, ranging from Churchill to Paul Getty and Jacqueline Onassis. Kipling, asked for his opinion of one of author de Chair's books, wrote: 'I've read your *Enter Napoleon* and, as you say, it is pretty bad.'

Through the park of St Osyth's echo the tragic cries of peacocks. Perhaps they have also been reading *Enter Napoleon*. But Mr de Chair and his peacocks are not too proud to let you have their great banqueting hall for your wedding – the very hall where the 2nd Lord D'Arcy entertained Queen Elizabeth I in July 1561 ('great rain till midnight'). The cost when I was there? A mere £450.

In the chancel of the parish church of St Osyth are the graves of the 1st and 2nd Lords D'Arcy and their wives – sarcophagus figures of marble and alabaster (after 1581). They lie there in magnificent robes, all set to enter heaven. Incidentally, the arcades in the nave and side aisles are unusual, being early 16th-century English Gothic brickwork.

When you leave St Osyth, the road will take you past the sailing port of *Brightlingsea*, and along the eastern bank of the Colne estuary to Colchester.

Colchester: The Roman Capital of England

Many years ago, a sentence in Fontane's novel *Stechlin* aroused my curiosity about *Colchester*: 'Russia, if you will allow me to make such idle comparisons, always has something of Astrakhan about it, and England always has something of Colchester. And I think Colchester stands higher.' How highly the locals think of their own town was clear from Mayor John Lampon's proud statement in 1987: 'We were the first Roman capital, when London was nothing but a few mud huts.'

Colchester lies between fields of roses and beds of oysters, Roman walls and ancient legends. Old King Cole, the merry old soul, was actually King of Colchester. His daughter is the bronze figure that crowns the tower of the Edwardian Town Hall (1898–1902) in the High Street: St Helena, legendary mother of the Emperor Constantine the Great. The town's coat-of-arms contains the crowns of the Three Kings together with the symbol of the Holy Cross which St Helena is believed to have found in Jerusalem. More solidly based in history is King Cunobellinus (Shakespeare's Cymbeline), who earned the ever-lasting gratitude of numismatists by minting large numbers of gold coins throughout his reign. Until his death, *c.*AD40, Cunobellinus ruled in Camulodunum, the capital town of the Catuvellauni at the mouth of the River Colne. According to the Greek geographer Strabo, these people used to export gold, grain, cattle, slaves and greyhounds, which even in those days were popular as hunting-dogs. They imported wine, glasses, enamel brooches, and other continental luxuries. Camulodunum prospered, and its wealth made the Romans greedy. After Caesar's unsuccessful foray, Claudius sent his troops across the Channel in AD43 – four legions, a total of 40,000 men. One year later, the Roman Emperor entered Camulodunum in triumph, to accept the surrender of eleven tribal kings.[1] The Twentieth Legion set up camp on a neighbouring hill, and from there organized the conquest of the rest of the country. It was the camp on the Colne, Colchester, and not Londinium that Claudius named as capital of his new province, Britannia.

Colonia Claudia Victricensis was the first of the great Roman *coloniae* on British soil, followed by Lincoln, Gloucester and York. Originally they were military bases, but then they became trading centres and settlements for retired legionaries. It was the beginning of England's Europeanization. But Britain's resistance, however divided it may have been, was not yet broken. In AD61, Boadicea – in an orgy of rage, despair and revenge – took up arms against the invader. The Queen of the Iceni in Norfolk, having been humiliated by the Romans (who took her land and were said to have ravished her daughters), gathered an army, burned down Camulodunum, destroyed Londinium and Verulamium (St Albans), massacred thousands, and finally took her own life in order to avoid capture. Her grave is believed to be in London, somewhere beneath Platform 10 at King's Cross Station. She became for the British what Joan of Arc was for the French – a symbol of national heroism. In her book *Boadicea's Chariot: The Warrior Queens* (1988), Antonia Fraser takes her as the archetype, tracing the line from Cleopatra right through to Margaret Thatcher.

After Boadicea's rebellion, central London became the administrative capital, and Camulodunum was given a defensive wall. Large stretches of this are still well preserved, as can be seen in Priory Street and on Balkerne Hill. Once it was sixteen feet high and more than nine feet thick, rubble and mortar, originally decorated with septaria alternating with bands of flat Roman brick. Of the six gates, only the ruined *Balkerne Gate* remains, built as a freestanding triumphal arch, but later incorporated into the wall as its west gate. What was once a deep moat below the wall is now a busy road. Opposite stands a citadel of modern culture – a massive car park, with corner towers, ramparts and crenellated gables, a postmodern echo of the Roman wall. On the foundations of this wall, near the Balkerne

---

1 Of the earthwork defences, Gryme's Dyke in Lexden Heath is still recognizable – some four miles long and ten feet high.

J. M. W. Turner: Colchester, Essex, 1827

Gate, stands a pub that dates from the 17th century, and since there was clearly a gap in the wall at this point, the pub rejoices in the name 'The Hole in the Wall'. Part of the Roman way of life adopted by Britons was undoubtedly the inn and the inn-sign. Chequered signs on painted wood were found in the ruins of Pompeii, and these may well have been the precursors of the many English 'Chequers' pubs.

The same chessboard clarity marked the lay-out of Roman Colchester: a walled-in rectangle, about 3,000 feet long and half as wide, divided by four roads running from east to west, and by seven from north to south, forming 40 *insulae* – apartment houses for 8,000–10,000 people. As you wander through Colchester, imagine that the streets are made of glass, and picture the reflections of the Twentieth Legion, veterans from the Rhineland, settlers from the Mediterranean, shivering in their togas; imagine Miccio, Minuso and Acceptus, potters stamping their names on the vessels they are making for export to the provinces, for at the time this was Colchester's main industry; imagine the traders with their large amphorae full of Falernian wine, fish sauces or olive oil from Greece and Italy; imagine dolphins and sea monsters painstakingly assembled in the beautiful, geometrical mosaic floors of the houses. The rude awakening comes when you find yourself standing in front of a barber's shop called 'Romans', appropriately in Headgate Lane.

Travellers from Londinium would enter the town through Balkerne Gate, which actually consisted of four gates. The main street – roughly corresponding to the present-day High Street – led to the area of the temple. This was no ordinary temple. It was the religious centre of the province of Britannia, dedicated to Claudius, Emperor and God. The imposing steps, the phalanx of Corinthian columns, the coloured, gilded sculptures in the gable – all this fell to ruin when the Romans left the country. Hundreds of years later, the Normans made good use of the favourable location. All around the site of the ruined temple they dug a massive ditch, and they piled the earth over the Roman walls to create a hill, and on this hill, on the very foundations of the Claudius temple, they built the mightiest Norman keep of the age.

Covering an area of 151 by 110 feet, *Colchester Castle* is even bigger than the White Tower in London. The two keeps have a similar ground plan: the dominant feature is the Great Hall, two storeys high; in the second storey is the chapel, with an apse instead of the usual rectangular end of the chancel. The third storey was removed by a 17th century property speculator, for use as building material. All that remains today is the brick shell, robbed of its stone dressing and surrounded by rosebeds, standing like a naked giant in the park. Throughout the Middle Ages until 1629, Colchester Castle was crown property. During the struggle for Magna Carta it was occupied by the barons, King John then won it back, it was the centre of a bitter siege during the Civil War, and finally it became a museum in 1860. Here you will find Roman statuettes, coins and jewellery, Colchester's stone sphinx, a bronze mercury with winged head, urns with carved faces, and burial gifts from more than a thousand Roman graves.

Colchester Castle is history's mausoleum – rubble with herringbone patterns, walls through which no sound could penetrate, not the groans of the prisoners nor the screams of the tortured. Many heretics, both Protestant and Catholic, were executed here – the Colchester Martyrs. On 28 August 1648, when the town fell to Parliamentary forces during the Civil War, the captured Royalist Sir George Lisle was taken into the courtyard to be shot. 'Shoot, Rebels,' he said, 'your shot your shame, our fall our fame.' For twelve weeks Colchester held out against the siege, and so great was the hunger among the 9,000 inhabitants that they killed and ate all their horses, dogs and cats (for any Englishman the worst form of cannibalism). A reminder of the siege is to be found at *Siege House* on East Hill – now a Steak House – where the timberwork still bears the scars of artillery fire.

Behind the Town Hall, but sheltered from the traffic, lies the *Dutch Quarter*: two-storey houses with pointed gables and tasteful extensions. Here in the 16th century Flemish weavers, religious refugees from the Netherlands, came and settled – 500 of them by 1573. They had their own *Dutch Church*, originally St Giles (now the Freemasons' Hall, St John's Green) on the southern outskirts of the town, the first parish priest being Johannes van Miggrode from Veere in Zeeland, who established the parish after his flight in 1563. Soon they also had their own trading centre, *Dutch Bay Hall* at the western end of the High Street, which is now the Corn Exchange, and specialized in 'boi' – a kind of flannel. They rented a watermill, *Bourne Mill*, outside the gates of the town. Originally this was an

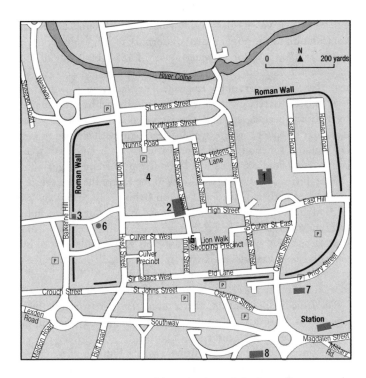

Colchester
1 Colchester Castle
2 Town Hall
3 Balkerne Gate
4 Dutch Quarter
5 Museum
6 Jumbo
7 St Botolph's
   Priory
8 St John's Abbey

aristocrat's fishing lodge, and with its Mannerist gable arabesques, it is the earliest example of the Dutch style in Essex (1591). Later it was used as a grain mill, and is now owned by the National Trust. By 1619, the richest people in Colchester were the Dutch, who worked as agents for merchants in England and Holland, and one of the wealthiest of them all, Sir Isaac Rebow, is commemorated by a baroque monument in St Mary-at-the-Walls. The Flemish immigrants were followed in the early 18th century by Huguenot silk weavers, who also made a substantial contribution to the prosperity of the town. They introduced new varieties of flowers, founded the first horticultural societies in England, and had a lasting influence on the British love of gardening. What had once been the privilege of the aristocracy now became a favourite hobby of ordinary people.

If you wander away from the Dutch Quarter, you'll find yourself confronted again and again by traces of the Romans: a Roman road-surface in the cellar bar of the George Hotel, Roman bricks in the tower of *Holy Trinity* – a fine example of Anglo-Saxon architecture, now a museum of social history. It is believed that the Elizabethan composer John Wilbye (see page 310) is buried here. He ended his days as music teacher to a noblewoman, and lived opposite the church in Trinity Street.

Not far from this medieval lane, on the corner of which are three giant goblets inviting you to slake your thirst in the pub, stands Colchester's new shopping centre, *Culver*

71

Square (1987): with its glass arcades, monumental round arches and gables, it is yet another contribution to the post-modern uniformity of English towns. Of far more interest is the exotic *Jumbo*, a Victorian water-tower of 1882, built out of one and a quarter million bricks and named after the great attraction of London Zoo at the time, an elephant whose name has become part of the language. The watery belly of this particular Jumbo stands on four pillars, discreetly supported by a central one; he is decorated with a frieze, crowned by a dainty pagoda, and has a golden elephant as a not-so-dainty weather vane. Long disused, this water tower – over 105 feet high, with a capacity for 200,000 gallons – has at last found a function befitting its loftiness: it's been taken over by a religious sect and converted to hold 200 souls, all of whom hope thereby 'to get closer to God'.

They form part of a long tradition. At the end of the 11th century, Augustinians founded in Colchester their first monastery on British soil: *St Botolph's Priory*, just a few yards beyond the Roman walls. It's built almost entirely out of flint and Roman bricks (plate 78), and I must confess that few ruins have made such a deep impression on me – above all, the west façade, with its colonnaded doorway and double row of blind arcades, the mighty pillars without capitals, the arches and galleries, all standing like massive rocks, bare and eroded against the sky. In the ruins of St Botolph's lie age-old sarcophagi that demand more respect than the crude graffiti now daubed on them ('Emma is a slag').

The Benedictines also founded a monastery here towards the end of the 11th century. Theirs is in the south of the town, *St John's Abbey*, of which only the gatehouse remains – a fine example of 15th-century flush-work.

The one good thing about Britain, wrote Pliny, is the oysters. For the locals it goes without saying that the Roman gourmet meant the oysters of Colchester. 'The best and nicest,' enthused Defoe, 'though not the largest oysters in England.' In Roman times, the oysters from the Colne Estuary were probably a basic food; in the reign of Elizabeth I they were traded by the barrelful, and today they are the town's speciality. Every year, in the third week of October, the dignitaries and the fishermen hold their oyster feast in the Town Hall.

In summer 1816, John Constable was visiting *Wivenhoe Park*, a country house east of the town; his host, General Francis Slater-Rebow, had commissioned him to paint a panorama of house and park, as was fashionable with the landed gentry of the time, who liked to have a permanent painted record of their estates.[1] Today Constable's painting hangs in Washington's National Gallery, while the General's house is a conference centre for the University of Essex. Instead of the Rebows' cows and sheep, the park is now filled with some 3,000 students. Six residential towers give a rather hard outline to this academic idyll, but what the university (founded in 1962) lacks in architectural glamour, it makes up for with its setting: this is an ideal campus, full of trees and lakes and sports fields.

1 The Georgian brick building of 1758 was extended in Neo-Jacobean style by Thomas Hopper (1846–9). The General also commissioned Constable to paint 'the beautiful little fishing house' – an 18th-century Chinoiserie pleasure-house in neighbouring Alresford ('The Quarters', 1816, now in Melbourne).

John Sell Cotman: St Botolph's Priory, Essex, c.1811

Colchester has little to offer in the way of entertainment, but such a setting should certainly be conducive to study. What are the favourite subjects here on the River Colne, apart from sailing, of course? Electronic engineering, comparative literature, and philosophy. As for Wivenhoe Park, what happened to its last owner? It was Charles Gooch who sold the family home to the University of Essex, and when he did so, he got the architect Raymond Erith to design a new and more comfortable house for him on what remained of the estate. You might have expected Wivenhoe New Park to be a modern building, but far from it. The new house holds fast to the classical ideals of all English country houses, combining practicality with a touch of grandeur. The 1964 building bears a remarkable resemblance to a Veneto villa of the 16th century. It has an attic storey and gable, and a two-storey, arcaded loggia – a Neo-Palladian villa of pink clinker brick, Portland stone and sun-seeking.

Coggeshall: Weavers, Barns and a Beautiful Countess

In the 19th century the farmers of Essex were mocked as the nation's country bumpkins. Essex calves they were called, and the dullest of them all were reputed to be those of *Coggeshall*. They would lower the customs barrier to keep out the smallpox, so the story went. In order to hold back a flood, they would stretch a rope across the field. They would even try to fish the moon out of the River Blackwater, because they thought it was a ball of gold. Such deeds were called Coggeshall jobs by Cockney highbrows, for whom the folk of Coggeshall were a standing joke.

I went there with high hopes, but alas, the people of Coggeshall are no different from anywhere else. The only man who might have restored the Coggeshall reputation was one who burned to death in his own house shortly after he'd arrived: Peter Langan was a legendary restaurateur in London, who used to spoil his guests with gastronomic delights and entertain them by biting their dogs or swallowing cockroaches; he was a Brendan Behan type, whose regular customers included such artists as Bacon and Hockney ('piss-elegant'). Now Langan's in Coggeshall provides the gastronomic delights of the region, but sadly without its eccentric founder.

You'd have thought that a place with a London gourmet restaurant, with sixteen antique shops, over 100 listed buildings and one star-turn half-timbered house would be a readymade tourist trap, but this little town west of Colchester has kept its character remarkably intact. There is a fine asymmetry in the streets that cross the triangular market-place in the town centre. There, in 1887, the people built a weatherboarded tower to celebrate the Golden Jubilee of Queen Victoria, and to tell the time. Near the church is a timber-framed inn, 15th-century, called the Woolpack Inn – a reminder of the town's main industry during the Middle Ages. In those days the weavers' village developed along the Roman Stane Street, which ran from Colchester to St Albans (now the A120), and became one of the textile centres of Essex. The biggest cloth merchant in Coggeshall was Thomas Paycocke, and in 1505 he built himself a magnificent timber-framed house, Paycocke's, in West Street.

With its oriel windows, overhanging upper storey, richly decorated beams and figured portal, Paycocke's is the very model of a medieval timber-framed house (plate 45). But the brick walls are neither original nor authentic. Originally the surfaces between the narrow oak uprights were filled with wattle and daub. 'Hideously overrestored,' was the verdict back in 1944 of James Lees-Milne, an inspector from the National Trust, to which the house now belongs. Much nicer than the face-lifted front is the rear of the house, with its staggered, many-cornered roofs and its little herb garden. There is some superb linenfold panelling in the dining-room, a favourite motif of the English Renaissance.

Sheep-rearing monks provided the basis of the medieval cloth industry, and not only in Essex. Of their Cistercian abbey, founded *c*.1140, on the southern outskirts of Coggeshall very little remains, apart from St Nicholas's (*c*.1225), an early Gothic chapel on the edge of the abbey grounds. The bricks that one can see there and in the abbey ruins by the river are among the earliest examples of post-Roman brick architecture in England. The large barn (see page 77) and a mill were part of the monastic economy. The present-day, very picturesque Abbey Mill is an extensive building with white weatherboards, a red pantile roof, and a golden trout as weather vane. It was built in the early 17th century for fulling and weaving, but after 1840 was used as a grain mill. The last miller is believed to have died in 1947. His father planted a lime-tree for each of his ten children, but the gales of October 1987 destroyed all except three of these beautiful trees.

Halstead, a few miles northwest of Coggeshall, was also a centre for the cloth trade in the Middle Ages. There the materials were delivered by weavers from neighbouring villages, and prepared for export to London, Italy and Portugal, the main markets for Essex. In Halstead, too, there is a watermill once used for cloth-making; it was built at the end of the 18th century, is three storeys high, and has walls of shining white weatherboard. It spans the River Colne like a bridge, with a gigantic warehouse whose square windows stand close together in long, perfectly geometrical rows that are doubled by their reflection in the water. Today, Townsford Mill houses craft and antique shops, and the large working areas are divided up into little studios. Only the façade remains as it was. This was where Samuel Courtauld manufactured his silk, and when the mill closed in 1982, it was – for Halstead – the end of an era.

The Courtaulds were among more than 40,000 Huguenots who emigrated to England when the Edict of Nantes (which granted religious tolerance) was rescinded in 1685. Their rise was exemplary. They began as silversmiths at Spitalfields in London, and then at the end of the 18th century turned to silk manufacture in Essex, where there were plenty of specialist workers left over from the fallow wool industry. In 1825 Samuel Courtauld took over Halstead's weaving mill in Bridge Street and made it into England's foremost silkmill. Halstead Crepe became a byword – indispensable for Victorian funerals. This black silk was also produced by Courtauld's branches in neighbouring Bocking and in Braintree – a town now stifled by traffic. When in 1836 the firm introduced mechanical looms, there were demonstrations akin to those that greet today's attempts at rationalization. Jobs were threatened, but as the *Essex Independent* observed, 'it must be recollected that it is by the perfection of our machinery alone that England can expect to maintain the proud position which she occupies.'

Courtaulds Ltd was for many years England's largest textile firm and the world's leading silk manufacturer. In 1970 it still employed 100,000 people, but by 1989 this had shrunk to 27,000 as a consequence of cheap imports from the Far East. From the Courtauld dynasty came one of the major patrons of the arts in Britain, another Samuel, a great-nephew of the founder, who in 1931 set up the Courtauld Institute of Art in London, donating his magnificent collection of Cézanne, Manet, Degas, van Gogh, Gauguin and other modern masters.

For thirty years, until his death in 1881, the Samuel who founded Courtaulds lived in a country house west of Halstead. Today *Gosfield Hall* is a retirement home, surrounded by a verdant peace and quiet that borders on the eternal. When I visited the house, James Thornhill's ceiling fresco in the entrance hall was in the process of being restored. Sir James Thornhill, Hogarth's father-in-law, was the first British artist to be ennobled (1720). His main works in London are the painted dome of St Paul's (1715–21) and the Painted Hall in Greenwich Hospital (c.1714). Gosfield Hall had once been a much bigger mansion, but all that remains of the mid-16th-century edifice is the Elizabethan west façade; the north side was modernized in the Palladian style (c.1730). France's emigré King Louis XVIII, under the assumed name of Comte de Lille, came to Gosfield Hall in November 1807, as guest of the Marquess of Buckingham. This hospitality was to be the ruin of the generous host, for the refugee king did not come alone: he was accompanied by an entourage of almost 300 hungry souls who were billeted throughout the village. His Majesty stayed until 1809, growing fatter as the Marquess grew thinner.

A beautiful path leads through the fields from Gosfield Hall to the church, and there I found one of the finest baroque sculptures in the county: Michael Rysbrack's 1756 monument to Sir John Knight and his wife Anne (plate 87). The two are seated beside each other like actors playing their last role, and the man has his arm around his wife, who is resting against an antique urn. The pathos of this tableau has been spoilt by the trivia with which it is now surrounded: the Georgian family chapel has become a vestry, and all around the marble monument are irreverent vases, chairs, ladders and bric-a-brac of all kinds.

Thanks to the proximity of Essex to London, some of its small churches contain big names – monuments made by the best sculptors of their time: Flaxman in Hornchurch, Leyton and Hatfield Broad Oak; Chantrey in Bradfield and Wanstead; Nollekens in East Horndon and Chipping Ongar; Roubiliac in Hempstead; Scheemakers in Faulkbourne. But far more characteristic of Essex than its churches and artists are its barns – the cathedrals of the countryside. In *Cressing*, southeast of Braintree, two barns stand in the fields, their steep roofs hanging down like folded wings, and their bulk as massive as dinosaurs. The Cressing Temple Barns once belonged to the Knights Templar, one of the great medieval orders (plate 40). The Knights Templar established their first English settlement here in Essex around 1135 – an estate complete with brewery, dairy, bakery, smithy, a chapel and accommodation for at least two knights and eight servants. Only the barns remain. Their size indicates the wealth of the order, which reached the peak of its power in the late 13th century, with some 9,000 estates and castles in a dozen different kingdoms – a financial empire of the Middle Ages.

The older and smaller of the two barns, the Barley Barn, dates from shortly after 1200, while the Wheat Barn is about fifty years later. Their brick and timber walls, with clay infill (originally plastered), were renewed in about 1520, as were the elm weatherboards of the Barley Barn. For each barn more than 500 oak trees had to be felled. About 70 per cent of the beams in the Wheat Barn are original, and about 50 per cent in the Barley Barn. The roof stands on massive supports and is beautifully structured with rafters, collar-beams and trusses. Both barns have naves and aisles, and so the comparison with cathedrals is not quite so far-fetched as it may seem. For over 700 years, right up until 1985, they were in continuous use for storing corn and hay, or more recently as sheepfolds in winter. Now there's just an old threshing machine in the corner. The last farmer sold house, farm and barns to the county for £300,000. The EC gave a grant of £70,000 for restoration, and now the barns of the Knights Templar are to be used as a museum or a craft centre. A good start was made in summer 1989, with a performance of Bizet's *Carmen* in the Wheat Barn.

In the old days, the church could draw on unlimited resources, and it did not hesitate to do so. Hence the need for large barns. They were called tithe barns, because here the church collected its *tithe*, ten per cent of the food produced – a medieval form of rural income tax. The monks of Coggeshall were the first to build such a tithe barn, the Grange Barn being the oldest surviving one in England, built around 1140 and renovated only once in all that time, at the beginning of the 14th century. It is in fact one of the earliest timber-framed buildings in Europe. It, too, has a nave and side aisles, with rafters and hipped gables – a fascinating space, archaic in effect but also refined in its structure and technically advanced for the age in which it was built. In the sixties it began to disintegrate, and hundreds of thousands of pounds were required to restore it; 75,000 old pantiles were used to re-cover the massive roof. Since 1989 it has been the property of the National Trust, and today it's used for all kinds of functions, from church conferences to art and flower exhibitions.

Essex was once England's granary, and nowhere in East Anglia are there bigger or more impressive barns. Each estate needed one big enough to hold the harvest of a whole year, especially as grain in the Middle Ages was not threshed until winter, as opposed to harvest time. The invention of the combine harvester at the end of the twenties meant that it was no longer necessary to store unthreshed grain, and as more and more smallholdings were absorbed into the larger farms, so many barns became redundant. Today EC-subsidized wheat is stored in concrete silos. In *Widdington* the farmer told me that he found it much easier to manoeuvre his heavy machines inside a corrugated iron shed than between the posts of his monastery barn, and so he had been happy to hand over his unwieldy heirloom to English Heritage. Priors Hall Barn in Widdington is one of the finest medieval barns in Essex, not quite as big as the one in Cressing, but still with its original, well-worn clay floor (not cement, as in Cressing), and with ornately curved beams, typical of 14th-century curvilinear Gothic.

During the Middle Ages, there were at least 1,400 barns in Essex. Of these there are still some 700 in existence, about 40 of them the size of Coggeshall Barn. Before the war, the monumental Tudor barn at Clees Hall in Alphamstone was taken apart and shipped to America, and after this and after the demolition or decay of many other historic barns, the conservationists stepped in to protect these long neglected victims of the agricultural revolution. This anonymous architecture of the countryside is as typical and as historical as the magnificent houses of the aristocracy.

Old barns, however, like all other buildings, can only be preserved if they are used. The most popular method was described long ago by William Morris as the ideal use: 'I would like a house like a big barn, where one ate in one corner, cooked in another corner, slept in a third corner, and in the fourth received one's friends.' Very few modern residential conversions, however, correspond to this medieval ideal of the large, open, timber-framed space that is the essence of a barn. All too often, the space is cut by partition walls, windows are knocked out of the masonry, fanlights break up the roofs. The barn may have been preserved, but it has lost its character. Another popular, and in gastronomical terms pretty ghastly conversion is the Tudor Barn Restaurant. In such places you will usually find coach parties graphically illustrating how, in more than one sense, one can eat like a horse.

There are many other possible uses for these barns, as shown by Mrs Pedley, wife of a furniture manufacturer in *Little Easton*. Her pink manor house next to the village church dates from the early 17th century, but she says that the barn is a lot older. 'We still have the original spiders,' she adds. Virtually every weekend, Mrs Pedley's barn is the setting for a wedding. She also rents it out to cricket and football clubs for their annual dinners, and there are fashion shows, chamber concerts, educational conferences, performances by the Cambridge Opera Company, or by the local amateur dramatic society. The latter is called the Barn Theatre Company, and it continues a great tradition in Little Easton: Lady Warwick's Barn Theatre.

Frances Evelyn, Countess of Warwick, was the last and loveliest blossom of the Maynard dynasty, an eccentric beauty who lived at the turn of the century, mistress of Edward VII, friend of G. B. Shaw, an aristocrat who took up Socialism, fought for reforms in health and education, and made her home into a kind of Labour University. Darling Daisy, as the Prince of Wales called her, was the radiant centre of a circle of artists, writers and radical politicians whom she gathered around her in Easton Lodge.[1] It was a kind of rural salon. Before the First World War, in the years of agricultural depression, Lady Warwick had her huge, crumbling barn converted into a theatre 'to amuse my growing family'. Soon it became the cultural focus of the village. Here people congregated for concerts, balls and whist drives, and in 1913 for the premiere of J. M. Synge's *Tinker's Wedding*, performed by the Dunmow Players. G. B. Shaw was one of the honorary members of this amateur group from the small neighbouring town. Plays were acted in Lady Warwick's Barn Theatre by gaslight, for fun and for charity. When Shaw directed *The Taming of the Shrew* in 1919, he was assisted by Ellen Terry. The famous Shake-spearian actress, who was a frequent visitor to Little Easton, brought some of her actor friends from London to take part in these village productions, and often gave recitations as well as acting.

A famous novelist also developed his thespian talents here: H. G. Wells moved from London in 1912 to take up residence in Darling Daisy's village. He rented the old rectory from Lady Warwick – a large, Georgian house built of brick. Easton Glebe, which remained his principal residence until 1930, had twelve bedrooms, six bathrooms, and its

1   Built in 1755, extended in 1847, northwest of Little Easton. Private.

Frances Evelyn 'Daisy', Countess of Warwick in fancy dress as the Assyrian Queen

own tennis court. Wells enjoyed having guests, and they included Joseph Conrad, Henry James, Somerset Maugham, other authors, publishers, government ministers, and on one occasion Charlie Chaplin. He would spend his weekends there with his wife Jane and their guests, playing bridge and tennis, and charades after dinner; during the week he would stay in his London house in Hampstead with his mistress Rebecca West. It was at Easton Glebe that Wells wrote *Mr Britling Sees It Through* (1916), an autobiographical portrait of a famous author living in the country – in a village called Matching's Easy, unmistakably based on Little Easton.

Today the village has some 200 inhabitants: lawyers, estate agents, insurance agents, TV people. It's a commuter village about 40 miles northeast of London. All very proper and very private. When I left Mrs Pedley, the furniture millionairess, the automatic wrought-iron gates closed behind me. I went across to the village church, and saw the memorial chapel to the beautiful Countess of Warwick. There, in baroque theatrical poses, stand her ancestors, the lifesize marble figures of the Maynards. And Darling Daisy herself is there, the great Edwardian beauty, wearing a plunging neckline, her head raised confidently as she surveys the worshipping world. Her marble bust was sculpted by Sir Edgar Boehm, Queen Victoria's court sculptor. The epitaph is short and sweet: 'Her Angel Face / As the great eye of Heaven shyned bright / And made a sunshine in the Shady Place.'

Death in Witham: Dorothy L. Sayers

What is there to see in *Witham*? Dilapidated shop fronts, and a never-ending main street with a never-ending stream of traffic. A small, noisy, and depressing town. The disaster began with the Romans. They built the road from Colchester to London, now the A12. When it used to take the coach two days to go from London to Harwich, Witham marked the halfway point, where horses were changed. And nothing has altered since. It's still a stopping-off place on the Great Essex Road, ruined by traffic and bad planning. The fact that in the meantime the A12 now goes round it instead of through it has not helped. It still stinks of diesel fumes and fishmeal. *The Times* called it 'Britain's smelliest town'. And yet it was to Witham that one of the greatest of all detective story writers came in 1926: Dorothy L. Sayers (photograph, page 43).

Two yew trees flank her house on the main road, 26 Newland Street,[1] a two-storey terraced house with a grey, Georgian brick façade.[2] Many years ago, an actor who played

---

1 Newland was the new settlement of the Knights Templar, founded c.1210–15, near the older Anglo-Saxon village of Chipping Hill, Witham's second centre.

2 Originally two 15th-century houses which were given a new façade in the early 19th century, as were many of the houses in Witham. This one is made of Gault brick, a sort of yellowish, silver-grey colour (baked out of chalky clay), which replaced the no longer fashionable red brick during the first half of the 19th century.

the part of Lord Peter Wimsey, her aristocratic detective, unveiled a memorial plaque to Dorothy L. Sayers, 'novelist, theologian and Dante scholar'. These last two terms may cause some surprise. 'I am a scholar gone wrong,' is what she used to say of herself. She only wrote detective stories because she needed the money, and when she had enough to live on, she would turn her attention to what she regarded as her 'real' work: great literature, and religion. She was the only child of a parish priest who was also a headmaster in Oxford, and she was one of the first women to take a degree there, in 1915 (at Somerville College, later attended by Margaret Thatcher). She was given her Master of Arts retrospectively, because initially the University did not bestow such degrees on women. Oxford remained her spiritual home – until she went to Witham.

Shortly after her marriage in 1926, she and Oswald Atherton Fleming, known as Mac, a war invalid and former journalist, moved to the grey house in Newland Street. At that time Witham had just 6,000 inhabitants (today, 26,000). In those days, women travelled by rail or by car – unless they were on foot or on horseback. But Dorothy, tall and slim, would ride her motorbike from Witham to London, where she was employed until 1931 writing slogans for an advertising agency, before she was finally able to live on her writing. The best known of the slogans she wrote for Bensons, her employers, was 'Guinness is good for you' – which was actually part of a four-line verse accompanying the picture of a toucan: 'If he can say as you can / Guinness is good for you / How grand to be a Toucan / Just think what Toucan do.'

Her first detective story was published in 1923: *Whose Body?*, beginning a line of thirteen Lord Peter novels. She regarded them as love stories with detective interruptions, but in 1950 they gained her an honorary doctorate of literature from Durham University. Just like her art- and cricket-loving amateur detective whose socks always matched his ties this daughter of an Anglican vicar dabbled in murder purely for intellectual and moral motives. Explanation of the crime, guilt and atonement were more important to her than action. All the tension in these social novels arises from the psychology of the characters and their social relations: Dorothy L. Sayers was the Virginia Woolf of the detective story.

Two of her novels take place in East Anglia: *The Nine Tailors* (1934), the mysterious death of a man in the belfry of a Fenland church (see page 30), and *Busman's Honeymoon* (1938). 'You have no idea,' she once complained to her readers, 'what a strain it is to be perpetually picking out new ways of killing people.' She seemed, however, to have no trouble doing it, and so it came as a shock to her many fans when one day she renounced Lord Peter and indeed the whole art of eccentric crime-fighting. After 1937, during the last twenty years of her life, she never wrote another detective story. The Mistress of Murder now wrote religious plays for the BBC – a series of radio plays on the life of Jesus, called *The Man Born to be King* – and translated some early French epic poetry as well as Dante's *Inferno* and *Purgatorio*. In her view, the Second World War and detective stories could not go together. And yet, one might ask, how could low crime and high church go together?

Here she found no anomaly. She wrote essays about the decline of the detective story, about proper English, and about male arrogance: 'Are Women Human?' 'I am occasionally desired by congenital imbeciles and the editors of magazines to say something about the writing of detective fiction "from the woman's point of view". To such demands, one can only say, "Go away and don't be silly. You might as well ask what is the female angle on an equilateral triangle."'

This sardonic wit always enabled her to cope with men, with her disabled husband, with life in general, and especially with life in Witham. At 26 Newland Street DLS lived so unobtrusively that even Lord Peter would have had difficulty finding out more about her than did her helpless biographers. During the war she kept a few pigs at the back of the house. One of them she called Francis Bacon. Mac, her husband, was the author of a cook-book and an alcoholic, and sometimes she would go over the road with him to the 'Red Lion', one of the old coaching inns. When asked how he would get home, Mr Sayers used to reply: 'By rail' – which meant hanging on to the railings on the way back to No. 26. While she was still writing detective novels, DLS would sometimes go to the nearby chemist's shop 'Stoffer & Hunter' to inquire discreetly about various poisons and their different effects. Her study was on the first floor, with a view onto the street. She often wrote till late at night, usually in the company of Timothy, one of her cats. She had no time for walks along the River Brain. She died in this same house in 1957, but her last resting-place is in St Anne's in Soho. Eternity in Witham would have been too much even for Dorothy.

'Here, where she lived,' says Eileen Bushell, 'nobody is in the least bit interested. I suggested erecting a monument to her in Witham, and got absolutely no support.' Mrs Bushell is a founder-member of the Dorothy L. Sayers Historical and Literary Society. While her literary estate is handled by the University of Illinois, which acquired all her unpublished manuscripts (some 12,000 pages of them), the Society deals with theses about her, as well as the occasional letter from Lord Peter Wimsey to *The Times*. Thus, for instance, we learned on 8 October 1985 that Lord Peter was celebrating his Golden Wedding. For Dorothy's hero and fictional substitute husband had, as everybody knows, finally – in her penultimate novel *Gaudy Night* (1937) – won the hand of the detective story writer Harriet Vane.

A few miles to the northwest of Witham is *Faulkbourne Hall*, standing in the midst of fields and pastureland, unchanged in centuries. Sir John Montgomery, one of Henry VI's knights during the Hundred Years War, had this country house built at some time after 1439. It was well protected against attack thanks to a massive keep at the north-east corner (the east wing dates from 1693, and the Tudor-style west façade from 1832). The present owner of Faulkbourne Hall is a banker – Colonel C. O. W. Parker. Before the Parkers it was owned by the Bullocks, one of whom was an MP, had his portrait painted by Gainsborough, and now lies buried in the little church on the estate itself. When I asked Colonel Parker about the professions of his ancestors, he informed me very succinctly: 'We run things in Essex.' The estate is some 3,000 acres in area – unusually large for such a densely populated county. Traditional crops are wheat and barley, potatoes and sugar beet, more recently joined by rape. How is it possible for a private person to maintain such a huge estate in this difficult day and age? 'We live very simply,' says the Colonel. He would rather do without state subsidies that throw his 40-roomed house open to the public. Only the garden is open on a few days every year. 'The National Trust would hate some of the changes I've made in the house,' he says, 'but after all, I'm the one who has to live here.'

Like the larger and better known Herstmonceaux Castle in Sussex, Faulkbourne Hall is one of the earliest examples of secular brick architecture in England. The decorations on the towers and windows show just how well the builders had mastered the art of brickwork. From Hampton Court, Cardinal Wolsey's palace, to the font in the village church of Chignal Smealey, brick was the most popular building material of the Tudor Age. But nowhere in Essex will you find it in more majestic form than in Layer Marney Tower.

From far and wide you can see the towers of *Layer Marney* rising up out of the fields southwest of Colchester. This massive building is nothing more than a gatehouse, with four corner towers, 82 feet high, taller and mightier than any other gatehouse that you will ever see (colour plate 19). Yet this is just a fragment, the ambitious beginning of a palace that was never completed. The Marneys were a Norman family who had lived in Essex since 1066. In the service of the Tudor kings, one of them rose to the pinnacle of power and honour: Sir Henry Marney, privy councillor to Henry VII and Henry VIII, Keeper of the Seal, head of the royal bodyguard, Sheriff of Essex, Knight of the Garter. The first Lord Marney wished to live in a residence that befitted his mighty status, a country castle with four wings around an inner courtyard. He died, however, in 1523, even before the gatehouse in the centre of the planned north wing had been completed. Two years later, his son John died, too, the last male heir. Layer Marney Tower had become the entrance to a house of the dead.

Two octagonal towers flank the gatehouse at the side of the planned inner court, with eight storeys full of windows, and two large perpendicular windows above the gate itself: towers designed for viewing, not for defence, for the owners wished to see and to be seen. When Layer Marney was begun in 1520, the gatehouse had long since ceased to be a functional fortification, and had become a popular status symbol, rather like a triumphal arch. From the late 14th to well into the 16th century, the supertower was in fashion. Tattershall Castle in Lincolnshire (*c*.1445), Oxburgh Hall in Norfolk (1483), Hadleigh's Deanery Tower in Suffolk (1495), Hampton Court (1514–25), Trinity College, Cambridge (1518–35) – magnificent though they are, they all take second place to Layer Marney Tower, thanks to its size and the beauty of its ornamentation: red Tudor brick with a rhomboid pattern of blue glazed brick; in addition – and this is something quite new – in place of the usual battlements, small, shell-shaped terracotta gables with dolphins, a motif from the Italian Quattrocento. The elaborate window frames in the gatehouse and the Tudor west wing are made of the same honey-coloured terracotta. Around 1510, Pietro Torrigiano (who was responsible for Michelangelo's broken nose and who made the

83

bronze monument to Henry VII and Elizabeth of York in Westminster Abbey, 1509–17) had introduced terracotta into England. Under his direction, or at least in accordance with Italian ways of moulding, an English artist created the terracotta patterns of Layer Marney, one of the very first examples of this form of decoration in Britain.

Unfortunately, the gatehouse does not stand in isolation. While the Tudor style of the west wing is in harmony, the Edwardian extension is certainly not. 'Horrible addition,' noted James Lees-Milne in his diary of 1944 (he was the doyen of English conservationists, a key figure in the National Trust during and after the war, and an informative, amusing and indiscreet diarist in the best Pepys tradition). 'If the place were mine I would pull down practically everything leaving the great perpendicular tower standing in a naked meadow.' Hear, hear, say I.

Nearby stands the parish church of St Mary, with the memorial chapel to the Marneys. Tudor brick and deathly still. On the sarcophagus is the black marble figure of Lord Henry, beneath a princely Renaissance canopy – his last, stone fourposter bed. One of the delights of this little church is the fresco of St Christopher on the north wall, dating from 1520; it was covered over during the Reformation, and rediscovered in 1870. Now it is urgently in need of restoration. The monumental scene is rich in detail. On the bank sits an angler with a large tub; the water teems with fish, and an eel is winding itself around the leg of the holy ferryman, the patron saint of travellers.

I took the hint, and resumed my journey, travelling through the strawberry-jam-fields of Tiptree in the direction of Chelmsford. Lord Marney had not been the only man to dream of a country home in Essex. Henry VIII had a similar plan, and as usual, was in luck. In 1517 he acquired New Hall in *Boreham* from Anne Boleyn's father. This house, northeast of Chelmsford, he then extended into a palace which he liked so much that he rechristened it Beaulieu. His daughter Princess Mary spent part of her childhood there, and the unfortunate Lady Jane Grey also lived there for a short time. Beaulieu was a place of great names and feudal feasts. George Monck, admiral during the Anglo-Dutch wars, created Duke of Albemarle, and immensely rich, entertained his guests on a lavish scale – Cosimo III de Medici came here, and Charles II was a frequent visitor. After the kings and the dukes, it was the moneyed upper class that took over Beaulieu in 1713. The banker Sir Richard Hoare actually bought it for his son, but the latter preferred a smaller, cosier modern place, the nearby Boreham House (1728, altered by Thomas Hopper in 1812, and bought by Henry Ford in 1930; it later became an agricultural college, and since 1981 has been an international training centre for the Ford Company). When New Hall was demolished, apart from its north wing with its impressive row of Elizabethan bay windows, the nuns of the Holy Sepulchre opened a convent school there in 1798. Today, with an ironic twist of history, Henry VIII's country palace is a boarding school for Catholic girls. Red school uniforms rush across green lawns in the shade of giant cedar trees.

Chelmsford is like Witham, but bigger, more depressing, and minus Dorothy L. Sayers. During the summer drought of 1989, aerial photographs revealed traces of a Roman camp on the outskirts of the town, which was probably the first archaeological evidence that Chelmsford was Caesar's base during his conquest of Britain in AD 54. The town was actually called Caesaromagus, 'Caesar's Market', and was administratively well situated halfway along the Roman road between Colchester and London. Since the 13th century it has been the county town, and until the thirties it was a quiet enough place with a weekly market. There were streets full of medieval timber-framed houses and Georgian brick façades, and the town had character and atmosphere. All that changed. In 1899 Marconi had set up the first radio factory in the world, but it was not until much later that industrial development, especially electrical goods, finally took over. At the beginning of the fifties, Chelmsford had 38,000 inhabitants; now it has 140,000. The planning department – if it ever existed – was hopelessly overstretched. In no time the town had been ruined by traffic, shopping centres, and ugly modern buildings.

In such cases, all the disappointed visitor can do is seek out the church. Or is it a cathedral? In 1913 St Mary's was given the status of a cathedral, though it retained the dimensions of a village church. This discrepancy preyed on the ambitious minds of the chapter. But instead of building a new cathedral, as had been done in Liverpool and Coventry, they decked out St Mary's in a bright and breezy barrel vault, a patchwork wall-hanging behind the high altar, and hideous wrought-iron grilles in the side chapels. Chelmsford Cathedral is a true reflection of the town itself – no style and no taste. Take the A414 out of it, and along the coast to Maldon.

Southend: The Costa Cockney

The Colne, the Blackwater, the Crouch, the Roach: these river mouths bite deep into the land, tidal estuaries full of creeks and channels, islands and peninsulas. There's Mersea Island, Foulness Island, Canvey Island, all off a watery maze of a coast, with no cliffs, hardly any hills, alluvial land, dike land, land-under-land, Holland-on-Sea, miles of saltings, flats and sands, sea lavender and oyster beds, curlews and shelducks which congregate every winter in their thousands on Foulness Island. The shallow tidal waters make these Essex marshes into perfect reserves for waders and wild duck. And this almost unspoilt stretch of coast, amazingly, is just an hour's drive away from Hyde Park Corner.

It's also, of course, a coast for sailors. Their ports are Brightlingsea, West Mersea and Tollesbury, Maldon, and Burnham-on-Crouch; their pubs are 'The Jolly Sailor', 'The Nelson', 'The Victory'. Burnham-on-Crouch has two Royal Yacht Clubs, two popular regattas in the summer, and the best fish restaurant on the entire coast – 'The Contented Sole'. But there is no place between the estuaries of the Stour and the Thames where I felt more at home than I did in *Maldon* (colour plate 32). Yet this little port on the Blackwater has no spectacular attractions, no architectural or artistic wonders to behold. It has, however, been spared all the horrors that have made other towns in Essex so unattractive: it has none of the seaside razzmatazz of Southend, none of the test-tube sterility of

Basildon, none of the expanding mediocrity of Chelmsford. For hundreds of years Maldon was the centre of this coastal region, and it is one of the oldest towns in the county. Fortunately, the Great Essex Road passed it by, so that the long arm of London failed to touch it. It has a Gothic church, All Saints, with a unique triangular tower, a 14th-century crypt, and a Washington Window donated by the town of Malden in Massachusetts to commemorate George Washington's great-great-grandfather, the Reverend Lawrence Washington, who is buried here. From this church, the road leads down the High Street to the port. Here too is a church, St Mary's, which dates back to the early Middle Ages. Its tower, with a small white wooden lantern, used to serve as a lighthouse, and is still a landmark for sailors. The quay is called the Hyth, an Anglo-Saxon word for landing-place. There are two riverside pubs, and alongside the quay are two beautiful old wooden ships with rust-brown sails. There used to be hundreds of these barges at Hythe Quay, and in the Blackwater Estuary, and indeed all round the coast of East Anglia: flat-bottomed sailing-boats generally with a crew of one man and one boy. They were ideal for navigating the shallow waters of these east coast estuaries, transporting some 70 to 80 tons of grain, stone, gravel or loam. The experts distinguish between spritties, mulies, boomies and stumpies, while Maldon's little shipyards specialized in stackies, which used to transport whole haystacks inland along the bays. Centuries ago these stackies took straw and fodder for London's horses, and they would return laden with 'London mixture' – manure for the fields of Essex. Today these barges in Maldon and elsewhere are being restored. Every June these beautiful sailing-boats – no fumes, no threat to the environment – come for a grand regatta on the Orwell and on the Blackwater.

Seen from a ship or from the end of the promenade, the town lies before you like a masterly painting: boats in the bend of the river, the little port, the church and the houses on the slopes above the marsh. From Maldon comes England's best table salt. The Maldon Salt Works, founded in 1777, is the only factory in Britain that extracts salt from the sea. It's an old industry. The mysterious Red Hills of Essex (200 hills of red earth, complete with fragments of brick and pottery, on the Colne, Crouch and Blackwater estuaries and on Skipper's and Canvey Island) are probably relics of salt manufacture during the early Iron Age (500 BC – AD 43).

When my hosts at the 'Blue Boar' recommended a visit to St Peter's, I was a little surprised, since all that remains of Maldon's third medieval church is the tower, to which is attached the town's library. But when I climbed up the spiral staircase, I was even more surprised, for here I found the Plume Library: it's a small room, with ten oakwood presses full of old books, the leatherbound survivors of a past culture. This is the almost perfectly preserved private library of a 17th century scholar, and it contains books on theology, astronomy, medicine, history, natural history, classical literature, and travel – almost all of them first editions, including rarities such as Sir Walter Raleigh's *History of the World* (1614), Sir Francis Drake's *The World Encompassed* (1628), John Milton's *Paradise Lost* (1667). The owner of this library was Dr Thomas Plume, born in Maldon in 1630. He studied at Cambridge, took orders, and was Archdeacon of Rochester when he died in

1704. It was he who established the Plumeian Professorship of Experimental Philosophy and Astronomy at his old college, Christ's. He left Maldon at an early age, but never forgot his hometown, and it was to Maldon that he gave his collection of over 5,000 books. The library was accommodated on the first floor over the grammar school which he had built next to the tower of St Peter's for twenty poor children from Maldon. In his will he left 20 shillings a year to provide for new books, little suspecting the effect inflation might have on prices. The Plume Library is England's second oldest public library – a little treasure chamber tucked away in the country.

From Maldon you go along the bank of the Blackwater to *Northey Island*. At ebb-tide you can cross a dam to the island, which is now administered by the National Trust as a nature reserve. In the summer of 991, a fleet of about 90 Viking ships sailed into the mouth of the Blackwater intent on plundering Maldon. They set up camp on Northey Island. On 11 August the battle began. 'Busy were bows / Shields met shaft / Bitter the battle.' When Brithnoth, Earl of Essex, fell, the fate of the East Saxons seemed to be sealed, but Brithwold managed to rally his weakened and exhausted troops: 'Courage shall the harder be, heart the keener / Mind shall be more, as our might grows less.' These much-quoted exhortations are even more powerful and moving in the Anglo-Saxon original: 'Hige sceal the heardra, heorte the cenre, / mod sceal the mare, the ure maegen lytlad.' It is assumed that this famous Anglo-Saxon epic, *The Song of the Battle of Maldon*, was written by an Essex man who fought in the battle. The Vikings were defeated. Now the mudflats off Northey Island resound with the shrill cries of the oyster-catchers, and on the site of the battle – on the bank opposite the island – are marshy fields and Maldon's rubbish tip.

A popular name hereabouts for elderberries is Danes' Blood. It's a sinister reminder of the time of these Viking invasions, when the skins of the heathen plunderers used to be nailed to the church doors in Essex. (The Norman south portal of St Nicholas in Castle Hedingham actually has the macabre name of Skin Door, though in fact it was not 'Daneskin' that was nailed to it, but the skin of a church thief, punished with typical medieval cruelty.) In 894 King Alfred had already repelled a Viking invasion near Mersea Island. But again and again they came in their longships, and twenty-five years after the Battle of Maldon, the Danish King Canute seized the throne. The village of Canewdon was once Canute's camp, set up to defend the River Crouch. The land between the Blackwater and the Crouch lies flat and green on the water, like a giant waterlily. This peninsula is called Dengie Marshes, or Dengie Hundred, because in times of war the local people had to provide 100 men for the Saxon king's army. When Daniel Defoe crossed Dengie Marshes in 1722, he found the area 'both unhealthy and unpleasant', but he also noted that these foul-smelling malaria swamps were good for farming and wild duck. 'For the pleasure of shooting,' rich gentlemen would come here from London, but would often go home with malaria – 'with an Essex ague on their backs, which they find a heavier load than the fowls they have shot.' In the marshlands Defoe often met men who had been widowed several times over and had had up to fifteen wives. The women were from the healthier villages higher up and further inland, and when they came to the marshes, they frequently died within six months. It is said that in 'this dàmp part of the world', in the hinterland of Burnham-on-Crouch, you will find the country homes of those successful entrepreneurs who have taken early retirement from London's underworld. (Strictly private.)

Dengie Marshes: arable and grazing land, fields full of rape and wheat, cows and sheep. On to Tillingham Marshes. On the northern tip of the peninsula, behind *Bradwell-on-Sea* and standing in splendid isolation between marsh and sea, is the chapel of St Cedd. Even the motorized pilgrim of today has to make the last part of this journey on foot, through fields of corn or fields of nothing, depending on the season. There are very few trees, and just a few bushes here. It can be stormy or still, and unless you're in a group of pilgrims or ornithologists, it's always lonely. If you were just out for a walk, you would still sense the spirit of pilgrimage in this desolate spot; the end of the path is like the end of the world, culminating in a humble, holy building: The Chapel of St Peter-on-the-Wall.

The chapel dates from the middle of the 7th century, and stands on walls that are even older, for below lie the ruins of the Roman camp of Othona. This was the only Saxon Shore Fort that the Romans built in Essex, back in the 3rd century, as a defence against Saxon pirates. Its walls were 520 feet long. The eastern wall sank into the sea, and on the western wall, of Roman bricks and rubble, the missionary St Cedd built his church in about 654. At that time it was by no means as isolated as it is today, for it stood in the middle of the Saxon settlement of Ythancaestir. It is one of the most perfectly preserved Anglo-Saxon churches of that time, with a single nave nearly 56 feet long, about 23 feet high, and almost as wide. Like St Pancras in Canterbury, the mission church of St Augustine (early 7th century), St Peter-ad-Murum originally had a chancel with a round apse and a small tower at the western end, which still served as a beacon for sailors in Elizabethan times. From the 17th century until 1920, the chapel was used as a barn (which helped to preserve it). Indeed its position in the midst of these marshy fields is more like that of a barn than that of a church. There is something simple and rustic about it, and yet despite its smallness and its isolation, it radiates a confident power, standing straight and solid like an olden-day prophet in the desert. The interior is without decoration, and the stillness of the stones is permeated with the prayers of centuries. Peasants and bishops have prayed here, fishermen and knights. Even if you have never prayed in your life and have come here only to look, you will not fail to sense the spirituality of the place.

As if the stones of Othona and St Peter were not enough, in 1985 three stones were added to the altar of the chapel: one each from Iona, Lindisfarne and Lastingham. Cedd attended the monastery school in Lindisfarne, Northumbria; his teacher St Aidan came from the Hebridean island of Iona, where the Celtic mission began; and in Lastingham, Yorkshire, Cedd founded a monastery, where he died of the plague in 664, after he had become Bishop of East Saxony in Essex and then Bishop of London.

Behind St Peter's Chapel lies the dyke built along the Dengie coast by a Dutch engineer, and behind this in turn is the salt marsh, or Saltings. Far out in the grey ooze of St Peter's Flat you can see the white glow of the sandbanks. In a copse behind the dyke are a few simple huts built by the Othona Community, and here people from all nations and all branches of Christianity meet in ecumenical celebration of St Cedd. Just two miles further away on the bank of the Blackwater stands St Peter's unholy neighbour, Bradwell Nuclear Power Station, a gas-cooled Magnox Reactor whose monstrous silhouette dominates the landscape. In the mid-eighties, Nirex planned to use this remote corner as a site for nuclear waste, which incensed the people of the peninsula. One member of the anti-nuclear movement was the rector of St Peter's Chapel, the Reverend Paul Booth: 'Anyone who says politics and religion don't mix, has never read the Bible.' The controversial rector has since been replaced, but the protests of the 850 inhabitants of the normally Conservative district of Bradwell were strong enough to earn them at least a temporary reprieve. According to Mary Marten, 'We want to live in Bradwell-on-Sea, not in Bradwell-on-Dump.'

Mrs Marten had invited me to tea. She is a journalist, and with her husband, a Turkish instrument-maker, lives in the most unusual house on the Dengie peninsula. Bradwell Lodge is a small Tudor house with a Georgian south wing, whose interiors are so elegant that Mrs Marten is convinced that none other than Robert Adam had a hand in them. For the original owner had money, taste, and close contact with the best artists of his day. He was the Reverend Henry Bate Dudley, owner and editor of the *Morning Post*, later the *Morning Herald*, playwright, journalist, and enthusiastic huntsman. Once, it is said, he killed a fox on the roof of the church, and twice he fought a duel. The Fighting Parson, later a knight and canon of Ely Cathedral, also drained the marshes on his estate, and commissioned the neoclassical architect John Johnson in 1781 to build the pavilion wing of Bradwell Lodge. There his guests included Gainsborough, Sarah Siddons, David Garrick, and many friends from London. Mrs Marten showed me the oval library, the frieze with rococo scenes by Angelica Kauffmann, painted on marble, and the crowning glory of the house, the belvedere with its panoramic view of the Blackwater, marsh and sea. The idea of the beautiful actress, the Fighting Parson, and his wife all posing for their Gainsborough portraits is part of the legend of houses such as these. The full-length portrait of Sir Henry (c.1780) and that of his wife, Mary White (c.1787) are in the Tate, while that of Sarah Siddons (1785) is in the National Gallery. In 1938, the house was bought by the Labour MP Tom Driberg . 'That sinister character', as Evelyn Waugh called him, was a central figure on the scene of English homosexuality and espionage, and he entertained many well-known guests at Bradwell Lodge, including Archbishop Makarios of Cyprus, and the spy Guy Burgess. Today this little gem of the marshes is in a sad state of decay, with cracks and damp everywhere. Alas, there is no money available for the necessary repairs.

Dengie Marshes – a strange mixture of land and water, farmers and crooks, chapel and nuclear power station. From there I went to *Southend-on-Sea*, which is like jumping from a hot bath into a cold bath. The contrast could hardly be greater. Two hundred years ago, Southend consisted of nothing but a few fishermen's huts. Today it stretches seven miles along the coast, from Leigh-on-Sea in the west to Shoeburyness in the east. George III made bathing fashionable, and Brighton became the resort for the upper classes; whereupon the fishermen on the north bank of the Thames Estuary saw their chance. It all began in the little village of Prittlewell, whose southern end became a seaside resort. It was in this South-end that the stout Caroline of Brunswick, 'Prinny's' unloved princess, took lodgings in 1803 (Royal Terrace, Nos. 7–9). Royal publicity, to be followed by literary. The whole family thoroughly enjoyed their autumn holidays in Southend, declares Mrs Knightley in Jane Austen's *Emma* (1816), and 'never found the least inconvenience from the mud.' Queen Victoria's future Prime Minister Disraeli also enjoyed the sea air here in 1833 (as well as enjoying the company of the beautiful Lady Sykes). By 1848, when the town had some 1,600 inhabitants, the steamer from London came five times a day to Southend Pier (which in those days was made of wood). The day-trippers from the East End would pour out onto the beach, even if they were bathing in grey Thames rather than blue sea. Later they would come in their thousands by train from Liverpool Street, enjoying the only holiday that most of them could afford. Southend became the cockneys' weekend paradise: Greater-London-on-Sea.

Today Southend has 157,000 inhabitants, and is the Essex equivalent of Blackpool – though Essex people would say that Blackpool is the Lancashire equivalent of Southend. From Peter Pan's Playground to the Chamber of Horrors in the replica of Francis Drake's Golden Hind, the place is bursting with tourist attractions: casinos, bingo, snooker, fruit machines, crazy golf, bumper boating ... even the roses along the promenade seem more garish than anywhere else. At weekends in the summer, the beach is as packed as that on Coney Island. I think Simon Carr must have been in Southend when he wrote his peerless description of English beach life in *The Independent*: 'We're good at desks, at dinner-parties, in crush-bars, restaurants and in the clever bits of bourgeois life. But we are no good at beaches. Beaches are fatally revealing. We really shouldn't be allowed on beaches. We haven't got beach bodies, or beach class. We haven't got beach style. We've got beach cricket.'

The nicest part of Southend is where it runs away from itself, far out into the sea: Southend Pier, one and a third miles long, the longest pier in the world. It was begun in 1829, renovated and extended many times, and given its present form in 1889 and 1923. On wrought-iron, Neo-Gothic columns it crosses the front, takes a little run-up, then steps over the water like a giant centipede. What is at the end of this pier? 'Not an awful lot, I'm afraid,' said the cashier at the entrance: 'a snack bar, an amusement arcade, another snack bar, and that's your lot.' Since Southend Pier seems to offer its visitors little but food and drink, one might say it's the longest bar in the world. And since it is so long, it needs an electric railway all of its own to take you to where it all happens – nightlife on three storeys and dozens of pillars, far away from the rest of the world, so that no neighbours can possibly complain about the noise. The dull rumble of the skittle alley mixes romantically with the hissing surge of the waves. Everyone loves this wonderful pier – the anglers, the roller-skaters, the pedestrians, the skittlers, the East Enders, the Southenders, and even the seafaring folk, though it does take them miles out of their way. The armed forces also loved this superpier, for it was naval command headquarters during the Second World War, and a meeting-point for hundreds of convoys.

Despite its popularity, Southend Pier was under threat of demolition during the seventies. Its most vociferous champion was Sir John Betjeman, Poet Laureate and then President of the National Piers Society. This pier, he said, was the only place where one could not be run over and where one could go to sea without getting seasick. Closing it would be like amputating a limb. 'Money doesn't matter,' he proclaimed, to the chagrin of the philistines. 'Beauty matters because beauty lasts.' The powers-that-be – shamed out of their normal vandalism – dipped their hands into their ratepayers' pockets, and shelled out some £3 million to restore their pier. Today there is a society specially devoted to caring for this rusting heritage. Every year it holds a Pier Festival, and once a month it holds meetings at the Palace Hotel (1901) – a building that looms like a giant ship's deck over the promenade (Pevsner calls it 'tasteless').

At one time Southend-on-Pier, London's most easterly suburb, had more than eight million visitors a year. The numbers have now gone down, partly because some Londoners came to stay. Quite a few large firms have moved permanently to Southend, including the headquarters of VAT. It's no longer a town of weekend bathers, commuters and pensioners. At the end of the eighties, George Walker told me about the future: 'The East Enders and the trippers, that's yesterday's world. We're fetching over tomorrow's world from America.' George was a multimillionaire whose father drove a beer-lorry and whose brother was a famous boxer, Billy Walker, the Blond Bomber (whom George managed for a while). He had big plans for Southend, including a holiday park with golf course, supermarket, thousands of holiday flats, a yachting port for 3,000 boats, and an astrodome in neighbouring Basildon, which was to be the biggest indoor sports arena in Europe. When I met him, he had already bought the Westcliff Pavilion, with its variety theatre, and the Kursaal (1902), whose red brick dome on the promenade had come to symbolize 'Amusements' for generations of East Enders. He even bought the pier itself, the very embodiment of Southend and its unending quest for pleasure by the sea. But like so many others, George Walker was riding the dangerous crest of a wave; at the time of writing the trough has almost swallowed him.

Leigh-on-Sea is the most westerly of the three parts of the town, and for a long time it held onto its character as a village of fishermen and shell collectors. But then Southend's planning department drove a new main road straight through the middle, and the old village disappeared. Now it merges seamlessly with *Hadleigh*, and if you follow a path from Hadleigh, you will cross cornfields and pastures on your way up into the hills above the marsh, and here you will come eventually to Hadleigh Castle. Little remains of the edifice which Hubert de Burgh, Earl of Kent, began c.1232 and which was still not completed by 1365. For a time it belonged to the Crown, and Henry VIII gave it to Anne of Cleves – probably aiming to get rid of both of them. Now it's all overgrown. When I was there, an Indian family were picnicking in the court, two fathers were flying their sons' kites, and a young couple were doing handstands. John Constable's dramatic painting of Hadleigh Castle, hanging in the Tate Gallery, bears no resemblance to this disappointing present-day reality. But for Constable the castle was not an end in itself, it was simply the

John Constable: Hadleigh Castle, c.1828–9

setting for something much deeper, an experience which he described after his visit in July 1814: 'the melancholy grandeur of a sea shore.'

The ruin itself is nothing; the view is everything. The windy and often stormy heights of Hadleigh Castle open up a broad and very English scene: the Thames Estuary. You can see the treeless marshes, Two Trees Island, the bay of Hadleigh, the houses and chemical works on Canvey Island, which was once grazing land for sheep and was dyked by Dutch workers under the direction of Joas Croppenbergh, an engineer then resident in London; from this time there remain two octagonal brick houses with thatched roofs, called Dutch Cottages (1618 and 1621). Behind Canvey are the rows of oil tanks at Shell Haven, which was not named after the Shell refineries of the fifties, but after the deposits which from the Middle Ages right up to the 18th century used to be processed into mortar. It's a river landscape and an industrial landscape, reflecting the flow of history. On a clear day you can look eastwards from Hadleigh Castle beyond Southend Pier and far out to sea, and there on the opposite, southern bank you will see the shining oil refineries on the Isle of Grain. But at other times the grey of the Thames and its marshes will merge with the grey of sky and sea, and then Hadleigh Castle stands like a solitary outpost in the grey, an island on an island, history in ruins, the still, sad heart of the past.

Joseph Conrad's *Heart of Darkness* opens with a group of friends waiting in their sailing-boat in the Thames Estuary for the tide to go out. Night falls, and a mist spreads over the marshes of Essex. Marlow begins a story, imagining how the Romans came to this land centuries ago. He visualizes a Mediterranean legionary setting foot on this inhospitable coast: 'Imagine him here – the very end of the world, a sea the colour of lead, a sky the colour of smoke, a kind of ship about as rigid as a concertina – and going up this river with stores, or orders, or what you like.' All this a thousand years before Hadleigh Castle was built. 'Sand-banks, marshes, forests, savages – precious little to eat fit for a civilized man, nothing but Thames water to drink. No Falernian wine here, no going ashore … cold, fog, tempests, disease, exile, and death – death skulking in the air, in the water, in the bush. They must have been dying like flies here.' Night has fallen, and the narrative ends with an evocation of the Thames as it was and indeed still is: 'The offing was barred by a black bank of clouds, and the tranquil waterway leading to the uttermost ends of the earth flowed sombre under an overcast sky – seemed to lead into the heart of an immense darkness.'

Tilbury Fort: 'Let Tyrants Fear'

I'm sorry, but I didn't go to *Basildon*. 'Depressin', bloody depressin' town,' is the description given by one of its inhabitants in Arnold Wesker's play *Beorthel's Hill*, written to commemorate its anniversary in 1989: 'borin', borin', borin'.' Beorthel's Hill was the Anglo-Saxon name for the district, and Wesker's work was a community play, developed and performed by the people themselves. The angelic chorus of amateur actors sings of the founders' Utopian plans: 'This was the dream … From the shadows into sunlight … From the pavements into parklands' – the dream of all the bombed-out East Enders in the over-populated wastes of postwar London. But the planners of Basildon New Town wrecked an existing Utopia, Cockney settlement like Jaywick (see page 65), transplanting the people from their fantastic, improvized dwellings into sterile, modern estates. Tensions rose when, during the eighties, they were joined by refugees from Idi Amin's Uganda, but Basildon has always been a town in search of an identity, in search of human warmth. 'You get used to the violence, you get used to any bloody thing.' No, I didn't go to Basildon.

A few miles away, on the bank of the Thames, stands *Tilbury Fort*. Nearby is a pub called 'World's End', further on are the stacks of a coal-fired power station, and in the marshy fields are a few asthmatic horses. Upriver you can see a phalanx of cranes at Tilbury Docks. And further still, beneath the smoke clouds of another power station, the M25 groans through the Dartford Tunnel, marking the border between Essex and Greater London. Is there a border? Administrators like things to be cut and dried, but it's a cartographical anachronism. With a ceaseless roar the city spreads itself day and night, polluting the air and eating up the land. Gunners of Tilbury, to arms! Defend your Essex,

Tilbury Fort, Water Gate, engraving by H. Adlard after a drawing by George Campion, 1831

fight off the invading Moloch, send these Londoners back from whence they came! But alas, Tilbury Fort has lost its one and only battle long ago.

Here in this dead corner of history, in this bleak industrial landscape east of Barking and Bexley, a picturesque procession floated downriver in August 1988. From Lambeth Palace, Queen Elizabeth I sailed down the Thames in a royal barge to Tilbury. There she stepped on shore and mounted her white horse – Gloriana in silver cuirass over a white silk robe. Crowds of people with cameras and Tudor costumes stood as guard of honour, the TV crew was there, too, and the armada-cum-jubilee reached its climax. 'Let tyrants fear,' cried the royal impersonator, addressing the multitude, and strengthening their resolve for the forthcoming battle against the approaching Spanish Armada: 'I know I have the body of a weak and feeble woman, but I have the heart and stomach of a King – aye – and of a King of England too, and think foul scorn that Parma[1] or Spain or any prince of Europe should dare to invade the borders of my realm.' It was a great speech, an inspiring speech, a highlight of English history and of the heritage industry. Many in the crowd thought of the Falklands and Maggie Thatcher, and their hearts beat a little faster. But all may not be quite

1   The Duke of Parma was waiting with his army on the Dutch coast, choosing his moment to join the invading forces of Philip II.

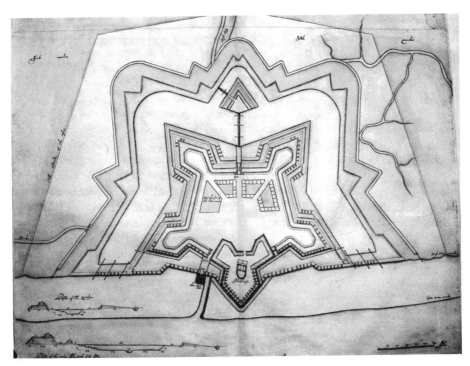

Tilbury Fort, ground plan by Sir Bernard de Gomme, 24 October 1670

as it seems. Historians are not convinced of the authenticity of these words, for they did not appear in print until 1654 – sixty-six years after the event – and contemporary historians made no mention of them. All that we do know for sure is that on 8 August 1588, when the Armada had already been repulsed though the danger was not yet over, Elizabeth I addressed her troops at West Tilbury, not far from the fortress of her father, Henry VIII.

A hundred years later, there was the threat of another invasion, this time by a Franco-Dutch fleet. The Dutch had already forced their way into the Thames Estuary more than once; in July 1667 they had got as far as East Tilbury, and destroyed the parsonage and part of the church. Now, in 1670, Charles II commissioned his chief engineer, Sir Bernard de Gomme – a Dutchman living in London – to design a new fort at Tilbury, incorporating all the latest developments in defensive techniques. At that time, it was artillery that had become the most important weapon, and so Sir Bernard made his fortress as flat as possible, with large underground stores of ammunition. Tilbury Fort is a pentagon, with star-shaped projecting bastions, earthwork walls reinforced with brick, and a double moat. In times of danger, the surrounding marshland could be flooded.

Sir Bernard's builders had to ram some 3,000 stakes into the soft ground to make the foundations secure. By 1683 it was ready, but it was never to hear a shot fired in anger. Such buildings were great deterrents. Tilbury Fort is the best preserved example of British military architecture from that period, along with the royal citadel in Plymouth.

To enter the fort, you have to cross a reconstructed drawbridge. On the broad cobblestone parade-ground are a few mortars and gun-carriages. There is an aura of tedium and futility about it all. The former officers' quarters contain a rather sad museum of gasmasks, medals, guns, grenades, and similar memorabilia. The Water Gate leading to the Thames stands like a kind of triumphal arch, with stone trophies carved into its gable; it was built as the façade of the guardhouse, on the lines of a baroque Dutch gatehouse. On the other side of the river, which narrows here, lay the batteries of Gravesend, directly opposite Tilbury's cannons. This was the Thames's first line of defence before London, and right up until the First World War a garrison was maintained here. Indeed it was then that Tilbury scored its one and only hit: a German Zeppelin succumbed to the flak.

In autumn 1776, however, there was bloodshed in Tilbury Fort. A cricket match between teams from Kent and Essex led to a fierce dispute. The men of Kent stormed the fort and seized some weapons. The result was two dead. It was definitely not cricket.

William Morris of Walthamstow: News From Nowhere

It's 1880, and the unfiltered sulphurous smoke is belching forth from factory chimneys. A man is travelling through England giving lectures on 'The Beauty of Life'. A madman? A cynic? An idealist? He fulminates against factory owners who call themselves patrons of the arts, and yet do nothing to stop the pollution of the air, and allow their profits to turn beautiful rivers into sewers. He decries the demolition of historic houses, warning that out of such brutality will new brutality grow. He is appalled by the rising tide of posters that deface the towns, and suggests that customers refuse to buy the products so advertised. His voice rings out loud and clear in the midst of the Victorians' economic miracle. He exhorts builders to save the trees on their building sites and to fit the house around the trees, for they are treasures to be preserved. A one-man Green Party in 1880.

The lecture became a kind of creed for the ecological movement that made its way around all the Anglo-Saxon and Scandinavian countries at the end of the 19th century. The author was the most versatile, most contradictory, most modern English artist of his time: William Morris, who came 'not from Heaven, but from Essex'. The Earthly Paradise where he grew up is now London E17. The village of his childhood, *Walthamstow*, has been swallowed up by Greater London, and the house where he was born – Elm House in Clay Hill – has been torn down. His father was a stockbroker, and he was the third of nine children. When he was born, in 1834, Walthamstow was still part of Essex, on the edge of Epping Forest and surrounded by pastureland: 'Scarcely anything but a few sheds and cots for the men who come to look after the great herds of cattle ... It does not make a bad holiday to get a quiet pony and ride about there of a sunny afternoon in autumn, and look over the river and the craft passing up and down.' This is how he describes the landscape of his childhood days, on the River Lea, in his Utopian novel *News from Nowhere*. He himself lived through the period of change, when the Victorian housing boom hit Walthamstow and turned a suburb of villas into a working-class slum: 'once a pleasant place enough, but now terribly cocknified and choked up by the jerry builder.'

Today the two-storey Victorian terrace houses of Walthamstow are homes to many artists, writers and media people, who cannot afford the top 'yuppie' areas like Islington and Chiswick. Morris would have difficulty now in recognizing the old village centre around St Mary's, the church in the village (where there is a monument to Sir Thomas and Lady Merry, 1633, by the Jacobean court sculptor Nicholas Stone). In the chapel at his old school, Forest School, he would now find only one of the three stained glass windows which his firm Morris & Co made for it in 1875: Samuel and Timothy, in the northern transept. He would also see Edward Burne-Jones's original designs for the David and Jonathan window, destroyed by a bomb in 1944. (The hospital chapel in neighbouring Ilford, however, does still contain stained glass windows by Morris & Co, designed by Burne-Jones in 1891.) All Walthamstow's Georgian houses along Forest Road have now disappeared, with one exception: his parents' home. Water House stands at the edge of a park on the A503 – an impressive clinker brick building, mid-18th-century, with two projecting bays and three storeys. The Morris family moved there in 1848, when William went to Marlborough. Today Water House is the William Morris Gallery, exhibiting his ideas and his products. There is no better place to get to know both the man and his time.

William Morris was a person who loved beauty above all else – beautiful houses, beautiful books, beautiful art. He was an aesthete who prized handicraft and hated machines, a poet who dreamed of the Middle Ages and fought for a new society, a revolutionary and a shareholder, a businessman and a socialist. He promoted art for all, but very few could afford his products. He longed to help the poor, but spent all his life 'ministering to the swinish luxury of the rich'. When he died in 1896, an obituary offered this praise: 'Strike him where you would, he rang true.'

Morris was a Victorian Renaissance man: he was a painter and poet, wrote verses, fantasies, aesthetic and political pamphlets, translated *The Odyssey*, *Beowulf* and various Icelandic sagas, demonstrated in streets and market squares, edited and financed the first socialist weekly in England, designed church windows, fabrics, carpets and wallpaper, dyed, wove and printed – there was very little that he couldn't do, and even less that he didn't try. 'If a chap cant compose an epic poem while he's weaving tapistry he had better shut up, he'll never do any good at all' (Morris's spellings).

He could never sit still at table. He always had to be doing something. He could get so worked up in a discussion that he would bite the table; he would sometimes kick doors open; if he didn't like the food, he sometimes threw it out of the window. Are these the manners you would have expected in the house of an ethereal Pre-Raphaelite? Here there was love and passion aplenty. Jane, his wife, daughter of a farm-hand, had a melancholy beauty – Shaw said it was as if she had emerged from an Egyptian tomb in Luxor – and she divided her life between her unloved husband and her neurotic lover Rossetti, whose wife Elizabeth Siddal committed suicide. Morris himself fell in love with Georgiana, wife of his friend Burne-Jones. There was a lot going on behind these respectable Victorian façades.

Morris was from the upper middle class. His father died when he was still a boy but left him a small fortune in copper shares. He grew up in what he called 'rich establishmentarian puritanism' – a bourgeois artist who cultivated the image of a manual worker. He usually wore a crumpled blue suit or overalls, his hands and clothes were always covered in paint, and over his mane of hair he wore a round proletarian hat. The things that most influenced the young Morris were the idyllic landscape of Epping Forest (see page 102ff.), where he grew up, the old manuscripts in the Bodleian Library at Oxford, where he studied theology with Burne-Jones, Carlyle's work ethic, Ruskin's apotheosis of the Gothic style, and the sight of French cathedrals. But the most decisive influence of all was the reality of English industrial society.

In 1856 Morris and Burne-Jones took a flat in London together. When they came to furnish it, they couldn't find anything they really liked, and so they made their own furniture. A few years later, Morris got the architect Philip Webb to design a house for

The M's at Ems (= the Morrises) by Dante Gabriel Rossetti, 1869

William Morris, pencil sketch by
Dante Gabriel Rossetti,
c.1856–7, study for King David,
Llandaff Cathedral

him, and his Pre-Raphaelite friends furnished and decorated it: this was the famous Red House in Bexleyheath, Kent, an oasis of beauty in the desert of Victorian taste 'Have nothing in your houses that you do not know to be helpful, or believe to be beautiful,' he declared – a maxim of Morris's which applies as much today as it did then.

He was quick to recognize the dictatorial power of the manufacturer and the helplessness of the consumer: 'goods are forced on him by their cheapness, and with them a certain kind of life which that energetic, that aggressive cheapness determines for him.' In order to counter the effects of mass production and mass taste, he founded the firm of Morris & Co in 1861. His employees were called 'fine art workmen', in keeping with the medieval image of the artist as worker and the worker as artist. It was the same ethos invoked by Gropius in his Bauhaus manifesto of 1919: 'Architects, sculptors, painters, we must all return to handicraft.'

At Morris & Co you could order virtually anything from an iron bedstead to a church window: tiles, wallpaper, carpets, embroidery, fabrics, furniture, kitchen utensils ... Soon it became fashionable to have your house and salon furnished by Morris & Co; orders came in even from St James's Palace. The lines were elegant, the colours glowed, and all over England there were stylized tulips, acanthus, jasmine – Blooms from Nowhere. This is the Morris we all know: the flowery fabrics and wallpapers that are still in production even today. You can buy them at Liberty's and at Sanderson's in London, even if they are the dearest wallpapers in Europe. Beauty can't be cheap, Morris used to say, and yet did he not

99

also say: 'What business have we with art at all unless all can share it?' Was it not Morris who wanted art 'which is to be made by the people and for the people', with better working and living conditions for all? And was this to be the outcome: art for the palace and promises for the poor?

In the year when Marx died, 1883, Morris attended a revolutionary cell of the socialist movement, the Democratic Federation. One year later he became co-founder of the Socialist League. He sold the party newspaper himself on the streets, went on lecture tours and held protest meetings, wrote political songs of battle, paid the fines of comrades who had been arrested, and was himself found guilty of taking part in an illegal demonstration, though the fine was merely token – preferential treatment for the socialist who was rich enough not to need socialism.

'There is no salvation for the unemployed,' he wrote, 'but in the general combination of the workers.' Not since the Communard Courbet had any artist been so politically engaged as Morris. He distrusted Parliament and its reforms, and was equally sceptical of the Fabian Society's subversive tactics. 'My belief is that the old order can only be overthrown by force; and for that reason it is all the more necessary that the revolution should be, not an ignorant, but an intelligent revolution.' After all, he didn't want Morris & Co's stained glass windows to be smashed.

His party colleagues must certainly have gazed in some astonishment at this socialist capitalist, who ran a high-class shop in Oxford Street, and decorated so beautifully the houses of the very people he attacked so vehemently. Friedrich Engels called him a 'settled, sentimental socialist'; his workers had little share in decision-making or in profits. Since, surely it was better that the manufacturer use those profits 'to further a revolution of the basis of society'. So much for the conscience of the socialist/capitalist.

When revolution is a long way away, you need Utopia. In 1890 Morris's *News from Nowhere* was published – a Utopian novel about the perfect Communist society. He set it in 1952, when at last England had succumbed to the Revolution: there was no more private property, no finance, no prison, no alienating labour; Trafalgar Square was an orchard, Parliament a dungheap, and scholars emerged from Oxford to do their little bit in gathering in the harvest.

News of *News from Nowhere* spread over the continent. Though it has little relevance for socialists today – the philosopher Ernst Bloch described the novel as 'a naive and sentimental mishmash of Neo-Gothic and Revolution' – the moralist and ecologist Morris that has been rediscovered for our time – a precursor of Friends of the Earth, a prophet of the environmental crisis, who more than 100 years ago asked his audience in Oxford: 'What kind of an account shall we be able to give to those who come after us of our dealings with the earth, which our forefathers handed down to us still beautiful?'

In 1890 Morris founded the Kelmscott Press. During the six years up till his death he designed and printed hundreds of title pages, initials and decorations, creating some of the most beautiful books of the 19th century, in particular the Chaucer edition illustrated by Burne-Jones. Was this the retreat into the ivory tower, revolt followed by resignation?

Should we point out, as one critic did, that the Kelmscott Chaucer cost just about as much as a miner would earn in six months down in the copper mines of Devon, the source of Morris's capital? Well, why shouldn't a socialist also be a bibliophile? It's just a pity that Morris did not attempt to illuminate Marx and give us a Kelmscott Kapital.

Morris, it must be stressed, was no ideologist. He never believed that the world could be saved through any one system. Even as a socialist, he always remained primarily an artist. This is what distinguishes him from those socialist artists whose unfortunate hybrid products masqueraded as Art for the People. In his 1894 essay 'How I Became a Socialist', he wrote that the dominant passion in his life was the 'desire to produce beautiful things'. When he died, two years later, he had designed over 500 patterns for fabrics, wallpaper and carpets, had worked on more than 500 stained glass windows, and had made over 600 designs for his press; he had published seven volumes of poetry and four fantasy tales, and had held over 250 lectures.

'Imagine,' he wrote to a friend in 1874, 'but look, suppose people lived in little communities among gardens & green fields, so that you could be in the country in 5 minutes walk, & had few wants, almost no furniture for instance, & no servants, & studied the (difficult) arts of enjoying life, & finding out what they really wanted: then I think one might hope civilization had really begun.'

What a life, and what a fascinating body of work. Walthamstow has finally done it

William Morris: designs for textiles and wall-paper (left: tulip 1885; right: willow, 1887)

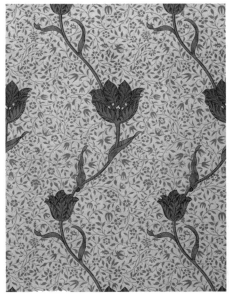

justice with a full refurbishment of the William Morris Gallery. The collection is not confined to Morris's work, but also includes that of his friends and contemporaries: there are pictures by the Pre-Raphaelites Burne-Jones, Rossetti and Ford Madox Brown; furniture by George Jack, who was so enamoured of marquetry; William de Morgan's tiles and dishes with their coloured glazing; works by C. F. A. Voysey, Walter Crane, and Frank Brangwyn; architectural and wallpaper designs by Arthur Mackmurdo, one of the great English designers, on a par with Morris – the London Savoy Hotel is his work (1889), and also some houses in Wickham Bishops, Essex. This is the only permanent exhibition of the Arts and Crafts Movement in Britain – one of the few movements in European art that found England at the forefront.

Epping Forest: How Even Royal Wood Can Shrink

It takes about 40 minutes on the Underground (Central Line) to get from Oxford Circus to the edge of *Epping Forest*. From 1840 to 1848 the Morris family lived in Woodford, a Georgian suburb of London, and as a child William rode his pony through the forest to his school in Walthamstow. Among the hornbeam thickets he saw the leaves and flowers which he later turned into stylized patterns for his tapestries and wallpapers. Epping Forest was his childhood paradise.

As London's suburbs gradually pushed deeper and deeper into the ancient forest, Morris wrote a letter to the *Daily Chronicle* on 23 April 1895, appealing for this paradise to be saved: 'the greatest possible care should be taken that not a single tree should be felled, unless it were necessary for the growth of its fellows ... We want a thicket, not a park from Epping Forest. In short a great and practically irreparable mistake will be made, if under the shelter of the opinion of experts, from mere carelessness and thoughtlessness, we let the matter slip out of the hands of the thoughtful part of the public; the essential character of one of the greatest ornaments of London will disappear, & no one will have even a sample left to show what the great north-eastern forest was like.'

In the early Middle Ages, the Forest of Essex, as it used to be known, came into the possession of the Crown. It was administered by the monks of Waltham Abbey. Until the middle of the 17th century, it covered an area of some 60,000 acres, reaching southwards to what is now West Ham, Barking and Ilford, and northwards as far as Roydon and Harlow. After the Civil War, many trees were felled to make warships, and by 1777 the Royal Forest had already shrunk to 12,000 acres. In the early 19th century, London's East Enders used to go out into the forest in their donkey-carts, and later they travelled by rail. On 6 May 1882 Queen Victoria declared that it was 'for the enjoyment of my people for ever.' In the meantime, the City of London had acquired it from the Crown and from various other landowners, and a law had been passed in 1878 prohibiting private use. But the forest was now under greater threat from the public hand than ever before, as is evident from the campaign waged by Morris and his friends. The ever expanding metropolis has gone on planting its houses and its roads in place of the royal trees, and now all that remains is a mere 6,000 acres.

Considering how near it is to London, the forest is remarkably well preserved, no doubt thanks in part to its status since 1953 as a Site of Special Scientific Interest. One very special feature is its hornbeams – trees with short, thick trunks that divide up into several tall, thin ones. The lightness of these woods, with their strange, elephant-grey trees, is the result of a particular technique of forestry going back to the Middle Ages: every four to six years, the trees are capped at a height of about six feet; the method is known as 'pollarding', and the wood is used as firewood. Today the trees are simply thinned out in order to retain the natural balance, and not for any practical purpose. Apart from the hornbeams, Epping Forest has an abundance of oak and birch, maple and ash.

It is not, however, a forest pure and simple. Originally the term Royal Forest denoted any royal hunting grounds, whether they were woods or fields, moorland or heath. One third of Epping Forest is actually pastureland. The royal hunting element is represented by Queen Elizabeth's Hunting Lodge, on the A1069 outside Chingford. This is a tall, three-storey, timber-framed house, a 'Greate Standinge', whose two upper storeys were originally open as a platform for the royal hunting party. Boar and red deer were driven towards this raised hide-away, from which the royal guns could fire down at them – a spectacle hardly worthy of the term 'hunting'. In 1602, however, a courtier remarked approvingly on the condition of the 69-year-old Queen Elizabeth I that she 'hunteth every second or third day, for the most part on horseback, and showeth little decay in ability.' The lodge bearing her name was in fact built by her father, Henry VIII, in 1543. The very best joiners used the very thickest timbers to accommodate the very greatest huntsman. Today, much restored and reconstructed, the lodge houses the Epping Forest Museum.

Writers also loved the old Royal Forest. When *Chigwell* was still a village, 'such an out of the way rural place,' Dickens used the 'King's Head', a Tudor inn, as a model for his 'Maypole Inn' in *Barnaby Rudge*: 'An old building, with more gable ends than a lazy man would care to count on a sunny day.' Only High Beech, where Lord Tennyson lived from 1837 to 1840, has retained the original character of an Epping Forest village. When Sir Arthur Blomfield built the Neo-Gothic parish church in 1873, the landscape was open heath. Today the little church is surrounded by tall trees and a romantic Victorian graveyard. Pubs in the forest bear such names as 'The Woodman', 'The Green Man', or 'Robin Hood', but no matter where you are, among beermugs or beech-trees, you will still hear the roar of the A104 going to and from London. For hundreds of years the road through Epping Forest to Cambridge was very dangerous. It was here that the notorious highwayman Dick Turpin plied his trade, until he was hanged as a horse-thief in 1739. The village of Epping grew up alongside this road, and by 1800 there were no fewer than 26 inns for the stagecoaches to stop at. Today it's a small town between the M11 and the M25, with a red brick Victorian water tower as its main landmark.

When in 1983 the M25 was being laid out southwest of Epping – to much local protest – it was not only at the expense of yet another stretch of forest, but it also sliced through the middle of the old, landscaped park of *Copped Hall* (plate 44). One year later, the rest of the park was placed under a preservation order. The house itself burned down in 1917, though one section survived and was inhabited until the Second World War. Since then, one of the great historic country estates in Essex has drifted inexorably into sad decay.

For a while, the Copped Hall estate belonged to Mary Tudor; it then passed to Elizabeth I, and then to the royal treasurer, Sir Thomas Heneage, who had a magnificent mansion built in 1568. Later the Earl of Middlesex received royal visitors there, including Charles II, James II, and William III. In the middle of the 18th century, the Tudor mansion was demolished and replaced by a Georgian building, designed by John Sanderson. Another hundred years passed, and the estate was acquired by a Victorian railway magnate, one of whose children, Ernest James Wythes, had the house extended and between 1883 and 1905 laid out the gardens for which Copped Hall became famous. They are formal gardens in Italian and Flemish style, with geometrical beds, parterres and balustraded terraces, obelisks, classical statues, and two incomparable Renaissance pavilions. The architect of this horticultural masterpiece was Charles Eamer Kempe, better known as a designer of stained glass windows. The gardens of Copped Hall were a virtuoso finale to the splendour and the sheer glamour of Edwardian society. But then, one Sunday in May 1917, there was a short circuit, and the house went up in flames. The heat was so intense that several days later, corks could still be heard popping in the wine cellar – strange music for the darkest days of the First World War.

Now the white Georgian shell is covered in graffiti. Neoclassical gable reliefs are a reminder of past glories, but the beautiful Edwardian gardens are overgrown, and the sculptures and most of the architectural features have long since been dismantled and sold. Between the trees and the stinging nettles, however, you can still see the two shining pavilions with their nymphs, satyrs and obelisks. Only Sleeping Beauty doesn't live here any more. 'A few years ago the pavilions still had their roofs,' I was told, 'but now it's all vandalized.' All too late SAVE Britain's Heritage recognized the seriousness of the situation – but the situation is not even serious: it's a scandal. For years the local people have tried in vain to rescue these ruins, and when I was there, a new hope had emerged. Copped Hall had been bought by a hotelier. If he can save the garden, he will have done the world a service. And if he celebrates such an event with a gala concert, he could do worse than invite one of his neighbours who lives on the estate: the pop-singer Rod Stewart.

Hill Hall is another burnt-out house that stood for many years all forlorn among the hills southeast of Epping. An Elizabethan scholar began it in 1557 – Sir Thomas Smith, Professor at Cambridge, Orleans and Padua, MP, and Elizabeth I's ambassador to Paris. The tombs of the Smith family are in the chancel of the little Jacobean brick church (1611–14) on the edge of the park. When I visited the house in the hills, there were two gigantic cedars lying uprooted in the park, two of the 15 million trees destroyed by the gales of October 1987. A watchman with four Rottweilers ('Be careful, they haven't had any breakfast') took me through the ruins. The walls of the inner courtyard are decorated with Tuscan and Ionic columns, and a Polish restorer was then working on a cycle of monumental murals dating from 1570 – tapestry style scenes with Raphaelesque motifs. After the war, Hill Hall became the most exclusive women's prison in the whole penal system, one of its most prominent guests being Christine Keeler. Today the house is being restored by English Heritage for use as a home for retired people.

Hatfield Forest also used to be part of the great Essex Forest; until 1446 it was a royal hunting-ground, and with its bridle paths, woodlands and game reserves it has retained far more of its original character than the larger, more popular Epping Forest to the south. Here too, in the open fields, are those typical hornbeams, pollarded down through the centuries – age-old trunks crowned with fresh, fine foliage. In his book *The Last Forest*, the Cambridge countryside historian Oliver Rackham describes this truly royal forest as the perfect ecological system, and as 'the only place where one can step back into the Middle Ages to see, with only a small effort of the imagination, what a forest looked like in use.' In the middle of the 15th century, the community of Hatfield contained eleven brewers, eight bakers, four butchers, two fishmongers, and one official hermit. Since 1924 the National Trust has been in charge of the remaining thousand or so acres of Hatfield Forest.

There are wild roses blooming on the edge of these woods, but above the treetops the birds have given way to airborne technology. Just one mile away from Hatfield Forest lies *Stansted Airport*, designed in the mid-eighties by Norman Foster. He is the minimalist among present-day British architects, and his passenger terminal is a large hall with steel scaffolding and a glass roof, light and airy and a brilliant feat of engineering. With Heathrow and Gatwick now bursting at the seams, Stansted is expanding, despite years of protest from the environmentalists. The airport administrators promised to preserve certain rare orchids in a special reservation – a token, not to say cynical, gesture when set against the pollution and overdevelopment with which Stansted Airport now threatens the very existence of England's last royal forest.

Going to Church: The Grave of John Locke

Once upon a time there was a carpenter in Somerset who dug a black crucifix out of a hill. The landowner, Earl Tovi the Proud, standard-bearer to King Canute, had the flint cross loaded onto a cart and taken by twelve red oxen and twelve white cows to his estate in Essex. Where his team halted, he founded *Waltham*, the 'settlement in the woods', and there he built a church. And because this black cross was soon found to have wondrous healing powers, the place became known as Waltham Holy Cross.

This all happened around 1030, and like many such stories, it may simply be a legend. But what is not legend is that around 1060, Harold, son-in-law to Edward the Confessor, built the first monastery of the Holy Cross in Waltham. From there, it is said, he went on to the Battle of Hastings. With a battle cry of 'Holy Cross' his Anglo-Saxon troops threw themselves upon the Norman invaders. Tradition has it that Harold's mistress, Eadgyth of the Swan Neck, brought his body back to Waltham Holy Cross, and in the garden there is a memorial stone where the high altar once stood, behind which the King is believed to have been buried: 'Harold Infelix' – Harold the Unfortunate. The last Anglo-Saxon king, buried in a Norman abbey: the smooth continuity of English history, though Harold would certainly not have appreciated it.

Waltham Abbey's prime period began under Henry II. As part of his penance for the murder of Thomas Becket, the King set up a new, much bigger monastery in 1177, which he raised to the status of a mitred abbey in 1184: this meant that the abbot had the rank of bishop, was given a seat in Parliament, and was subject only to the Pope and the King himself. This Augustinian abbey became one of the richest and most influential in the country, and the Holy Cross was a popular goal for pilgrimages. In the Middle Ages, when English kings went hunting in Epping Forest, which was then called Waltham Forest, they often stopped at the monastery. Waltham Holy Cross was Henry VIII's favourite abbey, and was the last of the 600 monasteries to be dissolved in the Reformation. Thomas Cranmer, later Archbishop of Canterbury, was a tutor here, and Henry VIII came to seek his advice. But some time after 1540, the legendary Cross disappeared, and the abbey church is now only a shadow of its former self. Apart from the seven bays of its original Norman nave, nothing remains. Before this demolition, it had been 370 feet long – four times the length of what has survived. In 1556 the stones of the former east tower were used to support the walls of a new west tower, famous for the sound of its thirteen bells.

Even at a second glance, the interior of this now stunted church remains a kind of hybrid: here you have the simple, powerful Norman arcades, the cylindrical columns with their carved spiral and zigzag patterns, a succinct language of form; and there you have the elaborate decorations of the Victorian east wall and the garishly painted ceiling (plate 83). The Victorian Romanesque was the work of the young William Burges in 1859–60. Using the ceiling of Peterborough Cathedral as his model, he designed the flat oak ceiling of the nave, which was then painted by Poynter: there are the four elements, the signs of the zodiac, labours of the month and, at the eastern end, allegories of the past and the future. Burges used the Norman crossing arch of the former tower as a frame, in order to give the church a new east end. Above the relief on the back wall of the altar glow the stained glass windows by Edward Burne-Jones – three lancets with the Tree of Jesse in the centre, Adam and Eve on the left, and Old Testament prophets on the right, with gloriously bright flowers. Above is a large rose window: Christ on a rainbow in the centre, surrounded by angels playing music; the roundels depict the seven days of Creation, in blue, green and dark red. Here Burne-Jones's designs (1861) were executed by Powell & Sons, and not by Morris & Co.

In the northern side aisle there is a magnificent 17th-century baroque sarcophagus. In death Robert Smith repeats what he was in life, captain and owner of a merchant ship. The marble relief of 'Industria', the allegory of hard work under full sail, is framed by a border of nautical instruments, with the heads of winged cherubs at the corners; the whole thing is so exquisitely sculpted that some people attribute it to none other than Grinling Gibbons. In much simpler, more direct fashion, though with a degree of Elizabethan theatricality, Sir Edward Denny and his family took leave of the world in 1600: Sir Edward lies there in full armour, his head on his hand, his mailed fist gripping the hilt of his sword which he wielded in Ireland in service of Elizabeth I; one level below is his wife, in similar pose; and below them both on the predella are their ten children at prayer – seven boys and three girls (plate 88). The tomb is a model tribute both to faith and to large families. The Lady Chapel, which was added to the southern aisle of the Norman church in the early 14th century, was used as a school and storehouse after the Reformation, while the crypt was used as a prison. When the plaster was removed from the walls, there emerged a monumental 15th century fresco of the Last Judgment.

Since the Reformation, Waltham Abbey has been without an abbey. For a long time it languished as a small, unimportant market town, and today it is a popular commuter area outside the gates of London, the centre of a landscape covered in glass – the greenhouses where the flowers and vegetables of Lea Valley grow.

Of all the churches in Essex, Waltham Abbey still stands supreme, but there are many other beautiful churches to be seen in the villages – most of them built of timber, since there is precious little stone in this county – and of all these my favourite is the Anglo-Saxon stave church of *Greensted-juxta-Ongar*. When I entered this little church east of Epping, it was being decorated by two old ladies who might have been preparing for the Chelsea Flower Show, though in fact it turned out to be a wedding. Greensted Church is the most popular in Essex when it comes to marriages. It has everything the romantic soul could wish for: roses all around the doorway, dormer windows like those of a country cottage, and that historic aura that promises a life of lasting marital bliss. And if the young couples can take their eyes off each other, they might also note with approval the picturesque combination of building materials, and the white weatherboards of the bell-tower with its pointed shingled broach spire and the red pantiles, and the Tudor brick with Norman flint foundations, and the Victorian dormer windows above Anglo-Saxon oak walls.

This *lignea capella* in Greensted is one of the oldest wooden churches in the world. Of the original, only the nave beams remain, which dendrochronological tests date back to approximately AD 850. During the restorations of 1848 these beams were given brick foundations. The oak trunks are split down the middle, with the round parts facing outwards, and the flat inwards. This gives the impression that the interior is wood-panelled. Originally there were no windows, only holes for ventilation. The church had a thatch roof and a rectangular chancel, which was the heart of the first Anglo-Saxon church on this spot – probably built in the middle of the 7th century at the time of St Cedd's mission. There were hundreds of these little wooden Anglo-Saxon churches during the 11th and 12th centuries, but the only one in Britain to have survived is that of Greensted. Its original, starkly simple effect has been almost ruined by Victorian restoration and the modern craving for decoration. Sir Hugh Casson, former President of the Royal Academy, set a better example in 1982, with a new oak font, whose simple geometrical form is entirely in keeping with the spirit of the old church. In the green hills southwest of Chelmsford is another village church, whose west tower is typical of the so-called 'boarding towers' of Essex. St Lawrence, in *Blackmore*, was originally an Augustinian church, and dates from the middle of the 12th century. Half pagoda, half Norwegian stave church, its tower begins with a timber-framed base, continues with two storeys of weather-boarding, and ends in an octagonal shingled broach spire. But even more impressive than the outside of this tower is its interior (plate 80). There are ten massive uprights and a Piranesian labyrinth of criss-crossing beams, all giving off a pungent odour of anti-woodworm spray. With these bell-towers, the master carpenter-engineers of the Middle Ages created the sacred, perpendicular counterparts to the great barns of Essex, with that same air of powerful, rough-and-ready simplicity. The diagonal supports were meant to absorb the swing of the bells and the pressure of the wind. St Margaret's, in neighbouring *Margaretting*, has a similarly intricate bell-tower, 15th-century, and there are others in Navestock, Bulphan and Mountnessing – 'the glory of Essex timber construction' according to Pevsner. The timbers of St Margaret's also hold four bells from the time of the Reformation (plate 77). They announced the death of Henry VIII and the victory at Trafalgar, and today they still ring out for all occasions great and small in Margaretting. No doubt they also rang in 1666, to accompany the sad events recorded on a gravestone in the churchyard. It marks the burial place of a happily married couple, Peter and Julia Whitcoombe: 'He missed her soone, and yet 10 months he trys / To live apart, and lykes it not, and dies.'

It took me a long time to find St Mary's in *Great Warley*, between Brentwood and Havering on the borders of Greater London and not far from the M25. It was worth the search. This is one of the most extraordinary churches in Essex. On the outside it looks like any other suburban Edwardian church, but the inside is a truly amazing display of Art Nouveau. The tunnel vault is decorated with silver bands and ornamental lilies, and the dome of the apse shimmers with silver, as if it had been papered with chocolate wrappers decorated with stylized vines and red grapes. On the altar, in front of the pale green marble wall of the apse, stands the figure of the risen Christ, made of copper and oxydized silver. The taste is Byzantine, and the style is Art Nouveau at its most eccentrically English. The pulpit stands on a black marble platform, cruciform, made of beaten copper with coloured enamel inlay. The walls are panelled in walnut and inlaid with ebony and mother-of-pearl. The lectern stands on bronze roses of Sharon.

The design of this church is as flowery as the language of the Bible itself. Its most luxuriant blooms are growing over the the rood screen. Out of moss-green Irish marble shoot six slender bronze pillars, which branch out to form a frieze of treetops with mother-of-pearl flowers and red glass pomegranates. Silver angels symbolize the fruits of the spirit. There is a second Art Nouveau screen of walnut, with elegantly curved poppy capitals, separating the side-chapel from the nave. There are bronze angels on the font, copper reliefs on the organ, a mother-of-pearl lamp above the organist's seat, and hanging lamps in the chancel with green glass knobs and mother-of-pearl borders,

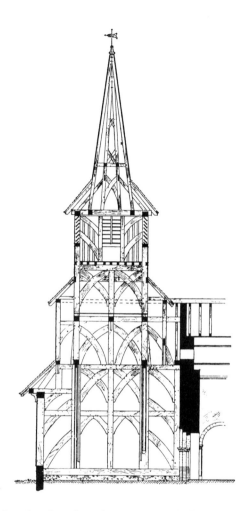

*St Lawrence, Blackmore,
section of belltower*

and every single detail is individually designed and made to harmonize with the whole. The lay-out of the church, though, is thoroughly conventional, and was designed by Charles Harrison Townsend in 1902 (he was also the architect of the Whitechapel Art Gallery). The overwhelming decoration was the work of the sculptor and interior designer Sir William Reynolds-Stephens, an American by birth. And it was all paid for by Evelyn Haseltine, a London stockbroker who lived in Great Warley.

In Cressing we saw the barns built by the Knights Templar; another order, the Knights of St John of Jerusalem, also known as Knights Hospitaller, built an unusual church (*c.*1335) in *Little Maplestead*, in northeast Essex. It is a round church, modelled on the Holy Sepulchre in Jerusalem, and is the smallest and youngest of the five round churches in England, the others being Holy Sepulchre in Cambridge (the oldest – 12th century),

109

Temple Church in London (the biggest), Holy Sepulchre in Northampton, and the chapel at Ludlow Castle (of which only fragments remain). The Knights Hospitallers had about sixty five settlements in Britain until they were dissolved in 1540. They are still active today, both here and in other countries, as the St John's Ambulance Association. Their round church in Essex had a hexagonal nave with a round ambulatory and a chancel with a semi-circular apse. The typically clumsy restorations by the Victorians (1851–7) largely destroyed the authentic nature of this church. Yet again one can understand all too well why the maxim of William Morris's Society for the Protection of Ancient Buildings, founded twenty years later, was: 'put Protection in the place of Restoration'. Robert Adam, no slavish restorer he, built two Neoclassical towers in 1776 for the village church in *Mistley*. The church was later demolished, but the towers have survived: square-gabled structures with slender drums and domes (plate 76) – monuments to the shattered dreams of George III's Paymaster, Richard Rigby, who wanted to turn the little village on the Stour Estuary into a bathing resort.

One spring day, I went to St Mary's in *Copford*, southwest of Colchester. There were daffodils and narcissi blooming all the way along the avenue that led to the little church. Nearby, in the midst of wide-sweeping lawns, lay Copford Hall, a Georgian house of red brick. In the Norman walls of the church you can see the typical flat Roman bricks, but the surprising thing is the frescoes, which date from the middle of the 12th century and originally covered the whole church. The restorers of 1870–2 only touched the painted apse: Christ in His glory, surrounded by angels, apostles, and geometrical patterns. In the nave are the remains of a Resurrection. Pevsner considers the murals 'by far the most important medieval wall-paintings in Essex',[1] but today they are dirty and faded, and if they are not restored soon, they will be totally ruined.

My spring tour of Essex churches ended in a village churchyard, beside the grave of a philosopher. In his *Letters from England*, Voltaire wrote of this man: 'Perhaps no-one had a cleverer, tidier head and no-one was a sharper teacher of reason than Mr. Locke.' When he returned from his exile in Holland in 1691, a year after the publication of his *Essay Concerning Human Understanding*, John Locke retired to the country, to the village of High Laver (east of Harlow). There he spent the last fourteen years of his life as a paying guest (for £1 a week) of Sir Francis Masham and his wife Damaris, daughter of a Cambridge Platonist. In Otes, the Mashams' country house, he had a library of some 4,000 volumes, a specially constructed chair on account of his chronic asthma, visits from Newton and other friends, and the peace and quiet he needed for thinking. What he thought about was the principles of empiricism and of representative democracy, the limits of the power of the state, and human understanding. Locke asserted (and this was

---

1 The village church in Bradwell (west of Coggeshall, A120) contains frescoes from *c*.1320; St Mary's in Great Canfield (southwest of Great Dunmow, B184) has a fresco of the Virgin Mary in the Norman choir arch, dating back to *c*.1250. There are also fragmentary remains of a 1250–75 fresco cycle in the over-restored Norman parish church of Wissington in the Stour Valley, Suffolk (southeast of Sudbury, A134).

John Locke, 1704, after Godfrey Kneller

fundamental for the Enlightenment) that everything we understand about the world arises from our perceptions. The emphasis on the experience of the individual led naturally to a theory of political action in which citizens have the right to revolt. In Otes, Locke wrote – among many other things – his four *Letters on Tolerance*, a plea for religious freedom. And yet even this enlightened Puritan considered Catholics to be traitors to the state.

Otes was long ago burnt to the ground. A trout pond in the fields and the old drive leading up to the house are all that remain of Locke's last home. It is raining, and the village church is barred and bolted. Thank Heaven for Mary Collins. She is the farmer's wife from next door, and she shows me some books about the great philosopher, makes me a cup of tea, and tells me all about the Japanese who came all the way from London by taxi just to put some flowers on Locke's grave. At last the rector comes, and opens up the church for me. All Saints has been freshly whitewashed – a simple, mainly Norman church. In the chancel are the memorials to the Mashams, and on the southern wall is John Locke's epitaph. Since he knew all too well what nonsense people often wrote, he composed his own – in Latin: 'Silte viator – Stay, Passer-by. If you ask what kind of man he was, he answers that he lived content with moderate means.' But even this modest thinker cannot resist a little self-advertisement: 'to truth his service was unparalleled. What else there is about him, learn from his writings which will set this forth in a manner more worthy of your belief than the suspect eulogies of an epitaph.' As if to counter his last insight, that this inscription will also fade, Locke's gravestone has been brought into the church, in order to protect it from the elements.

Today High Laver has about 400 inhabitants – less than in Locke's time. 'On Sundays we have about twenty four people at the service,' says the vicar of All Saints. 'We ought not to forget what churches are actually there for – not for their architecture or for their famous dead.' Locke would have approved.

'Sweet uneventful countryside': Where Foxes Play Cricket

'The deepest Essex few explore / Where steepest thatch is sunk in flowers / And out of elm and sycamore / Rise flinty fifteenth-century towers.' The elms are now dead, but the Essex of thatched houses and flinty towers hymned by Sir John Betjeman in 1954 still exists in reality and not just in old picturebooks. 'And as I turned the colour-plates / Edwardian Essex opens wide, / Mirrored in ponds and seen through gates, / Sweet uneventful countryside.' Beyond the urbanized, industrialized south, further inland, lies the other Essex, the good olde Englishe Essex. If that sounds sentimental, so be it.

Upcountry Essex is hill country and fox-hunting country. Next door, in flat Cambridgeshire, it used to be hare-coursing. But the real Essex sport is cricket. In the kingdom of cricket, Essex wears the crown. They say it's the home of 'grassroots cricket played on village greens and celebrated in country pubs.' I thought this might just be prospectus talk, until I went through Great Bardfield and Little Bardfield and arrived at Bardfield End. And there I saw twenty two men in white playing on the village green – and just as important, drinking Ridleys in the 'Butcher's Arms' afterwards. It was and is the same tale in Rickling, in Danbury, and all the other village greens in the county. For us Continentals, cricket is a mystery, but in Essex I finally understood it: it's the English love of green lawns, and the embodiment of the 'sweet uneventful countryside' (though no cricket fan will ever accept the second of those adjectives!). It was to Essex that the craftsmen came who for many a long year made the best cricket bats in England, carved from the wood that grows in the local meadows. People call their bats 'willows', and the village inn at Birchanger is called 'The Three Willows'. Three batsmen stand there on a beam, wearing the cricket gear of 1780, 1900, and 1946 – certainly the most original of all the many cricketing inn-signs.

It's ironic that of all the counties, cricket-mad Essex was one of the last to win any kind of trophy. A hundred years of effort were crowned in 1979 with their first ever county championship and for good measure, their first one-day trophy, all under the captaincy of Keith Fletcher, known as the Gnome. A marvellous decade under Fletcher was followed by triumphs under his successor Graham Gooch, the only batsman ever to score a triple century and a century in the same match.

One clear spring day, I drove to *Thaxted* along the road from Great Dunmow. From far away, beyond the green fields, I could see the tall pointed church spire on the horizon, and a little further away, the outline of a windmill. Thaxted reclines gracefully on the slopes of a gentle hill. On top is the church, halfway down are the market square and Guildhall, and curving over the rest of the slope are the houses. Thec stede, in the Saxon dialect, is the place where the straw comes from, but there are very few thatched houses left here. Instead there is medieval half-timbering, Georgian clinker brick, pastel shades and pargeting. The houses are simple, two-storeyed, and of varying shades and textures. They all maintain their individuality, but harmonize with their neighbours and with the surrounding landscape. It's this harmony that gives the town its charm and its air of quiet modesty. The conservationists call it an ensemble effect, and quote it as one of their favourite models. And yet it is here that they have committed a grievous sin.

The sin stands in the market-place and is the star of the show. Everyone, myself included, takes photos of the Guildhall (colour plate 27): oak supports, open arcades on the ground floor, two overhanging storeys above – all magnificent timber-framing. Built in the late 15th century, and messed up in 1910. That was when the Guildhall was restored: the walls were freed from their plaster, the timbers were laid bare, and in order to enhance the medieval appearance of the building, brand new wooden arches were inserted between the beams of the first floor, to harmonize with the arches below. This was more than a facelift; it was a starting-pistol. All over the country, medieval timbers were laid bare, and protective layers of plaster were stripped away – for ever since 1600 at the latest, timber-framed walls had almost always been plastered with stucco or clad in weatherboarding. What was the result? In no time the rain and damp waged war on the exposed walls, and sterile cement replaced the plaster between the timbers. It was because of this often devastating consequence that the art historian Norman Scarfe called the restoration of the Guildhall a national disaster.

I would love to know what the cutlers of Thaxted would have said about it all. It was they who built this house, and before it became the town hall in the 16th century – and later became a school before taking on its present function as a local museum – it was the headquarters of the Cutlers' Guild. As long ago as the 14th century, in the reign of Edward III, the cutlers were the richest guild in the town. The tax records of 1381 name two goldsmiths, four ploughshare-makers, eleven blacksmiths, and 79 cutlers in Thaxted.

Stony Lane bumps you over its cobbles past the Guildhall and up the hill to the church. Next to this, and almost encroaching on the churchyard, are two parallel rows of almshouses, one row thatched and the other tiled, all with roses around their doors. In the background, to make up the romantic picture, is a windmill of 1804, made of brick and with white sails. But one should not be misled by the picture postcard idyll: life for the poor people of the 19th century was not a tale of roses around the door.

When I visited the church on the hill, all the pews were missing. There were just a few odd benches and some large and ancient chests for chasubles. The interior seems remarkably spacious, the nave being lofty and bright, with noble Gothic arcades. There are also arcades on both sides of the chancel, and the spandrels are pierced with quatrefoil tracery. The windows are of clear glass – scarcely any stained – and there are very few monuments. There is a very special aura to this church: for me, it is the most beautiful in Essex. It was begun around 1340 and finished in 1510, the arcades are Decorated, the roof is Perpendicular, and the timbers are full of death-watch beetles. The beetles and carbonization have made heavy inroads in the flat oak roof and its cleats and bosses. A roof beam lay on the floor, eaten through by the *Xestobium rufovillosum* – an impressive illustration to accompany the appeal for restoration. The little community has to raise some £150,000 if it is to stop the church roof from falling on their heads.

Behind the church, in Monk Street, there was a cottage where the composer Gustav Holst lived from 1914 till 1925. The cottage has since burnt down. When he had done his teaching at the Royal College in London, he would always return to Thaxted, and it was here that he composed *The Planets* and much of his *Choral Symphony*: he conducted the church choir, and at Christmas he would play the organ of St John. He wrote a large number of works especially for the parish, in particular the ceremonial hymn 'Our Church-bells in Thaxted at Whitsuntide say / Come all you good people and put care away.' Holst died in London in 1934. His *Carols for Thaxted* are still sung every Christmas morning in Thaxted Church, including the most famous one of all, 'I vow to thee, my country'.

Spring in Essex. Daffodils along the way, fresh green sweet uneventful countryside. I'm driving past fields and villages to *Finchingfield*, a few miles east of Thaxted. It's a showplace which during the high season fills up with visitors like some great open-air theatre (plate 42). What's on? An English classic: *The Village*. The main characters: The Fox, a pub, and St John, a church. The set: a village green with pond and ducks, a sloping meadow with houses white as shirt fronts, and red-tiled roofs. In the background, tittle-tattle. The mighty hero, St John, a Norman, stands guard on the hill. This is the set and cast of our village masterpiece. Oh, and I almost forgot the white weatherboarded post mill on the road to *Steeple Bumpstead* – a name which Dickens might have invented – Steeple Bumpstead, where the church has a lifesize marble monument to Sir Henry Bendyshe and his five-month-old son (1717), lying in an almost theatrical pose, yet sad and strangely moving (plate 89). This is the lost art of public mourning, a masterpiece of Georgian monumental art by the London sculptor Thomas Stayner. Steeple Bumpstead – a name that rings out like the eight bells of St John. 'Music is medicine for the mind' is written on one of these bells. 'Percute dolce canto' says another – Strike softly and I sing.

The romanticization of country life, and the popularity of these Essex villages was almost involuntarily promoted by a number of artists. In 1949 Penguin published a paperback with 16 coloured lithographs: *Life in an English Village*. The model village depicted with such realism and with such loving irony by the painter Edward Bawden is Finchingfield's neighbour *Great Bardfield*. Bawden moved there in 1932, to Brick House, together with the painter and illustrator Eric Ravilious, who was a war artist in the Second World War and died in 1942. At the beginning of the forties, the painters Michael Rothenstein and Kenneth Rowntree also lived here, as did the art critic and painter Michael Ayrton, and John Aldridge, a member of the Royal Academy. They formed the Great Bardfield School, though their importance never reached beyond the county borders. A good selection of their pictures is to be found in the Fry Art Gallery in Saffron

Hedingham Castle, southwest view, engraving by Samuel and Nathaniel Buck, 1738

Walden (see page 123): impressionistic, realistic landscapes and still lives, all proving that the English countryside is beautiful – but it is not fertile ground for the avant-garde. Even a pop-artist like Peter Blake, when he turned to the Brotherhood of Ruralists, simply lost his edge. But that was in Somerset, and is another story.

During the fifties, Great Bardfield was still a colony of artists, potters, weavers and other creative folk, but those days are now past. Today there remain a few beautiful timber-framed and brick houses along the wide main street on the hill, some façades with pargeting, and in the parish church an impressive late 14th-century rood screen, which takes up the full height of the chancel arch like a monumental Gothic tracery window, with a Crucifixion right in the centre. There is a similar Gothic tracery screen (c.1350) in the village church at *Stebbing* (west of Braintree), which belonged to the Order of St John of Jerusalem until the Reformation.

If there is one place in Essex that corresponds to my ideal image of the Middle Ages, it's *Hedingham Castle*. The castle itself (Norman) stands on a wooded hill, at the foot of which lie the village and the church; if you add the history of the Earls of Oxford – one of England's great family dynasties – you have the perfect recipe. Don't go straight to the castle. The village, which is actually called Castle Hedingham, is a gem. It lies in the north of the county, on the Suffolk border, a little way off the main road to the Colne Valley. In the centre is a hillside graveyard leading up to the parish church, and all around it is a circle of flint and brick houses. It is as if the homes of the living were gazing up at the house of God and at the dead, in a simple but powerful expression of faith that has not changed down through the centuries. For this medieval aura and churchyard peace and quiet, well-heeled Londoners are prepared to pay: their second-home cottages – four tiny rooms and no garden – can cost a good £100,000. In the old days, weavers lived in these houses, but today the only looms are to be found in a former school on the edge of the village. The DeVere Mill is England's only silk mill that still uses the old handlooms of the 18th century. It was they that wove the silk wall coverings used for the restoration of Queen's House in Greenwich, the silk covers for the William III chairs at Hampton Court, and the wedding dress for Sarah Ferguson, Duchess of York: specialized commissions for the last specialists of an old craft.

A Norman portal with the macabre name of Skin Door (see page 87), and a much mended, age-old oak door with wrought iron fittings lead into the church at Castle Hedingham. St Nicholas is one of the surprises waiting in the shadow of the castle. The early 17th-century tower of red brick rises up like a Tudor gatehouse, and this architectural jewel of a church is almost completely Norman. Round and octagonal pillars alternate in the arcades, and they have exquisitely carved Gothic capitals; there is also a pointed arch in the chancel, with denticulated and zigzag decorations – all features of the transitional Norman style of the late 12th century. The magnificent hammerbeam ceiling dates from the early Tudor period, probably made by Thomas Loveday, who was buried in Castle Hedingham in 1535. Several East Anglian church roofs have been attributed to him, e.g. in Lavenham and Gestingthorpe, as well as that of the Hall in St John's College, Cambridge. Here in Castle Hedingham's church the light filters through three narrow lancet windows in the east wall and, above them, a Norman wheel window with eight columns for spokes

Edward de Vere,
17th Earl of Oxford, 1575

(substantially restored in the 19th century, as were the unusually complete sedilia in the chancel): the motif is very rare, and to be found in only five English churches, including Peterborough Cathedral. The misericords, if one can see them in the dim half-light, display the crude humour of their medieval carvers: the sun is putting its tongue out, a fox is carrying off a monk, and a wolf blows the trumpet. Beneath the chancel lie the tombs of the Earls de Vere, masters of Hedingham Castle.

'The de Veres, Earls of Oxford, were the longest and most illustrious line of nobles that England has seen.' Thus wrote the liberal historian Macaulay. They were known as 'the fighting Veres', for they fought in the Crusades, and in the Hundred Years' War, at Bosworth Field, and against the Irish in the notorious Battle of the Boyne. They possessed huge estates in ten counties, and enjoyed the favours of many kings. Even today the De Vere Gardens in Kensington recall the might of this Norman family. The first of them, Alberic or Aubrey de Vere, came to England with William the Conqueror and married the latter's half-sister Beatrix. Aubrey, a man of excellent taste and great piety, planted a vineyard at Castle Hedingham, and around 1100 founded a Benedictine priory downriver called Earls Colne, where he died as a monk. It remained the hereditary burial-place of the Earls de Vere until the Reformation, when it was demolished. Three of the de Vere sarcophagi were taken to the Gothic St Stephen's Chapel in Bures, Suffolk. Aubrey's son, Aubrey II, built the castle c.1140 (plate 19). His architect was William de Corbeuil, who was also Archbishop of Canterbury. Aubrey II took part in the First Crusade to Antioch, where the star now in the Vere arms miraculously appeared on his standard. In 1133, Henry I appointed him Lord Great Chamberlain of England, then an extremely powerful position, though later only an honorary title which was passed on to succeeding generations, right down to the present owners of the castle.

What a family this was. It included Robert de Vere, 3rd Earl of Oxford, one of the 25 Barons of the Magna Carta and an opponent of King John; Robert, the 9th Earl, who married Edward III's grand-daughter, thus becoming a member of the Royal Family, and was also made Duke of Ireland; then the richest and mightiest of them all, John de Vere, supporter of the House of Lancaster in the Wars of the Roses, godfather to Henry VIII, Privy Councillor, Lord High Admiral of England, Ireland and the Duchy of Aquitaine. When this 13th Earl of Oxford entertained Henry VII at Hedingham Castle in 1498, there were so many servants, attendants and guards of honour that the King had to wonder which of them was King. It is said that he fined his host the unheard-of sum of 15,000 marks for breaking the so-called Statutes of Retainers, a law devised to protect the Crown from the barons and their oversized private armies. The de Veres would have cared little about the fine – or the law.

The most brilliant of them all was Edward, nicknamed the Spendthrift. At his own expense, he fitted out a ship to fight against the Armada, but this was not the only reason why he was a special favourite of Elizabeth I. 'My Turk' was what she called the young 17th Earl of Oxford, with his brown locks and hazelnut eyes, and he was a veritable star of her court; at 16 he graduated from Oxford and Cambridge, he was a superb dancer and tennis-player, a horseman and a poet, a mixture of charm and cheek, a Renaissance man of extravagant style. It is reported by John Aubrey in his *Brief Lives* that once, at court, Edward let out a loud fart. He was so ashamed that he went travelling for seven years. On his return, he was greeted by the Queen with the immortal words: 'My Lord, I had forgott the Fart.' She made him Poet Laureate for life. For many years, some people believed him to be the author of Shakespeare's plays – an unlikely theory that still has some currency. With more than a hundred servants dressed in shimmering robes, a blue boar stitched to their left shoulders (the boar being the family emblem),[1] the handsome Edward rode forth and married Anne Cecil, daughter of Lord Burghley, and thereafter lost interest in the cold walls of Hedingham.

The 20th and last Earl of Oxford, another Aubrey, had the castle slighted in 1666 in order to prevent it being used as a military base during the war against Holland. On his death in 1703, the title finally became extinct. Ten years later, a former Mayor of London, Sir William Ashurst, bought the land and his son built a fashionable mansion next to the remains of the Norman castle. What is left now of the once mighty de Veres? The name of a street in Kensington, their emblem at the 'Blue Boar', a hotel in Maldon, and a sturdy Norman pile at Castle Hedingham.

The exterior grounds of the castle are now a perfect spot for picnicking at the foot of the hill. There are plenty of trees, but they have only been there since the beginning of the 18th century, before which time the fields were free and open. The castle did not stand alone, however; it was surrounded by a chapel, a bakery, a brewery, stables, granaries, and other outbuildings. All of them have long since disappeared, and the one survivor of the great days is the mighty keep: monumental, monolithic, free at last from the petty purposes of defence, it can unfold itself as a solid geometrical form, pre-minimal art which Sol LeWitt would have been proud of. Hedingham Castle is one of the finest, best-preserved keeps of its time in England, almost square in shape, and nearly 100 feet high.[2] The walls are divided up by pilaster-strips, and the windows are few and extremely narrow – just ventilation slits on the ground floor, where the stores were kept, broad enough on the first floor to allow archers to fire through, and then a little broader on the upper storeys and decorated with zigzag arches. The walls are made of flint and rubblestone, covered with Barnack – a Jurassic limestone brought from Northamptonshire. Most Norman castles only had such stone around their windows and doors, and it was extremely rare to have the whole façade covered in this way. The cost alone was a sign of the wealth and power of the de Veres. But for all their might, the castle fell to King John's forces in 1215, after a siege of several weeks.

If you go through the entrance – for security reasons, this was on the first floor – and

---

1 The Latin for boar is 'verres', a pun on the name de Vere, as is their family motto: 'Vero nihil Verius' – nothing truer than Truth.

2 The Hedingham keep was the model for the Neo-Norman keep at Penrhyn Castle, which Samuel Wyatt designed in 1782 for a slate baron in North Wales (see my *Pallas Guide to Wales*).

Hedingham Castle, Great Hall

climb a spiral staircase, you'll find yourself in the banqueting hall. A massive central arch spans the entire width of the hall, and at its apex is eighteen feet high – the epitome of Norman grandeur. The fireplace, windows and doors are all decorated with inset columns and zigzag arches. Halfway up, a gallery runs through the thickness of the wall (over ten feet) – and this was where the musicians and troubadors performed. The hall was the setting for all the banquets and receptions, and here the de Veres held court. Sadly there is little today to remind you of the grandeur and greatness of the de Veres.

Audley End: A Stately Home in Gardens of Saffron

In 1586 the historian William Camden noted that the fields all around *Saffron Walden* smelt sweetly of that plant, and indeed the giant crocus-fields of northwest Essex stretched almost as far as Cambridge in those days. The chalky soil was particularly suitable for cultivating *Crocus sativus*, and when the mauve flowers bloomed in October, the crokers would begin to harvest their saffron gardens. They would have to pick more than 4,300 flowers in order to extract a single ounce of the precious powder. Since the time of Edward

III it had been much in demand all over England as a medicine against pimples and plague, depression and seasickness, as an aphrodisiac, a dye, and a spice (and to help cakes set). Crocuses to Chipping Walden were like tulips to Holland, and they brought prosperity to the old cloth-making market town. Even in early Tudor times, it had begun to call itself Saffron Walden, and it flourished throughout the 16th and 17th centuries, until cheaper forms of yellow dye replaced the more exclusive saffron. Crocuses duly gave way to barley, and in the 19th century, the scent of saffron no longer wafted its way around Saffron Walden, but instead the air was filled with the odours of thirty or more malt-houses. Today the crocus is only to be found on the municipal coat-of-arms and in the Gothic spandrels in the southern aisle of St Mary's. And Mr Camden would now have to report that all around Saffron Walden the main smell is that of exhaust fumes.

The High Street takes you past propped-up plane trees, red and grey brick houses, Georgian and Victorian, down a long hill, up, down again, gently curving, a pretty route through a pretty town. East of the High Street, in the area between George Street and Castle Street, lies the medieval centre of the town. There was once a Norman castle, but of that only a few flint walls remain. At the foot of its hill, farmers and traders have been setting up their stalls ever since the end of the 13th century, and they still do so today. In the market place is the Town Hall, with Neo-Tudor half-timbering of 1879, diagonally opposite the Victorian Corn Exchange of 1848. Above its entrance is the head of a ram, harking back to the days when the Woolstaplers' Hall stood on this spot, and looms were clattering in the cottages of town and country.

It's been a long time since I lost my way so completely as I did in Saffron Walden. It happened on the edge of the Common. In the maze. This lies east of the castle and market, on the common where medieval people used to graze their cattle and present-day people walk their dogs. Saffron Walden's maze is one of only eight surviving lawn mazes in England. It consists of a large number of loops winding back upon themselves in a series of expanding concentric circles, with particularly large loops at each of the four corners. The total distance is about a mile, and for centuries the paths have simply been cut again and again in the grass, though now, in order to prevent it from being grown over, bricks have been laid. Originally there was a tree in the centre, though no doubt young girls have also stood there as the target for young men. It's probable that the maze dates from before the Reformation, but the first recorded mention of it is in 1699, when it was recut at a cost of fifteen shillings. The type was certainly known much earlier, since Titania in *A Midsummer Night's Dream* speaks of 'quaint mazes in the wanton green'. As one could get lost in them in the same way as one would be lost in legendary Troy, they were also known in the Middle Ages as Troy Towns. Most were made of stone, and these lawn mazes are a peculiarly English form,[1] with hedge mazes being a modern variant.

Saffron Walden's unmistakable landmark, visible for miles around, is the broach spire of St Mary's. Since 1831 it has crowned this late Gothic parish church (1475–1525). Tall,

1 Hermann Kern, a maze historian, believes that they were adopted before the Reformation from medieval French church mazes.

Saffron Walden, 16th-century maze

slender arcades, with Tudor roses in the spandrels, the fine clearstorey windows and broad side aisles – they all endow the church with a certain noble grandeur. For a change, we know who the architects were: the building contract names them as Simon Clerk, master stonemason at the Abbey in Bury St Edmunds, together with John Wastell, the ingenious builder of the fan vault in King's College Chapel, Cambridge. Around the church, Saffron Walden's medieval centre remains largely intact. You can almost imagine yourself back in 1500 if you spend the night under the open roof trusses of Nos. 1–3 Bridge Street, the most beautiful timber-framed house in the town, today used as a youth hostel. Behind the stucco plastering and Georgian brick façades of the town, there is more medieval timberwork than you would realize at first glance.

In Church Street, on the corner of Market Hill, is a particularly picturesque example of the stucco ornamentation known as pargeting (plate 46). Two huge and hulking figures are modelled in relief, filling the gable over the entrance to what used to be the 'Sun Inn'. They may be the legendary giants Gog and Magog, or the Wisbech Giant and the mighty carter Tom Hickathrift, but whoever they are, there is no doubt that they make up the most spectacular decoration in Church Street. Nearby there are birds and plants, including the saffron crocus, garlands of flowers, geometrical patterns, and one isolated leg. This is 17th century pargeting. The four strikingly decorative timber-framed houses, with their over-hanging gables, date back to the 14th and 15th centuries.

Pargeting, which is also known as pargetting or pargetry, developed in those parts of England where timber-framing was the dominant mode of construction, and local stone was rare. It was used most widely in Essex and the southwest of Suffolk. This was a case where practical and aesthetic needs went hand in hand. During the 16th century, and possibly earlier, it became fashionable to plaster the timber walls. Timber-framing was then regarded as medieval and old-fashioned, but there was also the problem of protection against damp. The year 1501 saw the foundation of the Guild of Pargeters. Previously these plasterers had been confined to decorating interior walls and ceilings, but now they also designed stucco façades. Sometimes they copied the motifs from Jacobean panelling, and sometimes they used the arabesques and grotesques they found in the pattern books of the Flemish Mannerists. What had begun with the fresco and stucco façades of the Italian Renaissance now flourished again during the reign of Charles II as an English speciality, above all in East Anglia. Some of the finest examples are Sparrow's House in Ipswich, *c.*1670 (see page 182); Crown House in Newport, Essex, 1692; Garrison House in Wivenhoe, Essex, *c.*1650; Bishop Bonner's Cottage in East Dereham, Norfolk, 1502; Ancient House in Clare, Suffolk, 1473. Most of these houses are in fact considerably older than their pargeting. Generally what we see today are reproductions of the frequently whitewashed and renovated originals of the 17th century. Around 1700, brick façades and neoclassical reserve became the fashion, but pargeting still held on in the simpler houses and cottages, and indeed enjoyed a renaissance in the middle of the 19th century.

The pargeters modelled their patterns with their fingers and few other tools, and most of their work was in high relief, using soft plaster reinforced with animal hair, straw and wood shavings. They also loved simple geometrical forms, semi-circles, zigzag and fan patterns, created with wooden moulds and repeated all over the façade. Most pargeting

Saffron Walden, 17th-century pargeting in Church Street

decorations were originally coloured. Even today, pargeting is still popular, as you will soon see if you travel around East Anglia. The technical and aesthetic standards, however, are for the most part lamentable. Shells, crowns, birds, Tudor roses are often slavishly reproduced without the slightest regard for the proportions of the façade. The stereotype geometrical motifs in Saffron Walden's Castle Street, or on the timber-framed houses at the end of Bridge Street, are prime examples of misguided modern pargeting. This dismal trend has not gone unnoticed by the authorities. In 1982 the Essex Planning Department issued an historical and practical guide on the subject of pargeting, in order precisely to put a stop to the 'visual anarchy' and 'mediocre standards' that all too often now prevail.

Saffron Walden has some 14,000 inhabitants and six Nonconformist chapels. The town owes much of its prosperity to the hard work of the Quakers, a community that is still very active here. One of them was the banker and patron of the arts, Francis Gibson. Among the artists whom he supported, the most prominent was John Sell Cotman, and he was also an avid collector of 17th-century Dutch masters, including a Vermeer ('Girl Interrupted at her Music' now in the Frick Collection, New York). For his collection, which has since been dispersed, Francis Gibson built a small private museum in Castle Street in 1856, and shortly afterwards he opened it up to the public. He also gave public access to the neighbouring park, Bridge End Gardens, which he himself laid out. Gibson's charming little Victorian museum was reopened in 1987 as the Fry Art Gallery[1], a private gallery which specializes in artists from northwest Essex (see page 114). The pictures hang in tightly packed rows, one above the other, as in Victorian times. They include works by Edward Bawden. This former teacher at the Royal College of Art, son of an ironmonger from Braintree, became well known during the thirties as a designer and illustrator. In the tradition of the Arts and Crafts Movement, he designed posters, wallpapers, tiles for the London Underground, and murals for ocean liners; he illustrated books and he made monumental linocuts; he painted watercolours of the Essex countryside and of 'The Private World of Edward Bawden', his cottage in Saffron Walden, where he lived with his black cat Emma Nelson until his death in 1989. He was in some ways an archetypal artist – a free spirit who shunned fashion, and for the most part shunned people as well. He was certainly far less of a public figure than another of Saffron Walden's star citizens, the writer and famous feminist Germaine Greer (author of *The Female Eunuch*).

Since 1967 the whole town has been a conservation area, and since 1974 has even rejoiced in the epithet 'outstanding'. This, however, has made little impression on car drivers, for the town is a brutalized victim of through traffic. The A130 between Chelmsford and Cambridge cuts right through the middle of the town, along High Street and Bridge Street. Car parks have flourished, taking over part of the common, and, worst of all, Swan Meadow.

---

1   A member of the Fry family, Francis Gibson's heirs, was the Cambridge art historian and amateur painter Roger Fry, a champion of modern art in England. He organized the first exhibitions of Post-Impressionism in London in 1910 and 1912.

A footpath leads from Abbey Lane through the fields to the park of *Audley End*. Here stood the Benedictine Abbey of Walden, founded in 1140. When Henry VIII dissolved the monasteries, he passed the Walden Abbey estate on to one of his most co-operative subjects, Sir William Audley (1538). This was a reward given to an out-and-out opportunist. Lord Audley not only presided over the trial of Sir Thomas More for high treason –the trial that ended in the execution of the great humanist – but he was also happy to become successor to the Lord Chancellor whose career he had helped to destroy. His grave is in the church at Saffron Walden, a sarcophagus of black Flemish marble, of which Thomas Fuller remarked in his *Worthies of England* (1662) that the stone was no blacker than the soul and no harder than the heart of the man who lay buried there. It was, however, Lord Audley's grandson Thomas Howard who built the palace of Audley End (plate 2).

He, too, stood high in royal favour, and set out to rise higher. When James I came to the throne, Thomas Howard was made Earl of Suffolk and steward to His Majesty, and in the same year (1603) he began to build his house, which was meant to symbolize his new rank and to exceed all other private residences in the country. Like Hampton Court, Audley End was a mansion with two inner courtyards. It was the largest of all the Jacobean prodigy houses, built in the express expectation of entertaining the King in the manner to which he was accustomed. This meant a suite for the King, a suite for the Queen, rooms for the servants, the stewards, the companions, the followers, and the whole entourage of a travelling court. In July 1614, when Thomas Howard was appointed First Lord of the Treasury, James I came to stay at Audley End. 'Too large for a king, though it might do very well for a Lord Treasurer,' said the King on processing through the two inner courtyards. The wealth and ambition of his host were evident from the choice of building material: limestone from Lincolnshire[1], and not the usual brick, which even Robert Cecil, State Secretary to the King ('my little beagle'), used for Hatfield House, built at the same time. Audley End was completed in 1616, and cost the Earl of Suffolk the then enormous sum of £200,000. It also cost him his career. For it transpired that the Lord Treasurer had siphoned off public funds in order to pay for his wonderful house. In 1619 he was stripped of his office and sent to the Tower for embezzlement. Pardoned, eventually, Howard retired to his estate, a broken man dwelling in a ghostly palace.

At a special knock-down price of £50,000, Charles II acquired Audley End as a stopping-off place on the way to Newmarket for the races. But His Majesty soon lost interest in the vast edifice ('too large for a king'), and in 1701 the house – still not fully paid for – was sold to the family of the Earls of Suffolk. The mansion could arouse the unsullied admiration only of those who did not have to live in it and maintain it – for example, the traveller Celia Fiennes: 'a noble appearance like a town,' she noted in 1697, and counted 'thirty great and little towers.' Finally the architect Sir John Vanbrugh, no less, offered the

---

1 During 18th-century renovations, this was replaced by Ketton stone, from Rutland, which was also used for most of the façades of Cambridge colleges. The core of the walls consists of brick.

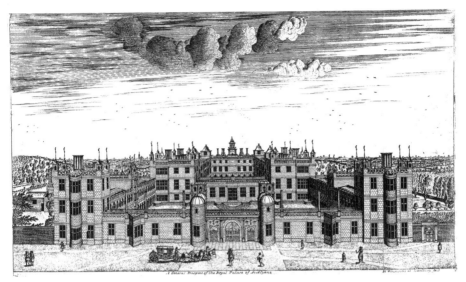

Audley End, Henry Winstanley's 'General Prospect of the Royal Palace of Auydlyene', c.1676

barbaric but sensible advice to the agonized owners: pull it down. And so, at the beginning of the 18th century, the three wings of the outer court (in front of what is now the west façade) were demolished, and in 1749 parts of the eastern inner court followed suit. Even now, reduced to a quarter of its original size, Audley End is still about as big as Hatfield House, and a masterpiece of Jacobean architecture, whose tall rectangular barred and bay windows are the embodiment of the Perpendicular glass-house ideal – the final phase of Tudor Gothic. The architect is believed to have been the stonemason Bernard Janssen, a pupil of the Strassburg master Wendel Dietterlin. The magnificent decorations on the two porches (1603) are an echo of designs taken from Dietterlin's book *Architecture* (1591), whose Mannerist motifs influenced many architects of early northern Baroque.

With pompous theatricality the entrance hall opens out to welcome the guests of Audley End. Beneath the heraldic stucco ceiling hang threadbare regimental flags, portraits of family ancestors, and various weapons. Against the end walls of the two-storeyed hall are two screens: one is made of wood, *c.*1615, massively solid, with Jacobean carvings, caryatids, arabesques, and a wealth of ornamental fantasy; the other is of stone, an arcade of six arches, of classical lightness and simplicity. Sir John Vanbrugh designed the latter in 1718, as he did the grand staircase that leads up to the first floor and the former state chambers. Let us stay for the moment, though, on the ground floor. When Sir John Griffin Griffin inherited Audley End in 1762, he engaged the leading interior designer of his time to modernize his all too uncomfortable inheritance. In the southern wing at least, Robert Adam was able to give the new owner what he wanted: comfort and elegance.

Robert Adam created a scenic succession of rooms and views, with columns, niches, and contrasting colours and decorations in accordance with his concept of 'the art of living'. All rooms had to give their occupants a sense of aesthetic pleasure. The vestibule is dominated by Naples yellow; the Dining Room is pea green; the Great Drawing Room, crimson. In the latter, the most magnificent room in the suite, the walls are covered with silk and damask. For dining rooms Robert Adam, for practical reasons, preferred stucco walls ('that they may not retain the smell of the victuals'). After their meal, the gentlemen would remain in the dining parlour, while the ladies retired to the sofas in the alcoves of the Little Drawing Room, which with its green-gold columns and pilasters stands out like the stage of a little theatre. Gold framed panels with arabesques and garlands, cherubs and sea nymphs decorate this precious drawing room, together with a mythological frieze in white and blue, Wedgwood style. The painted ceilings and the murals are by Biagio Rebecca, an Italian who had been working in England since 1761, and who also designed the Last Supper window in the chapel as well as painting some full-length portraits in the saloon. The sequence of rooms ends in the library, which was transferred to the first floor in 1826. Of Robert Adams' temple-style bookcases, only one is still in the house, as well as some of the book bindings he designed especially for Sir John, with scarlet and gold chequerwork patterns. In the library stands the supposed armchair of the poet Alexander Pope: it is a caquetoire, or 'gossip chair', from the 16th century. There are also portraits of Sir John Griffin Griffin himself, and his two wives, painted by Benjamin West.

Inspired by Adam's work, Sir John had a new chapel built on the first floor of the north wing (1768–72). The entrance is unusual in itself, for it was formerly the Jacobean music gallery behind the wooden choir screen, through which one can look down on the entrance hall. The chapel is beautiful Georgian Gothic, a sacred delight in pink and turquoise and cream – Strawberry Hill at Audley End. The fan and ribbed vaults are made of wood and stucco, while what appears to be stone is only painted. John Hobcraft, a joiner, designed and furnished this masterly chapel, including the chairs with backs like Neo-Gothic tracery windows.

The interiors of Audley End are the result of many different phases of rebuilding, and they reflect the changing tastes and styles of succeeding generations. The present appearance of most of the rooms, and the lay-out of furniture and pictures, is the work of the 3rd Baron Braybrooke, who created a remarkably homogeneous, early 19th-century ensemble. Lord Braybrooke was the editor of the first edition of Pepys' diary – Pepys having been a student at Magdalene College, Cambridge, which was founded by Lord Audley in 1542. Lord Audley's descendants, the Nevilles of Audley End, still have the right today as 'hereditary visitors' to nominate the Master of Magdalene College. Lord Braybrooke it was who restored and reproduced the Jacobean character of the house – hence the rather gloomy atmosphere of many of the rooms on the first floor, including the state chambers. The ceilings and friezes in the dining room and saloon are true to the original, and reveal the splendours of Jacobean stucco work: arabesques, still lifes, grotesque faces, fishes, water sprites, and sea monsters, all incorporated into geometrical patterns and fashioned in very delicate relief. It was in this saloon that Sir John, true to the traditions of the house, hoped to receive his King, and His Majesty was to sleep in a four-poster bed specially made in 1786 by the London cabinet-makers Chipchase and Lambert. But George III never came to Audley End.

The house is also full of stuffed creatures: birds and small animals in Victorian glass cases. It's almost like being in a natural history museum. Hanging above the 4th Lord Braybrooke's stuffed birds are portraits of the Cornwallis dynasty[1], of more historical than art-historical interest, and below these are paintings by the onmipresent Sir Peter Lely, the Carolean court painter from Soest in Westphalia, of whose portraits Samuel Pepys remarked: 'They are good but not like.' You can generally find a mediocre Reynolds and a dubious Rembrandt in most English country houses, but much rarer is a picture by Van Dyck's follower William Dobson, who made a name for himself during the Civil War. Another of the very few outstanding paintings at Audley End is a rare piece by the Flemish artist Hans Eworth. Between Holbein's death and Hilliard's rise, he was the leading painter of the Elizabethan court, and in 1562 he painted a portrait of Lord Audley's daughter Margaret. It was through her marriage to the 4th Duke of Norfolk that the Audley End estate came into the possession of the Howards (see page 240).

'There is a deal of indifferent stuff in the rooms,' noted James Lees-Milne, when he inspected the house for the National Trust in 1944. It 'makes Audley End a true English country house, and not a museum,' he continued. However, on a second visit in February 1945, he wrote: 'This time so much of it struck me as of poor quality,' and this no doubt contributed to the National Trust's decision not to take over Audley End. As one of the attendants said to me, the chances are that 'the family took all the good stuff with them.' And who could blame them? For when the two sons were both killed in the Second World War, the nation expressed its gratitude with a swingeing inheritance tax. And so the state collected the house and most of what was in it. The estate itself still belongs to the family, in the person of the 10th Baron Braybrooke, but the maintenance costs of Audley End have now made it into one of the most expensive gems in the English Heritage collection.

When you have absorbed all the history of the house, there is nothing better than to clear the tubes with a walk in the park. There are few houses with such a classically landscaped garden as Audley End. It was laid out by Capability Brown (1762–97) and furnished by Robert Adam – a great green open-air drawing room full of conviviality, Nature punctuated by a few antique-style temples. On the hill to the east of the house is a Corinthian Temple of Concord – the one park building not by Robert Adam, but designed by Robert Brettingham (1790). On the western hill is the Ionic Ring Hill temple, built in 1771 to commemorate the end of the Seven Years' War (1763). In the fields in front of the house, Capability Brown dammed the River Cam to form a narrow lake, and Robert Adam built a bridge at each end – one with three arches (1763), and the other with a

---

1 Jane Cornwallis, wife of the 3rd Baron Braybrooke, was the grand-daughter of the 1st Marquess of Cornwallis, who fought in the American War of Independence, and was Governor-General of India.

Palladian pavilion in the middle, an English teahouse bridge over the water (1782, plate 23). In 1840, there were plans to run the London-Cambridge railway line right through the middle of this Elysian garden. The then owner, the 3rd Lord Braybrooke, insisted however, that the landscape should stay as it was, and so the line was diverted to go round the back of the temple hill.

The transport vandals finally had their way, though. Today there are two roads separating the park from Audley End. And now the more distant sections of the park have run wild, while those that are nearer have been turned into grazing land. The glorious landscapes that Capability Brown had created in the meadows along the Cam are now sad shadows of their former selves.

25 THORPENESS   The House in the Clouds, water tower folly, 1925 ▷

26 FLATFORD MILL   Willy Lott's Cottage, 16th century

27 ALDEBURGH FESTIVAL   Musicians from Britten-Pears School in Snape

28 Twitchers on the shore at CLEY

29 On the beach at SOUTHWOLD

30   SOUTHWOLD   Beach theatre with Punch and Judy

31   SOUTHWOLD   Sailors' Reading Rooms, 1864

32 REEDHAM FERRY across the River Yare

34 KING'S LYNN Guildhall, 1421, and Town Hall, 1895 ▷

33 SNAPE The old Maltings on the Alde

35 IPSWICH   Willis Faber Building, 1975, by Norman Foster

36 SOUTHWOLD Market Place

37   Timber-framed houses in Lavenham

38   Lavenham   Tudor shop-front near Guildhall, 16th century

39 EAST BERGHOLT Belfry at St Mary's, 1531

40 CRESSING BARNS 13th-century barns of the Knights Templar

41 SAXTEAD GREEN MILL, 1796

42   Finchingfield   Showpiece village in Essex

44   Copped Hall   Dilapidated garden pavilion, c.1890 [

43   Cromer   Norfolk seaside resort

45 COGGESHALL Paycocke's door, 16th century

46 SAFFRON WALDEN Pargeting in Church Street, 17th century

47 House entrance in BURNHAM MARKET

SUFFOLK

Please don't rush me, I'm from Suffolk
(Car sticker)

My own Suffolk begins on the River Stour and ends at the Tate Gallery, where John Constable's water-meadows spread out in a green as endless as the cloudy skies high above the barges on the Stour. My Suffolk stretches from Sudbury to Vienna, from Gainsborough's birthplace to the Kunsthistorisches Museum, where there is one of his early pastoral scenes, recalling the landscape of his childhood. And Suffolk itself? It's between Essex and Norfolk, Cambridgeshire and the North Sea. Its boundary with Essex is the Stour, and with Norfolk the Waveney and the Little Ouse.

Just like the names of its rivers, Suffolk has a soft sound, gentle as the undulating land which locals say is 'easy on the eye'. There's nothing spectacular about this landscape – no dramatic rocky Cornish coasts, no romantic Cumberland lakes, no wild Scottish moors, but just undemanding slopes that won't raise a cyclist's sweat, and broad cornfields waving in the breeze. It's idyllic if all you want is a bit of peace and quiet. Orwell and Stour, Deben and Alde: Suffolk's estuaries reach far into the land, as if the sea wanted to take a good grip. The coastal roads keep their distance – which is good for the coast. Suffolk has very few high roads, but a maze of country roads and paths. There's only one really large town, Ipswich, and a host of little market towns, villages, hamlets, and isolated farmhouses of which all you can see is a roof peeping over hedges or the corn.

Despite all his travels Hammond Innes never forsook Kersey, his Suffolk village, and one day, as he returned home from London and crossed the Stour, he felt 'a sudden magic, the quintessential of an English landscape miraculously materializing before our eyes.' This English essence, captured so perfectly in Constable's paintings, has remained untouched in Suffolk even today, despite the many changes here and elsewhere. It's no coincidence that this peaceful region should also be the scene of many bizarre and puzzling crimes – particularly in the novels of P. D. James and Ruth Rendell.

Rendell (alias Barbara Vine) lives in an old farmhouse in Polstead, a village in the south of Suffolk, and P. D. James has a cottage in one of the county's tiny coastal towns. It was after a reading in Aldeburgh that I met the Queen of Crime, though in her bright, flowery dress she looked more grandmotherly than queenly. P. D. James grew up in Cambridge, and in the summer holidays often went camping on the sandy cliffs of Pakefield, south of Lowestoft. 'I love the wide sky, the wonderful sunsets, and the loneliness of the estuaries. I love the marshes, the birds, the reeds, and the smell of the sea everywhere. A landscape where the air seems to echo with the murmured litanies from ruined monasteries, and where you'd expect to find the hoofmarks of nightriders on the heath with their contraband. That's the sort of coast Suffolk has, between the A12 and the sea, from Kessingland in the north to Aldeburgh in the south.' This stretch of coast, says P. D. James, always seems to her to be one of the remotest spots in England. Here she feels 'the sense of history and a sense of timelessness.'

Behind the trees and the gentle hills, you can always see at least one and often several church towers on the Suffolk horizon. It's to these churches that the county owes its nickname Silly Suffolk, but 'silly' is not what you think it is. The word is a corruption of the Saxon 'seely', which means blessed. At the time of the Domesday survey in 1086, the county already had 417 churches. These were wool churches, built by rich clothiers of the Middle Ages. Without the wool trade and the rise of a prosperous middle class, the number and splendour of these village churches would have been inconceivable. The weavers' villages of Lavenham and Long Melford, Cavendish, Clare and Kersey made up what by medieval standards was a highly industrialized and densely populated region. When the Normans drew up their lists of land, churches, mills and people in 1086, Suffolk with some 70,000 inhabitants came near the top of the charts. For even before the great wool boom, and long after that, the land between the Stour and the Waveney nurtured a thriving agriculture. Suffolk was one of the kingdom's great granaries. And playing a leading part in this industry was the Suffolk Punch, the indefatigable carthorse which for centuries pulled ploughs through the heavy clay soil, and in the First World War dragged cannons through the mud of the Flanders battlefields.

Suffolk Punch, and Suffolk Pink – another speciality of the region. It's the traditional house colour, made originally from pig's blood and whitewash. Unfortunately, pink in recent years has enjoyed an inflated popularity in strident industrial paints. Only seldom will you see the real thing now, the pale salmon pink that makes such a sweet splash in the green countryside. Sometimes, as in Essex, you will find pargeting – geometrical patterns or figures in the plaster façades. The finest houses in Suffolk are timber-framed or brick. There was always plenty of wood and clay, as well as flint, and straw and reeds for the roofs. Bricks came later. These are the natural, typical building materials here, and they form the image of the villages and market towns, the churches, cottages and mansions, making the architecture harmonize with the landscape.

Medieval timber-framed houses are as natural to this county as trees – sturdy, practical, and beautiful. The manner in which the Gothic carpenters fashioned oak and chestnut into uprights, cleats and hammerbeams, into church roofs on angels' wings, into timbers without nails, joined only by wooden pegs – that is the wonder of medieval architecture in Suffolk. You will also find simple brick here in all its variations of form and colour: biscuit-orange in Kentwell Hall, pale yellow in Little Wenham, apricot Tudor bricks in Christchurch Mansion, Ipswich, white baked brick from Woolpit (very fashionable in Georgian times, for example in Bury St Edmunds), dark blue brick in lozenge patterns on the façade of Helmingham Hall. And was there anything the Tudor builders did not use brick for?[1] Vaults and ledges, stepped gables, curved gables, elegant pilasters, grotesque chimneys, turrets, towers and gatehouses. It's scarcely surprising that in Suffolk there are some 12,000 listed buildings – more than in almost any other county.

There are many people committed to preserving this ancient heritage. At the forefront is the Suffolk Preservation Society (SPS), an independent branch of the Council for the Protection of Rural England. The main problem facing this society is not the old farm and manor houses, but new buildings – the suburbanization of Suffolk, and the overdevelopment and destruction of the countryside. Suffolk's image as a quiet hinterland was rudely jolted during the seventies, when it was one of the fastest growing counties in England. Overspill estates went up in the west of Suffolk to relieve London, and industrial zones and new estates with big shopping centres were built on the outskirts of Bury St Edmunds, Sudbury, Hadleigh, Haverhill and Mildenhall. In the eighties there was still more pressure on the countryside. In 1988 house prices in Suffolk rose by 40 per cent. Up to a quarter of the newcomers were retired people, a fact which transformed village life.

Paul Edwards, director of the Suffolk Preservation Society, told me that East Anglia actually has the highest number of new buildings in England, particularly in the area between Ipswich, Woodbridge and Felixstowe. As a former architect himself, he is especially distressed at how badly designed they are – 'We believe that everyone has the right to live in a house that is well designed, well sited and suited in style and scale to its surroundings.' The slump of the early nineties has certainly put what is at least a temporary stop to this expansion, but it remains contrary to government policy to introduce stricter regulations and planning, since this would further debilitate the economy. There are other fields, too, in which the SPS – which can only act in an advisory capacity – has had to accept its own limitations. The most damaging have been the port extension at Felixstowe, and the construction of a second nuclear reactor at Sizewell – both projects situated on what is officially designated a 'Heritage Coast' and an 'Area of Outstanding Natural Beauty' – two labels which should have guaranteed double protection, but which, in an age when all things economic have absolute priority, count for suspiciously little.

Suffolk was the home of Constable and Gainsborough, and the birthplace of English landscape painting. It also gave to the world Humphry Repton and Arthur Young, the one a great landscape gardener, and the other a pioneer of British agriculture. Suffolk produced such contrasting characters as Cardinal Wolsey and Cromwell's plunderer of churches, William Dowsing. The musicians attracted here range from Benjamin Britten to Bill Wyman. The choreographer Sir Frederick Ashton lived here, and so did the educationalist A. S. Neill, the guru of Summerhill. Immigrants from the Continent also found what they were looking for to help them live and write: Arthur Koestler in his country house near Bury St Edmunds, and Michael Hamburger in a village near the coast.

1 Before the 15th century brick was rarely used in England for anything other than schools, colleges and some large country houses.

Thomas Gainsborough: Study of a Sheep, c.1757–9

I asked Michael Hamburger, who came originally from Berlin, what Suffolk people were really like. 'Heavy going, reticent, shy, very tolerant, very placid, very reliable,' he said. P. D. James called them 'sturdy people, stubborn and robust. They have a long fishing and farming tradition, and those are tough lives.' They say of themselves (if you can understand their dialect): 'We talk with our mouths shut because we don't want to let the east wind in.'

Constable Country: Across the River and Into the Frame

From the river all I could see was a knee in the grass, and next to it an easel, which was weighted down by a small sandbag. The willow trees were groaning in the wind. I tied my boat to a root and walked across the meadow. Of course the easel had to choose just that moment to fall over.

'It's all right,' he said. 'I must have fallen asleep.' Martin Chapman is a Suffolk painter, who finds his inspiration exactly where John Constable found it, 'under every hedge and beside every path.' Since Constable's day, two hundred years on, hardly anything has changed in the water-meadows of the Stour. 'If just one tree were felled,' says Martin Chapman, 'there'd be a national outcry.' *Dedham Vale* is an official Area of Outstanding Natural Beauty (plate 53). The meadows have been preserved as natural wetlands for cattle to graze in, and not for the more profitable cultivation of barley or rape. This is the most cherished and most often reproduced landscape in the history of English art. I've lost count of the number of times the 'Hay Wain' has appeared before me at the breakfast table, on mats, plates, tins and labels. It's Constable's most famous painting, done on the Stour, awarded a gold medal at the Paris Salon in 1824, admired by Delacroix and Géricault, lauded by Stendhal – and in London, at that time, unable to attract a single buyer. Constable's friend John Fisher wrote to him in that same year of 1824: 'The stupid English public, which has no judgement of its own, will begin to think that there is something in you if the French make your works national property.' But the stupid English public did not. Today, of course, his work has long since been fêted as 'national heartlands, inner countryside'.

I sat in my rowing boat and drifted through England's green soul, down the Stour from Dedham to *Flatford Mill* (colour plate 6). It was a warm summer's day, dragonflies hovered above the surface of the water, and the river meandered gently round its many bends. An occasional moorhen took off with a flutter, cows grazed on the banks, and in the distance one could see a few houses and the church tower of Dedham. There was nothing spectacular – just the quiet, everyday modesty of Nature. And yet this borderland between Suffolk and Essex was a piece of the world that fascinated Constable more than any of the countries that his contemporary and totally different fellow-genius Turner explored so restlessly. Constable's Grand Tour did not take him from England to Italy, but from Flatford to Nayland: nine miles which took him a lifetime to paint.

Constable's father was a miller, but also a businessman. He owned the watermills at Flatford and Dedham, and two windmills near East Bergholt. The fields of Dedham Vale yielded the corn for the father's mills, and the subjects for the son's paintings. The link continued until the very day John died, for the picture he was working on then was also of a mill: 'Arundel Mill', 1837, now in Toledo, Ohio. On the Stour, the young Constable would watch the barges transporting the flour down river to Mistley, stopping at his father's quay, and then going on to London. He watched the horses plodding along the towpath, and the locks with their mossy oak beams opening and closing for the barges. Here, as he helped his father, he learned to read the wind and the weather, such vital influences on the work of the miller, and which as a painter he was able to capture so profoundly and so truthfully, whether it was a fresh spring morning or the dark of an imminent storm. The realism was such that his colleague Fuseli once remarked that whenever he saw a Constable painting, he felt the need to reach for his coat and umbrella.

Flatford Mill, 200 years after Constable: The stump of a dead willow invites you to lunch at 'The Haywain'. A fisherman sits by the mill-pond. 'Are you fishing for herring?' asks an art-lover from overseas. 'It's just like the picture in Washington. There's a fisherman there too, and poplars on the right, and the lock-gate in front!' The similarity is not surprising. The whole thing has been reconstructed exactly according to Constable's pictures. Except that the 'old rotten planks' he so loved have been replaced by a concrete basin. There's the old wooden bridge over the Stour (asphalted), the pink thatched cottage by the bridge (with information and shop, riverside café and boat hire), the red brick mill, and the picturesque cottage of Willy Lott – 'too picture-postcardy for words,' wrote James Lees-Milne, when he inspected it for the National Trust in 1944: 'I love Constable, but I do not love this place. It has been made a travesty of the totally unpretentious, rural, domestic scene of one of England's greatest painters.'

'Flatford Lock and Mill', exhibited at the Royal Academy in 1812, was auctioned at Christie's in London in 1986, and bought by the media millionaire Lord Thomson of Fleet, for £2.64 million – then a record[1] for a painter who never earned more than £300 for any of his pictures, and who said of himself: 'My pictures will never be popular for they have no *handling*. But I do not see *handling* in nature.' What he saw in Nature was not the idyllic, the heroic, or the mythical that his contemporaries saw it, but simply the landscapes of the world around him; down-to-earth, everyday realities, working landscapes. The master of English Romanticism was in fact a great realist, induced by his very origins to be fascinated by the practical economies of the land. This practical side is evident from such paintings as 'Boat-Building' (1815), now at the V&A – a scene in the little boatyard that belonged to his father. When the National Trust began in 1987 to restore the riverside near Flatford Mill to the way it looked in the early 19th century, they found in the former dock one of the boats that Constable had so often painted: a 40-foot lighter with a flat bottom. It had been sunk at the beginning of the First World War to prevent it being used by the Germans in the event of an invasion. These lighters used to transport horse manure from London's streets to fertilize the fields upriver on the Stour, and then used to return carrying the corn ground by the Constables' mills, and bricks from Sudbury, Gainsborough's birthplace, which is only a few miles away. Flatford Dock, restored by the River Stour Trust, is the only surviving dry dock of its time on an English river. The Flatford Lock that Constable painted was built in 1706, and consisted originally of

---

1 Four years later, in 1990, Baron Thyssen-Bornemisza auctioned Constable's 'The Lock' (1824) at Sotheby's for £9.8m. – a world record for a British painting.

15 locks which made navigable the 25 miles of river between Sudbury and the sea. In those days there was a lot more traffic on the Stour, and there were fewer trees on the bank because of the towpath.

Constable country, with the gently undulating hills of the Stour Valley, is the very embodiment of the English countryside; Constable's work embodies the Englishness of English art. And *Willy Lott's Cottage*[1] is the English cottage par excellence (plate 26). Angular and whitewashed, with a neatly rhythmical set of roofs that seem to grow one out of the other, this is the late 16th-century cottage where Farmer Willy Lott was born. He is said to have lived there for more than 80 years, without spending more than four days away from his home. For Constable, he was the epitome of Suffolk's solid roots; for our

1   Among the many thousands who have photographed it is Bill Brandt, in 1976, whose winter image is far from picturesque, consisting only of the magic of light, shadows, and pure geometry. David Hockney also quotes Willy Lott's Cottage in an etching of the same year.

John Constable: Scene on a Navigable River (Flatford Mill), 1817

John Constable: The Hay Wain, 1821

mobile society, he seems more like a freak. Constable painted the cottage many times, and everyone recognizes it as the house beside the river which a farmer is crossing by horse and cart to fetch hay from the fields on the opposite side. This is the 'Hay Wain', 1821, the most famous working landscape of them all, yet still, in the words of Kenneth Clark, 'an eternally moving expression of serenity and optimism.' This is the essence of Constable's art and of his landscapes – an exalted harmony with earthly roots. His concept of Nature grows from a belief in the order of things, and it also reflects a social order not yet shattered by the unrest of the workers and the consequences of agricultural reforms that his contemporary William Cobbett was recording in *Rural Rides*, which included East Anglia. In Constable's pictures it is unthinkable that haystacks should burn or farm labourers wreck their machines, as they did in the East Anglian riots of 1821–2.

Today, Willy Lott's cottage offers accommodation for visitors to the neighbouring watermill. Flatford Mill was built in 1733, owned by the Constable family until 1846, and now belongs to the National Trust together with all the houses around it, including Valley Farm, an early 15th-century timber-framed construction, and Bridge Cottage, 16th-century. Since 1946, the mill has been used by the Field Studies Council as a centre giving courses of all kinds: botany, dendrology, ornithology, architecture, photography, painting, and conservation. During the fifties and sixties, the painter John Nash regularly gave courses in botanical illustration, and while his students were doing their drawings, he would go and fish in the millpond. Up in the attic studio of the Constable mill, I came across a group of would-be painters, young and old, busily doing portraits. 'Here you can forget everything, all the stress and the traffic,' said a Yorkshire businessman, 'and you've got everything you need all around you.'

Constable always came back to the Stour Valley from the busy London art world and also later, when he and his family took up residence in Hampstead, which was then still a village. The landscape of his childhood remained the permanent source of his inspiration. Like Wordsworth, he had reverence for little things; they shared a kind of religious love for Nature, seeing in the trees and flowers and clouds revelations of divine and spiritual forces. 'The light of nature,' was what Constable called it, 'the moral feeling of landscape.' This was the unity of origins and destinies, the small and the absolute: 'We exist only in the landscape, and are creatures of the landscape.' In the last of his six lectures on landscape painting, given in 1836, one year before he died, he said: 'The landscape painter must walk in the fields with an humble mind. No arrogant man was ever permitted to see nature in all her beauty.' His aesthetic credo can be found in the church at East Bergholt, along with other quotations on a plaque in the side aisle: 'Painting is with me but another word for feeling,' he wrote to his friend and collector, the Rev. John Fisher.

Constable was born in *East Bergholt* in 1776, and was baptized in the village church, where his parents (and Willy Lott) lie buried. 'Time passeth away like a shadow' is the message on the sundial above the door of the church, which he also painted many times. St Mary's has no tower. It is said that the money ran out when the community's patron, Cardinal Wolsey, was stripped of his office on the eve of the Reformation, and died. Instead of a tower, the church has something much more beautiful and very unusual: a wooden bell house, free standing, square-shaped, with a steep pyramidal roof (plate 39). Through the ingeniously interwoven timbers of this bell-cage of 1531, one can see five bells standing almost like funnels in a scaffold of oak beams. This is the only place where change-ringing is still done by hand and not by rope. In the bell-ringing guild, the handbell-ringers of St Mary's are a rarity indeed, and it was this same sound that Constable heard throughout his childhood, for his parents' house was just a few yards away from the church. Now all that remains of it is the stables, diagonally opposite 'Stour', the house where Randolph Churchill wrote his father's biography and, after a modest and cantankerous political career, ended his days gardening.

East Bergholt is not a particularly picturesque village, and without Constable it would scarcely have found its way onto the map. In his time it had about 1,000 inhabitants, now swollen to some 5,000. The museum in Ipswich contains two of his paintings of East Bergholt, showing his father's flower and kitchen garden, his wheat fields, the windmill and the old rectory – every detail depicted with tender but prosaic care. This is the view that he had from his window, over some forty acres of grazing and arable land – a view that recalled the days of childhood and of love. Looking out of that same window, he wrote to

John Constable: A Lock on the Stour, 1827

Maria Bicknell in the summer of 1812: 'I see all those sweet fields where we have passed so many happy hours together.' It was at the house of her grandfather, the Rector of East Bergholt, that he had first met Maria; he had to wait seven long years before he could marry her, because her family objected to having an unsuccessful painter as an in-law.

It was not until he was fifty-three that Constable was accepted into the Royal Academy, but even then he was to be humiliated when colleagues rejected 'Watermeadows near Salisbury' – 'that nasty green thing'. Yet it was precisely this work that so impressed Delacroix, who called him an 'homme admirable, une des gloires anglaises', and enthused over the manner in which Constable had set the green of the meadows free, by using the whole spectrum of greens. This free use of colour, anticipating Impressionism, was the revolutionary element in his local paintings. It is no coincidence that East Bergholt is twinned with Barbizon, where the French plein air painters used to meet in the 19th century. It was their rise and the success of the Impressionists that helped to give Constable's work its great posthumous breakthrough. The very things which today are regarded as his true strength and modernity – his oil sketches and large-scale oil studies, with their vibrant, spontaneous and liberated brushwork – were considered by his contemporaries and even by himself as rough and incomplete preliminary works.

Constable's real Royal Academy had nothing to do with art classes in London. It was here in East Bergholt, for this is where he began his 'laborious studies from nature', precisely observed, swiftly executed oil studies of the landscape. His realistically impulsive brush strokes were not an aesthetic whim, but were a reaction to what he called the 'chiaroscuro of nature' – the rapid changes of light and shadow, the continuous movement of water, leaves and clouds, basic appearances of Nature which were particularly striking in the coastal climate of East Anglia. 'The trees and clouds all ask me to do something like them.' The 'something' was to paint Nature's own movements in so direct a manner that the observer would actually think the wind in the trees was blowing in his face. Constable's painting, according to the writer Edward FitzGerald – also from Suffolk – is a constant effort 'to paint up to the freshness of earth and sky'. This is the atmospheric mastery that Constable himself admired so much in Ruisdael and Hobbema – aesthetic affinities born of the maritime climate. But for him even more than for the 17th-century Dutch painters, the sky was 'the key note, the standard of scale, and the chief organ of sentiment'. English artists were the first systematically to paint pure cloud formations, Constable more than anyone, apart perhaps from Cozens. 'Sky-ing' was the term he gave to what he had learnt as a miller's son – the 'natural history of the skies' which he observed and painted both as an empiricist and as a romantic. On the back of his open-air sketches, he would give precise meteorological information, such as: '5th of September 1822. 10 o'clock, morning, looking south-east, brisk wind at west. Very bright and fresh grey clouds running fast over a yellow bed, about half way in the sky.' If you are interested in the history of English weather in the early 19th century, tune in to Constable.

Wandering along the Stour, you will find Constable's clouds and Constable's pictures all along the way, for they are as much a part of this landscape as the meadows by the river and the ash trees that he loved more than any other tree. Fen Lane is the path that leads from East Bergholt into the valley and across the river to Dedham: the path that Constable always took to school. Every day he went this way – three-quarters of an hour there, three-quarters of an hour back, in sunshine and in rain. Imagine it in July: around midday, a flock of sheep wanders up the path, a farmer goes homewards from the fields, a boy in a red jacket lies in the grass and drinks from the stream. That is how Constable painted his route to school when he was fifty years old: 'The Cornfield', 1826. The only thing that is missing from this picture is the church at Higham – one of the rare occasions when Constable gave himself topographical licence. Despite the picturesque insertions which he himself admitted to making in greater abundance than normal, as 'eyesalve' for the beholder, no-one was willing to buy the picture. A group of friends and subscribers, including Wordsworth, acquired it after his death and donated it to the National Gallery – the first of his paintings to hang there.

Constable was born in Suffolk and went to school in Essex. With the Stour as border between the two counties, each can claim with equal authority to be Constable Country – an expression that was to gain currency even during his own lifetime. It was with some satisfaction that he reported, towards the end of his life, on a trip he had made by mail coach through Dedham Vale in the company of two strangers: 'One of them remarked, on my saying it was beautiful, "Yes, Sir, this is *Constable's Country*".' With the increase in popularity came a corresponding increase in fakes. The criminological satisfaction of tracking them down is matched only by the aesthetic satisfaction of finding the settings of his pictures. The hunt sharpens the eye for the special qualities of artist and landscape, and for the subtle differences between nature, art and life. Even in the seemingly timeless Constable Country, there have been some changes. Instead of the wooden bridge in his 'Dedham Vale' of 1828, there is now a four-lane highway (the A12) across the Stour near Stratford St Mary. The picturesque view from Gun Hill down into the river valley[1] is now blocked off; the watermill at Dedham has been converted into luxury apartments; Wivenhoe Park is no longer in splendid isolation, but forms a part of the University of Essex.

Upriver, in the village church at *Nayland*, I should have found Constable's altarpiece, but instead there was nothing other than high excitement. It had just been stolen. 'Isn't it a shame!' cried the brass-polishing ladies. 'And just imagine if we'd been here ourselves when the thieves came! Oh dear, what a business!' Fortunately, the business had a happy ending, because the local treasure was found unharmed. 'Christ Blessing the Bread and Wine', a relatively small, somewhat sentimental picture which Constable had painted in 1810 (wrongly dated 1809 in the church), was commissioned by his Aunt Patty[2] whose real name was Martha Smith. She lived in the neighbouring village of *Stoke-by-Nayland*. It hasn't changed a great deal since that time, and Constable captured it in paintings now to be seen in the Tate, in Chicago, and in the Metropolitan Museum, New York. On the crest of a hill above the valley you can see the tower of the Gothic church, surrounded by tall trees and Tudor houses. Nayland, Stoke-by-Nayland, Dedham – all these were villages that owed their prosperity to the cloth trade.

'Here I am quite alone amongst the oaks and solitude of Helmingham Park ...' I was surprised to find on the edge of the stream the very same oaks that Constable had drawn in July 1800 (the basis of his two paintings of 'Helmingham Dell', now in the museums of Philadelphia (1825–6) and Kansas City (1830)). I was, however, even more surprised to make the acquaintance of his great-great-grandson in *Dedham*. His name is also John, and he is also a painter, and he is also as unsuccessful as his great ancestor was originally (plate 49). It's not an easy inheritance, having Constable's deathmask on your shelf and Constable Country before your very eyes. 'Everybody expects me to paint just like him,' complains John Junior. He lives just outside the village with his wife, three cats ('Giotto is a nasty little trouble-maker') and three pugs, Phoebe, Rosy and Bertha. His studio is a

1 It was on the crest near Langham Church that Constable painted one of his most brilliant, small-scale oil sketches on 13 July 1812: 'Dedham from Langham' (Ashmolean Museum, Oxford), with a farmer ploughing in the foreground, and the Stour meandering as far as the horizon. Around 1830 he painted 'Glebe Farm' (Tate Gallery), the pink cottage near the beautiful little church just outside the village.

2 It is one of three altar paintings he did for churches in this area, the others being 'Christ Blessing the Children', *c.*1805, in St Michael's Church at Brantham (west of East Bergholt), and 'The Risen Christ', 1822, originally in St Michael's at Manningtree (on the Stour Estuary), but now in All Saints, Feering (west of Colchester).

John Constable: The Cornfield, 1826

converted pigsty, but he spends much of his time giving painting lessons to elderly ladies, while his wife Freda takes Japanese language students on tours of Constable Country. The marketing of the great artist with handkerchiefs, biscuit tins and calendars, has always been a source of annoyance to John Junior, since everyone else seems to make money out of the name, but the descendants themselves never see a penny of that money. Indeed, he had to pay so much tax on the paintings that he inherited ('legal robbery') that he was forced to sell five of them to the Tate Gallery, where they are not even on display.[1]

What about forgeries? 'The first ones already appeared during his lifetime,' says John, 'done by Charles Boner, who was a German private tutor to his children.' But the family don't like discussing this subject, which is scarcely surprising since at least five of Constable's seven children painted landscapes in their father's style – the most remarkable having been his youngest son, Lionel.[2] Some years ago, John and his brother Richard wanted to open a little museum to house the authentic paintings, documents, furniture and mementos still in the family's possession. Wouldn't Flatford Mill be the perfect place for this? 'Of course it would,' says John. 'You can house a Field Studies Centre anywhere, but that's the only place for a Constable museum.' The planning is absurd. Visitors come from all over the world – more than 250,000 a year – and all they ever see of Constable's paintings is postcard reproductions. The National Trust and the English Tourist Board have missed a golden opportunity. The potential of such a museum is clear from the success of the Gainsborough House Society in Sudbury (see page 174).

John Constable Junior has every reason to live outside the village. During the holiday season, it is simply overrun – and that is understandable, since it is a picturebook place. Dedham consists of a single, slightly winding street, a handful of old timber-framed and brick houses, a church behind chestnut trees, and the myth of a great painter. Long before Constable painted his father's watermill and the view of the tall flint tower in the distance across the river, Edward III established a colony of Flemish weavers here during the 14th century. Dedham had some 10,000 inhabitants in those days, and was a flourishing wool town, as can be seen from the fine houses of the clothiers (e.g. 'The Marlborough Head'). At the same time, around 1500, another clothier, John Webbe, built Southfields, a residence and warehouse south of the church, with an inner courtyard, and the church itself bears the initials of the Webbes, who were one of the families that built St Mary's (1492–1520). It is a Perpendicular building, with light, bright arcades, and a processional passage through the tower with the Tudor emblems of a portcullis and a rose in the ceiling. Opposite the

---

1 Since the retrospective of 1976, the Tate has been *the* centre for Constable research. The V&A is the second, older centre, with more than 400 paintings left by the last of the artist's daughters, Isabel, who died in 1888.

2 The (provisional) count of forgeries and false attributions, in which not only Constable's children but also his pupils and assistants were involved, has been tracked down by Jan Fleming-Williams and Leslie Parris in a real-life detective story: *The Discovery of Constable* (London, 1984). A lot of museums were affected, including the Neue Pinakothek in Munich: four of their five Constables have been discredited. A very apposite limerick was published in *The Times*, 4 June 1985: 'There was a young artist of Dunstable / Who once forged a painting by Constable. / His fraud was detected / Before he expected / As the paints he was using were unstable.'

John Constable: Stoke-by-Nayland, mezzotint by David Lucas, 1830

church is John Webbe's house, whose sundial and pilasters adorn a brick façade built over the older, half-timbered front in 1730. Sherman's Hall, as it is now known, shows that even after the decline of the cloth trade in Dedham, much good taste still went into the buildings. The spruced-up timber-framed bungalow on the road to the mill rejoices, of course, in the name 'The Haywain'.

The Stour Valley, where 'the endless beauties of this happy country' were more concentrated than in any other region, had been left by Constable and Gainsborough 'like a sucked orange' – complained the painter Walter Sickert. And yet the valley of pictures went on producing ever more pictures. You could easily cover all the meadows from Flatford Mill to Sudbury with them. Quite apart from the spare-time artists, the souvenir manufacturers, and millions of tourists with their cameras, the 20th century alone has seen three famous painters and one notorious forger settle in Constable Country.

Perhaps a genius like Constable could not have had geniuses for his heirs, but he had at least one genuine successor: John Nash. He followed in Constable's footsteps by painting working landscapes – and in his time, this meant the countryside of mechanized agriculture, with fields almost entirely devoid of people. In the Tate Gallery hangs a classic picture also entitled 'The Cornfield' (1918): the abstract pattern of a hilly East Anglian landscape. He too loved the Stour Valley more than anywhere else. 'Good river scenery – think we might stay here,' was the terse comment announcing his move in 1929 to

159

John Nash: The Cornfield, 1918

Wormingford, between Dedham and Sudbury, on the Essex side of the Stour. From 1943 onwards, he lived in a house on the eastern edge of the village (Bottengols, where the writer Ronald Blythe now lives) in modest circumstances and in the midst of a sumptuous garden. John Nash was one of the great English plant illustrators. With punctilious accuracy and geometrical abstraction he also painted the mills, barns and fields around him. When he died in 1977 in Wormingford, Nash Country was as unmistakable as the domain of his neighbour in Flatford Mill, where he was often a guest. For a time he was president of the Colchester Art Society, which he had founded together with the Welsh painter Sir Cedric Morris, who had lived in Suffolk since the thirties, painting his exotic garden at Benton End, south of Hadleigh. (One of Morris's pupils, incidentally, was Lucian Freud.) Nash and Morris strove all their lives to bring the conservative foundations of English art closer to the avant garde, and to gain international recognition for regional art. It was with this aim in mind that Cedric Morris founded the East Anglian School of Painting in Dedham in 1936, but he discovered that under every hedge and on every path, there was nothing but Constable's empty tubes of paint.

There was, however, another Dedham painter who became the darling of the nation, and that during his own lifetime: Sir Alfred Munnings. Like Constable, he was born a miller's son in Suffolk. He graduated from the Norwich School of Art, and in 1905 painted a farmer's wife on a white horse in a poppy field ('The Poppy Field'), after which he followed the safe English way to success. Epsom, Ascot, and wherever else the horses were running, there you would find Munnings, a 20th-century Stubbs, greatly valued, not to say overvalued as a British Impressionist. His 'Start at Newmarket' was sold at Sotheby's, New York, in 1987, and fetched a record $1.1 million. He became the most popular horse painter in the country, was made a knight, and became President of the Royal Academy. He resigned from this office in 1949, in protest against so-called modernism, which he denounced as 'all this damned nonsense', having delivered a sensational after-dinner speech in which he called Messrs Cézanne, Matisse and Picasso 'foolish daubers'. It must, alas, be said that this arch-reactionary had, as far as his fellow-countrymen were concerned, backed the right aesthetic horse. In 1920 he found 'the house of my dreams', on the outskirts of Dedham, and there he lived until his death in 1959. Sir Alfred's Castle House is now a memorial to him, so at least there is one of Dedham's painters whose pictures you can see in Dedham.

Tom Keating also wanted to be a great painter. He ended up, though, as England's greatest art forger – and he operated in Dedham. He first shook the art world in 1976 by confessing to having faked thousands of pictures: Impressionists, Expressionists, Turner, Samuel Palmer, and of course Constable – all as a protest against collectors and dealers who judge art only by its market value, and also as a vent for his frustration at the failure of his own pictures – which however increased considerably in value as a result. Poor Tom. How ironic that a great forger came to live in the home village of the most frequently forged painter in English art history. One can imagine a fascinating exhibition in Dedham one day: Keating's Constables in Constable Country.

Wool Churches, Tudor Mansions: From Lavenham to Long Melford

The streets of *Lavenham* are like timber-framed avenues, and the village itself might almost be a petrified forest, with windows and doors between the rows of silvery oak trunks. Walk downhill from the church, along the elegant curve of Church Street, and up the High Street to the market: it's like walking through a medieval world that is better preserved than any other in England (colour plates 25, 29, 30; plates 37, 38).

Lavenham is one of the old drapery towns, those Suffolk centres that used to export their materials in the Middle Ages via Ipswich to Holland and Spain. This hill town in the fields, which today seems more like a farming village, enjoyed its peak during the reign of

Henry VIII, when it was the fourteenth richest town in England. For almost 600 years the weavers flourished in Lavenham: first it was their famous blue cloth, then fine yarn, damask and flannel, serge and shalloon, and finally coconut matting, crinoline and horsehair mattresses. The last weaving mill closed in 1930. What remained were the houses of the clothiers and weavers, their old workshops, inns and guildhalls, all making up a little town that goes back to the Wars of the Roses.

Stalls go up in the triangular *Market Place* as they have since the market cross was built in 1502; you can picture the farmers selling their wares every Thursday, year after year, century after century; you can hear the cheers and the clattering hooves as Queen Elizabeth I comes to Lavenham, in 1578, escorted by 500 squires in black and white silk and 1,500 servants on horseback; you can shudder at the bull baiting that marked Guy Fawkes Day until 1842 – the last such show on British soil. In this nation of animal lovers, public executions (viewed no doubt as a more humane spectacle) continued for a good deal longer.

It's in the market place that you'll find Lavenham's most spectacular timber-framed house, the *Guildhall*, built *c.*1520 by the Guild of Corpus Christi, one of the town's four medieval guilds. This was where the clothiers met, fixed prices and wages, settled disputes and, on 3 February – St Blaise's Day – held a banquet in honour of their patron saint. In their heyday, during the 15th century, the weavers of Lavenham produced up to half a million square feet of finest cloth per year. After the Reformation and the decline of the guilds, the Guildhall served as town hall, prison, workhouse and almshouse, wool store and kindergarten. Today it is one of the National Trust's showpieces, with exhibitions of the cloth industry and wool processing, as well as first-class chamber concerts. Above all, though, it is the building itself that forms the focal point: it is a perfect example of Late Gothic carving and half-timbering. There is an extravagantly dense phalanx of oak supports, far more than the structure actually requires. The spandrels of the Tudor arches are richly ornate, as are the doorposts and the frieze on the beams of the projecting upper storey. Next door in the *Old Chapel* is a faithfully restored Tudor shopfront (plate 38). The little figure on one of the Guildhall's corner posts, holding a distaff, is John de Vere, 15th Earl of Oxford, patron of the guild and Knight of the Garter. One of his sons married the daughter of a local cloth merchant, niece of Thomas Spring, who was known as The Rich Clothier – a union between old aristocracy and new wealth. For centuries Lavenham was part of the de Veres' domain. They came from the town of Veere, in Zeeland, and accompanied William the Conqueror to England. There they became one of the mightiest families in the country. Hedingham Castle in Essex was their main seat (see pages 117 ff.), and there is a family monument in Lavenham church, while the family emblem can be seen above the entrance to the picturesque *De Vere House* in Water Street: the boar and the star, the latter of which shone forth from the crusader Aubrey de Vere's standard before Antioch.

Beneath Water Street there still flows the stream whose waters were once used by the clothiers to full their materials in the yards behind their houses. The latter reflect the whole range of Lavenham's development, from the 14th-century cottages of the hand-weavers to Roper & Sons' Victorian horsehair factory of 1891. However, no evidence has yet been found that the Weavers' Cottages (Nos. 23–6) were actually occupied by the Flemish weavers or 'Flemings' that Edward III brought to England in 1334. The three staggered roofs and pargeting decorations (including the fleur-de-lys, which was one of the Lavenham clothiers' emblems) denote the importance of *The Priory* in Water Street. At its centre is an early 13th-century hall, continually extended, which has been occupied by Benedictine monks, Protestant priests, Elizabethan Earls, Suffolk farmers, and now two enthusiasts called Alan and Gwenneth Casey. They have restored this wonderfully complex edifice as faithfully as could be. Only the originally open, medieval hatch windows have been replaced by sliding frames with glass. In the garden behind the house there are over 100 herbs. I was told that Water Street would soon hear the clatter of a loom again, because the Caseys' daughter is an artist in textiles.

Like the Priory, the *Old Wool Hall* (on the corner of Water Street and Lady Street) was originally a hall house with open roof trusses, built in the 15th century by the Guild of Mary. Later a clothiers' hall, it was torn down in 1911 but rebuilt after violent protests, and today forms part of 'The Swan', which is the oldest hostelry in Lavenham, and the very embodiment of Olde Englishe, timber-framed hospitality.[1] Here, after 13 hours, the exhausted travellers from London would climb out of their stagecoaches, which after 1763 made the journey three times a week. Another traveller also stopped for a last drink here in 1944: Glenn Miller. Shortly afterwards, his plane plunged into the English Channel.

Who could fail to love Lavenham? I love its half-timbered houses, with their magnificent simplicity, the natural proportions of their beams, their scars and cracks, their weathered strength. I love the clarity of this architecture, with its rigid and yet quite unmechanical order, and I love the pleasure it takes in its own variations, the fine balance between geometry and fantasy, the harmony between structure and decoration. I love the hand-made solidity, a completeness which takes its very life from the fact that it incorporates the irregular and incomplete. Shilling Street, Lady Street – the houses seem to exude a living, breathing warmth, the long breath of their history, centuries of work behind the aura of the picturesque. The beams creak and the cleats whine and the struts and braces create rhythms of their own, while the façades seem to be playing variations on a fugue. This is a magic forest made by man out of Nature.

There was once a time when timber-framed houses were out. Everyone thought they were old-fashioned – relics of rustic, medieval architecture. The good citizens of 17th-century Lavenham dutifully covered up all their timbering with a thick coat of plaster. The few who could afford it even put a Georgian brick mask in front of their old wooden façade, for example 'The Willows' in Church Street. Even the timbers of 'The Swan' were

---

1 Other prime specimens of timber-framed inns to be found in East Anglia are 'The Bull' in Long Melford, and 'The White Hart' in Great Yeldham, both in Suffolk, and the 'Fox & Goose' in Fressingfield, Essex.

covered in bricks until 1933. But after the war, people began to restore these houses, many of which were in a sorry state, and then the pendulum swung the other way: the threat of decay and demolition was replaced by a positive orgy of timbering – so much so that the Suffolk Preservation Society complained that there was far more timbering in Lavenham now than had ever been intended.

Little Hall, in the Market Place, is a beautifully restored timber-framed building (14–15th century), and it is the headquarters of the Suffolk Preservation Society (SPS), which was founded in 1929. This is the largest association of its kind at county level in all England, and has some 2,200 members. 'Lots of dukes and lords, old soldiers and writers,' the director Paul Edwards told me. When he gets up from his desk, he bumps his head on the ceiling of Little Hall. 'In Suffolk we've probably got the richest collection of historic buildings, and,' he adds tendentiously, 'the sorriest amount of state support.' There are about 12,000 listed buildings in Suffolk, with 300 of them in Lavenham alone.

Lavenham remains a model for all restorers. Even the Postmaster General made his contribution to the preservation of Lavenham's historical image: in 1967 he agreed to take down all the telegraph poles in the High Street and lay his cables underground. Another historical feature still to be seen on many houses is Suffolk Pink, a sort of pink whitewash that develops a patina of its own, much better than the normal shiny housepaint. Lavenham's outer appearance thus seems to be in safe hands, but the little town is not without problems of another kind: about two thirds of its population (about. 1,800) come from outside. They are mainly pensioners, commuters, or second home owners. Many of the locals live on the cheaper estates on the outskirts. There are posters in some of the windows: 'A working village. Let's keep it that way.' Lavenham does not want to become a museum piece, but nowadays there are few inhabitants engaged in agricultural work. Kitty Ranson, who owns a shop in the Market Place, remembers the days when the farmers used to drive their carts, drawn by their heavy Suffolk Punch carthorses, through the Market Place on their way to the fields. 'Now,' she says, with a rueful shake of the head, 'the local council wants to turn the Market Place into a parking area for tourist buses.'

One of the great sights that the tourists come to see stands triumphantly on a hill just outside the town: there, majestically, the soaring tower of *St Peter and St Paul* gazes down divinely over town and country. This is one of the great wool churches of Suffolk, built between 1485 and 1525, at the peak of the cloth industry's prosperity. The building material alone is clear evidence of Lavenham's wealth: imported Barnack limestone, set off by the homely local flint. The work of the stonemasons and woodcarvers is masterly: the ornate crennellations of the nave and side aisles, the porch with its fan vault, the exquisite wooden screen in the Spring Chantry (1525) with its carved foliage, columns and grotesques. For his chantry chapel and the completion of the tower, the clothier Thomas Spring paid £200, which at that time was a considerable sum. His coat of arms appears 32 times on the parapet, more even than the star emblem of the 13th Earl of Oxford, the other great patron of the church. Another well-loved feature is the sound of Lavenham's eight bells, while fans of gravestone poetry will admire the following: 'Hurrah! my boys, at the Parson's fall, / For if he lived he'd buried us all.'[1]

A few miles west of Lavenham is *Long Melford*, which was also a weavers' village and has a fine wool church. It was so rich in the Middle Ages that two Tudor mansions were built in close proximity to each other. 'Melford' is derived from 'mill' and 'ford', and 'Long' will be clear to anyone who dares to walk the length of the main street: it stretches for two and a half miles – the longest village in England. It's full of Georgian and Victorian façades, neoclassical doorways with columns, Venetian windows, and bricks of all sorts – early 19th-century white ones, and red and black ones in chequered patterns, as was the fashion around 1700. Less becoming is the modern trend of painting old bricks pink or green, and sticking old chimneys in front of the house as flowerpots. There's a great deal to see along this street, and also a great deal to drink, since you can divide your attention between thirty two antique shops and nine pubs. What 'The Swan' is to Lavenham, 'The Bull' is to this Antiquesville – it is the oldest of Long Melford's inns, built around 1450 by yet another rich clothier.

The long street of Long Melford leads to a broad village green, which was once a horse market and a camping site for gypsies (colour plate 11). A gentle slope, a magnificent green, a mansion on one side and a row of simple houses on the other, and, up above, the church and almshouse – all combining to form an unforgettably English scene. The green holds everything together and yet keeps everything apart: the feudal, clerical and civil powers of a society which, despite all its opposing elements, was always capable of achieving a balance. Melford Green is the perfect image of a social harmony and a centuries-old hierarchy which seems as natural here as the grass and the trees growing all around.

Long Melford's *church*, just like Lavenham's, stands on a hill on the edge of the village, and again its scale is in no way proportionate to the size of the community it serves (colour plate 12; plate 75). Its founders, the rich clothiers of Long Melford, built it (1460–96) to the honour of God and for the glory of themselves. It is a truly superb edifice, clearly laid out, rhythmically alternating between stone and glass, and flooded with light. The dark flint of the flushwork decoration and the bright limestone shine forth right up to the loftiest crenellation, particularly on the southern façade looking out onto the green. The church is built in the late Perpendicular glasshouse style, with long rows of tall, broad windows in the side aisles and the clearstoreys, while the slender piers supporting the arcades bring out the elegant nobility of this form of architecture. Unusually for parish churches, the Lady Chapel lies at the eastern end, as a prolongation of the chancel, an arrangement normally found only in cathedrals and monastic churches. The colourful splendours of the medieval church can be gauged from eight windows in the northern aisle – stained glass painted by Flemish or Norwich artists of the late 15th century. There, kneeling in the rich robes of their time, are noblemen, citizens, mayors, and judges – the pious founders of this church.

---

1 In the churchyard of neighbouring Long Melford is another classic epitaph to one William Willing: 'Death will'd that WILLING here should lie / Although unwilling he to die.'

Long Melford Church, 15th-century stained glass window: Elizabeth Talbot, Duchess of Norfolk (left), model for John Tenniel's illustration of the Ugly Duchess in Alice in Wonderland

The clothier John Clopton is also there, the chief benefactor, and so too is Elizabeth Talbot, Duchess of Norfolk. Her portrait, with its picturesque Gothic cap, is said to have served John Tenniel as a model for the Ugly Duchess when he was illustrating *Alice in Wonderland*.

One of the rarities in the church's stained glass windows is a little roundel with three rabbits: each has two ears, but the three rabbits only have three ears between them – a medieval joke that playfully symbolized the Holy Trinity to which the church is dedicated. Another noteworthy symbol is the Lily Crucifix window in the Clopton Chantry, where the cross and the lily are interwoven to give pictorial unity to the sufferings of Jesus and Mary. The alabaster relief[1] in the north aisle, the Adoration of the Magi, probably came from an altar, since it is coloured and gilded as all the altars, walls and ceilings were prior to the Reformation. In the floor are brasses of the Cloptons of Kentwell Hall, and their chantry is near the high altar. Opposite is the massive Renaissance monument to the other great benefactor, Sir William Cordell, master of Melford Hall. Thus the two local rivals and rulers of the Long Melford roost stand eternally united in death. If the church had patrons such as these today, it would never need to launch another appeal.

---

1 Alabaster from Nottingham was especially popular in the 14th and 15th centuries for altar reliefs and monuments.

In 1573 Sir William Cordell founded a refuge for 12 poor men of the parish: *Trinity Hospital*. There are four brick wings round a small inner courtyard, and it all stands right next door to the graveyard – suggesting a painless transition. This Elizabethan almshouse still has twelve occupants, 'but there aren't enough really needy people in Long Melford now,' says the warden, 'and so we also take people in from round about.' Until the Second World War, the men continued to wear frock coats and top hats – which had also been taken care of by the noble founder. Sir William did not, however, confine his building activities to housing the poor: around 1560 he built *Melford Hall* for himself (colour plate 17) opposite the church, and on the other side of the green.

Sir William made a career out of serving the Tudors. He was one of Henry VIII's legal advisers, rose to be Solicitor-General under Mary Tudor, became Speaker of the House of Commons and Master of the Rolls under Elizabeth I; he was an artist in political survival during these turbulent times. Unlike the Cloptons of Kentwell Hall, he was not one of the old landed gentry, but a nouveau riche. It was therefore with all the more pomp and

Michael Angelo Rooker: Melford Hall

circumstance that he welcomed Queen Elizabeth I to his new country house in August 1578. From the road, the modern visitor can see nothing more than the picturesque shapes of towers, domes and chimneys that glow in the warm red of Tudor brick as they rise up behind park walls and topiary. The mansion has six octagonal towers with onion roofs, rather like pepper-pots, an Italian Renaissance motif popular in the earlier 16th century[1] before Dutch influence on English architecture increased under the Protestant Elizabeth I. Apart from its Long Gallery, Melford Hall now has virtually nothing left of its Elizabethan interiors. The changes – including those to the west façade – were carried out by Thomas Hopper, who renovated the house between 1813 and 1820 for the family of Admiral Hyde Parker. Hopper, a much sought-after eclectic, worked with Georgian restraint except on the staircase, where he unleashed the full grandeur of the Greek Revival. There are some exquisite pieces of furniture, a few old Dutch pieces, and one absolute gem in the park: an octagonal Tudor pavilion with eight gables and sixteen octagonal turrets, which may well have served originally as a kind of sentry box for the house (plate 21).

Today the only thing that separates the two lordly domains of Long Melford is a busy road. I walked past the church and entered the shadows of an avenue of lime trees, planted in 1678, over half a mile long, the rustling drive to *Kentwell Hall* (plate 9). This, too, is a Tudor mansion of red brick, with towers similar to those of Melford Hall and perhaps even erected by the same builders and stonemasons (*c*.1550). And Thomas Hopper also modernized these interiors in a Georgian, neo-gothic style. The house is surrounded by a wide moat, and indeed the Moat House (*c*.1475) is all that remains of the original timber-framed building. While the heirs to Melford Hall gave their family home to the National Trust in 1960, the badly run-down Kentwell Hall was bought in 1971 by a young man named Patrick Phillips, a barrister. In due course he brought up a family of three children and became a highly successful lord of the manor. Room by room and year by year the Phillips have proved that it is still possible even today to preserve an estate of this size and, by one's own efforts, actually to make it pay. Their independence is far more precious to them than any state subsidy could possibly be.

For a long time Kentwell Hall was the site not of fine furniture and paintings, but of Herculean restorations. Now, however, the house is habitable, the moat re-dug, the fishpond full, and the park and gardens full of surprises. The Phillips breed rare farm animals like Tamworth pigs, Dorking chickens, Lincoln Longwool sheep and Norfolk Horn – all contemporary with the house. The courtyard is newly plastered and has a brick maze in the form of an enormous Tudor rose, which for a few weeks every summer sprouts the most lavish blooms. Knights and squires and court ladies, peasants and craftsmen – all in historical costumes – take over house and park: Tudor Kentwell is the name of the game,

---

1 Used at Hengrave Hall (Suffolk, colour plate 31), Layer Marney (Essex, colour plate 19), Sutton Place and Nonsuch Palace (Surrey, destroyed).

an authentic and happily nostalgic re-creation of the past, mixing history, folklore, English heritage, education, and a jolly good time for everybody. The performers are friends of the family and staff, and amateur dramatic societies from all around (plate 14). Sir John Clopton, the rich clothier, would have enjoyed it all immensely, and so do the school parties and the tourists, who flock here in their hundreds. And if you should say something to one of these Tudor folk, the response will come in good olde Englishe, as gallant or crude or poetic as in Shakespeare's day.

I don't know how many times *Cavendish* has won the Best Kept Village competition, but if you have to choose a village to put in a picture-book, this is it. The hillside village green is surrounded by church, pubs, and pink thatched cottages that used to be alms-houses. Behind the scenes in this tiny corner of perfection a remarkable charity is at work: the Sue Ryder Foundation. The woman who set up this whole operation in 1953, financing it through a chain of second-hand shops, now runs no less than 50 homes for sick and handicapped people, and for concentration camp survivors. Her husband, Leonard Cheshire, was an official British observer sent to witness the dropping of the atom bomb on Nagasaki, himself being a skilful and courageous bomber pilot. Having survived the traumas of the war, he saw it as his duty to help build a better world. His Cheshire Foundation now runs 260 homes for handicapped people in 49 different countries. In 1990, he began a new industry, producing ball-point pens out of scrapped Soviet medium-range rockets. The pen is indeed mightier than the sword. Every one of the 100 million or so pens is numbered, as a reminder of each of the 100 million or so war victims of the 20th century. The profits from this recycling of weapons are to help finance an international disaster fund that Leonard Cheshire set up.

Further up the Stour is *Clare*, a little town with a great past. All that remains, however, of the castle built by the mighty Earls of Clare are a few walls rising out of the bushes in the Country Park. The glittering feasts, the dramatic conflicts, the ambition and the glory of past generations have all faded away into information posted along the path, and the settings of power are now a picnic area. Clare College, Cambridge, has its roots here, for it was founded by Elizabeth de Clare, daughter of the 9th earl. Over on the other side of the river stands Clare Priory, the first Augustinian house in England, founded by Richard de Clare in 1248, and since 1953 once more run by Augustinians, though on a much more modest scale.

'Go about your Business' admonishes the sundial (1790) over the porch of the Gothic parish church. In the Middle Ages, the business of Clare was cloth-making, as it was in *Kersey*, too. In this village they produced a rough, ribbed cloth which was especially suitable for hosiery, and indeed Kersey was a famous name: 'Henceforth my wooing mind shall be exprest / In russet yeas and honest kersie noes,' says Berowne in Shakespeare's *Love's Labours Lost*. Today, Kersey is yet another of these picturesque villages: houses with roofs of red brick and tile, uphill and downhill, and right in the centre a road that fords the River Brett, where once the cloth-makers used to soak their materials (plate 71). Now it's cars that disturb the daily routine of the ducks and geese. 'My geese get a bit fed

Thomas Gainsborough: St Mary's Church, Hadleigh, 1748

up with the tourists,' complains one of the locals, as one gaggle is forced to give way to another. But Kersey too must march with the times. In the fifties they were even linked to the public electricity supply.

My last stop on this tour of Suffolk's cloth-making centres was *Hadleigh*. A 14th-century brick bridge with three elegant arches takes you across the River Brett. With varying roof heights and façades, some brick and some timber-framed, and the occasional pargeting, the High Street unfolds a fair range of the region's architecture (e.g. Nos. 62–6,

called the Coffee Tavern, 1676). The town council unanimously rejected a planning application for a supermarket here, as being totally unsuitable for such a protected area, and also bad for individual local traders.

In the centre of Hadleigh is a strange collection of medieval buildings, significantly assembled round the churchyard: St Mary's Church, the Guildhall, and Deanery Tower (plate 70). The church is flint, the Guildhall is timber-framed, and the Tower is Tudor red brick – a neat anthology of Suffolk's favourite building materials. The taller, central section of the Guildhall, with its overhanging storeys, was built in 1430 as an indoor market, and shortly afterwards it was extended to the sides and rear to accommodate the town's five guilds. Opposite stands the church, large and bright, with a tall wooden spire clad in lead – the only one of its type in Suffolk. Archdeacon Pykenham lived liked a prince next to his church, but now all that remains of his Deanery is the entrance,[1] a four-tower gatehouse built in 1495, with ornate crenellations, pinnacles, pilaster strips and Gothic trefoil arches (plate 18). This Deanery Tower is a miniature version of the gatehouse at Oxburgh Hall (1482), an example of how the architecture of defence could turn into the architecture of status symbols. The pomp of the clergy came to a sudden end with the Reformation, but in 1553 the English throne was once more occupied by a Catholic: Mary Tudor. During her short reign, Bloody Mary had 232 Protestants and Nonconformists executed as heretics, 70 of them in East Anglia alone. One of these was Rowland Taylor, Rector of Hadleigh.

Even in prison, Taylor retained his composure: 'There are a great many worms in Hadleigh churchyard, which should have had a jolly good feeding upon this carrion, which they had looked for many a day. But now I know we have been deceived both I and they; for this carcass must be burnt to ashes.' And one cold February day in 1555, that is what happened. 'Soyce,' said the condemned priest to the executioner, a well-known local drunkard, 'I pray thee come and pull off my boots, and take them for thy labour; thou hast long looked for them, now take them.' Then he recited the 51st psalm and was burned to death on the spot where today the obelisk stands on Aldham Common.

One of his successors in happier times was Thomas Tanner, who in 1748 commissioned a local young artist to paint a chimney-piece for the Deanery. Gainsborough's picture shows with pin-point accuracy the parson's residence and place of work, with a few graves and passers-by in the foreground. Their costumes apart, very little has changed since the young unknown set to work on his painting in 1748.

The Curs'd Face Business: Gainsborough in Sudbury

Suffolk is as much Gainsborough's Country as Constable's. He was born in *Sudbury*, on the Stour and just 12 miles upriver from East Bergholt. His early paintings, like Constable's, are Stour landscapes. 'It is a most delightful country for a painter,' wrote Constable. 'I fancy I see Gainsborough in every hedge and hollow tree.' Since then, many of the hedges have disappeared, but the broad water-meadows on the outskirts of the town have remained virtually unchanged, and the cows still graze there and drink from the river as they did in Gainsborough's day. Since the 13th century this has been 'The Freemen's Great Common'. The painter himself stands before the redundant Church of St Peter, a

---

1 The present Deanery is Neo-Tudor, 1831. It was here or in the Deanery Tower that Dean Hugh James Rose met his friends R. H. Froude, Palmer and Perceval in 1833. This so-called Hadleigh Conference was the beginning of the Oxford Movement, which aimed to restore the Catholic identity of the Anglican Church.

Thomas Gainsborough: Landscape in Suffolk, c.1748

lifesize bronze statue by Sir Bertram Mackennal (1913), depicting him in a wig and frock coat, his palette in his hand, gazing out over the market place and this 'age-old, loyal and patriotic community'. Sudbury was Dickens' model for the little town of Eatanswill, where Mr Pickwick stood for Parliament, with the Blues and the Browns vying for the voters' favours, much as they do today, using promises and presents, dirty tricks and glib slogans.

Gainsborough's name adorns a petrol station, a taxi firm, a night club, and a silk mill. Sudbury was the largest of all the old wool towns, and it still has three highly specialized textile mills. The American fashion designer Ralph Lauren produces the silk for his luxury ties in Sudbury, and the silk for Princess Anne's wedding dress came from here as well.[1] Gainsborough's father was also a clothier, but he went bankrupt, whereas his son became the best paid painter of silk robes in the whole kingdom. Do not miss No. 43 Gainsborough Street, where he was born in 1727, the youngest of nine children. This was originally two timber-framed Tudor cottages, which the father converted into a spacious

---

1   The ancestors of Stephen Walter, the silk-maker, were Huguenots like the Courtaulds, who emigrated to London, established workshops in Spitalfields, and from the middle of the 18th century onwards expanded to Essex and Suffolk.

weaver's house with a typical Georgian brick façade. This is actually the only house in England in which an artist was born and which is now open to the public. It nearly became a bicycle depot, but was saved by a few enthusiasts who bought it in 1958 and restored it. The Gainsborough's House Society is a purely private initiative which, in exemplary fashion, has ensured that the great artist's development has been accurately charted at the very place of his origin. As well as his palette knife, swordstick, and gold-framed lock of hair, one can see his 'colour cabinet', a mahogany desk with a slate top which he used for mixing his colours.

Now the Gainsborough House is filled with his work: drawings, etchings, a dozen paintings, more than in any other museum, and including a dazzling early work painted in London: the full-length portrait of a boy (c.1745). This is young William MacKinnon, dressed in the gentleman's outfit of the time – a frilly shirt, a frock coat, gold-coloured waistcoat with silk trimmings, knee breeches, and silver-buckled shoes. Next to the little cavalier is a girl with wild flowers in her lap, and one would love to see more of her, but her half of the picture has been cut off. This early, and still very formal costume piece foreshadows the sheer magic of Gainsborough's portraits of children: from the six double portraits of his daughters Margaret and Mary to the masterly 'Blue Boy' of 1770, the son of a rich ironmonger in Soho,[1] and right up to the 'Marsham Children' of 1787, a year before his death.[2]

The garden behind the house still contains the mulberry tree which was there in Gainsborough's time, and indeed had been there since about 1610, when it was planted for the silkworms. No genius comes without a childhood anecdote: looking out into this garden, the boy Gainsborough saw someone stealing his parents' pears, and drew the thief so accurately from memory that the culprit was instantly recognized. Thus the artist allied himself from the start with the enjoying classes. At school he showed more aptitude for drawing than for grammar, and when he was thirteen his parents sent him to London, to study under Hubert Gravelot, a pupil of Boucher. Gravelot's copperplate engravings were largely responsible for the spread of French influence in England, where taste in the early 18th century was still largely guided by classical Italian art. Unlike his rival Reynolds, Gainsborough never undertook the obligatory grand tour to Italy. The trees of Suffolk were his school, and the auction houses of London, where he first saw landscapes of Ruisdael and Hobbema, his academy. At the age of 18, Gainsborough moved into his own studio in London (1745). His earliest dated painting stems from this year – a quintessentially English subject: a portrait of a bull terrier named Bumper. The likeness of the dog delighted its master, and he was not alone in his admiration. 'Long-headed cunning people and rich fools are so plentiful in our country that I don't fear getting now and then a Face to paint for Bread.'

In London Gainsborough married the beautiful Margaret Burr from Scotland, the

1 Huntington Art Gallery, San Marino.
2 Gemäldegalerie, Berlin.

Thomas Gainsborough: The Artist's Daughters Chasing a Butterfly, c.1756

illegitimate daughter of Frederick, Prince of Wales. With her he returned to Sudbury in 1748 and took up residence in Friars Street. There he painted the wedding picture of another young couple: 'Mr and Mrs Andrews', the famous double portrait now hanging in the National Gallery. Frances, the sixteen-year-old bride, is dressed in blue satin and sits on a rococo bench; Robert leans next to her, his legs crossed and his gun hanging casually

Thomas Gainsborough: Mr and Mrs Andrews, c.1748–9

over his arm. Behind these fine specimens of the landed gentry is the timeless strength of an oak tree. The light is fresh as youth itself, and the neatly stacked sheaves appropriately suggest a universal fecundity. Gainsborough set this portrait on the young man's estate: this is the view from his country house, Auberies in Bulmer, across the Stour valley to Sudbury, with the tower of St Peter's in the background. The oak under which he painted the couple is still standing in the same fields.[1] However, unlike those of his neighbour Constable, Gainsborough's landscapes can rarely be pinned down to a precise location, apart from some of his early pictures around Great Cornard, on the outskirts of Sudbury, and 'Hadleigh Church' (1748), which he painted for the Rector (page 172).

When he failed to get the commissions he was hoping for, Gainsborough left his home town for good in 1752, and moved to Ipswich. For seven years he went on painting portraits of the clergy and the landed gentry, most of whom wanted nothing more than a cheap and simple likeness: head and shoulders, and plain background. Among his clients were the brewery family of Cobbold, the Mayor of Norwich, Sir Thomas Vere, the corporation lawyer of Ipswich, Samuel Kilderbee his lifelong friend, and the amateur flautist and MP William Wollaston of Finborough Hall. In addition to the portrait commissions, Gainsborough spent his time in Ipswich painting those early landscapes in which he developed a very personal way of combining Dutch realism with the new lightness of the Rococo. These are local scenes transformed into Arcadia, with Boucher's dallying shepherds beneath dramatic Ruisdael skies in the East Anglian countryside. But at that time the English public favoured a different type of landscape: either the precise reproduction of reality, or the heroic, mythological style of Poussin and Claude Lorrain. Besides, landscapes were regarded as an inferior genre – chimney-pieces they were called. Gainsborough knew that if he wanted success, it would have to be as a portrait-painter, and so he moved to Bath.

Bath in the 18th-century was the meeting-place in England for all those with name, rank, and a little bit of illness. 'A national hospital' is what it's called in Smollett's *Humphrey Clinker*: 'Every upstart of fortune, harnessed in the trappings of the mode, presents himself at Bath, as in the very focus of observation.' And if someone wanted to be noticed later, or even after his death, he had to have his portrait painted – preferably by Gainsborough. The studio at No. 17 The Circus became a centre for polite society, and Gainsborough made money. When the Royal Academy was founded in 1768, he was the only provincial portraitist to be appointed a founder member.

The sensuous pleasure of materials – shining robes, intricate lace, shimmering satin – which sometimes makes the faces themselves seem too smooth and flat, this was the influence of Van Dyck, whose work Gainsborough was able to study in the country houses all round Bath. 'We are all going to heaven and Van Dyck is of the party,' he said to Reynolds on his death bed. But the influence of Rubens lightened his palette and loosened

---

1 Almost 40 years later, in 1785, Gainsborough painted another wedding portrait, the romantic *Morning Walk* with a Pomeranian (London, National Gallery).

his brush, so that his landscapes became more animated and more impressive. His dramatic chiaroscuro is often the result of a predilection for painting by candlelight. Candles also illuminated the model landscapes which he designed in his studio. Cork and stones made up the rocky foreground, sand and moss the middleground, with a piece of mirror-glass for water, and the forests in the background were made of broccoli. He would then people his staged landscapes with tiny figures and animals modelled in clay. The model for one of his horses can be seen in the Gainsborough House in Sudbury – the only one to survive.

Gainsborough lived in Bath for fifteen years. The pictures suggest a portraitist of passion and conviction; the letters tell another story. 'I'm sick of portraits,' he wrote to a friend, 'and wish very much to take my viol-de-Gamba and walk off to some sweet village, where I can paint landskips and enjoy the fag end of life in quietness and ease.' He longed for the green banks of the Stour, away from the salons and under the lofty skies of East Anglia. 'But these fine ladies and their tea-drinkings, dancings, husband-huntings &c &c &c, will fob me out of the last ten years.' A visitor reported that Gainsborough's landscapes stood in long rows that reached from his entrance hall all the way to his studio, but the people who sat to have their portraits painted – 'people with their damn'd faces' – scarcely glanced at them as they passed by. 'Damn gentlemen … they have but one part worth looking at, and that is their Purse.'

'The curs'd Face Business' it may have been, but seldom can an artist's frustrations have been as fertile as his, either financially and aesthetically. In 1774 Gainsborough moved to a house in London's elegant Pall Mall, and he already had a country house in Richmond (where his patron George III occasionally came to visit him), a cottage in Essex, and his own carriage. Incidentally, he had all his fees paid to his wife Margaret. Actors and musicians were among his special friends, and he liked best to paint them, particularly the women: Sarah Siddons and Mrs Sheridan were two of the most famous beauties of the London salons. David Garrick sat for him, and so did Johann Christian Bach and his partner Karl Friedrich Abel, German composers at the Court in London; another sitter was Johann Christian Fischer, who had been oboist to Frederick the Great and was to become Gainsborough's less than beloved son-in-law. He portrayed James Christie, founder of the famous auction house, with a smile on his face as he leans on a Gainsborough landscape. It is, however, Sotheby's who have set the pace today with a record price of £1.5 million for the portrait of the young Mrs Drummond. His family portrait of the Gravenors was sold by Sotheby's in 1972 for what was then a record of £280,000. The picture went to America. There the New York art dealer Joseph Duveen (who was actually born in England) had already ensured that such collectors as Henry C. Frick, Andrew Mellon, and Henry E. Huntington acquired their own Gainsboroughs – a prerequisite for anyone who aspired to 'the millionaire taste'. Duveen sold his American customers a past, for anyone who bought a Gainsborough portrait was adopting an ancestor from the English upper classes.

In London Gainsborough painted some of his finest, most colourful pictures – conversation pieces by an English Watteau: *The Mall*, for instance, where the ladies promenade with their beaux, a 'fête galante' in St James's Park, in the Frick collection in New York; or the Duke of Cumberland walking with his wife under the trees at Windsor – one of the prize pieces of the Queen's collection, the largest private collection of Gainsboroughs in the world. They are, of course, glamour portraits, but Gainsborough was never a purely representational artist or mere costumier. For him, the landscape was not just a background setting for his subject, but an essential part of what he was trying to express. Mrs Sheridan's hair blowing in the wind and the leaves trembling above her together form a synthesis between humanity and Nature which makes Gainsborough a genuine precursor of the Romantics. The backgrounds were so important to him that he never employed any assistants – with the single exception of his nephew Dupont – to work on them. The relaxed, sketchy impressionistic brushwork knits his pictures together and endows them with that incomparable, poetic atmosphere. No-one has described it better than Constable, Gainsborough's successor in the art of landscape painting: 'The stillness of noon, the depths of twilight, and the dews and pearls of the morning, are all to be found on the canvasses of this most benevolent and kind-hearted man. On looking at them, we find tears in our eyes, and know not what brings them.'

Gainsborough used to dilute his paint with turpentine and to apply it in subtle layers, almost like varnish. This is what gives his subjects a tactile elegance, and his oils the lightness and transparency of watercolours. In Gainsborough's pictures you find the same soft pastel shades and tender curves so typical of the interiors designed by his contemporary, Robert Adam. But you can never see from Gainsborough's people what they are thinking. The often extraordinary blandness of their faces, however, does not mean that they are without character, any more than their portrayer is without powers of expression. On the contrary, his work is the ideal expression of what Jane Austen called the 'true English style', which means 'burying under a calmness that seems all but indifference, the real attachment'. Both the need for understatement and the desire to show 'the real attachment'. Both the need for understatement and the desire to show 'the real attachment' are fulfilled in the great open-air portraits, where the true feelings of the subject are transposed into the changing moods of Nature. This is what gives the pictures their shimmering aura of inaccessibility combined with intimacy. They reflect the new approach to life of a society that was stepping out of the constraints of rigid courtly etiquette and formal French gardens into the freedom of open spaces, English gardens, and an era of natural rights and natural poetry. Gainsborough's people are the heralds of a new and Romantic vision of Nature.

In 1788, one year before the French Revolution, Gainsborough died of throat cancer in his house in London. His lifelong rival Reynolds offered this noble eulogy: 'If ever this nation should produce genius sufficient to acquire to us the honourable distinction of an English school, the name of Gainsborough will be transmitted to posterity in the history of the art, among the very first of that rising name.' The master from Sudbury left behind some 800 portraits, as well as hundreds of landscapes and a great deal of confusion in the art market. He seldom signed his pictures and only dated one. Copies and forgeries abound, and John Hayes, director of the National Portrait Gallery, in his two-volume catalogue raisonné *(The Landscape Paintings of Thomas Gainsborough*, London 1982) accepts only 187 of the landscapes.

In 1980, Gainsborough's lords and ladies travelled from Boston, New York, Malibu, and all the great museums and galleries of the world, to a reunion in London's Tate Gallery, and together they formed the portrait of a whole class, a retrospective of Britain's former might and glory. This exhibition was 'a ceremony of national taste' *(Time)*, a résumé of a style of life that is past but not completely lost. The presence of the young Henry, 3rd Duke of Buccleuch, in Gainsborough's 1770 portrait was matched by the presence of the lender, the 9th Duke of Buccleuch. This historical continuity can be felt even more strongly in the great houses of East Anglia than in Gainsborough's own birthplace in Sudbury. There is scarcely one where you will not find on the walls 'the Gainsboroughs and Lawrences / and some sporting prints of Aunt Florence's', as Noel Coward put it. About one third of all Gainsborough's pictures are in the possession of individual families, despite the ravages of death duties and auction houses.

It should not, however, be forgotten that Gainsborough did not confine himself to portraying only the enjoying classes. He also painted farmers, shepherds and woodcutters, often lifesize, representatives of the simple life, though he showed them in circumstances somewhat divorced from reality. 'Fancy pictures' he called them, and they catered to the picturesque taste of the time. His models for these pieces would be, for instance, beggar children brought in from the streets, or even pigs. He painted farmers on their way to market or on their carts, or outside their hovels in the twilight. This was country life from the perspective of the landlord – pastoral idylls on the eve of the agricultural and industrial revolutions. Even Gainsborough's contemporaries saw this Anglo-Arcadia with nostalgic eyes – the townsman's eternal, bourgeois longing for an alternative way of life.

What could be more English than this countryside, and these tall, excessively slender figures, and these ladies in silks and satins, occupying Gainsborough's Nature as if it were a salon, and taking their place in Society as if it were a part of Nature – in the true spirit of Rousseau? Gainsborough did not invent the full-length open-air portrait, but one could say that he perfected it. That is the basis of his fame. What he really wanted, though, was not portraits in a landscape: he wanted landscapes without portraits. That was his dilemma.

To follow Gainsborough's life and pictures, go from Sudbury to Ipswich. In the museum at Christchurch Park, are a number of the early journeyman portraits, and right next to them is an outpouring of sheer poetry from his last years: 'A Country Cart Crossing a Ford' – perhaps it is the Stour. Farmhands in a horse-drawn cart cross the river; the willows gleam on the banks under a brilliant, stormy sky.

Orwell's Orwell, or Who Flows Through Ipswich?

The most beautiful thing about *Ipswich* is Chapter 22 of *Pickwick Papers*. Dickens's hero stays in an inn which, because of its monstrous size, is 'famous in the neighbourhood, in the same degree as a prize ox'. This is 'The Great White Horse' in Tavern Street: 'Never were such labyrinths of uncarpeted passages, such clusters of mouldy, badly-lighted rooms, such huge numbers of small dens for eating or sleeping in, beneath any one roof, as are collected together between the four walls of the Great White Horse at Ipswich.' Mr Pickwick loses his way and ends up in the room of a lady. Miss Witherfield, 'a middle-aged lady in yellow curl-papers', proves to be an even greater disappointment to Mr Pickwick than the wine he had drunk earlier ('a bottle of the worst possible port wine, at the highest possible price').

At this hotel on the coach route between London and Norwich Dickens himself stayed in 1835, when he was reporting for the *Ipswich Chronicle* on the election in Suffolk. But evidently no criticism can be so damaging that it can't be used later for publicity. The 'Great White Horse' is thick-skinned enough to deck itself out in Dickens illustrations and a 'Pickwick Room'.

Chaucer's grandfather came from Ipswich, as did Cardinal Wolsey, and England's first lawnmower. The town was founded by Anglo-Saxon settlers around AD 600, and with its naturally protected port on the upper course of the Orwell, it developed during the Middle Ages into an important trading town. Queen Elizabeth I visited it in 1561 (and complained about the dirty streets), Gainsborough spent seven lean years here early on in his career, and in 1741 the great actor David Garrick made his début here. Ipswich is a fine illustration of the fact that famous people are of little use to a town if the people of that town don't watch what the planners are up to. 'They massacred it,' said a local, and undoubtedly the most successful businesses in Ipswich include the demolition companies.

Since the days of Victorian prosperity, the story is one of pulling down and building up, following all the changing fashions, with little individual inspiration and absolutely no collective planning. The old Ipswich no longer exists, and of a new Ipswich there is nothing but odd beginnings. Tower Ramparts, Westgate and Northgate Street – only these street names denote what used to be the medieval town walls. There is a crude mixture of styles and indeed of non-styles in the centre around Cornhill, the old market place. Not far from the Victorian Town Hall (1868) and the Corn Exchange (1882) – now a leisure and conference centre – is Ipswich's one eye-catcher: the *Sparrowe's House* in the Butter-market. There are carved wooden posts on the ground floor, and magnificent bay windows, garlands of fruit and animated scenes on the overhanging first floor. Few more opulent, more baroque houses of this period (*c.*1670) are to be seen anywhere else in England. The pargeting includes the royal coat of arms of Charles II, and naive allegories of the Continents: America with a tobacco pipe; Europe with a Gothic church; and, sitting astride a crocodile with sunshade and spear, Africa, stark naked. It's also worth taking a look at the interior, especially as it is now occupied by a well-known bookshop. For two

Mr Pickwick in 'The Great White Horse' in Ipswich, illustration by Phiz for Chapter 22 of The Pickwick Papers

hundred years the house was lived in by the Sparrowes, a family of merchants, one of whom – John Sparrowe – was a councillor and was painted by Gainsborough. The artist's own house, at 34 Foundation Street, has been demolished.

A few 16th- and 17th-century merchants' houses have been preserved in Fore Street, and there are some older timber-framed houses in Silent Street. This was where Thomas Wolsey was born in 1472. Son of an Ipswich butcher and inn-keeper, he rose to be Cardinal Archbishop of York, and Henry VIII's Lord Chancellor. York Place in London, later called Whitehall, and Hampton Court were among his palaces, and it was he who initiated the Dissolution of the Monasteries, as well as dreaming of one day becoming Pope himself. In 1528 he founded the Cardinal College of St Mary in this, his home town, a rival to the elite schools of Eton and Winchester. Wolsey's college was meant to train pupils for his other great foundation, Cardinal College at Oxford, now Christ Church. But in 1529, after his failure to support Henry VIII in breaking with Rome, the unco-operative Lord Chancellor fell from favour, and almost all his property was seized by the King. He died only one year later, a broken man. All that remained of his ambitious project in

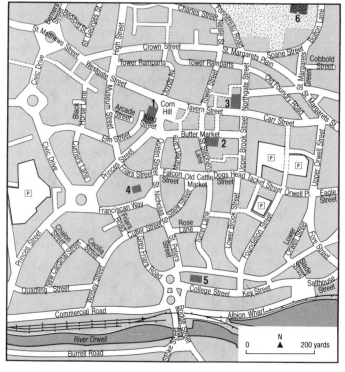

Ipswich, Town Plan
1 Town Hall and
   Corn Exchange
2 Ancient House
3 Great White
   Horse Hotel
4 Unitarian Meeting
   House
5 Wolsey's Gate
6 Christchurch
   Mansion

Ipswich was a modest, red-brick Tudor gate with Henry VIII's coat of arms: Wolsey's Gate, standing in College Street, on the edge of the Docks. A street, a school, the Wolsey Theatre and the Wolsey Orchestra are further reminders of the man who embodied the might of the church during the Middle Ages.

In the nave of *St Lawrence's* are long poles from which hang large numbers of theatre costumes. About half of Ipswich's ten medieval churches are redundant and now used for secular purposes or are preserved by a trust. A real discovery, though, is the *Unitarian Meeting House* in Friars Street, one of the earliest and finest Nonconformist chapels in England, and remarkably unaltered down the years. A local carpenter named Joseph Clarke built it in 1699 at a cost of £257: half-timbered, with plastered walls, and a double hipped roof. The façade is beautifully proportioned, with two oval windows above the two entrances, and three rectangular ones between them; the door frames have pediments on consoles decorated with doves and cherubs' heads. The playful ornamentation and the severe geometry are in perfect balance. The interior, too, is simple and clear-cut: a square-shaped room with galleries on three sides, supported by massive wooden columns. Pine box pews enclose the worshippers (and keep them warm), and all the seats face inwards towards the open centre of the room, emphasizing the family spirit of the

Cardinal Thomas Wolsey,
by an unknown painter

congregation. The dominant feature of the end wall is the richly decorated pulpit; opposite is the organ which has an octagonal clock crowned with cherubs. The hours are struck sweetly and gently.

'The interior is the best finished I have ever seen, London not excepted,' was Defoe's verdict in 1720. Indeed the quality of this church is so outstanding that one could suppose that colleagues of Christopher Wren or Grinling Gibbons had had a hand in it. A chapel like this could by no means be taken for granted in 1699. It was only ten years since the Act of Toleration had officially allowed the Nonconformists to build their own meeting houses. Before the Declaration of Indulgence (1672, but rescinded just one year afterwards), Dissenters had only been able to meet in secret. The fact that Ipswich's Nonconformists still felt insecure in the face of this new tolerance is indicated by the spy-hole built into the door: there a member of the congregation would keep watch during services.

You can see a reflection of this chapel in the most ultramodern façade in Ipswich: the black glass front of the *Willis Faber & Dumas Insurance Company building* (plate 35). This was designed by Norman Foster in 1975, and is the town's one and only outstanding modern building. Its elliptical elegance is not just an aesthetic end in itself but is actually the optimal use of space between two streets of the town centre. Smoothly the architecture follows the given line, as organic as an Arp sculpture. Escalators climb from the central well to the upper floors, whose open ceiling construction is rather like Foster's Sainsbury Centre in Norwich (page 385). An environmentally friendly roof garden with a restaurant for the employees crowns the building, which reflects the surrounding houses by day, and by night seems like a dark transparent vault. This was Norman Foster's first major public commission, and it is a masterpiece of high-tech architecture well deserving its listing in 1991.

The insurance palace and the Dissenters' chapel – these were the only attractive buildings I found in Ipswich. *Christchurch Mansion*, for all its fourteen Gainsboroughs and its eleven Constables is a musty place, though it does contain enough treasures to be memorable: furniture, porcelain, domestic items from Tudor times through to the 19th century (with many interiors from houses that have been demolished). One rarity is the early Jacobean Porch Chamber from Hawstead Place, whose wood panelling is covered with allegorical scenes, mostly concerning the vanity of the world; they were painted by Lady Drury, who was grieving after the death of her young daughter. Among the portraits of local personalities is one of Admiral Edward Vernon, nicknamed Old Grog because he always wore a camel-hair coat, or grogram. In 1740 Old Grog gave orders that the sailors' rum should be diluted, and grog has been the name for the hot mix of rum and sugared water ever since.

Christchurch Mansion (1548–50) was the Elizabethan country home of a London merchant. The Flemish gables were added in the 17th century. Later the house, together with its beautiful park, passed to the Fonnereaus, a Huguenot family. It was threatened with demolition, but was saved by the banker and mayor Felix Cobbold, a member of the local brewing family. He bought the mansion in 1894 and gave it to the town, together with money to build up an art collection. But now, before this museum is totally swamped by household equipment dating from the Year Dot, it desperately needs to be reorganized. Especially now that grandiose plans for a European Arts Centre in Ipswich docks have had to be abandoned.

When they were built in 1839–45, *Ipswich Docks* were the largest on the east coast, and they were crowned by a Custom House of 1844 hailed by Pevsner as 'remarkably original'. But the docks fell into disuse when new docks for bigger ships were built further upriver. The main exports were grain, animal feed, fertilizers, coal and stone. Locally, leather goods, textiles and cigarettes have generally replaced the traditional heavy industry of agricultural and hydraulic machinery, while modern technologies, and the relocation of businesses from London, and the arsenal of major international insurance companies have brought new commercial life to Ipswich in recent years.

Stratford, as everybody knows, lies on the Avon and not on the Shakespeare. But Ipswich lies on the Orwell. When Eric Blair was looking for a pseudonym in 1932, he did not call himself, for instance, George Thames, but he took the name of a river that was as little known as himself. The River Orwell is, in its turn, the pseudonym of another river which is actually called Gipping and which only assumes any real significance – under the name of Orwell – when it flows above Ipswich (the Anglo-Saxon Gippeswic) and forms a delta which runs out into the North Sea between Harwich and Felixstowe, and is absolutely perfect for a regatta. Why, though, did Eric Blair call himself Orwell? Alas, it had nothing to do with his love for Ipswich's river. He once told a friendly bookseller that it was better for an author to have a name beginning with a letter from the middle of the alphabet, because then his books would be placed in the middle of the literature section, just about at eye level.

Orwell Bridge is nearly a mile long, and since 1982 its reinforced concrete pillars have carried the ring road south of Ipswich across the River Orwell. On either side of the river are the gentle slopes of green hills. John Kirby in 1735 declared that 'to speak cautiously [this] is *one of the most beautiful Salt Rivers in the World*. The Beauty of it arises chiefly from its being bounded with High-land on both Sides, almost the whole Way. These Hills on each Side are enriched and adorned with almost every Object that can make a Landscape agreable; such as Churches, Mills, Gentlemen's Seats, Villages and other Buildings, Woods, noble Avenues, Parks whose Pales reach down to the Water's Edge, well stored with Deer and other Cattle, feeding in fine Lawns, &c &c. all these and more are so happily disposed and diversified, as if Nature and Art had jointly contrived how they might most agreably entertain and delight the Eye.' I went walking through Woolverstone Park, under ancient oaks and chestnuts, and across cornfields full of poppies to *Pin Mill*, a hamlet on the southern bank of the Orwell. The peak period for the waterside pub, the 'Butt and Oyster', is at high tide. At Pat Watt's bar there's a fine mixture of sailors, punks and ladies of all sorts. There was a pub here as long ago as 1553, the first and the last refuge of the coaster men. Right up until the start of the 20th century the great ocean-going clippers would drop anchor downriver of Pin Mill, and transfer their loads to the cargo vessels which carried them the rest of the way to Ipswich. These picturesque barges with their rust-red sails also used to transport hay for the coach-horses in London, and on the return trip they would bring back the city's manure to fertilize the fields of Suffolk. Today there are about 50 of these barges still to be found on the East Anglian coast, and during the first week in July they hold a traditional regatta in the estuary of the Orwell – a glorious reminder of the river's heyday. There are quite a few barges around Pin Mill, either broken up or restored as houseboats. In one of the latter lives Robert Bryant, generally known as Fat Bob, the tattoo artist. His customers include sailors, prostitutes, and all sorts of other people. 'Churchill's mother had a tattoo,' he remarks with the dedicated seriousness of the true craftsman. 'A snake on the wrist it was.'

On the bank of the Orwell between Pin Mill and Ipswich stands a strange tower of red brick. *Freston Tower* was built in 1549, and when you look at this six-storey belvedere, whose windows get bigger the higher up they are, you can't help asking whether it really was meant to be just a watch-tower. Personally, I prefer the other, more eccentric account, which is that it was a High School for Lord Freston's beautiful daughter Ellen – a pedagogic ivory tower. Each storey was specially laid out for each day of the week. Monday was weaving on the ground floor, Tuesday was music on the first floor, Wednes-

Christchurch Mansion, Ipswich, Jacobean emblems in Hardwick House

day was Latin on the second floor, Thursday was English Literature, Friday painting, and Saturday took the young lady high enough to study the stars. On Sunday the beautiful Ellen was let out of the tower, only to resume her laborious climb the next day. Not much time for this Rapunzel to let down her golden hair.

We are on pedagogically firmer ground when we enter the neighbouring *Woolverstone Hall* (1776). The Neoclassical mansion on the Orwell was for many years a boarding school for boys, run by London's educational authorities. This 'poor man's Eton' mainly took in problem children from the inner city – children from minority groups or broken families. The commitment was enormous, and so was the cost, and so was the volume of criticism; so now it is a high school for girls. One very successful Old Boy of Woolverstone is the writer Ian McEwan. The government tends to look with rather more pride on the Royal Hospital School, also for boarders, and founded in 1712 in Greenwich for the sons of Royal Navy personnel. It moved in 1933 to *Holbrook*, into a monumental modern building in a Neo-Wren style, designed by Buckland & Haywood in 1925–33, and with a

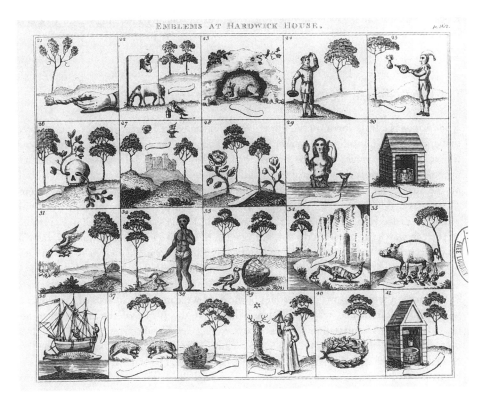

chapel that has frescoes by Eric Gill. In this institution the 700 pupils are made to feel something of the spirit of the Old Empire. It's half educational, and half military training camp, for where the Orwell and the Stour flow into each other, near Bloody Point, the Royal Navy has its cadet school.

On the other side of the Orwell Estuary, on the horizon over Trimley Marshes, tower the cranes of *Felixstowe*. At the place where, early in the 7th century, St Felix stepped ashore to accomplish his mission in East Anglia, today there is a gigantic, computerized container port. Two thirds of all Britain's trade with the Continent now passes through Felixstowe. Liverpool has long since been left behind, and this, England's largest and Europe's fifth largest container port is still expanding. With each addition to the docks, the main landowner of the area rejoices – Trinity College, Cambridge. But with each addition, the wading birds lose yet another of their precious habitats, even though the salt marshes of the Orwell Estuary have been officially designated an Area of Outstanding Natural Beauty and a Site of Special Scientific Interest. To their credit, however, the Felixstowe

189

Dock Company did balance out one of its recent extensions by financing a nature reserve in Trimley Marshes.

Journey to the Land of Shadows: The Burial Ship of Sutton Hoo

Woodbridge is a little town on the upper course of the River Deben. In 1724 Defoe noted that apart from a considerable market for butter and grain there was nothing special about it. But since then, much water has flowed through the Deben, the old salt-works basin has become a sailing port, and at least one building is now a sight worth seeing – the tidal mill on the quay, which was still in operation until 1957 and is now an industrial monument. There was a tidal mill here as long ago as the 12th century, but the present one, with weatherboarding and a high hipped roof, was built in 1793, the last of its kind in England.

You can watch the boat-builders at work on the river, browse in the antique shops, stroll up Church Street and down Angel Lane, and enjoy all the provincial charms of this modest little town – its market place on the hill, its Town Hall with a fine flight of steps and a Dutch gable, surrounded by Georgian brick houses, and right next to them the churchyard of St Mary's, almost as if the gravestones of the dead were in the backyards of the living. It was in this pleasant and respectable place that there dwelt one of the colourful minor characters of the Victorian literary scene: Edward FitzGerald, who from 1860 to 1873 lived on Market Hill, and from 1874 to 1883 lived at Little Grange, Pytches Road. He earned his fame in 1859 with a book that he didn't even write himself. His translation, though, was so brilliant that his English version became one of English literature's most famous poems, and will forever be associated with his name: *The Rubáiyát of Omar Khayyám*. FitzGerald took the verses of this 12th-century Persian poet, and repolished them into 75 quatrains of wisdom about love, wine, and death. These were the poetic meditations that Thomas Hardy read as he lay on his deathbed, and FitzGerald's translation remains one of the most popular of all 19th-century poems.

Edward FitzGerald grew up on his parents' estate north of Woodbridge, in Bredfield House and Boulge Hall – both of which were demolished in the fifties. His mother was a millionairess from the Irish aristocracy, and used regularly to go to London in a canary-yellow coach drawn by four black horses. Her son, known to everyone as Fitz, enjoyed a reputation as something of an eccentric, especially after he had left Cambridge. He used to go sailing in a top hat and flowery silk waistcoat, and reading Dante and Calderón and the ancient classics en route. Occasionally he would fall overboard, book in hand, and when fished out of the water, would still be wearing his top hat, which he had lashed to his chin with a handkerchief. Such anyway are the tales told of this amateur yachtsman. His yacht was called 'Scandal', named apparently after what he considered to be the main product of Woodbridge. His own contribution was not inconsiderable. Edward FitzGerald liked handsome, manly men, for instance the fisherman 'Posh' Fletcher from Lowestoft, 'who looks like one of the Phidian marbles dressed in blue Trousers and Guernsey Jacket'. Sometimes the 'self-contented stupidity' of the little town got on Old Fitz's nerves. Sarcastically he wrote to a friend 'that I see, however, by a Handbill in the Grocer's Shop that a Man is going to lecture on a Gorilla in a few weeks. So there is something to look forward to.' The intellectual life of Woodbridge took place once a month in the Bull Hotel, where the twelve members of the 1760 Book-Club would meet for a roast beef dinner. The Woodbridge Wits included (in addition to FitzGerald) a parson, a bank clerk, and the lawyer Thomas Churchyard, who made a bit of a name for himself as a landscape painter.

Old Fitz, vegetarian, socialite recluse, was the prototype of the eccentric, creative idler. He was buried in 1883 in an idyllic churchyard near Boulge Hall, but not far from the cottage where, as a young man, he began his Persian studies. 'So bury me by some sweet Gardenside ... / That ev'n my buried Ashes such a Snare / Of Perfume shall fling up into the Air, / As not a True Believer passing by / But shall be overtaken unaware.' His grave is a simple stone sarcophagus near the church tower, with his name and dates on one side, and his own choice of epitaph on the other: 'It is He that hath made us and not we ourselves.' Ten years after his burial – for it takes that long for the English to honour their poets – his friends planted on his grave a cutting from the rose-tree that grows on Omar Khayyám's grave in Nishapur. But it is not only the pink of the Omar Khayyám roses that brings back memories of Old Fitz. Every ten years the members of the Omar Khayyám Appreciation Society gather for a commemorative meal at his local pub in Woodbridge, 'The Bull'. 'They always order the same,' says the landlady, 'boiled salmon, strawberries for dessert, and Kir.' Of course, everything in pink.

Edward FitzGerald spent most of his life in Suffolk, which he loved and always defended. Once, when the east wind was blowing a gale, he remembered the completely still but already rumbling night some 72 hours before the storm: 'What little wind there was carried to us the murmurs of the waves circulating round the coasts so far over a flat country. But people here think that this sound so heard is not from the waves that break, but a kind of prophetic voice from the body of the sea itself announcing great gales. Sure enough we have got them, however heralded. Now, I say that all this shows that we in this Suffolk are not so completely given over to prose and turnips as some would have us. I have always said that being near the sea, and being able to catch a glimpse of it from the tops of hills and of houses, redeemed Suffolk from dullness; and, at all events, that our turnip-fields, dull in themselves, were at least set all round with an undeniable poetic element.'

When night is falling and the owl begins its flight, when the last sailors on the Deben make their way back to the port in Woodbridge, 'with the first of the flood gurgling round the dinghy, and the bottom of the river seeming to clasp you in its mud-banked arms' as Hammond Innes writes, 'where but on this strange east coast of England can hardness of light so combine with the dying day to produce an hour of total magic?'

For the sailor, these eerie moments recall a strange longboat buried not far away. The *Sandlings*, east of Woodbridge were once a heath that stretched all the way along the coast of Suffolk. From the Middle Ages, this was traditionally a sheep-rearing area, but more and more of the grasslands then came under the plough. From the 18th century onwards, the Sandlings were used for raising and shooting pheasant, and there are still more pheasants to be found here than in any other part of England. The Sandlings themselves, however, have almost completely disappeared, thanks to intensive agriculture, reafforestation, housing estates and golf courses. The conservationists are now trying to preserve the meagre remains of the heath.

The way to *Sutton Hoo* is across the fields on the northern bank of the Deben. You follow the sign of the stag – a symbol of majesty on the sceptre of the buried king. Suffolk's pyramids are green and as unprepossessing as molehills. But what a young employee of Ipswich Museum found there, when in 1939 he opened the biggest of these fifteen mounds, was simply breathtaking: a magnificent helmet with facemask and copper reliefs, a wooden shield with a gold buckle, a sword and chain-mail coat, ornate gold clasps, silver bowls, bronze kettles, drinking vessels made from aurochs' horn, a three-legged beeswax lamp, spoons and lyres. It was the richest archaeological find in Britain this century, and also the most mysterious: a grave without a body, a sceptre without a king.

Who was the dead man of Sutton Hoo? There can be no doubt that he was a mighty ruler, for he was buried with all the insignia of his power, well equipped for the long journey to the land of the dead. He had two leather shoes, an otter-skin cap, three combs, a blanket and goosefeather pillows on which to rest his head during the eternal sleep. Piece by piece the archaeologists reconstructed a ship from the remains and imprints that they found in the sand. It was 89 feet long and 14 feet wide, with a flat bottom, clinker-built and stabilized with ribs, a rudder on the starboard side. The damp sand of the barrow had preserved only the dark colours of the wood, which had rotted away leaving just the imprints of ribs and boards, along with the rusted iron rivets that had held them together. This was a ghost ship. From triangular discolorations in the sand, the archaeologists also reconstructed gable-shaped rowlocks and 20 benches for the oarsmen. And just as Charon was always given money for ferrying his customers across the Styx, and the Greeks always buried their dead with a coin in the mouth, so too did the burial ship carry its fare: 37 gold coins for the oarsmen, and three unmarked gold bars for the helmsman.

Although only its shadow had survived, the ship of Sutton Hoo is considered to be the best preserved ship prior to the Norman Conquest of 1066. It was built in virtually the same way as the so-called Nydam boat, which was sunk c.AD 400 in the bog on the island of Als in Denmark. It is typical of the craft used by the Angles and Saxons, Jutes and Franks when they crossed the sea to invade and colonize Britain. This boat would have been dragged overland from the River Deben for half a mile onto the 100 foot high ridge of

1   A summer's day in SOUTHWOLD   ▷

3 CROMER   Pier with bathing beauties
◁ 2   Fishermen's huts on the Blyth Estuary near WALBERSWICK
4   ALDEBURGH   Beach with readers

6   Constable Country: on the River Stour near FLATFORD MILL ▷

5   SOUTHWOLD   Synchronized sipping

7　Windmill on the RIVER THURNE

8　ST BENET'S ABBEY　Ruins on the River Bure

Ousden   Rape fields in Suffolk

0   Blythburgh   Perpendicular church on the River Blyth

11   The long High Street of LONG MELFORD

13   HELMINGHAM HALL   Moated mansion in Suffolk

12   LONG MELFORD   15th-century Perpendicular church

14   BLICKLING HALL   Jacobean manor house, *c.*1620

15   EAST BARSHAM HALL   Tudor country house, *c.*1520

16 ERWARTON HALL   Gatehouse, *c*.1550
              18   HEVENINGHAM HALL   Georgian mansion in park by Capability Brown ▷
17 MELFORD HALL   Tudor country house, *c*.1560

19 LAYER MARNEY TOWER   Gatehouse, *c*.1520

20   ST OSYTH'S PRIORY in Essex

21 BARTON TURF   Victims of post-Reformation iconoclasts

22 BARTON TURF   Saints on 15th-century choir screen

23 NORWICH CATHEDRAL   Norman crossing tower

24   Suffolk Pink: Cottage and church in HARLESTON

25   Street in LAVENHAM

26 Church in park on FELBRIGG HALL Estate

28 Bay windows in ALDEBURGH ▷

27 THAXTED 15th-century Guildhall

29, 30   Timber-framed Tudor houses in LAVENHAM

31   HENGRAVE HALL   Heraldic bay window, 1538

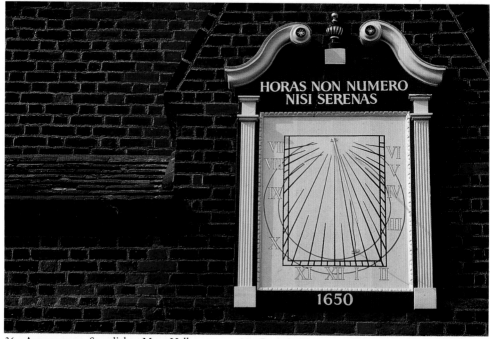

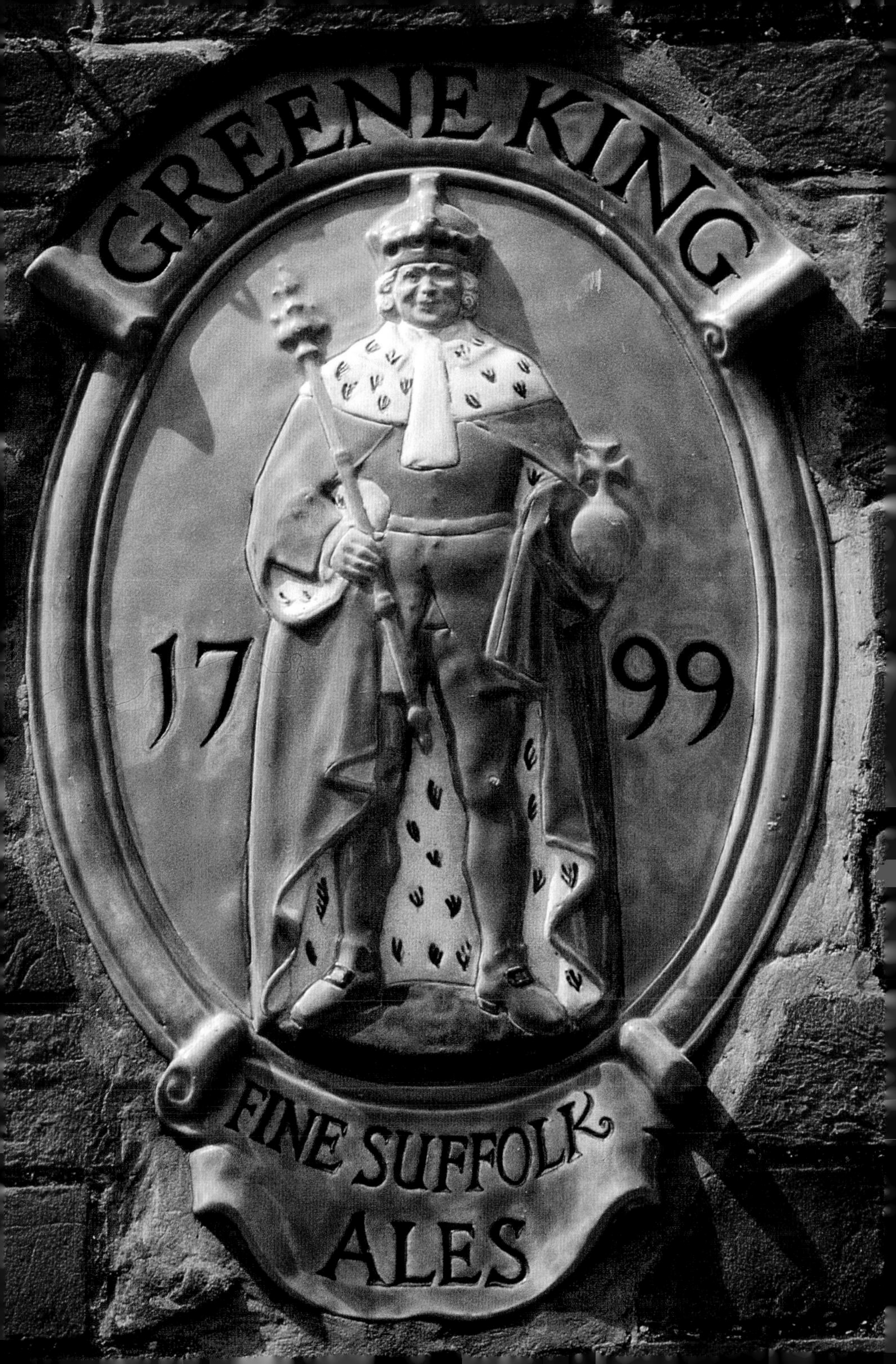
GREENE KING
17
99
FINE SUFFOLK
ALES

Sutton Hoo. Amidships they built a burial chamber, a cabin for the dead man. The gifts were covered with ferns, the ship filled with sand, and an oval mound of earth piled on top. Such ship-burials have been found in the Viking settlement at Haithabu in Sweden and at many Scandinavian sites; they correspond to the description of the Danish King Scyld's last journey in *Beowulf*. The king buried at Sutton Hoo was probably Raedwald, King of the East Angles, who died *c*.625.

The body, however, has disappeared like a wave in the sea, decomposed in the acidic sand, and washed away by centuries of English rain. No trace has been found either of burial or of cremation. Only from the burial gifts, their origin and their dates, can one reconstruct an image of Sutton Hoo's ship king. He was certainly more than a tribal chief. He was a ruler whose domain had trading links as distant as Uppsala and Constantinople. His silver utensils came from the Mediterranean, his gold coins from Merovingian Franconia, and his sword was a product of some early European Community, since the blade was made in the Rhineland, the richly enamelled hilt was made in Sweden, and the weapon was assembled in England. The burial gifts also included two silver spoons with the Greek names of Paulos and Saulos – baptismal spoons. And indeed King Raedwald was the first of his line to be converted to Christianity, although his widow had him buried according to heathen rites. As in *Beowulf*, nothing is certain in times of such upheaval.[1]

The grave is empty, the hero's last resting place has been desecrated, and the treasure has been taken to the British Museum. In the summer of 1987, archaeologists began to excavate another of the barrows, layer by layer, using computers and sonar machines and all the latest electronic and forensic technology to wrest its secrets from the bitter sand. What they found were the shadows of dead people: bodies that had disappeared, but had left their shapes behind, filled with sand. 'Sand-bodies' is what the archaeologists call them, rather like the dark matter which the astrophysicists call the long dead stars they discover. Traces of habitation beneath the Anglo-Saxon graveyards of Sutton Hoo reach back to two thousand years before Christ. This unspectacular field of molehills means mountains for the burrowing academics, for herein lies the key to the origins of the Kingdom. Sutton Hoo was the burial ground of the East Anglian dynasty of the Wuffingas, the first kings of the region. Their ancestral home was probably East Schleswig, and Raedwald was the only ruler to become 'Bretwalda', i.e. to rule over a wider community, and be king of all the other English kingdoms. Recently, the discovery of human sacrificial victims buried around the royal graves has suggested a growing sense of Englishness amongst the East Anglians since. Such pagan rites asserted kinship with Scandinavia, and defiance of the Christian Frankish empire. 'Sutton Hoo is a theatre in which the longest running theme is the defiant pagan politics of East Anglian kings trying to resist European Christianity,' says Professor Carver about these latest excavations. 'The late 6th century marked the

---

1   Since the discovery of the Sutton Hoo burial ship, East Anglia has been regarded as a more likely place of origin for *Beowulf* than the hitherto favoured kingdom of Mercia. The date is still variously placed between the early 8th and the late 10th centuries.

beginning of a debate over whether England should opt for political integration with the Continent.'

The first kings of East Anglia lived in *Rendlesham*, four miles north of Sutton Hoo. That was where Raedwald also held court, though the precise place is not known. I found two follies there: the first was the strange gatehouses of Rendlesham Hall.[1] The second was the American airbase RAF Bentwaters: 'Welcome to the 81st Tactical Fighting Wing'. Thus they hunt over Stour and Styx. If they have their way, Raedwald, not even a trace of us will be left in the acid sand when the neutron blitz has ended – just a world of burial gifts.

Sutton Hoo, then, was where the Anglo-Saxon kings were buried, but if you want to know how the ordinary people lived, you should go to *West Stow*. This little spot in the Brecklands, northwest of Bury St Edmunds, is also an archaeological sensation. While the ghost ship of Sutton Hoo has been reconstructed in fibreglass, West Stow has reconstructed an entire Anglo-Saxon village. The huts stand on a slope on the bank of the River Lark, the thatched roofs descending low down as a defence against wind and cold. Life was probably grim around AD 410, at the time when the Roman legions went home, and later, when mass migration began from the Continent. Catastrophic floods that ruined the homelands of the Angles and the Saxons, and a power vacuum in Britain combined to create a refugee problem comparable to those facing us today.

West Stow, a settlement some 5 acres in area, was discovered quite by chance when it was decided to put a rubbish tip there. What emerged during excavations in 1957–61 were the foundations of 80 houses, and over 2,000 objects in a so-called culture layer, including 120 combs and weaving implements made of bone. The ancient inhabitants of West Stow bred sheep, and kept cattle, pigs, goats and chickens, as well as horses, dogs and cats. This was one of many small Anglo-Saxon farming communities. Their houses could be reconstructed from the ground plan mapped out by the holes that had held the supporting posts. There were six large halls, up to 35 feet long, and these were the centres of family life, each having its own group of smaller huts, all made of wood and thatched with straw. The huts were rectangular, about 18 feet long, and had cellar-like rooms beneath the wooden floors, which were at ground level. (These sunken rooms are the origin of the technical name for these huts, *Grübenhäuser*.) It is impossible to say whether these sunken rooms were stores, workshops for the weavers, or bedrooms for women and children. West Stow was inhabited around AD 400, and abandoned around AD 650. Drifting sand covered the ruins, then moorland, and after that forest. This was how West Stow was preserved, and there is no other Anglo-Saxon settlement in England that is so complete.[2]

---

1 There were originally five gatehouses (*c.*1790), of which two survived the demolition of the Hall: Ivy Lodge, a sham Norman ruin, and Woodbridge Lodge, a Neo-Gothic cappriccio of buttresses, pinnacles, traceried windows and crenellations – two perfect follies. Part of Humphry Repton's landscaped park is now an RAF runway.

2 In Mucking, in Essex, over 200 *Grübenhäuser* have been found – the largest known Anglo-Saxon settlement of this type.

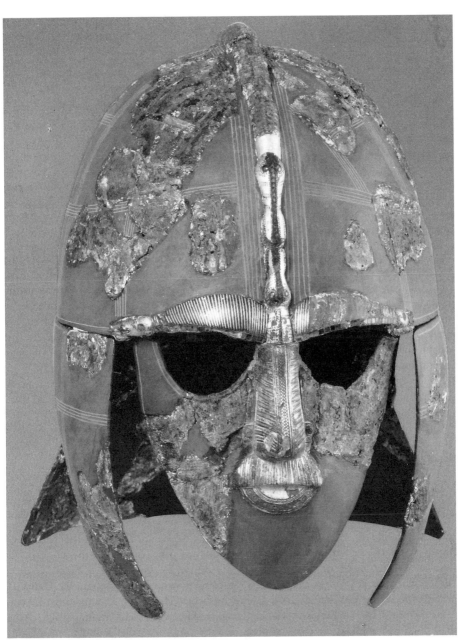

Anglo-Saxon helmet from burial ship of Sutton Hoo, c.625

In 1973, archaeologists began to rebuild some of the huts as authentically as possible, using only the tools and techniques available in this crucial period that laid the foundations of English village life and rural society. During the summer, members of the Dark Ages Society give demonstrations of how the Anglo-Saxons lived in West Stow. They camp out in their cloths and skins with their ponies and poultry, set up markets, and do battle with marauding Vikings. History is fun, they say, and indeed the British heritage industry would be poorer without them.

Helmingham and Heveningham: Houses of the Landed Class

Sometimes you come across links with your own history where you least expect them. When the old man at the gatehouse of *Helmingham Hall* heard where I was from, he began to tell me his story. He was a Polish Jew who had fled from the Warsaw Ghetto in 1940 and had made his very roundabout way to England. Now he was a supervisor here – the odd job man on Lord Tollemache's estate. 'It's a beautiful park,' he said, 'and don't forget the rosegarden.'

Helmingham Hall lies in the countryside north of Ipswich. At the end of an avenue of tall oak trees, you will see the dull red glow of the brick mansion. It's surrounded by a broad moat with two drawbridges, and just like the double majesties of kings and queens on old playing-cards, the bay windows, stepped gables, ornate chimneys and the sky double themselves in the water (colour plate 13, plate 4). The house is built round an inner court, and was begun in 1510 in traditional Tudor half-timbering, but then altered in 1760 to a Georgian style. The timber-framed façade – clearly recognizable in the protruding upper storey over the entrance – was completely covered with bricks, and around 1800 was again modernized. The Regency architect John Nash clad the whole façade in grey plaster (which, thank Heaven, has long since been removed). Nash or his assistant also added the bay window over the gatehouse, the wrought iron bridge, and the battlements to give the whole thing a bit of 'a castle air'.

For eighteen generations, Helmingham Hall has been the family seat of the Tollemaches, who like the Herveys, Gurdons and Rouses constitute one of the few great landed families that have lived continuously in Suffolk from the Middle Ages to the present day. The Tollemaches came originally from Avranches on the Normandy coast. Shortly after the Norman Conquest, they came to England, bearing the name 'Talemache', which means 'Keeper of the Great Seal'; and indeed this was the very office that one of them held in the service of King Henry I. At the Battle of Crécy, during the Hundred Years War, the Tollemaches actually fought against their old compatriots, and they fought for Henry II against the Welsh, and for Edward I against the Scots. This feudal loyalty to the Crown never wavered. During the Civil War, Helmingham Hall was a secret meeting place for the Royalists. Twice Elizabeth I stayed here, and she was godmother to one of the Tollemaches. On her second visit in 1580, the Queen presented her hostess with a lute which had been made in that same year by the London instrument-maker John Rose and which is still in the family's possession. Four hundred years later, Queen Elizabeth II also came here, and planted an oak tree, and in 1976 Prince Charles became godfather to Edward Tollemache, the future heir to Helmingham Hall.

Lord Tollemache, the present owner, received me in jeans and a blue pullover. He's in his mid-forties, and holds his family history out in front of him like a screen behind which he can discreetly hide himself. He didn't want to talk about his own education, though methought it smacked of Eton and Oxbridge. In earlier days he served for a time in the Coldstream Guards, the family's traditional regiment, but then he went into the brewery business. Today he's on the board of Tolly Cobbold – an amalgamation that took place in 1960 of the two rival family breweries in Suffolk, Tollemache and Cobbold. They own something like 400 pubs in Suffolk.

His Lordship's real occupation, though, is agriculture. 'Our family has always lived on the land,' he says, 'and the only other career was the army.' The Tollemaches own 6,000 acres of the best arable land in Suffolk, plus another 4,000 acres in Cheshire round their second family home, Peckforton Castle. Ham House in Richmond also belonged to them until the National Trust took it over in 1948. Helmingham has good soil, 'the driest in England'. In Suffolk they grow corn, and in Cheshire they raise cattle. The fields in Helmingham have an average area of some 20 acres, and Lord Tollemache is particularly keen to preserve the hedgerows. He feels that in the past people have not given enough thought to preservation, because they are 'too greedy'.

'Without such estates you just couldn't maintain a house of this size unless you were a very rich banker.' When Lord Tollemache's father took over the house in 1953, it still had no electricity and no running water. 'He restored it at a time when a lot of other people were demolishing their houses. After the War there were few skilled workers around, not many building materials, and no subsidies.' What does it cost to maintain Helmingham Hall today? 'I could tell you, but I won't.' Even running an ordinary house costs enough, and with a house like his ... well, 'it costs a bit more.' The Tollemaches can still manage by opening their gardens to the public, but not the mansion itself, which means they cannot claim any tax concessions.

'If you're not a born showman, you really don't want to see a lot of strangers wandering round your house!' He makes no secret of which part of Helmingham Hall he loves the most: the drawbridge. 'We pull it up every evening, as we've done for the last 500 years, and then in the morning we let it down again. The moat has always been an excellent form of defence.' It is said that this routine proved somewhat disadvantageous to Prince Charles during one of his visits: after a night out, he didn't want to cause a fuss, and since the drawbridge had already been raised, the prince simply swam across the moat, somewhat to the surprise of his companions.

The garden is the province of His Lordship's wife: 'She's the gardener. She speaks Latin.' In 1982, Lady Tollemache began to lay out a herb and knot garden on the east side of the house – an Elizabethan concept mirroring the Tudor architecture. She only plants flowers that were familiar in English gardens before 1750, and herbs that are mentioned in a recipe book written *c.*1600 by one of her predecessors, Catherine Tollemache – an ever-useful asset from Helmingham Hall's library. In Lady Tollemache's rose garden bloom Félicité et Perpétue, Rosa Mundi, and Tuscany, roses from the Tudor period. This garden 'in progress' is still private, but what is open to the public is the other, historic garden on the southwest side of the house, and indeed this is one of the few East Anglian gardens to be listed Grade I.

A gate with two winged horses' heads – the heraldic crest of the Tollemaches – leads into this walled garden. As in Elizabethan times, it is divided into four large beds enclosed in flower borders and protected all the way round by brick walls. There are lilies and lavender, scabious and speedwell, cosmea and campanula, larkspur and hollyhock. You must see it all in June or July, when the colours and scents are at their finest. Or come in spring, when the old garden is full of wild orchids, marguerites and cowslips. In the summer, you can walk in the cool shade of the avenue of yew trees, past the *Daphne laureola*, and into the shadows of the cedars.

Even the walled garden in Helmingham has the added protection of a moat – smaller than the 60 foot one around the house, and considerably older. It probably dates from Anglo-Saxon times, and was dug to protect the cattle from marauders. It's very unusual to find two moats at one house, even in Suffolk. In the Middle Ages, moats were used not only to defend castles and manor houses, and sometimes even farms, but also for drainage purposes and for fish-breeding. Quite apart from the houses of the gentry, Suffolk alone is known to have had some 500–600 farms with moats – a clear sign of past prosperity. (Essex, though, was the champion moat county, with more than 760 known to have been in existence from the 12th to the 14th century.)

Moats are not without their drawbacks, however. When Lord Tollemache was looking for a new coachman a few years ago, he set the applicants a test: how close to the moat could they drive his coach? He gave the job to the man who kept the horses furthest away from the water.

In the park there are Soay sheep, Highland Cattle, and large numbers of fallow deer. And near the bridge on the way to the church is the oak with the crooked trunk which Constable painted when he visited the parsonage in the summer of 1800. There is also a pond beyond which stands the church where the Tollemaches lie buried in idyllic peace and quiet. Baroque epitaphs praise their virtues, their accomplishments and their adventures, as well as recording the fact that most of them were called Lionel. I had tea in the coach-house with Desmond, the aged caretaker at Helmingham; his father worked here for 70 years before him, and incidentally Lord Tollemache let Desmond have the best cottage on the whole estate rent-free. It pays to be a good and faithful servant.

If you're travelling round Suffolk, you should take your time. Give yourself the chance to see the little things, and to go down the hundreds of side roads. Go and see *Crowfield*, for instance, where there's a tiny church on the outskirts, standing like a farmhouse in the middle of the fields – the only church in Suffolk with a half-timbered chancel. Give yourself time to go and see the Reverend Anthony Wingfield at *Stonham Aspal*, lying on his sarcophagus outside the church, his elbow on a cushion, his eyes turned up to heaven, pathos in every angle, right through to the folds in his garments, his pose, his serenity – in Pevsner's perfect description, 'the design is so unlike anything one is used to in churchyards that one feels a monument in Westminster Abbey may be taking a country holiday.' This classical marble sculpture by Francis Bird (1715) is a monument to all those English country parsons who for centuries have played such a worthy role in the life of the nation.

Then there are the angels in all the glory of Gothic carpentry: the hammerbeam roof of St Mary's in *Earl Stonham*; and the Perpendicular roof of St John's in *Needham Market*, where the hammerbeams, braces and crossbeams are like the ribs of a great sailing ship on its way to heaven, with angels as figureheads (*c*.1460–78). These are some of the village churches and churchyards around Helmingham. Whichever you visit, sooner or later the route will lead you to *Shrubland Park*.

The surprise here is not the house, but the park: it's an English version of the gardens at the Villa d'Este: Tivoli in Suffolk. It began with a modest country house built in 1770 by a parson on a hill north of Ipswich. This villa was extended in 1848–52 by no less an architect than Sir Charles Barry, who designed the Houses of Parliament. He gave the house an Italianate style, in the high Victorian fashion adding balustrades and an asymmetrical corner tower like that at Prince Albert's Osborne. The most important addition, however, was on the west side of the house, where Barry designed a terraced garden on a grand scale – which was remodelled in 1888 by the landscape gardener William Robinson. A triumphal flight of steps goes down the slope to a 'gloriette', cascades of stone in the green. On both sides are broad lawns with geometrically shaped box-hedges, tall trees, and moss-covered classical statues. There is no finer park in East Anglia. Victorian society loved these ceremonial theatres of Nature, and Barry created similar grandiose terraces at Harewood House (Yorkshire) and Trentham Park (Staffordshire). Today the guests of Shrubland Park bathe in peat and seaweed, for Lord de Saumarez has turned it into a health clinic. There is also a folly here – a Swiss chalet with a classic German greeting: 'Seid mir willkommen meine theureren Freunde / Zur guten Stunde führe euch das Schicksal' (Welcome to me, my dear friends, / May Fate give you some happy hours).

England's stately homes have become cases for treatment. The natural cure seems to be for them to be used as retirement homes or health clinics or other such institutions. One use that is rather less beneficial to these old houses is the strenuous one of being turned into schools – and especially boarding schools. Of course if you are lucky enough to have your home chosen for the set of *Brideshead*, or you set up a safari park all around you, it won't be necessary for you to sell off the Leonardo for a while. Quite a few of these always hospitable mansions have succeeded in setting themselves up as country house hotels, renting out their historical aura at horrendous prices. The Americans are particularly eager to combine the four-poster bed with the helicopter pad. One of the more felicitous of these conversions is *Hintlesham Hall*, west of Ipswich: its centre is Elizabethan, its façade early

Georgian, and its cuisine French – a gourmet Mecca for London's yuppies. This is where David Watson, a graduate of 'Le Gavroche', celebrates (on good days) the culinary wonders of Suffolk. Elsewhere there is an 18th-century house that produces East Anglia's best cider – the dry Aspall Cider. Ever since 1728 this has been produced at Aspall Hall, north of Debenham. Still a family concern, it was founded by C. B. Chevallier, a Huguenot immigrant from Normandy.

One has to admire the mixture of enthusiasm, expertise and fantasy, idealism and business acumen with which the English always manage to cling to, preserve, and exploit their heritage. It's never easy, it's usually expensive, and it's not always successful. Sometimes the owners go under, and sometimes they gamble their heritage away. In Suffolk I know of no sadder case than the demise of *Heveningham Hall*.

When the French nobleman François de la Rochefoucauld made his grand tour of East Anglia in 1784, he visited this 'magnificent modern house', which had just been completed, and wrote that of all the fine houses in the county, Heveningham Hall was 'the only one that is really worth seeing'. This was no exaggeration at the time, for Ickworth was not built until twenty years later. Even today, architectural historians still regard Heveningham Hall as 'without question the grandest Georgian mansion of Suffolk' (Pevsner).

It stands in the green hills south of Halesworth, overlooking a hamlet down in the valley from where you can see the bright façade in a framework of old trees (colour plate 18). Nature mirrors Art in a park laid out by Capability Brown in the style of classical landscape-painting, one of his finest pastoral designs (1781–2) which even incorporates the practical: in order that the aristocracy should enjoy the benefits of cool food and drink right through the year, Brown constructed an ice house, a bowl-shaped brick construction with a thatched roof, which was in use right up to this century.

Heveningham Hall is completely within the Palladian tradition: above a rusticated storey is a central projection with Corinthian columns and entablature, while the sides consist of two corner pavilions with columns and pediments. The whole of this neo-classical façade, 25 bays wide, is of brick and stucco, and its monumental symmetry is said to have been the model for John Nash's terraces in Regent's Park. Heveningham's architect was Sir Robert Taylor, who was also George III's architect; the client was Sir Gerard Vanneck, MP and a London businessman of Dutch extraction. The Hall was built between 1777 and 1784, at the peak of this age of elegance. It was the period of Robert Adam, Gainsborough and Reynolds, Chippendale and Sheraton, Dr Johnson and Horace Walpole. A dazzling period, which was reflected in the interiors of Heveningham, designed by James Wyatt, thanks to whom the house is famous.

Wyatt was the son of a timber merchant and builder from Staffordshire. His two best known buildings no longer exist: the Pantheon in London, and Fonthill Abbey, the eccentric palace built for William Beckford. When Wyatt accepted the commission to design all the interiors of Heveningham Hall, in 1781, he was 34 years old and was one of the most successful architects in England. His adaptation of Adam's style transcended the model. Robert Adam was interior designer to the Age of Sensibility, and James Wyatt was the ingenious plagiarist. The rectangular, box-shaped neoclassical rooms created by Robert Taylor in Heveningham were reshaped by Wyatt through semi-circular apses, domes and niches. Edges were rounded off, and corners modified, so that the rooms became as soft as cushions. Wyatt favoured pastel shades, like apple-green, biscuit, Wedgwood-blue, and he liked antique decorations in coloured stucco – arabesques, fans, and garlands of leaves and flowers. He was more reserved than Adam, leaving wide expanses free in order to give more emphasis to the individual medallion or frieze. And so the interiors of Heveningham Hall are like subtle variations on Robert Adam's rooms in Syon House or Osterley Park.

Even the entrance hall is perfect in proportions, elegance and rhythm. Dominating both ends are the yellow scagliola columns, while pilasters line the long walls. The floor is marble, the tall doors mahogany, the walls apple-green, and in the niches are marble statues, with stucco medallions up above. The fan motifs in the spandrels of the Roman-style barrel-vault anticipate Wyatt's typical, later Neo-Gothic style. The dining-room is equally magnificent, divided off from the library by a row of columns. The walls are pale blue, with stucco reliefs against a dark red background. The murals and ceiling frescoes are in Pompeiian style, and were painted by Biagio Rebecca, who was of Italian origin and who specialized in historical scenes and decorative painting. He worked on many of the houses designed by Wyatt and by Adam. It was also Rebecca who created the profiles of famous authors in the oval medallions in the library, as well as the figures in the Etruscan Room, painted in the terra cotta colours of Greek vases. The Etruscan style had been fashionable ever since the excavation of Pompeii in the middle of the 18th century, and this room had no function other than that of a showpiece and a passage – a decorative testimony to the classical education of its owner. Osterley Park and Ickworth both have Etruscan Rooms. These might not correspond too closely to our own ideas of education, but for Lord Vanneck and his contemporaries they were the New Wave, and no sooner had Wyatt finished his work in 1784 than the first culture vulture was knocking at Heveningham's front door. La Rochefoucauld's verdict was: 'A masterpiece of good taste.'

For some 200 years the Vannecks lived at their family home. Then in 1970 they sold it, because of swingeing death duties, and emigrated to Australia. The Department of the Environment took it over, and the National Trust was given the task of running it, not having had enough money to buy it outright. In 1980, one year after taking office, Margaret Thatcher decided it was a liability, and put it on the market. There was no profit to be made from Wyatt. And so what the State had acquired, with a view to preserving for the nation, was now privatized for the absurd sum of £726,000.

In 1984, there was a fire in Heveningham Hall, a disaster in itself. (There had already been a fire in 1949, but then the dining room had been beautifully restored.) Repairs were slow, and security inadequate: in came burglars and vandals, ripping out one of Wyatt's fireplaces. The new owner, an Iraqi businessman, failed to understand that a commitment to a beautiful house and lavish lifestyle would not be enough to impress England's vociferous conservationist lobby. Communication failed, enemies were made, and the house was virtually closed to the public. The businessman died, some said of grief, and the house is now in the hands of the Receivers.

Built at the peak of England's age of elegance, cast off in England's monetarist age of Thatcher, that is the story of Heveningham Hall. I was lucky enough to go there long before the fire of 1984. Over the fireplace in the morning room hung Reynolds' portrait of Sir Joshua Vanneck, who acquired the estate in 1752. Most of the other paintings and original furniture had already been sold off, but there was still a rich glow in Wyatt's rooms. And on the slopes there were sheep grazing, while down below there were cows drinking from the lake. In the water Heveningham Hall, Englishness itself, perfectly reflected.

Lots of Fun in Light and Shade: Angus McBean in Debenham

I shall always associate *Debenham* with laughter – the laughter of Angus McBean (plate 69). When I met him, he was already over 80, the Grand Old Man of British theatre photography. In the little town on the Deben north of Ipswich everybody knew Angus, with his snow-white beard, his Pop-Art cravat and his silk shirt. 'I'm one of the ancient monuments,' he said. He lived in the High Street, opposite 'The Angel'. In his hall under the roof hung the photograph that first made him famous: Vivien Leigh with a large hat, 1937; below it was the postage stamp that was based on his photo. It was this portrait by Angus McBean that set the then unknown English actress on her way to Hollywood and to Scarlett O'Hara.

'My camera and even I fell in love with her.' He photographed her in almost all her film and stage roles, for thirty long years. And he photographed Charles Laughton, Maggie Smith, Laurence Olivier as Hamlet, and the young Richard Burton donning the crown as Henry V. In the golden years of British theatre, Angus McBean was court photographer to the stars. Some of his pictures are in the National Portrait Gallery, but he sold most of them – some 48,000 negatives – to Harvard University. The stars strutted their hour upon the stage, but he created the icons of their glory. His method: sophisticated lighting, a spot of black-and-white magic, and perfect retouching. His creed: 'People want to be beautiful.' It was not only the stars of Stratford-upon-Avon and the Old Vic that came to him; the Beatles employed him to do the sleeve of their L.P. *Please, Please Me.*

In 1951, he told me, he discovered another star in London: 'I was doing a cosmetics advertisement, and went to a West End revue to try and find a model. I chose the third girl in the chorus line. She was eighteen, and her name was Audrey Hepburn.' On his photo all you can see are the naked shoulders and the head emerging from the sand, and nearby are the miniature columns of ancient ruins. It was one of the very first surrealist advertisements – and all for cold cream. 'At the time it went all over England, on display in every chemist's shop. I got a £50 fee, and MGM in Hollywood made *Funny Face*. Audrey Hepburn was a bookseller, and Fred Astaire was a young photographer who made her famous as a model.'

An old photographer looks back in laughter. A chest of drawers is covered with surrealistic props from the thirties: a miniature temple, and various kitschy antiques from the Caledonian Market. He loves to make bizarre portraits of himself – one with a wide open eye where the mouth ought to be. At one of his exhibitions, a German ('Germans take everything so seriously') asked him what it meant. 'I did it for my dentist,' said Angus.

He was born in the same year as Dalí, 1904. Proud of his Welsh origins and his Scottish grandfather, he became the perfect example of the English Eccentric. With a laugh he told me about his latest comeback. At the age of 80 he was commissioned by Vogue – 'to my utter amazement' – to photograph the new Yves Saint-Laurent models in the style of his old pictures: beautiful women among fake ruins – his surrealistic trademark. But it was to be in colour, not black and white (though he insisted that the best colour photos are hand-coloured). And then a few days before I went to see him, the McCartneys had rung him up to do a portrait for their office. Paul wouldn't be a problem, but Linda, 'who's never been exactly a beauty', would be tricky without retouching.

He went on reminiscing, sitting on the end of his four-poster bed, whose canopy was fastened under the covers. He designed a similar oddity of a bed for Mick Jagger. There was also a little bedside cabinet with Gothic folds. 'Original McBean Tudor,' he explained. 'The Tudors never made anything like it, so I had to make it.' Restoring and retouching, copying and decorating, they always went together as far as Angus was concerned. Making people up for the theatre, setting the stage for his photos, designing interiors for himself and others[1] – it was all part of the same process of acting out realities and identities, combining (just as Cecil Beaton did) the twin arts of photography and life.

Angus opened his wardrobe. Silk shirts, brocade and Jacquard waistcoats, cravats of his own design – Beau Brummel would have had a field day. There was also a Sherlock Holmes cape, and a black-and-white striped cotton waistcoat, such as servants wore in the 19th century. 'Horizontal stripes for indoor servants, vertical stripes for outdoor servants. I wear them both.' He was wearing them, among other things, on one of his legendary Christmas cards – ironic self-portraits – which he always sent every year to his friends. 'Not long ago, one of my photo collages was auctioned at Christie's, and it fetched 250 quid. I couldn't believe it!'

The virtuoso photographer lived above one of the six antique shops in Debenham. 'My friends Emeric and Norman run the antique shop, and I make the antiques.' That's something he learned in London's Liberty's back in the twenties. There he worked for seven years in the antiques department, before becoming a photographer. It proved to be a useful experience when in 1966 he bought Flemings Hall, near Bedingfield north of Debenham, 'a wonderful old timber-framed house', originally 14th-century, but extended

---

1 His glamorous decoration used to be one of the attractions of the gourmet restaurant at Hintlesham Hall (see page 231).

c.1550. After his third hip operation Angus, instead of sitting down for a good rest, climbed up the ladder and started a complete restoration job. Panelling, doors, stairs were all renewed, made out of old parts from elsewhere. 'At that time a lot of historic houses were being pulled down, so you could pick up a staircase or a roomful of wooden panels for £25.' He also designed a lot of the furniture himself – pastiche pieces put together from various sources, like his surrealist photos. Thus Flemings Hall became the historical collage of a modern Elizabethan. When Angus and his friends had finished restoring the house, after some twenty years, it was time to leave it. 'We bought it for £10,000, and sold it for £180,000. Now it's just gone on the market again – for £350,000.' And with some satisfaction he added: 'It's gone up to Grade One.'

When I met him, Debenham's 'ancient monument' had just started on a new project: photographing redundant and endangered churches. 'In Suffolk we've got 600 medieval churches and four people who still believe in God.' Fritton, Denton, Ufford, Icklingham – Angus loved the old churches as much as he disliked religion ('Christ was a great teacher, but St Paul ruined him.') Every week, he said, some young photographer would come and ask to do his portrait, as if he himself were some kind of icon. His success, like so much else, caused his 'utter amazement', and indeed his whole life seemed to amaze him and to make him laugh. He died in 1990. 'The Nadar of English Upper Bohemia' was how the *Independent* described him. One can imagine him now, having to his 'utter amazement' got to the heaven he didn't believe in, laughing away and photographing the angels.

If Angus McBean was a guru of British photography, Sir Frederick Ashton was the guru of British ballet. He too came to spend his old age in this part of Suffolk. Born, just like Angus, in 1904, Ashton was a dancer, choreographer, and Director of the Royal Ballet. He lived in *Eye*, a little town north of Debenham, where he always returned after working at Sadler's Wells and Covent Garden (he created his *Cinderella* there at the age of 83). In his country house, Chandos Lodge, he surrounded himself with a world of artificial forms and rhythms in the green shapes of the topiary. His hedges of box and yew were cut into pyramids, balls and skittles to create a kind of geometrical garden ballet. And along the street, like a drunken chorus line, ran an undulating, wave-like brick wall. These crinkle-crankle walls, probably originating in Holland, were all the rage in 18th- and 19th-century Suffolk gardens. In their niches, fruit trees and flowers find protection and warmth. There are more than 50 of these walls in Suffolk, some fine examples being in Hadleigh, Long Melford, Bramfield and, especially, in the former kitchen garden at Heveningham Hall. In addition to Sir Frederick Ashton's crinkle-crankle wall, Eye has some fine Georgian houses and a Perpendicular church, the whole of whose western tower is decorated with flushwork.

'Silly Suffolk' with all its churches: you keep coming across them, and you keep coming back to them, and often it's in the smallest churches that you get the biggest surprises. For instance, in *Thornham Parva*, southwest of Eye. St Mary's is one of the few remaining thatched churches, even the tower being covered with a reed pyramid. In earlier times a lot of village churches had thatched roofs, but now there are only about twenty left in Suffolk, though even this is more than in any other county. But what is really special about St Mary's is its Gothic altarpiece – a Crucifixion, flanked by eight saints, slim and elongated figures, painted in a linear style on a gold background, *c.*1300, perhaps in the royal workshops of Westminster Abbey. Known as the Thornham Parva Retable, it was only discovered in 1927 among the belongings left by a Catholic family who had lived on a farm. It is one of the few surviving masterpieces of its time in England, and it is quite astonishing to find it in this tiny church in the middle of a Suffolk field.

St Mary's in *Dennington*, north of Framlingham, is another must for any church-crawler. In the south chapel is a tomb chest on which lie two lifesize alabaster figures, side by side, their hands folded: they are Lord Bardolph, in full armour, who died in 1441 (he fought at Agincourt with Henry V) and his wife, who has a richly embroidered Gothic bonnet. Angels hold the pillows on which their heads are resting, and an heraldic dragon keeps guard at their feet. These alabaster figures have been delicately painted, showing up the precious gold of their rings and of the borders. This is monumental sculpture of the highest quality, capturing perfectly the nobility of a long-lost world.

Superb tracery parclose screens divide off the north and south chapels, prime examples of late Gothic wood-carving – an art which reaches its zenith in the 'poppy-heads' for which Dennington Church is famous. The 76 bench-ends are lavishly decorated with foliage, birds, and mythological and allegorical figures. Specialists always head straight for a row of benches on the right of the nave, where there is an exceptionally rare carving of the rather unattractive and peculiar creature known as a sciapod. This is a long-haired, bearded creature of the Libyan desert; it likes to lie on its back, holding its giant feet up in the air as a sunshade while it comfortably munches its prey. Such sciapods, somewhat unusual in our part of the world, were a vivid myth for St Augustine and for medieval thought generally, but today the last of them eke out a shadowy existence (as befits the name, which means shadow-foot) in a few French churches. The only known English specimen, apart from one or two found in libraries, is the one at Dennington.

Just a few miles further north is *Laxfield*, the village of William Dowsing. Cromwell's chief iconoclast was given the task of 'defacing demolishing and quite taking away all images altars or tables turned altar-wise, crucifixes, superstitious pictures, monuments and reliques of idolatry out of all churches and chapels' throughout the Commonwealth. Punctiliously this Puritan vandal noted his successes in his diary – for instance, the destruction of the church windows in Clare, 1644: 'We brake down 1,000, I brake down 200.' He was known as Smasher Dowsing, and he and his men took just two days to purge all the churches in Ipswich. The scratched faces of saints, heads knocked off choir screens and fonts – the iconoclasts left their trail all over England (colour plate 21).

In Laxfield lives an artist who might even have made the grim Dowsing laugh: Ron Fuller, the toy maker (plate 51). With Pop-Art colours and a subversive sense of humour, Ron creates a whole world of wood, metal and laughter: Yellow Submarines for the bathtub, Red Baron aeroplanes with saluting pilots, hens that lay wooden eggs, circus artistes and all kinds of comic automata. When I visited him, he was working on two lifesize, computer-operated figures in plywood for a shopping centre in Sheffield. Ron's wife Moss Fuller is a painter in the tradition of Cotman: she does watercolours of the fields and barns around her home and of farm machinery – a poetic but realistic record of rural East Anglia.

The Renaissance of Dead Souls: Wingfield College, Framlingham Castle

Northwest of Laxfield, right on the Norfolk border, is a hillside church in the middle of the fields, as remote as its history. *Wingfield* was once the ancestral castle of the de la Poles, one of the mightiest dynasties in the country. Today, this village with its tiny population of 250 is the setting for the most intimate festival in Suffolk: Wingfield Arts and Music. The man who woke this Sleeping Beauty (but in no way damaged the fairytale atmosphere) is Ian Chance. He was just 30 years old, a graduate from the Slade School in London, when he came to Wingfield in 1971 and bought the property next to the church from a local farmer. 'Everyone thought it was an 18th-century house – even Pevsner. But what I found was a medieval college.'

Ian Chance, a modest bachelor, took me and his black cat Betty on a tour of Wingfield College. The house within a house which he discovered and laid bare room by room is a 14th-century timber-framed building which was covered up completely in about 1760 by a Georgian stucco façade, with twelve real and seven blind windows. Very carefully he restored the Great Hall with its open roof trusses, the heart of the house (*c.*1300). Until the Reformation, twenty to thirty pupils had lived here, with six teachers and four priests. The College had been founded by Sir John de Wingfield, a friend of the Black Prince. During the Hundred Years War, Sir John was chief of staff of the English army in France, and he returned to his estate in Suffolk with rich booty. Before his death in 1361 he established a college and a church, where he was buried and where the students were to say daily masses and prayers for his soul. During the 15th century Wingfield College was one of the three leading schools in the county, and its head was also chaplain to the Dukes of Suffolk.

'If this is a college, it must be run like a college.' And so hardly had Ian Chance finished his ten-year labour of restoration when in 1981 he proceeded to organize a festival of concerts, exhibitions, readings and workshops. When I was there, the Medici String Quartet were giving a guest performance in the church, to be followed a little later by the Indian sitar-player Imrat Khan. The Spanish concert guitarist Ernesto Bitetti held a guitar workshop, and the best-selling author Malcolm Bradbury gave a reading at the end of a story competition for local schoolchildren. As artist in residence, the Brazilian painter Ana Maria Pacheco held a course in wood engraving, using a handpress of 1840, and as composer in residence the Hungarian György Kurtag demonstrated the theory and practice of contemporary music. In the house itself, Kabuli kilims and Moroccan ceramics were on display, and in the garden there were sculptures by Norwich artists. Wingfield

Arts and Music is East Anglia's most personal festival, and it combines its rural roots with a cosmopolitan range. What began simply as a restoration became a true renaissance, bringing the medieval college back to life as a centre for summer visitors to find a relaxed *studium generale*.

Ian Chance organized all this during the first five years without any subsidies or sponsors, because he wanted to have complete control over the programme. Regional authorities and commercial sponsors now bear a part of the costs, while the founder himself finances the rest from his own pocket. He teaches at the Norwich School of Art – 'I have to teach in order to pay for the Festival.' He is the embodiment of a British success story, though in some ways it is a two-edged success. As a young man he moved to the country in the seventies in order to realize his own ideas about art and life; in the eighties he became, involuntarily, a paradigm of Thatcherism: an arts entrepreneur. Ian Chance himself regards the main aim of Wingfield as being 'to put people in a position to strive for excellence, and to find their own cultural identity.' His example shows that the Super-Festivals are not the only creative centres; great things come out of the little arts foundations, like the Fondation Maeght in Saint Paul de Vence, or Kettle's Yard in Cambridge – or Wingfield College.

Soon after he had moved in, the new owner of Wingfield planted a rare weeping oak. He also laid out an Elizabethan topiary garden, with angular hedges that defy the laws of geometry and of gravity: toppling pyramids, asymmetrical balls, corkscrew shapes – bizarre variations on the normal relationship between Art and Nature.

Ian Chance, then, made a new beginning to the history of Wingfield, which seemed to have ended forever with the great name of de la Pole. The de la Poles lie buried in the village church, and one of them – 'Sweet Suffolk, proud Pole' – even plays a part in Shakespeare's *Henry VI*: William de la Pole, 1st Duke of Suffolk. He fought against Joan of Arc, arranged Henry VI's marriage to Margaret of Anjou, and himself aspired to power: 'Margaret shall now be queen, and rule the King; / But I will rule both her, and King, and realm.' It was not to be, for he was murdered on the beach at Dover: 'They lips, that kissed the queen, shall sweep the ground.' Now 'Sweet Suffolk' rests in one of the fine sarcophagi in Wingfield, next to his son John, the 2nd Duke, and the latter's wife Elizabeth Plantagenet, a sister of Edward IV and Richard III (plate 86). Not far from these truly royal alabaster figures lie two rare wooden monuments, originally painted. They are Michael de la Pole, 2nd Earl of Suffolk, and his wife Katherine – the parents of the 1st Duke.[1] Sir Michael built Wingfield Castle in 1384 on the outskirts of the village. Of all the greatness of the Earls and Dukes of Suffolk, nothing remains but a three-storeyed gatehouse. The timber-framed house that is there now was built in the middle of the 16th century.

'Look on my works, ye Mighty, and despair!' said Ozymandias, and a few miles further

---

1 The restoration of Wingfield College uncovered part of the linenfold panelling of *c*.1525, including two panels with portraits of Mary Tudor and her second husband, Charles Brandon, whom Mary's brother Henry VIII made Duke of Suffolk, after the execution of the 5th Earl of Suffolk, Edmund de la Pole.

south, the Dukes of Norfolk might well despair too, seeing *Framlingham*, once the seat of their power, now just a little village. Its castle has thirteen towers, and its church has the finest Renaissance monuments in East Anglia. On the hill opposite the castle is Framlingham College, a Neo-Gothic citadel built as a public school in 1864. When the pupils look out of the window, and cast their eyes three arrow flights across the valley, what they see is an exemplary piece of local history, chivalry, and tourism.

Once a castle, now a picnic spot. Once the pride of Norman military strategy, now a picture postcard. When all is said and done, history is just a tale of disarmament, destruction, and decay. The result, it must be said, is not always as pleasing to the soul as Framlingham Castle. It's sheer pleasure to wander over the ramparts, and to look down over the little town, the church, the lake – once dammed for defensive purposes – and the peaceful hills of Suffolk all around. There have been no enemies in sight since Cromwell's day. The domain was a gift from Henry I to his Norman follower Roger Bigod. A century later, between 1190 and 1213, a second Roger Bigod, 2nd Earl of Norfolk, built the castle in its present form. The concentric curtain wall, with corner towers and gatehouse, was at that time the most up-to-date military architecture, imported by the homecoming crusaders after their encounters with Saracen fortresses. Windsor and Dover are the earliest English examples of this type of castle, which replaced the keep. The walls and trenches laid out by the first Roger Bigod at the beginning of the 12th century surround the inner and outer courts of the castle. The Tudors gave the thirteen towers a domestic look by adding elaborate brick chimneys, nearly all of which are dummies (1530–40).

The last of the Bigods was yet another Roger. He was the 5th Earl of Norfolk, and was one of the driving forces behind the barons' conflict with Edward I. In 1297 it came to a test of strength, when the gallant knight refused to go and fight in Gascony. 'By God, Sir Earl, you shall either go or hang,' said the King. 'By God, O King,' said the Earl, 'I will neither go nor hang.' Whether true or false, it has gone down in history as a classic piece of dialogue. Bigod was eventually stripped of his position, and his castle reverted to the King.

The story of the Howards at Framlingham Castle also oscillates between faithful service and high treason. Under Richard III they became Dukes of Norfolk and Lords Chamberlain; under Henry VIII they lost their castle and their heads. But before they were buried in the church at Framlingham, they enjoyed their feasts in the Great Hall. On 30 December 1526, the 3rd Duke of Norfolk entertained 235 guests, including 35 knights, nobles and priests, the rest – according to the household accounts – being 'persons of the country'.

Framlingham Castle saw its last days of glory in 1553. That year, the year of his death, Edward VI gave the castle to his unloved Catholic half-sister Mary Tudor. The crown, however, did not go to her, the legitimate heiress, but to the eighteen-year-old Protestant Jane Grey, daughter-in-law of the Duke of Northumberland, Lord Protector of the realm. Mary Tudor fled to Framlingham. The Howards were, and still are, staunch Catholics, and at Framlingham, Mary had herself proclaimed Queen by the landed gentry of East Anglia, and marched on London. Lady Jane Grey reigned for nine days, before Northumberland was forced to yield to Bloody Mary. Both he and Lady Jane died on the scaffold.

Framlingham Castle continued to mirror the changes of power and faith when Mary Tudor's Protestant sister and successor, Elizabeth I, used it as a prison for recusants. Then in turn her successor, James I, gave the castle back to the Howards, who had supported the Catholic Stuarts. By then, however, the family had moved to Arundel Castle in Sussex, after the marriage of the 4th Duke of Norfolk to the daughter of the Earl of Arundel. Arundel Castle now belongs to the 17th Duke of Norfolk. Framlingham Castle passed to Pembroke College, Cambridge in 1635. In place of the Great Hall, the academics built a poor house in the bailey, and allowed the rest of the castle to fall into decay. Even today, the College still has the title 'Lords of the Manor', though Framlingham has been state property since 1913. The remains are looked after by English Heritage.

On the south portal of Framlingham Church, where the Dukes and the Earls lie buried, hangs the key to the castle, ready and waiting for the Resurrection, perhaps. The Perpendicular Church of St Michael has an unusual roof of 1475, whose hammerbeams are concealed by the ribbed coving, and a famous Baroque organ which was originally built for Pembroke College. Built in 1674, it is in almost original condition. Above the high altar hangs the helmet worn by Thomas Howard, Earl of Surrey, at the Battle of Flodden in 1513, when the English under his command slaughtered the flower of Scottish knighthood. His son lies buried in the grandest tomb below, guarded by the twelve Apostles. This is one of the finest monuments of the Early Renaissance in England, and one of the last of pre-Reformation piety. Not that Howard was an otherworldly man: he boosted his family's power by launching two of his nieces towards the throne – first Anne Boleyn, then Catherine Howard – and when their heads were on the block, he looked the other way. He escaped losing his own head only because Henry VIII died the day before it was due to be chopped off. Howard spent six years in the Tower of London before Mary Tudor let the eighty-year-old free. He was a cruel man who lived in cruel times. The very fact that he died in his bed, and at a great age, having survived all the ins and outs of the power game, shows that what an extraordinary person he must have been.

His son also lies buried in the chancel of Framlingham Church:[1] Henry Howard, Earl of Surrey. A Renaissance tomb, and for the Renaissance man par excellence. He loved court intrigue, heroic verse, and riotous living, and he died young enough to maintain the reputation of the romantic hero, a virtuoso of the sword and the pen. The swashbuckling Raleigh brought the potato to England; Surrey brought blank verse. And what is more, through his translation of Petrarch he changed the Italian sonnet into the English sonnet by transforming the two tercets into a quatrain followed by a final, epigrammatic couplet – the so-called 'heroic couplet'. Many editions of his poems and his pioneering blank verse translation of Books 2 and 4 of Virgil's *Aeneid* are in the library of Arundel Castle, where there is also a brilliant portrait of him painted in 1546 by Guillim Scrotes. We have, of

---

1 After the dissolution of Thetford Priory in 1540, which had hitherto been the hereditary burial place of the Earls and Dukes of Norfolk, the chancel of Framlingham Church was extended to hold the tombs of the Howards (1547–53).

course, been spoilt by Shakespeare, but it is well worth listening also to the voice of the Earl of Surrey:

> When other lovers in arms across
> Rejoice their chief delight,
> Drowned in tears to mourn my loss
> I stand the bitter night
> In my window, where I may see
> Before the winds how the clouds flee.
> Lo, what a mariner hath love made me!

Anyone who could sing so passionately of true love, and could so self-indulgently play the power game was taking a big professional risk if he had any connections with Henry VIII and his court. Before he had reached the age of thirty, he was charged with high treason. 'The most foolish proud boy that is in England' was one contemporary's description of him. The short and dazzling career ended in January 1547 on Tower Hill. Portrayed by Holbein, beheaded by Henry VIII: only a real virtuoso could put that in his c.v. And so in Framlingham Church, symbolizing his execution, his coronet lies next to the head of the alabaster figure on the tomb-chest of poor, handsome Henry. By his side lies Frances de Vere, his wife, daughter of the 15th Earl of Oxford. Kneeling behind them are their three daughters, and before them are their two sons. They wear purple, ermine-lined robes, and one of them was to follow in the Howards' trail of blood: Thomas, 4th Duke of Norfolk. Elizabeth I had him beheaded for high treason. His own son also died in the Tower, 24 years later, in 1595: Philip, Earl of Arundel, likewise attainted as a Catholic of high treason. They lie there in state, these dead Howards in Framlingham Church, facing the other world in all their heraldic splendour, participants and victims in an age which seemed to revel in its coronations and executions as if they were simply plays and mummery. The Earl of Surrey's tomb was not built until 1614, more than half a century after his death, and two years before Shakespeare died.

The illustrious dead of Framlingham also include an illegitimate son of Henry VIII's, Surrey's childhood friend Henry Fitzroy, whom the King was said to have loved 'like his own soule'. Henry Fitzroy escaped the more violent demonstrations of a father's love by dying at the age of seventeen.

This was a bloodthirsty age, but it was also an age that thirsted for beauty, harmony, and eternal peace, and this was expressed in the stone monuments they erected to their dead. Four kneeling angels bear on their shoulders a black marble slab, beneath which stands the burial urn of Sir Robert Hitcham, who bought the castle from the Howards and shortly before his death in 1636 bequeathed it to his college in Cambridge. The sculptor Francis Grigs designed the monument in 1638 (plate 90). When I visited Framlingham Church, it was spring. A woman was placing flowers on Sir Robert's tomb – daffodils, reflected in the black marble.

That evening I went to neighbouring *Saxtead*. There's a windmill on the edge of the

242

broad village green, spotlessly white, with four massive sails (plate 41). The movable, weatherboarded post rests on a brick roundhouse, and is as aesthetically pleasing as it is functionally efficient – a rural mobile that really works. This is where the corn was ground for the lords of Framlingham Castle. Saxtead Green post-mill[1] is regarded as one of the finest of its type in Europe. There is documentary evidence that a windmill has stood on this site since 1287. The present one was built in 1796. It remained in operation until the First World War as a corn mill, and then afterwards was used to grind cattle feed. Today the sails only go round to entertain the customers of English Heritage.

Britten in Aldeburgh: Festival on Curlew River

The ventilation shafts of the Maltings shimmer white over the marshes, like the funnels of a stranded ocean liner. From within come the sounds of a harp and soprano, rehearsing Schoenberg's *Herzgewächse*, opus 20. People in evening dress are already strolling along the dyke, their opera glasses trained expectantly: 'Oh look, a redshank!' Redshank, black-headed gull, oyster-catcher – they are all traditional inhabitants of the Alde estuary. A little water music, a pint of of Adnams Bitter (or a glass of champagne, perhaps), before the concert begins.

Everyone has heard of Glyndebourne, but what about *Aldeburgh*? To tell the truth, a Britten opera in an old maltings doesn't have quite the same jet-set appeal as, say, 'Aida' in the temple ruins of Luxor. The attractions here are rather more homespun, mixing urbanity with fresh country air, and without the 'drilled smartness of Glyndebourne' (E. M. Forster). Aldeburgh is a big family gathering in the English countryside, with guests from all over the world. Janet Baker, Heather Harper, Lutosławski, Henze, Menuhin, Anne-Sophie Mutter, Colin Davis, Clifford Curzon – all of these have sung, played or conducted here. Some of the guests are regular, like the great 'cellist Rostropovich – known as 'Slava' – who now has a house in Aldeburgh, where he lives with his wife Galina Vishnevskaya, the star soprano at Moscow's Bolshoi Theatre until she emigrated in 1974. There is also a place here for younger, lesser known musicians. For all of them, the famous and the aspiring, the intimate atmosphere of the Maltings is a far cry from the great halls of the metropolis.

'The hardy sea-faring music-lover' will come to the festival aboard the 'Ethel Ada', a restored barge (who wants Glyndebourne's Rolls Royces?). With its rust-brown sails, the old vessel used to carry malt and barley from the Maltings to London. As for the Maltings themselves, they were built in the middle of the 19th century and were still in operation until 1965; they stand by the bridge to Snape, and it is up to this point that the Alde is navigable (plate 33).

1   Other historic post-mills in Suffolk are at Drinkstone, 1689, Friston, and Holton, 1752.

On the lawn in front of the Maltings, you enter the world of pure forms, for you are greeted by a group of bronze sculptures by Barbara Hepworth. The concert hall of unplastered red brick, with open roof trusses, is regarded by the cognoscenti as one of the finest in Europe, thanks to its magnificent acoustics. On the other hand, in the summer of 1980 the rain made such a noise on the roof that Mozart's Piano Concerto K413 had to take an unscheduled break. The concert hall was created out of the Maltings by Derek Sugden, who has also worked with Ove Arup, and it was officially opened by the Queen in 1967. By then the Festival was already 20 years old, having begun six miles away in the little Jubilee Hall in Aldeburgh. This hall had been donated to the town in celebration of Queen Victoria's Jubilee in 1887 by Newson Garrett, the owner of Snape Maltings. His daughter, Elizabeth Garrett Anderson, was the first woman to practise medicine in England, and she was also the first lady mayoress in England – taking office in Aldeburgh in 1908.

Aldeburgh consists of three streets that run parallel to the beach, with a few shops and a few pubs. It's famous for its herring, its sprats, and its Britten. 'Slow please,' says a hand-painted sign, 'Cats Crossing'. On Crag Path the houses have balconies and bay windows like ships' bridges looking out into the sea (colour plate 28). What the locals enthusiastically refer to as a beach looks as if it's a receptacle for all the gravel-pits in Suffolk. Maybe it's a way of deterring the trippers (colour plate 4). Aldeburgh never was one of the fashionable resorts.

'That miserable, dull sea village' was what Virginia Woolf called it. In Henry VIII's time, it was a flourishing trade port, and in those days Moot Hall, the town hall with its half-timbered and brick walls (1520–40), still occupied the centre of the town, instead of standing in isolation on the promenade as it does now (colour plate 36). As at Dunwich, the sea has taken a large chunk of the land, thanks to creeping erosion and terrible floods. Where the yachts now anchor used to be Slaughden Quay. The quay disappeared beneath the sand, and the houses disappeared beneath the sea. It was here, during the mid-18th century, that the poet George Crabbe grew up, in a town that was already impoverished and dying.

'Here a grave flora scarcely deigns to bloom, / Nor wears a rosy blush, nor sheds perfume …' With grim verses Crabbe captured the grim reality of the coast, the harsh conditions under which the farmers and fishermen of Aldeburgh lived. Poems and letters to counter the popular and false image of the simple country life (*The Village*, 1783; *The Borough*, 1810). Unlike his contemporaries, the Romantics, 'the poet of the poor' gave a truthful account of the other side of the village idyll, describing the alms houses, for instance where 'you / Have placed your poor, your pitiable few; / There, in one house, throughout their lives to be, / The pauper palace which they have to see: … It is a prison, with a milder name, / Which few inhabit without dread or shame.' As a parish priest, and for a while chaplain to the Duke of Rutland, Crabbe led a generally quiet and uneventful life. He died in 1832, 'the poet of nature and truth' according to the marble bust in Aldeburgh Church.

In the summer of 1941, a young English composer who had gone to America two years before came across Crabbe's works in a bookshop in Los Angeles. At the same time he read an essay by E. M. Forster which began with the words: 'To think of Crabbe is to think of England.' The young composer found himself strangely moved by the sound of these verses, and in particular by the fate of the cruel fisherman, Peter Grimes, the outsider of Aldeburgh.

> Thus by himself compell'd to live each day,
> To wait for certain hours the tide's delay;
> At the same times the same dull views to see,
> The bounding marsh-bank and the blighted tree;
> The water only, when the tides were high,
> When low, the mud half-cover'd and half-dry;
> The sun-burnt tar that blisters on the planks,
> And bank-side stakes in their uneven ranks;
> Heaps of entangled weeds that slowly float,
> As the tide rolls by the impeded boat.

Suddenly Britten realized where he belonged, and what he was missing. He returned to England, and composed the opera *Peter Grimes*. Its first performance, with Peter Pears in the title role, marked the reopening of Sadler's Wells Theatre in 1945, and it also marked the beginning of Benjamin Britten's glittering career as an opera composer.

He was born in Lowestoft, a child of the Suffolk coast, and his life was as close to the county as a bow to a violin. Eight of his operas were given their first performance in Suffolk, and back in 1937 he had already lived for a short time in a converted windmill in Snape. After his return from America, he and his friend, the tenor Peter Pears, took a house in Crabbe Street, Aldeburgh. In the same year, 1947, they went with the librettist Eric Crozier and the English Opera Group to the Lucerne Festival. They were all weary of being on tour, and perhaps also feeling a little homesick or nationalistic. Whatever the cause, Peter Pears suddenly suggested: 'Why not start our own little festival?' His idea was to invite their friends to give a few concerts back in Aldeburgh.

By June 1948, arrangements were in place. In the parish church, Britten's cantata *Saint Nicolas* had its world premiere, with the audience as choir since there was no money to pay for professionals. The Schumann piano concerto was played in the cinema, accompanied halfway through by two cannon shots: a yacht was in distress, and that was the signal for the lifeboats to go out. In the evening, Peter Pears sang the part of *Albert Herring*, and in the interval, everyone went to the beach. 'It was a very modest beginning,' recalled Eric Crozier, the only surviving founder of the Festival. 'At that time, just after the war, petrol was still rationed here, and the great question was whether enough people would actually come.' Conditions could scarcely have been more difficult, and success could scarcely have been sweeter. Aldeburgh became a little Salzburg by the Sea. For the fortieth anniversary of the Festival, British Rail named its London-Amsterdam night express 'Benjamin Britten'.

'At the beginning we gave open-air concerts,' said Eric Crozier, as we drank tea in his

Peter Pears, E. M. Forster, Nipper, Benjamin Britten and the fisherman Billy Burrell, 1949 (from left to right)

cottage. 'The audience sat on the shore of the lake at Thorpeness, and Imogen [daughter of the composer Gustav Holst] conducted from a rowing boat, with the musicians also sitting in boats.' Eric wrote librettos and was in charge of lighting and organisation. His wife Nancy Evans sang the part of Lucretia and various other roles in Britten's operas, and the painter John Piper created the sets. A Jewish immigrant from Berlin became the unofficial Festival photographer[1] – Kurt Hübschmann, who called himself Kurt Hutton and was one of the best photo-journalists on the magazine *Picture Post*.

'The artists could have earned a lot more in other places,' said Nancy Evans. 'But they came out of friendship for Britten.' Today she directs the training of singers at the Britten-Pears School in the Maltings (plate 27). Solo pianists and string-players, as well as graduates from music colleges all over the world come to the master classes on the Alde, to be given a final polish before launching their careers. Several times a year, participants in these courses come together to form the Britten-Pears Orchestra, in which young musi-

---

1 This 'quiet and sympathetic German gentleman', much admired by King George VI for his portraits, died in Aldeburgh in 1960. There are also several photographic studies of Aldeburgh by Angus McBean *(Shrine of Music)*, as well as by Bill Brandt and George Rodger, co-founder of the photographic agency Magnum.

E. M. Forster, Benjamin Britten and Eric Crozier (from left to right) working on the libretto for
Billy Budd *in Aldeburgh, 1949*

cians gather their first orchestral experiences under prominent conductors, either going on tour or playing at the Festival concerts in Aldeburgh. The school was founded in 1972, is 'shamelessly elitist' in its demands, and is a living national monument to Benjamin Britten and Peter Pears.

'Well, he loved me,' Sir Peter openly confessed, 'and he also loved my voice.' From 1937 onwards, for forty years, they lived together, the composer and the singer – a unique partnership in the musical history of this century. Britten became England's 'new Purcell', and Pears was his finest interpreter. Pears, who began his career in the chorus at Glyndebourne, sang the title roles in nearly all Britten's works, and when he went on tour to sing Schubert, Britten accompanied him at the piano. Together they edited old English vocal music, and together they supported the peace movement, Britten as founder of Musicians for Peace, and Pears as patron of Musicians Against Nuclear Arms. Their artistic success ensured them a degree of latitude which in those days especially was usually denied to 'ordinary' homosexuals. The Queen even knighted the pair of them.

Britten was a shy, introvert man. No-one ever saw him in an Aldeburgh pub. But at his home he would entertain such people as Dmitri Shostakovich, Aaron Copland, musicians from all over the world, and writers like W. H. Auden, E. M. Forster, Edith Sitwell. He would work in the mornings, and often go for a walk in the afternoons, along the coast or across the marshes. He loved going for picnics in the country, or church-crawling with Pears or with John Piper. Sometimes he would play tennis with the painter Mary Potter, who moved into his house in Crabbe Street and let him have her Red House – the brick house on the edge of the golf course. 'I belong at home – there, in Aldeburgh. I have tried to bring music *to* it in the shape of our local Festival; and all the music I write comes *from* it.' In this respect Britten's music diverges from modern trends, for it derives from the spirit of the countryside. 'I believe in roots, in associations, in backgrounds, in personal relationships. I want my music to be of use to people, to please them, to enhance their lives.' He succeeded. With a wealth of operas, orchestral works and cantatas, he was an avant-garde composer who never lost touch with his audience: a modern classic. He even wrote music for the Court – the opera *Gloriana* for the coronation of Elizabeth II, and the shattering *War Requiem* for the opening of the rebuilt Coventry Cathedral ('I am the enemy you killed, my friend').

His friend John Piper made the Britten memorial window in Aldeburgh Church (1980), with motifs from *Curlew River* and other parables by Britten. The composer and his singer lie buried in the churchyard. Their house in Golf Lane is now an international research centre. The Britten-Pears Library owns most of Britten's original scores, together with hundreds of unpublished compositions, his voluminous diaries and letters, scores by Gustav Holst, Michael Tippett and other British composers, and a growing collection of British songs from the 16th century to the present day. 'This is a place of work,' says Peter Wilson, the librarian. 'We are very anti-shrine.' Britten-worship is discouraged, but the Great Britten Industry is flourishing.

Thanks to a continuous flow of royalties, the Britten-Pears Foundation can help to finance the Festival, but unlike its counterpart in Bayreuth, the Aldeburgh Festival is not only designed to promote the local hero. Other composers are also celebrated, from Henze back to Haydn, and even further back to Elizabethan court music. There is also a composer in residence, who ensures that every summer there are new ideas and a busy workshop atmosphere. Among the acclaimed guest composers of recent years have been Alfred Schnittke from the then Soviet Union, and Lukas Foss, the American composer, pianist and conductor.

'How did you find the concert?' is the standard question at the breakfast table in the Wentworth Hotel. 'Terrific stuff!' gushes Lady Margot, pushing her crossword puzzle to one side. 'But Horszowski's got a finger infection.' It's almost as bad as saying that the Queen has died. Mieczyslav Horszowski, the 96-year-old Polish pianist, had had to cancel his concert. 'Never mind,' says Lady Margot, 'he's sure to be back next year.' And so is she – for the fifteenth time. 'With my taxi-driver from London.' And like all the regular customers, before she leaves she books her room for next year.

As indispensable as the Glyndebourne picnic basket is the Aldeburgh walking shoe. Walks are a firm feature of the programme. Sometimes the art lovers wander through the Stour Valley along Constable's route to school, or they cross the marsh to Dunwich – three and a half miles of pure beauty. A walk along the Sailors' Path from Aldeburgh to Snape is part of the ritual, but if you don't want to get wet feet, follow the official line: Wellies advisable.

Festival days in East Anglia, and the countryside is full of music. You hear Britten's *Curlew River*, and you know it's the Alde or the Blyth, and you hear the cry of the gulls, the rustling of the reeds, the grinding shingle on the beach, and you know that this too is the music of Aldeburgh.

To the distress of the locals, however, very few of the Festival's events actually take place in Aldeburgh now. The whole thing has spread far and wide to the villages, towns and manor houses all around. I heard the finest chamber concerts in various churches: music by Gainsborough's friends in the old Nonconformist Chapel in Ipswich, and Britten's *Hölderlin Fragments* in Blythburgh Church under the angel roof. The main problem for the Aldeburgh beginner, though, is eating. Not where, and not what, but when. Most concerts take place shortly after lunch or precisely at dinner time. Serious concert-going is extremely difficult to combine with serious eating and serious drinking. The best solution might be the old standby of the picnic, but if you do manage to get the odd hour free from music, there are some good pubs you can try: 'The Plough & Sail', Snape Maltings; 'Cross Keys Inn', Aldeburgh; 'The Jolly Sailor', Orford; 'Eel's Foot Inn', East Bridge. I can also recommend the fish & chip shop in Aldeburgh's High Street, at No. 226, with home-smoked salmon. Even Rostropovich has been seen queueing here.

The Festival has become increasingly popular with yuppies from London's Docklands, though the music sometimes takes second place to a meal at Hintlesham Hall or in the Old Rectory at Campsea Ash (where you can comfortably land your helicopter in the garden). But such serious eating costs serious money. These young whipper-snappers, complain the Festival old-hands, couldn't tell a Schnittke from a Schnitzel.

The first Festival lasted for nine days; now it's spread over the whole year: 160 days of music on the Alde, from Easter to the New Year. What has remained unspoilt, however, is the uncommercial character of the place, and the intimate atmosphere of the Festival. Things can happen in the Maltings that would be unthinkable in London's Festival Hall. When a Schoenberg song went particularly well, the conductor Oliver Knussen turned to the enthusiastic audience and asked if they wanted to hear it again. 'Play it again, Oliver!' they cried.

On the beach you can see the blue and white fishing boats of Aldeburgh – Suffolk Beach Boats of larchwood. In the middle of the 19th century there were over 100 fishermen here; when I was there, the number was just 22. When they bring their catch ashore, and adroitly cut up their Dover sole, plaice and skate, the festival guests gather admiringly in front of the black tarred huts. The biggest crowd will be watching a man with a red woollen cap. His name is Billy Burrell, and he's the best known fisherman on the east coast. Billy was a friend of Benjamin Britten. Billy remembers 'Ben' bringing him tea on the beach, enjoying his salmon, going out to sea with him to watch the avocets. 'I was never interested in his music, though,' says Billy. 'It wasn't my sort of thing. My wife likes it. She was in the choir.' Britten once played one of his pieces to Billy on the piano. 'Fancy people paying money to listen to that rubbish!' was Billy's comment. But it didn't affect their friendship. Britten gave Billy a score of his opera *Billy Budd*, with the inscription: 'To BB, from BB, for BB'. Billy knows what stories the 'arty people' like to hear. He sits outside his hut, a fifth-generation fisherman, splicing ropes and telling his tales. He's an integral part of the Festival, a natural actor for the stage of Aldeburgh. 'Last week Lord Snowdon came by. The Queen's also been here. Everybody comes to my hut.' The Queen wanted to know where he caught his fish. 'Over there, ma'am,' he said, and pointed to the sea.

On the beach just outside Aldeburgh stands a massive tower. Made out of nearly a million bricks, the Martello Tower of 1815 was the last and the biggest link in a chain of more than 100 coastal defences against the dreaded French invasion. But Napoleon never made it to Aldeburgh, and the brick block with the cloverleaf ground plan became a painting (watercolour by J. M. W. Turner, *c*.1825, now in the Tate Gallery) and a holiday home.

If you look for the Alde Estuary near Aldeburgh, you'll have to look for a long time. The bank of shingle that blocks it reaches far to the south. For almost ten miles the Alde flows parallel to the coast, and by the time it finally reaches the sea, way beyond *Orford*, it has changed its name and become the River Ore. Shaped like a boomerang, Orford Ness curves between river and sea, leaving a broad promontory at its centre. The isolation here has a thousand voices, all as old as stone, and the sea murmurs and rolls and grinds its teeth on the shingle. Known as the Spit, Orford Ness has been generally silting up since 1170, as a result of strong tidal currents southwards along the coast. The Spit expands on average about fifty feet a year.

With a miniature oar of silver, only the town regalia carry memories of the fact that in the Middle Ages Orford was a flourishing port, particularly for the export of wool. But at the end of the 16th century, the sea built a barrier of shingle across the entrance to the harbour. In those days the 'Jolly Sailor' in Quay Street was a waterside pub, and where there are now vegetable gardens, there used to be trading vessels at anchor.

One summer morning I wandered over the dyke alongside the river. The broad mouth of the Ore was full of sailing boats. Inland, on a gentle slope, I could see the houses of Orford in the morning haze, sheltering beneath the castle and the church, just as they do in Turner's watercolour of *c*.1825, with shrimpers in the foreground.

Laughing children tumble down the grassy slopes surrounding Orford Castle. Only the keep with its septaria walls, 10 feet thick, remains from this, the first royal castle in Suffolk, built by the Plantagenet King Henry II in 1165 to counter the threat of the barons. Eight years later, just after its completion, it passed its first test: an attack by the rebellious barons and his own son, Prince Henry. With its unusual, 18-side ground plan, Orford Castle was one of the most advanced pieces of military architecture of its time and the first in England to depart from the rectangular form, whose corners were always vulnerable to sapping during sieges.[1] The three side towers, which act simultaneously as buttresses and staircases,

---

1 Chilham Castle in Kent (*c*.1171–4) and Odiham Castle in Hampshire (*c*.1207–12) are the only other polygonal Norman keeps in England.

J. M. W. Turner: Orford, Suffolk, 1827

lead to the two-storeyed balconies of the keep. The view from the battlements of this castle is breathtaking. For hundreds of years the great tower served as a landmark for ships, and in the two World Wars it was still used by the army as a watch-tower.

The arcades of the ruined chancel at the east end of Orford Church bear witness to the skills of late Norman stonemasons; alas, this is all that remains of the original church, which was begun at the same time as the castle. The 'new Church' of St Bartholomew dates from the early 14th century, and in addition to its Gothic font and many fine brasses (*c.*1480–1520), has an important Renaissance altarpiece: a 'Sacra Conversazione' by the Lombard painter Bernardino Luini (*c.*1520). Four of Benjamin Britten's works received their first performance in this church: three of his parables, and *Noye's Fludde* (1958), a musical adaptation of the Chester miracle play. Every year, some of the Aldeburgh Festival concerts take place here as well. But you don't need to be a Benjamin Britten fan to enjoy the culinary masterpieces performed at the 'Oysterage' in the Market Place: oyster soup, prawns in garlic sauce, smoked eel or Irish salmon. Even Noah would have licked his lips.

'Neill, Neill, Orange Peel': The Heritage of Summerhill

Deep in the Suffolk hinterland lies a myth called *Summerhill*. Even people with no interest in education have heard of Summerhill. Isn't that the school where there were no reports? The school where pupils only went to lessons if they felt like it? Next to the mini-skirt and the Beatles, Summerhill in the sixties was England's most sensational export – and the most scandalous school in Britain. Its founder was Alexander Sutherland Neill, son of a Scottish village teacher. His maxim was 'I would rather see a school produce a happy street cleaner than a neurotic scholar.' This sentence comes from Neill's book *Summerhill, A Radical Approach to Child Rearing* (New York, 1960). It was a signpost for a generation in rebellion against parents, State, and every kind of authority. Summerhill was like a drug to the left-wing revolutionaries of 1968, and Neill was their guru; the school was overrun by sightseers from all over the world – an educational zoo. The inveterate rebel died in 1973 at the age of ninety. The children of Summerhill have long since spawned children of their own, and today they prefer to send their offspring to Eton. So what happened?

Even long after the death of the founder, the road to Summerhill is still not called Neill Street but Westward Ho!, after the Victorian best seller by Charles Kingsley. The school is a red brick building on the outskirts of Leiston, and the setting is green, though to call it a park would be an exaggeration. The grounds are full of what one would have to say are shacks rather than bungalows, and there's a vegetable garden, rabbit hutches, a tennis court and a swimming pool. In the lounge-cum-assembly-room-cum-disco are five torn chairs, tipped over at various angles. Up on a scaffold rather like a raised hide, a boy switches on the amplifiers and out come the tones of the 'Talking Heads'. Next door an older girl is practising on the piano with a little Japanese boy. 'Smile Summerhill Style' says a notice on the wall, and another says 'Summerhill School Food is a Killer'. The children are not in the least shy. They happily show me round their school, friendly, full of information and self-confidence. They are obviously enjoying their schooldays. One is wearing a T-shirt with a quote from Neill: 'the closest thing here to a uniform.'

The next day I meet Zoe Redhead, born in 1946, former pupil at Summerhill. She lives on a farm nearby – a pink, thatched house with a black swan in a pond and a white Mercedes at the door. Zoe is Neill's daughter, and since 1985 has been head of Summerhill. What is her greatest debt to her father? 'Self-determination right from birth. Neill brought me up precisely according to his Summerhill philosophy, and in that sense I had the same advantages as all the other pupils – and that applied to the holidays as well.' She left the school without any particular career in mind, did this and that, and for a time gave riding lessons at Summerhill. 'I wanted to work with horses.' Then she married a farmer from the neighbourhood. Now her children Amie, William and Henry also go to Summerhill. The fourth child has been respectfully named after her father: Neill Alexander Sutherland, born 1987.

Education through freedom, which is based on sexual freedom, self-determination, and personal responsibility. Neill's basic principles are firmly adhered to by his daughter.

252

Summerhill when I visited it had 70 pupils between the ages of six and seventeen, six classes, eight teachers, and two house parents for the boarders. A typical day: breakfast between 8.15 and 8.45 a.m., lessons start at 9.30 a.m. 'by which time everybody should be up and about' (including anyone who doesn't want to go to lessons). Lunch for the younger pupils is at 12.30, for the older ones at 1.15. Then everyone is free. At 4 p.m. there's a cup of tea, then at 4.30 p.m. lessons start again. Supper is at 5.30 p.m. The evenings are free. There is a pub, and the pupils brew their own beer. They can all smoke if they want to, with no age limit, but they mustn't smoke in the house or in their rooms. Not even Neill allowed smoking.

It was Zoe who lifted her father's ban on smoking and alcohol. 'He was always afraid that the authorities would find an excuse to close his school.' Today society is far more tolerant, and life is much freer and easier, including attitudes towards sex. 'People don't worry about it so much.' Up until now no pupil has ever become pregnant. And furthermore, the proportion of smokers is smaller here than in most other schools. The school community has always been small enough to settle its own problems. 'There's a strict distinction here between freedom and promiscuity. That is basic to our school.' Freedom of the individual is balanced by respect for the freedom of others. In order to protect that, one needs rules, in a free school even more than in any other kind of school. Violation of the rules often has painful consequences. For instance, if you disturb people at night, you forfeit your pudding; if the offence is repeated, you will only get bread and butter for lunch. 'Or an hour's weeding – we have all kinds of punishments here, and they're especially severe for drunkenness.' But then she corrects herself, and changes the authoritarian term for a more sporting one: 'Well, not really punishments, more like a penalty.'

The pupils have their own governing body which meets twice a week. Some years ago they demanded the right to give their own examination grades, which horrified Neill. He was outvoted – but was then delighted by the success rate. Teachers, pupils and head-mistress, children and adults, have equal votes in the so-called 'tribunal'. These early exercises in democracy, free speech, and social conduct still constitute the spirit of Summerhill and the myth of the 'children's republic'. But there are two elementary things the children have to swallow and can do nothing about: the food, and the teachers. Summerhill's budget and staff policy is the province of the headmistress alone, and is not subject to a community vote.

Summerhill is one of the very cheapest independent boarding schools in England. Since there is no other form of income, the teachers' salaries are ridiculously low: just 60 per cent of what state teachers earn. 'That really is our problem. Teachers who would like to work here often find out that they simply can't afford to,' says Zoe Redhead. 'Today especially we need even better teachers and facilities than we did in Neill's day, if only to prove to our critics that even though the children don't have to go to lessons, when they do, they find the best possible conditions.'

One third of the 70 pupils come from Japan. 'It's a bit of a fad,' said Zoe. Neill's books have been translated into Japanese, and in such a highly competitive, hierarchical society they are bestsellers among those who are seeking alternatives. But former pupils rarely send their own children to Summerhill. Anyone who wants to take A-Levels can do so, but very few pupils ever go on to university. People used to ask Neill: 'Does Summerhill prepare children for the real world?' His answer was: 'Summerhill *is* the real world.' Of course he knew, as everyone else did, that this was not quite true. The school that he founded in 1924[1] has remained an educational island, and has never been accepted as a workable model for other schools. In the last thirty-odd years, only Kilquhanity in Scotland has followed the Summerhill example.

Neill began with the modest, difficult and wholly admirable aim of letting people live their own lives; his school then became known as the Eton of anti-authoritarian education and, against his will, was politicized; now it is nothing more than 'an international rural youth hostel of the very best kind' (R. W. Leonhardt). Neill's daughter is watching over a fading myth. There are no longer any new pedagogic ideas radiating out of here, and as for the question of success: 'Maybe our example has helped to make English schools a bit more human,' hopes Zoe. And she hopes, too, that 'children who were at Summerhill at least had a happy childhood.' That would be no mean achievement, and would be totally in keeping with Neill's own preference for happy people rather than successful people.

Summerhill became known the world over, but nobody has ever heard of *Leiston*. The local people have only themselves to blame for that. The school on the edge of their town might as well be on another planet as far as they are concerned. They prefer to send their children elsewhere, and not to what they used, somewhat vulgarly, to call the 'free fuck school'. 'A few are proud of Summerhill,' says Zoe, 'but others think we're crazy.'

Leiston is a small country town, and once upon a time it, too, was famous – as East Anglia's only centre for heavy industry. At the end of the 18th century, Richard Garrett built an ironworks here. It became the leading manufacturer of agricultural machinery in eastern England, alongside Ransomes of Ipswich where Queen Victoria bought her lawnmowers. Garrett & Sons were initially known for their drills and horseshoes. Later they specialized in threshing machines, steam rollers, ploughs and tractors, exporting their machines as far afield as Africa and Australia, and until 1914 they even built railway engines for the Tsar. In the mid-19th century, Garretts had about 500 employees; by the turn of the century this had risen to over 1,000, which was very substantial for a rural region like Suffolk. During the First and Second World Wars they produced hundreds of thousands of grenades. But in 1980 they had to close. Fortunately someone in Leiston realized that this factory, which had never been modernized and was virtually in its original condition, still had all its machines, tools and documents, and would make an ideal industrial museum. Since 1983 this redundant industrial complex on Main Street has been fully restored, partly by its former employees. The Long Shop of 1855, the central area of

---

1 It was preceded by the so-called Neue Schule [New School] which Neill and others founded in 1921 in Hellerau, near Dresden.

production, is a prime specimen of industrial architecture – a functional and beautifully proportioned hall, 85 feet long, 43 feet high and 43 feet wide, one of the earliest assembly line factories for steam engines in England.

There is something touchingly nostalgic about these relics of the Industrial Revolution, not least if one walks east out of Leiston. Two miles along the beach stands a monstrous, aluminium-grey block: England's biggest nuclear power station. When this gas-cooled Magnox Reactor (1961–6) was supposed to be joined 20 years later by a second reactor, *Sizewell* became the centre of a national controversy, and a test case for the Conservative government's nuclear policy. Labour declared that it would not build Sizewell B (Britain's first heavy water reactor) and would discontinue the whole programme of fast breeder reactors. Mrs Thatcher, though famous as TINA ('There is no alternative'), set up a commission of inquiry, thus beginning a lengthy process of acceptance or non-acceptance. Sellafield, Harrisburg, Chernobyl – weren't these names frightening enough? At Three Mile Island the accident involved a Westinghouse heavy water reactor, precisely the type to be used for Sizewell B.

Opponents ranged from local farmer Robin Hare to Lord Somerleyton, from inshore fishermen and the Miners' Union to environmentalists, writers, musicians and artists (including Sir Peter Pears and the Suffolk-born Elisabeth Frink), from Friends of the Earth to the Council for the Protection of Rural England. Eventually supporters and opponents of Sizewell B came together at a public hearing in the area's biggest hall: Snape Maltings. There, in the concert hall of the Aldeburgh Festival, on 11 January 1983, there began the longest hearing in British history. It lasted over two years, cost some £20m, called on over 200 expert witnesses, and ended in a 2,000-page report – '24 times longer than War and Peace' (*The Times*). The findings of the Layfield Report: the planned reactor was 'sufficiently safe to be tolerable'. In the judgment of Sir Frank Layfield, chairman of the inquiry, national economic advantages were great enough to justify the risk. His report did not deny that Sizewell B meant a totally inappropriate excrescence in the landscape, but national interests were of greater importance than the local interests of the environmentalists.

The safety risk was cold-bloodedly set against expected profits, and in that sense Sizewell B was a perfect example of the Thatcher government's economic absolutism. The whole thing had nothing to do with safeguarding the electricity supply or with conserving coal and oil reserves (some 80 per cent of Britain's electricity was then produced by coal-fired power stations). Above all, this was a matter of business for the British nuclear industry – safeguarding fast breeder export contracts with China, Egypt, and other countries interested in developing nuclear power. As always in such cases, the interested party – the state-run Central Electricity Generating Board (this was before privatisation) – was offering plenty of sugar with its mighty pill: the intruder on Heritage Coast would be camouflaged behind a wall of grass and trees, and the inshore fishermen would be handsomely compensated for the inconvenience caused by the construction process. Sizewell B, at a cost of £2.03 billion (and 56p), will be in operation by 1994. The 1,175

Sizewell B: Protest against nuclear power station, 1988. The demonstrators are carrying names of surrounding villages

megawatt reactor will cover most of East Anglia's electricity requirements, though only for the next 35 years. Then they will need a new nuclear reactor. Sizewell C, however, also included in the long-term planning, will not be built. After the fiasco of privatization, the government drew a line after its 16 nuclear reactors. Nobody wants to take over these uneconomic and incalculably dangerous monsters.

In Sizewell there is a nicely named pub: 'The Vulcan Arms'. It is, I suppose, human nature that the people of neighbouring Leiston are still more suspicious of the Summerhill experiment than they are of the nuclear volcano on their doorstep. When the machine factory closed down, the town had 9 per cent unemployment, and so the possibility of a new power station meant new jobs. What else mattered?

I went for a leisurely stroll along the beach at Sizewell. By turning the head just an inch further south, I could shut Monster A and incipient Monster B right out of sight. All I saw then was sky and sea and a few fishing boats, just as it was hundreds of years ago. One could have imagined that nothing had changed.

But it appears that even conservationists should in fact be grateful for Sizewell B. It's not only the many supply firms but also the fish and bird life that regard it as an undisguised blessing. The cooling water pumped out of the reactor warms the sea by several degrees, and according to an official information sheet, the fish are absolutely delighted. They all come flocking – or shoaling – to the area, and so do the anglers. The not-quite-so-fast breeders – the winged ones in the nearby nature reserve at Minsmere – are equally delighted by their new bathing facilities: 'Some species are now nesting in the area for the first time and others are attracted to the warm water outfall for feeding.' We visitors should perhaps also be grateful for the free heating of the sea around Sizewell, but for some reason the people in power make no mention of that.

The hub of one of P. D. James's most recent, most elegiac detective stories, *Devices and Desires* (1989), is a nuclear power station: 'That concrete bastion on the edge of a polluted sea.' Her Sizewell is called Larksoken, and lies on the coast of northern Norfolk. There 'The Whistler' – a psychopathic woman-killer – goes about his grisly business. When the universally hated woman director of the power station is murdered, everyone in Larksoken comes under suspicion. A case for Chief Inspector Dalgliesh, but it's also a case dealing with dangerous technology, which threatens more than just a few lives in a small coastal community.

Further along the coast to *Thorpeness*, is the strangest water tower in the British Isles. 'The House in the Clouds' (plate 25) holds 30,000 gallons, is disguised as a wooden house, and looks as if it has been run through by its chimney. This extraordinary piece of architecture dates from 1925. The nearby post-mill (1803) serves as a pump for the water tower. As for Thorpeness itself: around 1910 the writer G. Stuart Ogilvie hit on the idea of establishing a holiday village for London's upper middle-class, with golf course, artificial lake, and timber-framed, Tudor comforts: Merrie Englande by the Sea.

Quite a different kind of England is that of the poet Michael Hamburger (plate 50). He lives with his wife Anne and their tom-cat Oskar on the edge of *Middleton*, one of the many unprepossessing villages between the A12 and the coast. Born in Berlin in 1924, son of a Jewish paediatrician, he, his parents, and his brother (the London publisher and multi-millionaire Paul Hamlyn) emigrated in 1933. Michael went to school in Edinburgh and London, studied at Oxford, and has been a British citizen since 1939. A recent collection of his poems is entitled *Roots in the Air*. But where are the roots? Michael Hamburger is a tall, gaunt man. He showed me round 'Marsh Acres', a labyrinth of rooms and staircases and hidden corners, with a few pieces of Biedermeier furniture left over from his childhood in Berlin, and Anne told me about the haunted staircase, where a ghost sometimes announces his presence with a mysterious scent of lily of the valley.

In his place of exile which eventually became his home, Michael Hamburger translated Hölderlin into English during the war, and later translated Büchner, Trakl and Celan, Benn and Brecht, Grass and many others. Thus he became the most important champion of German literature in England, along with his friend and fellow émigré Erich Fried. As an essayist and poet, Hamburger wrote only in English for a long time, and not until the sixties did he also write in German. But instead of belonging, as he had hoped, to two cultures, he had the feeling that he was 'stateless in a No-Man's-Land'. His has been a life between two languages, which in his memoirs he describes as *A Mug's Game*. But he loves Suffolk, with its many different landscapes, its sky, its light and its wide open spaces – these he finds inspiring, and here he feels at home. Middleton has about 400 inhabitants. When the Hamburgers moved here in 1976, the village still had a blacksmith, various craftsmen, and a post office. Now they've all gone. Practically everyone here votes Conservative, 'because that's what they've always done – not because they like the government.' Anne runs an amateur dramatic society, and Michael is a passionate gardener. He takes me past his roses, hollyhocks, mint and balm to his 'wilderness' where the yellow iris blooms.

At the house there's a pump dated 1770. 'It's the year Hölderlin died, and Beethoven and Wordsworth were born,' he announces cheerfully, as if somehow the coincidences bode well. 'Goodbye, words. / I never liked you, / Liking things and places, and / Liking people best when their mouths are shut.'

Fish and Chips in Dunwich: A Trip to Vineta

'The corpse without hands lay in the bottom of a small sailing dinghy drifting just within sight of the Suffolk coast. It was the body of a middle-aged man, a dapper little cadaver, its shroud a dark pin-striped suit which fitted the narrow body as elegantly in death as it had in life.' These sentences begin P. D. James's detective story *Unnatural Causes* – which deals with the murder of a writer in the fictional town of Monksmere Head, 'just south of Dunwich'. Fortunately, as far as the solution of this macabre case is concerned, Scotland Yard's Chief Inspector Adam Dalgliesh happens to be spending his autumn holiday there with his Aunt Jane, an amateur ornithologist who lives in a house on the cliffs. Not so fortunately, even Dalgliesh cannot prevent the dastardly deed from taking place: in Minsmere nature reserve – beware, you bird-lovers – a dead man lies in the observation hut on the beach. 'It was a lonely shore, empty and desolate like the last fringes of the world.'

Of course all English people like to think that when they are standing on the shores of their beloved isle, they are standing on the edge of the world. But on this particular part of the coast, there really is an additional something, a peculiar feeling of 'Land's End'. For what we see in *Dunwich* is not Dunwich, but its myth: the town that sank into the sea. This is the sight that lures thousands of people every year to the lonely shore, and the fact that they don't all lapse into deep melancholy and hurl themselves into the sea is due solely and simply to Flora's Tea Room, the best fish and chip shop on the entire eastern coast. The reputation of this classic English seaside caff has long been established even in London, and when it burnt down in 1988, it was immediately rebuilt in its original style, which was that of the tarred fishermen's huts. It's my belief that Flora's is the real reason why people come to Dunwich now, and not the old story of Vineta. But no doubt you'd like to know the story. It began with St Felix and ended with the wild North Sea.

The name Dunwich comes from the old Celtic 'Dubno', meaning deep water, and the

Anglo-Saxon 'wic', meaning settlement or port. Around 632 a missionary from Burgundy, St Felix, founded East Anglia's first see at Dunwich. When the Norman conquerors conducted their great survey of populations and incomes in 1086, the Domesday Book recorded that Dunwich had some 3,000 inhabitants (Ipswich only had 1,300), three churches, a Benedictine abbey, and a house each for the Franciscans and Dominicans. It was a prosperous place, and every year paid a tax of 68,000 herring. At its peak in the 13th century, it had 18 churches and monasteries, and was the second biggest town in East Anglia, after Norwich. Dunwich had 80 trading vessels, compared to Ipswich's 30. It competed with Yarmouth, exporting wool to Flanders and importing wine from Gascony; the people were merchants, fishermen, pirates, and heaven knows what else. But already, in the 11th century, the sea was gnawing away at the low sandy cliffs on which the town was built.

The end of Dunwich port came on the night of 19 January 1328. A terrible storm, more devastating than anything hitherto experienced, resulted in some 400 houses and three churches being swallowed up, while the entrance to the port was totally blocked. The sea had made the town rich, and now it took back everything that it had given, and buried it under sand and shingle. During the centuries that followed, 13 more churches sank beneath the waves. At the end of the 17th century, the Market Place also disappeared. Trade continued, as Defoe noted, 'particularly for the shipping of Butter, Cheese, and Corn' – Suffolk butter being famous. But the ships had to dock at Walberswick, since the ruins of Dunwich made the harbour unsafe. The seamen hated it, as Defoe records in their 'rude verse': Swoul [Southwold] and Dunwich and Walberswick / All go in at one lousie Creek.

Dunwich, writes Paul Theroux, is 'famous for no longer existing.' It's a place of the imagination, visited by poets, historians, and melancholics. Edward FitzGerald came in 1855 with Thomas Carlyle, and Swinburne came, and so did Henry James and P. D. James, and Jerome K. Jerome often spent his holidays at Mrs Scarlet's guesthouse at the turn of the century. In the early summer you sometimes get divers here, looking for the remains of the sunken town. And in September you get the faithful who gather on the shore for the so-called blessing of the sea, though you'd have thought there'd be more reason to curse her. And during the holiday season you get everybody joining together at Flora's Tea Rooms, savouring their Dover sole and telling the children that on stormy nights you can still hear the bells ringing beneath the sea.

Dunwich, or what's left of it today, has 160 inhabitants. At the local museum near the 'Ship Inn', the North Sea dozes before the next storm. On the high shingle beach lies 'Fred's Last', one of Dunwich's six fishing-boats. To the north is Southwold lighthouse, beyond the marsh is Blythburgh Church, to the south is the Sizewell monster, and ahead, a quarter of a mile out to sea, is old Dunwich. The rest is hardly worth mentioning: the ruins of the leper hospital in St James' churchyard, or the ivy-covered walls of Greyfriars, which used to be the Franciscan monastery, was an ack-ack station during the war, and is now a paddock. There's a lovely path along the cliffs, where you can pick blackberries and look

John Sell Cotman: Covehithe Church, Suffolk, 1804–5

out over the sea, and on the steep edge of the shore lies the body of John Easey, buried in 1826. He is not likely to rest in peace for much longer. His is the last gravestone in the churchyard of All Saints, which was the last of Dunwich's medieval churches, and began to crumble into the sea back in 1904.

'This town is a testimony to the decay of public things' wrote Defoe. 'The ruins of *Carthage*, of the great city of *Jerusalem*, or of ancient *Rome* are not all wonderful to me; being the capitals of great and flourishing kingdoms, when those kingdoms are overthrown, the capital cities necessarily fell with them; but for a private town, a sea-port and a town of commerce, to decay as it were of itself (for we never read of *Dunwich* being plundered or ruined by any disaster, at least not of late years); this I must confess seems owing to nothing but to the fate of things, by which we see that towns, kings, countries, families and persons have all their destruction in the womb of time and the course of nature.'

In the last 400 years, the coast has fallen back an average of a yard a year. Every flood, every winter storm, every rolling wave takes away another piece of land, delivering it to the sea 'which moves forever, like a ruminating beast, an insatiable, indefatigable lip' (Henry James). The history of this coast is the history of the rise and fall of its ports, of the fishermen's fight for survival, of the heroism of the lifeboatmen, of brief triumphs and protracted helplessness. Orford, Aldeburgh, Dunwich, Blythburgh, Walberswick, Southwold – all of them were once flourishing ports that fell victim to erosion and that insatiable sea. Only the grey towers of their churches remain like unlit lighthouses gazing nostalgically out to sea.

Covehithe is another lost soul of a place, languishing between sea and sky. Just a few sad houses. A church without a village. The last road comes to an end here, but you can follow the path past hawthorn hedges and cornfields, through a sparse wood, and along to where you can see the steep coast and the shining sand. It's a beach without beach-huts and without souvenir stands, but after every winter storm there's enough driftwood to brew a kettle or two. Here the sea claims 13 feet of land a year – which is four times as much as it takes from the Dunwich coast. Covehithe also had a port in the old days, and when the port went, the town went. When the dwindling community could no longer maintain its large Perpendicular church, much of St Andrew's was torn down, and the stones taken from the ruined nave were used to build a new and smaller church with a thatched roof in 1672. Now one feels that, like the Babushka dolls, this church could do with a smaller one inside it, for the Reverend Laurence Spratt never has more than nine souls in his congregation. But if the erosion of the coast continues at the same rate, the sea will have solved that problem anyway by the year 2030.

For those who love the romance of ruins, these melancholy sites are places of pilgrimage. In summer 1804, John Sell Cotman met his lifelong patron, the banker Dawson Turner (see page 387), for the first time, and they spent a few days together in Covehithe. There Cotman painted the ruined church, then ivy-covered, as a silhouette against a dramatic sky – like the fragile architecture of his own soul. As a place of mystery, Covehithe ranks second only to Dunwich in the works of P. D. James: 'To see Covehithe by moonlight is to be entranced by a nostalgic beauty which is both eerie and majestic.' It is no coincidence that her detective hero writes his only known verses in one of these poetic coastal churches, before he becomes involved in the serial killings of *Unnatural Causes* – 'sitting in the silvery peace of Blythburgh Church'.

I shall never forget *Blythburgh*. The first time I saw it, many years ago, I was driving along the A12 from Ipswich to Yarmouth, and now, whenever I take this route, I'm eagerly looking forward to the view as one would to seeing an old friend. Holy Trinity stands on a hill above the marsh, at the old tidal estuary of the Blyth. It's almost like an anchored ship stranded by the retreating tide. This is the Cathedral of the Marshes (colour plate 10). It is one of the great sights of Suffolk. I first saw it gleaming in the sun, its flint walls flashing, as if they were dissolving in the blinding light of the great windows. But I've also seen it on an autumn evening, standing guard over the fields like a mysterious dark watchman. I've been in this church when it has been filled with concert-goers, and has echoed to the sounds of madrigals or the mighty organ. And I've been there when it's been empty and so still that one could hear nothing but the ticking of the church clock and the creaking of the rafters, as if the angels were flexing their wooden wings.

That angel roof is Holy Trinity's pride and joy (plate 93). But the basis of the church's beauty is its simplicity: its white walls, its spaciousness, its clear proportions, and the gentle rhythms of its piers and windows. And all this simplicity is illuminated by an extraordinary light, which animates even the tiniest figures in the stalls right through to the folds in their garments, and floods upwards into the very domain of the angels. Blythburgh glows, even on the most miserable of days. It is a late Gothic light that bathes the church like a glasshouse. The 18 closely-set windows in the clearstorey spread the glow evenly over the whole interior – the glow of the East Anglian coast and of the Holy Trinity.

Blythburgh Church was built in the middle of the 15th century, at the same time as the other great Perpendicular wool churches of Suffolk, Long Melford and Lavenham. Art and craft and the service of God still went together in those days, and what we now admire as superb carving was then taken as a direct lesson in faith and morality. On the poppyheads of their stalls, c.1475, the congregation were confronted with the striking personifications of Gluttony, Pride, Avarice and the rest of the Deadly Sins, as vividly portrayed as the hard grind of their own everyday routine through allegories of sowing and harvesting, ploughing and threshing, or the slaughtering of pigs. And above all this hovered the messengers of heavenly glory. To people in the Middle Ages, angels were still real beings, for it was not until the so-called Enlightenment that dull eyes and minds shrank them into mere images, though they have occasionally returned since then, 'almost fatal birds of the soul' in Rilke's melancholy verse.

In pairs, back to back, at the intersections of beams, linked by painted bosses, gazing east and west – thus the Blythburgh angels cover the entire length of the nave's flat roof. Each one of the twelve (but one is missing) holds a coat of arms, for the Hoptons and other local families who financed the building of the church: Glory to God in the Highest, and also to the Donors. The rafters of this self-supporting beamed roof are painted with garlands, a gentle red and green on a bright background. Beneath this firmament, the angels majestically spread their long and slender wings. Their lightness seems to take the weight off the mighty oak beams, and their grace lightens the church and the hearts of the worshippers down below. 'Who, if I cried out, might hear me – among the ranked angels?' Rilke exclaimed. In such churches, beneath these medieval angel roofs, any despair finds an echo and an answer, and beauty is nothing more than a reflection of the eternal.

On 8 April 1644 Cromwell's trusted henchman William Dowsing came to Holy Trinity. How infuriated he must have been by those angels in their lofty, untouchable glory. His iconoclasts destroyed the saints, ripped the brasses from the gravestones, and fired hundreds of shots up at the ceiling. When the angels were taken down for restoration in the 19th century, Puritan bullets were found in the wood (though a less warlike explanation is the fact that here as elsewhere, it is known that people sometimes fired shots into the roof to try and drive away the birds that were nesting there). The 19th-century restoration of Blythburgh Church, incidentally, was quoted by William Morris as a model during his campaign against Victorian cosmetic surgery. In the mid-seventies, though, a new threat emerged: woodworm had eaten away so much of the roof that it was in danger of total collapse. But happily the new, and very expensive restoration succeeded in preserving Holy Trinity just as it has always been.[1]

Shortly after the opening of the 1969 Aldeburgh Festival, the concert hall in Snape burnt down, and so all performances were transferred to this church. Janet Baker, Dietrich Fischer-Dieskau, Rostropovich and many others have since returned to perform below the angels of Blythburgh. These great stars of the music world fully appreciate not only the marvellous acoustics provided by the wooden beams, but also the unique atmosphere. I was privileged to attend a concert given here by the American pianist Murray Perahia, playing Alban Berg's piano sonatas in front of the Gothic choir screen. It was a warm afternoon in June, and in the interval we sat outside on the grass between the gravestones, enjoying the fresh air and the view across the marsh. Blythburgh Church is also the venue for some concerts in the Wangford Festival, begun by the rector of the neighbouring village in 1966. With a white dinner jacket over a black cassock, the Reverend Miles Copley says a few words of introduction, the audience-cum-congregation stands to the sounds of the National Anthem, and then the church concert begins.

There is room in Holy Trinity for 600 people. The size of this village church – it is over 130 feet long – was commensurate with the importance of Blythburgh in the Middle Ages. It was a centre for fishing and the cloth trade – a harbour town with two annual markets, its own coinage, and its own prison. But the economic decline began as early as the 15th century, when the proud church was barely completed. It was typical of this treacherous and malign coast. When the port of Dunwich sank and the River Blyth sought a new path to the sea, Blythburgh's port silted up, and a new port was established at the mouth of the river: Walberswick. And then that, too, disappeared. It's a never-ending story.

From Holy Trinity you can follow a path along the river through the reeds and meadows to Walberswick and Southwold, where you will find the other two Perpendicular churches on the Blyth.

Sunny Periods in Southwold

Beloved little *Southwold* smells of hops and malt and sea. It lies in a dead end on the Suffolk coast, and most people – thank Heaven – pass it by. There are no sights in Southwold, no castle, no cathedral, and not even any ruins (colour plate 1). There's no reason at all to turn off the A12, cross the marsh, and head towards the white lighthouse and the bright beach huts that are lined up between fields and foam like a row of colour charts. So, please, leave the place to me.

---

1   One detail to be noted is the Clock-Jack of painted wood, 1682; he hits the bell with his battle-axe when the priest enters. These bellringing figures, also known as Jack-of-the-Clock or Quarter Jack, used to be more popular on the Continent than in England, but there is one in Southwold and also one in Wells Cathedral, c.1390.

Stanley Spencer: Southwold, 1937

The High Street ends in a small, triangular market place (plate 36), in the middle of which is a Victorian pump with a glass ball and gold crown, wrought iron dolphins and the motto 'Defend Thy Ryghts'. 'The Swan' hospitably reaches out its bay windows and its gables, and opposite are the bank, Denny the Tailor, and Norman the Butcher ('over 300 years and still going strong'). It all looks as if it's always been like this, and always will be.

The first person to see us arrive is probably Ginger. He stands at his front door, blinking into the sun. Ginger wears rubber boots, one black and one green. He always wears rubber boots, in summer and in winter. People say that's where he keeps his money. Certainly he was in 'The Nelson' once, and when it was time to pay, he pulled a £50 note out of his rubber boot. His real name is Ernest Newson, but he's got this tobacco-coloured beard, which is why he's known as Ginger. How long has he lived here? 'Seventy-five years, three months, and one week. And this is the house where I was born.' His father was a baker, one of seven bakers in Southwold. Today there's just one. Ginger sells lottery tickets. His pension is too small for him to be able to do any repairs on the house. If he were to sell it, he'd be a rich man, for Ginger lives on South Green.

South Green is on the cliffs overlooking the sea, and on a hill overlooking the marsh. The wild lupins bloom yellow, and the view takes your breath away, until the storm breaks and sends you scurrying off into 'The Red Lion', which is the pub on South Green. 'They're all rich people, my neighbours – seriously rich,' says Ginger, looking seriously poor in his ragged tweed jacket. 'But even a millionaire can only drink one Guinness at a time.'

There are only four local people still living on South Green. The rest are 'newcomers', though some have been here for years, and some have been here before. The latter may have been here for their holidays when they were children, and have come back again to spend their old age here. Most are from London – retired judges, colonial officers, 'resting' actresses. They form a highly conservative and extremely eccentric little society. Thus Southwold has quietly evolved into the coastal suburb of Hampstead. Half the 2,000 inhabitants are over 60, and every sixth house is a holiday or second home. It's no coincidence that there are four estate agents here. Many of the local people, especially the young ones, can't afford these expensive houses, and so they move inland to neighbouring Reydon.

Southwold's history as a seaside resort began at the end of the 18th century. The landed gentry built themselves some modestly elegant Regency villas beside the sea. Then around 1830 there came the row of neoclassical houses on Centre Cliff. Swinburne spent a few summers here. In 1879 the railway reached Southwold, but the great boom never materialized, and the last train puffed sadly away only 50 years later. The herring industry also left, and so the charms of the little town were left just for the likes of me.

There's a nice summer breeze today, and everyone's heading for the beach. But if you think the beach means sand, then you are barking up the wrong parasol. All the stoic bathers sit on the pebbles like fakirs on a bed of nails. Cowering behind solid breakwaters and flapping windbreaks the English holidaymaker bravely defies the elements (colour plate 5). And if the breeze gets to gale force, the last and finest refuge is the beach hut. Like a row of little Victorian terraced houses, 248 of them line up at the foot of the cliff, bright beacons against the grey sea, lashed down to defy the grasping winds, mini-fortresses and tea-houses, where the life-saving brown liquid is being constantly brewed as first aid and last aid in between the sunny periods (plates 29, 30).

The huts all have names, of course. Patriotic ones: 'Britannia', 'Lady Nelson'; social ones: 'Chatterbox'; philosophical ones: 'Take It Easy' and 'Happy Days'. They are the fixed pole of seaside life, the permanent box at the theatre of the sea. You catch a glimpse of a leg or a wet snuffly nose between the boards, and over there two old ladies are reading Jeffrey Archer, while their husbands stand with rolled-up trousers and silly grins, testing the water. 'Nice and warm, darling!' Then back they come to the nicer, warmer shelter, and scan the horizon through their binoculars, as if awaiting the Spanish Armada. Nothing happens, of course, and that's the beauty of it all. Then around five o'clock, a lady steps onto the shore with a fully laden tray, catches her foot in the pebbles, and falls headlong. Pity about the tea, but at least it's something for everyone to look at.

The beach at Southwold boasts no bingo halls, no amusement arcades, no lowbrow, Blackpool-type entertainments. At Southwold everybody has to entertain himself. Charley, for example, the dog of our neighbour Sir John: for hours and hours he's been scraping and scratching a tunnel under 'The Blue Dragon'. Sir John thinks there may be a rabbit there. If Charley goes on tunnelling like this, 'The Blue Dragon' will fall flat on its face tomorrow.

We buy our sole from Arthur Swan in Victoria Street. At 14 'Swanney' went to sea, at 40 he became a fishmonger, and now he's nearly 80. His buckling, smoked over oakwood, are surpassed only by his kippers. Some customers even write poems about him: 'Whenever I am lonely / Homesick for Hertford only / I'll buy some fish / For a supper dish / From faithful Mr Swanney.' Even in London his fish is famous. Rumour has it that in Soho they sell his mackerel as smoked salmon.

In the middle of the town is the brewery. The sweet and heavy smell of Adnams' malt and the aroma from Mr Swan's smoke-house combine to create the heavenly scent of Southwold. There's a heavenly sound, too: at half-past-eight in the morning, you can hear the hooves of the horses pulling the beer-cart along the road, and at midday they come trotting back across the market place to their stable. 'Prince' and 'Sovereign' have the afternoon off. Nobody overworks in Southwold.

Nobody, that is, except John Adnams. He is manager of the brewery, estate agent, auctioneer, pig-farmer, town councillor – a man with his fingers in most of the town's pies. With a staff of 140, Adnams is by far the biggest employer in town, and his is one of the last family breweries in England. Without Adnams, Southwold would be little more than an old people's home, especially in winter when the holiday homes are empty. Adnams' trademark is the Jack-of-the-Clock that hits the bell in Southwold Church with his battle-axe – a delightful link between going to church and going to the pub. Our Father followed by our Adnams.

John Adnams is a sober man, and a thrifty one. He uses the yeast waste from his brewery to feed his hundreds of pigs. 'Adnams' pigs are happy pigs'. His partner in the family business is Simon Loftus, who deals exclusively with wine and runs a flourishing wine bar at 'The Crown'. Simon, a Cambridge graduate, also organizes dinner concerts in the winter, with champagne, candlelight and the London Chamber Orchestra. Music and wine to balance the beer and swine.

After dark the beam from the lighthouse strokes the roofs of the tiny town. Don't be afraid if you should then meet the Black Man. He walks around in a ragged cloak, with blackened face, like a creature from the time of the plague. His name is Robert. He has lived for many years alone on the marshes, in Tinker's Barn, which is knee-deep in waste paper and old tin cans. Sometimes Robert sits by the churchyard wall in Southwold, spreading pieces of paper from his plastic bag out on the grass before him and writing on them. Local people say he's composing. He never does any harm to anyone, and nobody interferes.

The greatest eccentric of them all, however, is the Earl of Stradbroke. His Rolls-Royce tells you who he is. It says: 'Call me Keith'. He's what some people call a parvenu. He was a sheep-breeder in Australia before he inherited Henham House and his title. The Aussie Earl had little time for the family silver, so he auctioned it off, but he did restore Humphry Repton's magnificent park.[1] By conservative estimate, he now has 15 children, and in his

1 The auction took place in 1988, and in addition to furniture and paintings, one of the items that came under the hammer was the Axminster carpet which James Wyatt designed for the library at Heveningham Hall in the late 18th century.

Mr Bottomley, headmaster of Eversley School in Southwold, with pupils and teachers, 1988

own enterprising way has, according to Mr Denny, opened a seed bank, 'so that he can charge for spreading his blue blood.'

Jack Denny used to measure old Lord Stradbroke up for his trousers. He is the owner of the wood-panelled clothes shop in the Market Place, founded by his great-grandfather in 1851. When Mr Denny began as an apprentice here in 1927, the family business employed no less than 28 people – 'enough to field our own football team'. Denny's of Southwold is a famous name in East Anglia. All the local gentry, and Benjamin Britten, and Peter Pears and many other celebrities had their suits made for them by Denny the Master Tailor. Once he even had an office in Savile Row. Another of his customers was Eric Blair, better known as George Orwell.

At the beginning of the thirties, Orwell's parents lived in Southwold. 'Their house in High Street, Montague House, belonged to my aunt,' said Mr Denny. 'Eric used to like going fishing, and he also went to parties. But he never used to dance. He preferred to entertain himself. He was a lone bird.' Once again, Mr Denny took measurements. 'Eric was quite tall – about six foot four. I made him a pair of trousers for two guineas. West of England Flannel. He ordered another pair from us later, when he was living in the Hebrides.' In Southwold, George Orwell taught the neighbours' children how to hunt eel with a gun and how to make little explosive devices – which earned him the nickname of Blarry Boy.

'In Southwold one feels that escapism is a positive virtue' wrote P. D. James. London's Queen of Crime has for many years had a cottage in Southwold. She, too, loves the unpretentiousness of the place, its picturesque but unvarnished beauty. The cannons of Gun Hill that are trained on the sea should rather be swung round inland, suggests P. D. James, 'to protect this civilized little community against the shibboleths and encroaching vulgarities of our age.'

'We in Southwold,' says Mr Burke, 'use the front entrance and not some sheltered back door – even in a force 10 gale.' John Burke is also a writer, and has lived here for over twenty years. 'In those days there used to be the Blythe Club. Only gentlemen could become members – men of leisure, that is. Meetings were held in a house that belonged to Denny the builder. Of course Mr Denny also wanted to join the club, but the honourable members refused. Unfortunately, he wasn't a gentleman. So Mr Denny gave them notice to quit their club rooms. Which proved he really wasn't a gentleman.' After that, the members met in the back bar of 'The Crown' in 'God's Waiting Room'.

The gun-smoke of history swirled once over Southwold. The date was 28 May 1672. Off the very shores of our little town, the British and Dutch fleets met together in a battle without a victor but with hundreds of dead. A footnote to the Battle of Sole Bay is the tale of the Ghost of Sutherland House. In this house on the High Street, now a restaurant, the Earl of Sandwich is said to have spent the night. The Earl, captain of the flagship 'Royal James', fell in love with a young red-haired serving girl, overslept, went on board ship when the battle was already raging, and was killed. Since then, on the eve of the anniversary of the great battle, footsteps can be heard in the corridor of Sutherland House – the footsteps of the unfortunate young lady.

On the way to the Sailors' Reading Room, I go past Misty, the mist-grey Persian cat from 'The Nelson'. Even dogs are afraid of Misty. The Sailors' Reading Room lies up on East Cliff – half brick chapel and half shelter – built in 1864 by the widow of a Victorian ship's captain, in the hope that the fishermen of Southwold would spend more time reading and less time drinking. It is thanks to this wild dream that Southwold has the smallest and loveliest maritime museum in Britain. It's a room full of model ships, figureheads and pictures, portraits of 'hardy old salts', photos of floods, shipwrecks and record catches. Is it really a museum? Well, sort of. It's also the place where the old Southwolders meet to play poker and (members only) billiards in the back room (plate 31).

What shall we do tomorrow? We'll collect hagstones on the beach – they're stones with holes in them, that protect you against the Evil Eye. After that we'll catch crabs and have a crab race on the River Blyth. For crabbing you need a cord, some bacon fat, and a lot of flair. You wait till the crab bites, and then before he knows what's bit back, you pull him ashore. When you've got enough crabs in the bucket, you either cook them, or you let them run. But it has to be a race. The race is to the river, and the winner is the one that falls in last.

Towards eleven o'clock, a red flag is hoisted outside the town: that means the fishermen are back, and there's fresh fish. Off we all go to the port – another of those ports that centuries of storms have driven further and further away from the town. Now it's way off in the marshes where the herons breed, in the Blyth estuary. During the 16th century, more fishing and merchant ships went from Southwold to Iceland than from any other port on the east coast. Today there are no more than a couple of dozen fishing boats. You can live on it, they say, 'if you've got a pound in your pocket'.

The harbour walls are crumbling, like bulging bulkheads. How long can they hold? Remorselessly the tide washes the mouth of the river. Bobbing boats are moored to bobbing landing-stages. Nets, planks, lobster pots, and the smell of the sea and the fish. Black-tarred fishermen's huts with blue and red doors, small ones, big ones, crooked ones, handsome ones: 'Billy Boy', 'Jackamina', 'Night Owl', 'Wyenot'. We go and eat a few cockles at 'Willie's Plaice', cockles with pepper. Billy himself tells us the crazy tale of the marina: 'They wanted to build a yacht club here – pull down our huts. Unbelievable!'

Of course it was inevitable that one day Mrs Thatcher's investment sharks would swim ashore at Southwold. A place straight out of *Pickwick Papers*, a Victorian Sleeping Beauty of a port. What an opportunity. 'Redevelopment' was the keyword. They would redevelop the river, and build their yachting club and sailing harbour and holiday complex ... But the planners had reckoned without the people of Southwold. The only place big enough to hold them all was the church, and the hearing turned into a tribunal. We want the huts, we don't want palaces, we love Southwold, we don't want the developers. Even John Adnams, mighty town councillor and honest broker, had no chance against 'these damned conservationist people'. 'We're not Brighton,' said Susan Hicklin, one of the fighting ladies of Southwold, 'and we don't want to look like Bournemouth either, with flower beds all over the place and a palm tree stuck in the middle.' Who wants to be a holiday camp for continentals? 'Absolutely mad. Let them go to Italy or Spain!' On this occasion, it was power to the people. All the same, it must be said that Southwold has become worryingly popular with the English themselves. First the BBC made a film here called *East of Ipswich*, and then the yuppies and everyone else seemed to discover 'the new Mecca of the East Coast' (*Sunday Times*).

As ever, the red flag of the fishermen flutters beside the Blyth (colour plate 2). Ourd Bob the ferryman is still there. For 15p he rowed me across to *Walberswick*. He's been ferrying people for some 50 years, though by now he must be eighty if he's a day – a thin, quiet man (plate 52). He used to have his dog with him, sitting on the lifebuoy in the rear of the boat, but poor Bonnie has rheumatism now, and stays at home.

According to the Southwolders, Walberswick is the home of 'the top twenty who speak only to each other'. You are more likely to meet artists and media people here than on the other side of the river. Southwold's summer theatre comes from Walberswick, run by Jill Freud, wife of the journalist and ex-MP, Sir Clement Freud (a grandson of Sigmund, and brother of the painter Lucian). At the end of the 19th century, this little fishing village was a flourishing artists' colony. In the Tate Gallery you will find three Walberswick paintings

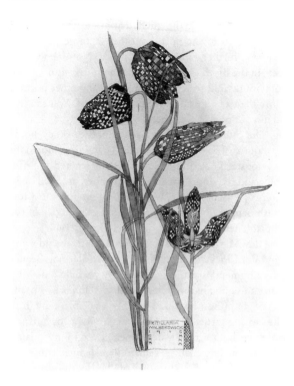

Charles Rennie Mackintosh:
Fritillaria, Walberswick, 1915

by Philip Wilson Steer, who spent several summers there from 1884 onwards.[1] In glowing colours, fascinated by the light of the East Anglian coast, Steer painted children playing on the beach – 'Girls Running; Walberswick Pier 1894' – pictures from the Indian summer of Impressionism. Between 1914 and 1915 the Scottish Art Nouveau architect Charles Rennie Mackintosh and his wife also lived in Walberswick, as guests of the director of the Glasgow Art Academy, who had a holiday home here. In Walberswick Mackintosh painted over 40 plant watercolours, pictures of flowers with a fine filigree use of colour. The couple used to go for long evening walks, which aroused the suspicions of the locals, for the Great War had already begun. And when it was discovered that these strangers had received letters from the Vienna Secession – post from the enemy! – it was crystal clear that spies had come to Walberswick. Fortunately, Mackintosh was able to prove his innocence before the nation was alerted.

Once you have savoured your cream tea at Mary's Garden Café, go and have a look

1   The beach at Southwold was painted by Stanley Spencer, who was married in the neighbouring church of Wangford in 1925.

Philip Wilson Steer: The Bridge, Walberswick, 1887–8

round St Andrew's. Consecrated in 1493, this Perpendicular church was once just as imposing as its neighbours in Southwold and Blythburgh. But the port lost its importance in the late Middle Ages, the community grew smaller and poorer, and in the end they tore down part of their church in 1695. Just 30 years later, Daniel Defoe went to a Sunday service in Southwold, and 'was surprised to see an extraordinary large church, capable of receiving five or six thousand people, and but twenty-seven in it.' The believers, however, had been unfaithful only to the church, and not to God; Defoe found hundreds of them in the neighbouring Nonconformist chapel.

One mild winter's day, when the broom and the mimosa were already in bloom, a farmer's wife opened up Walpole Old Chapel for me, the loveliest of all the rural Nonconformist chapels in East Anglia. It lies south of *Halesworth*, on the edge of the road and the village, and so much on the edge of time that it has remained quite unchanged for 300 years. In those days the high-backed benches and galleries would be packed with nearly 500 farmers, farm labourers and their families, to hear the Word of God spoken from the three-tiered pulpit and impressively amplified by the tester above. The simple pine benches, oil lamps and candelabra are all just as they were in 1689, when this farmhouse was converted into an independent chapel. Today as a home for summer concerts, it's a meeting-place for Puritans and lovers of chamber music alike: 'Summer Music at Walpole Old Chapel'.

Chateaubriand in Bungay, or The Love of Round Towers

The finest view of Lowestoft is to be seen at the British Museum in London: Turner's watercolour 'Lowestoffe' (c.1835), a triumph of grey and the sea rescue service. In this picture of a storm-tossed sea, the town forms a sketchy background – much to its advantage. In more modern times, it was badly hit by the bombs of the Second World War, and even worse hit by the rebuilding process. The outskirts have been over-developed, and the centre is devoid of character. What can be said in its favour, however, is that its long, broad esplanade is traffic-free, and it has avoided the fair-ground atmosphere of its neighbour Great Yarmouth. And what is indisputable is the fact that Lowestoft is the most easterly town in England, and is also the site of the Royal Norfolk and Suffolk Yacht Club.

The great age of the herring boom – those 'silver darlings' – is over. Shortly after the turn of the century, there were over 700 trawlers operating from Lowestoft; now there are just 40. But in 1987 a dream-boat emerged from the stocks – the $20-million superyacht 'Stefaren'. It was built for the New York business tycoon Bennett S. LeBow, who then proceeded to buy the whole shipyard, Brooke Yachts International. Sadly the hopes that this small, highly specialized firm would help to bring about the rebirth of Britain's once world-famous luxury yacht industry fell victim to the recession.

In June 1878, when the port of Lowestoft still smelt of herring and coal, a ship from Marseilles was moored to the quayside. Among the passengers was a 21-year-old Polish immigrant, who with muted expectations set foot on English soil for the very first time. Eight years later, Jozef Konrad Korzeniowski was a captain in the British merchant marine. Out on the high seas, he began to make new voyages inwards, into the Heart of Darkness. We know him as Joseph Conrad – like his hero Marlow, 'an English captain who told stories'. In the work of this great novelist, alas and alack, there is not one single quotable sentence about Lowestoft. And so the town was all the more grateful to celebrate with plaques, an honorary citizenship, and the naming of a shopping centre, the arrival of another truly great artist: Benjamin Britten, born in Lowestoft in 1913. His mother, who sang in a choir, managed to get her fourth child to enter the world on 22 November, the feast day of St Cecilia, patron saint of music. Britten's father was a dentist, and even today the parental home at 21 Kirkley Cliff Road houses a dental practice. Until his fourteenth year, young Ben enriched Lowestoft musical life in the kindergarten and then the elementary school. Then he left for Holt and Gresham's School, London and the Royal College of Music, and after that, America. It was on his return from the States that he founded his famous Festival – that at Aldeburgh (see page 243).

The man who really did do something for Lowestoft was Samuel Morton Peto, a

Joseph Wright of Derby: Artist's Model (An Academy by Lamplight)

Victorian entrepreneur on a grand scale. He built railways in Africa, Australia, Argentina, Canada and Russia, set up supply lines during the Crimean War, linked Norwich to Yarmouth, financed Nelson's Column in Trafalgar Square, developed Lowestoft into a seaside resort as well as extending the port, became an MP, got himself knighted, and in 1857 moved into a new house northwest of Lowestoft, called *Somerleyton Hall*. Five years later, Peto went bankrupt. He sold his country house to a carpet manufacturer from Halifax, the great-grandfather of the present Lord Somerleyton, who has five children, holds the office of Lord in Waiting to the Queen, and keeps an open house.

Somerleyton Hall is pure Victoriana, a Jacobean pastiche with a large campanile at one corner (1846–57), and was designed by John Thomas, architect and sculptor, and a favourite of Prince Albert's. He also reproduced a typical estate village with thatched cottages, based on John Nash's picturesque Blaise Hamlet near Bristol. Paintings by Edwin Landseer and Clarkson Stanfield, the star painters of the time, adorn Somerleyton's interiors, but there are no really outstanding works apart from a picture by Joseph Wright of Derby, England's 18th-century master of chiaroscuro. You can take tea beneath the arcades of the former winter garden, in the park there's a maze of yew, and for the children there's nothing finer than a trip on the miniature railway – an unintentionally ironic reminder of Sir Morton Peto, the railway speculator who started it all.

By *Fritton Decoy*, the long lake north of Somerleyton, a thatched church stands in the fields, with a Norman chancel and a mysterious round tower. Not far away is another round tower – that of St Margaret's in *Herringfleet*. Time and again as you travel through East Anglia you'll come across these little, often remote village churches with towers that are round and not rectangular. There is a man who specializes in these round tower churches, and as is so frequently the case in England, he's an amateur: William Goode, retired butcher. He lives in a row of terraced houses in Oulton Broad, a suburb west of Lowestoft. He's a rather frail old gentleman who collects round towers the way some people collect triangular postage stamps. It all started in a prosaic way: one day in 1965, he bought himself a new camera. In order to try it out, he snapped some of these strange churches with round towers. There seemed to be an extraordinary number of them in the area, and the further afield he went, the more he found, and the more he photographed, the more he wanted to know about them. 'They just took over,' he explained. Eighteen years later, William Goode – now retired – issued the results of his personal researches: *East Anglian Round Towers and Their Churches*, a private publication the size of a doctoral thesis.

He has counted 175 round tower churches in East Anglia, and only five in the rest of England.[1] He has seen each one at least twice, and climbed nearly every tower in order to measure it exactly. This Mr Goode does with the help of his piece of string and the parson,

---

1 Others come up with different figures: Alec Clifton-Taylor says there are 180 round tower churches in England, of which 119 are in Norfolk, 41 in Suffolk, and 5 in Essex. In Cambridgeshire there are just two – Bartlow and Snailwell.

who usually holds the ladder for him. For round towers have no steps, and if they do have steps, then they are not *old* round towers. 'Almost all of them are Anglo-Saxon in origin, although most experts think they're Norman.' It's difficult to date them precisely because there are never any documents. 'You have to have a close look and do your detective work,' he said. But even he can't identify all the Anglo-Saxon round towers straight away by their typical motifs: long-and-short-work, lesenes, or tower windows with triangles instead of round arches. Most of these towers were constructed between 950 and 1066. Goode considers the one in East Lexham, Norfolk, to be the oldest (*c*.950) and that in Bardfield Saling in Essex to be the last medieval one (*c*.1380).

This diligent amateur archaeologist also discovered something else that goes against current expert opinion. 'The romantic theory is that round towers were built as watch towers to give warning of Viking attacks, and the churches themselves were only added later. But my research shows that that's wrong. They were designed as bell-towers, often built onto the older wooden churches and only Normanized later when the new churches were built. Often the original towers are only as tall as the nave, and so they couldn't have been watch towers.' It is undeniable, though, that there are particularly large numbers of round towers in those areas of East Anglia where Viking attacks were especially frequent. Furthermore, many of them only had embrasure-type windows on the lower floor, and originally had no entrance at ground level. In times of danger they could serve as refuges.

On the other hand, the twin Romanesque towers of Gernrode in Germany are also round, and there are round towers in Italy and Ireland, many of them taller and older than those in East Anglia. The question is: why are there so many in East Anglia – and why are they round? At least the experts agree on this: it's all because of the building material. In those days, East Anglia's main material was flint, and this lent itself particularly well to the form of the round tower. For rectangular constructions you need to have stone or brick.

Bill Goode's love of round towers led him in 1973 to form the Friends of the Round Tower Churches. 'Many of them were in a terrible state, and I thought somebody ought to do something about it. There are people to take care of the great churches like Blythburgh, but no-one looks after the little village churches.' The Friends aim to help preserve the round towers and to promote further research on them. The members come from all over England, and even from Scotland.

Of all the round towers in East Anglia, Bill Goode has one particular favourite – *Hales* in Norfolk. 'Pevsner calls it Norman, but it's quite an early Saxon tower,' he says triumphantly. The little church lies dreaming in the fields between Beccles and Norwich: thatched roof, nestling amid trees and shrubs, no village, no congregation, shut off from time and from the worship of God. St Margaret's has a single nave and an apse, and is an almost perfectly preserved 12th century village church. For some years now it has been looked after by the Redundant Churches Fund. The door is locked, but there are signs directing you to the key-holder ('The key is by the back door'). Such diversions are worth the effort – also in the neighbouring villages of *Heckingham* and *Haddiscoe*. They too have round towers of Anglo-Saxon origin, with ornate Norman columned portals, probably made by the same stonemason as the one in Hales.

Bill Goode's round towers[1] lured me across the Waveney to Norfolk, and I found myself wandering deeper into the maze of fields, along the great loop of the river to *Burgh St Peter*. Some distance from the village, past the yachting harbour, on the edge of the marshes at last you come to the church. But it hasn't got a round tower. What it has is a folly, made up of five step-like storeys of brick, one heaped on top of the other. Next to this early 16th-century tower-telescope is the nave, older, with flint walls and thatched roof.

I went back across the river into Suffolk. In the fields between Beccles and Bungay is an absolute gem: *Barsham* church. I'm quite happy to leave the round tower to Bill Goode, because what is far more unusual is the east wall of this thatched church (plate 73). The diamond pattern of the window tracery is continued as flushwork over the entire surface, in a latticework of flint and stone: op-art by a virtuoso of the 14th (or 16th) century. The terra cotta tomb-chest inside the church, with its Early Renaissance (*c.*1530) decorations, is one of a group of seven similar tombs in East Anglia, presumably all made by the same Flemish workshop. Holy Trinity is set in a gloriously overgrown churchyard, and is surrounded by tall old trees. Next door, in Barsham Rectory, Catherine Suckling was born in 1725. She was Nelson's mother.

No English county has more beautiful borders than Suffolk: in the south is the River Stour, and in the north the River Waveney. Why is it that so many more people know and love the Stour? Broad water meadows, weeping willows on the banks, cows going down to the river to drink – the Waveney has all of that, and villages that are even more serene than those on the Stour. But the Stour has one all-important birthright: Constable was born in East Bergholt. If he'd been born in *Harleston* (colour plate 24) or *Homersfield*, it would all have been a different story. The Stour Valley is art history, landscape in a gold frame with tourist buses, the river polluted with the oils of a thousand Sunday painters. The waters of the Waveney still reflect the clouds in the sky and not the clouds of Constable.

Before it flows into the River Yare, beneath the walls of the Roman camp at Burgh Castle, the Waveney makes a wide curve through the marshes near Lowestoft. In Defoe's time it was still navigable for big lighters all the way to Beccles and Bungay. As on the Stour, these barges were pulled by horses along the tow paths through the meadows. Their main cargo was grain, coal and bricks. The village inn at *Geldeston* (Norfolk) is called after

---

1 A few notes about round towers in Suffolk: Blundeston (near Lowestoft) is the tallest in East Anglia, Anglo-Saxon origin, *c.*990, restored in commemoration of Dickens' hero David Copperfield, who was born in 'Blunderstone'; Bramfield (southeast of Halesworth) is the only round tower that stands alone as a campanile next to the thatched church; Holton and Wissett (near Halesworth) both have Norman portals with demons and zigzag ornamentation; Thorington (near Blythburgh) has Anglo-Saxon blind arcades; Little Saxham (west of Bury St Edmunds) has Norman round arch windows and a blind arcade all round the tower; Wortham (near Diss) is the biggest Anglo-Saxon round tower in England. One of the most beautiful Anglo-Saxon round tower churches in Norfolk is St Mary's, Beechamwell (near Swaffham).

'The Wherry', the type of barge that was used in the old shipping times. Nowadays the cabin cruisers of the Broads crowd together on the banks of the Waveney in *Beccles*, which used to be a flourishing river port. On a hill overlooking the river is the Perpendicular church of St Michael, whose most striking features are its location and its sound. The ten bells of Beccles stand high in the charts of the apostles of change-ringing. The rest of medieval Beccles was largely destroyed by fires between 1580 and 1680, but there are some fine Georgian houses in Northgate and Ballygate Street.

Gently the Waveney eases its way through the meadows. Even the name has a silky caressing sound. Gentle green meadows spread all round *Bungay*, another little town with no great sights to see: most of its Tudor houses suffered the same fiery fate as those in Beccles, and were replaced by Georgian houses that were extended in Victorian times. There are no raucous redevelopments in the old town, no modern monster blocks – it's all simple and wholesome and beautiful.

Bungay unfolds its charms round its Market Place (plate 57). The Butter Cross was erected in 1689, when William and Mary came to the throne. It's a rotunda with eight arches and eight columns. During the reign of George II, in 1754, a lead figure of Justice was added to the dome; it may not necessarily have advanced the cause of justice in Bungay, but it made the place more decorative. The Butter Cross has remained a welcome shelter for the ordinary people of the town – a large umbrella for the market and the gossip. This is where housewives meet as they do their morning shopping, pensioners and the unemployed sit and watch the world go by, and the young folk do whatever young folk do in the evenings. The Butter Cross is the home of Bungay's stories, and over the years there are few that have not been told beneath its eight arches. This would not, of course, be an English market place if it had a monument only to the Goddess of Justice; there also has to be, and is, one to a dog (a weather vane on the lamp-post in the middle of the roundabout). His name is Black Shuck, and he belongs to the Devil. It is said that during a storm in August 1577 the Devil, in the form of this black hound of hell, roared into Bungay Church, killed two worshippers with one swipe of his paw, and burnt a third with his fiery breath. From that day to this the forsaken monster has roamed the heath 'twixt Aldeburgh and Southwold.

Bungay Market lies between the 'King's Head' and St Mary's – pub and church, the classic twin poles of little old towns (colour plate 35). The Perpendicular tower soars high above the roofs of the houses, but this once proud church of a Benedictine nunnery is yet another that now depends on the Redundant Churches Fund. Nearby is a second, smaller church with an Anglo-Saxon round tower. Its eastern end faces a stretch of land which for centuries has remained open and uncultivated. It was in this town, deep in the English countryside, that the parson's daughter set her cap at a Breton aristocrat.

It happened in 1794. He was 26 and had fled from the French Revolution, a royalist, a romantic, and a penniless émigré. Under the name of M. de Combourg he lived for a while in Beccles, and gave French lessons to the young ladies of the area. One of the young ladies was Charlotte, the 15-year-old daughter of his landlord, Parson Ives. One day, after a riding accident, the young Vicomte was brought into the parsonage at Bungay, No. 34 Bridge Street. Here Mrs Ives took care of him, and when she saw the extent of the Anglo-French alliance, she suggested that he should marry Charlotte and settle down in Bungay. At this prospect, the noble Frenchman turned pale. He was, he declared, already married (which was true), whereupon Mrs Ives fainted clean away and the perhaps-not-so-noble Frenchman took his leave. He left behind him a weeping Charlotte and a town legend.

The young man was indeed none other than François-René de Chateaubriand. He became famous through a book which he actually began during his seven-year exile in England: *Le Génie du Christianisme*, an apologia for the Catholic religion, seen from a Romantic standpoint. One can hardly imagine that a man with those views would have been welcomed with such open arms in an English parsonage. All the same, Charlotte would no doubt have been metaphorically swept off her feet when she read his sensational love story, written in London and published in 1801: *Atala, ou l'amour de deux sauvages dans le désert.* They were to meet once more, in 1822 in London. Charlotte was now Lady Sutton, and Chateaubriand had been sent officially by King Louis XVIII as French ambassador to the Court of St James.

We do not know what they said to each other. Perhaps they had a good laugh, or a Romantic cry, or puzzled over the popular rhyme from the region of their past: 'Beccles for a puritan, / Bungay for the poor, / Halesworth for a drunkard, / And Blythboro' for a whore.'

At the end of the 19th century, on the Norfolk side of the Waveney in Bungay's neighbouring village of *Ditchingham*, there lived another author: H. Rider Haggard. East Anglia was his home, but South Africa the spur to his imagination. R. L. Stevenson and his contemporaries regarded Haggard as a classic adventure writer, while both Graham Greene and Henry Miller idolized him, the first for *King Solomon's Mines,* and the second, unsurprisingly, for *She.* Rider Haggard was born at Wood Farm, West Bradenham, west of Norwich in 1856, went to school in Ipswich, and at nineteen shipped to South Africa. There he rose to be a master of the High Court in Pretoria, but during the Boer War he returned to England, worked as a lawyer in London, and began to write.

He wrote over 40 novels, many of them in Ditchingham House, the Georgian home of his wife. He lived there from 1889, but at the turn of the century he bought the former coastguard station, 'The Grange', up on the cliffs of Kessingland, south of Lowestoft. There he named each room after an English admiral, and wrote further exotic and highly successful novels like *Ayesha,* as well as detailed studies of the life of farm-workers (*The Poor and the Land,* 1905). For the vivid expression of his colonial fantasy and his social conscience, George V rewarded him in 1912 with a knighthood. A good place to drink to the memory of Sir Henry Rider Haggard is 'The Falcon' on the Waveney.

Rider Haggard's 'Rural England' is no more. But how it used to look before the great machines drove through the fields, you can still gauge from the hinterland southwest of Bungay. Saints' Country is the name of this desolate area, for even the tiniest hamlet has its own church and incorporates its patron saint into its name: *St Peter South Elmham, St Mary South Elmham*, and all the other saintly South Elmhams (nine in all), not to mention four holy Ilketshalls.

In *St Cross South Elmham*, there's an old farm surrounded by trees and ditches. In the 13th century, South Elmham Hall was the hunting lodge of the Bishops of Norwich, who kept a game park there. Today you'll see Oxford Down sheep grazing, together with rare British White cattle – white cows with black ears, noses and feet. Along the hedgerows and fields the farmer has marked out a path that leads through the meadows to the ruins of South Elmham Minster. Whether this was an abbey, a church, or a bishop's seat the archaeologists do not know. There is ivy creeping up the flint walls, and hornbeams and oaks all around. The remains of a Roman moat enclose this sad and solitary place. When I walked back through the fields, on a still December evening, the farmer was burning his dead elms. The tall, rotten trunks were blazing upright in the twilight.

I followed the Waveney, the gentle green Waveney, upriver to where the Little Ouse relieves it of its border duties, west of Diss. In the No-Man's-Land between the two rivers lie *Redgrave* and *Lopham Fen*. This is the one area in the British Isles where you can still find the Great Raft spider. Motionless it lurks in the water meadows, waiting for its prey – a predatory creature that can even dive into the water and catch little fish. But the water-meadows are to be drained, and so environmentalists, supported by the World Wildlife Fund, are digging little ponds to house *Dolomedes fimbriatus*, the rare and endangered robber of the marshes.

Bury St Edmunds: Where the Magna Carta Was Born

'"Delightful prospect, Sam,"' said Mr Pickwick. '"Beats the chimbley pots, sir,"' replied Mr Weller, touching his hat.' In Chapter XVI of *Pickwick Papers*, Dickens has his hero travel to *Bury St Edmunds* in order to unmask the deceitful Mr Jingle. In those days, the mid-19th century, it took eight hours to get from London to Bury. 'The coach rattled through the well-paved streets of a handsome little town, of thriving and cleanly appearance, and stopped before a large inn situated in a wide open street, nearly facing the old abbey. "And this," said Mr Pickwick, looking up, "is the Angel. We alight here, Sam."'

The old inn on Angel Hill is still there, its imposing Georgian façade covered with vine-leaves. 'And this,' says Caroline, the innkeeper's daughter, 'is where Dickens spent the night.' Twice in fact, on his reading tours of 1859 and 1861, and he stayed in Room 15. The Dickens Room has remained unchanged, apart from the electric light. It has a large four-poster bed, and *Pickwick Papers* lying on the bedside table. There are Dickens characters all over the inn: Dolly Varden and Mr Micawber adorn the walls of my own room. Guests, incidentally, can confidently follow the procedure set out in the novel: shortly after his arrival, Mr Pickwick sat down to 'a very satisfactory dinner'. This is one of those rare and happy cases where reality lives up to fiction. Daniel Defoe also praised 'The Angel' and its clientèle, 'people of the best fashion, and the most polite conversation'. The owners are not content to live on the literary reputation of the past, but also look to that of the future. Since 1982 the Goughs have been making annual Angel Literary Awards to authors in East Anglia – the only hotel in England to offer such a prize, which incidentally is also the most generous outside London. Thus through their laureates and through such famous guests as Edward Bond, Harold Pinter, and Ruth Rendell, the Goughs have ensured that the literary fame of 'The Angel' at Bury St Edmunds will not fade.

Defoe praised the place as 'the Montpellier of Suffolk', because of its healthy air and beautiful location. 'Sacrarium Regis, Cunabula Legis' is the town's motto: Shrine of a King, Cradle of the Law. It's a town with royal connections: Magna Carta was hatched here, the martyred King Edmund is honoured here, and the Greene King is venerated. The Greene King, of course, is the majestic beer brewed by the family firm of Benjamin Greene of Bury, founded in 1799 (colour plate 38). Bury St Edmunds also has the biggest sugar-beet factory in England, and the smallest pub: 'The Nutshell'. The landscape gardener Humphry Repton was born here, and Queen Mary Tudor was buried here. And Mr Pickwick, after his nocturnal adventure in the garden of the girls' boarding-school, suffered an attack of rheumatism here.

From my window in 'The Angel' I can look across at the great gate of the abbey, a view which Edward FitzGerald recommended to a friend 'with a biscuit and a Pint of Sherry'. (FitzGerald [see page 190 ff.] went to the King Edward VI Grammar School here, 1819–26.) In the morning you can see the school-children going through the gate, and at lunchtime it's the salesgirls and the secretaries, off to eat their sandwiches in the abbey garden. *Abbey Gate* is a massive, almost square tower, the monks' bastion against the rebellious citizens of Bury. They had torn down the old gate in 1327 and plundered the abbey in their violent resentment against their aggressive landlords. And so the new gate, in the Decorated style, presented itself in 1353 as a rather more strongly fortified construction, with a portcullis below the ogee arch, and embrasures behind the figures of saints that once stood in the niches of the façade. Just a few paces away is the Abbey Gate's companion piece, the Norman Tower (1120–48). It has a portal with a fish-scale pattern in the gable, flanked by buttresses with blind arches and pyramids, above which is a triplet of round arches and circles – the whole thing amounting to a celebration of Norman geometry. Behind the Abbey Gate and the Norman Tower lay one of the richest and mightiest Benedictine monasteries in the land – one of the great pilgrimage churches of the Middle Ages, and an English national shrine.

Like a picture puzzle the town's coat of arms encodes its whole history: two gold crowns on a blue background with two crossed silver arrows – the emblems of the old Kingdom of East Anglia, the insignia of the martyr and patron saint of Bury, St Edmund. The story begins in the middle of the 9th century, probably in Nuremberg. There, at the court of the Saxon King Alkmund, King Offa met young Edmund, Alkmund's son. He nominated him to be his successor as King of East Anglia. On Christmas Day 856,

Edmund – just turned 15 – was crowned King of the East Angles in Bures. At that time the Vikings were constantly raiding the country, pillaging and murdering as they went. Edmund took arms against the invading army, was defeated, and in 869, when he refused to renounce his faith, was executed. An illuminated manuscript of the 12th century, now in the Pierpont Morgan Library, New York, shows King Edmund's end: like the martyred St Sebastian he was bound to a tree and used as a target by the Viking archers. One of the legendary elements of his death is the wolf which kept watch over the decapitated head of the King – this is the good wolf also in the Bury St Edmunds coat of arms,[1] the English cousin of Romulus and Remus's wolf.

The King was dead, and proceeded to show that he was indestructible. His corpse, reburied several times, remained in both wondrous and macabre fashion free from decay. His beard and nails continued to grow, and had to be cut – welcome relics for the guardians of his shrine, the Benedictine monks of Beodricsworth. King Edmund was canonized, and his burial place renamed St Edmundsbury. Killed in the flower of his youth for his people and his religion, King Edmund became a political symbol like King Arthur, as the unifying power of an English kingdom. Many churches all over the country were dedicated to St Edmund, and for a while he was as popular as St George himself.

His fame spread beyond the Channel, and with unfortunate results. About the beginning of the 13th century the Abbey of St Sernin in Toulouse declared 'S. Eadmundus Rex Angliae' one of the patron saints of their town. It now seems certain that the dead saint was abducted from Bury to Toulouse in one of the most spectacular grave robberies of the Middle Ages. At the beginning of our own century, the French monks gave Edmund's corpse back to England, minus the head. The bones of the saint – which some claim not to be genuine – are now kept in Arundel Castle, the family seat of the Catholic Dukes of Norfolk.

'One of the chief architectural glories of the kingdom,' was the verdict of John Leland, England's great topographer, when he visited the Abbey of Bury St Edmunds in 1538, a year before the Reformation. 'A man who saw the abbey would say verily it were a city; so many gates there are in it, and some of brass; so many towers and a most stately church upon which attend three other churches also standing gloriously in the same churchyard, all of passing fine and curious workmanship.' Leland, a humanist and Henry VIII's librarian, could only watch – and record – the Reformation with horror. The abbey, a masterpiece of medieval architecture, became a stone quarry for houses in the town, until all that remained was a gigantic pile of rubble. One needs a strong imagination to reconstruct from these ruins the power and the glory of St Edmund's Abbey.

It had begun around 633 with a wooden church and a little monastery on the River Lark. The founder was Sigbert, the first Christian king of the East Angles. In 1020 King Canute installed twenty Benedictines at the shrine of St Edmund, and c.1080 Abbot Baldwin began to construct a third, Norman, abbey church. Completed a century later under Abbot

1   One of the many depictions of this scene is on a 17th-century poppyhead in the south chapel of Hadleigh Church: it shows the head of St Edmund in the mouth of the wolf.

Samson, this was the largest church in England, longer by 100 feet than the Norman cathedral church of St Albans, and with a west front 243 feet wide, a third again as big as Lincoln. St Edmunds had transepts with two chapel apses, a chancel ambulatory with three radiating chapels, like the cathedrals of Canterbury and Winchester, a crypt and a cloister, a western central tower, and a crossing tower whose piers still reach towards the sky like the gnawed bones of a giant. The ruins show typical features of Norman architecture: the core of the walls is made of flint and mortar, and the exterior is of hewn limestone, gleaming white after centuries of rain (plate 82).

On 20 November 1215, the 25 mightiest men in England met together in this church. It was St Edmund's Day, but the mighty men had not gathered to offer up prayers at the shrine of the saint; they were there to seal a secret pact against the King. Under the leadership of Stephen Langton, Archbishop of Canterbury, the Barons took an oath to adhere to a proclamation of 61 articles: the Great Charter, or in Latin *Magna Carta*. 'To no one will we sell, deny or delay right or justice,' King John would be forced to say. Equally famous is Article 39: 'No free man shall be taken, imprisoned, or outlawed ... except by the legal judgment of his peers or by the Law of the Land.' Everyone should have equal rights before the law, and protection against abuse by the Crown; the Church should have the right freely to elect its own bishops and abbots, and many other rights were to be guaranteed by the Great Charter of Liberties. These liberties were, however, only feudal precursors of basic civil rights, for the charter was designed primarily to protect the barons, and ordinary people were by and large excluded. Six months after the conference at the altar in Bury St Edmunds, Magna Carta was signed at a much more famous and secular place: a cow-pasture on the Thames named Runnymede. In the mid-19th century, when English historians were endowing Magna Carta with the legendary status of a constitution, two plaques were put up on one of the pier-stumps of the Abbey chancel, commemorating the names of the 25 barons and their descendants.

The political pilgrimage of 1214 is not the only sign of the importance of St Edmund's Abbey. The illuminated manuscripts and books of hours from the Bury scriptorium now adorn the great libraries of the world: the Metropolitan Museum in New York, the Bodleian in Oxford, the Vatican Library, and the British Library among others. One of the finest pieces is kept at Corpus Christi College, Cambridge: Master Hugo's *Bury Bible*, of the mid-12th century. The 'Bury Cross' of *c.*1155 is also attributed to him or to his workshop – a little ceremonial cross of ivory, with exquisite reliefs. In 1963 the Metropolitan Museum paid $600,000 to acquire the cross from an arms dealer who kept it in the safe of a Zurich bank, but arguments still rage among medievalists about the true value of the piece. Far more modest, indisputably genuine, and of immense documentary value is the diary of a monk named Jocelyn de Brakelond: a remarkable picture of everyday monastic life towards the end of the 12th century.

The land around St Edmund's Abbey is now a large municipal park. Next to what used to be the cloister is a bowling green, and behind the church are tennis courts. After the dissolution of the monastery, houses were built directly into the arches and walls of the

St Edmund arrested and led into captivity. From: The Life of St Edmund, 12th-century

Norman west façade. Much as some restorers would like to purge the ruins it must be admitted that houses in the west front, however, have themselves long since become a picturesque monument to the Reformation.

On the grassy forecourt stands St Edmund, a bronze statue by Elisabeth Frink (1976). Behind it is the *Old English Rose Garden*, where behind the high hedges the pensioners of Bury quietly doze, drugged by the scents of the 'Duke of Windsor', 'Honeymoon', 'Chicago Peace' and a thousand other old roses donated by John T. Appleby of Arkansas. Stationed here in the war with the 94th US Bomber Squadron, Appleby wrote an enthusiastic book about his host country, *Suffolk Summer* (Ipswich 1948).

Only St Mary and St James, the two Gothic parish churches on the edge of the monastery grounds, remained generally untouched by the Reformation. *St James*, with a freestanding Norman tower, became St Edmundsbury Cathedral in 1914. Since then, alas, it has been trying to build up to its new status. The results of these pretensions include a dubious extension to the east, a new chancel, and the beginnings of a cloister and a crossing tower – all this since 1960, in the style of an insipid modern Perpendicular. This serves to highlight all the more poignantly the nave and its tall, slender piers (*c.*1510–30), probably the work of the master builder John Wastell, who spent most of his life in Bury and died there in 1515.[1] The simple elegance of the arcades, however, is somewhat overwhelmed by the modern fairground colours of the hammerbeam roof – itself part of the restorations carried out by Sir George Gilbert Scott (1865–9) – and of more than a thousand eye-catching 'kneelers', which pious fingers have embroidered with symbols of all the parishes in the diocese of Suffolk (1952–66). It's a bit showy, this carnival of cushions, but it's also good fun. My personal favourite is the one depicting the nuclear reactor at Sizewell.

In neighbouring *St Mary's*, an old lady is sitting in the entrance doing a crossword puzzle. 'It's a lovely place,' she says. 'Put 10p in to light up the angels.' It's worth doing. Your 10p will catch not only the angels in the late Gothic hammerbeam roof, but also the spandrels with their carved dragons, birds, fish and a unicorn. The roof of the choir is also wood-panelled; on one of the bosses there are dogs fighting, and on another Reynard the Fox is preaching to some chickens. Near the high altar is the tomb of Henry VIII's sister, Mary Tudor, Queen of France. At the age of 17 she was married to King Louis XII, but very soon became a widow, whereupon she secretly married her childhood sweetheart Charles Brandon, Duke of Suffolk, and lived at Westhorpe Hall, near Bury, until she died in 1533. Mary was buried in the Abbey Church, but after the Reformation Henry VIII had her moved to St James. According to the verger, Edward VII enclosed her grave in an awful marble frame because he didn't want any priests treading on the grave of a Queen. The verger was also unhappy about the window that Bertie's mother, Queen Victoria, gave to the Lady Chapel in 1881: 'No biblical scenes at all, just pictures of Mary's life, along with

---

1 John Wastell also built Canterbury Cathedral's Bell Harry Tower. Other work attributed to him includes such magnificent churches as those of Lavenham and Saffron Walden, and the fan vault of the retro-choir of Peterborough Cathedral. His masterpiece is the fan vault of King's College Chapel in Cambridge.

Fat Henry. You'll recognize him straight away.' One of Fat Henry's councillors is also buried here: Sir Robert Drury, once the richest man in Bury. London's Drury Lane is named after his family.

The hemlock blossoms white in St Mary's churchyard, and the old stones are overgrown with weeds and grass. Some of them tell a sad tale. Two young girls are buried near the ruins of the charnel house: Mary Haselton, who was struck by lightning in 1785 while she was at prayer; and Sarah Lloyd, executed in 1800 for assisting in a burglary and fire-raising. The good and the bad all rest at peace now in this green stillness. I wander down an avenue of elms, and head back to the town.

Bury St Edmunds is probably the first example of town-planning after the Norman Conquest of 1066. Abbot Baldwin laid out his model Norman settlement on a gentle slope west of the Abbey. The ground plan follows the Roman grid system, and has remained essentially unchanged right up to the present. The streets run from north to south, parallel to the west side of the Abbey, and are crossed by the two main streets, Abbeygate and Churchgate. Abbeygate Street led through the gate itself into the great courtyard of the Abbot's palace, while Churchgate Street went through the Norman Tower to the entrance of the Abbey Church; and when the gate was open, you could see all the way to the high altar and the shrine of St Edmund, the goal of your pilgrimage. Thus monastery and town were linked together architecturally, economically, and spiritually, as inseparable as Siamese twins. The Jews also had their place in the Christian plan for Bury: a sidestreet between Abbeygate and Churchgate, named Hatter Street, 'Hatter' being derived from 'Heathen'.[1]

William the Conqueror's Domesday Book, the first English record of property and taxes (1086), gives precise information about the prosperous Norman market town. Living there at the time were 30 parish priests and deacons, 28 nuns and paupers ('who daily pray for the king and for all Christian people'), 34 knights with 22 smallholders, 75 bakers, brewers, tailors, shoemakers, laundresses, cooks, carriers and middlemen, and 13 monastic administrators with five smallholders. William's royal inspectors recorded a total of 342 houses under the jurisdiction of the Abbey, which extracted a handsome tithe as well as continually whittling away common rights – a source of bloody conflicts between citizens and monks.

In the Middle Ages Churchgate Street was the processional main street of the town, while today Abbeygate is its commercial centre. The windows of these little shops are an aesthetic pleasure in themselves: the pointed-arch, Neo-Gothic mullion windows of Toots the baker's; the Georgian front of Ridley's grocery store; Savory & Moore, a chemist's since 1781, with glorious Tudor beams peeping out between the soap and the toothpaste. In the late 18th century, many of Bury's houses covered their half-timbered façades with grey brick from Woolpit, which was both cheap and fashionable. In a lot of entrances you

1 The Jews were rarely popular. On Palm Sunday 1190, nearly 60 of them were massacred in Bury, and the survivors driven out of the town on the orders of the abbot. There were similar murders and pogroms in the same year in King's Lynn, Norwich, York and other English towns.

can still see niches with iron boot scrapers, left over from the days before streets had proper surfaces. Some 980 houses are listed, virtually the whole town centre. It is not so much a matter of special, individual buildings as of complete units that make this old area so worthy of preservation and indeed so pleasant to be in. Narrow streets run between the squares, some big, some small, the variety adding to the charm. In 1843 Thomas Carlyle found the town both flourishing and lively, and a pleasant change from the 'grassy face of Suffolk'.

There are, of course, notable individual buildings as well: *Market Cross* on Cornhill was designed in 1774 by Robert Adam[1] as a theatre and indoor market, though it later became the Town Hall and is now an art gallery. There is also *Cupola House*, from whose belvedere Celia Fiennes admired the fine view in 1698. The classical *Nonconformist Chapel* in Churchgate Street is a brick building with high, round-arched windows and an original interior dating from 1711. In the *Theatre Royal* on Westgate Street you can still sense something of the rather threadbare luxuries of a provincial town in the Regency period. William Wilkins, architect of the National Gallery, designed this intimate little theatre in 1819, with a gilded frieze of sphinxes on the balcony. For their balls and banquets, the gentry used to gather in the *Athenaeum* on Angel Hill (1789–1804), behind whose Queen Anne façade is a Regency hall with elegant stucco decor, attributed variously to Robert Adam or Francis Sandys (the architect of nearby Ickworth – see page 288 – who lived on Angel Hill 1799–1803, and probably designed some of the Regency houses in Bury). In the Athenaeum, their social and cultural meeting-place, the gentry managed for a long time to keep themselves to themselves: 'tradespeople, however respectable and opulent, are rigorously excluded' – an observation made in 1813. But the audience that attended one of Dickens' readings, at which *David Copperfield* was apparently well received, was already mixed. Today the more exclusive events take place nearby in 'The Angel'.

All paths in Bury lead back to *Angel Hill*. This beautiful, wide-open space was the seam that joined monastery and town, the stopping-place for the London coach, the intersection of metropolis and province, and once a year the site of the Bury Fair. This was the event of the season, as much of an attraction as the shrine of St Edmund itself. Even Henry III sent his royal tailor to Bury Fair in July to buy fur robes and coats from Ghent and Ypres. Trade fair and fun fair, public festival and social forum, fashion show and marriage market, Bury Fair was famous all over 18th-century England – not, of course, for its wares, but for its women. Daniel Defoe, in 1722, was overwhelmed by the number of lovely ladies, raved about 'the bright appearance of the beauties', and was appalled by the vulgar rumour that 'the Daughters of all the Gentry come hither to be pick'd up'. In 1731, the *Gentleman's Magazine* wooed the beautiful daughters of the Herveys and the Fitzroys at Bury Fair with the gallant rhyme: 'Could Bury the Whole Year these Nymphes retain / Venus would keep her Court here, they her train.' Other attractions included The Invisible Girl, the

---

1 Robert Adam also designed Moreton Hall in 1773, a country house on the other side of the River Lark. It is now a school.

Giant of Norfolk, and The Smallest Man - a dwarf only 29 inches high. Bury Fair was incomparable street theatre, and Angel Hill was its stage. The Duke of Grafton's players appeared here, and so did the eccentric Earl of Bristol, who lived on Honey Hill. Naturally the landed gentry also had their town houses in Bury, and at one time even Mary Tudor used to come yearly from Westhorpe Hall to the great fair. The last one took place in 1871. And what is Angel Hill today? A car park. 'Bury has the tradition, Ipswich the money' – and so at the beginning of the seventies, Ipswich replaced Bury St Edmunds as the county town of Suffolk.

In autumn all the roads to Bury are suddenly covered in mud. This is the time when the farmers bring their beet to the factory. Bury St Edmunds is still a rural town and centre of the region's agriculture. Every Wednesday there's a cattle market in the centre, and there's a constant bleating, mooing and snorting from the aluminium pens behind St Andrew's Street, while men in tweed jackets and wellington boots mill round the little arenas where the auctioneers from Lacy Scott or Simpson & Sons take bids at machine-gun speed for 2,000 pigs, 800 cows and hundreds of sheep a week. The Bury St Edmunds cattle market is the biggest in East Anglia – bigger even than those in Norwich and King's Lynn. When the sales are over, it's time to tour the pubs – off with the boots, and bring out the bottles.

Agriculture is still Bury's main industry, but after the war a number of new firms did move into the town, creating jobs for unemployed farm workers. Thousands of Londoners also moved into the outskirts of Bury, and in the last 25 years, the population has risen from 30,000 to 86,000. At the end of the eighties, before the grim recession, the unemployment rate was one of the lowest in England (6.7 per cent). The crime rate was also low, and there were few problems of vandalism or drugs. The neighbourhoods are well-planned, transport connections are good, and there's countryside aplenty – all major advantages which enabled Bury St Edmunds to attract business, most notably in electronics. The old market town has thus enjoyed a new boom, not thanks to its abbey or its textiles, as in the Middle Ages, but thanks to computers and chips. Soon no doubt they will also replace England's last horsehair processing firm, the main suppliers of judges' wigs.

Wednesday is not only market day for cattle in Bury, it's also market day on *Cornhill*. At the corner of this seething square stands a house with round-arched windows and a flint façade, built around 1180. This is *Moyses Hall*, the house of a rich Jew, once the bank (or synagogue) of Norman Bury, and now the town's museum. Among all the Anglo-Saxon and Roman items, the jewels and the gems, the ancient pots and pans and bits and pieces, are the severed ear and scalp of William Corder. In May 1827, William Corder murdered his mistress Maria Marten in a barn. The Red Barn Murder was the sensation of its day, and there were even Staffordshire porcelain souvenirs of the bloody location. Corder himself ended up on the scaffold in Bury's Buttermarket in 1828. A display case in the museum contains a report of the crime, bound in leather tanned from the skin of the murderer himself. No more gruesome relic ever graced St Edmund's town.

Ickworth: How the Bristol Hotel Got Its Name

It was one of those little social announcements that even the more serious British newspapers are reluctant to pass over. For the possession of cocaine, it was reported in the autumn of 1988, Frederick William John Augustus Hervey, Earl Jermyn and 7th Marquess of Bristol, must go to prison for one year. 'The downwardly mobile embarrasstocrat', as the Tatler once called him, born in 1954, is a multimillionaire, owner of an Australian sheep-farm, American oilfields, and thousands upon thousands of acres of good British soil.

This honourable member of the gossip-column aristocracy comes from one of the best families in the land. His father Victor, the 6th Marquess of Bristol, was Chancellor of the International League of Monarchists. From his office in Norwich and his home in Monte Carlo he supported the notion of the monarchy and those of its representatives who were in need. Almost all Europe's dethroned kings and queens were received as guests in the Marquess's London residence in St James's Square or in his country house of *Ickworth*, three miles southwest of Bury St Edmunds (plate 5). That was where Victor grew up, and helped his Uncle Frederick William 'to run the show'. When the uncle died in 1951, the 'show' was over. The house was given to the Treasury in lieu of death duties, and responsibility eventually passed to the National Trust. Thus it came to pass that the present 7th Marquess of Bristol was left with nothing but 7,000 acres of land, a heated prison cell, and – on his release – just the east wing of the mansion to live in (which we are not allowed to visit, as it is guarded by a fearsome sign that says PRIVATE).

Solemnly the cedars spread their sunshades over the lawn. When you leave the park and stand in the oval forecourt, you find yourself confronted by a monumental rotunda with a shallow dome and extended side wings which are joined to rectangular, two-storeyed pavilions. But where these wings end, how they end, or even if they end at all, you cannot see. The house is so hidden by trees and hedges that you can never get a view of its entire length. Ickworth is 700 feet long – longer than Ely Cathedral. It's more a royal palace than a family mansion, and its massive rotunda makes it more a mausoleum than a home.

This was just one of the houses built by Frederick Augustus Hervey, 4th Earl of Bristol and Bishop of Derry. He commissioned it in 1795 from the brothers Francis and Joseph Sandys, working to a design by the Italian neoclassicist Mario Asprucci with additional ideas by himself. The Earl-Bishop, classically educated and much travelled, was obsessed by round and oval shapes. After seeing the Colosseum in Rome and studying Piranesi, he had had a 'doghouse' in the form of a rotunda sketched for him by the young architect John Soane. John Plaw's Belle Isle (1774), a rotunda on an island in Lake Windermere, was the model for his Irish country house, Ballyscullion on Lough Beg, begun in 1787, but

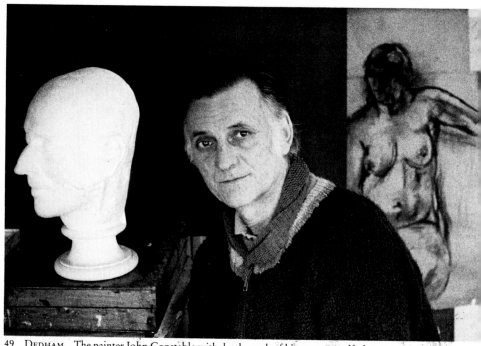

49 DEDHAM The painter John Constable with death-mask of his great-grandfather

50 MIDDLETON The poet Michael Hamburger with his wife Anne and his cat Oskar

51 LAXFIELD   Ron Fuller with Fruitmachine Man

52 WALBERSWICK   Bob Cross, Ferryman on the River Blyth

53   On the Stour at DEDHAM VALE ▷

54 Wymondham   Market with Market
          Cross, 1618
55 Swaffham   Georgian market rotunda, 1783

57 Bungay   Market Place with Butter Cross of 1689
56 Newmarket   Tattersalls' monument to the
          Fox and George IV, 1824

58 NORWICH Cathedral, begun in 1096

59 NORWICH Cathedral nave, c.1150

60 NORWICH University of East Anglia, Sainsbury Centre, 1976, by Norman Foster

61 NORWICH Cathedral cloister, begun in 1297

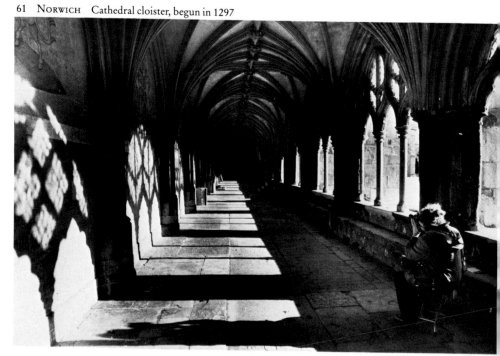

62 NORWICH Market and Norman Castle

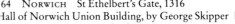

63 NORWICH Royal Arcade, *c*.1905,
by George Skipper 67 NORWICH Marble Hall of Norwich Union Building, by George Skipper ▷

64 NORWICH St Ethelbert's Gate, 1316

65 NORWICH Elm Hill 66 NORWICH In search of the past

taken down again in 1813. It was an oval central building with cupola and portico, flanked by curved side wings – the prototype for Ickworth.

Brick walls with ochre stucco, behind rows of columns like those of the Colosseum – thus sits Ickworth, enthroned in the fields of Suffolk, the Earl of Bristol's very own Pantheon. He commissioned the brothers Casimiro and Donato Carabelli, sculptors from Milan, to create the terracotta frieze between and above the columns, looping endlessly round the rotunda (1799–1803): reliefs of scenes based on John Flaxman's illustrations to Homer[1] – a comic strip for the connoisseur. You go through the high, four-columned portico, which seems somewhat uncomfortably stuck onto the rotunda, and enter the Earl-Bishop's palace, which he never actually occupied. He died in 1803, and it was not until 1829 that his family finally moved into the Roundhouse. The inside of the dome, is still incomplete, as it lacks the lantern from which the Earl Bishop had hoped to enjoy a full view of his great estate.

What a house, and what a man! There he sits in his Drawing Room – or at least a portrait of him, the Bishop dressed as man of the world. It looks as if he's sitting in a theatre box, his arm draped loosely over the balustrade, but in the background is a smoking Vesuvius. That was how he had himself portrayed in 1790 by Madame Vigée-Lebrun in Naples; in Rome he was painted by Angelica Kauffmann. He liked women and art and all the earthly pleasures, and seemed to be rather less enamoured of heavenly promises. 'His conversation ran generally in support of atheism,' reported a contemporary. 'His conversation was obscenity itself, no modest woman could talk with him or go up his staircase at Rome, where the frescoes were most indecent …' For years this most unepiscopal bishop and model eccentric lived in Italy, a patron of the arts and of the Neoclassical. Flaxman thought highly of his 'noble patronage', and said that he had 'reanimated the fainting body of Art in Rome'. From Madame Vigée-Lebrun he also commissioned the enchanting self-portrait now hanging in the Smoking Room at Ickworth, and from John Flaxman he commissioned a monumental marble sculpture: *The Madness of Athamas* (1790), one of those horrific family tragedies of Antiquity. The young artist, who lived in Rome, swore that no-one in England would ever have commissioned him to make such a group – seven foot high, with a man, woman, and two children. His patron was equally delighted, and considered that his *Athamas* 'exceeded the Laocöon in expression and was indeed 'the finest work ever done in sculpture.' Flaxman's group stands between two gigantic pairs of scagliola columns – the imitation marble of coloured, polished plaster so popular in the period – and forms the heroic centre point of the entrance hall at Ickworth.

Lord Bristol, the part-time Bishop, believed in Beauty and left God to look after Himself. He spent far more time in Rome and on his travels than he did with his Irish

1 Flaxman wanted to renew the tradition of the antique bas-relief, and regarded his outline drawings as models.

Frederick, 4th Earl of Bristol, 1790
by Louise Elizabeth Vigée-Lebrun

flock. As the 48th Bishop of Derry, he enjoyed the richest diocese in the whole of poverty-stricken Ireland, quite apart from the 30,000 acres of his family estates in Suffolk and Lincolnshire. He blatantly raised his prebends, and gave them out in quite extraordinary manner. He once arranged a race among his curates, the winners to be given a free living in his diocese. Scandalous, you may think. So it was. And so were many of the other things that he did. Yet the Irish seemed to prefer a scandalous lively Bishop to a pious boring one: in 1817, the people of Derry paid to erect an obelisk in honour of their outrageous spiritual leader, and there it stands proudly erect on the distant horizon of Ickworth. But we are digressing, for you are waiting to hear how Lord Bristol got to Goethe and how the Bristol Hotel got its name.

Flaubert complained that one can never be merry on journeys, and perhaps that is hardly to be wondered at. In those days travel was a good deal more hair-raising and uncomfortable than it is today. People didn't just rush from one site of culture to the next; they regarded the journey itself as a cultural event. But wherever they went, even to the most far-flung corner of the most far-flung country, they would always be sure to find that someone had got there before them, and that someone was always an Englishman. And there was no Englishman in the late 18th century who was more itchy-footed or more hard to please than the Bishop of Derry cum Earl of Bristol. The further away he went from

England, the more – understandably – he craved for English hospitality. What did he think he was entitled to expect? Actually, not all that much, and yet more than one often gets even today: a comfortable bed, a good cup of tea, and pleasant company. Any accommodation used by Lord Bristol was soon noted down by the travelling echelon of European society, and if the mitred Earl actually went back to the same place several times, its reputation was made for ever. And so it was that not only England's grand tourists bumped into one another in Lord Bristol's hotel, but the name became synonymous with luxury hotels in general, long before Michelin studded them with stars. Karl Baedeker led the traveller from one sight to another, and Lord Bristol showed him where he could most comfortably recover. There are many hotels between England and Italy that still bear his name (quite a few without any justification for doing so). But there is only one that the Earl actually went to in person: the Vienna Bristol, which has the Earl-Bishop's coat of arms above its entrance.

He seldom stayed long in one place. 'A vagabond star' is what he called himself, and he had to keep moving if his star was to keep twinkling. Thus it was that he saw Voltaire in Ferney, and Goethe in Jena. The latter meeting took place on 10 June 1797, and over 30 years later, Eckermann recorded Goethe's memories of Lord Bristol's visit: 'He sometimes took pleasure in being vulgar; but if you replied in an equally vulgar manner, he would be quite tractable. In the course of our conversation, he wanted to give me a sermon about *Werther*, and to lay it on my conscience that through that book I had led people to commit suicide. "*Werther*," he said, "is a totally immoral and damnable book!"' Then the Poet read the riot act to the Man of God, and in the end – as was so often the case – Goethe was very pleased with himself. Eckermann summarizes Goethe's verdict: 'Lord Bristol, vulgar though he could be, was a man of the spirit and of the world and thoroughly capable of grasping the widest variety of subjects.'[1]

In Ickworth you can see which subjects, or rather which objects, the Bishop most enjoyed grasping: paintings, sculptures, furniture, silver. Yet Ickworth's treasure is only a fraction of what he collected over the years in Italy: paintings by Raphael, Guido Reni, Annibale Carracci, ancient statues, marble busts, mosaic floors, and vast quantities of other art treasures – 'gran Dio che tesoro' – where was it all to go? This problem of all great collectors was not solved by the new house at Ickworth. No, the solution was in fact none other than Napoleon. When the French occupied Rome in 1798, Lord Bristol's collection fell into their hands before he could ship it off to England. And the man who built palaces at Ickworth, and Ballyscullion, and Ireland's first country seat, Downhill Castle (c.1775–85, now a ruin), though he never really lived in any of them, finally died in 1803 in a peasant's outhouse on the way to Albano – the peasant being unwilling to have a heretic bishop in his home. The corpse was taken to the family grave at Ickworth, but since

---

1 Goethe himself gives a detailed description of 'this remarkable man' in the *Biographischen Einzelheiten*, 10 June 1797.

the superstitious sailors were not willing to have a dead body on board, it had to be packed as an antique statue: a final irony of a collector's life.

There are only three rooms around the entrance hall of Ickworth: the Dining Room, the Drawing Room, and the Library. It was here in the Rotunda that the Earl wanted to live, surrounded by his collections in the side pavilions. In July 1796 he had written to his friend John Symonds, in Cambridge, describing his vision of the house that had just been begun: 'I wish to mark magnificence with convenience and simplicity with dignity – no redundancy – no superfluosity – no one unnecessary room, but the necessary ones to be noble and convenient, to have few pictures but choice ones, and my galleries to exhibit an historical progress of the art of Painting both in Germany and Italy, and that divided into its characteristic schools – Venice, Bologna, Florence etc.' But as so often happens, his heirs had other ideas. His son Frederick William preferred to live in the gallery in the east wing (which is still used as living quarters), and he had the rooms of the Rotunda fitted out as reception rooms. There is nothing to regret here, with all the Portuguese mirrors, furniture by Boulle and other French and English cabinet-makers, and one of the finest collections of family portraits that you will ever see anywhere. The Herveys had themselves painted by the very best artists of their time – by Gainsborough and Reynolds, Lawrence, Ramsay and Romney, and Jean-Etienne Liotard, the pastel virtuoso of High Society between Rome, Geneva, and Constantinople.[1] Angelica Kauffmann portrayed not only the Earl-Bishop himself, but also his daughter Elizabeth, who later became Duchess of Devonshire. there are two other Herveys shown leaning casually on anchor and cannon, dressed in gold-embroidered naval uniforms: they are Lord Bristol's brother, Vice Admiral Augustus John, and John Augustus, Lord Bristol's eldest son. These are two full-length portraits by Gainsborough.

From 1467 the Ickworth estates belonged to the Herveys. Over and over again they were employed in the service of the Crown, as ministers, ambassadors, viceroys of Ireland. In this manner they preserved and indeed extended their possessions through all the storms of English history. There is at least one who deserves our special attention: John, Lord Hervey, father of the 4th Earl of Bristol. He was MP for Bury St Edmunds, a supporter of Walpole, Lord Privy Seal, and a confidant of Queen Caroline. Lord Hervey kept a diary about life at the court of George II, recording the intrigues, the major activities and the minor ones in the royal household – upper class gossip mixed with national history. William Hogarth portrayed Lord Hervey in one of his conversation pieces (c.1738), surrounded by his friends, the famous Holland House Group. The picture now hangs in the Library, near four busts of English Prime Ministers by Joseph Nollekens.

In civilized times, long gone, anyone who wanted to smoke at Ickworth went far away from the Dining Room to the Smoking Room. This too contained typical Hervey

---

1 Liotard also worked successfully in London in 1754, but Horace Walpole wrote of him: 'his crayons and his watercolours are very fine; his enamel hard and in general he is too Dutch and admires nothing but excess of finishing.'

showpieces: Chippendale chinoiseries, a classical Poussin landscape, a brilliant Velasquez portrait of the Infante Balthasar Carlos, a dubious Titian, and a studio copy of the celebrated 'Death of Wolfe' by the court painter Benjamin West, 'the flattering, feeble dotard West / Europe's worst dauber and poor Britain's best', as Lord Byron called the successful American.

Not until 1879 was the companion-piece to the Smoking Room completed. This is the Pompeian Room. The trompe-l'oeil decorations by John Diblee Crace[1] are based on the antique frescoes of the Villa Negroni in Rome – historical scene-painting so beloved by the Victorians. In the western one of the two long, curved corridors, where the Earl-Bishop had intended to display his sculptures, you can now admire some of the Bristol silver, made by Huguenot silversmiths in London during the 18th and early 19th centuries – one of the most magnificent private collections in England.

From the terraced path behind the southern façade the view stretches far across the fields and wooded hills, where sheep graze in the shade of ancient oaks. It's a pastoral scene in the style of Capability Brown, who certainly left a few marks on this landscape (1769–76). If you look carefully, you'll also see the little church, where the Earls of Bristol lie surrounded by trees, in a picturesque solitude.

Since the Middle Ages, many aristocratic families and church dignitaries have had their country houses around Bury St Edmunds. On a more modest scale than Ickworth was the Queen Anne house that the Bishop of Ely had built between Bury and Newmarket (1704–5): *Dalham Hall*, which is now linked to a famous stud farm (see page 324). *Culford Hall*, north of Bury, was once the country mansion of the first Marquess of Cornwallis, a general in the American War of Independence; later it became the family seat of the Earls of Cadogan. The park was designed by Humphry Repton c.1794, and in the church is a complex baroque monument by Thomas Stanton, 1654. Culford Hall has now been taken over by a school.

Opposite Culford Hall, on the other side of the River Lark, is one of the most important Tudor houses in Suffolk: *Hengrave Hall*. Despite drastic restorations at the end of the 19th century, the long, low south façade has retained its symmetry, with polygonal corner towers, a central doorway, and turrets crowned with tiaras. The pride of Hengrave Hall is the spectacular bay window above the entrance – heraldic splendour unequalled anywhere (colour plate 31, plate 15). The trefoil form of the bay[2] is late Gothic, but the decoration is Early Renaissance. Below the royal coat of arms on the gold-edged base of the window, naked cherubs hold the coat of arms of the Kytson family,[3] containing three fish which

1 J. D. Crace came from a family of cabinet-makers and interior decorators, and his style was Neo-Renaissance: other work includes the staircase at the National Gallery, and the Library at Longleat.
2 There are similar bay windows at Windsor Castle, in the Henry VII Tower (c.1500) and at Thornbury Castle (c.1511).
3 For many visitors, another coat of arms in one of the (newer) windows of Hengrave Hall will be more important: the family coat of arms of George Washington. One of his ancestors married a sister of Sir Thomas Kytson. Winston Churchill was also related to the Kytsons.

recall the family's ancient fishing rights in the River Lark. Hengrave Hall was built by a rich London clothier, Thomas Kytson, who was knighted by Henry VIII. He began it c.1525, and according to the date on the window, it must have been finished in 1538. Mary Tudor was a guest here, as was Queen Elizabeth I. After the Kytsons, the Hall was taken over by the Gage family, one of whom – Sir William – brought the reine-Claude plum from France to England and cultivated it on his estate. Since then, in his honour, it has always been known as the Gage plum or greengage.

The Gages were Catholics who rejected the Anglican communion for nine long generations, defying all adversities and clinging to the hope expressed in their family motto: 'Bon temps viendra'. Thus Hengrave Hall became one of the great recusant houses in England. During the French Revolution, the Gages rented their house to nuns from Bruges, and for some years they ran a little boarding school here. In 1952 Hengrave Hall once again became a convent school. Today Catholic nuns, together with married and unmarried members of various Christian groups form the Hengrave Community, in a model centre of ecumenical understanding and exchange. A few years ago, this Tudor mansion in a Suffolk park won first prize in the *Out of This World Guide*, which lists the quietest, most contemplative places in the British Isles.

'Flora, give me fairest flowers.' For many guests, a night in the Wilbye Room is a revelation. John Wilbye, son of a tanner from Diss, lived for 30 years as resident musician at Hengrave Hall, Lord and Lady Kytson's Chief of the Minstrels. Here he wrote many of his songs, such as 'Adieu, sweet Amarilis', and 'Weep, O mine eyes', which made him, next to John Dowland, the leading madrigal composer of his time. Only 64 of Wilbye's madrigals have survived, songs of love ('Sweet honey-sucking bees') and melancholy ('Draw on, sweet night').

At about the same time as Sir Thomas Kytson was busy with Hengrave, his neighbour Sir John Crofts was building *West Stow Hall* (plate 16) scarcely two miles to the north. It must have been a highly prestigious house, bearing in mind Sir John's position as Queen Mary's Master of the Horse,[1] and also bearing in mind the scale of what remains: a gatehouse with four towers leading over a moat (all timber framing and red Tudor brick in a beautiful combination). Today, however, West Stow owes its fame not to the Hall (which is private), but to the archaeological discoveries made here: a complete Anglo-Saxon village has been excavated and reconstructed (see page 226).

There's one more Tudor mansion we must talk about – one of the finest in Suffolk, built c.1550 – and that's *Rushbrooke Hall*, southeast of Bury. After a fire, it was simply demolished in 1961, and Pevsner was not alone in describing that as 'a tragedy'. Anita and Amschel Rothschild lived here for a time, and in the tradition of the very best Lords of the Manor, Lord Rothschild – incidentally, a passionate racing driver and cricketer – had the old village of Rushbrooke rebuilt as a model estate (1955–63): two-storey brick cottages, every one with a different ground plan and setting, joined together by high walls in a

---

1 One of Mary's residences was Westhorpe Hall, northeast of Bury St Edmunds.

perfect balance between privacy and communal village life. This classic model village is the latest, and perhaps the last in the line of estate villages that go back to the early 18th century.[1]

It was the day after Steffi Graf won Wimbledon in the rain (the 'Raining Queen', as *The Observer* dubbed her). Germans don't forget days like that, and I certainly shan't forget it, though I was not at the Centre Court myself. I *was* in the rain, though. To be precise, I was standing amid the beet fields of *Felsham*, some way off the main road southeast of Bury. It was there that I met a farmer named Stanley Steadman. He stood at the front door of Moores Farm, and next to him on the wall the ocean liner 'Queen Mary' was busily steaming to nowhere, while between the yellow window frames the wall had turned into a proud Union Jack – the whole of this lovely thatched farmhouse, and the barn and the garage as well, are covered with brightly painted pictures.

'It all started one drizzly day,' says Stan – a day like today, in fact. He'd finished work in the fields, felt bored, and began to paint. He hadn't got any canvas, but he had plenty of wall space, and so he painted his farm. He filled it with views of Windsor Castle, Tenerife, Willy Lott's Cottage, Scottish glens – subjects from calendars and picture postcards, all enlarged in the same format and painted in the gaudiest colours. Once he'd started, he couldn't stop, and when I was there, the number of pictures had gone up to 112. 'To amuse my grandchildren', Stan also made some cut-out figures, sawn out of planks, nailed together, and painted. And so they are all standing around the house as well, the brightest of dumb animals: a cow with a horse's head, a pheasant, a peacock, chickens, cat and dog, a crocodile in the pond, a snowman in the dungheap, and a wooden guard of honour at the vegetable patch, comprising a village boy, a fox, and the postman in blue uniform. And thus Farmer Steadman surrounds himself with a colourful world of his own, full of fantasy and good humour. He's not interested in naïve art or exhibitions in galleries. On his grass-green garage, he wrote: 'Common sense is not so common', and next to it, 'Everyone is funny, but some are more funny than others'.

Euston Hall: A Duke for the Environment

For five long and bloody years the Sikhs fought against the British colonial rulers. Then in 1856 the British annexed the whole Punjab. The King of the Sikhs, Duleep Singh, was banished from India for life, to *Elveden Hall*, on the edge of Thetford Forest. The Maharajah had lost his home and his power, but not his wealth. Between 1863 and 1870 he had the architect John Norton convert this modest Georgian country house into an oriental palace, with dome, onion-shaped arches, richly decorated ceilings, wrought iron

---

1 Bill Wyman, rock guitarist and a Rolling Stone, also has a country house southeast of Bury: Gedding Hall, a Tudor gatehouse (*c*.1530) with Victorian extension and moat.

balustrades, doors covered with beaten copper, and tons and tons of Carrara marble. Elveden Hall was the most sumptuous, most bizarre place of exile in British colonial history: Indian Neo-Gothic, or How the East Came to East Anglia. The banished Punjabi prince surrounded himself with hunting friends, ballet dancers, and bittersweet memories of his palace in Lahore. By the time Queen Victoria became Empress of India in 1876, the Maharajah was already dazzling the world as an English Super-Squire. It is said that in one day he shot no less than 789 partridges, single-handed.

After the death of the Maharajah, the Guinness family, of brewing fame, acquired Elveden Hall in 1894. The first Earl of Iveagh again enlarged the palace, and changed the Indian fairytale into an Edwardian extravaganza: Taj Mahal interiors were enclosed in Italianate brick façades (1899–1903). He also extended the parish church (1904–6) with a mixture of neo-Gothic and Art Nouveau, and in 1937 added a west window by Sir Frank Brangwyn. Since the Second World War, the house has been uninhabited, as the last Lord Iveagh, head of the Guinness clan, lived on his estate near Dublin. In May 1984, however, Elveden Hall made headlines, when Christie's auctioned off the entire contents of the house: 3,297 lots, which fetched a total in the region of £6 million. Chippendale furniture, Persian carpets, tapestries, silver, paintings: all went under the hammer. In his gatehouse, one of Lord Iveagh's gamekeepers showed me an album of colour photos taken shortly before the auction, when employees and tenants were allowed for the very first and very last time to see the magnificent interiors of the house. 'Many of us had worked here for decades and had never been allowed inside.' Now the windows are dark and the rooms are empty. In the fields, the pheasants trumpet, just as if King Edward VII were once again coming to shoot at Elveden Hall. With some 23,000 acres (estimated value approximately £50 million), Lord Iveagh's property is still one of the largest shooting estates in England, and is more than twice as big as that of his neighbour, the Duke of Grafton.

Duke's Ride is a dead straight track across the heath to the Duke of Grafton's estate. Sheep graze peacefully in the fields around *Euston Hall*, a brick house of modest dimensions. I have an appointment to see the Duke. I go through the half-open door and find myself being scrutinized by Van Dyck's Charles I. All is still. No-one in sight – not even a butler. Eventually, a man comes from the garden, watering-can in hand, a Hawaiian shirt hanging loosely over his trousers. Problem: is it the Duke, or is it the gardener? 'I've been watering,' he says, with the precise, upper-class voice that removes all doubt. He's a big man with a Roman head and cool, bright blue eyes: Hugh Denis Charles, 11th Duke of Grafton, born in South Africa in 1919, cousin of the Queen, godfather to Prince Andrew, Knight of the Garter (plate 13). His Grace takes me through to the drawing room, and there, under the watchful gaze of a black retriever, we sink into soft flowery armchairs.

If you ask the Duke of Grafton which of his ancestors he most admires, he'll name the founder of the family, none other than King Charles II. His Majesty had a large number of mistresses, and treated his 'natural' children with absolutist discretion. When Barbara Villiers, later Duchess of Cleveland, presented him with a son, he made the bastard a duke. Henry FitzRoy, 1st Duke of Grafton, married Lord Arlington's only daughter, Isabella

Bennet. Lord Arlington himself had been with Charles II in exile and was Lord Chamberlain after the Restoration; he married a Dutch member of the House of Orange and had a residence in London (on the site now occupied by Buckingham Palace) and a country house on the Norfolk Border, Euston Hall (1666–85). In October 1671, Charles II came to Euston Hall on a visit, and if one can believe all the royal bedtime stories, it must have been a fairly informal visit, too. In any case, the following July, Louise de Kerouaille, a lady-in-waiting, presented His Majesty with a love-child from Euston Hall: Charles Lennox, later to be Duke of Richmond.

All the royal company of the Stuarts, those free-and-easy Lords and Ladies with or without their Orders of the Garter, are still to be seen today, asembled in the drawing-room of the Duke of Grafton, as portrayed by the various court painters – Daniel Mytens, Peter Lely, Godfrey Kneller, Van Dyck – in a unique combination of social and art history, and of power politics and the family. Every picture in the house, says the Duke, is more or less related, 'either by blood or by interest'. Most of them were collected by Lord Arlington himself. His favourite, Van Dyck, was also the King's favourite. In Euston Hall you can see Charles I in romantic hunting costume (a replica of the original in the Louvre), his double portrait with Queen Henrietta Maria, and the most popular of all Van Dyck's pictures of children, 'The Five Eldest Children of Charles I', which was often copied even during his lifetime. The Euston version is believed to be a copy he made himself of the original (1637) which is in the Royal Collection. It shows the seven-year-old Prince of Wales (Charles II) in the centre, with his left hand on a huge mastiff; to the right of him are Princess Mary and the Duke of York (James II); to the left, the Princesses Elizabeth and Anne, with a little King Charles spaniel at their feet. In wonderful harmony of colour, Van Dyck has here brought together a mixture of court ceremonial and the enchantment of childhood. The Duke of Grafton also has two sons and three daughters – a happy, royal coincidence. Which is his own favourite picture? 'Mares and Foals' by George Stubbs, who was commissioned by the third Duke to do several portraits of horses in his stud. This particular portrait is set on the bank of the Little Ouse, not far from the house, and one of the foals was later to win the Oaks at Epsom.

The Duke would also like to collect paintings, but where would he put them? The walls of his house are already 'so stuffed with pictures'. Only on the piano and the tables is there still room for a contemporary continuation of these celebrity portraits, the present ones being signed photos of VIP's in silver frames: Emperor Hirohito, the Pope, the Reagans, Kings, Presidents – many of them trophies acquired by the Duchess of Grafton during her frequent journeys with the Queen. Since 1953, Her Grace has been Lady of the Bedchamber, and since 1967 Mistress of the Robes, the oldest and most high-ranking position for a lady-in-waiting to the Queen.

The fact that Euston Hall's art collection has generally remained intact is due to the English system of primogeniture. 'Everything goes to the eldest,' explains the Duke – 'so long as the eldest can pay the death duties.' Back in 1923, the 8th Duke had had to auction a Van Dyck self-portrait through Christie's (now at the Metropolitan Museum, New

Anthony van Dyck: The Five Eldest Children of King Charles I, c.1637

York), and in the mid-thirties the present Duke's father had unfortunately had to sell to Thyssen père the most valuable painting in the whole collection: a portrait by the Renaissance master Sebastiano del Piombo. In order to pay these very heavy death duties, the 10th Duke had also had to sell 2,000 acres of land in 1938, at a ridiculous price of about £10 per acre. During that last agricultural depression, everyone advised him to sell the house, which in those days was three times the size it is now. In 1952, on the advice of the present Duke, his father demolished almost everything that his grandfather had rebuilt after a disastrous fire in 1905. Only Matthew Brettingham's North Wing of 1750–6 and a small part of the West Wing remain. Thus the family survived.

So far the 11th Duke of Grafton has managed to make ends meet without selling the family silver. But it gets harder every year. At the beginning of the century, his grandfather had a staff of about twenty servants and twenty gardeners. During the thirties, his father still had twelve servants and nine gardeners. And now? 'Well,' mumbles His Grace, 'I don't want to go into that,' but one gets the feeling that he has to polish his own shoes. The only member of the household that's living in luxury now is the little Norwich terrier on which the Duke lavishes a continual supply of chocolate biscuits.

In the 19th century, the Euston estate gave a living to over 200 workers. Today there are no more than 40 farm and forest workers to cope with 11,000 acres, of which 9,000 are arable land (the soil on the edge of the Brecklands is not particularly fertile). 'Prospects are not very good. A lot of houses like this one, which depend on the income of the estate, are heading for hard times.' What does it cost to maintain Euston Hall? 'No figures,' insists the Duke. But the house has to be painted every five years, which costs him something like £20,000 a time. 'Absolutely appalling.'

The home of the Dukes of Grafton was once considered to be admirably modern. 'Very magnificent and commodious' enthused John Evelyn on his visit in 1671. Evelyn, the great diarist and garden enthusiast, gave the Lord of the Manor advice on the layout of his park, and he especially admired 'the invention of Sir Samuel Morland,' the ingenious water supply system, 'that provides for the family, and reuses water for the fountains and offices.' Sir Samuel Morland was an engineer who experimented with pumps and steam-power, was *magister mechanicorum* at the court of Charles II, and adviser to Louis XIV on the waterworks at Versailles. Euston Hall is believed to have been the first country house in England to have running water – one of the great accomplishments of the 17th century.

The blessings of flushing toilets, however, remained a thing of the future. A young nobleman from Paris, François de la Rochefoucauld,[1] indignantly described his experiences (on the eve of the French Revolution) at the table of the Duke of Grafton: 'On the sideboard stand innumerable chamberpots, and it is generally normal to relieve oneself whilst the others are drinking; people do that totally without inhibition – a custom which I find exceedingly embarrassing.' The daily routine appears to have been equally contrary to French taste: breakfast at nine, with everybody buried in their newspaper; at precisely four o'clock, dinner with two hours of eating, followed by two to three hours of drinking by the gentlemen on their own. Such social intercourse seemed to La Rochefoucauld to be among 'the most boring of all things that are English'.

And your own daily routine, Sir? 'No different from Mr Smith's,' says the Duke of Grafton, 'except that I'm lumbered with this rather large house.' Breakfast, work in the office, do the rounds with the steward – 'a thousand and one things, so I scarcely even have time to go to the House of Lords'. But several times he has spoken to their Lordships on his favourite topic, which is also his life's work: preserving the heritage. Ever since his father took over Euston Hall, the Duke has fought above all for the preservation of historic houses. In the beginning, people like him were 'the lone boys fighting a lone battle', with no money and no help from the law. Today there are hundreds of conservation groups, and the problems are common knowledge. Even the Labour government withdrew their threat of a wealth tax. 'If they hadn't, within one single generation many of these houses and art collections would have been completely ruined.' Of course, their future is never assured. 'For their owners they always mean responsibility and worry.'

1 The 18-year-old son of the Duc de Liancourt, together with his brother and a tutor, used Bury St Edmunds as a centre from which to visit all the great country houses of the area in 1784. His account, *Mélanges sur l'Angleterre*, conveys a vivid impression of English provincial life at that time.

The Duke of Grafton, who advised his father to demolish two-thirds of their family home, has more honorary preservation posts than anyone else. They call him the Duke of Preservation. He's a member of the Georgian Group, the Victorian Society, English Heritage, the Royal Fine Arts Commission, is actively involved in the National Trust and the Historic Houses Association (a lobby group for the owners of such houses), and for decades has been the leading light of the Society for the Protection of Ancient Buildings, the oldest such movement in England, founded in 1877 by William Morris. 'With all these endless meetings and committees, I don't even have any more time now for my hobby.' His hobby is painting – just like his father, who coloured the tableware in the Dining Room. In addition to all these activities, the Duke is President of the East Anglia Tourist Board. Promoting tourism and conserving the countryside can sometimes lead to a conflict of interests which may be 'somewhat embarrassing'. Holiday camps, for instance, with up to 700 chalets dotting the green. 'A completely new threat to the countryside ... ugh!' says the Duke, as if someone had put ketchup in his tea.

On Thursdays His Grace makes the supreme sacrifice: his privacy. Allowing people into the house is 'an exceedingly alarming step'. But so far people have always 'behaved extraordinarily well', only you just never know 'who's casting an eye over the contents of your house'. You actually have to show them your own four walls, 'the bit we live in', and that makes him very uncomfortable. Fortunately, Euston Hall doesn't get more than 4,000 visitors a year. The Duke uses the entrance money for charitable purposes, and he has 'ten wonderful volunteers' to do the supervising and to chat to the visitors and give them a discreet account of the family history, which they know as precisely as their own. They like to describe the Queen Mother's visits, and the evil influence Barbara Villiers had on her lover, the King, and how His Grace found his grandfather's robes for the Order of the Garter hidden away in an attic. 'All he had to get for the ceremony was a new hat!'

Meanwhile, the Duke's fat little Norwich terrier has wolfed down the last chocolate biscuit. The audience is over. I walk through the park to the church. The unspectacular façade of St Genevieve hides an elegant interior of 1677, comparable to Christopher Wren's town churches, with beautiful stalls and plaster ceilings – one of the few surviving Restoration country churches. The rector is gathering up the silverware from the altar (nothing is safe here either), and shows me the Graftons' pew, and the family vault. The latter is now full, and so the next applicant will have to go out into the churchyard.

In *Pakenham*, northeast of Bury, the parson sits at his library window in his full-bottomed wig, reading. He doesn't move. He's an anachronism, and he's also an illusion. Window and parson are by Rex Whistler, the master of trompe-l'oeil, who was stationed in the neighbourhood shortly before he was killed in Normandy in 1944. 'Whistler painted it all in one hour. It was raining, and someone held an umbrella over him,' explains the owner of the old vicarage next to the church. In nearby *Stowlangtoft*, Whistler's medieval colleagues entertained the community in their own way, with burlesque scenes and allegorical figures on the poppyheads in St George's. There's a pig playing the harp, a dog catching a wild duck, a hedgehog, an owl, a camel, a unicorn, a pelican – in fact a complete bestiary carved in wood round about 1500.

Of all the village churches in northwest Suffolk, there's one I'm particularly fond of. It has no art treasures, no baroque tombs, no unusual brasses, no special features, and yet something that's worth more than all those. With its thatched roof and its rough flint walls, All Saints in *Icklingham* has been the house of God and of God's farmers since the early 14th century. The benches are low, many without backs, and the hassocks are partly filled with straw, with none of the obsessive embroidery beloved of later generations. There's not even an organ – just a harmonium in the corner. The Gothic font stands on four shafts, and there's a black bier on wheels below the bell-tower (plate 84). Everywhere these concise symbols of life and death, or rural labour and simple piety. Icklingham has two churches, but even in the 19th century the community could only afford to maintain one. And so All Saints escaped the attentions of the Victorian restorers, for it was closed and forgotten. The fact that today it can once more display all the charms of a medieval village church is due to the Redundant Churches Fund.

Downriver on the Lark, in *Mildenhall*, a farmer was ploughing his field in 1942, when he struck gold – well, silver. What came up out of the earth was a treasure consisting of 34 late Roman artefacts, including some dishes with exquisite reliefs of bacchanalian dances. The Mildenhall Treasure is now in the British Museum. A more sacred treasure is in the magnificent church of Mildenhall, for high up in the distant timbers of the roof fly angels superbly carved by the master carpenters of the early 16th century. They are matched only by the angels flying further north in the church at *Lakenheath*. But angels are not the only creatures flying over Lakenheath and Mildenhall. Over the heath and over the fens and over the forests of the Brecklands thunder the mightiest wings the world has ever seen. RAF Lakenheath and RAF Mildenhall were for years two of the biggest American airbases in Europe. It was from here that the F111s took off for Tripoli in 1986, as part of Reagan's retaliation against Ghaddafi. Many English people were horrified at being implicated in such a policy. But the local people have come to depend on these bases: there are some 15,000 members of the American armed forces, plus their families, living in Mildenhall and Lakenheath, compared to a local population of 10,000. The Americans spend over $220 million a year in Mildenhall alone. They have leased the two bases from the RAF since the early fifties, though not without incident. On 27 July 1955, a US bomber crashed near a hangar in Lakenheath where atom bombs were stored; later the commandant expressed an equal degree of astonishment and relief that the whole of East Anglia had not been made into 'a desert'.

For some years the dramatist Edward Bond has been living in an idyllic village near Cambridge. He wrote to me from Great Wilbraham that he sees East Anglia as nothing but an outpost for American strike forces. 'We have the killing capacities of a hundred thousand Auschwitzes: many people don't seem to mind.'

Peter Tillemans: The Newmarket Watering Course

Newmarket: Heroes and Hunters, Painters and Punters

They hunt on the heath, they pad round the paddocks, they're on top of the Victorian clock tower, all over Ladbroke's betting shop, lifesize in bronze on the streets, bony idols in the museum, and edible exhibits in the cake-shop window. There are pubs named after them, and pubs that are full of them. Wherever you go, there are horses. Painted ones, printed ones, heroic ones, humble ones, horses in the stable, horses on the hoof, horses on the ground floor, horses on the roof. You feel like Gulliver in the Land of the Houyhnhnms.

Newmarket has 15,000 inhabitants and 3,000 horses. This is the domain of the horsey people, the Promised Land of the English turf. Every fourth inhabitant of Newmarket is connected one way or another with the racing industry,[1] as stable lads, jockeys, trainers, saddlers, dealers, bookies. This is where tomorrow's Derby winners are bred, and where the Rothschilds train their horses, and it's here, not Ascot, that you'll find the National

---

1 There are about 100,000 people in England whose jobs are connected with racing. At the 5,600 races held each year, more than £3,000 million change hands in bets, and more than £30 million are paid out in winnings.

Horseracing Museum. When there were still sheep bleating all over Epsom heath, Charles II was already sending his horses to race over Newmarket Heath. It's at Newmarket's National Stud that the Queen's horses are covered. Here Prince Pückler, the great gardener and traveller, kept one eye on the horses and one on the women, and George Stubbs painted, and Lester Piggott lives, and the legendary jockey Fred Archer lived and died. Here you'll find the portrait of Gimcrack, the skeleton of Eclipse, the grave of Mill Reef, the nation's saintly horses and their relics. This is the headquarters of the Jockey Club, the ultimate authority of British racing, and here too you will find Tattersalls, England's oldest and Europe's biggest auctioneers of thoroughbreds. Newmarket means horses – it's as simple as that.

I took a room at the 'Rutland Arms', a coaching inn dating back to 1815. Once upon a time, Charles II had a house on this spot. The fact is recalled by the name Palace Street, and behind my hotel there is a timber-framed house with a modern terracotta portrait of the King and his last wish: 'let not poor Nelly starve ...' Nell Gwyn was the most popular whore of her time. At 13 she was selling oranges at the Royal Theatre, at 15 she was an actress, admired by Pepys and Dryden, and at 18 she was the King's favourite courtesan. The Merry Monarch billeted her here ('I think there's no hell / Like loving too well'), but

*Mr Fellowes, General Secretary
of the Jockey Club, Newmarket*

unlike his other mistresses, she was never given a title, on account of her cockney origins. He did, however, make her son Duke of St Albans. Charles II, patron of science, art and pleasure, came regularly to the races at Newmarket from 1665 onwards, together with the Duke of Buckingham, the Earl of Rochester, and other Restoration playboys. He once said that the only creatures in whose company he could really relax were horses, because they alone treated him as an equal – namely, as a king. His favourite horse was called Rowley, which gave rise to his nickname of Old Rowley and the name Rowley Mile for the truly royal racecourse. It is a mile and a quarter long, 58½ yards wide, and has the longest straight 'across the Flat' in the world. Two of the five English Classics take place here: the 1,000 Guineas (since 1814) and the 2,000 Guineas (since 1809) right at the start of the season in May.

Charles II started his own stud in Newmarket and remained patron of the races until he died: 'The greatest monarch we've ever had – on a racecourse' (Lord Northcliffe). But the royal tradition began before Old Rowley. His grandfather, the Stuart King James I, had realized while coursing hares in 1605 that the flat heath offered ideal conditions for horseracing. His son, later Charles I, when he was still Prince of Wales had a suitable residence built by Inigo Jones in the then obscure village of Newmarket. It fell victim to the fire that destroyed most of the old town centre in 1883. Since then Newmarket's stables have been rather better-looking than its houses.

Prinny and Tub Tum, two Princes of Wales, both whiled away some of their almost sixty-year wait for the throne with racing and betting at Newmarket. By the time they became George IV and Edward VII respectively, their racing days were almost over. 'The Old Peacock', as Kaiser Wilhelm II called his uncle Edward, has a special place in the

National Horseracing Museum. From behind a stable door peeps the stuffed head of his 1896 Derby winner, Persimmon, while two of his passions are innocently linked together in the form of hairs from his favourite horses, mounted in silver frames, and the racing boots of his mistress Lillie Langtry. Cigar in hand, top hat at a saucy angle, Bertie would stand on the racecourse with his Lillie just as King Charles had once stood with his Nelly. Lillie had her own stud farm at Newmarket, and exercised considerable influence on Edward's betting. The descendants of his horse Perdita II alone earned the royal breeder a fortune in just 26 races.

At the museum in Newmarket, you can get to know Tregonwell Frampton, 'Father of the English Turf'. It is said that Frampton hated women, but loved cockfights, hunting with hounds, and anything and everything to do with horses and gambling: the perfect combination for a court appointment which he was the first to occupy: Keeper of the Running Horses. William III and Queen Anne had their horses trained by Frampton at Newmarket. Their successors, George I and George II, were completely uninterested in the sport, but Frampton still kept his job. Daniel Defoe describes him as a pokerface, 'as perfectly calm, cheerful, and unconcerned, when he had lost one thousand pounds, as when he had won it.' For thirty years Tregonwell Frampton remained in the saddle as the highest authority at Newmarket, until the reins were taken over by the Jockey Club.

The Jockey Club is the Holy See of British racing. Its home is in the High Street, in a Victorian brick building which was extended in a Neo-Georgian style in 1933. Protected by heavy red silk curtains from the inquisitive eyes of passers-by, the Coffee Room of 1771 is the historic centre of the Club. In the entrance hang some leather fire buckets with the initials C.R. 'Charles II gave them to us,' explains Mr Fellowes, 'and they were used for feeding the horses.' Robert Fellowes is a greying gentleman in grey tweed, and he was General Secretary of the Club at the time of my visit. He was born in the same year as Hyperion, he says proudly – 1930. Hyperion was Lord Derby's famous Derby winner which came from Newmarket and now stands in a lifesize bronze on the road to Snailwell. On this same road, in Balaton Lodge, the Animal Health Trust has its Equine Research Station.

The Jockey Club is the biggest landowner in Newmarket. 'The whole area belongs to us,' says Mr Fellowes – the racecourse, 30 miles of gallops, and a total of some 4,300 acres. Much of this was given by a generous member of the Club and of the aristocracy, the 4th Duke of Portland. For permission to use the heath, trainers pay the Jockey Club a monthly 'heath tax' for each of their horses. The Club itself employs about 45 groundsmen to look after the precious turf. 'Gallopmen' take care of the gallops, the training area east of the town, and 'heathmen' are in charge of the racecourses on the other side. They mark out the ever-changing courses (in the old days this was done with bundles of pine branches, but now it's all plastic), repair the turf with grass from the hothouse, and check every inch of the ground as if it were a minefield. The fact that William III died when his horse tripped over a molehill was regrettable. But if Shahrastani, the Aga Khan's Derby star, had broken a leg while training here, it would have been a catastrophe. The July course, as flawless

*Edwardian racing dandies,
by Sem, c.1908*

as a Persian carpet, can only be used in summer, and the Rowley Mile only in spring
and autumn. Irrigation holes have been bored alongside both courses so that even
during prolonged dry spells, the turf will always be in peak condition. Newmarket's turf
is as holy as Wimbledon's Centre Court, in wartime as well as peacetime. It's true that
during the war part of the area was used as an airfield, but there was never any question
of putting in a concrete runway. In both world wars, the Derby was transferred
from Epsom to Newmarket. Nothing could be allowed to interfere with such a national
institution.

Of course the Jockey Club does more than mow the lawn. 'We run and rule the races,'
says Mr Fellowes. Without them, not a hoof would pound on Newmarket Heath or on
any other of Britain's 58 racecourses. They make all the laws and pass all the judgments on
every case connected with the Turf. The authority of this self-elected, self-regulating body
even extended over the future George IV, for after a dubious victory in 1791, Prinny's own
jockey had to appear before an inquiry. In disgust, the Prince sold his stud and never
returned to Newmarket. The dreaded Stewards' Room is the only one in the Club without
any pictures. Anyone who broke the rules had to stand on the carpet before the stewards:
'So-and-so's been carpeted', they used to say. But nowadays, Mr Fellowes told me, 'the
offender is allowed to sit down, bring a lawyer, and even lodge an appeal. It's all very
democratic – unfortunately.' Since 1977 women have been allowed to become members

(just 100 years after the admission of the first Jewish member, Baron Meyer de Rothschild, who owned a stud, 'Palace House', in Newmarket). Jockeys are still not admitted, however, with just one exception: the late Gordon Richards, who starred in no less than 4,870 victories. But even he was just an honorary member – and that only came about after he had become the first English jockey to be knighted.

There are good reasons why jockeys have no place in the Jockey Club. Racing began when one gentleman bet that his horse was faster than another's. Then they got together with other friends, and rode their own horses in order to try to win their bets. Professional jockeys were not engaged until later on in horseracing history. To start with, it was a purely amateur sport for aristocrats. These gentlemen founded the Jockey Club in 1752 in Pall Mall, the heart of London's Clubland. (The Charleston Jockey Club in Virginia, USA, is the oldest in the world, founded in 1734.) Twenty years later, they moved to a coffee house in Newmarket's High Street. The 'Coffee Room' has remained unchanged ever since, with leather sofas worn smooth, mahogany tables, and the incomparable atmosphere of cultivated idleness. On the walls are cut-out caricatures (c.1908) of Edwardian racing dandies by Sem (Georges Goursat), the most famous French cartoonist at the turn of the century. They include Lord Rothschild, Lord Howard de Walden, and other eccentrics from the 'belle époque' of the Jockey Club. This is where they sat, gossiped, drank and dozed, laughing and joking and placing their bets – notorious gamblers like Old Q, the Duke of Queensberry, and great racing dictators like Admiral Rous and Lord George Bentinck, who left the Club his binoculars.

'The beginning of October, one is certain that everybody will be at Newmarket, and the Duke of Cumberland will lose, and Shafto[1] win two or three thousand pounds,' noted Horace Walpole in 1763. Some kept horses in order to pay off their gambling debts, and others gambled in order to keep their horses. Every year they would all go the rounds and meet up at Epsom, Ascot, Doncaster, Goodwood, and the other stops on the great social merry-go-round. Other places may have had more glamour, but Newmarket was always the Mecca of the experts, and the Jockey Club was always the focal point. It ensured that the 'enjoying classes' coul ' enjoy the class privilege they had long since lost on the racecourses themselves, for the sport of kings had now become the sport of the people. Thoroughbreds, with family trees going back further than those of their owners, became the entrance ticket for the nouveaux riches to enter the grandstands of the aristocracy. It is said that all men are equal on the racecourse and six feet under, but anyone who wanted to be more equal than others became a member of the Jockey Club. Your average middle-class man had no chance. For instance, Dennis O'Kelly, an 18th-century Irish self-made man. He began his career as a litter-bearer in London, made a fortune through racehorses and betting, married a well-known courtesan, acquired the country house of the Duke of

---

1 Jenison Shafto owned racing stables and was an MP, and he was famous for his bets: in 1759 he bet that he could ride fifty miles in less than two hours. He used ten different horses, and won with 43 seconds to spare. Shafto commissioned George Stubbs to paint Snap (1762–3), the first of Stubbs' portraits of Newmarket winners.

Chandos ... but could never get into the Jockey Club. The nearest he did get was through one of his horses: Eclipse, painted by George Stubbs in about 1770.

'To get into the Jockey Club, you have to be a relative of God's, and a pretty close one at that,' said a modern industrialist on the rejection of his application. 'Until about twenty years ago,' says Mr Fellowes, 'our people were all members of the Establishment, elected by their peers because their fathers were already members, or because they were major landowners, or simply because they were the right people in the right place. In those days, the owner of a chain of shops, for instance, would never have been accepted, but today, well, yes – because they know how to run a business.' And racing, now more than ever, is big business. Thus people like McAlpine, the building contractor, have become 'clubbable', and Freddie Laker of cheap airfare fame, or David Sieff of Marks and Spencer. The hundred members now include whisky distillers, property developers, Philip Oppenheimer, Evelyn de Rothschild, and the Aga Khan. The Dukes of Sutherland and Devonshire are still in the race, as are the multimillionaires, Lord Cadogan, Lord Derby (descendant of the 12th Earl of Derby, who founded the Epsom Derby in 1780), Lord Howard de Walden (owner of three stud-farms), and of course the Duke of Edinburgh and the polo-playing Prince of Wales. Perhaps the Jockey Club is no longer the most exclusive club in England, but it is certainly the richest. This is guaranteed by the presence of such exotic-sounding members as Sheikh Maktoum bin Rashid al Maktoum, and Prince Khalid bin Abdullah. 'The Arabs,' explains Mr Fellowes, 'are the new aristocrats of English racing. They invest enormous sums here.'

Six of the 72 stables and stud farms in Newmarket, and 20 per cent of the horses, belong to Arabs. Here they breed their own Derby winners. When Shahrastani won at Epsom for the Aga Khan in 1986, barely ten per cent of the starters had English owners. It's a pity, reckons Mr Fellowes, but the situation is not hopeless. The Americans may have the best stallions, and the sheikhs may have the most money, but the English have the best grass. Why else would the Sons of the Desert bring the Stars of Kentucky to train at Newmarket? Besides, the Arabs recently donated several hundred thousand pounds to build a new racetrack. 'And if they ever decided to close down their stables in Newmarket, they could hardly take those with them!' The most important of their stables is at Dalham Hall. This is a country house east of the town, built in 1704 for the Bishop of Ely, later owned by Cecil Rhodes, and now the property of Sheikh Mohammed el Maktoum, Defence Minister of Dubai. He and his brother Hamdan not only run the historic racing stables, but have also built a maternity wing for 250 mares. In this monumental wooden edifice, the mares wait for their appointment with Dancing Brave, stallion Number One, the great hope of the thoroughbred world. Successful meetings at Dalham Hall Stud incur cover charges of up to £120,000. In his short racing career, Dancing Brave won something approaching £1 million in prize money. He's a Kentucky stallion, and for about £14 million he came under the ownership of an international syndicate which includes the Maktoum brothers, the Aga Khan, and the billionaire Paul Mellon. The expected yearly capital gain on their shares is about £6 million. In 1987, the star of Dalham Hall fell ill with Marie's Disease, and the nation held its breath. The fall of the dollar could soon be forgotten, but the loss of Dancing Brave would have been a tragedy for ever. Fortunately, he recovered, and is hard at work again.

Mr Fellowes showed me round the Jockey Club. The house was so still that you could almost hear the horsey pictures whinny. It's only at the major race meetings in spring and autumn and at Tattersalls' auctions that all the honourable members assemble here. In the Jockey Club – and this is a very positive distinction between it and most other clubs – you generally won't find portraits of the members, but only of their horses. The Dining Room is an élite gallery for all hippophiles: 'All Derby winners, all owned by our members, and all painted by Adam.' That was Emil Adam, a Bavarian painter at the turn of the century, who found fame and fortune here. In the Jockey Club, one of Eclipse's hooves also found its final resting-place, encased in gold and mounted on a silver plate; it was a gift from William IV. The National Horseracing Museum, right next door, keeps the complete skeleton as if it had belonged to one of the Pharaohs. Eclipse, the wonder stallion, was born during the great eclipse of 1 April 1764, which gave him his name, but he also eclipsed all other horses by his amazing deeds. In the legendary words of the Irish gambler Dennis O'Kelly, prophesying another dazzling victory: 'Eclipse first, the rest nowhere.' He won all his races, usually by about twenty lengths. In due course, O'Kelly bought the horse from the Duke of Cumberland's stud, along with the portrait by George Stubbs, and the undefeated champion proved to be equally indomitable in retirement: eight out of ten thoroughbreds are descended directly from him, including no less than 90 Derby winners. Even the director of the Royal Academy of Veterinarians in London failed to find the secret of this phenomenal success when he dissected the horse of horses after its death in 1789. Eclipse was simply supreme. So, in their day, were Flying Dutchman and Diamond Jubilee, Nijinski and Macaroni, Dante and Blücher, all great Derby winners, like Gainsborough and Pretty Polly, Arctic Prince, Magic Mirror, Never Say Die – the names are poetry, the race is run, the cheers echo down the years, and of those for whom the cheers were loudest there remains a hoof or a tooth, a saddle or a bridle in the reliquaries of Newmarket. My own favourite is the tail of Gladiateur, the Derby winner of 1865: 'his tail was the view enjoyed by the other runners'.

Of course the place is also a Valhalla for jockeys, the 'Giants of the Turf': Frank Buckle, who won five Derbys, Charles Trigg (Hellfire Jack), Elijah Wheatley, known as The Whippet because he was so thin that the wind blew through his ribs. 'Little old men,' Prince Pückler called them, 'as small and weedy as possible, continually reducing themselves as much as they can through artificially induced sweating, purges etc.' Prince Pückler in his better times was himself owner of a stable, and had a jockey from Newmarket 'who among other things won an important bet for me in Vienna'. Jockeys were the idols of the nation, much as footballers are today, but there was one star who outshone them all with his triumphant victories, though it ended tragically. Fred Archer was a myth in a sport of myths. The 1,000 Guineas, the 2,000 Guineas, the Oaks, the Derby, Fred Archer rode from one victory to another. He often rode in more than 600

O. Brower: Frederick Archer, 1878

races a year, and at the peak of his career, he was earning some £10,000 a year. 'Archer's up,' the taxi-drivers would shout in London, and that meant everything was all right. Some months after his fifth Derby win, in 1886, the 29-year-old jockey at his home in Newmarket picked up a revolver which a friend had given to him, engraved with the words 'T. Roughton, Trainer of the good horse Stirling', and shot himself. Fred Archer epitomized the glamour and the misery of the jockey's life. It was often one long starvation diet, and before every race came the nightmare of the weighing room, with a permissible maximum weight of just eight stones. Lester Piggott was once asked what he would do when he retired from racing. His reply was one word: eat.

Lester Piggott is the most famous resident in Newmarket, the shooting star in the firmament of The Turf, the 'Rider of the Century' (*The Observer*). His forebears were jockeys and trainers down through two centuries. At 12 he rode his first race, at 18 he won his first Derby, on the outsider Never Say Die. After 38 years in the saddle, he had won 9 Derbys, 29 English Classics, and 4,389 races on 19,806 horses in 28 different countries.[1]

1 Exceeded only by William Lee Shoemaker, known as 'The Shoe'. Between 1949 and 1979 the American jockey won 7,766 races and some $75 million in prize money.

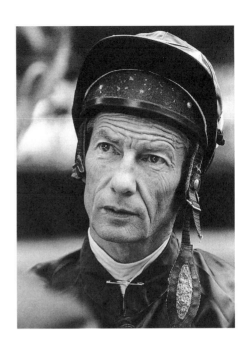

Lester Piggott, 1985

He has ridden with a broken foot, broken ribs, eye problems, a punctured lung, a stitched-up ear, and renal colic. 'You can only win if you always want to win.' Only in the saddle does Lester Piggott truly come to life; otherwise he is shy, taciturn, and totally introverted. You hardly ever see him smile. He's also unusually tall for a jockey – five foot seven. He has always been regarded as a hard, often ruthless rider with an instinctive understanding of his horse and of its chances. The man with the golden whip became a multimillionaire, retired at the age of fifty in 1985, and began a second career as a trainer in Newmarket. Shortly afterwards, however, there was a humiliating reverse: he was found guilty of tax evasion, involving millions of pounds. The national hero and holder of the OBE was sentenced to three years' imprisonment. On his release, he withdrew to his home, Florizel, in Hamilton Road, Newmarket, near his racing stable 'Eve Lodge' – and then proceeded to stun the world by announcing his comeback as a jockey. At the time of writing, he has already expanded his vast list of winners, and injuries.

Every Wednesday and Saturday morning between 6.30 and 7 a.m., everyone goes out on the heath for training. Through inconspicuous town-centre doors that one unsuspectingly passed by the previous day, and out of the great stud farms on the outskirts of the town, and from every angle and every corner they come in their hundreds, the riders and the horses, with red, yellow, blue saddlecloths – the colours of their respective stables – and off they trot in long rows to the 'gallops' on either side of Bury Road. When they've warmed up, they go galloping in little groups over Warren Hill, up the long slope, racing past with thundering hooves, their silhouettes then disappearing over the crest. It's one of the classic sights of the English countryside, unchanged since the days of Old Rowley. 'You've just seen seven and a half million dollars run past you,' says David, an aficionado, pointing to Jareer, the Derby hope of one of the sheikhs. There's big money on Newmarket Heath. One rider sits motionless, scanning the track – 'a trainer on his hack'. His name is Michael Jarvis. David points them all out to me: the ex-champion jockey Doug Smith, the only man ever to win Classics for two British kings; Michael Stoute, trainer of the Aga Khan's Derby winners; the great Henry Cecil, whose stable 'Warren Place' looks after more than 200 horses, and whose best jockey, Steve Cauthen, the Kentucky Kid, is the latest star of Newmarket. The latest star trainer is a former apprentice of Henry Cecil's, Luca Cumani from Milan, who set up on his own and now trains horses for Arab princes and English millionaires at 'Bedford House'.

After two hours on the heath, everyone trots back to the stables for breakfast. Then there's another hour of training, a break for lunch, and two more hours of galloping in the afternoon. 'It's a hard life,' says David. A stable lad, whose job it is to clean out the stables, though he will generally ride the horse as well, earns only three or four hundred pounds a month. In their spare time, these youngsters go to their club, the 'New Astley' in Fred Archer Way, where they can play billiards or snooker, or do some boxing. Some of them keep pigeons. All of them dream of becoming the next Lester Piggott.

There are about 100 trainers working in Newmarket. In the 19th century, the rich Lords of the Turf used to have their own stables, which included a trainer. Now most trainers run stables with a hundred horses or more belonging to different owners. Gavin Pritchard-Gordon, for instance, is a trainer who owns 'Fairhaven' stables, which Lord Derby built in 1902 in Newmarket near his country home Stanley House, where the present Earl of Derby (owner of 18 racehorses) lives when the races are on. Successful trainers nowadays can earn up to £100,000 a year, though that is pin money compared to what the horses cost and what they can win in prize money.

On the edge of Waterhall Gallop, by the road to Bury St Edmunds, stands a little wooden cross with the inscription: 'Joseph the Unknown Gypsy Boy'. In the 19th century, Joseph guarded sheep on Newmarket Heath. One day a sheep escaped, and Joseph killed himself out of fear that he would be punished for stealing it. Since then, fresh flowers always appear on his grave, and no-one knows who puts them there. The story goes – and it has often happened too – that on Derby Day, the winner wears the colours[1] of those flowers that are on the gypsy boy's grave that day. But sometimes the legendary floral oracle gets it wrong. 'This year there was a bunch of lilacs on the grave,' says David, 'but the winner was wearing green and red. The next day, though, there were red carnations and evergreens – Shahrastani's winning colours.'

---

1 There are hundreds of colours or 'silks' registered with the Jockey Club. They have the same importance to the world of racing as tartans have to the clans of Scotland.

Richard Tattersall, 1788,
by an unknown painter

God created the horse, and the English created the racehorse. Newmarket is the living proof. On a visit in October 1826, Prince Pückler wrote to his wife that after breakfast, people went 'to the horse auction which is held by the universally known Mr Tattersall, and which takes place almost every day out in the street, and then they ride or drive to the races.' Tattersalls' December auction is attended by horsey people from all over the world, for Tattersalls is the Sotheby's of the turf. You'll find it on a hill in the centre of town, not far from the Jockey Club and only a few years younger.

Richard Tattersall was the son of a wool merchant from Yorkshire. In 1766 he began to sell horses, coaches and hunting dogs at Hyde Park Corner to gentlemen from the great city. This was the origin of England's first and Europe's biggest auctioneering firm for thoroughbreds (started in the same year, incidentally, as Christie's). With his street trading, Old Tatt made a fortune. His best customer was the Prince Regent, later George IV. On the occasion of the coronation in 1824, the firm showed their respects as well as their advertising acumen by erecting at Hyde Park Corner a fountain in the form of a rotunda with Ionic columns, with the bust of the King at the top, and a fox under the canopy – symbolizing the royal and the national love of hunting. This has remained Tattersalls' emblem right through to the present. The poor old fox, the most persecuted animal in the country, and its eccentric, utterly English monument have accompanied the firm wherever they have gone: in 1865 to Knightsbridge Green, and when the town-planners drove out the horses from there, off they all went to Newmarket in 1939 (plate 56). But Tattersalls

Horse sales at Tattersalls in Newmarket, 1887

had already been holding their auctions outside the Jockey Club in the High Street since the end of the 18th century.

Today the thoroughbreds parade in Park Paddocks, a Neo-Georgian brick arena (1965), surrounded by stables with room for 700 horses. The smell is of big business, in more senses than one.

In a good year like 1984, Tattersalls sold some 3,100 thoroughbreds for a total of 82.6 million guineas (only in the horse world do people still calculate in guineas). Each horse therefore cost an average of about £28,000 – 'top prices for the best British blood'. A gilded Pegasus on the roof of the auction arena shows which way the wind blows. When in 1982 the Greek shipping magnate Stavros Niarchos bought the three-year-old Tenea, he paid what was then a record price of £1.02 million. Of course you can also get bargains at Tattersalls. 'He was cheap at £20,000,' they'll say. And that is cheap if you think, say, of Shergar. The Guinness family's Derby winner and stallion disappeared in 1983 and was never seen again, and with him vanished some £13 million worth of horseflesh. But such astronomical sums are more realistic than the prices paid for art. A Van Gogh is not going to win races or reproduce. Those are the two vital factors in the horse world: victory in the Classics, followed by successful breeding, can net the owners prize money and stud money amounting to many millions. Tattersalls, which remained a family concern until 1942, has sold over 70 winners of the Derby and other Classics in the last 60 years, which is a record they are proud of. Most of the animals they sell, though, are yearlings – between one and two years old, for junior races. There are about 110,000 thoroughbred foals born every year worldwide, with far too many weak horses according to Tattersalls ('overproduction at the bottom end'). Their best customers are the Arab millionaires, but since these are also breeders, they now constitute the main competition to England's flourishing bloodstock industry.

In 1939, the Aga Khan got Tattersalls to sell two of his Derby winners – Bahram and Mahmoud – to America, whereupon there was a national outcry. A member of the Jockey Club had dared to export an exclusive part of the British Heritage. For thoroughbred patriots, this was as dastardly as spying for the KGB. Fortunately there is now a bulwark against the sale of national breeding interests: the National Stud. The basis of this industry is Tattersalls' motto: 'Match the best with the best and hope for the best'.

The National Stud is on the Cambridge road, beyond Devil's Dyke. This Bronze Age earthwork is almost eight miles long and twenty feet high, and it runs across the Heath from Reach to Ditto Green, going right through the racing territory of Newmarket. The Ditch, a natural grandstand, separates the Rowley Mile from the July Course, with its dead straight Bunbury Mile. Even in prehistoric times, according to the Jockey Club, horses were reared in the Newmarket area: the Iceni were renowned for their riding skills, and actually exported horses to Rome. But the English bloodstock industry did not really begin until much later, when three Arabian stallions were imported in the late 17th and early 18th centuries, to be crossed with local mares. The 'Byerley Turk', the 'Darley Arabian' and the 'Godolphin Arabian' are generally regarded as the founding fathers of English thoroughbreds. Indeed all thoroughbreds the world over are descended from these. How do we know? The information comes – more or less definitively – from James Weatherby of Newmarket. In order to ensure the continued purity of this highly success-ful mixed breed, he was commissioned in 1791 by the Jockey Club to keep a precise record of official and even unofficial breeding in the stables. His *Stud Book*, the Bible of British thoroughbred enthusiasts, is still published today by the Weatherby family. Of course, despite all the systems of the breeders and the efforts of the trainers and jockeys, the horses still go on doing the unexpected – much to the despair or delight of the punters. In this risky, ridiculous but eternally fascinating mix of sport and genetics, Newmarket's National Stud represents the most ambitious and perhaps even the most likely step towards producing the perfect horse, the born winner of the Derby.

Everything is on a large scale here, clinically clean and as quiet as a rest home. Gone are the military beginnings of the National Stud, which was set up during the First World War in Ireland (1916) to breed horses for the cavalry. It moved to new stables in Newmarket in 1967, on land which also belonged to the Jockey Club – 500 acres of it. Those who graze on this hallowed grass are destined for higher things. Final Straw, Star Appeal, Royal Palace: they are the elite of the thoroughbred world. 'These are the Duchess of Norfolk's mares,' says my companion, 'and those are guests from the Schlenderhahn stud.' Names are put together here with even more care than those of a dating agency. As for prices, to have your mare covered here will cost you about £80 a week for lodgings, and you must reckon on ten weeks, plus a stud fee of up to £12,000 down from £70,000 before the recession. There's room in the stables for about 140 mares. The Queen also has her horses covered here, in the hope that one day she'll get a Derby winner. At present there are six stallions hard at it in the National Stud, 'for the British bloodstock industry'. The nation's stallions do not, however, belong to the nation or to any individual, but to international syndicates of various owners. Each stallion has its family tree emblazoned on its stable door in gold lettering. I greeted Royal Palace, Derby winner of 1967, 'who's retired now. So we give him six mares a year just to keep him happy.'

When Royal Palace died, he was laid to rest next to Tudor Melody, in the National Stud's own graveyard. Never Say Die, on which Lester Piggott began his career, is also here, as is the unforgettable Mill Reef, equally successful as stud and as Derby winner (one of his descendants is the 1987 Derby winner Reference Point, a star of Henry Cecil's stable and valued at around £15 million). Mill Reef's bronze statue stands on the main path through the National Stud. He belonged to the American billionaire and arts patron Paul Mellon, who founded the Center for British Art at Yale. A collector of great discernment, it was he more than anyone, with his purchases, that helped to bring about a reassessment of an artist who found some of his finest subjects in Newmarket: George Stubbs.

Sometimes just one picture captures the entire spirit of a place and the history of a passion. Such a picture is the Jockey Club's 'Gimcrack'. Stubbs painted it around 1765. It's an everyday scene on Newmarket Heath: horses and riders galloping in the background; in the foreground a grey has just finished running, and is being held by its trainer, while the jockey stands nearby, and a stable lad kneels on the ground drying the sweating horse with straw. 'Rubbing down', this work is called, and it is done outside the rubbing-down house, which is made of brick. Everyone is depicted in profile. The horse stands with its coat shimmering like silk, the head and neck long and narrow, tensed like a bow to launch the arrow-swift body, whose power seems enhanced by its motionlessness and by the parallelogram framework of house and roof. There is immense subtlety in the geometrical lines, the figures and the gaps, and the whole composition is beautifully balanced. The relationship between man and beast is a piece of sublime observation: the network of looks and gestures, the natural distance and social gulf between trainer, jockey and stable lad, the three acting as a frame for the horse. Stubbs painted them all both realistically and sympathetically in muted ochre tones against the cool, light blue sky of Newmarket Heath. It's a piece of everyday racing life, but also an historic chapter of turf history, and the portrait of a winner. For Stubbs was not portraying any old horse. This was Gimcrack, a superstar of his time; and this was not any old race, but that of 10 July 1765, Gimcrack's spectacular victory for the 3rd Viscount Bolingbroke. He owned the horse, and he commissioned the picture, as one of Stubbs' early patrons. Seldom has a victory been celebrated in a more succinct or more matter-of-fact manner than in this painting.

George Stubbs: Gimcrack on Newmarket Heath with a Trainer, Jockey and a Stable Lad, c.1765

Gimcrack's victory won the Viscount a bet of 1,000 guineas and earned the bookmakers well over ten times that amount. It was the event of the season. Among the spectators at Newmarket that day was Lady Sarah Bunbury, full of admiration for Gimcrack, 'the sweetest little horse that ever was'. And she added, 'I was more anxious about the horse than the ministry' – a reference to the fact that on the same day her husband had lost his ministerial post. Three years later, Sir Charles Bunbury, President of the Jockey Club, bought the sweetest little horse himself. But his love of horses was to ruin his marriage, for Lady Sarah, daughter of the Duke of Richmond, was bored to death in far-off East Anglia, Gimcrack notwithstanding. The latter passed into the hands of the 1st Earl of Grosvenor (such horses can collect a whole catalogue of illustrious names), one of the richest men in England and a notorious horse fanatic. On 17 March 1761, Horace Walpole reports that Sir Richard Grosvenor has just been made 'a Viscount or a Baron, I don't know which, nor does he, for yesterday when he should have kissed hands, he was gone to Newmarket to see the trial of a race horse.' Next to horses, the new peer's great love was the fine arts, and in particular, of course, the paintings of George Stubbs. Grosvenor had at least eleven of his pictures, including a second version of 'Gimcrack', which today hangs in the Jockey Club. The continued popularity of the horse, incidentally, is shown by the fact that there is still a Gimcrack Club in New York.

The patrons of George Stubbs were the Lords of the Turf. They organized the great race and hunt meetings, and they determined the cultural life of the country estates. They had their wives painted by Gainsborough and Reynolds, and their horses by Stubbs. No-one portrayed them more accurately or more vividly than did the tanner's son from Liverpool.

But his realism went far beyond mere representation. Instead of the works of Antiquity, Stubbs studied anatomy, on a remote farm in Lincolnshire. He bought dead horses from local farmers, hung them from a beam, dissected them and drew them, layer by layer: skin, sinews, muscles, bones. And he varied the gait of his dead models, fixing them in a step, or at a trot, so that he could capture every aspect of their pose and their movement. The bodies hung there for six or seven weeks, while Stubbs made his drawings amid the sickly smell of decay. It was lonely and nauseating work. His only assistant was his wife, Mary Spencer. For a year and a half Stubbs lived with his dead horses. By then he knew them quite literally inside out, right down to their tiniest bones. This was his Academy, the bloody prelude to the apotheosis of the horse.

'Mr Stubbs, Painter of Horses' set himself up in London in 1758. His etchings 'Anatomy of the Horse' made his name known all over England, and there were plenty of commissions – ranging from William Wildman, a London slaughterer and cattle-dealer, to the Prince of Wales, later George IV, who got Stubbs to paint his new carriage and pair complete with coachman and horses. His hunting and horse pictures are part of a traditional, typically English genre of sporting art. Some of its early 18th-century pioneers can be seen in the National Horseracing Museum. A racing centre such as this was as attractive to painters as it was to bookmakers, for here they could find their best models

George Stubbs: Self-Portrait, 1781

and their richest patrons. Together with the self-taught James Seymour, a racing connoisseur and gambler, John Wootton ran a flourishing studio for horse pictures in Newmarket. His friend Peter Tillemans from Antwerp also worked here for a time, as did John Nost Sartorius from Nuremberg[1] and John Frederick Herring, who rose from being a coachman to being one of the most popular painters of horses in the 18th century. But it was George Stubbs who gave a new dimension to this otherwise rather dry and conventional subject matter.

'Thy pencil, Stubbs, no rival need to fear; / Not mimic art, but life itself is here.' So wrote Horace Walpole, who was otherwise seldom moved to verse. Stubbs painted with a precision and intensity never seen before. Together with the anatomical accuracy goes the absolute autonomy of the horse, which entails a revolutionary change of role: now the horse is more important than the rider, who becomes a marginal figure allowed only to hold the reins; man may sit on the horse, but he is no longer the crown of creation – that status belongs to the horse. Of course the high-born patrons of the artist did not see themselves as being in any way dethroned by such pictures; on the contrary, they felt ennobled, for the magnificent creatures that Stubbs had painted were, after all, products of their breeding and of their galloping capital investments, made glorious by art, and presented as the very embodiment of the cultured country life and the harmony between Man, Nature and Society. This, in the words of Robert Hughes, was 'Order on four legs'.

'Dukes, Lords, stable lads, rogues all shout at the same time and make bets with each other,' wrote Prince Pückler in October 1826, describing the betting post at Newmarket. In Stubbs' paintings, the noise of course is stilled, just as the moving horse is frozen. There is no crowd, and there are no tales being told. Instead there is an almost surreal peace and harmony. The statuesque effect of the horses is enhanced by what appears to be merely a topographical detail: the rubbing-down houses. These brick buildings stand there like monuments, a realistic component of the racehorse's working day, but also a symbol, the temple of the cult of the horse. There used to be four of these houses on Newmarket Heath, but now there is only one on the edge of the July Course, used as a toolshed, and a landmark on the horizon. In the 1930's, another great horse painter, Sir Alfred Munnings, used it as a studio.

In George Stubbs' last grandiose picture of Newmarket: 'Hambletonian, Rubbing Down', the brick houses mark both the setting and the rhythm of the painting. Measuring nearly twelve foot by eighteen, it is his largest and, in terms of expression, his most radical work. The whole width of the picture is taken up with Hambletonian, seen from the side with his flanks heaving, his ears pinned back, his mouth foaming as he pants. This is an

---

1   The Sartorius family, which emigrated c.1770 from Nuremberg to England, produced three generations of British painters of hunting scenes and horses.

George Stubbs: Studies for 'The Anatomy of the Horse', 1766

exhausted, not a triumphant winner. The picture is monumental, and is unprecedented in its realism. It was commissioned by the 28-year-old baronet, Sir Henry Vane-Tempest, who then rejected it. The artist, 75 at that time, had to go to court to get his fee. Stubbs had painted not the glorious victory of the owner, but his own sympathy with a horse, and the reality after a race over more than four miles, which Hambletonian had won by half a neck thanks to the brutal goadings of spurs and lashes, shocking even in those times.[1] This was on 25 March 1799 – the race of the century, which brought the owner a prize of 3,000 guineas, and the artist a fee of 300 guineas.[2] A farm labourer's wage then was about five guineas a year. Stubbs left the anatomizing of society to Hogarth, though his own

1   The yearly trotting race in Goshen, New York, is named *Hambletonian* in commemoration of this horse.
2   Stubbs' pictures of horses are now hot favourites on the art market. His *Baron de Robeck Riding a Bay Cob* was auctioned at Sotheby's, New York, in 1987, and fetched a record price of $2.2 million.

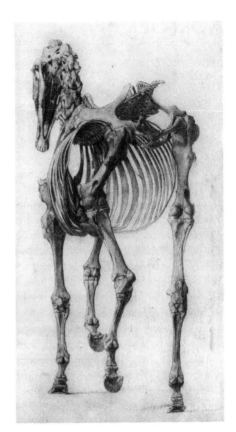

observation of people as vivid but always marginal figures, remained sensitive and incorruptible.

Stubbs was highly respected as a painter of horses, lordly dogs, and all sorts of exotic animals. But he never attained the wealth or the honours heaped upon Gainsborough. By comparison with portraits and historical scenes, Stubbs' animal paintings – for all their brilliance – were regarded as an inferior genre. In his old age, he was again seized by his earlier passion: dissecting and drawing. He died in 1806, aged 81, working on 'A Comparative Anatomical Exposition of the Structure of the Human Body with that of a Tiger and a Common Fowl'. His meagre estate included one white Persian cat.

NORFOLK

Norfolk? Oh, flat Norfolk
(Noël Coward)

In the thirties the whole of London was laughing at Sir Noël Coward's little platitude. Norfolk, they say, is so flat that on a clear day you can see the domes of St Petersburg. I must admit, I went right across the county, and it wasn't till I got to Cromer on the coast that I saw the first hills that you could really call hills – moraines left over from the Ice Age. And if you go to the top of the few hills that there are, you'll see all the more clearly just how flat the country is. Between the Fens[1] and the Wash on one side, and the Broads and the North Sea on the other, Norfolk just about manages to keep its head above water. The splashing of the Bure that Sir John Betjeman heard from his cabin at night was the basic melody of this Waterland: 'A whispering and watery Norfolk sound / Telling of all the moonlit reeds around.'

Fifty to sixty years is the life expectancy of roofs thatched with Norfolk reed, the toughest in the land. Even more typical are the walls, houses and churches built out of hard and gleaming flint.[2] This is flint country, and as clear and cold as the stone is the flinty light of the coast. Cotman, Crome and the artists of the Norwich School all painted this light, on their unsentimental journeys through a landscape that is anything but picturesque. Norfolk is rougher and cooler than Suffolk. While the latter envelops us in the atmosphere of its medieval clothiers' villages, here we feel the earlier spirit of the Saxons and the Normans. England's most easterly county is far beyond the Central Heating Belt of London.

Norfolk, say the locals, 'is cut off on three sides by the sea and on the fourth by British Rail.' The railway does in fact only go as far as King's Lynn in the northwest, and Cromer in the northeast. In between, throughout the whole central area of the county, you can only walk along the disused tracks, and dream of steam engines. Especially inland, Norfolk has remained as remote and untouched as Suffolk used to be before the war.

To get to Mannington Hall, you have to go along narrow, winding country lanes. When eventually I arrived at Lord Walpole's country house, the owner diplomatically agreed that the main roads really ought to be improved, but on the other hand he thought the minor

---

1 The major part of the Fens lies in Cambridgeshire, which I will be covering in another book.
2 Apart from flint, the only local stone used for building in Norfolk is carstone, a chalky sandstone also called gingerbread stone on account of its golden-brown, rust-red colour. It is often found in the northwest of the county, in the villages around Snettisham, where it is cut.

roads were 'delightfully inadequate – long may they stay that way!' Clearly they have been specially designed to protect the holy British right of privacy, although even Lord Walpole – a descendant of the first British Prime Minister – does confess to occasionally feeling a little cut off from the world.

Norfolk's centuries of isolation have had their effect on the character of the local people: they are proudly independent even to the point of rebelliousness, as personified by Queen Boadicea, the Warrior Queen of the Iceni, and the Kett brothers who led the last English peasants' rising. 'Norfolk do different,' they say in these parts. The pronunciation of some of the placenames, for instance, can be a problem to English folk from elsewhere: you have to be different to pronounce Costessey 'Cossy', or Hunstanton 'Hanstn', or Wymondham 'Windem', or Happisburgh 'Haysbrr'. What's more, these people are even more taciturn than their Suffolk neighbours, to the point where 'they may occasionally appear unfriendly' (Lord Walpole). 'Norfolk Dumplings' some people call them. It's very much Tory country, even though it's Nonconformist, but it's the Toryism of a rural, feudal heritage and not of a monetarist philosophy.

Norfolk beyond Yarmouth consists of lonely shores, even in the high season, with miles and miles of uninhabited marshland. There are churches without villages, and villages quiet as churchyards. Of the 44 counties in England, Norfolk is the fourth largest in area, and 23rd in terms of population. In the Middle Ages it was the most densely populated county of them all. At the time of the Domesday survey, 1086, it had 125,000 inhabitants (the same as the county town of Norwich today). Of the 726 settlements listed by the Domesday Book, 130 have disappeared altogether. It was not just the plague that thinned the population. Daniel Defoe, on his travels around England, noted that no other county could boast of three towns 'so populous, so rich, and so famous for trade and navigation' – namely, Norwich, Yarmouth and King's Lynn. That was in 1723, before the decline of coastal trade, and long before the great agricultural depression.

In the Middle Ages, Norfolk was wool country. Thousands of sheep grazed in the north of the county and in the Brecklands, to the southwest. From Norfolk came the wool that made the weavers and clothiers of Suffolk so rich. Norfolk also produced outstanding agrarian reformers like the Cokes, the Townshends and the Walpoles, who wrested extraordinary yields from their sandy soil. Holkham, Raynham and Houghton estates were centres of agricultural progress during the 18th century. It is still 'the greatest barley county in the kingdom' (Arthur Young), and it also has the biggest fields of sugar beet. But the great rural revolution has long since disinherited its children.

At the time of my last visit, the unemployment rate in the north of the county was 14 per cent, far above the regional and national average. 'Very alarming,' said Lord Walpole, 'but if the estates are to survive, they have to cut down their work force.' At Mannington Hall alone, almost three-quarters of the staff have gone in the last 25 years. 'Tourism helps, but it's not the solution. We need more light industry to fit in with the region: food factories, breweries, potato crisps.' The former centres of agricultural progress have now become a Rural Development Area, which means state-subsidized development of land.

In the mid-sixties, huge reserves of natural gas were discovered off the Norfolk coast. Since then, the gas has been transported through pipelines to the refineries at Bacton, a flint village north of the Broads. And as far as industry is concerned, that's all there is. Motor-racing fans might take note of the name Hethel, a village near Norwich, which is the home of Britain's most successful racing-drivers' stable (Stirling Moss, Jim Clark and others) as well as being the production site of Lotus International, the sports car firm founded by a former Grand Prix driver Colin Chapman. Chapman joined the landed classes when he built himself East Carleton Manor, though he chose the colonial mansion of the Deep South as a model. The house was designed by James Fletcher-Watson, the Lutyens admirer who also built two Neo-Georgian brick houses in Norfolk: Watlington Hall (1965) and the Bishop's Palace in Norwich (1959). Chapman's is one of the very few new country houses in the county, but this is modernity looking backwards.

When the Queen needs a break from the stresses of London court life, she goes to see her horses at Sandringham (plate 22). Having only bought the estate in 1861, the Royal Family must be regarded as mere newcomers to Norfolk. The Cokes and Walpoles, Townshends and Fountaines are the real 'landed families' here, and have lived on their estates for centuries. Holkham and Houghton, the most splendid of them all, are still lived in and managed by the families who built them (plates 3 and 8). Just how proud they are of their heritage, and how hard they work for it, was made clear to me again and again on my travels. It was the same at Heydon Hall (plate 12). 'Norfolk is a man-made landscape,' declared the owner, William Bulwer Long. 'As a landowner one has the good fortune actually to create the landscape which the painters of the Norwich School could only paint. It's a huge privilege.'

In the 16th century, there were more than 600 Lords of the Manor in Norfolk. Even today, Burke and Savill's *Guide to Country Houses* still lists 462 large and small estates here, most of them private. Among the architectural treasures that *are* open to the public, however, are the churches. There are churches in the marshlands between King's Lynn and Wisbech that hardly anyone knows about, bathed in a medieval glow.[1] There are countless churches in the villages, over 50 of them thatched (more than anywhere else in England), where you'll find a Norman font,[2] or a Gothic screen,[3] or monumental brasses.[4] And then there's Norwich, the Cathedral city with a wealth of old parish churches. The indefatigable Pevsner listed over 50 monasteries and over 650 churches from before 1830. Again, that's more than in any other county. And that is why Sir Nikolaus, in his survey of the *Buildings of England*, needed two volumes for Norfolk alone ('the biggest county job I have had to do').

---

1 For example, Terrington St Clement, Walpole St Peter, Walsoken, West Walton (see page 532f).

2 For example, Burnham Deepdale, Castle Rising, Fincham, South Wootton.

3 The finest are in Ranworth and Attleborough, filigree tracery with painted wooden panels.

4 Impressive examples in Elsing, King's Lynn and Walsoken.

John C. Joy: Ship's crew rescued at Gorleston

It's a county of churches, and a county of windmills: post mills, tower mills, brick mills, weatherboard mills, grain mills, drainage mills – nowhere (except in Holland) will you find so many, and nowhere will you find such weatherbeaten solidity as in this windy county. And nowhere does the beer stream more heroically from the taps than it does in the Nelson pubs around Burnham Thorpe (plate 48). No Norfolk, no Nelson; and no Nelson, no British mastery of the seas. The heroic Horatio, victor of Trafalgar, was the son of a Norfolk clergyman. What a coast this is, with its salt marshes and lavender, its channels, dunes, bays and crumbling Ice Age cliffs, lonelier and wilder than its Suffolk neighbour, Arctic, melancholic, beautiful, treacherous, with sandbanks and quicksands, storms and floods, and never-ending erosion. This is a coast, warned Defoe, 'which is particularly famous for being one of the most dangerous and most fatal to the sailors in all England.' I love this coast. I'm not a sailor, and I'm not even an ornithologist,[1] but if I were, I'd love this coast still more, if that's possible.

1   The Holme Bird Observatory, which is the information centre for Norfolk's north coast, has recorded over 280 different types of bird here.

Horatio, Viscount Nelson, by William Beechey, 1801

NORFOLK DUMPLINGS or ~~his~~ G̲R̲A̲C̲E̲ before MEAT.

George Cruikshank: Caricature of the Duke of Norfolk, a notorious Regency roué

The Wash is the broad, shallow bay between Norfolk and Lincolnshire. At low tide it's a docile lake, but in a north or northeasterly gale it's a raging sea. Four rivers flow into the Wash: the Ouse, the Nene, the Welland and the Witham, but what they flow into is constantly changing. As for the treacherous sands, their natures are reflected in their names: Pandora, Thief, and Bull Dog Sand. Once upon a time you could often see horse-and-cart-fishermen going out at low tide and collecting mussels, but now they're a comparatively rare sight. Around the Wash the isolation stretches for fifty miles – the longest uncultivated coast in England. There are more than 160,000 wading birds and 51,000 wild duck living in these internationally recognized wetlands, which were declared a National Nature Reserve in early 1993.

'Oh! rare and beautiful Norfolk,' enthused John Sell Cotman, journeying with his paint brushes around his native county. The coast, the pictures, and the scents of Norfolk reign supreme. To the west, the lavender fields of Heacham; to the east, the bloaters of Great Yarmouth. Middle class beaches here, the Queen's country home there. And I'll bet the Windsors have Yarmouth bloaters for their breakfast.

Norwich: Provincial Queen

For years I bought my tea from Mr Wilkinson in *Norwich*.[1] His shop used to be a beer tavern; it was an old house in Magdalen Street, narrow and sweet-scented with aromas from Assam, Sikkim, Yunnar and countless other exotic places. Mr W., as his colleagues called him, had about 150 different sorts of tea, all packed in large wooden containers with handwritten labels. Whenever I went in, he'd open up dozens of boxes for me, let me look and smell, hold out a handful of rich leaves, rub them gently together between his fingers, breathe on them, and with half-open hand invite me to fill my nostrils with the heavenly perfume. Always in an apron and a tie, Mr W. was a 20th-century Victorian merchant, dispensing the ultimate, priceless fragrances of the lost Empire. He died last year, and his shop has moved to Lobster Lane: but it is typical of Norwich that nothing much will change. People here value good things in life too much to throw away Mr W.'s hard work. 'Modern' may not be a dirty word in Norwich, but nor is 'old-fashioned'.

In the mid-eighties, a new generation set itself up in the middle of old Norwich. They were the young bankers, computer designers, hi-tech entrepreneurs, and media people, the smart and the successful whom Malcolm Bradbury christened 'Mrs Thatcher's children'. You might meet them in 'The Last Wine Bar', for instance, a restored Edwardian shoe factory, downtown in Merchant's Court. As in Cambridge, the enterprise-culture upswing of the Thatcher years found fertile ground in Norwich: a university city without the ruins of the Industrial Revolution, and without the traumas of a decaying inner city. This is a place with the unaltered charms of an age-old provincialism.

'Norwich has the most Dickensian atmosphere of any city I know,' wrote J. B. Priestley in his *English Journey*, 1933: 'What a grand, higgledy-piggledy, sensible old place Norwich is!' This, however, is not just a provincial city; this is the old capital of the whole of East Anglia. Priestley sensed that something had got lost in Norwich, and the loss was a general one as applicable now as it was then: '... government in this country is now far too centralized.' Priestley ends his declaration of love with a half-serious, half-ironic cry: 'Home Rule for East Anglia!'

Norwich has about 126,000 inhabitants. It's no longer a small city, but it's not a large city either; it's a bit of both, and it's more than both – a happy kind of mini-metropolis. In an EC league table of the 'most habitable' cities of Europe, Norwich was the top British town, ahead of far more famous and prestigious ones like Bath and York. It has one of the oldest cathedrals in the country, and one of the youngest universities. On my last visit, it had a Labour controlled City Council in the middle of an overwhelmingly Conservative county. Norwich produced some of the finest English landscape painters of the 19th century, and the pioneers of wire netting. Colman's Mustard comes from Norwich, and so did England's most passionate mystic Julian of Norwich. You can't help admiring a city where the practical and the poetic are held in equal esteem, and which takes in the ideas of

1 For city plan, see inside back cover.

John Thirtle: View of Norwich from Mousehold Heath

the radicals as readily as it accepts the beet from the fields. When, in the 17th and 18th centuries, religious refugees fled in large numbers first from Holland, then from France, Norwich showed everyone just how such refugee problems should be solved: through a policy of open doors and active integration. Of course even then, the process was not without strife or injury, but it succeeded, and in the end, everybody gained – the locals as well as the newcomers.

'A fine old city, truly, is that, view it from whatever side you will.' And what is still the finest of the fine views of Norwich is described by George Borrow in his autobiographical novel *Lavengro* (1851): the view from St James's Hill on Mousehold Heath, northeast of the city (though the heath is no longer a heath). 'Yes, there it spreads from north to south, with its venerable houses, its numerous gardens, its thrice twelve churches, its mighty mound. which, if tradition speaks true, was raised by human hands to serve as a grave-heap of an old heathen king, who sits deep within it, with his sword in his hand, and his gold and silver treasures about him.'

The roads from Norwich form a star as they reach out towards southern and central England; those to the north and east soon come to a halt at the coast. That's something the writer Malcolm Bradbury loves especially about Norwich – the fact 'that there is almost no way to go from here except to London one way and to Amsterdam the other way. So imaginatively this place encourages a kind of solitude and separatism of mind and spirit; I find it attractive.' It takes one and three-quarter hours by train to London, and just one hour by plane to Amsterdam.

The first known mention of the name Northwic is on a silver penny, minted between 920 and 940 during the reign of King Aethelstan I. Even when the Vikings were masters of East Anglia, Norwich, the settlement (*vicus*) in the north, controlled the bridgehead on the River Wensum, which was navigable up to that point above its confluence with the Yare.

Robert Dixon: Back of Magdalen Gates, Norwich, 1809

It was an ideal inland port and trading centre. At the market near Tombland, the Anglo-Saxons used to buy their luxury articles: furs from Russia and Scandinavia, fine woollens from Flanders, pottery from France. This flourishing settlement in the bend of the Wensum formed the nucleus of the Norman diocese.

With some 5,500 inhabitants, 21 churches, and 43 chapels Norwich was listed in the Domesday Book of 1086 as the third biggest city in England, after London and York. The Castle and the Cathedral, the Norman centres of power, still mould the image of the city (colour plate 23, plates 58, 62). In spring *Castle Hill* is yellow with daffodils, and certainly this is one of the most impressive of all medieval escarpments, built shortly after 1066 on an already existing hill. Not until a century later, though, was the stone castle constructed, not much smaller than the White Tower in London, and also a hall-keep as opposed to just a tower-keep. Although it is only 70 feet high, it makes up for that in width, being 95 by 90 feet across. What sets Norwich Castle apart from all other Norman fortresses is the richness of its façade: there are blind arcades all round, between three and four rows of them one above the other, of different heights and widths, interspersed with flat, pilaster-style buttresses. One can't help asking what a military fortress is doing with all this decorative finery. Could it all be sham – a piece of 19th-century theatre? Well, in actual fact the architect Anthony Salvin, the Victorians' great expert on castles and fortresses, did restore Norwich Castle between 1833 and 1839 (just as he restored the Tower and Windsor Castle), and he reconstructed the façade almost totally – but he remained faithful to the original designs; the only deception is the materials he used: the flint walls had been clad in Caen stone, but Salvin dressed them up in Bath stone – rather too elegant for such a military establishment.

Of the original interior nothing remains. There were two halls on the main floor, with passages and stairs running through the thickness of the wall. The castle lost its military importance early on in its life, and from the 14th to the late 19th century served as the county's prison. Since 1889 it has been a museum. It's thanks to this continuous use that it has remained in such an excellent state of preservation. Kings have been welcomed here, and rebellious peasants imprisoned and hanged at public executions which took place until 1867 at the lower end of the medieval bridge leading to the outer courtyard. It was there that for centuries the city's horse and cattle market was held, which since 1960 has been at Harford Bridges, on the southern outskirts of Norwich. For a while now it's cars that lay siege to the castle, but there is to be a park and shopping centre, with the cars banished underground.

Norwich Castle is one of the liveliest provincial museums I have ever come across. In the cellars you'll find death masks of executed murderers, and in the galleries are the most delicate watercolours by Cotman and his friends – but let's not go to the museum yet (see page 386 ff.). Between it and the Cathedral, beating just as it has done since Norman times, is the very heart of the city: the *Market*. From Castle Street you get to it via a passage called the Royal Arcade, full of Art Nouveau motifs and designed at the beginning of this century by George Skipper, a local architect (plate 63). The market itself is as bright and bustling as a beach in the peak season. The red, blue, green and yellow awnings of the stalls cover the whole square like a single, giant tent, and there is nothing you can't buy here: goat's cheese, wellington boots, second-hand books, hot dogs, pink slippers, sea fish, game from the great estates, fruit and vegetables from the Fens and marshes. A hundred scents mingle in the air, and bodies swarm over the square like bees over a honeycomb. For nearly 900 years, farmers and dealers have been bringing their wares to this market, and with over 200 stalls it is both the oldest and the biggest in England. It's everything a market should be, with the Norman castle towering over one side, the modern City Hall on the other, and all around are Georgian houses, together with the parish church and the medieval Guildhall.

King George VI opened the *City Hall*, a spare, Nordic building of greyish red brick, based on the Stockholm City Hall, with a tall tower and the monumental beauty of (I'm sorry to say) a public convenience. This is where the city regalia are kept – the rich trophies, silver dishes and insignia, together with portraits of the (so far) 530 mayors. Until 1938, the City Council used to meet beneath the Tudor beams of the neighbouring *Guildhall* (1407–13), which had successively or simultaneously served as lawcourt, prison,

John Sell Cotman: Norwich Castle, c.1808–9

centre of the cloth trade, and municipal library; today it is a tourist office. The wall of the east gable is magnificent, with its flushwork diamond patterns of flint and stone – a 16th-century harlequinade.

In the old days, people who went to market also went to the market church, *St Peter Mancroft*. Its splendid Perpendicular tower bore witness both to the blessing of God and to the blessings of commerce. Norwich has many churches, but none finer than this. Built in 1430–55, it creates a space that is full of light and Gothic clarity; there is no choir screen or arch to separate the nave from the chancel, and so the view and the light remain unbroken. The light comes from the large windows in the side aisles, the 34 windows in the clearstory, and especially from the magnificent east window, which fills the whole end wall with the colourful glow of the mysteries. It was local stained-glass painters who created this radiant pictorial Bible, with scenes from the life of Jesus, the Passion, the life of the Virgin, and legends of the saints. Above the high Gothic arcades stretches a glorious hammer-beam roof, covered by wooden fan vaulting whose piers rest on the heads of kings and prophets. Angels flank the roof, and Tudor roses bloom among the timbers. St Peter Mancroft, which is still the principal parish church in the city, has a valuable collection of Elizabethan church silver, a tapestry of 1573 – probably the work of Flemish weavers in Norwich – and a seven-sacraments font of 1463 with a wooden canopy, one of the few Gothic ones to survive. On the wall of the baptistry hangs the charter of the Norwich

John Sell Cotman: Norwich Market Place, c.1806

bellringers (1716), an icon of campanology. To play the thirteen bells of Mancroft just once in a Gransir Bob Triples – that is the dream of every marathon bell-ringer in England (see page 30 ff.).

Buried in St Peter Mancroft is a man whom Charles II knighted during his visit to Norwich in 1671. His name was Sir Thomas Browne. He was a humble doctor with a European-wide reputation, a contemporary of Milton and of Harvey, a believer in science and a believer in miracles, a man of paradox: a Baroque man, in fact. The world is 'not an Inn, but an Hospital; and a place not to live, but to dy in', he said in his *Religio Medici* (1642), a masterpiece of religious tolerance. In the square next to the church there is a lifesize bronze of him, seated with his Van Dyck beard and in his knightly garb, in the mood and attitude of a melancholic. He clasps a broken urn in his hand, the motif of his famous book *Urne-Buriall* (1658). Inspired by the discovery of some burial urns in Walsingham, he wrote an extraordinary meditation on death and eternity, the metaphorical and rhetorical power of which made John Cowper Powys call him 'the greatest of all our stylists'. Browne grew his medicinal herbs in the garden of his house, which was on the Haymarket. He also wrote a book on gardening and an essay on the quincunx; flowers with five leaves, mistletoe, artichokes, hands and feet – everywhere he saw the magic five at work, the quintessence of all things living. He would certainly have welcomed the five-day week as the pinnacle of modern civilization, not to mention Chanel No. 5. And so the brick pentagram set in the plaster next to the church has less to do with warding off witches than with the memory of Sir Thomas Browne.

St Peter Mancroft used to be the actor's church. Not far away stands the *Theatre Royal*, founded in 1757, and rebuilt after a fire in 1935. David Garrick and Fanny Kemble trod the boards here, as did Charles and Edmund Kean, all stars of the London stage. Today, even though it does not have its own company, the Theatre Royal is one of England's most successful provincial theatres. The very best companies perform here, and many West End hits are first previewed in Norwich.

Nearby, the modest brick façade of the *Assembly House* once concealed Norwich's high life. This is where the city's top brass and the county's landed gentry held their balls and banquets and beanfeasts, or delicately sipped their tea in Georgian salons whose elegance could be matched only in Bath. In October 1805, some 400 bejewelled guests danced the minuet here to celebrate victory at Trafalgar. Recitals were given here, too, by Liszt and Mozart's pupil Hummel, among others. The Assembly House was built in 1754 by Thomas Ivory, a local carpenter and architect, and it is a masterpiece from the days of a highly social High Society. Whenever I go to Norwich, I always return to this pinnacle of good taste. Today the former ballroom is the setting for concerts, lectures and exhibitions, while the banqueting hall houses the most stylish self-service restaurant in the whole city.

Even in the days when progress came at coach-and-horses speed, back in Georgian times, Norwich already had traffic problems. Since there were no conservationists, however, the solutions were not too difficult to find. Between 1791 and 1801, all the medieval city gates were removed, to make way for the traffic. And the walls of the city also crumbled away. The best preserved parts are to be seen at the end of *King Street*, near Carrow Bridge in the south of the city, where the wall runs from the Boom Towers uphill to the Black Tower. But much more impressive than these ruins are the actual dimensions of the city walls. If you follow the ring road, which itself follows the line of the old moat, you'll get some idea of the size of the medieval walled town. The walls built c.1297–1334, were well over two miles long, and enclosed an area as big as the City of London.

Norwich's economy flourished during the Middle Ages, thanks to its weavers and its cloth merchants. *St John Maddermarket*[1] was where the weavers bought their vegetable dyes, particularly the red dye derived from the madder root. On his visit in 1723, Daniel Defoe wrote that on a weekday the town seemed dead, presumably because everyone was sitting at their looms. He estimated that some 120,000 people in and around Norwich were working at home for the wool and silk industry, and that the merchants themselves owned upwards of one thousand ships. They exported their worsted to Russia, India, China, and the American colonies. In those days, textiles were England's main export, and Norwich was the second biggest city in the kingdom, after London.

---

1 On the corner of Pottergate Street is the Maddermarket Theatre, home of the Norwich Players, an amateur society founded in 1911. They have a professional director, and perform in a converted Catholic chapel of 1794.

John Thirtle: Devil's Tower near King Street Gates – Evening, c.1809

Only when the Industrial Revolution began did Norwich lose its key position. The worsted weavers, who had organized themselves into an efficient union, fought long and hard against the introduction of mechanical looms, but after 1833 the competition from the big factories in the north of England proved to be overwhelming. For a while, they turned to silk-weaving, but then that too went under, thanks to French imports that were more fashionable and were made from the cheaper Manchester silk. Only the attractive Norwich shawl, of silk and cotton in elaborate designs and glowing colours, managed to defy the competition in the art of draping Victorian ladies' shoulders. By 1900 there were no more worsted weavers in Norwich, and a great tradition had come to an end.

A hill with a slight bend in it, cobblestones, pastel-coloured fronts, timber-framed houses with pointed gables: that is *Elm Hill*, which is as narrow a lane as you'll find in Norwich (plate 65). It's a short street with a long history. In the late medieval heyday of the weavers' city, rich merchants used to live in the fronts of the houses, and down in the direction of the river they had their warehouses and workshops. In their back-yards were the cramped quarters of the workers. Many of the mayors of Norwich also lived in Elm

John Sell Cotman: Interior of St Peter Hungate Church, Norwich, 1810

Hill in the 16th and 17th centuries, and in those days it was a busy thoroughfare. When the cloth trade went into decline, craftsmen and small firms moved into the merchants' houses, and the back-yards, ever more densely populated, turned into 19th-century slums, where typhus and cholera were rampant. At the end of the nineteen-twenties, the city set about the task of cleaning up Elm Hill, and today it is the conservationists' showpiece and the tourists' promenade. Here you'll find flint and brick, Tudor half-timbering, Georgian fronts, antique shops, residences, craft studios, art shops, all together in a fascinating mixture of styles and occupations. Only the elms which gave the street its name have disappeared. Ever since the reign of Henry VIII they had grown in the little square next to the communal pump, but the last of them had to be felled in 1979 and was replaced by a plane tree. It was one more act in the national tree tragedy that has resulted in the destruction of virtually every elm in England: Dutch Elm Disease.

The corner house at the top of Elm Hill is 'The Britons Arms', and it is believed to be the only house in the street that escaped the great fire of 1507. It is also one of the few straw-thatched houses in Norwich. If I can find a seat, I always have a cup of coffee in 'The Britons Arms', but otherwise I go to the 'Crypt Coffee Bar' opposite, the crypt being that

St Peter Hungate,
late medieval brass

of the former Becket Chapel. In the Middle Ages it was part of the extensive property of the Dominicans, the Black Friars. Their great church (1440-70) is the only one of its kind in England that has been so completely preserved, but after the Reformation it became an assembly hall. Here, in St Andrew's Hall, the councillors entertained their royal guests, Charles II and Edward VII, George V and George VI. It was here too that in 1824 the Norwich Triennial Festival began, which since 1989 has become an annual festival of art and music. In Blackfriars Hall, which is the former choir of the Dominican church, hang the portraits of mayors and other prominent citizens. A contribution to this unusually large collection of municipal portraits was made by a German immigrant named John Theodore Heins, who ran a studio in Norwich from 1720 until his death in 1756. He made portraits of many of East Anglia's estate owners, including the family of Gainsborough's uncle, a successful clothier who lived in Sudbury.

Elm Hill, like so many other streets in Norwich, is richly endowed with churches. At the bottom stands *St Simon and St Jude*, which is now the Boy Scouts' headquarters; at the top is *St Peter Hungate*, now a museum for ecclesiastical art. Angels adorn the hammer-beam roof of this Perpendicular church (1431-60), two of whose benefactors were John

353

and Margaret Paston, made famous by their letters to each other (see page 412f.). They had several houses in Norwich, including Nos. 22–26 Elm Hill (burnt down) and Music House in King Street, formerly called Jew's House, one of the city's, and indeed England's oldest inhabited houses (12th century).

The *churches* of Norwich are a marvel. Of how many towns outside London could it be said that there was a different church for every Sunday in the year? And how many towns can boast a different pub for every workday? Even today, from any street corner you can expect to see at least three church towers, and the 200 or so pubs should suffice for anyone's dry throat. Around 1500 Norwich had some 10,000 inhabitants and at least 50 parish churches. Every area and every community within the city competed with the others in trying to demonstrate its piety and its prosperity by building its own church. Along the 500 yards of St Benedict's Street alone there are no less than five churches: St Gregory, St Laurence, St Swithin, St Margaret, and St Benedict. There were once three St Peters, three St Michaels, and three St Georges. Today Norwich still has 32 parish churches from before the Reformation, more than any other town in England, though twenty of them are redundant. The city bears maintenance costs and tries to find new tenants, sharing responsibilities with the Norwich Historic Churches Trust. The church where Cotman was married, St Mary's, is now an arts and crafts centre; St Martin-at-Oak is a shelter for the homeless; St Etheldreda is an artist's studio; St Mary-the-Less is a furniture warehouse; St James is a puppet theatre. Every one of these medieval churches has its own special qualities, its own atmosphere, and some detail or the other that deserves attention: the angel ceiling of St Giles; the flushwork decorations of St Michael at Coslany; the terra cotta sarcophagus of 1533–4 for the merchant and mayor Robert Jannys in St George's, Colegate; the 14th-century doorknocker in the south chapel of St Gregory – the head of a lion swallowing a man.

In this town of churches and monasteries there lived one of the great mystics of the Middle Ages: Julian of Norwich. She led the life of a recluse in a cell near the little church of St Julian, from which she took her name, above the old Wensum ford, between King Street and Rouen Road. When Julian was thirty, in 1373, she fell seriously ill, and had a vision. In her little cell she wrote down her sixteen *Revelations of Divine Love*, a classic work of spiritual life in the Middle Ages, and one of the first known books by a woman in the English language. The original text, alas, is lost, and the oldest copy is a 15th-century manuscript now in the British Museum. The first printed edition appeared in 1670. With what vividness, and yet with what earthly simplicity Julian expresses her spiritual message. The core of her experience she describes in terms of the hazelnut, which seems to incorporate the whole of God's creation: 'In this little thing I saw three truths: the first is that God made it; the second is that God loves it; and the third is that God sustains it.' God's love is the first and highest principle: 'Of this needs each man and woman to have knowing that desires to live contemplatively – that it pleases Him to like as naught all thing that is made, for to have love of God that is unmade.' Convinced as she is of the all-encompassing and all-preserving love of God, Julian does not even fear evil, which the people of the Middle Ages, and the theologians as well, dreaded like the plague. Sin, she declared, is necessary, 'but all shall be well, and all manner of thing will be well.'

For forty years she lived in her cell, to the right of the altar in the present-day Church of St Julian, with only her cat for company. Through one window she took part in the mass, and through another she received her meals. One of the many people who sought advice from the 'Recluse atte Norwyche' was Margery Kempe, the eccentric pilgrim from King's Lynn (see page 464ff). The latter threw herself into more and more pilgrimages all over the world, and the former shut herself up in a cell: two different ways of finding God and oneself, and two equally extraordinary medieval women. 'Set all your trust in God and fear not the language of the world,' the recluse advised the restless wanderer. 'Patience is necessary for you, for in that shall ye keep your soul.'

Today people sometimes cite Julian of Norwich as an early instance of feminist theology, because she talked of God as 'Mother'. Her *Revelations* have been reissued in paperback, and evidently their optimistic mysticism and spirituality meet needs that are alien to the sober orthodoxy of the Anglican High Church. 'Britain's increasingly powerful desert-trained religious voice,' is what the writer Ronald Blythe calls her. The German writer, Ernst Herhaus ('a churchless crypto-Catholic') found that Julian's 'light of courage' gave him practical assistance, and he is one of many to have visited her shrine in Norwich, and to have shared and rejoiced in her acceptance of God's love.

In 1942, during one of the Luftwaffe's bombing raids on historic towns (the infamous 'Baedeker raids'), St Julian's Church was destroyed. In 1954, the little flint building was reconstructed opposite the Norwich Brewery, and Julian's cell was also rebuilt, on the foundations of the medieval structure. A bare room, and an altar with a quotation from the recluse herself: 'Thou art enough to me'. Visitors write their requests on slips of paper, which together form an anthology of human suffering and faith: 'Pray for Ruth Flood, Sydney, short time to live with cancer.' 'Please pray for Eva who is old, losing her sight, and very frightened.'

When I went to see the grave of the painter John Crome at *St George's* in Colegate, I came upon two churches that embody the other, Nonconformist tradition of Norwich. Colegate was the street of the rich clothiers on the other side of the river, opposite Elm Hill. Between its three medieval churches are the two oldest Nonconformist chapels in the city: the *Old Meeting House*, hidden at the very end of a lane – a red brick house with Corinthian brick pilasters, founded in 1643 by Protestant refugees from Rotterdam – and nearby the *Octagon*, formerly a Presbyterian but now a Unitarian chapel. 'The Devil's Cucumber-frame' is what local people used to call it. The Octagon is a brick building with a columned portico and a pyramid roof, designed in 1754–6 by Norwich's Georgian architect Thomas Ivory, with such an elegant interior of Corinthian columns and galleries that the Methodist leader John Wesley found it quite astonishing: 'How can it be thought that the old coarse Gospel should find admission here?' Yet find admission it did, and so too did the ideas of the French Revolution.

'I am truly amazed and half alarmed to find this County filled with little Revolution

Societies,' wrote Fanny Burney on 27 November 1792. At that time the Octagon Chapel was a meeting place for the intellectuals of Norwich, and 'the Jacobin city' was one of the most radical Nonconformist centres in England. It also had a flourishing colony of painters (see page 386ff.). Among the free thinkers of Colegate were the notorious 'bluestockings', the writer and social reformer Harriet Martineau, and the Quaker Amelia Opie, a successful novelist whose most characteristic work is perhaps *Father and Daughter*, 1801. Amelia's husband John Opie was a member of the Royal Academy. Paintings of his in Norwich include a self-portrait in the Strangers' Hall Museum, and a 'Christ in the Temple', in the Bauchon Chapel of the cathedral. The Opies lived at the foot of the castle mound, in the street now named after them. In 1806 John Opie painted a portrait of the Romantic poet Robert Southey, who visited the Octagon Chapel twice and enjoyed his visits so much that he wrote: 'For society, of all places I have ever seen, Norwich is the best.'

One of the leading figures of the Octagon community was the journalist William Taylor, who was an enthusiastic translator of German literature. George Borrow learnt German from him, and even more important – as he describes in *Lavengro* – he learnt the close connection between smoking, philosophy and suicide. 'It is good to be a German, the Germans are the most philosophic people in the world, and the greatest smokers,' says Borrow's teacher. Whoever smokes can withstand the adversities of life with dignity, which explains why 'suicide is not a national habit in Germany as it is in England.' 'But,' Borrow objects, 'that poor creature Werther who committed suicide, was a German.' 'Werther is a fictitious character,' answers Mr Taylor. 'I should say that, if there ever was a Werther in Germany, he did not smoke.' Billy Taylor, the great defender of the German way of life and death, lies buried in the graveyard behind Octagon Chapel.

It was not by chance that around 1800 Norwich was one of the culturally and politically most active provincial cities in England. There was a long tradition of Dissent here, connected with a liberal attitude to foreigners. Thousands of religious refugees from the Continent sought asylum in England during the 16th and 17th centuries: first Dutch Protestants, then French Huguenots. Many of them found a new home in Norwich. The first Flemish weavers had already been brought across by Edward III back in 1336, but the first wave of refugees came in 1556: twenty four Flemish and six Walloon weavers with their families, fleeing from the Spanish Counter-Reformation. When the Duke of Alba invaded the Netherlands, more and more people fled across the water to Norwich, and by 1580 the city had about 16,000 inhabitants of whom a third were cloth-makers of the highest quality, who introduced new methods and techniques. Worsted and exports of textiles enjoyed a new boom.

At first, then, these foreigners were welcome, since they were so good for Norwich's economy, but they also provided considerable competition as far as the local people were

Rembrandt: Reverend Johannes Elison (1634) [

concerned, and this greatly soured the welcome. There was a good deal of tension and discrimination, with laws passed forbidding the immigrants to work as shoemakers, to bake white bread, and even to go on the streets after curfew. Not until 1598 were the 'strangers' given the same rights as ordinary citizens. In time they integrated, but they also maintained their own culture. They would meet in the Strangers' Club[1] on Elm Street, and they also had their own churches. Since 1565 the Flemish community had been granted the use of Blackfriars Hall, and right up until the beginning of the 20th century, you could still hear Dutch sermons in the Dutch Church. In St Mary-the-Less, the Huguenot church, services were held in French until the mid-19th century.[2]

In 1634, the Reverend Johannes Elison, preacher to the Dutch community in Norwich, and his wife Maria went to Amsterdam. During their visit, their full-length portraits, almost lifesize, were painted by their fellow-countryman Rembrandt. This marvellous memento of the Dutch Connection remained in the possession of the family in Norfolk until 1860, and is now in Boston, Mass. What other influences, apart from the Dutch gables, did the strangers have on Norwich? There is the Flemish street name 'Plain', and there are the canaries which supply Norwich City football club with its nickname. It is said that the first refugees from Holland brought their canaries with them to Norwich; by the early 18th century, keeping canaries had become a popular pastime, and indeed Norwich canaries soon became a coveted export. Why were they yellower than canaries everywhere else in England? Because they were fed on cayenne pepper.

Some years ago, I was walking along *Bridewell Alley*, one of the many lanes that wend between castle and river, and a bull's head enticed me into a shop where there is only one item for sale, and that is the sharpest thing in Norwich. Mustard. No, not just mustard. Colman's Mustard. Incomparable Colman's, with horseradish, or with tarragon and thyme, spicy, English, Norwich Mustard. Once it's hit your tongue, and you've wiped the tears from your eyes, nothing will ever taste quite the same again. Jeremiah Colman started up in 1804; in 1823, his nephew James also acquired the taste; and 150 years later, the firm of J & J Colman celebrated the jubilee by opening a mustard shop. The marble counter and mahogany shelves ensure a thoroughly Victorian atmosphere. This Old Curiosity Shop is both a shop and a mustard museum – the only one in the world. You can see mouth-watering containers and advertisements with a bite. In the twenties the whole kingdom was entertained by a culinary detective story involving key characters named Lord Bacon of Cookham, Baron de Beef, and Miss Di Gester: this was Colman's Mustard Club advertisement written by none other than Dorothy L. Sayers. But today Colman's does not live on mustard alone. The firm, which since 1854 has been based on the site of the former Benedictine Carrow Abbey in the southeast of the town, has over 1,500 employees

---

1 The Strangers' Club still exists: half the members must come from Norwich, and the other half may consist of newcomers. It is not to be confused with the Strangers' Hall in Charing Cross, which is a medieval merchant's house in which émigré Catholic priests were given refuge during the French Revolution. Since 1922 this has been a museum of everyday life.

2 Among the prominent Huguenot families of Norwich were the De Hagues, the Columbines, and the Martineaus.

producing a variety of drinks and foods. The yellow mustard fields lie all around East Poringland, and the old wives say that when the plants are in full bloom in the month of June, they shine all the way up to the moon.

Right next to the mustard shop is *Bridewell Museum*, which displays everything else that Norwich produces: shoes, beer, chocolate, silk scarves, wire netting, and Mackintosh's confectionery. This museum of regional industries and crafts is in one of the oldest merchant's houses in Norwich. In 1583 it became a 'bridewell', a workhouse for beggars and tramps. One of the exhibits you can see there now is the first wire-netting machine in the world, made in Norwich in 1844. Charles Barnard's invention was an export sensation, and even today Australian farmers still order miles and miles of galvanized wire fencing from Barnard, Bishop and Barnard of Norwich. Some of the firm's more upper class products, such as their splendid gates of cast or wrought iron, are to be found decorating the estates of the aristocracy, including that of the Queen at Sandringham. Meanwhile, at Wilkinsons they are busy mixing their Royal Blend of teas – a loyal offering to the Queen Mother for her 80th birthday.

The shoe industry, which relieved the played-out cloth industry in the 19th century, is still flourishing, but of the great breweries only one has survived – the Norwich Brewery. As for the media, Norfolk's county town is a centre for the whole of East Anglia, with Anglia Television, the BBC, Radio Broadland (a private radio station), and the *Eastern Daily Press* (whose predecessor, the *Norwich Post*, founded in 1701, is believed to have been the oldest provincial newspaper in Britain). The region's leading printers and publishers are the Jarrold family, who originally settled in Norwich in 1823, printing and publishing biblical tracts. In 1877 Jarrold & Sons published a book that was to become a children's classic: *Black Beauty*, the fictitious autobiography of a horse. The authoress, Anna Sewell, was paid a fee of £20. When she died just five months later in Norwich, her book had already sold 100,000 copies. Today *Black Beauty* has been translated into more than twenty different languages. Anna Sewell's grave lies between Irish yew trees in the Quaker cemetery at *Lamas*, a hamlet north of Norwich. Not far from her house in Catton is the *Sewell Barn Theatre*.

Norwich is dominated by its Cathedral, Castle and churches, but that is no excuse for ignoring the few good examples of industrial architecture. The Jarrold press is situated in the former cotton factory near Whitefriars Bridge, a five-storey brick building on the River Wensum, designed by John Brown in 1834 – functional but beautiful as well. Also worth seeing is A. F. Scott's former cloth factory in Botolph Street, whose façade is a kind of latticework of windows and brick pilasters. This was built in 1903, the same year as George Skipper's palatial Edwardian offices for *Norwich Union* in Surrey Street, with interiors of marble and mahogany – a successful piece of Revival architecture for an insurance company that was founded in 1792, and today is the city's biggest employer, with a staff of 4,000 (plate 67).

Wherever you are in Norwich, there is a signpost that is visible from almost every angle: the great spire of the Cathedral. I walk through Prince's Street to Tombland, which has a kind of dark medieval ring to it but in fact has nothing to do with tombs – it's derived from 'toom', an old word for wasteland. From there I cross the timber-framed courtyard behind St George's, and pass the two baroque giants of 1657 that flank the entrance to the Samson & Hercules House, which is diagonally opposite the Maid's Head Hotel on the edge of the Cathedral close. The hotel is older than its Georgian and pseudo-Tudor façade might appear; from 1762 onwards the Norwich Machine, the first regular mailcoach to London, used to leave from here. And in the late afternoon, I am standing in front of the Cathedral itself, at the hour of Evensong, when the very stones seem to glow and sing.

When the Normans conquered England, there began a building boom without parallel in English history. Castles and churches were the poles of their power, and the builders were often knight and priest in one. One of these mighty, glamorous men was Herbert de Losinga, known as 'the fighting bishop', and he it was that built *Norwich Cathedral* (plate 58). He was abbot of Fécamp in Normandy, came with William the Conqueror to England, and from the latter's son William Rufus he bought, for the then massive sum of £1,900, the title of Bishop of East Anglia. Simony is the name given to the practice of buying titles, and it was as blatant as it was customary. Shortly afterwards, Herbert de Losinga transferred the bishop's seat from Thetford to Norwich, and in 1096 he began the construction of the Cathedral and of a Benedictine abbey. By the time he died, in 1119, the choir and transepts had been completed, and the nave and crossing tower followed over the next few decades. The mighty abbot-bishop, who also founded churches in Lynn and Yarmouth, was buried in the choir of his Cathedral. There is a sarcophagus relief in the south ambulatory, an early Norman sepulchral portrait of an 11th-century bishop, and it is possible that this is Herbert de Losinga himself. His bishop's throne is the oldest in England, and the only one still in its original place in the apse behind the high altar.

Norwich Cathedral always glows, in the daytime as well as in the evening floodlights. The creamy stone comes from Caen in Normandy, supplemented by Barnack stone from Northamptonshire. The core of the walls is made from local flint. The Norman builders imported the ground plan of the edifice from France: a choir ambulatory with side chapels and additional chapels east of the transepts. It is the same plan as that of the cathedral in Rouen, Norwich's twin town. Nowhere else in England has this Norman outline been so perfectly maintained, and rarely is there such an harmonious link with the Gothic. On the Norman crossing tower is a Gothic spire; above the Norman nave is a Gothic vault – different architectural styles inspired by the same spirit. The tower, completed c.1145, is the tallest Norman tower in England (140 feet) (colour plate 23). Blind arcades, circles and lozenges cover it like stone crochet-work. The timber spire of 1145 was destroyed by a hurricane in 1362 and replaced in 1490 by a Gothic stone spire which, at 315 feet, is almost as tall as Salisbury.

The massiveness of the walls and the elegance of the decorations are matched in the interior of the Cathedral. The Late Gothic fans of the vault spread out like palm leaves from the Norman columns. Here too timber was replaced by stone: the vaults of the nave in the middle of the 15th century, the choir c.1480, the transepts after 1509. The arcades

*Norwich Cathedral,
north transept, before 1149*

and galleries are the same height, and above them is a three-part clearstorey with a wall-passage. There are two contrary movements that interpenetrate and reach a climax in the nave: the horizontal rhythm of the round arches and the vertical rhythm of the slender half-columns that continually urge their way upwards (plate 59). The choir screen and the organ[1] break the view and the magnetic pull of this extraordinary space, separating the nave from the presbytery, the people's church from the monks' church.

The crossing arches soar up beneath the tower, and the choir too is unusually high, a triumphal highlight of Norwich's marriage of Norman and Gothic. The arcades of the choir ambulatory are echoed and enhanced by the gallery with its stilted arches, above which are the Gothic tracery windows and ribbed vaulting – the late but perfect completion of the whole space. Clerics, pilgrims, tourists, one generation after another down through the centuries, have trodden these floors, until the tiles of the ambulatory have been worn smooth beneath their steps; the memorial slabs shine like soapstone, the names and dates faded with time, the dark stone cracked and scarred.

On the north side, the choir ambulatory leads you under an arch where there is a glittering glass cabinet. This is the Cathedral Treasury, formerly the Relic Chapel – a solid

---

1 First-class concerts of choral and church music are held in Norwich Cathedral, ranging from Byrd to Britten, during the Summer Festival and at other times.

manifestation of faith for medieval pilgrims to gaze on. Amongst the treasures of Norwich Cathedral are the Gothic altarpieces in both of the choir side chapels: in the northern one, the Jesus chapel, is Martin Schwarz's 'Adoration of the Magi' (1480); the southern one, the Luke chapel, contains the so-called Despenser Reredos. This altarpiece, contemporary with Julian of Norwich, c.1380–90, was probably given by Bishop Despenser and painted in Norwich. The retable is in five sections, depicting the Passion, the Resurrection and the Ascension. The elongated Gothic figures are set against an ornamental gold background, and the piece is an unusually fine and rare example of medieval painting in East Anglia.It escaped the attentions of the Reformation iconoclasts only through a trick. It was turned upside down, with the painted surfaces underneath, and used as a worktop by the Cathedral's carpenters. Thus it remained perfectly preserved, and indeed the trick was so successful that the painting was not rediscovered until 1847. Bishop Henry le Despenser, with whose time and name the work is associated, lies buried in front of the high altar. He is known to have been a 'warlike' bishop, who brutally suppressed the Norfolk peasants during Wat Tyler's Peasants' Revolt of 1381. And what sort of man is the present, 70th Bishop of Norwich? The Right Reverend Peter John Nott is a former tractor salesman who is well known for his abstinence and his championship of women in the priesthood.

In the choir stalls, a monk has laid a Cathedral pupil across his knee. This is one of more than sixty carved misericords from the 15th century. At every step you will find a piece of history, art, religion. There are carvings, stained glass windows, sculptured monuments

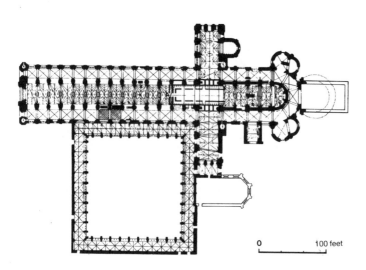

0   100 feet

Norwich Cathedral
Plan

Norwich Cathedral, St Luke's Chapel:
Despenser Reredos, centre panel of altarpiece,
c.1380–90

everywhere.[1] Such places are inexhaustible, and alas they also demand inexhaustible funds. The inevitable appeal informs all visitors just what it costs to maintain the Cathedral of Norwich: over half a million pounds a year, which works out at roughly £1 per 'Minute of History'.

If you leave the south aisle through the Prior's Portal (*c.*1310), you'll find yourself in the cloister (plate 61), a large green courtyard of stillness and stone beauty. The sun draws the silhouettes of the tracery windows on the tiles in a Gothic shadow play. The cloister was begun in 1297 with the east wing, and finished around 1430 with the north wing. Here you can see the whole range of ornamentation, from Decorated to Perpendicular. In the northwest corner, where the tracery changes, the Black Death of 1349 brought about a long interruption in the work of the stonemasons. Norwich's surviving grandees left their coats of arms on the cloister walls. 'For that courtesie of theirs shall remayne in perpetuall memorie, whiles the walls of their citie standeth,' wrote the local chronicler Thomas Churchyard.

There's another treat for us in the cloister: up in the vaulted ceilings are the keystones, nearly 400 coloured bosses, and each stone tells a different story: scenes from the lives of

---

1 Just two details from the northern transept: Chantrey's marble monument to a bishop, 1841; and the west window by Burne-Jones and Morris & Co., *c.*1901, depicting the Archangels Michael, Gabriel and Raphael in harmonies of blue, red and green.

Norwich Cathedral, nave bosses, second half 15th century

Jesus, Mary or the saints, and in the south and west wings the Apocalypse, with allegories and grotesques in between, even, somewhere, an owl in a pear tree. There are similar treats back inside the Cathedral, in the nave and transept, but if you want to enjoy the stonemasons' heavenly fantasies up there, you'll have to take your bird-watching kit along with you, because you'll see nothing without a good pair of binoculars. Again there are almost 400 of these coloured bosses, spread all over the ribs, stars and lozenges of the ceilings. They depict scenes from the Old and New Testaments, ranging from the Creation to the Last Judgment – the last visible remnants of the Norwich Mystery Plays that took place in the Middle Ages. Above the cloister is the Cathedral Library, which with its 7,000 old books and incunabula is one of the most important of its kind in England.

Outside, in front of the choir wall, a simple cross decorates the grave of a clergyman's daughter: Edith Cavell. A nurse during the First World War, Cavell was executed in Brussels in 1915 by a German firing squad for helping Allied soliders to escape. Her last words before she was shot were: 'Standing as I do in view of God and Eternity, I realize that patriotism is not enough. I must have no hatred or bitterness towards anyone.'

Chasing around the playground in their navy blue uniforms are the pupils of a school that dates back to 1553. Once the King Edward VI Grammar School, it saw such notables as Lord Nelson, George Borrow, and Humphry Repton[1] busy at their Latin, and before them were generations of monastic schoolchildren. During the Middle Ages up to 60 Benedictine monks used to live in *Cathedral Close*, and although the Cathedral precincts lay within the city, they were beyond the city's jurisdiction. This soon led to tensions between the citizens and the monks, and so high walls were built – you can still see them along Bishopsgate – to protect the abbey against attacks like that of August 1272. On that occasion enraged citizens laid waste to the abbey, to atone for which they later paid for the rebuilding of *St Ethelbert's Gate* (1316, plate 64), with its three large flushwork rose windows. About 100 years later, its Perpendicular counterpart was built opposite the west end of the Cathedral – the splendid *Erpingham Gate* (1420). It was named after the benefactor who, in Shakespeare's *Henry V*, lends the King his cloak: Sir Thomas Erpingham, 'a good old commander and a most kind gentleman', who led the Welsh

1   Before becoming a landscape-gardener, Humphry Repton was apprenticed to a cloth merchant in Norwich, and after his marriage for several years he ran his own, none-too-successful textile business here (1773–8).

archers at the Battle of Agincourt in 1415. He now lies buried in the Cathedral choir. There is no more idyllic spot in Norwich than the Cathedral Close. It's like a village in the city. The last monks left the abbey in 1535, and there are now about 80 houses on the site, some of them medieval, like the Deanery, and many of them Georgian. The houses are small and utterly charming, the majority still lived in, but a few used as offices. There are no cars to break the peace, and neither you nor I will disturb it either, for we're off again, on our way down to the river. There's an old ferry house, and near it an even older gatehouse: *Pull's Ferry*, part of what used to be the abbey walls. Beneath the larger of the two arched gateways, a canal once branched off from the River Wensum, but that was filled in long ago. Most goods were taken along this canal to the abbey – food, peat from the Broads, and in the very earliest days stones from Normandy to build the Cathedral with.

From Pull's Ferry a path goes alongside the Wensum. Downriver it leads to *Carrow Bridge* at the southern end of the city walls, and upriver to *Bishop Bridge*, the only remaining medieval bridge,[1] dating from 1340. You wander past the statuesque anglers and the boats from the River Yare to the ruins of *Cow Tower* (*c.*1378), the most massive of all the old city towers, and from there to *Hellesdon Mill*. This is a truly picturesque path[2] in all senses, for it's full of the views painted by the artists of the Norwich School. And now you're standing in Cotman Fields. One of the painter's favourite water meadows, you might think. Well, no, it's a part of a new housing estate in *Bishopsgate*,[3] with brick houses and pleasant courtyards and corners – a successful continuation of the medieval line of estates. It's perfectly possible to integrate temperate modernity with historical surround- ings, as Norwich's city-planners have also shown with Fye Bridge and in Anchor Quay. The inner city has once more become an attractive place to live in, and this is not due just to the building firms' invitation to come and live in their new houses on the Wensum, please, but also to the excellent restoration work that has been done in the twenty or so conservation areas. That is no small achievement when you consider the notorious inner-city problems of many other English towns.

What Hampstead Heath is to London, *Mousehold Heath* is to Norwich – an oasis on the outskirts of the city. Here you'll meet joggers and walkers and people taking the dog out, and dogs taking the people out. But what has happened to Cotman's Mousehold Heath? Those bare open spaces so beloved of the Norwich painters in the 19th century have been filled up with oaks and alders and birches. Just occasionally you come across the odd clearing with gorse and ferns. Ever since the Middle Ages, people have come here to dig for gravel and clay – hence the many little hills and valleys. The heath has also been the site of brickworks, firing ranges and cavalry training. Today the Britannia Barracks – from

---

1   Others are the Neoclassical St George's Bridge, 1783 by John Soane; St Miles Bridge, 1804, Norwich's earliest iron bridge, by James Frost.

2   As well as Riverside Walk along the Wensum, there is Yare Valley Walk in the west of the city, from Earlham Park to Eaton Street.

3   Part of the monastery precinct was the Great Hospital in Bishopsgate, founded in 1249 as a poorhouse, and now used as an old people's home. Attached to it is St Helen's Church and cloister (*c.*1450).

John Sell Cotman: St Ethelbert's Gate, 1817

where you get the very finest view of the city – are a regimental museum and prison. The gypsies used to camp on Mousehold, and this is where the young George Borrow first met them – the beginning of a lifelong passion. Romani Road, Crome Road are names that recall the area's intimate association with the gypsies and the artists. There is also Kett's Hill, commemorating the bloodiest event in the history of Mousehold Heath and Norwich: Kett's Rebellion.

In July 1549, thousands of peasants rose up in revolt and besieged the county town of Norfolk. At their head were Robert Kett and his brother William. Simmering resentment had been fanned into flames by three successive bad harvests and inflationary prices, but now the peasants' very existence was under threat. 'Enclosure' was the familiar keyword: the common land was to be fenced off. More and more of the land that belonged to everyone and to no-one was being annexed by the landowners, and fenced in as grazing land for their sheep. Kett's Rebellion was the struggle of these peasants for the right to use the commons. Their demand was: 'No lord of the manor shall common upon the commons.' Mousehold Heath was their headquarters.

On August 1st they stormed Bishopsgate. For almost a month, Norwich was in the hands of the rebels. Then the Earl of Warwick's army moved in, among them over 1,400 German mercenaries. After bloody street fighting, Warwick retook the city. Over 3,000 peasants were killed, 39 of the rebels' leaders were hanged, drawn and quartered, while 300 others were merely hanged. In December 1549 Robert Kett was chained to the tower of Norwich Castle and left to starve. Warwick was made Duke of Northumberland for his pains. Thus ended the last great peasants' revolt on English soil.

One of the leaders of Wat Tyler's Rebellion in 1381 also came from East Anglia: John Ball, a clergyman from Colchester and the eponymous hero of William Morris's historical and philosophical tale *A Dream of John Ball* (1886–92). Ball wrote the most famous rhyme in the history of medieval Christian class warfare:

> When Adam delved, and Eve span,
> Who was then the gentleman?

The enclosures of Tudor times were only the beginning of a long and painful process of social restructuring, which in the 17th and 18th centuries made independent small farmers into tenants, then into labourers without land, and finally into factory workers.

'Kett's Rebellion, and all the Nonconformists – Norwich is proud of its radical heritage,' says Malcolm Bradbury. This Yorkshire-born writer had only intended to stay in Norwich for a few years, but having arrived in 1965, he is still there. 'I've never enjoyed any city more than Norwich,' is the explanation. He lives in Heigham Grove, a quiet area on the edge of the inner city. On his mantelpiece are busts of John Milton and Abraham Lincoln, in his hand is a pipe, and as always he's in a hurry. Malcolm Bradbury is a novelist, essayist, film writer, political satirist, and chronicler of a changing society. One of his recent TV

70 HADLEIGH   Parish church of St Mary, 15th century, and Deanery Tower, 1495

71 KERSEY Village street with ford and parish church

72 SNAPE St John's churchyard

73 BARSHAM Trompe-l'oeil east wall and round tower of Holy Trinity
75 LONG MELFORD Perpendicular church of the Holy Trinity, 1460–96 ▷
74 BORLEY Topiary in village churchyard

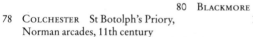

76 MISTLEY TOWERS by Robert Adam, 1776

77 MARGARETTING West tower of St Margaret's,
15th century

80 BLACKMORE 15th-century timber-framed tower of St Lawrence

78 COLCHESTER St Botolph's Priory,
Norman arcades, 11th century

79 WEST WALTON Early Gothic arcades
of St Mary's, c.1240

81 CASTLE ACRE Ruined monastery, late Norman west front with blind arcades

82 BURY ST EDMUNDS Ruined abbey

83 WALTHAM ABBEY   Arcades of Norman monastery church, begun *c*.1105

84 ICKLINGHAM   Bier at All Saints

85 PASTON Katherine Paston, monument by Nicholas Stone, 1629
86 WINGFIELD St Andrew's: monument to John de la Pole, 2nd Duke of Suffolk, and his wife
Elizabeth Plantagenet, after 1491

7   GOSFIELD   St Katharine's: Baroque monument to John and Anne Knight, 1756, by Michael Rysbrack

8   WALTHAM ABBEY   Monument to Sir Edward Denny and his wife Margaret, 1600

HERE LYETH BURYED THE BODY OF
Sᵗ HENRY BENDYSHE BARᵗ
WHO DEPARTED THIS LIFE THE THIRD

10   FRAMLINGHAM   St Michael's: monument to Sir Robert Hitcham, 1638, by Francis Grigs

9   STEEPLE BUMPSTED   St John's: Georgian monument to Sir Harry Bendyshe and his son, 1717, by Thomas Stayner

91 RANWORTH   Gothic choir screen at St Helen's, 15th century

92 GREAT WARLEY   Art Nouveau choir screen at St Mary's, 1902, by Sir William Reynolds-Stephens

93 BLYTHBURGH   Angel roof at Holy Trinity, 15th century

plays was entitled *Anything More Would Be Greedy*, and showed academics becoming millionaires in a new hi-tech class of entrepreneurs. It was a satire on the Cambridge Phenomenon and the sex-appeal of money. 'The price of lifestyle is destroying certain people who think because they do not have a lifestyle they don't have a life at all.'

Bradbury made his name in 1975 with the novel *The History Man*. His hero is Howard Kirk, a Marxist sociologist at a provincial university. Having already experienced campus life in America, Bradbury found the ideal model for this classic academic satire on his own doorstep: the *University of East Anglia*. There he became the first Professor of American Studies in a department which since 1989 has been named the Arthur Miller Centre for American Studies, after the great dramatist and honorary doctor of the University. In 1970, together with Angus Wilson, he inaugurated the first MA course in Creative Writing, for many years the only one of its kind in Britain. One of its best-known graduates is Ian McEwan (*First Love, Last Rites*; *A Child in Time*; *The Comfort of Strangers*). Until his retirement in 1978, Sir Angus Wilson was Professor of English Literature at Norwich, another 'poeta doctus' and novelist-cum-social-critic in the tradition of Dickens. His masterpiece is *Anglo-Saxon Attitudes* (1956), whose hero is a retired history professor.

The University lies on the western edge of the city, on the site of a former golf course near Earlham Park, which was once the country home of a banking family, the Gurneys, on the River Yare.[1] One of Britain's brave new universities, it was designed by Denys Lasdun (1962–72). The buildings that house the lecture-rooms have an almost brutal zig-zag half-timbering, while the halls of residence are on terraces to the south, going down to the river valley. It's a compact little town-within-a-town for the brainworkers on the banks of the Yare. One of the University's strong points is its School of Environmental Sciences, started in 1968. At that time no other university in Britain held a degree course in this subject.

On the edge of this green campus stands a hall made of aluminium and glass – a silver hangar with three Henry Moore sculptures around it. This is the *Sainsbury Centre for Visual Arts* (plate 60). It houses one of the few major private art collections of the 20th century in England, and is itself an outstanding example of modern British engineering. Designed by Norman Foster in 1974–8, it is an unsupported hall of welded steel tubes clad in aluminium panels sealed with neoprene. It's 440 feet long, and 114 feet wide – exemplary minimal architecture with not a squiggle in sight. What is especially delightful is the witty contrast between the hi-tech construction and its parkland setting, the functional aesthetic of the museum and its contemplative purpose. Norman Foster brought together all the activities of such a centre in a single, variable space, so that it can be used for exhibitions,

◁ 94   KING'S LYNN   Gothic misericord in choir stalls at St Margaret's

1   The Gurneys were a Quaker family, and their Norwich bank was one of a group of private banks that merged in 1896 with Barclays. It was in the family's town house, Gurney Court, at No. 31 Magdalen Street, that the prison reformer Elizabeth Fry was born in 1780.

seminars, as a library and as a restaurant. It's a space on a grand scale, to match the grand gesture of the Sainsburys, who have displayed here the results of a lifetime's collecting.

There are Benin bronzes next to Picasso and Epstein – ancient primitive art standing shoulder to shoulder with the moderns. These are the two poles of the Sainsbury Collection. You will find sculptures and pictures by Henry Moore, Bacon, Giacometti, and John Davies; and there are Egyptian, Etruscan and Roman bronzes, African and Pre-Columbian artefacts, sculptures from the Cyclades, the South Seas, the Orient, and medieval Europe, and works by Indians and by Inuit. This is a collection of world art, not just western art, and it was gathered together by someone who called himself, not a collector but a 'passionate acquirer'. For over 50 years he 'acquired' what he (and his wife) liked, judging more by the heart than by the head, obeying an instinct and a taste that was as eclectic as it was sound.

In 1973 Sir Robert and Lady Lisa Sainsbury donated most of their collection to the University of East Anglia, in order to give young art students the chance 'to learn the pleasures of visual experience – of looking at works of art from a sensual, not only an intellectual point of view.' The collection was the gift of the parents, and the museum was the gift of their son David. It was a magnificent act of patronage from a family whose name is known to all English people in a totally different context. With their chain of some 300 supermarkets, the Sainsburys have an estimated fortune of about two billion pounds, which puts them in third place behind the Queen and the Duke of Westminster in the league table of Britain's super-rich. Another member of the family, Sir John – former Chairman of the Royal Opera – clubbed together with his brothers to donate £30–40 million for the Sainsbury Wing, an extension to London's National Gallery, designed in 1987 by Roberto Venturi. In these penny-pinching days when the State turns a blind eye to all but the balance sheet, it's good to know that that Sainsburys tin/loaf/bottle you've just bought may help to finance the next art gallery.

Cotman & Co.: The Quiet Revolutionaries of Local Art

Some folk say the British lag behind in the visual arts. It's not only Suffolk's heavenly twins, Gainsborough and Constable, that demolish the lie, for in the period from the end of the 18th century until about 1840, England enjoyed a Golden Age of landscape painting that was without equal anywhere on the Continent. And the most dazzling of all these pictures came from the heart of East Anglia. For a long time they were almost completely overshadowed by the genius of Turner, and even the finest of these painters has never been given a one-man exhibition outside the British Isles. His name was John Sell Cotman, and he came from Norwich. Here better than anywhere else, you can get to know him and his fellow painters of this undervalued Norwich School.

To begin the story, we must return to the Norman Castle, which is now such a versatile and stimulating museum. Could there, for instance, be a more English introduction to the history of English china than the 2,600 teapots of the Bulwer & Miller Collection? Scarcely less eccentric are Mrs Langton's collected cats – about 100 of them, of porcelain, jade, ivory, bronze, wood, and glass; cats from Egypt, China, Japan, Dresden, Derby and Staffordshire. And what about the sublime obsession of the lepidopterist Margaret Elizabeth Fountaine, daughter of a Norfolk clergyman, who during her travels around the world caught no less than 22,000 butterflies and gave them all to the Castle Museum, together with her diaries (published as *Love Among the Butterflies* and *Butterflies and Late Loves*). Then there was Mrs Bulwer's Victorian brother, who collected mustard pots from all over Europe and left them to his native city. And if you're going to talk of mustard, you are bound to talk of Colman's, which brings us back nicely to the subject of painting, for it is thanks to Norwich's art-loving mustard-maker Jeremiah Colman and his son that the little city possesses the biggest Cotman collection in the world.[1]

The Colmans handed over their collection on one condition: the pictures must never leave the Castle. Cotman fans would have to come to Norwich to see his work. Is this a subtle way of promoting the city and its mustard, or a narrow-minded local pride that hinders international recognition? Or is it a far-sighted measure to hold off the consequences of uncontrolled distribution? Andrew W. Moore, curator of the museum, pulled a face like a man who has just swallowed too much mustard, but perhaps that wasn't only due to my questions. Another problem that weighs heavily on him is the fact that of the 48 oil paintings and 882 watercolours and drawings, only just over half are regarded as indisputably genuine Cotmans. 'He had a lot of pupils,' said Mr Moore, 'and good pupils means good copies.' But what remains is quite overwhelming.

Cotman was not a painter of large-scale masterpieces or dramatic subjects; nor did he portray society like Gainsborough, paint representational landscapes like Constable, or use visionary colours like Turner. Most of his work was in watercolour, his sizes were small, and his subject-matter modest. But in his best paintings he is more brilliant and more modern than any of his contemporaries. Cotman's life went by without any major highlights, so gently and undramatically that one of his biographers found it 'unsatisfactory'. There were no dazzling triumphs, and no tragic disasters. When he died in London in 1842 (he is buried at St John's Wood Chapel in Marylebone), there was not a single obituary – not even in Norwich, his birthplace.

Like Turner, Cotman was the son of a hairdresser. In 1798, at the age of sixteen, he went to London, where he coloured engravings for an art dealer and copied pictures at the home of a collector. That was the full extent of his training. He soon went to Wales, which was the epitome of the picturesque landscape, and it was there as well as in Yorkshire that he produced some of his finest watercolours. But the Old Water-Colour Society in London rejected his application for membership. Disappointed, he went home to Norwich in 1806, and became an art teacher, which he said was precisely what he had feared most. Nevertheless, he did have a patron: Dawson Turner, Quaker, banker, botanist (specializing in seaweed) and archaeologist from Yarmouth. And so that was where Cotman went in

1   Far bigger than the other principal collections, in the British Museum, the V&A and Leeds City Art Gallery.

1812, to give drawing lessons to his patron's wife and their six daughters; he also began his 'Herculean' task of making topographical etchings which he hoped would bring him a wider reputation. He was a virtuoso architectural draughtsman, and in ten years he made some 400 etchings of castles, churches and towns in Norfolk and Normandy, where he went three times. He published several volumes of these copper etchings, including one entitled *Architectural Antiquities of Norfolk* (1818), and another on *Sepulchral Brasses in Norfolk and Suffolk* (1819). During this time he gave up oil painting almost completely, and he also gave up hope of ever becoming an English Piranesi.

In 1823, Cotman moved back to Norwich, into a brick house near the Cathedral – No. 7 St Martin's-at-Palace-Plain. There he lived with his wife, their five children, and their dogs Titian and Rubens, in ever increasing poverty and depression. 'The sun has set for ever on my career and all is darkness before me,' he wrote on 3 August 1826 to Dawson Turner. 'My pupils diminish to such a degree that it is impossible for me to live in any, save a *Workhouse* or a *Prison.*' His one hope was to get to London, away from the provinces: 'London, with all its fog and smoke, is the only air for an artist to breathe in.' In vain he applied for the post of drawing teacher at the School of Military Engineering in Chatham. 'My views in life are so completely blasted that I sink under the repeated and constant exertion of body and mind.'

But then things took an upward turn. In 1834 he was at last offered a post as art teacher, at King's College in London. One of his pupils was soon to become more famous than he was himself: Dante Gabriel Rossetti. He described Cotman as 'an alert, forceful-looking

John Sell Cotman: Boat on the Beach, 1808

man, of modest stature, with a fine well-moulded face, which testified to an impulsive nature, somewhat worn and worried.' For Cotman, recognition came too late: 'Age has overtaken me perhaps prematurely, without my having accomplished what I hoped to have done – but this is but the lot of millions.' In the cold and stormy autumn of 1841 he once more enjoyed the 'wilderness of Norfolk', drawing the Devil's Tower, Aylsham Church, and the trees of Blickling Park. Just a few months later he was dead.

A life in dark aquatints. But the colours stand out against the dark background. Cotman's subject-matter is limited, and as modest as his formats: a wooden fence, a peasant's hovel, a river scene with cows, boats on the shore, a ruined monastery, and trees, trees, and more trees. Trees on the Greta, trees on the Yare: 'Oh! rare and beautiful Norfolk.' He was wont to say that he made 'close copies of that fickle Dame', referring to Mother Nature, but these were not just copies: he painted much less than he saw, and yet at the same time much more. Beyond the fleeting appearance of things, he captured their structure, and beyond the mere structure of things, he captured their changing yet unmistakably individual atmosphere.

'Leave out, but add nothing,' was the advice Cotman gave his son Miles, who was also his assistant. With just a few strokes of his pencil he would sketch the outlines, and then with broad sweeps but in thin layers apply his watercolours in an endlessly subtle mixture of greens and browns, greys and blues. Cotman's style is simple and clear, light and lucid. His monochrome watercolours, with masterly variations of grey or brown, are a development of methods he learned from Thomas Girtin, whom he had got to know during his early days in London among a group of artists known as 'The Brothers'. He had an unerring instinct for the nuances of light, for substance and space, and for the balance between form and colour. A perfect example of this watercolourist's art, bordering on the abstract, is 'Kett's Castle' (c.1809–10) in the Castle Museum. Here we have the structures of an atmospheric evening on Mousehold Heath. For all the precision of detail, the places he shows here are also the charts of a feeling, so that the scenes are totally real and yet at the same time dreamlike. Cotman paints pictures in which the eye can wander while the soul remains at rest. Turner loves dynamic movement, and elemental contrasts. Cotman seeks to balance such opposites in one great harmony.

His silhouette technique of setting dark forms against light, and light against dark, creates fields of colour which were not seen again until the Symbolists. His flat, almost geometrical style anticipates Cézanne and Cubism, and herein lies his modernity. It also explains his lack of popularity among his contemporaries, for in their eyes his compositions were not sufficiently naturalistic; they were too spare, too abstract, too cool and dull in their colouring. And so masterpieces such as 'Drop Gate' and 'Mousehold Heath', both in the British Museum now, never found a buyer during his lifetime. It is little wonder that Cotman began to have doubts about his work: 'My poor Reds, Blues and Yellows ... nonsense & stuff.' He used to mix his watercolours with ink and coloured chalk, and his pigments with flour or paste in order to achieve a sort of impasted expressiveness that went beyond the range of ordinary colours. In his later work he tried in vain to emulate Turner in

John Crome, by Hannah Gurney   *John Crome: The Poringland Oak, c.1818–20*

his use of brilliant colour, and to attain popularity by depicting historical figures or spectacular subjects. His best pictures are certainly those he produced between 1805 and 1812, and they are highlights not just of British but also of European watercolour painting. The prices are perhaps an accurate reflection: a watercolour like 'Mousehold Heath' (1810), withdrawn at an auction in 1862 when only £5.15 was bid, would now fetch around £30,000.

· Even in Norwich, the city of his birth, England's greatest watercolourist is still not given his due. Of more than 400 pictures, barely one tenth are on permanent exhibition. Even allowing for the fact that the watercolours are changed at regular intervals because of their sensitivity to light, this is a sad case of hidden treasure. If in the end London managed to build a museum wing especially for Turner, then why can't Norwich build one for John Sell Cotman? Why, even the Colmans created a museum for their mustard.

However singular an artist he may have been, though, Cotman was not the isolated genius of the provinces. He was one of a group of local artists, amateur and professional, who came together in 1803 to form the Norwich Society of Artists. There were similar associations in other towns, but nowhere else did they attain the national importance of the Norwich School. It is difficult to find a rational explanation for this. Of course at the end of the 18th century, Norwich had a lot of clubs and societies, an open and stimulating political and cultural climate, some rich patrons, and a public that was generally well enough disposed towards the arts that many painters were able to earn a living. But there were plenty of other provincial cities that could claim the same – Bath, Bristol and Liverpool, for instance. So why was it that Norwich was the first city outside London to stage regular art exhibitions? Why was Norwich the setting for this triumph of regionalism?

'I arrived here a week ago and find it a place where the arts are very much cultivated,' wrote the miniaturist Andrew Robertson in a letter from Norwich (1812): 'The studies of landscape about the town are infinitely beautiful and inexhaustible. The buildings, cottages, etc. are charming, and have invited people to the general practice of drawing, or rather painting in watercolours from nature …' The Norwich School in fact had two fathers: Cotman and Crome, the city's two dominant painters. Without their influence, it would scarcely have been possible for so many talents to flower in so fertile a fashion, amateur as well as professional.

For some thirty years they met for discussions, exhibitions and excursions with sketchbook and brush. They were inspired by everything they saw around their city. Like Constable (who ignored them) they felt a close affinity to 17th-century Dutch landscape painting rather than to the more sentimental Victorian art. The breadth of the East Anglian coast, the Norfolk Broads with their rivers, canals and windmills, and the Dutch character of the landscape would seem to explain what Pevsner calls their 'Dutch genius' for landscape painting. Dutch ships are constantly turning up in the pictures produced by the Norwich School, and not just in Cotman's 'Dutch Boats off Yarmouth' in the Castle Museum. The traditional trade links between East Anglia and the Netherlands also resulted in Dutch paintings finding a place in local collections.[1] Cotman was able to study some of them at the home of his patron Dawson Turner in Yarmouth, and John Crome copied them in Catton Hall, where his (and Gainsborough's) patron Thomas Harvey lived. Harvey was a master weaver, married to the daughter of a merchant in Rotterdam, and on his country estate near Norwich he surrounded himself above all with 17th-century Dutch paintings: Hobbema, Ruisdael, Teniers, Rembrandt – a revelation for John Crome, then a young provincial painter.

Crome learnt his trade from a coach and sign painter in Norwich. The inn signs that he painted for 'The Lame Dog' and other local establishments have unfortunately not survived. His father was a journeyman weaver and inn-keeper of doubtful repute, and he himself was known as a notorious drinker, gregarious and business-minded – the exact opposite of Cotman, who suffered a good deal from the competition. George Borrow, who had drawing lessons from Crome, described him as 'the little stout man whose face is very dark and whose eye is vivacious' and went on: 'he has painted, not pictures of the world, but English pictures such as Gainsborough himself might have done; beautiful rural pieces, with trees which might well tempt the birds to perch upon them.' They might perhaps have landed on 'Poringland Oak' (1818, Tate Gallery), whose strange branches are flooded by the clear light of East Anglia. As an art teacher, which was the most lucrative job a

---

1 Some of them now form part of a small collection of Dutch paintings in the Castle Museum: Avercamp, Pieter Breughel II, Jan van Goyen, Hobbema, Isaac van Ostade, Rubens and Wouwermans. One of the treasures here is the so-called Ashwellthorpe Triptych (see page 42).

provincial artist could do, Crome was so successful in Norwich and with the landed families all around that no less than six of his eleven children became painters themselves.

Crome was one of the first to make his pupils work out in the open air directly from Nature. During lessons on the banks of the Yare, this self-taught master would sometimes cry: 'This is our Academy!' Crome used Gainsborough's technique of applying oils as thinly as watercolours, and he also emulated the naturalism of Dutch landscape painting. Dutch influence is to be seen in pictures like 'Moonrise at the Yare' in the Tate Gallery, or 'Yarmouth Jetty' in Norwich Museum – a study in browns, with a single glowing red point in the middle: the fisherman's jacket. Crome was also a master of monochrome: the church at Whitlingham in grey watercolour hills, the glistening silver-grey willow branch over the waves of the Yare, painted on a little piece of mahogany. The subject-matter is nothing special – just a happy moment. In the finest of his pictures,[1] Crome achieves a lightness almost akin to that of Corot. His etchings seem like soft pencil drawings, sketch-like, and with a shimmering atmosphere. Only 34 of these 'softground etchings' have survived. Cotman also used this technique, which was to be perfected by Whistler.

John Crome was a provincial artist all his life. Wider fame did not come until long after his death, when seven of his pictures were displayed in London at the World Exhibition of

---

1 Some of them are now in deplorable condition because of the excessive use of bitumen. There are also many copies, forgeries and false attributions.

John Crome: Moonrise on the Yare, c.1811–16

Alfred Stannard: On the River Yare, 1846

1862. Monet, Pisarro and Van Gogh all admired his work, but he himself at the end of his life had admiration for one artist in particular, if one can judge by what are believed to have been his last words: 'Oh Hobbema, my dear Hobbema, how I have loved you!' Dawson Turner, however, reported a different set of dying words – Crome's advice to his eldest son: 'John, my boy, paint; but paint for fame; and if your subject is only a pig-sty – dignify it!' He is buried in the Church of St George, where he was baptized. He has his own room in the Castle Museum, with some twenty pictures. After his death in 1821, his eldest son John Berney Crome took over his art school and also became President of the Norwich Society, thereby furthering the influence of his father. His 'Great Gale at Yarmouth on Ash Wednesday' (1836) in the Castle Museum is ample evidence of his heritage.

The continuation of Cotman's influence also had its roots in the immediate family: Miles Edmund, his eldest son, was already exhibiting at the Norwich Society when he was just thirteen, and both style and subject-matter are sometimes indistinguishable from his father's. He and his brother John Joseph – the more original of the two – also continued the tuition that their father had given. The artist sons of 'Cotty' and 'Old Crome' were not the only ones to ensure the survival of the Norwich School and the confusion of the experts. The Stannards, too, were an art dynasty, active in Norwich over not two but three generations. Joseph Stannard, the most important of them, painted his masterpiece after a trip to Holland: 'Thorpe Water Frolic' (1824–5), a festival on the Yare in front of the city gates – an afternoon scene that is full of life and light and gaiety. (Equally masterly is his 'Boats on the Yare, Bramerton, Norfolk' (1828), now in the Fitzwilliam Museum, Cambridge.)

The Stannards and Cotmans and Cromes had wives, daughters and sons who painted, and there were other members of the Norwich School with in-laws and brothers and sisters who painted, and so there was a sort of mushrooming effect rather like the Pre-Raphaelites. Robert Ladbrooke married the sister of Crome's wife, and John Thirtle married Mrs Cotman's sister. Thirtle, son of a shoemaker, lived in Norwich as a miniaturist, gilder and art teacher. His watercolours in the Castle Museum often show Norfolk's trees, boats, houses and clouds sublimely reflected in the waters of the Yare and Wensum. Robert Dixon, like Thirtle, was a Norwich man and an art teacher. He also painted sets for the theatre and was an accomplished watercolourist, specializing in picturesque village and street scenes. A series of Dixon's softground etchings ('Norfolk Scenery', 1810–11) match Crome's in quality. The Norwich School was not, then, confined to watercolours, and Andrew W. Moore is quite right to point out that the 'etchings remain the least recognized aspect of the quiet revolution that the Norwich artists achieved.'

Give yourself time also to study the work of the Norwich School's second generation, whose pictures hang in tightly packed rows, one above the other, in the Castle Museum. Crome's pupil James Stark is there, the son of a Scottish dyer but born in Norwich; another, George Vincent, painted panoramic views of the water meadows near Trowse and of the fish auctions on Yarmouth beach; Henry Bright's dramatic chiaroscuro landscapes herald the new and spectacular visions of the Victorians. Bright had over a hundred pupils from all over England, the most gifted being John Middleton, a watercolour painter of quiet river and forest landscapes who died very young. The vitality of the Norwich School is also evident from the range of its amateur members: Thomas Churchyard was a lawyer from Woodbridge; Robert Leman was an employee of the Norwich Union, and travelled and painted in Cotman's footsteps; his friend Thomas Lound, a watercolourist, was a brewer and pupil of Cotman's. There were also two clergymen who exhibited work at the Norwich Society: the Reverend James Bulwer, a friend and patron of Cotman's with whom he travelled through Norfolk drawing churches, and E. T. Daniell, who became well known as a copper engraver and travelled widely in Europe and the Far East. So eagerly did the amateurs devote themselves to art (and Norwich was not the only hotbed) that the painter Thomas Uwins wrote to a friend in 1830: 'If gentlemen all take to painting for themselves, what is to become of us poor professional brushmen?'

The professionals and amateurs of the Norwich School all influenced one another, but although they had the same interests and often the same subjects, there was no uniformity

John Thirtle: Self-Portrait

Reverend James Bulwer, by Frederick Sandys, 1863

of style. Their pictures celebrate the beauty of the countryside, but they also realistically depict the everyday lives of the farmers and fishermen of Norfolk. Local art has been much abused, and often rightly so, but here you will find none of the sentimental clichés that give the genre such a bad name. The Norwich School represents a peak of achievement by artists who travelled around, precisely and lovingly capturing the essence of their homeland in all its rich variety. After years of war with Napoleon, and after the perils of possible revolution and invasion, these pictures mark a return to peaceful times and to the traditional values of a rural society. They are pictures of a social and national harmony, and that is not the least significant reason why they are once more so popular in England after having long been misunderstood and misrepresented as mere imitations of Dutch landscape painting. Yet for a long time the Norwich School was the least known of all English provincial schools of painting, for even if it was the most intensive and the most vigorous, it was also the most isolated. Some of its members did occasionally exhibit in London's Royal Academy, but for the most part the pictures were sold only to local people in and around Norwich. In 1933 the 27th and last exhibition by the Norwich Society took place, and although this did not mark the end of the school itself, it was the end of the school's most vibrant period.[1]

As in Constable Country, you can locate many of the Norwich School's subjects on your art-hunting hiker's map: the market and churches, Devil's Tower and Bishop Bridge – Norwich's medieval scenery on the River Wensum – and Mousehold Heath, which used then to be open heathland on the hills overlooking the city, with a windmill, now gone, that was a favourite subject for Cotman, Crome and Co. On you go to the round tower of Whitlingham Church, to Postwick Grove, to the banks of the Yare, and to Cotman's birthplace Thorpe, once called 'the Richmond of Norfolk'; on next to Trowse Hythe, where the Yare and the Wensum join together, and to Reedham Ferry (plate 32), where the chain ferry still goes across the river just as it does in the pictures of Joseph Stannard. And from there head for the Broads, and the lonely ruins of St Benet's Abbey (colour plate 8). Could there ever be a more beautiful guidebook than these pictures? Irresistibly they draw you into comparing places and times. In Thirtle's Norwich watercolour of 1812, boats are being repaired in a boatyard near Cow Tower; today there's a riverside café with boats for hire. One of John Crome's early masterpieces shows the ruins of Carrow Abbey; they now form part of the site of Colman's mustard factory.

You can imagine the artists still sitting there before the same scenes, pencil or brush in hand, all with different eyes, all with the same pleasure. The Norwich School's picturesque subject-matter soon attracted the tourists, and the artists' topographical and architectural illustrations became welcome features of the guidebooks. Seventy-six of Cotman's water-colours, turned into copper engravings, were used to illustrate *Excursions through Norfolk*, a two-volume guide published in London in 1818–19. 'Oh! rare and beautiful Norfolk.'

The Broads: A National Park in All but Name

Fens and fields, and a few windmills in the distance. Now and again a white sail glides smoothly through the meadows, like a shark fin cutting through a green ocean. Grey and motionless as Egyptian statues, herons stand on the riverbank. Dragonflies swirl noise-lessly over the water, their wings glittering. Some coots chatter away as they disappear into the reeds. The air is heavy with the smell of burnt stubble.

Moments on the Broads, memories of a late summer's day on the River Bure. Drifting downriver past Horning, which in the holiday season has as many boats as the port in Shanghai; following the bends in the river, branching off into narrow passageways that seem to lose themselves in the strange and whispering world of the reeds, but then suddenly open up again into a lake that's framed with alders and willows. Malthouse

---

1 The Norwich School of Design, founded in 1845, produced a minor figure of the Pre-Raphaelite movement, Frederick Sandys, son of a Norwich dyer. Some of his pictures and almost lifesize portrait drawings are to be seen in the Castle Museum. There is also a monumental tapestry by Edward Burne-Jones, *The Star of Bethlehem*, designed in 1890 for Exeter College, Oxford. The tapestry in the keep of Norwich Castle is a replica, woven in 1906 by Morris & Co. in Merton Abbey for Carrow Abbey in Norwich. Two well-known contemporary painters come from Norwich: Colin Self and Michael Andrews.

Broad: not to stop here would be a sin. On the shore is a pub, and on the hill is a church with a gold crown for a weather vane. A moment ago you were watching the bitterns, and now you're gazing in wonderment at the apostles of Ranworth, the most beautiful Gothic choir screen in Norfolk. Then you climb up to the top of the tower to gaze out over the vast expanse of the Broads, like a giant pool full of little toy boats. Then back we go to our own boat, and down the Bure we drift in this dreamlike, timeless, amphibious, laby-rinthine world of lakes and rivers, past the anglers at St Benet's, the only abbey with a windmill in its ruins, though the poor creature has lost its wings in the battle against the remorseless wind. Past bobbing boats with people on deck drinking tea or dangling their legs in the water. 'Proud Lady', 'Cheshire Cat', 'Silver Gem', 'Free 'n' Easy', these are the holiday boats of the Great British holidaymaker in the dreamiest of all holiday resorts: the Norfolk Broads.

Broadland, northeast of Norwich, covers an area of about 220 square miles, richly watered by the Rivers Yare, Bure and Waveney, and their tributaries the Thurne, the Ant and the Chet. It's a fascinating landscape, unique in its origins but typical in its problems (colour plate 7). This is England's largest stretch of wetlands, and its marshes and waters are a refuge for many endangered species of birds and plants. It's also one of England's favourite holiday resorts, boasting the biggest fleet of boats-for-hire in all the canal systems of Europe. This is where Nelson's countrymen can sail to their hearts' content. At the same time, the local farmers also have a living to make from the Broads. And so *Aeshna isoceles*, the rare Norfolk hawker dragonfly, has a hard time just surviving.

Nature reserve versus holiday resort, conservation versus agriculture. It was a classic case of conflicting interests, and even Parliament has had to step in. The Norfolk Broads became a national issue. And yet this region that needs protection from human inter-ference is actually the result of humans interfering. The Broads are, for the most part, an artificial and not a natural creation. Quite unlike the Lake District, they did not emerge from geological history, but from the social history of the early Middle Ages. Their creators were not the glaciers of the Ice Age, but the peat-cutters of Norfolk.

The history of Britain's splendid isolation, as everybody knows, began late and wet. Up until 6,000 BC, England was part of the European mainland, and it only became an island when the sea-level rose. Most of eastern Norfolk was flooded at the time, and became a flat, extended bay whose older layers of peat were then covered with new layers of mud and sand. Then gradually the bay became land again, and new peat formed in the marshes. There were very few trees in this region, and so peat was the most convenient fuel. Roman mercenaries, Saxon settlers, and Norman conquerors all took what they needed, but it was not until the Middle Ages that the monks first organized peat-cutting on a large scale. The Benedictines of St Benet's (colour plate 8) managed to acquire all the rights as well as the services of the peasants, and the abbey on the Broads became rich with its brown gold. A city like nearby Norwich needed masses of fuel – the episcopal monastery alone burnt 200,000 bales of peat a year. Within two hundred years, some nine million cubic feet of peat had been cut from the Broads, and the scars stretched wider and wider, and deeper and

P. H. Emerson: Ricking the Reed, 1887

deeper, sometimes to a depth of fifteen feet. Then in the 14th century, the sea-level rose, rainfall increased, and the great holes filled with water. By 1400 most of the cutting had ceased. And thus came into being the broad waters that we know as the Broads – relics of a medieval energy crisis.

Early 19th-century cadastral maps of the fields often show the geometrical lines of these flooded pits, but today the only remaining signs of the Broads' origins are place-names like Barton Turf, and the narrow strips of land that were left between individual diggings, used as dams and boundary markers. It was not until the fifties, in fact, that the painstaking detective work of English landscape historians pieced together the true story. Until then, people had assumed that the Broads were the work of a fickle climate, the natural remains of a shallow bay that had developed into marshland during Roman times, like Pevensey Levels in Sussex.

As is so often the case in East Anglia, the water reclaimed its share of the land. The Broads became the territory of the eel-fishers and reed-cutters, the basket-makers and the wild-duck-hunters. The reeds are used for thatching, and wild duck is a staple food for the farmers and a delicacy for London's markets and restaurants. King George VI used to go wildfowling every year from Sandringham to Ranworth and Malthouse Broads, where he was the guest of Colonel Cator, who gave both lakes to the Norfolk Naturalists' Trust.

Attempts to drain the marshes go back a long way, but the first successes were not until the 18th and 19th centuries. As in the Fens, windmills were used all over the Broads to pump the water from the marshes into the higher, dyked rivers. Initially, most of these wind-pumps were simple wooden constructions. Among the few surviving ones are Boardman's Mill on the River Ant (west of Ludham), and Herringfleet Mill on the Waveney, a weatherboarded Dutch mill, c.1830, near Somerleyton. The later and bigger mills were of brick. Two of the finest specimens are on the Thurne: the Thurne Dyke Windpump (colour plate 7), glowing white all over, with white sails, and diagonally opposite, a second mill of red brick – the two together making up a perfect 17th-century Dutch landscape painting. Many of these windpumps and cornmills have been restored by the Norfolk Mills and Pumps Trust (see page 503), with both private and public money.

It's on the Broads that you will find England's biggest windmill – eighty feet high, a dinosaur of brick: *Sutton Mill*. It was built by Tom Worts, a prosperous farmer and businessman, in 1789. After it had become redundant, Chris Nunn, an unemployed mechanic, bought it in 1976, and for years he has been single-handedly restoring his gigantic toy, in an act of pure and passionate devotion. ('Otherwise I'd have restored a viaduct.') Right up to the ninth storey, Chris explained all the machinery (perfectly preserved) to me. Sutton Mill was able to grind twenty tons of grain a day. Shaped like a ship's hull, the revolving cap of cedar braces itself against the wind, with mighty sails of Canadian pine. Once upon a time there were hundreds of these windmill wings turning on the Broads, and you can just imagine the creaking and clattering, humming and pumping, and droning and turning that used to go on day after day, as if armies of gigantic flies were swarming across the marshes. Now only a few are left, some decayed and some restored, frozen into pictures, looked at by the tourists, pictures of melancholy.

Like the windmills, the wherries are part of the Broads' archaic image. They are barges with black sails, and were once the most important means of transport between Norwich and the coast, carrying coal, timber, manure, reeds, fish and malt. Their heyday ended with the advent of the railway. The Norfolk wherry was specially designed to manoeuvre in the wind on the extremely shallow and often narrow waters of the Broads. It is about fifty feet long, and has a flat bottom and single mast, some forty feet high, with a gaff-topsail which can easily be tilted with counter-weights when the boat is passing under a bridge. Of the once great fleet of these barges, only a handful has survived,[1] plus the model in 'The Wherry' in Norwich.

1 One trading wherry remains afloat on the Broads, called Albion. It is owned and sailed by the Norfolk Wherry Trust. The only other trading wherry alive is Maud which is under restoration at Upton Dyke and hopes one day to return to her native waters. There are two pleasure wherries – Hathor and Solace; and three wherry yachts – Olive, Norada and White Moth. Note for underwater archaeologists: on Ranworth Broad (and some other lakes as well), a number of these gaff-topsail boats were sunk during the Second World War in order to prevent German seaplanes from landing.

P. H. Emerson: Coming Home from the Marshes, 1887

There is no better record of the marshdweller's life in East Anglia than that made by a Victorian gentleman named Peter Henry Emerson. He was a photographer, and in his pictures we see the reeds being cut and bundled in knee-deep water; the fowler stalking his wild duck, lying in his gun-punt with shot-gun cocked in the bow; fishermen taking in their eel-traps, and two children going home to their lonely farm in the marshes. The man with the camera even persuaded poachers to pose for him. *Life and Landscape on the Norfolk Broads* (1886) is one of seven books of photographs that Emerson published on this strange and then still remote world between land and water. He was born in Cuba, where his father had sugar plantations, took a degree in medicine at Cambridge, and in 1884 bought a cottage in Southwold. From there he explored the Broads, lived for weeks on a painter-friend's houseboat, gave up his medical practice, and devoted himself exclusively to his photography. But then he gave that up, too, dissatisfied with the limitations of the medium, and spent the last forty years of his life on such existential matters as writing detective stories, genealogy, and improving the rules of billiards.

P. H. Emerson was one of the pioneers of documentary photography in England. In his most important work, *Naturalistic Photography* (1889), he argued for photography that would correspond to natural perception, as opposed to pictorialism. 'Simplicity and sentiment are at the foundations of all true art' was his comment under his picture of a thatched house. He greatly admired the naturalism of Millet, and just as the latter painted the farmers of Barbizon, Emerson photographed the Broadmen. His *Birds, Beasts and Fishes of the Norfolk Broadland* (1895) is one of the first natural history books to have been illustrated entirely with photographs. He combined the precision of the scientist with the curiosity of the newspaper reporter, and artistic composition with technical brilliance. With full self-awareness, he warned his fellow-photographers against calling themselves artists: 'call yourself a photographer and wait for artists to call you brother.' The soft, impressionistic nuances of his platinotypes (some of the originals are in Norwich Library) endow the harsh working world of the Broads with a poetic aura not altogether free from elements of the Victorian idyll. But his record of a landscape and its life is also a swan song. At the very time when he was capturing the seemingly untouched world of the marsh people, the railway had already reached Wroxham, soon to be the site of the Norfolk Broads Yacht Club. Sailing became the Victorians' new hobby, and Broadland was the ideal place for it. Now, as well as transporting goods, the wherries began to carry tourists. And what did the tourists do as they sailed amongst the reeds? In Emerson's photo of 1886, they were busy picking waterlilies.

Such carefree enjoyment of Nature is a thing of the past. Here, as elsewhere, the conservationists try to save whatever *can* be saved. Of the 52 lakes on the Broads, 30 are completely ruined, and only four have anything approaching the rich plant life of former times. So, at any rate, concluded Timothy O'Riordan, a professor at the University of East Anglia, in the 1983 report for the Countryside Commission. What had caused this 'dramatic' decline in the natural beauty and the scientific importance of the Broads over the last fifty years? Were they, as he warns, 'a biological timebomb'? If so, who was guilty? The armada of motorboats, the greed of the farmers, Blakes (the holiday people), or *Myocastor coypus*, the coypu?

When a highly complex ecosystem like the Broads falls apart, the causes are many and varied. For years, sewage and chemical fertilizers have been swelling the amount of nitrate and phosphate on the Broads (the waters of East Anglia's rich arable land have the highest nitrate content in the whole of Britain). The water has been supersaturated, the growth of algae overstimulated. Dead particles of algae that have settled in the mud are constantly being stirred up by the propellors of the motorboats, the water becomes soapy and soupy, and plants are unable to grow. Furthermore, the dead algae in the mud form an ideal breeding-ground for bacteria. What is the result? In rivers once full of pike, perch, bream, roach, trout, carp, the fish are dying in their thousands. Waterfowl suffer the same fate, and the otter is almost completely extinct. The over fertilized algae are also responsible for the rapid disappearance of the reeds: in the last fifty years, more than half have been lost, and with them the irreplaceable habitat of warblers, marsh harriers, snipe, frogs and insects. There are only ten pair of bittern left. On the other hand, until recently there were far too many coypus, which had been introduced from Argentina in 1929. Instead of letting themselves be turned into fur coats, some of them had the cheek to escape from their farms, multiply at top speed, and go on the rampage among the reeds. During the sixties, there were about 200,000 of them, and it took an intensive campaign during the eighties to bring them under control. Now they are almost extinct.

Where the reeds die, the banks crumble. Natural protectors have to be replaced by iron bulkheads. But if the coypus gnawed away at the Broads, motorboats and holidaymakers positively devour them. The invasion of the wild ducks in autumn is nothing compared to the invasion of the leisure people in spring. In their dinghies, fibreglass yachts and plastic cabin cruisers, they are here, there and everywhere, enjoying ever more sophisticated mod cons, with galleys, heating, fridge, shower and chemical toilet. Boating on the Broads is fun – but not for the Broads. There are 12,000 vessels operating here, with ten times more motorboats than sailing boats. During the peak season, the River Bure near Horning is the Broads' equivalent of the M1. By far the most intensive users are the 2,714 hire boats, nearly two thirds of which are motor cruisers. Nevertheless, David Court, managing director of Blakes Holidays, expresses his fear that the conservationists might gain the upper hand and ruin the fun (and the business) of the boat people. Blakes of Wroxham, founded in 1908 by a London accountant, is the oldest boat agency on the Broads, and one of the most successful of its kind, with a range of solid and floating holiday homes from Norfolk to Florida. David Court does not dispute the fact that erosion in some places is 'serious'. 'But the boats are blamed for a lot of damage that they don't cause.' There are speed limits, aren't there? Well yes, but there's no-one around to enforce them. A lot of the Broads are closed to boats, aren't they? Well yes, fortunately, but that simply means more boats on the others.

Business with Nature can only flourish if Nature flourishes. If Blakes support measures for the preservation of the Broads, that can only be in their own interests. But things are different as far as the farmers are concerned. Obviously *their* interest lies in the fertility of the soil more than in the quality of the water. Drainage was always the name of the game – everyone knew that. Until eventually people began to see the degree and the consequences of this process: in the postwar years alone, a quarter of all the marsh meadows were ploughed into arable land, and the flora and fauna of the area were decimated. In 1984, the landscape historian Richard Muir warned that the destruction of the Broads through drainage and the transformation of cattle pastures into prairie-type wheatfields was proceeding at an alarming rate. One exemplary case was the Battle of Halvergate Marshes.

Halvergate is a village in the large, wet triangle between the Bure and the Yare: rich grazing land, dykes, ditches, the remains of old windmills. As late as the 19th century, farmers from the Scottish Highlands would drive their thin cattle to Norwich, where they sold them to the farmers of Halvergate Marshes for fattening. But eventually the Norfolk farmers decided to make better use of their land, and to cultivate grain (we have now jumped to the present). This, though, is the territory of the curlew, the snipe, the grey heron, marsh orchids, and no less than fourteen different varieties of grass. Once ploughed, gone for ever. There erupted a storm of indignation. Conservation groups, private citizens, the Council for the Protection of Rural England, all protested vehemently. The farmers got ready to do battle. Members of Friends of the Earth chained themselves to the first bulldozers as they came to plough up the marshes. No-one would give way, and no-one could win. *The Times* called Halvergate the 'Flanders' in the great war between the interests of agriculture and the goals of conservation.

The only way out at the time was compensation on the unions principle of 'profits foregone' – high profits indeed in view of the richness of the land here. Instead of this clearly unsatisfactory scheme, the Broads Authority devised an alternative voluntary incentive system to encourage farmers to stick with traditional grazing and to protect flowers and birds. Even the Ministry of Agriculture contributed funds for this new approach, which has been successful enough to give real hope for the future of the Broads. Further afield, the scheme has been a blueprint – or green print – for the Environmentally Sensitive Areas Scheme now in use throughout the county.

The truly amphibious organization responsible for these improvements is the Broads Authority, set up independently by the local councils to protect their countryside. Now it consists of two county councils, six local councils, the Anglian Water Authority, the Association of Inland Shipping and the harbour authorities at Great Yarmouth. In March 1988 the Boards Act gave the Authority statutory powers, in particular one designation. The Broads are now a National Park in all but name, and their regeneration continues at a considerable pace.

Just how successful, though costly, the purification and revitalization of polluted water can be, I saw for myself on *Cockshoot Broad*. In the last few decades, this little lake south of Horning had become more and more silted up, and the quality of the water had increasingly deteriorated. To start with, the lake was dammed off from the River Bure, and then the polluted water and mud were pumped out. The aquatic plants proliferated, and water-fleas,which eradicate algae, returned. Today Cockshoot Broad is once more an oasis, barred to pleasure boats and to be reached only by way of a corduroy road. Similar work has been done at Belaugh Broad and Hoveton Little Broad. The hope is that by the middle of the 21st century, all of the Broads will have been revitalized in this way – certainly one of the most ambitious projects in the history of the English countryside and its restoration. Expensive, laborious and technically pioneering, this work is 'a marathon, not a sprint' (Broads Authority).

In charge of Cockshoot Broad is the Norfolk Naturalists Trust (see page 503), which is doing magnificent work with its information centres, nature trails and bird-watching observatories. This is preservation through enlightenment. On the triple-forked upper reaches of the River Thurne are *Martham Broad* and *Hickling Broad*, parts of which are also administered by the Trust as nature reserves. Here there are still bitterns and marsh harriers – more often heard than seen – and another typical inhabitant of the Broads, the bearded tit. Occasionally you may even see an osprey as you make your way to Hickling Broad. This is the largest of the lakes, though it's only about three feet deep, and one of its special attractions is *Papilio machaon*, the swallowtail butterfly. Here the caterpillars of this rare species find the milk parsley they need to feed on. You may also catch sight of an even rarer species: a man in the uniform of the Napoleonic Wars, skating swiftly across the water as if the lake had frozen over. He is, of course, a ghost. To be precise, he is the Skating Soldier, the Ghost of Hickling Broad. There was once a young soldier who was stationed with his regiment near this lake, and he fell in love with a farmer's daughter on the other side of the lake. Whenever he could, he would go across to see her, and that winter he would often skate across the ice to his beloved. But one night, the temperature rose slightly, and in the middle of the lake he fell through the ice and drowned.

Stiff and still and grey, a heron poses on the shore. The reeds thrust their dark lances up into the twilight. Near the windmill at the quay of *Horsey Mere*, a boatman moors his boat and wends his way back to the village. A few houses, a church, a pub, a pillar-box – that's Horsey. The little church is made of flint and has a thatched roof. On the wall is a list of all the parsons since 1315, and next to it are photos of the barn owls that nest in the round tower. And why shouldn't the house of God also be the house of birds, especially on the Broads? The choir window contains a portrait, but it's not of a saint. The figure stands at an easel, wearing a long, red, highnecked dress. Her name is Catherine Ursula Rising, and she was a Victorian painter, forgotten by the history of art, but remembered here in the small eternity of the church in the village where she was brought up.

After the stillness of Horsey Mere, just a mile away from the sea, you can go upriver to the hurly-burly of *Potter Heigham*: boatyards, corrugated iron sheds, shops for boating equipment and provisions, and dominating everything, the navy blue 'Tower Shop'. For many skippers on the Broads, this is the start or end of the journey. Ever since the Middle Ages, a low stone bridge has ensured that only the smaller boats can pass through the eye of this needle.

October is the time when the cormorants come. They spend their winter on the northern edge of *Ranworth Broad*. Towards evening these black rock-birds gather in their hundreds among the trees on the shore. Here, between Ranworth and Malthouse Broad, the Queen opened a floating museum in 1976, the *Broadland Conservation Centre* of the Norfolk Naturalists Trust. As you walk through the marsh on a corduroy road a third of a mile long, you will learn literally step by step just how the vegetation develops, from open water right to dry land. Another nature trail of a very special kind, dedicated to the glory of God and the joy of the community, is in *Ranworth*, and it's been there for centuries: yellow irises, buttercups, and other marsh plants, painted on the ribbed coving of the Gothic choir screen of St Helen's, under its crown of filigree tracery. This is the most beautiful and best preserved screen in Norfolk. It separates the full width of the nave from the choir, and also forms two niches for the side altars. On the wooden panels of the central section are full-length figures of the twelve Apostles, flanked by the Archangel Michael and St George, the patron saint of England. Amongst this gallery of saints and martyrs are Thomas Becket, Archbishop of Canterbury, Queen Etheldreda of Ely, and St Felix, the first Bishop of East Anglia. This screen is a wonderful combination of graceful movement, elegant dress, expressive spirituality, the courtly world and the heavenly, the realism and the ardent faith of the Middle Ages – all depicted in glowing red and green and gold. Forming the background to these figures are stylized flowers, taken from the earthly paradise of the Norfolk Broads. The Ranworth screen is probably the joint work of local carvers and Flemish or German painters. The fact that this masterpiece of English ecclesiastical art, dating from the early 15th century, is so well preserved is not due only to the restorers. Puritan zealots scratched out only a few of the faces, and instead they attacked these hated popish symbols with brown paint – an excellent method of preservation.

In Norfolk alone there are at least 86 painted screens, in a more or less fragmentary state. Two of the finest are in churches on the Broads: *Barton Turf* (mid 15th-century, colour plates 21, 22) and *Ludham* (1493); in the choir arch of the latter hangs a Crucifixion painted on wood, probably from the time of the Catholic Queen Mary Tudor (1533–58), as a replacement for the Crucifixion group on the rood screen which had been destroyed by the Reformers shortly before she came to the throne.

When I visited St Helen's, shortly after Harvest Festival, there were sheaves of wheat in front of the screen and bundles of reeds around the pulpit, and next to the pre-Reformation oak lectern lay a giant pumpkin. This village church has yet another treasure, which you would expect to find in a museum rather than in a church: an illuminated manuscript dating from about 1400. Premonstratensian monks from Langley Abbey created this antiphonal, which contains their daily prayers and hymns and is decorated with nineteen superb miniature paintings. Next to it, though, is a bitter relic of our own times: a field altar from the First World War, together with a photograph album containing portraits of those who fell – some fifty men just from this one small community. I climbed up the spiral staircase to the top of the tower, and was greeted by a truly regal view: the Broads all around, and a gold crown weather vane, with the initials ER (Elizabeth Regina), plus the date of the Coronation, 1953.

In the marshes far from the villages and the roads lies a strange double ruin – a windmill in the gatehouse of an abbey: *St Benet's Abbey* (colour plate 8). Benedictines founded a monastery on the north bank of the Bure, Vikings destroyed it in about 870, and England's Danish King Canute rebuilt it in 1020. It became one of the richest abbeys in all East Anglia. By the end of the 13th century, the monks of St Benet's owned estates in 76 Norfolk parishes; they had control over numerous parish churches as well as substantial sections of the medieval peat industry. A nice fat bag for the Reformers, you might think. But Henry VIII preferred to do a deal: he made the last Abbot Bishop of Norwich in 1536, and in return the latter handed over the estates belonging to the Cathedral while he kept those of the Abbey. Thus St Benet's was the only English monastery to escape dissolution. Even today, the Bishop of Norwich is still Abbot of St Benet's – England's only Abbot-Bishop in the House of Lords. On the first Sunday in August every year, he comes from Norwich, making the last part of his journey by boat, and holds an open-air service next to the ruined abbey. He is an abbot with no monks, for the last one left the abbey way back in 1545. St Benet's fell into ruin, providing a cheap source of stone for the peasants in the region.

John Sell Cotman: St Benet's Abbey, Norfolk, 1831

Since the wind whistled constantly through the gatehouse, it seemed a good idea to build a windmill there in order to help drain the marshes. That was in the late 18th century. And then along came the artists from Norwich, including John Sell Cotman. From him alone came four variations on the theme of St Benet's Abbey: an etching, an oil painting, and two watercolours (1813 and 1831). It was a subject straight from the Romantic textbook: the lonely ruins on the riverbank, Gothic abbey walls, and a windmill growing out of them and reaching its sails up into the sky. It was also the perfect pilgrimage for Victorian picnickers until in 1863 a gale blew the cap and wings off the body of the picturesque prayer-mill, leaving only this strange, lonely wreck.

The abbey and its grounds now belong to the Norwich Union, the insurance company, and have been leased to a farmer. There are reeds growing in the monks' fishponds, and cows graze on the foundations of the church. And here lies the body of Shakespeare's Falstaff: Sir John Fastolf of Caister Castle (see page 411f.), one of the Abbey's great benefactors.

From the riverbank I could see flint glistening in the water, and in the distance a red sail gliding through the marshes. I walked on along the river, and up above me the sky was imitating Cotman's watercolours.

Bloaters from Yarmouth: The Smell that Conquered the World

'It looked rather spongy and soppy, I thought as I carried my eye over the great dull waste that lay across the river; and I could not help wondering, if the world were really as round as my geography-book said, how any part of it came to be so flat. But I reflected that Yarmouth might be situated at one of the poles; which would account for it.'

That was how it was when little David Copperfield first came to Great Yarmouth, and understandably he expressed the view to Peggotty that he 'hinted to Peggotty that a mound or so might have improved it; and also that if the land had been a little more separated from the sea, and the town and the tide not been quite so mixed up, like toast and water, it would have been nicer.' Incidentally, Ham's houseboat evidently enabled Master Davy to feel a lot happier in Great Yarmouth than I ever did, despite my enjoyment of Dickens. How can one feel good in a seaside resort that's been ruined by tourism and has an unemployment rate of 16 per cent? 'Try your handa at winning a panda.' There are two miles of fatuous promenade entertainments, from the piers through to Joyland. Bathing? According to official figures, the beach at Great Yarmouth does not come up to EC health

J. M. W. Turner: Great Yarmouth, Norfolk, 1829

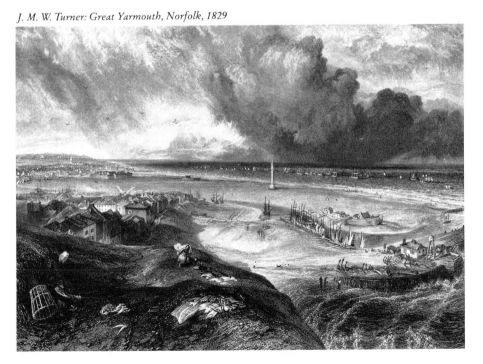

regulations. I really don't think Mrs Peggotty would still be 'proud to call herself a Yarmouth bloater'.

In the Second World War, Great Yarmouth was badly damaged by bombing. The damage by reconstruction is just as bad. Some places were spared, and some were restored, but all too many have been rebuilt without any plan and without any imagination. St Nicholas, for example: this was a 12th-13th-century parish church dedicated to the patron saint of fishing; it was burnt out in 1942, and rebuilt in 1960, as a Neo-Gothic imitation. They didn't even have the courage to use modern forms. A completely wasted opportunity. Yet in spite of it all, you can still see that once this was a town of character.

Yarmouth developed on a long and narrow bank of sand and gravel between the sea and the mouth of the Yare, which flows for nearly three miles parallel to the coast before it discharges itself into the sea. The location of the town also determined its layout: three long main streets running from north to south, crossed by numerous lanes going from west to east, at most six feet wide. These medieval alleys were called The Rows, and there were over 200 of them prior to the war. You can imagine the hustle and bustle, the smells, the Hogarthian scenes and Dickensian characters that filled the Rows of Yarmouth. This ancient pedestrian zone behind the South Quay was the home of seamen, craftsmen and merchants. You can still see two restored merchants' houses of the 17th century in Rows 111 and 117. The stately middle-class houses on South Quay itself, which Defoe rated as the most beautiful quay in England, were inhabited by the richer merchants: Benjamin Cooper, for instance, at No. 4 South Quay (1596), and John Andrews, 'the greatest herring merchant in Europe' at No. 20, built c.1720.

This is the town of the herring. Three lions with herring tails leap through the coat of arms of Great Yarmouth. Herrings made Yarmouth great, and for centuries the whole town smelt of smoked herrings. That is the unmissable, unmistakable, unmatchable smell of the most English of English breakfasts. Even the continental nose is tickled into surrender by that smell. From Great Yarmouth the scent spread all the way across the British Isles, thence to Malta and Gibraltar, and across to Rhodesia, India, New Zealand, and onto the furthest breakfast tables of the British Empire, and into the nostrils of the entire English-smelling world.

John Woodger from Great Yarmouth was the man who transformed the common herring into the majestic kipper. Before smoking it, he split and gutted it and deluged it in salt and spices. Meanwhile, his colleague Mr Bishop merely smoked it, but smoked it so perfectly that he is glorified as the inventor of the bloater. These two geniuses of the art of herring-processing are the only geniuses Great Yarmouth ever produced.

For centuries the autumn brought huge shoals of herring to the Norfolk coast, and the herring fishers and the herring dealers would come from far and wide to the port, where the annual fish market was held – the Free Herring Fair. They came from Rye, Dover and

◁ *John Sell Cotman: Yarmouth Fisherwoman, c.1812*

the other Cinque Ports, and from Scandinavia and the Baltic; the whole of northern Europe flocked to medieval Yarmouth in order to buy the salted herring. Defoe says they were even exported to Italy, Spain and Portugal, and he quotes the number of ships that were registered in Yarmouth in 1697: 1,123 – more even than in London. For a long time it was the Dutch who dominated the herring industry (in 1571 there were 104 Dutch families living in Yarmouth, mainly fishermen from Seeland), but then Charles I and his successors banned all foreign competition in their Majesties' waters. After 1815, however, Dutch trading and fishing vessels again became part of the everyday scene in Great Yarmouth – and a colourful scene it was, as painted by J. S. Cotman and other artists of the Norwich School (e.g. George Vincent, 'The Dutch Fair on Yarmouth Sand', in Norwich Castle Museum). Cotman lived in Great Yarmouth from 1812 till 1823, at No. 83 Southtown Road. Among his Yarmouth pictures are 'Dutch Boats off Yarmouth', c.1823, 'Yarmouth Fisherwoman', c.1812 (British Museum), and one of his most brilliant sea watercolours, 'Storm on Yarmouth Beach', 1831 (Norwich Castle Museum).

In 1913 alone, over 900 million herring were brought ashore in Great Yarmouth. Little wonder, then, that with all this overfishing, the North Sea withdrew its herring favours. Great Yarmouth is still a commercial port, but now it's a supply base serving the gas and oil fields off the coast of Norfolk. One of the last fishing boats, the 'Lydia Eva' has lain since 1973 at South Quay, to recall the good old days. It's a floating museum of the herring industry.

Daniel Defoe had good reason to laud the port of Yarmouth for its safety as well as its economic efficiency. Fresh in his memory was the disaster of Winterton Ness, north of the town, where one stormy night in 1692 more than 200 ships and 1,000 men were lost. Devil's Throat was the name the seafarers gave to this coast. Survivors of later disasters were taken to the Shipwrecked Sailors' Home of 1861, which is now the maritime museum of East Anglia. There we can learn about Captain George W. Manby, who in 1807 invented a lifesaving apparatus that fired a rescue line from the shore to a shipwreck. Captain Manby was a patron to local marine painters, a fellow-student and admirer of Nelson, and an indefatigable inventor. One of his more out-of-the-way plans was to assassinate Napoleon.

West of Great Yarmouth, the Waveney and Yare join together in a broad lake of an estuary, almost as if they wanted to stay inland for a while rather than take to sea, and here, at the western end of Breydon Water (and therefore just in Suffolk), lie the ruins of the Roman fortress of Gariannonum. This is history in a natural state of abandonment, Piranesi in an English marsh: *Burgh Castle*. From the village church with its Norman round tower you go through fields of turnips; the Roman walls are gleaming in the sun – flint with bands of red brick – and in the distance a windmill is flexing its wings. A few children and dogs are playing among the walls of the ruined Roman camp, and at the foot of the hill you can see the white holiday cruisers gliding by. On the other side of the river, infinitely green and flat, Halvergate Marshes stretch out into the Norfolk mist.

When the Romans built their stronghold here in the 3rd century, the marsh was still

Joseph Stannard: Boats on the Breydon, 1825

under water, and Burgh Castle stood on a broad bay, a naval base for the Comes Litoris Saxonici to defend the region against invading Saxons and marauding Vikings. The walls of alternating flint and brick, reinforced with round bastions at the corners and in the middle, enclosed an area of some six acres. At some points the walls are still up to 15 feet high and over 11 feet thick at the base. In about AD 408, the Romans vacated Gariannonum. In the early 7th century, the itinerant preacher St Fursey, one of the Irish *peregrini*, founded a mission monastery within the abandoned ruins. During the Middle Ages, however, they were used as a quarry to provide building materials for churches.

North of the Yare Estuary, in present-day *Caister-on-Sea*, the Romans had already set up a trading post in about AD 125, much bigger than Burgh Castle. This walled Roman town was inhabited until well into the 4th century, but only a few foundations and remains have been uncovered. The rest is buried beneath bungalows and holiday camps. In the fields further west stands the castle of Sir John Fastolf, one of the legendary sources of Shakespeare's Falstaff, the most cowardly, boastful, witty and lovable fat man in world literature. The real-life Sir John was one of the most colourful characters to emerge from the Hundred Years War. He led the English bowmen at Agincourt, was the King's governor in Normandy, and a veritable old warhorse, and when he returned from the French campaign he was so rich that he was able to build Caister Castle (1432–5), a brick building originally surrounded by a moat, and now used to house a collection of veteran cars.

When Sir John died in 1459, the castle passed to a family whose name is for ever linked to a famous collection of letters from the late Middle Ages: the Paston Letters. They give a vivid picture of everyday life in East Anglia at the time of the Wars of the Roses. It's a family correspondence over several generations, and precisely because it is so private and so personal, it offers a good deal of fascinating information about the social, economic and political conditions of that period. The letters go from 1425 right through to the beginning of the 16th century – sober ones, worried ones, angry ones, tender ones, on Valentine's Day, or about the administration of the estate, or the dirty tricks of powerful neighbours, or the weather, the harvest, or what they had for dinner. They are not about the fate of a nation, but about the problems of a family, with all their hopes, fears and ambitions during this troubled time. On 28 February 1449, Margaret Paston warns her 'Right worshipful husband' John: 'I pray you beware what ye eaten or drink with any other fellowship, for the people is full untrusty.' And Agnes Paston advises her son: 'In little business lieth much rest.'

The Paston Letters are an important example of early written English, spanning the period shortly before and after William Caxton introduced printing to England (1475). More than a thousand of these letters have survived, the majority of them now kept in the British Library. *Paston* is also the name of the village on the northeast coast of Norfolk, where the Pastons came from. Another magnificent legacy from this family is the barn that Sir William Paston built in 1581, almost 60 feet high and 160 feet long – the longest barn in Norfolk. This monumental flint building with the open trusses of its thatched roof is now to be used as a crafts centre. Nearby, the village church displays the elegance of this landed family in the form of Katherine Paston's alabaster tomb (plate 85). She lies there in her Jacobean dress, with ruff, embroidered bodice, puffed sleeves and pearl necklaces, a lifesize sculpture by Nicholas Stone (1629), who was the Stuarts' court sculptor (other monuments of his in Norfolk churches are at Holkham, Oxnead, Emneth and Tittleshall). The epitaph was written by John Donne. Another of the Pastons to have been buried with great ceremony in his village church was John, in 1466. Shortly before he died, he had asked his wife for a jerkin of 'fine worsted, which is almost like silk'. Flemish immigrants helped to make this cloth popular all over medieval England. Its name came from the weavers' village of Worstead in northeastern Norfolk.

Until the Civil War, the Pastons were one of the most influential families in all of East Anglia. There are still many traces of them, especially in Norfolk: Sir Edward's Jacobean house *Barningham Hall* (1612), southwest of Cromer; Sir William's alabaster tomb in the parish church at *North Walsham*, where he founded a grammar school. While the Pastons were penning their letters, there were many craftsmen exercising their own skills in some of the local churches. In St Peter and St Paul at *Knapton*, there are about 160 angels, archangels and prophets – carved and coloured wooden sculptures of 1503 – holding up the hammerbeam roof of Irish oak. The font of St Botolph's in *Trunch* is crowned by a two-storey canopy with six richly decorated posts and miniature fan vaults – a masterpiece of late Gothic woodcarving (c.1500).[1] The choir screen dates back to the same period, and was originally painted in gold, red and green. Almost all the faces of the Apostles were scratched out by the iconoclasts of the Reformation.

Crabs and Roses: Cromer's Beach and Repton's Park

For a long time I used to think that Cromer only existed for the sake of Edward Lear's limerick: 'There was an old person of Cromer / Who stood on one leg to read Homer; / When he found he grew stiff, / He jumped over the cliff, / Which concluded that person of Cromer.' A classic demise when you consider how short a limerick has to be, and how badly Cromer's cliffs have been eroding, especially since Lear's day. Even the deckchair attendant warns his customers: 'When you come back next year, there'll be less.' And he doesn't mean fewer deckchairs. Every year, a few more inches of cliff disappear, dug away by the rabbits, and washed away by the winter storms.

'Going to the edge' was what they used to call it in East Anglia when you travelled to the Norfolk coast. And for centuries, people, houses, churches and whole villages have gone right over the edge. The miles of glorious sands that make up the beach near *Trimingham*, southeast of Cromer, are the result of continuous erosion. I once spent a night there, in a house on the cliffs, and it felt as if the waves were already pounding at the door. 'In a few decades,' said my host, a retired sea captain, 'the sea will have swallowed this place up as well.' In neighbouring *Sidestrand*, the church was in danger, and so it was rebuilt further inland in 1880. But the coastal village of *Eccles* has long since disappeared, and of its church all that remains is a few fragments of flint in the sand. Let us then hasten to *Cromer* while Cromer is still there.

There are a few fishermen's cottages grouped around the church, some Victorian brick houses and hotels, and a rather stunted pier (colour plate 3, plate 43). Cromer is as far from Brighton's sleek elegance as it is from Blackpool's messy hullabaloo. The only loud things here are the seagulls. Cromer has the faded charms of an Edwardian bathing costume. Since the war there has never been enough money available to cause more damage through new buildings.

'Perry was a week at Cromer once, and he holds it to be the best of all the sea-bathing places,' writes Jane Austen in *Emma* (1816). Perry is a champion of the good, fresh English summer. He is a man made for Cromer. Less hardy souls might find the Norfolk coast just a bit too harsh and a lot too remote. That, perhaps, is why despite Jane Austen Cromer's rise to the status of seaside resort was somewhat delayed, until in 1877 the first trainful of

---

1 There are only four other font canopies of this sort remaining in England: St Mary's, Luton (1370), St Peter Mancroft, Norwich (1450), Lower Ufford Church, Suffolk (c.1450), and Durham Cathedral (1680).

holidaymakers arrived from London. Shortly afterwards, *The Daily Telegraph* described how one should spend the day at this 'pretty little watering place'. It was best 'to go on the sands during the morning, to walk on one cliff for a mile in the afternoon and to crowd upon the little pier at night.' Amazingly, Cromer became fashionable. Lord Tennyson came to have a look, and so did the Duchess of Marlborough, and Princess Adolfa von Schaumburg-Lippe. Even Queen Victoria's dashing grandson from Germany, the Kaiser himself, came across in his white yacht 'Hohenzollern'. The best people stayed in the 'Hotel de Paris' on the promenade – Lord Suffield's former summer residence, extended to become a Victorian Grand Hotel and a somewhat bizarre outpost for the upper echelons of society. Goose-pimpled Edwardians got together for the last beach-parties in Cromer and in the villas at Overstrand, and since those days the 'Hotel de Paris' has sunk from caviare to ketchup. The only thing that hasn't altered is the fine sea view.

'Still raining?' – 'Yes, still raining.' – 'Ah well, it's good for the garden.' On such days, the Life Boat Tea Shop soon fills up, and so do the parish church, the local museum, and the Life Boat Museum. The interior of the church is 'somewhat meagre' (Pevsner), but its tower is the highest in Norfolk. The 'Number One Lifeboat' is legendary. Another of the town's attractions is the pier (1901), and especially the Pavilion Theatre at the end of the pier (colour plate 3). Here you can still see the popular *Seaside Special*, harking back to the golden age of the End-of-the-Pier Show. You'll find a happy audience, the Birmingham Brothers Gordon & Bunny Jay, and a host of courageous clowns. Television has killed off the variety theatre, and with it most of these pier shows that were once as much a part of the English seaside as the dirty picture postcard.

Defoe's verdict on Cromer is still more or less valid today: 'I know nothing it is famous for except good lobsters.' Lobsters, crabs and shrimps, perhaps. Cromer crabs are indeed reputed to be the best in England. The banks of crabs are about three miles out, and they are caught between April and September in boats manned by two men with 200 pots. The blue and red boats are heavy, and are pulled to the shingle beach by tractor. Once Cromer had fifty of these crab-boats, but now there are just fifteen. Seven of them belong to the Davies family, the head of which is Henry, known as 'Shrimp'. In his youth, recalls Shrimp, 'women had more on when they went bathing than they did when they went to church.' In those days his grandfather drove the horse-drawn bathing machines, from one of which the Austrian Empress Elisabeth lowered herself into the waves of Cromer in 1887.

Neighbouring *Sheringham* never rose to these dizzy heights. Even its crab fishers were relegated to the second division by the reputation of Cromer crabs. As consolation, however, one can travel with the old steam engine of the North Norfolk Railway from Sheringham into the countryside, three whole blissful miles as far as Weybourne Heath, and soon even as far as Holt. This historic stretch, restored by devoted railway fans, has the poetic name of 'Poppy Line', recalling those distant times of smoke and steam and poppy-red fields before the farmers deluged Norfolk's landscapes with herbicide.

In the hills southwest of Sheringham lies the home of a Regency gentleman, a house of

John Thirtle: Cromer, c.1830

grey brick in a setting of trees, azaleas and rhododendrons. This is *Sheringham Hall* (1812–17). The park was designed by Humphry Repton, one of the great landscape gardeners who followed Capability Brown. He and his son John Adey Repton also designed the house. In his theoretical writings, Humphry Repton was the first to coin the term 'landscape gardening'. In all, he created some 200 gardens and parks, but Sheringham was his 'favourite and darling child in Norfolk'. He regarded it as essential for the landscape gardener to have detailed knowledge of architecture, and although he himself was not one of the great architects, with Sheringham Hall he achieved exactly what he always strove for: complete harmony between building and landscape.

In contrast to the picturesque fashion of the time, Humphry Repton surrounded his houses with flowerbeds, trellises, terraces and kitchen gardens. Only then would he allow a carefully composed Nature to take over his park. 'In whatever relates to men, propriety and convenience are not less objects of good taste, than picturesque effect,' he wrote in 1794. He used watercolour plans that could be folded over one another in order to show his clients the before-and-after effect of his suggestions for reshaping their estates. 'The first object of improvement ought to be *Convenience*; and *Beauty* should adapt itself to that,' he wrote in one of his sketchbooks, called *Red Books* because of their red morocco bindings. In the Red Book for Sheringham Hall, 1812, Repton also appealed to the social conscience of his client: Abbot Upcher, the young landowner, should let poor people collect wood from the park, and should organize hare coursing on the beach with them in order to bring the social classes closer together 'in a happy medium between Licentious Equality and Oppressive Tyranny'. In 1986, the National Trust acquired Sheringham Hall and arranged one of the drawing-rooms as a Repton Room.

Repton grew up in Bury St Edmunds, was apprenticed to a cloth merchant in Norwich, and spent most of his life in Sustead Old Hall, near Aylsham (Norfolk), and in Hare Street, near Romford (Essex). East Anglia's gentle slopes and undulating oak and ash hedgerows had a strong influence on his landscaped gardens. He had his first commission in 1788 for the park at Catton Hall, which belonged to the Mayor of Norwich. His most important client, however, was the Duke of Portland, through whom he gained connections with the landed class. His clients included the 1st Marquess of Cornwallis (Culford Hall, Suffolk), who was a general in the American War of Independence, the Pitt family, and dozens of MP's.

Humphry Repton had sixteen children, of whom only seven survived into adulthood. He himself died in 1818, and is buried in the churchyard at *Aylsham*, a little market town between Cromer and Norwich, where he lies beneath the roses by the south wall of St Michael's. He wrote his own epitaph, which is also his creed as a landscape gardener: 'Not like Egyptian Tyrants consecrate, / Unmixed with others shall my dust remain; / But mold'ring, blending, melting into Earth, / Mine shall give form and colour to the Rose, / And while its vivid blossoms cheer Mankind, / Its perfumed odours shall ascend to Heaven.' A Romantic, pragmatic, very English farewell.

A hundred years after Humphry Repton, another landscape gardener came to the Norfolk coast: Gertrude Jekyll. In Overstrand, a suburb of Cromer, she laid out one of her intimate parterre gardens, for which the architect Edwin Lutyens designed an arcaded passage and alcoves. They were both commissioned by Lord Battersea, Chief Whip in Gladstone's cabinet, who was married to one of the Rothschild daughters. In 1897-8 they had their villa 'The Pleasaunce' redesigned by Lutyens, with an elaborately inlaid Moorish door and a fireplace with tiles by the Arts and Crafts potter William de Morgan. From what remains of this interior, one can gauge Lord Battersea's love of travel and collecting. His rather whimsical Edwardian summerhouse is now used as a Christian Endeavour Holiday Home, which is not exactly to the advantage of the architecture. Lutyens designed two other buildings in Overstrand at around the same time: a Methodist church with a Roman-style stepped porch in brick – his only Nonconformist chapel (1898) – and Overstrand Hall (1899-1901), a 'pasticcio' of brick, flint and timber, with Elizabethan and Roman motifs. The rooms are wood-panelled, the tiles are Delft, and no expense was spared on materials or indeed on staff: five gardeners and three butlers were permanently employed just in case the owner wanted to have a holiday in his summerhouse. And Lord Hillingdon, a London banker, did precisely this, for about two weeks of the year.

Rooms with a View: Blickling and Felbrigg

'My woods are my joy and pride,' Wyndham used to say. He was the last Squire of *Felbrigg Hall*, which lies two miles west of Cromer. Before Robert Wyndham Ketton-Cremer died, in 1969, and made over his estate to the National Trust, he planted some 200,000 trees, and since he was not only a passionate gardener but also a patriot, he laid out two long, V-shaped bridle-paths at the end of the war, running through Victory Wood, to celebrate VE Day. Not until 1954 did he install such new-fangled conveniences as the electric light, and until shortly before his death he regarded central heating as a luxury.

From the windows of his library, where he wrote his biographies and histories, Wyndham could look out over the park, and between the old oaks and chestnut-trees see the church tower of St Margaret's. The church stands completely isolated in the park (colour plate 26), for the village that used to be all around it in the Middle Ages was abandoned – though nobody knows exactly when or why – and rebuilt some distance away. The lords and ladies of Felbrigg Hall are buried in this little flint church, beneath brasses, or a bust by Joseph Nollekens, or putti and marble garlands from the workshop of Grinling Gibbons. On one of the brasses, almost lifesize, are Sir Simon Felbrigg and his wife Margaret, looking visitor and eternity straight in the eye, their hands folded, beneath ogee-arched canopies. Sir Simon is dressed in helmet and armour, with the Order of the Garter and the royal standard, for he was standard-bearer to King Richard II.

In the middle of the 15th century, the Felbrigg estate was bought by an ambitious merchant from Wymondham. The Windhams, who took their name from their place of origin, made their way in the world through good marriages and sheer industry. One of them rose to be an admiral, another a minister, and another climbed Mont Blanc. And one of them, William Frederick, was known as Mad Windham because that's what he was. He lived in Victorian times, and what he was mad about was railways; he only wanted to travel by rail, sold tickets in his railway uniform, ruined the estate, and ended up earning his living by driving buses between Norwich and Cromer. The Windhams were a splendid family.

GLORIA DEO IN EXCELSIS cry the capital letters on the balustrade at the front of the house – an exhortation as eccentric as it is pious, for much of the glory was certainly intended for the builder of Felbrigg Hall. Thomas Windham was his name, and he built the south wing (1620–4) of brick, flint and ashlar, with a typically Jacobean grid façade: three rectangular projecting bays and porches, stone mullion windows, and three sets of three tall brick chimneys. Just fifty years later – and the contrast could hardly have been greater – the gentleman architect William Samwell added a west wing of red brick (1674–87), smooth-fronted with high windows and a hipped roof, in classical Charles II style. Finally, around 1750, the popular country-house architect James Paine added the east wing (later gothicized) for the servants, with a central projection and clock turrets. Dating from more or less the same time is the octagonal dovecote in the kitchen garden, domed accommoda-

Felbrigg Hall, south front, engraving by J. Hawksworth after John Sell Cotman, c.1820

tion for 2,000 doves, which were a welcome delicacy for the table as well as providing useful fertilizer for the garden.

Past the Great Hall are the salons of the West Wing. The ceiling and walls of the Dining Room were decorated by James Paine, *c.*1750, with Rococo plasterwork; there are hunting trophies above the doors, and garlanded frames for family portraits by Kneller and Lely. Next door, in the Drawing Room – originally used as a dining room – is a Jacobean plaster ceiling of 1687, probably by Edward Goudge, to whom the plaster ceilings in neighbour- ing Melton Constable Hall (same year) are also attributed. The Felbrigg ceiling is covered with sumptuous fruits, flowers, pheasants, partridges and wild duck – a mouth-watering ceiling that any table would find hard to match. In this room and the next hang the paintings that young William Windham II had collected in the course of his continental tour between 1738 and 1742: seascapes by Willem van de Velde, gouaches by Giovanni Battista Busiri, Dutch landscapes and especially classical views of the Campagna. The manner in which these pictures are framed and displayed – virtually unchanged in 200 years – makes Felbrigg into a rare and authentic illustration of early 18th-century taste as influenced by the Grand Tour. (The only comparable collections are in John Parker's Red Room at Saltram House, and – much superior – the Methuen collection at Corsham Court.)

For four years the heir to Felbrigg Hall wandered through Europe. The young gentleman's educational journey brought him the loftiest of experiences – Antiquity, love, and the Alps. Young Windham climbed the glaciers round about Chamonix, and also went up Mont Blanc – a piece of trail-blazing before England's crown princes became accustomed to risking their necks with similar feats. William's friend and tutor on this tour was Benjamin Stillingfleet, son of the Bishop of Worcester, a man of broad education and pleasant eccentricity. At Lady Mary Wortley Montagu's London salon, he did not wear the normal black silk stockings of the day, but his own blue worsted stockings, which is why literary ladies have, ever since then, been called bluestockings. After his return, William Windham led the life of the cultured landowner, going to London clubs and theatres, and entertaining his artistic friends at Felbrigg Hall, including David Garrick and Dr Johnson. Books from the latter's collection are among the treasures of Felbrigg's library, which was designed by William's friend James Paine in the Gothic Revival style (1752). One of William's descendants, Thomas Wyndham Cremer, also left his mark in the form of fifty cases of stuffed birds – a lifelong passion – most of which he had shot himself – the bird-lover as bird-killer. Many of these birds were stuffed by Thomas Gunn of Norwich, the most famous Victorian taxidermist.

I shall never forget my first sight of *Blickling Hall* (colour plate 14). I was driving past fields of beet and barley northwest of Aylsham. Suddenly, right beside this country road,

Blickling Hall, south front, by J. C. Buckler, 1820

Sir Henry Hobart (d.1625) by Daniel Mytens

on the far side of a broad stretch of lawn, there was this glorious house. The red brick glowed warmly in the afternoon sun, great green walls of yew, over sixteen feet high and close to 400 years old, lined the path. These hedges lead the eye to the former stables and servants' quarters which flank the forecourt – brick buildings with curved Dutch gables of 1624, said to be the first of their kind in England, undulating all the way up to the main building. That was my first sight of Blickling Hall.

Two rectangular corner towers, two bays, and the entrance in the middle: it's a perfectly symmetrical façade, measured but animated by its contrasts. Rectangular Elizabethan bays and windows, and baroque curved Dutch gables; strictly geometrical corner towers with bright and breezy ogee roofs. Above the entrance, lording it over the gallery of chimneys, is a three-storey timber clocktower with an open lantern. Behind this front stretches a house with two inner courtyards, much bigger than the narrow southern façade might lead you to expect. Who was the architect? He has left his initials in the Baroque decorations over the entrance: RL, Robert Lyming, carpenter and stonemason. At the same time as he was building Blickling Hall (1619–25), he was probably also hard at work in neighbouring Felbrigg Hall. An even clearer affinity is to be found with Lyming's gable front at Hatfield House (c.1611), from the dominating clocktower to the perforated balustrades. Blickling Hall is one of the last great Jacobean country mansions to have been built in England; the double inner courtyard had already become old-fashioned, and had been supplanted by the new Palladian style. A portrait of the original owner, painted by Daniel Mytens, later court painter to Charles I, hangs over the fireplace in the state bedroom: Sir Henry Hobart, dressed in the furred robes of his office as James I's Lord Chief Justice.

Blickling Hall,
'Auditus', allegory of
the sense of hearing,
detail of the ceiling in
the Long Gallery, 1620

With even greater majesty than before, Sir Henry could today go from his entrance-hall up to his state apartments by way of a magnificent double staircase, for the original single staircase was replaced in 1767 by one in Jacobean style. The banisters are of oak, with ornate arcades and carved figures on every newel post: a courtier, a musketeer, ancient heroes. This splendour was created by William Ivory[1] of Norwich, who also made the two lifesize Rococo reliefs in the niches beside the staircase: Elizabeth I and her mother Anne Boleyn, the latter with the inscription 'Hic Nata'. The claim that this unfortunate queen was born here is legend rather than fact, but there is no disputing that the Blickling estate did belong to her family right up to her execution. The Boleyns were smallholders from Norfolk. Their rise began with Anne's great-grandfather Geoffrey, a protégé of the mighty Sir John Fastolf (see page 411), who had owned the Blickling estate since 1431 and sold it to his follower. Later, Hever Castle in Kent became the main seat of the Boleyns. There are some brasses of the family still in Blickling Church, but Anne's heart is said to have been buried in the village church at *Salle*, a radiant Perpendicular building in the remote fields southwest of Blickling, and worth a detour even without this somewhat morbid attraction. (In fact two other churches also claim to have Anne's heart: All Saints, East Horndon in Essex, and St Andrew & St Patrick, Elveden Park in Suffolk.)

The Long Gallery in the East Wing of Blickling Hall is about 123 feet long, and is one of the last of its kind – the end and the high point of a great tradition. It's a gallery to walk in

---

1   His father Thomas and cousin John also worked on the alterations to the house, particularly the North and West Wings (1765–85).

and to look out of, at the parterre garden and the park. But better than looking out is looking up – at the superb ceiling overhead, an amazing Jacobean plasterwork ceiling that has no equal: it's a densely woven, undulating pattern of ribs, arabesques, pendants, plant and geometrical decorations, and between them all, 31 panels of heraldic motifs and symbolic figures, including allegories of the five senses, various virtues, and learning. The designer of this plaster ceiling (1620) was one Edward Stanyan, probably a Londoner, and it is without doubt the most stunning show-piece in Blickling Hall. Originally the Long Gallery was used to display paintings, but in the 18th century it became the Library, with over 12,000 books bound in calfskin, including many early rarities.

The Long Gallery, with its books and its marvellous decor, leads to the scarcely less impressive Peter the Great Room, named after the tapestry depicting the Tsar riding his horse into victorious battle against the Swedes at Poltawa. This tapestry, woven in 1764 in St Petersburg, was given by Catherine the Great to the 2nd Earl of Buckinghamshire, who was George II's ambassador to the Tsarist court. On his return, the Earl had this room in Blickling Hall redesigned in order to accommodate his precious souvenir, and as a companion piece to it, he commissioned John Wootton to paint a monumental portrait of his king on horseback. Twenty years later, he was finally able to gaze in admiration at himself, for there on the wall he hung, full length and draped in ermine, while nearby hung his beautiful young wife Caroline – both of them painted by Gainsborough. A truly royal room, for all its vanity. Also captured for eternity is the Earl's sister, in pink and silver silk, with a flowered hat and décolleté: Henrietta Howard, Countess of Suffolk, friend of Swift, Pope, Horace Walpole, presumed mistress of George II, and certainly one of the most dazzling ladies of her time.

Blickling Hall effortlessly combines court scandals, glorious interiors, the history of art, and the history of a family. In such a place, specialists can study Jacobean plaster ceilings, European inlaid furniture, or 17th- and 18th-century weaving: Axminster carpets, Brussels tapestries based on Teniers motifs, and monumental Mortlake tapestries. It is no coincidence that the National Trust has set up its textile restoration centre at Blickling Hall, as well as its East Anglian headquarters. Apart from Gainsborough, Reynolds, Benjamin West and Canaletto[1], what particularly impressed me was a series of large sepia drawings by Christoph Heinrich Kniep, Goethe's companion on his Italian journey. Typifying the artistic taste of the time is Blickling's Print Room, with Piranesi's Vedute of Rome, and engravings after Raphael, Claude Lorrain, Richard Wilson and others, stuck directly to the wall next to or above and below one another in the 18th-century fashion.

John Hobart, 2nd Earl of Buckinghamshire (1723–93) ▷

1 The Blickling Canaletto, *View of Chelsea from the Thames* (c.1746–8) is only the left half of a painting whose right half is part of a private collection in Cuba.

John Earl of
Buckingham
Lord L. of Irela
from Jan. 1772
to Dec. 1780.

Rooms with a view. Again and again you find yourself looking out onto the garden and the pictures painted by the landscape. The now waterless moat is filled with old roses and camellias, protected against the wind and flourishing. From behind the East Wing with its five Dutch gables come the scents of herbs, laid out in the evergreen geometry of a Victorian parterre garden[1] with terraces, balustrades, and topiaries laid out in thirties. Beyond the garden lies a 'wilderness' – an early 17th-century arboretum, star-shaped, with avenues running through it. There are bluebells beneath the old trees, and a Doric temple provides a classical touch as well as a bit of shelter from the rain. From here you can see Blickling Hall in all its glory, blending in with a man-made composition of Nature that has grown and developed over the centuries. If you walk along the lake and through the park with its various traces of Humphry Repton (the orangery southeast of the house, c.1785, is also attributed to him), and continue far enough to the northwest, you come to the Blickling pyramid (by Bonomi). This is the Earl of Buckingham's last monument, as stylish as everything else that he created. Beneath the dome of the round interior are three marble tombs containing the Earl and his two wives. Farewell, Egyptian style, 1794.

The last owner of Blickling Hall was also a diplomat in the service of the Crown. The 11th Marquess of Lothian was British ambassador to Washington, and before he died there in 1940, he made his family seat over to the National Trust. It was Lord Lothian who was the first to introduce laws into Parliament making it possible for historic houses to be saved for the nation (1937). At the time it had seemed as if massive death duties would also herald the death of England's great estates. In 1900, Norfolk alone had over two hundred large family estates, of which about half are still in existence. About one hundred and ten stately homes were sold or split up, and fifty of these were demolished. The most important of them, however – Holkham, Houghton, Raynham Hall – are still in the hands of the families that built them (plates 3, 8), and indeed many of the medium-sized houses are still lived in by old Norfolk families such as the Bacons, Buxtons and Birbecks, the Fountaines, Barclays and Gurneys. The Walpoles of Mannington Hall are still there, too, their estate actually bordering on that of Blickling. Their house, though, is a great deal smaller and older, and above all it is very, very private.

Country roads with no traffic, paths with no signs – this is the heart of Norfolk. Down in a shallow valley, surrounded by fields, lies *Mannington Hall*. Somewhere a pheasant blows his trumpet. A drawbridge takes you across the moat, and between the waterlilies shine the reflections of house and sky. A 15th-century house of flint, with crenellations, Tudor windows, and … a swimming pool. The owner shows me graffiti written in the entrance by an eccentric ancestor: 'A tiger is worse than a snake, a demon than a tiger, a woman than a demon, and nothing worse than a woman'. The Victorian misogynist was the 4th Earl of Orford.

---

1 The fountain comes from Oxnead Hall, the family home of the Pastons which was demolished in 1731; so too does the statue of Hercules in the orangery and of Diana in the information centre, as well as sculptures by Inigo Jones's master stonemason Nicholas Stone (c.1640).

'When I took over Mannington Hall in 1969,' said Lord Walpole, 'it was in a really bad way. We tore down quite a lot of it, right to the medieval nucleus that we're sitting in now.' By drastically cutting out all that was superfluous, and carefully restoring the basic essence of the house, Lord Walpole has been able to preserve his heritage as a family home. The National Trust, he says – with the greatest respect – cannot avoid making such houses into 'fossils'.

His family comes from the Walpole villages in the Fens. One was England's first Prime Minister: Sir Robert Walpole (see page 467 ff.), whose younger brother Horatio, a successful ambassador, acquired Mannington Hall 'more for the land than for the house'. Two miles away he had a new house built, in 1727–41, the Georgian Wolterton Hall – designed by Thomas Ripley (who also designed the Admiralty in London), and with a landscaped park by Charles Bridgman. This is still a family home of the Walpoles, and is likewise private. Robert Horace Walpole, known as Robin, was born there in 1938. He had a 'classical' education – Eton and King's, where he studied Natural Sciences and Land Economy, with a view to running the family estate: 'about 1200 acres, which is a bit less than 500 years ago.' Lord Walpole has a staff of eleven to work in the fields and the office. In 1963 he had forty. 'Somehow you have to survive and get through to the next century. You can only do that if you try to keep the best and get rid of the rest.'

It's no easy task to conserve the countryside and yet at the same time exploit it, especially if you hold Lord Walpole's view that 'we should give the public far more access to the estate and to the countryside than they've had in the past.' But who actually wants to come to Mannington Hall? 'Horace Walpole never came here,' laments his descendant. 'He never wrote a word about this house, which is really a shame.' And yet the Lord of Strawberry Hill wrote about everybody else's houses that he visited. 'Every guidebook of every house in the country quotes something that Horace said, that's virtually taken for granted.'

People who open their homes up to the public have to have some sort of attraction to offer them: veteran cars in the courtyard, or tigers in the park. The Walpoles collect roses. The Heritage Rose Garden of Mannington Hall was begun in the eighties, and even for the connoisseur, it is something really special: a new garden with over a thousand different sorts of old roses. The Walpoles have transformed the former kitchen garden behind the stables into a series of historic gardens. You walk through them as you would walk through the rooms of a house, and each one illustrates a different historical period of rose-growing: you pass from the medieval to the Tudor, the Georgian, and the Victorian, and the gardens have their own special layout, with the roses of that particular time. You'll find the creamy *Rosa pimpinellifolia* of the Middle Ages, the tender pink Maiden's Blush of the Plantagenets, the *Rosa Alba maxima* of the Jacobites, the dark red Portland Rose of the Georgians, the mauve Balle de Crecy of the Victorians, the Edwardians' Snow Dwarf, and the red Lilli Marlene of 1959. The list is endless, from the bloody roses of York and Lancaster to the pure innocence of Burnet Double White.

I wonder if Poppy and Lambton are still alive. They were already old and grey, though still very alert, when I walked past their baskets as I entered *Heydon Hall* (plate 12). They were growling at me in lurcher language: strictly private. The public are only allowed in on two days in the summer, and that's only to the park, not to the house. This is where Captain Bulwer Long lives with his wife Sarah and their three children. It's an Elizabethan manor house, which was built by an auditor of the royal treasury in 1581–4. A prominent relation, the best-selling Victorian author Edward Bulwer-Lytton (*The Last Days of Pompeii*), spent part of his childhood here, in a house that has an atmosphere and a history all its own. 'A very pleasant burden' is the half-proud, half-groaning description given by the present owner. William Bulwer Long was born in 1937, went to Sandhurst, became a cavalry officer, and then in 1968 inherited Heydon Hall.

'Everyone in the family kept saying: 'Tear it down! Sell it! It's too big, so turn it into a school!' The house was really on its last legs – woodworm and dry rot.' So why did he move in, against all economic reason? 'It's my family home,' is his reply. 'My family lived in this area for 600 years.' His own immediate family had to start off in the stables, while they set about restoring Heydon Hall. 'Whenever we ran out of money, we sent the workmen home.' But after ten years, they'd done it: they'd saved the Elizabethan Hall, taken down the Victorian extensions, reduced the house to a quarter of its previous size, and made it habitable. 'Unfortunately, no butler.' The Bulwer Longs live off the land, cultivating vegetables, sugar beet, grain, with a few cattle and horses. Production is sufficient to cover the running costs of the house. 'If I had a farm of similar size and lived in a bungalow, I could probably afford to go skiing for two months in the year or run a Mercedes 500.'

On the edge of the park lies the village of Heydon: some thirty houses, not one of them built in this century. There's a church, a post office, a village green, and it all adds up to the idyllic estate village. 'Of course it still belongs to my family,' says Captain Bulwer Long. The rent paid by the forty tenants helps to maintain and modernize their houses. 'Large country estates seem completely anachronistic, but for villages like this, they're still a key element. Certainly the village squire as such is out-of-date, and you'll probably do a lot more damage to village society by getting rid of the parish priest and the schoolmaster. They used to be the leading lights in the community. Whenever the different governments and the Church of England closed village schools and rectories, they took the heart out of the villages.' But in such a vacuum, country houses at least offer a degree of continuity. The lord of this particular manor is chairman of the local council, and his wife works at the Women's Institute, and whenever something has to be done in the village – from the mowing of the green to the arrangements for the yearly fête – it is generally left to them to do the organizing. 'If I don't fix the fire for Guy Fawkes Day, then there *is* no fire for Guy Fawkes Day.'

Estate owners like Captain Bulwer Long are respected and even loved by their villages, and form the conservative backbone of a conservative, rural society. The durable link to the land and the family which has grown through the centuries like the oak in the fields continues to uphold their social position, and increasingly influences their sense of responsibility towards the environment. 'Perhaps I've turned more arable land back into pastureland than I ought to have done, but I want to maintain the character of the park,' says William Bulwer Long. He is appalled by the callousness of the big farmers, who kill off the hedges. 'There's no excuse for greedy farming.' In the Country Landowners Association his principles are well known, and many agree with him. 'If we want to keep our land and not have it nationalized, then we must preserve it in a way that is acceptable to everybody.'

There is a long, broad avenue leading from the south to Heydon Hall. 'One of my ancestors cut all these trees down in 1801, so that he could form his own regiment to counter the threat of Napoleon's invasion. Fortunately, he replanted too, though chestnuts, not oaks.' William Bulwer Long was not going to be able to take a holiday in the year when I met him. The north façade needed to be restored. And who can tell which of the walls will start crumbling next? We went outside. Poppy and Lambton were blinking in the October sunshine, and I looked back at Heydon Hall, and gazed over the park, as so many generations had done before me. 'It's worth all the effort and all the work,' said the owner. 'It's worth preserving.'

Just what can happen if there is no-one to put in all the effort and all the work became clear to me shortly afterwards. I was in the remote countryside of northern Norfolk, amid an abandoned, overgrown park, a terraced garden with rotting balustrades and broken amphorae, plinths robbed of their statues, statues robbed of their limbs, fountains falling to pieces – the whole park in a state of heartrending decay, exceeded only by that of the house itself. The beautifully proportioned front was totally dilapidated, the rooms were gutted, the wooden panelling ripped away, the carpets in tatters, and in the middle of it all, mysteriously spared from all this havoc, a few mahogany doors, plaster ceilings and marble fireplaces – the last remnants of past glories. How could this happen to a place like *Melton Constable Hall* (plate 20)?

This is not just any old country house, but 'one of the most perfect examples of the so-called Christopher Wren House' (Pevsner). It's a rectangular block of red brick, with windows and porches framed in ashlar, three storeys high, nine bays long by seven wide. There is a central projection with a pediment, and the whole Baroque façade is resplendent with symmetry and dignity. It was built in baroque, neoclassical style by Roger Pratt in 1664–70 for Sir Jacob Astley, but of its original 17th-century interiors there remain only a few superb plaster ceilings, attributed to Edward Goudge, just like the ceilings at Felbrigg and at Hintlesham in Suffolk.

From 1236 the Melton Constable estate was owned by the Astley family – and they remained the owners for more than 700 years. The last of them, the 21st Lord Hastings preferred to live in a Victorian extension, obviously not just for reasons of comfort and convenience. When James Lees-Milne inspected the Hall for the National Trust in May 1942 he noted that the ignorance of the owner was 'alarming'. Instead of the National Trust, it was the Duke of Westminster who acquired the estate, but in 1959 he sold it again to Geoffrey Harrold, a local farmer who was only interested in the land. He left the house

Melton Constable Hall, detail of marble chimneypiece in the Red Drawing Room, 18th century

empty, and let it rot. Only once, very briefly, did it return to its old glamour, and that was as the setting for Joseph Losey's film *The Go-Between* (1971).

Melton Constable Hall became the nightmare of the preservation groups. For years they looked on in horrified helplessness, from SAVE Britain's Heritage to the Duke of Grafton, the 'Duke of Preservation'. 'It should never have been allowed to happen,' he said to me. 'It's the worst case of its kind in East Anglia.' The worst perhaps, but not the only one. There are far too many wealthy farmers who, like the owner of Melton Constable, own large tracts of land with ancient houses which they allow to go to rack and ruin if they can't actually demolish them. But since there are some listed 10,000 buildings in north Norfolk alone, the authorities simply can't cope. Only when it was almost too late did they at last compel the owner of Melton Constable Hall to sell. It was bought by an unknown businessman from Norwich in 1986, for £250,000. The cost of repairs are estimated at five times that amount. The stables were to be converted into flats, and the house itself into an arts and conference centre. But Melton Constable Hall is more than a house. There is also the park, designed by Capability Brown in 1764–9, and with a late 18th-century menagerie in the style of the Gothic Revival, a little church, a temple, and various follies, the whole thing constituting a work of art in itself. It would be tragic if such beauty were lost for ever.

Blakeney Point: Twitchers and Avocets

'We're an island folk,' says Ann, my Norfolk hostess. 'At the weekend, everyone rushes to the sea like a lot of lemmings. Three hours' drive, and then they sit there, their cars facing the sea, and they stare at the water, read the paper, or go to sleep because they're worn out by the long drive. And then they drive back to their towns.' Perhaps that's why you see so few people between the car parks in even the most densely populated places on the British coast.

England's loneliest coast lies in the north of Norfolk. No cliffs, no white beaches, just banks of sand and shingle and endless marshes, with innumerable coves, channels, canals forming an amphibious, labyrinthine landscape. It's a wild, rough coast, strangely beautiful, but cold and hard as flint. This is England's Arctic coast, where storms can sometimes go on for days on end, so violent that the solid sign of 'The White Horse' in Blakeney hangs horizontal. If you learn to sail here, not even the name Trafalgar will frighten you. From this coast came Horatio Nelson, the Hero of Norfolk.

The coastal road runs between Weybourne and Holme, a mile away from the sea. It separates the marshy meadows from the hills in the hinterland, which were once cliffs of an earlier shore. Along this road are the marsh villages with their flint houses and churches: Cley-next-the-Sea, Blakeney, Stiffkey, Wells-next-the-Sea. The old fishermen's and farmers' cottages are now occupied by pensioners, commuters, and summer visitors. Most of the locals have moved to the cheaper council flats or to the towns, where there is more chance of a job. There are some parts of Norfolk where the unemployment rate is as much as 14 per cent higher than the national average.

Houses with curved gables, Flemish bricks and pantiles, and a windmill on the edge of the marsh – this is *Cley-next-the-Sea*, but it could easily be a little port in Holland. What are now the meadows next to the windmill used in the Middle Ages to be the harbour, until it became silted up. It was from here that north Norfolk's wool was exported, as well as salt from neighouring Salthouse. Cley's former prosperity can be gauged from the grandiose Perpendicular church on a hill outside the village, overlooking Glaven Valley beyond which stands the hillside church of Wiveton. In Cley churchyard the ancient gravestones are decorated with vine leaves and anchors, winged hourglasses and crowned skulls. A short, sharp epitaph for an olden-day pathologist: 'He lived and died / by suicide.'

From Cley there is a path that leads out into the marshes, past peacefully grazing cows, and across to the sea. The tide has thrown up banks of rock, and upon these, as if they were the terraces of some football ground, stand the densely packed spectators, binoculars in hand, or telescopes mounted on tripods, the faithful thermos flask at the ready. For hours they stand there, gazing out to sea. Is it a regatta? A shipwreck? An Armada? 'Avocets,' says one of them, without turning his head or batting an eyelid. Now what sort of people would stand for hours in the hope of seeing avocets? I'll tell you. Twitchers. Twitchers are not ordinary ornithologists. Twitchers are sportsmen and women (plate 28), whose great aim in life is to see as many rare birds as possible. They have their own telephone service, called Bird Line, which keeps them in a constant state of readiness, and no sooner has a rare bird been sighted than off they rush in their hundreds to the vital spot. And the most popular vital spots are the marshes and coves between Cley and Holme.

This is where the cormorants fly, and the wind cuts in from the northeast, and the light is as clear and silvery as Norfolk flint. I walk westwards along the water's edge, and with every step and with every wave the stones are ground and washed, ground and washed, in the never-ending, melancholy music of Norfolk's coast. *Blakeney Point* juts out three miles into the sea, a spit made of rock and sand, resounding with the voices of the sea and a thousand birds. It's the northernmost point of this coast, East Anglia's Land's End. Terns and other sea birds nest here in the early summer, the migratory birds come in the autumn, and in winter it's the turn of the shelducks and various waders.

Blakeney Point belongs to the National Trust, which owns over 6,500 acres of this coast. The Norfolk Naturalists Trust is in charge of the Cley and Holme marshes, while the NCC (now English Nature) runs England's biggest coastal nature reserve, the marshes and dunes between Stiffkey and Burnham Overy (owned by the Cokes of Holkham Hall). The whole North Norfolk coast has been designated an Area of Outstanding Natural Beauty, and is under the auspices of the Countryside Commission, with twelve distinct nature reserves. And as if that is not enough, these precious wetlands have also been given the honorary title of Heritage Coast. Here you will find the 'green wellie people', the guild of the rubber boot and the windcheater, friends of the sea aster, guardians of the bittern. In the evening they sit with wind-reddened cheeks in front of their Norfolk bitter, at 'The Harnser' (local dialect for 'heron') in Cley, or at 'Moorings' in Wells.

You'll see the finest yachts at Blakeney quayside. Once this was a fishing and trading port, but now it lives off its well-to-do pensioners and its yachtsmen. The warehouses in Ship Street have become shops or holiday flats, and more than a third of the houses are people's second homes. On a hill overlooking the marsh stands the church of St Nicholas, patron saint of fishing, with an Early English choir vault, lancet windows, and angels up in the rafters. The little turret at the east end was built for the beacon which still guides the inshore fishermen.

Wells-next-the-Sea, or at least it used to be. Where is the sea now? Two miles away at ebb-tide. There are a few freighters at the quayside, and animal feed is being loaded onto them from a silo. Wells is the only trading port in the marshes not yet completely taken over by the weekend sea-captains. But it is also a holiday resort, and with its souvenir stands and amusement arcades is definitely more downmarket than Blakeney. The 'Local Shellfish Bar' is a camper on the quay, and you can get fresh crabs, mussels and gossip there. I learn from this local mine of information that an Irish lady named Marion Cartwright has opened a little jam factory in Wells, and every Tuesday she delivers twelve buckets of top-class strawberry jam to the Ritz Hotel in London.

Far into the hinterland, between fields of beet and grain, stands Norfolk's most unusual museum, a gigantic hall full of old tractors, steam engines, and fairground organs. A farmer from *Thursford*, George Cushing, collected all these vintage machines of work and pleasure, beginning shortly after the war when everyone was scrapping their old farm vehicles. 'In 1946 one ton of tractor cost one pound.' Nobody wanted these rusting, rattling, coughing and sneezing old dinosaurs of the fields, and so George took them in and nursed them back to health: 'Fearless', 'Victory', and the 20-ton daddy of them all 'Edward VII', King of the steam-driven tractors, 1905, shining red, with a top that rests on columns of twisted brass.

In the mid-fifties the farmers of Thursford had renewed reason to shake their heads: George had started filling his barn with old fairground organs and merry-go-rounds. Actually, it wasn't all that strange. The machinery was driven by the same steam-engines that powered the old tractors. 'When I was young, the only music you heard on a Sunday was the church organ, and once a year the fairground organ.' When George Cushing was born, in 1904, Norfolk's villages were as remote as the Scottish Highlands. 'You could only

John Sell Cotman:
Little Snoring Church,
south door, 1812

431

travel as far as you could walk in a day. A lot of people who lived just ten miles or so from the coast never saw the sea in their entire lives.' What an event it was, then, when the fair came to the village, with its colourful roundabouts and organs and monsters and mechanical wonders. For many of the villagers, who only had gaslight, it was the first encounter with electric lighting. And how they would shout and scream on the big dipper, with its eight Venetian gondolas of gold revolving round a Gavioli organ, the showpiece of George's collection. The big dipper is driven by one of those steam engines with which the engineer Frederick Savage of King's Lynn revolutionized fairgrounds in the 19th century. At three o'clock every afternoon, George lets his organs play: the Art-Deco dance organ from Antwerp; the Belgian Hooghuys, with drums and glockenspiel; the ornate Marenghi organ from Paris, 1911, with gold dragons and girls and flowers in sweet pastel, pure fairground rococo. Of all these shake-rattle-and-roll machines, the most amazing is the 1931 Wurlitzer, which has 1,339 pipes that can make any noise you can think of: horses' hooves, fire-engines, thunder, the sea, or the toot-toot of an old railway engine. This virtuoso music machine was rescued by George from a Leeds cinema that was due for demolition. Now it is flourishing in the dreamland of a farmer, happily housed in his Thursford barn, where the instruments of work and play live together in perfect harmony.

Deep in the heart of rural Norfolk lie the villages of *Little Snoring* and *Great Snoring*, which by definition just have to be sleepy. But the name is actually derived from Snear's people, who used to live here. Given the choice, I think most people would prefer Snoring to Snearing. Also of Anglo-Saxon origin is the round tower of Little Snoring's idyllic church in the fields outside the village. Two little old ladies are sitting there among the gravestones, painting. With their straw hats, they look like characters from Beatrix Potter. I see them again in the evening, at the Old Rectory of Great Snoring, a house that specializes in the art of rural living. They only have one menu, but what a menu! Thus revived and refreshed, the pilgrim makes his way to *Little Walsingham*. In medieval England, this remote little spot was the most important place of pilgrimage after Becket's shrine in Canterbury.

In about 1061, the Holy Virgin appeared to Lady Richeldis de Faverches in Walsingham. She was to build a house, Mary told the pious widow, modelled on the Holy House of Nazareth. This was the time of the Crusades, and for those of the faithful who stayed in England, the Walsingham shrine became a symbol of the Holy Land regained. Here in Norfolk, as was to happen later in Italy's Loreto, the pilgrims could feel the atmosphere of Nazareth, where Jesus spent his childhood. Archaeologists have located the legendary house and measured it. It was made of wood, like the only other remaining Anglo-Saxon stave church, in Greensted, and was small in area, 13 feet by 23, later enclosed in a Norman stone chapel on the north side of the abbey church. When Erasmus of Rotterdam visited the Walsingham shrine in 1511, the modest timber chapel had long since been transformed into a unique chamber of wonders, shining and shimmering all over with jewels, gold and silver.

Erasmus was an enlightened humanist, and in his *Peregrinatio religionis ergo* (1526), he

John Sell Cotman: Walsingham Abbey Gate, 1812

criticized the veneration of relics and the commercialization of the place, and mocked such 'authentic' relics as 'Virgin's milk'. In those days the Augustinian abbey on the River Stiffkey was one of the richest in the country. Every English king since Richard I had made the pilgrimage to Walsingham, Edward I more than twelve times, and even Henry VIII went there, actually walking the last mile barefoot. But it all came to an end with the Reformation. The abbey treasures were confiscated, the shrine and holy spring were destroyed, and the monks pensioned off. As for Walsingham's statue of Mary, Thomas Cromwell had it publicly burned in Chelsea (1538) as being an instrument of the Devil.

'Weepe, weepe O Walsingham, / Whose dayes are nightes, / Blessings turned to blasphemies, / Holy deeds to dispites,' sighs a 16th-century lament on the fate of this holy place sometimes attributed to Philip Howard (see page 242). In the aftermath of 'the wrackes of Walsingham', all that remains of the Augustinian abbey church is the east wall, with a high Gothic window. The pathetic ruins languish in a magnificent park just behind the High Street. There you will also find a 15th-century gatehouse, which was the old entrance to the abbey. Tudor houses, Georgian façades, timberwork, flint and brick all mingle together here as if it was the most natural thing in the world. Common Place, opposite the 16th-century octagonal pumphouse, is where the Shirehall is situated, originally housing the lawcourts but now a local museum. Even the pious folk of Walsingham had to have a jail, and it's a Bridewell of 1787, built according to designs by the prison reformer John Howard: eight roomy cells, a hospital, a chapel, and four treadmills for grinding corn: at the time a model of a progressive penal system.

Little Walsingham now has a population of 525, and receives half a million visitors a year. There is 'Pilgrim Accommodation' everywhere. England's Nazareth has once more become a flourishing place of pilgrimage, and lives on scarcely anything else but its host of visitors – just as it did in Erasmus's day. The renaissance of Walsingham's religious importance began with the Catholic Revival of 1833, the so-called Oxford Movement. Both theologians and laymen protested against the State's authority over the Church, and wanted to go back to the rites that had existed before the Reformation and the great religious split. It took almost a century for the Norfolk pilgrimage to regain its former status, but then Catholics and Anglicans venerated Our Lady of Walsingham at their own separate altars.

In 1931–8, the Anglicans erected a new pilgrimage church – brick, flint, and not an ounce of imagination. 'Weepe, weepe O Walsingham.' Anyone who has seen the noble abbey ruins will understand Pevsner's view that the new building is like 'a minor suburban church'. Inside there is merciful gloom. Fifteen chapels, one for each of the mysteries of the rosary, surround the reconstructed Holy House containing a replica of the statue of Mary. Praise be to the guardians of the shrine for at least creating a beautiful garden. There one can sit and peacefully meditate on the fact that the glories of religious faith today rarely bring forth any glories of religious art.

What is glorious, however, is the path running south through the fields, the Holy Mile between Walsingham and the Slipper Chapel. This Decorated Gothic building (c.1325–50)

Great Walsingham, Norman font: The Four Seasons, work in the fields

is dedicated to St Catherine of Alexandria, the patron saint of pilgrims. According to tradition, the pilgrims were supposed to leave their shoes at this chapel, and walk the last mile barefoot to the shrine. After the Reformation, the Slipper Chapel was used as a smithy, cowshed, and barn, but in 1897 it was restored on the private initiative of a local woman, and in 1934 was declared as a Roman Catholic 'National Shrine of Our Lady'. It's a proud title, but all too often it left the faithful standing out in the rain, and so the Catholics built a new pilgrims' chapel right next to the old one. The style is that of local barns, made of flint, and with a low, steep pantile roof and a name with a message: 'Chapel of Reconciliation'.

Reconciliation was a long time coming to Walsingham. The very first Archbishop of Canterbury to visit the Norfolk shrine since the Reformation was the Most Reverend Robert Runcie in May 1980. The first member of the Royal Family to come here since Henry VIII was the Duchess of Kent, in the same year. But even then, all was not well. In May 1988 the Catholics made their annual national pilgrimage, to be greeted by Christian

Fundamentalists brandishing black bibles in protest against 'Mariolatry'.'Crown Him,' sang the Protestants. 'Ave Maria,' sang the Catholics. 'Wine bibbers! Priests of Baal!' shouted the Protestants. And the more popular the pilgrimage has become, the more vehement are the protests. At the same time, though, Anglicans and Catholics do mix together (after their initial rivalry over the shrine) and have long since embarked on joint pilgrimages. Knights of Malta, Marists and Methodists, the Sons of Divine Providence and the Little Sisters of Jesus, all have places in England's Nazareth. And when in 1964 the railway line was closed, the Russian Orthodox Brotherhood of the Holy Seraphim of Sarov moved into Walsingham Station, which is now the only station in Britain to sport a gold onion tower.

Down in the valley of the River Stiffkey lies the manor house of *East Barsham* (colour plate 15). That is where King Henry VIII stayed on his way to Walsingham. As you come down the hill, it is suddenly there before you, like a fairytale castle. Through the trees and shrubs you can see the warm glow of its red bricks, towers, turrets and chimneys; the chimneys are like a forest of pepperpots, each one differently decorated with lilies, lozenges, hexagons. The battlements and buttresses too are superbly decorated with ornamental bands of brick. This is an early Tudor country house (*c.*1520–30) with a two-storey gatehouse as a triumphal status symbol.[1] Some of Norfolk's top families lived in East Barsham – the Calthorpes, the L'Estranges, and the Astleys. During the thirties, a Hapsburg duke used to give giant parties here, until one day he disappeared with giant debts. For a time, the Tudor gem belonged to the pop group 'The Bee Gees', but today it is owned by a London business man, and is strictly private.

Holkham Hall: Farming and Art

Triumphal archway and obelisk, a long avenue of ilex trees, fallow deer and sheep wandering through a wide park – it's like a pastoral overture, with every tone and every nuance precisely attuned to the rise of the curtain on the approaching masterpiece. And suddenly, from behind an undulation of the ground, there it is: *Holkham Hall*, the country home of the Earls of Leicester (plate 8). It's as if history has come to a standstill here, frozen at a moment when art and Nature have joined together in perfect harmony.

Before William Kent laid out this park in 1727, there was nothing but salty marsh and a wind-swept, treeless coast. It was an amazing thing to do here, to build a house, but what a house it is. A Palladian palace in a marshy wasteland, a single resplendent jewel to crown the northernmost tip of Norfolk. With his palace almost complete, Thomas Coke[2] looks round for his neighbours, and where are they? 'It is a melancholy thing to stand alone in

---

1 One of the best examples of early 16th-century brick architecture in Norfolk is the neighbouring Tudor manor house of Thorpland Hall, two miles northeast of Fakenham.

2 Coke was created Earl of Leicester, but the title died with him, to be revived in another branch of the family in 1837.

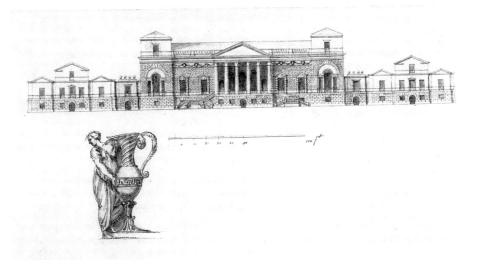

Holkham Hall, south front, sketch by William Kent, c.1735

one's own country. I look around, not a house to be seen but my own. I am Giant of Giant Castle, and have ate up all my neighbours – my nearest neighbour is the King of Denmark.'

Thomas Coke inherited a large fortune at a very early age. When he was fifteen, he embarked on the obligatory Grand Tour of Europe, accompanied by his tutor, a Cambridge professor. He returned five years later from this educational trip, and in his luggage was one of the most valuable private collections of antiques in the country. In purchasing the various works of art, the young milord took the advice of a coach painter from Yorkshire who happened to be studying the fine arts in Italy at the time – William Kent. The result of this friendship is Holkham Hall, a piece of Italy in East Anglia.

Matthew Brettingham, an architect from Norwich, built Holkham Hall (1734–62) using designs by William Kent and by the owner himself. Thomas Coke's friends the Duke of Bedford and Lord Egremont were also busy with houses at the same time, Woburn and Petworth, and ideas were certainly exchanged. This was the time when the baroque style of Wren and Hawksmoor was giving way to a purer, more classical style, and the keyword here was 'Palladio'. Lord Burlington was the chief champion, and Colen Campbell the chief architect. It was he who designed Holkham's neighbour Houghton Hall (plate 3).

Today the visitor comes to the house from the wrong side, the north. It was the south that was conceived as the front, facing on to the garden. The main block has four rectangular corner towers (as in Inigo Jones's Wilton House), flanked by wings with a triad of gables. The size and proportions of Holkham Hall are beautifully rhythmical, and its 350 foot of length are set in a tableau of green. The little hatch windows on the ground floor, the large surfaces of wall above the windows near the portico, and the cool greyish yellow of the bricks all combine to give this façade an almost Puritanical severity. This is the architecture of practical reason, which Nigel Nicolson calls 'as functional as a Prussian riding school'. Architecture for Thomas Coke, however, also meant 'commodiousness'. Everything had to be easily accessible – drawing-rooms, galleries and state apartments in the main building all round the two inner courts; the wings contained kitchen and chapel, family and guest rooms. The model for the ground plan was Palladio's Villa Mocenigo, and the motif of the Venetian windows also came from him, though it was Inigo Jones who first introduced it into England.

If Holkham's façade is simple and unadorned, the rooms behind it are extravagantly splendid. The contrast was in keeping with the spirit of the age, and in some ways also with the national character. Asceticism and luxury come together under one roof, the Puritan and the Epicure are one and the same person. Where in England will you find a more triumphal entrance than the Marble Hall of Holkham (plate 7)? A flight of steps is framed by a semi-circular colonnade, with columns of ivory and pink Derbyshire alabaster; above is the richly ornate coffering of a domed ceiling. This entrance hall, half Roman basilica, half Roman baths, contains a number of pieces by English neoclassical sculptors, including busts and bas-reliefs by Sir Francis Chantrey and a plaque for two woodcock which he killed with one shot during his visit in 1829. The steps take you up to the first floor, and here the rooms express all the glamour of the age and the elegance of the people who lived in them. The main reception room is the Saloon, which contains paintings by Van Dyck and Rubens ('The Flight into Egypt', 1614), mythological pictures (Italian late baroque) over the fireplace, some splendid furniture by William Kent, including side tables with ostrich legs (the ostrich was the Cokes' heraldic beast); there are also two beautiful mosaic tables from Hadrian's Villa in Tivoli. The walls still have their original covering of crimson and wine-red velvet from Genoa. There are splendid gold plaster ceilings and semi-domes, partly based on designs by Inigo Jones, and monumental tapestries from Brussels and Mortlake (17th century). For all the lavishness of the materials and the design, nothing exceeds the bounds of neoclassical decorum. The proportions of the rooms reflect this same intellectual discipline, with wealth and taste perfectly balanced.

Each of the rooms has its own special features. In the Brown State Dressing Room is one of Holkham's rarities: the only surviving contemporary copy of Michelangelo's cartoon for the frescoes for the Great Council of Florence. In the Landscape Room is an exquisite collection of mythological landscapes by Claude Lorrain, Lord Leicester's favourite painter, together with pictures by Nicolas and Gaspard Poussin. Also exquisite is the view from the high Venetian window with its columns and pilasters, an elegant frame for the real-life landscape outside. This unity of landscape, architecture, art and craft is what gives houses like Holkham Hall their incomparable charm.

The paintings in the Drawing Room include Claude Lorrain and Hondecoeter, whose naturalistic though often symbolic pictures of poultry were very popular in 18th-century English country houses. In this room, there is one portrait that deserves a special mention, though not specifically for artistic reasons. It shows a man with an Elizabethan goatee beard, a ruff, and red ermine robes. Sir Edward Coke came from an old Norfolk family, and rose to be Attorney General and Lord Chief Justice. He was Chief Prosecutor in the cases against Sir Walter Raleigh and Guy Fawkes, and served his King loyally, but became the King's sharpest opponent when he saw a threat to those fundamental democratic rights that we now take for granted – the independence of Parliament and of the courts: 'The liberties, franchises, privileges and jurisdictions of Parliament are the undoubted birthright and inheritance of the subjects of England.' For such insubordination, James I had him locked up in the Tower. Even when he was 77, now opposing Charles I, this incorruptible lord was one of the initiators of the Petition of Right (1628), an important step in the struggle between Crown and Parliament. It was Sir Edward who founded the fame and the fortune of the Coke family.

The lords of Holkham had a lot of rooms at their disposal. The barest were for the servants (footmen slept four to a bed), and the finest were for the statues. The long gallery in the west wing was conceived by Lord Leicester specifically for the Greek and Roman sculptures in his collection. An educated gentleman was one who knew something about horses, cricket and Antiquity, and so in those days the British marble-hunters flocked to Rome and Athens – coachloads of little Lord Elgins – and come back and fill their cold houses with trophies of southern culture. It was then, in the middle of the 18th century, that the great private collections were assembled; at Petworth House, Castle Howard, Arundel Castle, and Houghton Hall. Among the showpieces of Lord Leicester's collection, still displayed much as they were at the time of his death, are the lifesize statues of Diana and Marsyas (2nd century AD).

Such collections had great influence on contemporary taste, especially as there were no public museums in those days. People often used to visit Holkham Hall, even during Lord Leicester's lifetime, especially to look at his collections. Once a week the house was open to 'every decently dressed person', regardless of class. People were offered sherry and biscuits, and there were often large crowds. Even the King wanted to come. That was at the time of the American War of Independence, and the Thomas Coke of that period was, as a Whig, bitterly opposed to the King's colonial policy. And so when George III sent him a note to say that he would like to visit Holkham Hall, back came the succinct message: 'Delighted. We are open to the public on Tuesday.'

The Coke who sent this classic reply was Thomas William, who had himself portrayed by Gainsborough in 1782 – not as a Knight of the Bath, as his predecessors had done, but as a Knight of the Shire, in the simple clothes of a farmer, surrounded by his dogs, standing in an open woodland landscape cleaning his shotgun. You might think this was the portrait of one of the landed gentry who happened to be a passionate shot. In fact this brilliant late work of Gainsborough's depicts the historic role played by Thomas Coke. This is a political stance in pastoral dress. In these very clothes, which as a Knight of the Shire he was even allowed to wear at court, Coke presented himself to George III in February 1782 and, on behalf of Parliament, handed him a resolution that had been passed by a majority of just one: The King should end the war in the American colonies and officially recognize the

United States. And shortly afterwards, the King did precisely this. The Norfolk farmer's clothes in which the young Whig member of the Opposition had snubbed both the King and the King's party, the Tories, were ennobled by Gainsborough's painting, and indeed became a model for Regency dandies, who all wanted to wear the Country Look à la Coke. But even this was not the reason for Coke of Norfolk's fame.

At the age of twenty-two, he inherited the Holkham estate. He had left Eton, but instead of going on to further studies, he went on the ox-cart tour of the estate followed by a Grand Tour of Europe. The young milord became more interested in improving the infertile land than in admiring the art treasures of his mansion. He planted trees and hedges in order to stop the erosion of the soil, and he employed experts from Holland to drain his fields. He got his tenants to enrich their light soil with marl, and persuaded them to rotate their crops by cultivating wheat, potatoes and beet instead of leaving the fields fallow. In place of the antique statues his great-uncle had imported from Italy, he imported Italian breeding pigs, and he introduced new machinery, built a huge barn (1790–2), and also built better houses for his tenants. They were to profit from these improvements, too. In forty years, Thomas Coke increased the productivity of his estate about tenfold, which for those times was a spectacular success. Equally unusual was the fact that the landlord also worked on the land himself, which was unheard-of for a gentleman – gentlemen always left that to their tenants. It was another tradition broken by Thomas Coke, and it endowed agriculture with a new prestige.

Every year when the farmers met for sheep-shearing, Coke of Norfolk would demonstrate his newest methods and products. The Holkham Sheep Shearing was the ancestor of the Royal Norfolk Show and other agricultural shows. Experts came from France, Sweden, Poland, Russia and America, and the many hundreds of visitors all had to be accommodated in the Hall and in the villages around.

When he was 68, Thomas Coke married the 18-year-old Anne Keppel, became a father, and was cheered in Parliament. Queen Victoria came to the throne in 1837, by which time Thomas Coke was 83, and she made him Earl of Leicester, the first peerage of her reign. When he died, five years later, his tenants erected a memorial column to him, on the lines of Nelson's Column, almost 120 feet high; on its plinth are the four basic elements of his agricultural reforms: a Devon ox, a Southdown sheep, a plough, and a mechanical seeder. Since then, the legend of Coke of Norfolk has grown, although in fact there were others who were the real pioneers of the agricultural revolution in England: Jethro Tull, who had introduced the seed drill a century before; the cattle-breeder Robert Bakewell from Leicestershire, whose advice Thomas Coke often sought; and 'Turnip Townshend', of Raynham Hall (see page 476 f.). What they had begun provided the broad base of Thomas Coke's success.

Holkham Hall is still owned and run by the same family. The Gainsborough is still there, hanging in the South Dining Room, and the oldest son is an Edward. Edward, Viscount Coke is a powerfully built, athletic man. He received me in his estate office. At his feet was Shrimp, a spaniel, and on the walls were pictures of cows and sheep, his illustrious ancestor's ideal breeding animals. He was born in South Africa in 1936, and learned on the Queen's estate at Sandringham how to run such concerns. The Queen, incidentally, has a private beach on the stretch of coast that belongs to the Cokes. Lord Coke inherited Holkham in 1976, exactly two hundred years after Coke of Norfolk, but the estate, which had remained almost intact since the 17th century had been reduced in only 35 years from 42,000 acres (1941) to 25,000, by death duties. Another round of them forced Lord Coke to sell even more of his heritage. Instead of selling land, however, he sold Raphael and Leonardo. 'One had to do it, you see. Land is something that's always there, and no-one can take it away. The land finances the house.'

Thus it was that in spring 1986, Raphael's *Belle Jardinière*, a preliminary sketch for the famous painting in the Louvre, was sold. The first Lord Leicester had bought this drawing in 1713, when he was in Rome during his Grand Tour. It had been the first Raphael in any British collection. For almost three hundred years it had hung in Holkham Hall, but now it went to the National Gallery in Washington for something in excess of one million pounds. Even more spectacular, though, was the sale of the *Codex Leicester*. This was the last of Leonardo da Vinci's notebooks still to be in private hands. His notes, in mirror writing and illustrated with some 360 drawings, cover subjects as the building of canals and sluices, the light of the moon, and submarines – an invention which Leonardo feared would be misused, for he knew all too well 'the evil nature of man'. This notebook is one of the great treasures of art history; it was written in 1508, acquired by Lord Leicester in 1717, and sold by Christie's in 1980 in just one minute for £3.4 million. Leonardo's *Codex Leicester* is now called *Codex Hammer*, for it was bought by the late American oil tycoon and collector Armand Hammer.

'Instead of the Leonardo,' says Viscount Coke, 'I could have sold 2,500 acres of land, which would have been the equivalent then. But I like the land, I walk over it, I see it, I enjoy it, I farm it. The Leonardo was locked up in a safe, and nobody saw it.' Put that way, the argument was unanswerable, and one couldn't help but like and admire this Norfolk countryman who just happens also to be curator of a family museum of national importance. How can one expect such people to preserve the cultural heritage of the nation when their own heritage is falling apart? 'My predecessor died ten years ago and we're still paying off the inheritance tax. I don't think that's unjust, but if the nation wants to preserve estates like Holkham, they should give us a bit more help, for instance with tax concessions. If the state were to be solely responsible for such places, it would have to pay out far more than it does when they're in private hands.' If the worst comes to the worst, he says, he will have to sell something else – but it will be a work of art rather than a single inch of that precious land. True to his word, he auctioned over sixty old master paintings in 1991 for £3.2 million.

The yearly running costs of Holkham Hall come to something like half a million pounds, only a fraction of which is covered by entrance money from the 30,000 or so visitors. 'Every day of the week except Sundays, all through the year, we have one or two workmen in the house repairing something.' For major restorations there are state subsidies from English Heritage (up to a maximum of 40 per cent of the costs). 'Running a place like Holkham is a question of philosophy. Either you find it's too much and you're afraid to do anything, or you take it as a great challenge and a great opportunity – and that's how I see it.' Has he never thought of handing the whole thing over to the National Trust? 'That would be a declaration of bankruptcy. Holkham is viable.'

The Coke estate also contains 267 houses. Lord Coke – Eddy to his friends – has 84 employees: farm and forest workers, gamekeepers, gardeners, masons, plumbers, carpenters. Each of his 30 tenants farms 500 acres, and he himself farms 5,000 acres, mainly of wheat, barley and sugar beet, though he also has sheep and cattle. 'Where you had twenty men working on the estate in 1968, you now have five – we just get bigger machines.' Bigger machines, and bigger fields, which presumably means fewer hedges. 'My tenants aren't allowed to take down any hedges without permission from me. I'm very concerned about protecting the countryside. When you've got four hundred years of history behind you, you're very careful about what you do. Farmers who have no emotional or historical ties to their land just want nothing but bigger fields and bigger profits, so they simply tear down the hedges.'

The Lord of the Manor ... you can just imagine him riding across his fields, or gazing admiringly at his Old Masters, or sailing in the Caribbean. 'I spend most of my time in the office,' says this modern lord. From eight in the morning till six at night. His 19th-century forebears had forty servants for the house alone. Lord Coke thinks himself lucky if the cook arrives and the three cleaning ladies turn up. When he has visitors, he hires a butler. He is on the local council, and is chairman or vice-chairman of several associations: The Country Landowners, the Historic Houses, and the trust for the preservation of the coast. His most unusual position, however, is as Her Majesty's Postmaster. Since the 1st Earl of Leicester was made Postmaster General, all his descendants have inherited the office of sub-postmaster, which gives him the privilege of having his own post office at home. 'Families like ours have always been active in public service.' Does he have any political ambitions? 'No. Not yet.' Eventually, of course, he'll take his seat in the Lords, but in the meantime he's collecting donations to 'keep the Conservatives in power.' Lord Coke a Tory, and not a Whig like his combative ancestors? 'I'm a Conservative,' he confesses – because Socialism means state control over everything, and that is anathema to him.

Lord Coke has three children. The eldest, also a Thomas, read art history at Manchester. Not Oxbridge? Nothing is quite what it used to be. In these enlightened times, it's ability that counts, and not social rank. Lady Coke has also rolled up her sleeves. Together with twenty fellow workers, she produces very popular pottery in the former brickworks of the Hall. There is even an official sign: *Holkham Pottery*. 'When eventually I retire,' says Lord Coke, 'I'd like to leave this place in a better condition than when I took it on.' He gazes out over the park. A few golfers here, a few anglers there, and people picnicking by the lake. On the edge of the woods, some young people from London have pitched their tent – free of charge. 'I like it. I enjoy giving the public pleasure.'

Saltmarsh and Lavender: Where Nelson Learnt to Sail

Lord Nelson came from a God-forsaken spot in the turnip fields of Norfolk. *Burnham Thorpe* lies off the coastal road in the gently undulating hills southwest of Holkham Hall. It consists of a few flint houses and the fine smell of the sea and the not-so-fine smell of manure. On the tower of the village church, even on peaceful summer days, the White Ensign flutters in Nelson's honour. All Saints is the only church in the realm that is allowed to hoist the flag. The lectern and crucifix are carved out of oak boards from the 'Victory', his flagship at the Battle of Trafalgar. Patriotic ladies in the community have embroidered the hassocks with pictures of the ship, though the saintly relic itself lies in Portsmouth harbour.

Nelson's forebears were country parsons and not sailors. Horatio was the sixth out of eleven children, and was born in Parsonage House at Burnham Thorpe. Since this house was demolished even while he was alive, Nelson fans tend to congregate sooner or later in the 'Lord Nelson', the only pub in the village, next door to a junk shop called 'Trafalgar Stores'. There are in fact over 200 Nelson pubs in England, many called simply 'The Hero' or 'The Norfolk Hero'. The pub at Burnham Thorpe, though, is unique. 'It's where I live,' says Les Winter, the landlord, as I search in vain for a bar in this little room (plate 48). 'Every village used to have pubs like this one, and every one used to brew its own beer.' I sit on one of the high-backed benches. 'You're sitting on the same wood as Nelson did,' says my host. Les Winter has covered the walls of his pub with marine pictures, battle scenes and portraits of his hero, as if this was a branch of the National Maritime Museum in Greenwich.[1] Even Nelson's last prayer before the great battle is hanging on the wall. The only person who occasionally dares to contradict this self-appointed guardian of the Nelson legend is the retired rector of Burnham Thorpe. Their favourite argument is over where Nelson was born. 'In Parsonage House,' says the Reverend Cecil Isaacson. 'In the Shooting Lodge,' says Les. He claims that the former barn on the River Burn is where Catherine Nelson gave birth to the hero, when she was on her way to the Rectory and was taken by surprise.

Nelson went to the Royal Grammar School in Norwich and the Paston School in North Walsham. When he was scarcely thirteen years old, he joined the merchant navy – a delicate child who suffered badly from sea-sickness. 'What has poor Horace done, who is so weak,' mused his Uncle Maurice, captain of the 'Raisonnable', that he above all the rest should be sent to rough it at sea? But let him come, and the first time we go into action a cannon-ball may knock off his head and provide for him at once.' Poor Horace, as his family called him, was determined to become a hero. For years he plied the route between England and the West Indies, and got married – not without his bride being given the classic warning 'that salt water and absence always wash away love'. He returned once

---

1   There are also Nelson memorabilia in museums in Norwich, King's Lynn and Monmouth (Wales). The Royal Navy's cadet school at Shotley Gate (Suffolk) has a little Nelson museum of its own.

more to Burnham Thorpe, a captain with no ship, and for five frustrating years tilled the land, visited relatives – sister Susannah in Wells, and the high-ranking Walpoles in Wolterton Hall (Nelson's mother was a great niece of Sir Robert, the first British Prime Minister) – thought deep thoughts about the miserable lives of the farm labourers, and hankered after one thing and one thing only: glory at sea.

At last, in 1793, England was at war with France, and Nelson was made captain of the 'Agamemnon'. In Burnham Thorpe's one and only pub, then called 'The Plough', he celebrated his farewell to family and friends. He was never to return to his native village, but even in the great ports of the world, he never forgot his origins. From the Mediterranean he wrote to his wife in England: ' "Agamemnon" is as well-known through Europe as one of Mr Harwood's boats is at Overy.'

Overy Staithe was the port that served Burnham Market and all the other Burnhams. Large ships used to drop anchor here, but then the port silted up, and today it's a holiday village for the yachting people. In 'The Hero' you can get fresh crab salad, while the obligatory Trafalgar etching decorates the wall. The yachts lie prettily in the mud of the meandering estuary, and from the quay a dam stretches way out into the marsh, along the water's edge, and as far as the open sea. The last dune is called Gun Hill. It was on this coast, with its treacherous currents and banks of sand and gravel, that Nelson learnt to sail. Here he acquired the experience that gave him sufficient confidence to manoeuvre even in shallow waters, and to attack Napoleon's fleet at Aboukir Bay in 1798 from an inshore course. For this victory, the King made him Baron Nelson of the Nile and of Burnham Thorpe. Bloody battles, and agonizing victories: at the siege of Calvi he lost his right eye, and he lost his right arm in an attack on Santa Cruz. Thus he became a cripple and the hero of the nation: 'Saviour of the silver-coated isle / Shaker of the Baltic and the Nile' (Tennyson).

Les Winter's pub-museum in Burnham Thorpe is not, of course, without its pictures of the beautiful Emma Hamilton. The daughter of a blacksmith became a *fille de joie* in Vauxhall Gardens, the artist's model became the star of the salons, and the wife of the ambassador and connoisseur Sir William Hamilton became the mistress of Horatio Nelson. Goethe raved about her in Naples ('A beautiful woman, the masterpiece of the Great Artist'), Tischbein painted her as Niobe, Romney as Circe, Cassandra and Iphigenia. Nelson was lost without her. In vain he begged his 'King and Country' in his will to provide for his mistress, and her last years were darkened by alcohol and poverty. But Nelson's 'Beloved Emma' has remained part of popular folklore. When the latest biography appeared, Harrods devoted a whole display window to her. Edward Bawden (see page 123) calls his black cat after her.

In 1798, one of his captains presented Nelson with a coffin carved from the main mast of the French battleship 'L'Orient', which Nelson had sunk off Aboukir Bay. It was a

◁ *Nelson, waxwork by Catherine Andras, 1805*

macabre souvenir, but he took it with him in his cabin wherever he went. In 1805, the victor at Trafalgar was taken on shore in this coffin. He had wanted to be buried in his own village, but had specified in his will: 'unless the King decrees otherwise'. King George III did decree otherwise: the Norfolk Hero was taken to the crypt of St Paul's, and his wooden coffin was placed in a marble tomb that had originally been intended for Cardinal Wolsey. Meanwhile, on a granite column 170 feet above Trafalgar Square, Admiral Nelson now fights his last battle against the pigeons, tourists and exhaust fumes of London.

Nelson ensured England's mastery of the world's seas, and Burnham Thorpe acquired a Nelson Hall. There, in front of the gilded bust of the great man, members of the Nelson Society come together from all over the world to celebrate Trafalgar Day, 21 October. Their President is Peter John Horatio, 9th Earl Nelson, a direct descendant of the Admiral, and a retired CID officer. After the Trafalgar memorial service, the members – mostly retired naval officers – go their separate ways to picnic in the neighbourhood: perhaps to Burnham Market, where Nelson's daughter Horatia got married, or to Wells-next-the-Sea, where his wife Fanny lived for a while, or best of all to Overy Staithe, where the Duke and Duchess of Kent keep their yacht. The more elevated members, however, tend to go to the exclusive Royal West Norfolk, a golf club in the marshes of *Brancaster*. The club-house stands marooned amongst the sand dunes and straggly grasses. The sea has retreated a long way from Branodunum, the coastal fort of the Romans. Today the National Trust looks after large sections of the marshes as well as the offshore island of Scolt Head, with its long stretch of shifting sands.

Brancaster Marsh and Titchwell Marsh reach out endlessly between sea and sky; here the sun always seems to be setting in a no-man's-land of changing tides and lonely shores that contain nothing but sea asters, sea lavender, and a thousand-voiced choir of seabirds. If I had to name the most beautiful marshlands in England, I would go for the saltmarshes of Brancaster Bay.

Near *Holme-next-the-Sea*, the Norfolk Coast Path meets the prehistoric Peddars Way, which cuts southwards through the fields of West Norfolk in so straight a line that you'd think the Romans themselves had made it, instead of simply fitting it in with their own network of roads. Another sight is the cliffs of *Hunstanton*, the Victorian resort on the Wash, with their three layers of red and white lime and rust-brown sandstone, glowing like some vast prehistoric tricolour. Don't miss *Heacham* either, with its incomparable orgy of colour when the lavender fields bloom in summer. One hundred acres of glorious scents: *Lavendula angustifolia*, or blue Norfolk Lavender – a veritable landscape of perfume. The amber-coloured lavender oil is distilled in an old watermill, producing that royal essence of a million herbal pillows, bars of soap and bath oils whose aroma spreads all over the world, the beguiling and bewitching fragrance of Olde Englande.

Sandringham: Where The Queen Sees In The New Year

The carpark is full of buses from all over the country, and the park is full of picnickers. You'd think it was Derby Day at Epsom. There are long queues at the entrance, but then this is *Sandringham* in the summer – the Queen's country home, south of Heacham's lavender fields (plate 22). There is nothing the English middle class like seeing more than the houses of the aristocracy, and in particular the palaces of its Queen, from Osborne House on the Isle of Wight to Balmoral Castle in the Scottish Highlands. During the holiday season, Sandringham becomes the target of 2,000 royalist pilgrims and tourists a day.

'Please wipe your feet,' requests a notice in the entrance. I shake the petit bourgeois dust off my shoes, and go in. The very first exhibit – a set of Victorian scales with leather-upholstered seat – is comforting: Their Royal Majesties must certainly have had worse weight problems than their subjects, since they ate so much more lavishly, not to mention frequently. Mahogany tables and glass cabinets display the china that is still used today: Dresden, Copenhagen, Royal Worcester. There are Brussels tapestries from the 17th century, plaster ceilings, large mirrors, and lavish Edwardian elegance everywhere. If the Queen were to come in now, wearing a tartan skirt and polo-necked sweater, as she is on the picture postcards being sold at the royal kiosk, or with a scarf on her head, somehow it would ruin the Sandringham illusion. Fortunately, she only comes for the New Year and the pheasant shooting in January.

Once upon a time, the house had 365 rooms. Rather too many, thought the Queen, so she had a wing removed. The house was not actually opened to the public until 1977, but it seemed a democratic thing to do. (The profits go to charity.) Today Sandringham has just 274 rooms, of which no less than six are open to visitors. They are rooms which the Royal Family themselves also use. The others are for guests and staff. There are 70 people employed here, but if you think that's feudal, you should hear R. S. French, one of the stewards, recalling the good old Edwardian days: 'Then we had fifty gardeners alone, and now we only have twelve.' Edward VII, known as Bertie, was the first royal owner of Sandringham. Queen Victoria gave it to her eldest son in 1862 as a twenty first birthday present, in the vain hope that it might distract him from the sinful temptations of London life. Shortly afterwards, and newly married to Princess Alexandra, the Prince of Wales moved in. And shortly after he moved in, he decided that this old Georgian place was too small, so he sent for an unknown London architect, A. J. Humbert, and got him to build a bigger, neo-Elizabethan residence (1870) with lots of gables and chimneys. It's not unlike a Victorian station hotel. Unfortunately, in the sixties Queen Elizabeth II turned down her husband's proposal that they should demolish the old house and build a new modern one. Instead, she commissioned Sir Hugh Casson, President of the Royal Academy, to do some discreet modernizing of the interior.[1]

---

1   The park was designed by the doyen of English landscape gardeners, Sir Geoffrey Jellicoe.

King Edward VII at Sandringham, 1902

In order to gain more privacy, Edward VII had the road moved a mile away from the house. He received Kaiser Wilhelm and Tsar Nicholas in Sandringham, and hold glamorous balls and shoots. His guns, together with those of his successors, fill several cupboards. The Royal Family have always been eager shots, and the things that they've bagged over the years in Norfolk and on their tours round the British Empire – antelopes, tigers, rhinos, elephants, and other big game – used to hang in tightly packed rows on the walls of four rooms of what used to be the coach house and fire station. Now there is a more politically correct exhibition of royal snapshots and a commemoration of the Sandringham Estate Fire Brigade. Also banished were the tails, hooves and jaws of famous thoroughbreds that bear witness to another of the Royal Family's passions: racing. Shirley Heights is the Queen's best stallion in the Sandringham stud. In front of the stables is a bronze statue of Persimmon, the legendary Derby-winner which brought its owner, Edward VII, prize money totalling exactly £34,706, a huge sum in those days. The polo-playing Prince Philip has earned rather less with his short-lived Carriage Driving Centre, where his trainer gives lessons for about £20 an hour.

They're a hunting, riding and driving family, the royals, and in the museum you can see Queen Victoria's wheelchair, and her son Edward's two-cylinder Daimler Tonneau, made in 1900,the first car to be bought by a member of the Royal Family, and still in good working order. There's also the wood-panelled Daimler shooting brake owned by George VI in 1937, and Queen Mary's black and green six-cylinder 'Shopping Daimler', in which she drove round London's shops.

In those early days, the Windsors constantly expanded their territory, which now covers some 20,000 acres. Edward VII gave each of his children a house in or near Sandringham.

His favourite daughter, Princess Maud, was given Appleton Hall (1863) as her wedding present, and it was there that her only child was born – Olaf V of Norway. When Edward's son, the Duke of York (George V) married the German Princess May of Teck in 1893, he was presented with York Cottage, which was once used to house Sandringham's guests and is now the estate office. The future George VI was born there. The neighbouring estate of Anmer Hall belongs to one of the Queen's cousins, the Duke of Kent. Princess Diana was born nearby, in Park House. Her father, Lord Spencer, was at that time in charge of the Queen's horses. The Spencers had the only heated swimming pool for miles around, and it was there that Prince Charles and Lady Di first met. It's a small world, even for the royals.

'Dear Old Sandringham, the place I love better than anywhere else in the world,' gushed George V. Here he could shoot to his heart's content. He would think nothing of knocking off a thousand partridges and pheasants in a day. Critics complained that the King did nothing but kill defenceless birds and stick stamps in his album. He did, however, make a speech to the nation on radio at Christmas 1932, from Sandringham. Twenty-five years later, Queen Elizabeth made her first television speech, and it was also from Sandringham. A very strange chapter in court and media history occurred when George V lay dying. He was a heavy smoker, and had a very painful disease of the respiratory tracts. The family were waiting in an adjacent room. The 71-year-old King deserved to die in dignity and peace, thought his doctor, Lord Dawson. 'I therefore decided to determine the end.' Dawson had a telephone call put through to *The Times* to tell them to hold publication. He

The Queen and the Duchess of York at Sandringham, 1987

King George V broadcasting his Christmas Day speech from Sandringham, 1934

injected the King with morphine and cocaine. Shortly before midnight, the King died – just in time for the headlines the following morning, 20 January 1936. It is clear from the diary of this publicity-conscious physician that one of his considerations in timing the moment was 'the importance of the death receiving its first announcement in the morning papers rather than in the less appropriate evening journals.' Fifty years later, *The Times* expressed its gratitude and its apologies in a leading article: 'Even in those days it was a bit above the odds to be tipped off that the King was about to die by the man who was killing him.' One can just imagine the scene as the deadline approached, and the patriotic men of *The Times* waited anxiously to see if the King could meet it. What a relief when the tragic news came through. A popular rhyme at the time ran: 'Lord Dawson of Penn / Has killed many men / That is why we sing / "God Save the King".'

Under the sun-dial at Sandringham ('My time is in thy hand') lie Queen Alexandra's favourite dogs: 'Facie and Punchie my darling faithful little companions in joy and sorrow.'As for the village church, it glitters like an Edwardian ballroom. The solid silver altar was given by an American in 1911, and is covered with gilded angels. Even if we are all equal in the sight of God, royalty has to be specially equal in the sight of the congregation, and so the red upholstered bench front right in the choir is reserved for the Queen and her family. Sir Alfred Gilbert, creator of the Eros statue in Piccadilly, made his own contribution to the edifying patriotism of this church with a virtuous St George of ivory and aluminium (1892).

The estate of Sandringham includes seven villages, together with fields of grain and sugar beet, orchards, forests, and the Queen's own shooting dogs and labradors, which she breeds here. Her Majesty's pick-your-own apples are extremely popular. In the park are the oaks that each generation has planted, and the magnificent Norwich Gates are here too, the wrought-iron wedding present given by the city of Norwich to Edward VII (made by Thomas Jekyll *c*.1860). At the end of your visit, you'll come to another queue, from which the visitors depart happily bearing their pots of begonias, gloxinias and other flowers from the royal gardens, to be planted in their own front gardens with as prominent a label as possible.

Many British passions come together in Sandringham: gardens and parks, racehorses, veteran cars, and that rare species, the royals. This is how the ordinary man imagines his monarchs to be, and in the most natural, democratic and socially acceptable way, he can actually step into the fairy tale himself. All he has to do is get there during official opening hours, and pay his entrance money.

If you go through the woods, you'll come to *Wolferton*. Between the trees the rhododendrons burst forth in royal profusion. Fenrir, the mythical wolf of the Vikings, stands guard on the Wolferton sign, and before the houses are lanterns with gold crowns, once part of Wolferton Station. 'Through these doors passed all the Kings & Queens of Europe,' it says at the entrance; 'all others, please use the next door!' An empty platform with a white wooden roof; a few forgotten leather cases; rolled up on a handcart, the red carpet from the Royal Train. This used to be the terminus for the London–Sandringham royal line. It was to Wolferton that they came, princes, kings, prime ministers – to bring reports, to go shooting, to dance at the royal ball. And this is where they said goodbye, the guests both wanted and unwanted. 'Thank God, he's gone,' said Edward VII, having waved goodbye to his nephew Kaiser Wilhelm II. The little Victorian station saw it all, from private parties to state visits, from weddings to funerals. And whoever died in Sandringham, like George V and George VI, went on one last journey with the Great Eastern Railway from Wolferton to Windsor, to be buried in the family vault.

At 4.20 p.m. on 23 March 1863, the very first Royal Train stopped here. The Prince and Princess of Wales, Edward and Alexandra, were back from their honeymoon on the Isle of Wight. The very last Royal Train stopped here in 1965. One year later came the vital moment for Eric Walker, an employee of British Rail. He was to make an inventory of everything, before British Rail closed the line and demolished the station. Eric Walker took one look at the royal waiting-rooms, unchanged since the days of Queen Victoria, and at once he took a decision: he would buy Wolferton Station and save it for ever. The station became his home and his life's work. He even owns the old wheelwright's shop now as well. He took early retirement so that he could devote himself completely to restoring the station and collecting all the memorabilia of his royal railway. 'It's not that I'm a monarchist. If it had been Karl Marx, I'd have done the same thing. This is a place of major interest, and it's small enough for little people like us to cope with. Here we can do something for our historical heritage.' When Queen Elizabeth first opened Sandringham to the public in 1977, Mr Walker opened Wolferton Station as a museum. 'Why shouldn't I do the same as the Queen, so that I can also cover the costs of maintaining my home?'

Once the opaque glass of the station's windows kept out the curious gaze of the ordinary folk, but now anyone can go into the Royal Retiring Rooms. The King and Queen had separate waiting rooms. Queen Alexandra would take tea in upholstered armchairs of blue satin brocade – her favourite colour – while King Edward stood next door by the fireplace, enjoying the benefits of a screen that kept the draught off his back. Discreetly tucked away in one corner is His Majesty's pissoir, a porcelain basin sporting the Union Jack. Eric Walker has labelled everything, with a mixture of affection and irony: Queen Victoria's travelling bed, timetables, tickets (even Their Majesties had to have tickets), and innumerable souvenirs from the great days of the railways. When the last visitors have left Wolferton Station, the Walker family relax in Queen Alexandra's waiting-room. Does their Sandringham neighbour ever drop in? 'No, we don't get on too well with the Queen.'

Just a few miles further south, more than 600 years ago, there lived another English queen, Isabella, known as the 'She-Wolf of France'. She was the daughter of a French king, and widow of Edward II, having assisted in his brutal murder in 1327. Her son Edward III deprived his ambitious mother of all power, had her lover Roger Mortimer executed, and banished the 'She-Wolf' from the London court to Norfolk, where she lived at *Castle Rising*, which belonged to the Crown (plate 24). Even as a ruin, this Norman keep still seems like a medieval high security prison. But the deadly widow spent 27 years here living in queenly style, with complete freedom of movement, and with a state pension provided by her son. She was not a prisoner, but was a Queen Mother. Only she wasn't a Queen Mother to put on display.

Massive earthworks and trenches, one inner and two outer courts, all surround the mighty keep of Castle Rising. It is one of the biggest and best preserved Norman keeps in England, but like those of Norwich and the Tower of London it is a hall-keep (i.e. residential) and not a tower-keep (defensive). It is 50 feet high, and 78½ by 68½ feet wide. Although the shape is almost rectangular, the effect is by no means squat. The long sides are divided up with flat, pilaster-like buttresses, and the west wall has three large blind arches. The porch on the east side seems more like the entrance to a palace than to a fort, with its columns, ornamental strips, medallions and blind arcades. The decoration is deceptive, however. This porch is the only entrance to the castle, and anyone who wanted to conquer the castle would have had to fight his way up the long flight of steps, then go along another path through another gate to the entrance on the first floor. It is a brilliant example of aesthetic medieval military architecture.

What splendour must have met the eyes of Queen Isabella when she stepped through the grand Norman doorway (now blocked off) into the two-storeyed Great Hall of Castle Rising. A railing is there now to prevent us from falling straight down into the cellars. Her boudoirs too have lost their ceilings, and indeed everything else that would have made her life here bearable or even enjoyable. The keep was unusually roomy, and details like the

Castle Rising, aerial view of Norman castle

scalloped capitals in the chapel reveal the quality of the interiors. The walls are over eight feet thick, of rubble that was originally covered with Barnack stone. In Isabella's day the oval courtyard would not have been so green or so spacious, since this was the site of the bailiff's house and the wings that housed the servants and all the services. One can just imagine the hustle and bustle – rather like a weekend in the holiday season, when the knights of the White Society march up for their yearly conquest of the castle.

When I visited Castle Rising, the battle had already begun. Fierce fighting was going on at the gatehouse, and the first victims had got up again, and then gallantly died again, to the

John Sell Cotman: Castle Rising Castle, 1818

applause of the onlookers. In the courtyard there was the clashing of swords, halberds and chain mail, while people sat on the walls all around and enjoyed the spectacle. Occasionally small children would go rolling down the slope, shrieking with laughter. By the end, everybody had won, a few people were tending their scratches, and most were picnicking amid the gunsmoke. The heroes of this Sunday show are the members of the White Society, who keep alive the traditions of medieval knighthood – young English people who by sheer bad luck happened to be born in the 20th century instead of the 15th. These computer-age Plantagenets bring their armour in the boot of the car, all very authentic, though generally home-made. Such historical re-enactments are enjoying a boom in England. It's historical, open-air theatre: fans of the Romans join the Ermine Street Guard; Cavaliers and Roundheads join the Sealed Knot (originally the secret society that played a decisive role in restoring Charles II to the throne), which with 5,000 members is the biggest of these societies, and specializes in the battles of the Civil War. There are also mobile armies that restage the Wars of the Roses, the Napoleonic Wars, and even the two World Wars. It would be nice if future wars were confined to this sort of spectacle.

The man who built Castle Rising was William de Albini II. His ancestors from Martin d'Aubigny in Normandy had conquered England alongside William the Conqueror, and he himself conquered an English queen: Alice of Louvain, widow of Henry I. Thanks to this marriage, William de Albini climbed to the very top of the Anglo-Norman aristocracy.

He came into possession of the Rising estate, as well as Arundel Castle and the title of Earl of Sussex, and shortly after his marriage he began to build Castle Rising in 1138. It remained in the powerful Albini family's possession for two hundred years, and then returned to the Crown.

After Queen Isabella's death, Edward III gave the estate to the Black Prince, Edward Duke of Cornwall, and stipulated that for all time it should remain part of the Duchy of Cornwall and a permanent possession of the heir to the throne or the king. But of course along came Henry VIII, who was no respecter of other people's stipulations, and he gave the estate to his uncle Thomas Howard, Duke of Norfolk, in 1544. English lawyers have proved that the present Duke of Cornwall, Prince Charles, would have a legal right to Castle Rising if he cared to take the current owners to court. They are, as before, the Howard family, the head of which is the 17th Duke of Norfolk, Earl Marshal and Chief Butler of England. Not really a man that Prince Charles would wish to pick a quarrel with. As the royal master of ceremonies, he will eventually be responsible for organizing the next coronation.

We have already met the Howards. You may remember them from Framlingham Castle (see page 240 ff.): knights, courtiers, and traitors, supporters of the papacy and of poetry. They had plenty of castles elsewhere, and neglected Castle Rising, which is now run by English Heritage. On the other hand, though, they also did some good in the village. Henry Howard, Lord Privy Seal and member of the Crown Council, founded the

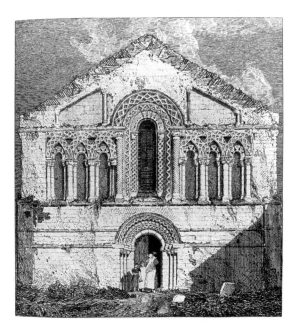

John Sell Cotman:
Castle Rising church, west front, 1813

455

Hospital of the Holy and Undivided Trinity in 1614, to house eleven needy spinsters and their governess. 'They must be of honest life and conversation, religious, grave and discreet,' he wrote in its constitution. Each one must also 'be able to read, if such a one may be had, single, 56 at least, no common beggar, harlot, scold, drunkard, haunter of taverns, inns or alehouses.' That the ladies of Trinity Hospital still fulfil these demanding conditions is beyond doubt, as I was assured by Doris, Gladys and Dorothy, all single ladies of over 70, and three of the present eight occupants of the house.

The sisters of Castle Rising are one of the sights to be seen (colour plate 34). When they cross the street on Sunday to go to service in the Norman village church with its famous blind arches, they wear their Jacobean capes of scarlet serge with the Howard coat of arms, just as they did nearly 400 years ago. The tall, pointed black hats, or 'steeple hats', are worn only on Founder's Day at the end of February. The founder's descendant Greville Howard is still living in the village. For their single rooms in this historic old folks' home, with kitchen, bath and TV, the ladies pay a monthly rent of £80. Their idyllic surroundings are, however, priceless. Four brick wings extend around an inner courtyard with tall chimneys, a little gatehouse, and a lot of variety. Journalists, tourists, and even the Queen come to gaze, and everyone loves the ladies of Trinity Hospital.

God Save King's Lynn: The Royal Streets of a Trading Town

In 1985, Nastassja Kinski and Al Pacino went through a number of adventures during the American War of Independence. The 18th-century sets for the film 'Revolution' were not built in the studio. They were all *King's Lynn*. Georgian town houses, commercial offices with Dutch gables, warehouses on the quay, markets, medieval customs houses and guild houses – they are all together here as if time had simply passed King's Lynn by. It's right on the edge of Norfolk, deep in the heart of the province, and off the beaten tourist track. Perhaps that is why this old port and trading town has remained so intact and so little known. On the Continent, everyone knows Lübeck or Delft or Bruges, and so perhaps in this European age it is time people got to know the English equivalent on the Great Ouse.

Lynn means lake, and it was the water that gave everything: fish, the salt of the marshes, olden day prosperity, catastrophic floods. Before the merchants came the monks. In 1101 the Bishop of Norwich founded a Benedictine monastery on the bank of the Ouse: Lenne Episcopi, or Bishop's Lynn, was its name, until Henry VIII dissolved the monasteries and the town renamed itself King's Lynn. During the Civil War the town also remained true to the King, one of the few in East Anglia not to join Cromwell's side. Baroque figures pay homage to Charles I and II on the front of the Customs House (1683) and of the Bank House (1685), and today this royalist town is a Tory stronghold. King's Lynn's history, however, is not one of kings but one of trade and water.

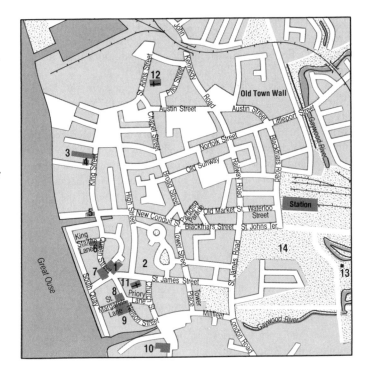

Friars Fleet, Millfleet, Purfleet, Fisher Fleet – only the rudiments and the street-names remain to mark the existence of the four branches of the Ouse between which the town arose, and which it controlled and used like canals, finally building almost completely over them. By the middle of the 12th century, the first settlement had already become too small. Newe Londe was added to it, between Purfleet and Fisher Fleet, with its own market and church. Saturday Market and Tuesday Market, St Margaret's and St Nicholas are the two extremes of the medieval town, firmly linked by the trio of patriotically named King, Queen and Nelson Streets, with their long rows of houses running parallel to the Ouse, slightly curved like the bank of the river.

As a trading port, King's Lynn competed in the Middle Ages with towns like Bristol and Bruges. Goods used to come from many counties along the Ouse and its tributaries, to be exported from Lynn: cereals from the marshlands and the Fens, wool and cloth from the East Midlands, lead from the mines of Derbyshire, and salt from the salterns of Norfolk and Lincolnshire. The merchants of Lynn imported luxury items such as wine from Gascony, furs from Siberia, and Flemish and Italian cloths. They also brought in large quantities of coal, timber and herrings from Scandinavia, and dried cod from Iceland. Timber and cereals are still the most important goods handled here, and as before, the

Baltic countries are the main trading partners. The import of Skoda cars from the Czech Lands also comes through King's Lynn. The main industry here, though, is canning and freezing fruit and vegetables. There is also old Frederick Savage's factory, which built England's first steam-driven merry-go-round. Since then, his home town has risen to be the market-leader in building fun-fair machines.

An impressive witness to Lynn's importance in the Middle Ages is the *Hanseatic Warehouse* (1428) in St Margaret's Lane. From 1475 onwards this long brick building with its projecting timber-framed storey was one of the four Hanseatic establishments in Britain. The mayors of Lübeck, Hamburg and Bremen kept their common counter here until Edward Everard of Lynn bought it in 1750 for £800. Everard and Thoresby, Bagge, Browne and Hogge were the great merchant dynasties of the town, and each had its own quay and its own crew of ten to fifteen sailors. For generations they lived here, first in the High Street and at Tuesday Market, then later beside the river, until in the 18th century these oligarchs of Lynn married into the aristocracy, became landed gentry, and spent the rest of their days in country houses far away from the noisy, smelly quays that had brought them their fortunes.

King Street and *Queen Street* are the royal roads of the merchants and their architecture. The area between street and river was divided into a series of long, narrow plots. The merchants had their shops on the street itself, and lived either above or behind them. From there they could see all the buildings that stretched out along the different plots for 60 to 90 yards right down to the quay: offices, warehouses, workshops, stables and gardens, and even bakeries and breweries. Nowhere in England are the residential and business quarters so tightly knit or so well preserved as they are in King's Lynn, a quite fascinating piece of social and architectural history. 'The finest old streets anywhere in England,' was the verdict of James Lees-Milne, the authoritative voice of the National Trust. By the 19th century Lynn was already too poor to tear down its old buildings and replace them with new, but now the town is strong enough to resist the vandalism of the developers.

King Street, Queen Street ... between the mud of the Ouse and the cries of the gulls, there stand the houses, just as they were in Hogarth's time. Georgian fronts concealing Tudor beams and balance sheets and the rise and fall of Lynn's Buddenbrooks. Partly out of curiosity, and partly drawn by the baroque doorway with its corkscrew columns, I suddenly found myself in one of these walk-through houses: from the cool entrance to *Clifton House* I walked across the courtyard, through another, neoclassical doorway with a white bust in the pediment, across worn-down sandstone paving slabs into a second courtyard leading down to the river. All the time, I was being observed by Mr Foster, from the first floor of his Elizabethan watch-tower, as he proudly informed me while at the same time inviting me to put 50p in the box (to help maintain the house). 50p is very reasonable if you consider the size of this house, and its 12th-century fireplace, 13th-century floor tiles, 14th-century cellar and ribbed vault, and 16th-century granary and brick tower. 'I'm 25 per cent of the sights of Lynn,' says Mr Foster, putting on his bowler

BVRSA LINNENSIS

The Exchange at Lynn Regis in Norfolk

King's Lynn, the Customs House, 1683, engraving by the architect Henry Bell

hat, 'and 100 per cent on Sundays when the others are shut.' He's a retired businessman from London, and once sold vacuum cleaners ('I can sell anything'); he bought this crumbling merchant's house in Queen Street (maybe someone else could sell anything, too) some years ago. He'd intended it to be a place for retirement and an investment, but now he finds he has to keep on investing, and there's precious little hope of retirement. He spends most of his time restoring the house and digging up its history, for he's now become an amateur archaeologist – one of those magnificent eccentrics without whose undying enthusiasm Clifton House, King's Lynn, and England itself would never be the same.

What Roland Foster does in his own eccentric way, the King's Lynn Preservation Society does systematically. Founded in 1958, it can take most of the credit for preserving essential areas of the old town. 'We save them by buying them,' explains Miss Bullock, who runs the society. The society buys houses that are in danger of collapse or demolition, restores them, and then sells them again to people who will use them properly. A fine example of their work is *Hampton Court* in Nelson Street, a building with four wings round an inner courtyard; the south wing is 14th century, one of the earliest fully preserved merchant's houses in Lynn; next to it is a brick warehouse with arcades that formerly opened out on the quay. This is industrial architecture at its functional and aesthetic best. Today Hampton Court is an idyllic residential complex. Just as impressive is *Thoresby College* in Queen Street, opposite the Town Hall. Behind the Georgian front is a much older, very spacious building, c.1500, given by the merchant and mayor Thomas Thoresby as a college for the thirteen priests of the Trinity Guild and for his own two chaplains. This too is a building with four wings – a classic piece of college architecture, and since its restoration by the Trust, two of the wings have been converted into a retirement home, one is a youth hostel, and the open-roofed Great Hall is used for all kinds of events. The Preservation Trust also has its offices here.

Miss Bullock showed me one more example of the Society's successful work – one which even enjoys the patronage of the Queen Mother. We entered No. 32 King Street, which from outside looks Victorian; inside, it is a late 12th-century Norman house with round arch windows – the oldest surviving merchant's house in King's Lynn, exposed in all its glory by the careful restorations of the Trust. It is now the office of a firm of solicitors. Once it was a 'one-up one-down' cottage, with a shop below and the residential quarters above – typical of the smaller businesses in King Street, by contrast with the large-scale concerns on the posher side of the street.

Even in Lynn the anonymous architecture of the ordinary folk has almost completely disappeared. It was always unobtrusive anyway, just like their work and their everyday lives, not worth a second glance. Only in *Pilot Street*, on the northern edge of the medieval part of the town, has the Trust been able to restore six of the fishermen's and workmen's cottages. In 1841 there were 91 of these cottages here, with 444 people living in them. But the old fishermen's quarter was brutally destroyed at the end of the fifties by development and road-building. 'We couldn't save everything,' lamented Miss Bullock. Even George

Vancouver's birthplace was destroyed.'[1] When I met her, Diana Bullock was nearly 80 years old – a retired teacher and founder member of the Preservation Trust, awarded the OBE for all her work. She lived in Greenland Fishery House, which was built in 1605 for the merchant and mayor John Atkin. Brick and timber-framing with ornate cleats, bay windows, allegorical murals, and in the evening, when everything is quite still in the house, you can hear the voices of the Greenland fishermen whose pub this was, and who used to meet here before sailing from Lynn to the Arctic where they would hunt their whales.

There are still a few dozen inshore fishermen here. Their brightly coloured wooden cutters lie in the Docks at Fisher Fleet: 'Daphne' and 'Andy', 'Jenny Rose' and 'Harmony'. 'We don't make a fortune, but you can earn a living,' they say. In the great bay of the Wash there are no more fish. Dow Chemicals are allowed to discharge their waste into the sea when the tide is going out – and when the tide comes back in, so does the waste.

Thanks to a typically English holy alliance between natural inertia and natural conservatism, King's Lynn has been generally spared the evils of urban development, and happily it has not made any special effort to attract the tourists. Since 1951, however, there has been an exquisite festival every summer with concerts, theatre, and a composer in residence. Yehudi Menuhin has performed here, and Janet Baker, Colin Davis, and many of the stars of tomorrow. There are also exhibitions which for a long time were in the hands of Sir Geoffrey Agnew, the London art dealer. It all takes place in the King's Lynn Arts Centre, which remains extremely active all the year round. It is situated in the *Guildhall of St George*, King Street, which was built shortly after 1400, with open roof trusses, vaulted storage rooms, and a long row of warehouses stretching right down to the river. This is one of the few completely preserved complexes of a medieval merchants' guild. After Edward VI had dissolved the guilds in 1547, the Guildhall of St George served as a court, a corn exchange, an arms and gunpowder store – and very early on, a theatre. Shakespeare's company is known to have performed here, and he may well have been here in person.

The guilds were the medieval equivalent of our chambers of commerce – professional, co-operative associations, but rather more than just that, they were also political and religious centres, with social functions, economic muscle, and an early penchant for worker participation. They were important enough for Richard II to have a statistical record drawn up in 1389. The county with the largest number of guilds (164) was Norfolk, and the town with the largest number (51) was Lynn. In 1421, the richest of all the guilds built a house at Saturday Market, which has remained one of the great sights even today: the *Guildhall of the Holy Trinity*. It has a chequerwork front of flint and stone, and the Elizabethan extension is also black and white. The same pattern – clearly a favourite – made its way across to the house next door, which is the Victorian *Town Hall* of 1895

1 One of the highly efficient seafaring men from Lynn, who served as an officer under James Cook, and was the first to chart the coast north of San Francisco. Vancouver Island in British Columbia was named after him. He also explored the south-west coast of Australia and New Zealand.

(plate 34). The overall effect is of the town's architectural dignitaries dressed up in their very best check suits.

In the lofty hall of the Guildhall, you can hold your wedding feast, while in the cellar of the Town Hall you can admire the town's regalia. The finest jewel in Lynn's crown is King John's Cup. Traditionally it was said to have been part of the King's treasure which on 13 October 1215 was lost in the Nene Estuary west of Lynn, when the King's baggage-train tried to cross the treacherous sands at low tide. This is impossible, since the cup was not made until 1340, more than a hundred years after King John's death. The kingless cup is nevertheless the earliest to survive, and a royal piece of secular art produced by the very best of medieval goldsmiths. Its coloured enamel scenes are set in gold: falconers, knights and their ladies, courtly elegance, courtly love, courtly hunting – this is a cup like an Ode to Joy. There is another magnificent cup here too, by Martin Dumling, court jeweller to the Emperor Rudolph II in Prague and later in Nuremberg (c.1600). And there are baroque maces, shining chains of office, charters and chronicles and many more priceless gems in the treasure chamber of this self-confident royalist town of trade and commerce. Twice a year the ceremonial sword – symbol of justice – is brought before the Mayor of Lynn and with blade held high is carried in solemn procession to the Priory Church of St Margaret with St Mary Magdalene and all the Virgin Saints.

The columns of St Margaret's are as crooked as a drunken sailor. The church was built in 1101 by Bishop Herbert de Losinga, but its site on the bank of the Ouse was unstable. Somehow, miraculously, it has survived all the floods, iconoclasts, and the hurricane of 1741 which tore the spire off its southwest tower. High above the columned balustrade of the tower, St Margaret's dragon shows the tide times: LYNN HIGH TIDE, with twelve letters instead of numbers, each one two hours away from the next. Up above is the Baroque moon dial (17th century), and down below on the doorway are the flood marks: 11 March 1883, 31 January 1953, and above that the latest in the line, 11 January 1978. When the wild North Sea comes to church, Lynn is in trouble. St Margaret's has been shaped by many hands: Norman, Gothic, Victorian, some skilful and some not so skilful. The pulpit is a revelation of Early Georgian artistry, while the platform in the choir is an aesthetic crash-landing in the shape of an RAF bomber. How much more discreet was the artist who carved the Gothic screen, hiding his Lilliputians in the delicate tracery (14th-century); in the choir stalls, there are heads supporting the oak seats, like Atlas holding up the earth – misericords for the comfort of the clergy (plate 94).

Many people go to St Margaret's just to see the brasses. These are two massive monuments, dating from the middle of the 14th century, both dazzling and rare examples of the brasses made in Flanders – plates, not cut-out figures. One depicts Adam de Walsokne, who died in 1349, together with his wife and allegorical scenes of everyday rural life: a man carrying corn to the mill, and workers in the vineyard. The other, the Peacock Brass, depicts the dead man, lifesize, and his magnificent 'Peacock Feast'. The man is Robert Braunche (died 1364), and he is shown with his first and second wives Letitia and Margaret. They are all wearing long robes with embroidered borders, and pointed Gothic shoes. They stand next to one another, their hands folded, facing us and God, with angels above their heads under heavenly canopies, while at their feet there is no earthly vale of tears but, on the contrary, a lavishly loaded table of roast peacock, with musicians and twelve guests. This is the famous feast which Robert Braunche held for his sovereign Edward III in Lynn (1349). It is a royal banquet and a last supper, life feasting death. Even the host is only one of the guests, leaving his house and hoping for a place at the Lord's table. It is a monument created out of the fullness of life and faith, and its beauty even 600 years later is enough to make even the unbeliever yearn. I touch the brass, and it is cold. We go outside, into the shade of the chestnut trees, and picnic among the graves.

Later I walked along the river, past the warehouses on Kings Staithe Lane, to the *Custom House* at Purfleet Quay. It was built in 1683 as the Merchants' Exchange, with arcades (originally open), pilasters, a hipped roof, and an almost rectangular ground plan similar to that of Dutch buildings of the period (e.g. the Alte Waage in Amsterdam). This fine, functional building was designed by a local architect, Henry Bell, son of a merchant and Mayor of Lynn. He also built what is still the first port of call in this square, the *'Duke's Head' Hotel* (1685), and the parish church of All Saints in North Runcton (1703–13) is also attributed to him. The front of the 'Duke's Head' has a romantic appeal, all in pink with gold letters, very Barbara Cartland. Opposite is the Victorian *Corn Exchange*, which Pevsner calls 'jolly and vulgar'. The houses are all of different types and heights, adding to the variety of a square that is full of market-women, townswomen, farmers from the Fens, fishermen from the Wash, traders from Pakistan. For this is *Tuesday Market.*

Beyond the square, at the other end of the medieval town, lies *St Nicholas Chapel*, which is a daughter church to St Margaret's. Despite its size, it only has the status of a chapel and not of a parish church. It's situated in what used to be the fishermen's quarter, and was dedicated in 1146 to the patron saint of fishing. This was always the church of the ordinary folk, whereas St Margaret's was for the middle classes, including the merchants. Today St Nicholas Chapel is popular with everyone, as the Festival concert hall. Angels spread their wooden wings over the high, bright room, while the mayors make their last official appearance on the walls, surrounded by their families in baroque abundance. The church was finished in 1429, and among its special features is a Neoclassical burial urn designed by Robert Adam in marble with reliefs (*c.*1757) for Sir Benjamin Keene, George II's special envoy to Spain. There is also a hand that reaches out from a pillar into empty space. It is not, however, a piece of 18th-century surrealism, but a swordrest (1757) for the mayor's ceremonial sword. Alas, this church like so many others is in imminent danger of closure.

There is a beautiful path through St James' Park called the Walks, and here on the former walls of the town stands a Gothic chapel which from far away looks like a water tower; this is *Red Mount Chapel* (1485), an octagonal building of red brick, with buttresses at each of the eight corners and a recessed, cruciform roof. Two staircases lead between the outer and inner walls to the upper storey, which was where the services actually took place, beneath a lovely fan vaulted ceiling. 'Our Lady of the Mount' is now a favourite meeting-place for tramps, but once it was the pilgrims' church as they made their way to Walsingham (see page 432 ff.)

Talking of pilgrims, we must mention one in particular, for she was one of the two most extraordinary women in the history of Lynn. Margery Kempe was her name. She could neither read nor write, and yet she left behind the first English autobiography (c.1435). The other famous lady, however, was a bona fide lady of letters named Fanny Burney. Her thousands of letters together make up a fascinating chronicle of Georgian society. Fanny was born in 1752, either at St Augustine's House in Chapel Street or at 84 High Street (no-one knows for sure), and was baptized in St Nicholas. Her portrait can be seen in the Town Hall Card Room. Her father, the great writer on music Dr Charles Burney, was an organist in Lynn, and in 1754 he ordered the organ of St Margaret's from Snetzler in London. Even after the family had moved, Fanny often returned to Lynn for her holidays, and it was here that she began her lifelong habit of keeping a diary. She would sit beside the river and write, until she grew tired of the 'annoying oaths of the watermen'. At 25 she wrote a best-seller, the novel *Evelina*, and at 40 she married a French immigrant. She was Mistress of the Robes to Queen Charlotte, a favourite of Dr Johnson's and of Reynolds, and a star of the London salons. Her description of her cancer operation is classic: the doctor, Baron Larrey, a surgeon in the Napoleonic army, was famous for amputating up to 200 limbs a day (he was the scalpel hero of Borodino), and in 1811 he amputated not only her tumour but also her entire breast without anaesthetic. Throughout this twenty minute operation, apart from one short fainting fit, she was fully conscious. 'Ah, Messieurs, que je vous plains!' [Gentlemen, I'm so sorry for you!] Fanny Burney died at the age of 87.

It was not only her birthplace, King's Lynn, but also London, Paris and Bath that were Fanny Burney's social and intellectual centres. Margery Kempe was far more deeply rooted in her hometown. She was the daughter of the mayor of Lynn, was married to a merchant, is believed to have had 14 children, and also had strange visions. When the priest raised the Host, she saw the sacrament flutter like a dove. She threw herself full length onto the tiles of St Margaret's, praying and weeping without restraint, and her tears flowed like the Great Ouse itself. She was a religious exhibitionist, whose ecstasy aroused strong feelings in the town. During the great fire of Lynn in 1421, she prayed so ardently that the snowstorm which saved the town was attributed to her. Some called her a mystic, others a swindler, but she herself, in all humility, believed that she had been called to sainthood. That was a dangerous belief at a time when women like her could easily be burnt as witches. It was the age of the Lollards, who trusted in the Gospels rather than in the Pope, and frequently ended up being burnt at the stake. Margery Kempe was also attacked and several times arrested for heresy, but she was also released – a fact which she took as confirmation that she was among the chosen.

Unlike Julian of Norwich, whose advice she sought, Margery did not retire to meditate in a cell, as the recluses did. She was a contemporary of Chaucer, and like the latter's *Wife of Bath*, she set off as a pilgrim. But not just to Canterbury. In the winter of 1413 she went to the Holy Land via Holland and Venice, returning via Assisi and Rome. Again and again she sallied forth, to Santiago de Compostela and various other places where true miracles had taken place. But she always returned home to her John, who looked after the house and the children while she was away. In about 1433, at the age of 60, this emancipated woman set out on her last journey: through Danzig to Aix-la-Chapelle, then back on foot from Dover to London. She remained intrepid, defying all the difficulties and dangers of travel in those times – the born tourist. Back in Lynn, and still illiterate, she dictated her life story, a unique account of the adventures of a medieval woman: her everyday life, her spiritual life, realism, fantasy, religious tract, objective report, it's all combined in this, the first autobiography in the English language. *The Book of Margery Kempe* was published in London, in an abridged version, in 1501, but then disappeared and was forgotten. It was not rediscovered until 1934, and the manuscript is now in the British Library. Was she a mystic, or a fraud? She was certainly arrogant, humble, moody, attractive – 'an honest woman with a high opinion of herself,' writes her biographer, Louise Collis, 'she was the victim of religious mania, deceiving herself as to the nature of her dreams and hallucinations.' Her religious exaltation was part of the great unrest which permeated Europe at that time and took possession of many lay people. Dogma was replaced by personal revelation, and the secularization of the church was countered by a new form of piety, and that was what Margery Kempe sought too. Her life shows how a person who is determined enough can miraculously make her way through the world, and thus perhaps even come to God.

I hunted in vain for Margery Kempe's grave in King's Lynn. How she died, *c*.1440, is as unknown as the year of her birth. And nothing is left in this her hometown to recall the existence of one of its most remarkable women.

Houghton Hall and Raynham Hall:
Prime Minister Walpole and the Lord of the Turnips

Lena doesn't like me. I can tell from the way she's yapping. Lena is the dachshund guarding the lap of the Dowager Marchioness of Cholmondeley. In the circumstances, it would be highly unwise for me to kiss the hand of the lady of *Houghton Hall*. Sybil, Lady Cholmondeley has received me in the Coffee Room, where there is a bunch of mauve hollyhocks beside her, and a portrait on the wall of an Edwardian beauty, lifesize. The beauty is Sybil Sassoon, 1913, the year of her marriage to the Earl of Rocksavage. Now, more than seventy years later and long since widowed, she is sitting opposite me, the old Marchioness so touchingly close to the young one. But the old one is full of life still.

She was painted by an American in Paris, John Singer Sargent, who became famous for portraying the famous. In thirty years this 'Van Dyck of our times' (Rodin) painted more than 600 portraits, after which he had simply had enough. 'No more mugs!' But he made an exception for Sybil Sassoon, the rich and beautiful daughter of a businessman and Rothschild granddaughter, and he gave her the portrait as a wedding present. In 1922, three

The Countess of Rocksavage, 1919,
by John Singer Sargent

years before he died in Chelsea, he painted her again, with a plunging neckline and a dress of many folds. Now the widow guards her Sargents among the treasures of Houghton Hall, and Lena the dachshund guards the guardian.

'I don't collect. I have a collection,' she explains, with all the matter-of-factness of the landed class. The Cholmondeleys are one of the few Norman families to have maintained possession of their land uninterrupted since the 12th century. Their family seat is Cholmondeley Castle in Cheshire, but at the end of the 18th century they linked themselves by marriage with the Walpoles of Houghton, and shortly afterwards with the Dukes of Ancaster. Thus they came into possession of the house in Norfolk and the office of Lord Great Chamberlain. The greying gentleman in the red uniform with gold braid who every year precedes the Queen when she solemnly opens Parliament is the Lord Great Chamberlain, and until recently was Hugh, Lady Cholmondeley's eldest son. When I visited her, Lady Cholmondeley herself was 92, but neither her age nor her rank (she is also a CBE) stopped her from occasionally taking her seat to sell entrance tickets to her house. She was not so keen on giving interviews, and totally forbade photographs. Lena growled and looked meaningfully at the door. It was clearly time to leave.

Mr Baldwin is – or was – an agent on the estate. He has worked for Lady Cholmondeley for fifty years, has been officially retired for ten, but still works for her. He takes me round the park. 'That is our border with Sandringham,' he says, with a westerly wave of the hand that covers lawns, meadows, woods and a broad expanse of green that reaches as far as the horizon. Sometimes the Queen pops in for tea ('quite informal'). Peacocks parade in front of the house, their crests bobbing. There is a honey-coloured glow from the Aislaby sandstone (Yorkshire) in which the brick walls are clad – a stone that is as noble as it is weatherproof. This is one of East Anglia's very greatest country houses, as imposing and as powerful as the man for whom it was built: Sir Robert Walpole, Britain's first Prime Minister.

The main building is a rectangular block with massive corner towers, flanked by two lower wings which are linked to it by colonnades. The basement is rusticated, the piano nobile is marked out with Venetian windows, a columned portico holds the centre, and strict symmetry reigns. It presents itself as an Italianate palace, in the style invented by English followers of Palladio, and it is very much a companion piece to its contemporary neighbour Holkham Hall (plate 3). The original design of 1721 was by Colen Campbell, the 'Vitruvius Britannicus'. But he died before it was completed, in 1735. Even before his death, Thomas Ripley – successor to Grinling Gibbons as court carpenter - had taken charge of the building. Campbell had planned a high attic storey with gables, but instead Ripley built a variation designed by James Gibb (himself following a German pattern-book): domes on the four corner towers, with lanterns – a Baroque finish to a Palladian concept.

The paying public, made welcome since 1976, enter Houghton Hall through the West

Houghton Hall, west front, design by Colen Campbell, c.1723–4

Front Door, which is on the garden side, with its flight of steps and its handsome columned portico. It was already apparent to people at the time that the design of the house was extremely functional. The ground floor, noted Lord Hervey, was reserved for 'huntsmen, hospitality, noise, dirt and business'; the first floor, with its state rooms, was all 'taste, expense, state and parade'. Little has changed since. For his interiors, Walpole engaged the services of William Kent, the leading interior decorator of that period. What Inigo Jones had been for Lord Arundel and his circle a hundred years before, his most original follower William Kent was now for Lord Burlington and the high society of his day. He was the principal promoter of the Palladian taste in England.

The gold-decorated carvings on the mahogany doors, the decorative murals and painted ceilings, the furniture – heavy with gold and scrolls and covered in faded silk velvet– all stem from William Kent. His furniture is at one and the same time as corpulent and as elegant as the people who used it – often pompous and stiff, wallowing in its garlands and putti and bacchanalian masks. The style is courtly and ceremonial, reaching its apogee in the fourposter bed, which has a gigantic shell at its head (Kent's favourite ornament). Here Robert Walpole could feel the flattering caresses of the green velvet all around him, and shining down at him fourfold from the ceiling was the golden star of his Order of the Garter.

The splendour of Houghton Hall begins on the staircase with the great crescendo of the mahogany banisters and Kent's grisaille murals – scenes from the myth of Meleager and Atalanta; it culminates in the Stone Hall and the neighbouring Saloon. The Stone Hall in the piano nobile is a perfect cube, 40 x 40 x 40 feet, the same measurements as the hall in Inigo Jones's Queen's House in Greenwich, but far more lavish in its decoration: gabled doors, a ceiling frieze with putti and garlands by the Venetian plasterer Artari, a Neo-classical fireplace with caryatids, a relief and the bust of Sir Robert, all by Michael Rysbrack. (This naturalized Flemish sculptor who also made one other antique-style relief, for the fireplace in the dining room, now called the Marble Parlour – the finest examples of his art, as are the reclining figures of Britannia and Neptune above the central window at the front of the house.) Before the fireplace of the Stone Hall is an Aubusson carpet from the time of Louis XV. A magnificent columned doorway leads to the Saloon: the walls and furniture are covered with Utrecht silk of Burgundy red, there are huge family portraits by Reynolds, gilt mahogany chairs and sofas by Kent, and between the windows his typical bracket tables with baroque volutes and tall mirrors which redouble the splendour of the room (plate 6).

For a particular treasure of English weaving, Kent designed a special room. It was to house a unique series of Mortlake tapestries with lifesize portraits of the Stuart Kings: James I and his wife Anne of Denmark, Charles I and Queen Henrietta Maria (both based on Van Dyck), and Christian IV of Denmark, James I's brother-in-law. Between the full-length portraits of the monarchs are head-and-shoulders of their children in the medallions round the borders. The contrast is charming, and it all goes to make up a breathtaking gallery of Stuarts, woven in 1670 by Francis Poyntz with vegetable dyes

Houghton Hall, Mortlake Tapestries in the Tapestry Dressing Room

that are as fresh today as they were three hundred years ago. The Tapestry Dressing Room also contains two Victorian showpieces that seem a little uncomfortable in this setting: A. W. Pugin's Neo-Gothic thrones from the House of Lords, specially made on Queen Victoria's orders for her Prince Consort and her Prince of Wales, and granted by Edward VIII, who had neither wife nor son, as a perquisite to the 5th Marquess of Cholmondeley as Lord Great Chamberlain. They are lent out every year for the State Opening of Parliament so that Prince Philip and Prince Charles can attend the ceremony appropriately seated.

Houghton Hall's treasures have been accumulated over generations, and you need far more than a single visit to take them all in. Look at the gilt garlands of fruit and foliage above the fireplace in the Common Parlour, attributed to none other than the virtuoso Grinling Gibbons himself. There are superb collections like the chinoiseries in the Cabinet Room: hand-painted Chinese wallpaper, Rococo mirrors, Chippendale cupboards, black and gold lacquered furniture, all in the fashionable Chinese style of the mid-18th century. They were very rich people, the Walpoles and the Cholmondeleys, and they had taste; that is clear not least from the choice of portrait artists: Reynolds, Hoppner, Rosalba Carriera, John Singer Sargent – high society painters for high society people. My own favourite portrait, though, is of a duck, the white one in the White Drawing Room, painted in 1753. It's a still life in grey and white whose forms and colours are immensely pleasing to the eye. There is no important man or woman posing here for eternity, but only one dead duck, hanging by one leg from a limestone wall, its head resting on a damask cloth next to which is a china dish full to the brim with cream, and a silver candlestick holding a white candle. That is all. A soft and gentle picture of the end of life, conveyed by the end of colour; it is a triumph of pure painting, a still-life masterpiece by Jean-Baptiste Oudry, court painter to Louis XV and director of tapestry manufacture in Beauvais. The candle on the kitchen table burns in honour of this unknown bird, sacrificed on the altar of good eating. It is all done with sublime pathos, a typically French *Vanitas* painted with Cartesian discipline, coolly coded, with none of the anecdotal self-indulgence you find on the tables of Dutch still-lifes. It is a *Memento Mori* as the apotheosis of the culinary principle – the duck is dead, long live the roast. I enjoy, therefore I am. (Or not, since the painting was recently stolen.)

The Lords of Houghton would certainly have understood the message of Oudry's white duck. The spirit of Nouvelle Cuisine would have been as alien to them as a continental breakfast. Sophisticated they may have been, but they loved their food, and Houghton's tables would have been like those of Hogarth's genre pictures, groaning under the weight. 'They lived up to the chin in beef, venison, geese, turkeys, etc., and generally over the chin in claret, strong beer and punch,' says Lord Hervey, heir to Ickworth, describing Robert Walpole and his guests. Twice a year the Prime Minister invited his London friends and the neighbouring lords of the manor to his famous 'congresses' at Houghton. These were political parties in a purely social sense, an orgy of food and drink in grand style, with hunting and gossip, and no women to spoil the fun. One of the guests, the future Austrian Emperor Francis I, slept off his hangover in 1731 in the great Embroidered Bed, snoring in his four-poster between English embroidery and Brussels tapestries.

The most valuable of Houghton Hall's paintings now hang in the Hermitage in St Petersburg. What Robert Walpole collected, and his son Horace catalogued (*Aedes Walpolianae*, 1747), was scattered to all four corners by Robert's grandson George. George, the 3rd Earl of Orford, was an eccentric who so ran down the estate that in 1779 he was forced to sell much of the famous collection. The lion's share was bought by Catherine the Great, who was busy snapping up paintings from all over Europe for her Winter Palace and various country houses. Thirteen Rubens, twelve Van Dycks, four Teniers, and works by Guido Reni, Salvator Rosa, Murillo and Rembrandt (*Abraham's Sacrifice*) form the basis of the Hermitage collection. Horace Walpole was bitterly disappointed to see all these Old Masters leaving the parental home: 'It is stripping the temple of his glory and of his affection ...' Altogether Catherine, the Great Collector, acquired 79 Italian, 75 German and Flemish, 22 French, 7 Spanish and 5 English paintings and drawings for the sum total of £35,000. As a token of her gratitude, she presented the

Robert Walpole, 1st Earl of Orford, by John Wootton

unhappy Earl with her portrait – a chimney-piece for the Saloon. Highly appropriate in view of all that had just gone up in smoke.

The family portraits were spared this commercial carnage,[1] and so Sir Robert is still to be seen several times over in the Stone Hall: in oils, as a marble bust, and high up in the ceiling as a plaster relief in one of the oakleaf-crowned medallions. The Stone Hall was where Walpole kept his antiques, surrounding himself with the great men of old, and in particular with the busts of Roman emperors. They set the example by which he measured his own ambitions and achievements. For this was also a display cabinet of his own glory, Walpole's Valhalla. His portrait on the easel near the fireplace has much more to do with an English sense of realism than with any classical ideal of beauty, for the figure we see here is not the connoisseur on his Grand Tour, but Falstaff out in the open. Here we are confronted by the love of bodily pleasures rather than the exquisite artistic taste of Houghton Hall. The lord of the fields poses like a commander in the field, resplendent in his gold-braided coat, whip in hand, tricorn on head, and his hunting hounds panting and wagging their tails at his feet. This is how John Wootton portrayed him, in the green uniform of Master of the King's Staghounds and Warden of the Royal Park. This is Sir Robert after retirement, a man at the end of his career, but the stolid, portly Norfolk squire

1 One picture was bought back in 1974: Kneller's portrait of the Spanish poet Carreras, court chaplain to Catherine of Braganza.

Horace Walpole, 4th Earl of Orford, 1795,
by Thomas Lawrence

had only recently been the most powerful political figure in the land, The Great Man as his contemporaries called him, the 'English Colossus'.

The Walpoles took their name from a village in the Fens. Ever since the 12th century they had lived in and around Houghton, East Anglian squires who worked their estates and steadily expanded them. Some even became members of Parliament, but Robert Walpole was the first to rise to really great heights. As leader of the Whigs he headed the government of 1721, and became Prime Minister under both George I and George II. Initially he was First Lord of the Treasury, then became the first to be known by the title of Prime Minister, and remained in office for longer than anyone else, right up until 1742 (almost twice as long as Margaret Thatcher). He was a skilful diplomat, did not shy away from corruption or intrigue, was both subject and master of the Court, and in the political chess game could manipulate his king and queen in court just as adroitly as his knights and bishops in Parliament and his pawn-tenants at home on the estate. His opponents called him the Norfolk Trickster. He was a provincial parvenu who crowned his career with a house in the country, financed by speculation on the Stock Exchange. He was as popular as all those who have, enjoy and use power to their own advantage. On the other hand, though, Walpole contributed in large measure to bridging the old gap between Crown and Parliament, and to bringing about a new harmony between the executive and the legislative powers. Indeed, as the Oxford historian Paul Langford puts it, 'in practice Walpole subtly transformed the basis of the Hanoverian regime. The politics of coercion gave way to those of consensus.' Instead of promoting war, he promoted trade, and provided an internal stability that was the basis of Britain's prosperity and rise to world power.

The *Pax Walpoliana* ended with victory for the hawks in 1742. Walpole retired to his estate to enjoy the pleasures of the hunt and of the countryside. The picture that John Wootton painted was the image that Walpole himself wanted to convey. The old political fox is now the honest squire, the embodiment of peace and prosperity in all its baroque fullness, an oak in uniform. Here I am Squire of Houghton Hall; in London I was merely Prime Minister. It is, perhaps, the final trick of the Norfolk Trickster. He is a man in harmony with nature, above all with his own nature, no longer concerned with the power struggle between Crown and Parliament, but relaxed in the role of the benign landowner. So benign was he that his tenants had the roof taken from over their heads because their homes were in the way of his park. He then calmly built them a replacement in 1729, the model village of New Houghton, which stretches like a guard of honour along the road to Houghton Hall. The 50 inhabitants still pay their rent to the Marquess of Cholmondeley.

What of Horace Walpole, who today is perhaps even more famous than his once mighty father? His picture is also to be seen in Houghton Hall: a youth with soft but alert features, dressed in silk embroidered with flowers – the head of a thinker and dreamer, a child of the Age of Reason, with the soul of a Romantic. Clearly enchanted by her model, the Venetian painter Rosalba Carriera has depicted young Horace Walpole in the gentle, wavering pastel tones which she could handle so masterfully. He was a child of delicate constitution, quite unlike his vigorous father – the massively dominant figure of his childhood – and although

Raynham Hall, 1819, ▷
engraving by F. R. Hay
after J. P. Neale

Charles, 2nd Viscount Townshend,
c.1695, by Studio of Godfrey Kneller

he was politically highly gifted, he was both unwilling and unable to enter the power struggle, and so in addition to a brilliant career in the service of the state, he happily sought refuge in another world that was secret but exciting – the eccentric one of Strawberry Hill, of Neo-Gothic palaces, and of deep, dark fantasy.

When he was a student at Cambridge, and also later, Horace would always spend the long and often agonizing summer weeks in his father's country home. He found it 'picturesque' on the outside, but 'bad and inconvenient within'. His description of the atmosphere in August 1743, when he wrote to a friend about it, seems almost like a Fellini film: 'Only imagine that I here every day see men, who are mountains of roast beef, and only seem just roughly hewn out into the outlines of human form, like the giant-rock at Pratolino! I shudder when I see them brandish their knives in act to carve, and look at them as savages that devour one another.' With such a symbiosis between cannibalism and culture, and with the gluttony of the collectors and the hunters, Houghton Hall could never be a place for Horace Walpole, and so he built his own strange castles to suit his own taste: *The Castle of Otranto*, scene of his Gothic novel of 1765, and Strawberry Hill, his real-life dream-house in Twickenham. Houghton Hall was the Neoclassical, respectable old world, the golden cage of Realpolitik, perfect for the father, anathema to the son. His departure from his father's house took him into a new, Romantic world, of the sublime and the picturesque.

Horace Walpole died in 1797, unmarried, witty to the last. He now lies buried, with

his father, in the place where he could not bear to live. Their graves are in the park, in the little church which is the sole survivor of the old village of Houghton and which the landscape gardener Charles Bridgman incorporated into the park as a picturesque but practical element, as he did with the Water House (designed *c.* 1733 by the 9th Earl of Pembroke) – a pavilion with a tank holding 20,000 gallons of water for house and stables, with a garden temple on the first floor.

I walked across to the former orangery, to be greeted by the sounds of a military band. Here the battles of Waterloo and Balaclava are still being fought – by Lord Cholmondeley's model soldiers. This is one of the biggest collections in Europe, some 22,000 men. 'The Marquess himself positioned every single one of them,' Mr Baldwin the agent assured me. There's tea available nearby. First it was a chapel, then it became a sports hall, and now it's a tea-room. Such is the progress of many a stately home. Others, however, have managed to maintain their privacy and remain as splendid as they were when they were first built. Such a one lies southwest of Houghton: *Raynham Hall.*

Houghton, Holkham and Raynham were the three great 18th-century country houses of Norfolk, and their owners were the three leading families in the county. The Walpoles, Cokes and Townshends owned the whole of the northwest; Sir Robert and Horace Walpole, Coke of Holkham, and 'Turnip' Townshend were major figures in the worlds of politics, art and agriculture, hereditary domains of the British aristocracy. They were part of the history of their times, and their importance can be gauged from their houses.

The least known of these is Raynham Hall, which has remained strictly private right up to the present day.

Splendid isolation in a park: an Augustan pastoral. There is an unforgettable moment when you stand in the centre of the house and through open doors on both sides you can suddenly see the landscape – a grandiose green view of a life form that links isolation and openness in a unity that is as natural as it is lavish. It is a classically symmetrical house, brick covered with sandstone, slightly projecting wings, Dutch gables. It radiates warmth and homeliness rather than its own importance. Nevertheless, Sir Horatio Townshend gave a right royal welcome here to Charles II in September 1671. The details are faithfully recorded in the family archives: 17 pigs, 10 calves, 40 geese, 25 turkeys, 351 pounds of butter, 1,400 eggs, 1,600 walnuts, 9 oxen, 22 sheep, 6 barrels of ale, 14 barrels of beer. Not everyone could afford to entertain the king, and indeed many went bankrupt doing so.

Raynham Hall was begun in 1622, at the peak of the English Renaissance. It was probably designed by the owner himself, Sir Roger Townshend. The immaculate Palladian style of the east façade with its Venetian windows suggests that Inigo Jones may have had a hand in the design. In any case, a century later Inigo Jones's ideas found a Baroque echo in William Kent's interiors, just as they had done in Houghton Hall. Between 1720 and 1730 he created some of the finest rooms in the house: the white entrance hall, one and a half storeys high, gleaming with marble and plaster, lit by gilded lampstands, caryatids for four candles, which Pevsner calls 'Kentissime'. The Dining Room with its triple arches; the Belisarius Room (named after a Salvator Rosa painting that used to hang in it and was presented to the 2nd Viscount, 'Turnip' Townshend, by Frederick William I of Prussia) with its ornate fireplace and ceiling. The grandeur and the grace of William Kent's work here stand on a par with his designs for Chatsworth and Kensington Palace.

The Townshends came to prominence as judges under Henry VI. Charles Townshend was a disastrous Chancellor of the Exchequer in Pitt's government, but a passable model for a portrait by Reynolds. His brother George succeeded Wolfe as the English commander at Quebec. Their grandfather had been Walpole's partner in office for over ten years before being forced out in 1730. From then on, the 2nd Viscount Townshend defended the national honour with his turnips. He thereby earned the nickname of 'Turnip' Townshend and was said to have introduced the turnip to England. That, of course, is nonsense.

Turnips had been grown in England back in the 16th century, introduced by the Dutch, and Jethro Tull had improved methods of cultivation. Following his example, 'Turnip' Townshend simply expanded the uses of the turnip – for cleaning the soil, for feeding cattle in winter, and as a basic element in quadruple crop rotation. Norfolk Four Course Rotation became a set term, and it spread from Norfolk all over England. The alternation of wheat, turnips, barley and clover ensured that the soil was exploited in different ways and so regenerated through particular nutrients – a big advance on the open-field-system inherited from the Romans, whereby the fields were left fallow every third year. Lord Townshend's crop rotation system was, however, just one further step along a much longer and more difficult road than the simple concept of 'agricultural revolution' might suggest. Better soil produced more forage, more forage produced more cattle, more cattle produced more fertilizer for the cornfields. Now the cattle had enough to eat in the winter, whereas previously they had generally had to be slaughtered towards the end of autumn and salted. 'Turnip' Townshend and later Coke of Norfolk at nearby Holkham brought their hitherto backward county to the very forefront of English agriculture. Thanks to their reforms, there was a huge increase in the production of cereals and cattle, and in view of a rapidly rising population, this was a blessing for the entire country.

If the Turnip Lord of Raynham Hall does deserve a special title, then it ought to be 'Marling' Townshend. The introduction of marling really was an innovation on his part, and it was through this mode of fertilization that the wild sheep pastures between Raynham and Holkham actually became the most fertile arable land in East Anglia. Today the 7th Marquess of Townshend cultivates mainly wheat and barley on his estate. Turnips are out. But Raynham is now famous for something else: the Sky Arabian Stud. At the beginning of the sixties, the Marchioness began to breed Arabian horses 'just for pleasure'. Now everyone knows of her stud. In the old stables[1] stand stars with heavenly names: Sky Crusader, Sky Wings, Sky Solitaire, Song of the Sky, Nirvana Sky. In the paddock are the mares and foals, peacefully grazing as if posing for a picture by Stubbs.

Mary Stuart in Oxburgh Hall: Embroidery in a Golden Cage

'Come! Come! Come! ye admirers of Beauties …!' Thus did the painter John Sell Cotman advise his patron Dawson Turner and the whole Dawson family in August 1804; they should leave the 'escape from these galling chains of fashioned follies' in Yarmouth, the balls and card-games, and come to *Castle Acre*. What so inspired Cotman was the uniquely concentrated medieval atmosphere of this place southeast of King's Lynn – an atmosphere you can still enjoy today. He later made five etchings of the ruined Norman monastery, but his enthusiasm was not confined to the ruins. Nor was that of the authorities who, in 1971, followed his example and gave the village their official seal of approval by making it the very first in Norfolk to be made a conservation area.

Prehistoric settlers had already made use of the strategically well-positioned hill in the water meadows. Shortly after the Norman Conquest, at the point where the Celtic Peddars Way and later the Roman road crossed the River Nar, William de Warenne – the Conqueror's son-in-law – built the castle that gave the place its name. Castle Acre was a fortified settlement for the colonists, completely enclosed by the earthworks that marked

1   The stables at Houghton Hall have also preserved their original interiors.

the outer boundaries of the castle. It was one of the great 'motte and bailey' fortresses in England, surrounded by a flint wall with a sentry walk, a deep moat, the steep castle mound in the centre (again walled round), and right in the middle of this, the massive rectangular keep. Of all this, nothing remains except the mighty earthworks and a 13th-century gateway. Castle Rising has the more impressive castle, but Castle Acre has the more famous ruined priory.

Castle Acre Priory lies outside the village, in the fields by the River Nar. It was a Cluniac establishment, founded in 1090, and for nearly 300 years was controlled by the mother-house in Cluny. With its five apses, only to be seen now from their foundation walls, the English priory church followed the ground plan of the mother church in Burgundy (Cluny II). Only the west front has survived, but even without its two towers it is a triumphal relic of late Norman architecture (plate 81). Its three sections correspond to the nave and side aisles of the church. There are several rows of blind arcades surrounding the great round-arched doorway in a seemingly endless sequence of interlocking arches – a much-favoured motif of Anglo-Norman stonemasons. Their mastery is to be seen in the cube-shaped capitals, the demons on the ledges, and above all the graduated portal with its ornate doorcase. The sense of proportion and rhythm, combining stillness and movement, is truly astonishing. In the evening, when the last visitors have left, the peace of these ruins is perfect. It was among these relics of flint that Roger Corman chose to shoot some of the more ghostly scenes of his Edgar Allan Poe film *The Tomb of Ligeia*.

Only 25–30 monks lived in the priory during the Middle Ages – far fewer than one would imagine, looking at these vast ruins. Best preserved is the Prior's House, which was in the west wing during the early 16th century. He had his own bath with a built-in wash-basin, and thus enjoyed considerably more of the mod cons than most lay people of his time. Norfolk's most important Cluniac priory lay on the pilgrims' route to Walsing-ham, and as a rival attraction was able to offer the pilgrims the arm of St Philip. After the Reformation, however, the priory disintegrated, and like the castle became a stone quarry for the grander houses being built all around.

The village is almost entirely of flint, from the 15th-century parish church up to the 20th-century old people's home. Only in recent years have the traditional flint cottages been joined by houses of brick, though there are still no bungalows. Since the conservation order, Castle Acre has become a popular place for commuters to King's Lynn or Swaffham, and that led to the usual problem of house prices soaring, so that the younger local people could no longer afford to live in the village and had to move to rented accommodation on the outskirts.

In the fields northeast of Castle Acre stands an extraordinary group of four late 10th- and 11th-century Anglo-Saxon village churches: *Newton*, *Great Dunham*, and the two round-tower churches of *East Lexham* and *West Lexham*.[1] Their simple, straightforward forms are in stark contrast to the sophistication of Late Norman monastic architecture and

---

1 Further west in North Elmham are the ruins of an Anglo-Saxon cathedral (see page 529).

John Sell Cotman: Castle Acre Priory, west front, 1813

to the ornamental richness of Castle Acre. The central tower of Great Dunham stands solidly between the narrow single nave and the tiny choir (renovated in the 15th century). The axial ground plan is typical of Anglo-Saxon churches, as are the west entrance with its triangular lintel, the twin windows in the tower with the inserted columns, and the two round louvres above them. Originally there were only a few small windows. The round arches are decorated with a number of Roman bricks, the walls are of unhewn flint, and the corners are bonded with long and short work. Equally typical are the blind arcades in Great Dunham Church and the pyramid roof of the central tower at Newton. These are all rural churches of wonderful simplicity, all the more striking for their directness of expression.

On the hand-carved sign that welcomes you to *Swaffham*, south of Castle Acre, is a man in medieval dress. His name was John Chapman, and he was known as The Peddlar. John had a dream: he was to go to London, and on London Bridge he would meet someone who would bring him luck. John took his dog, and went. He did indeed meet a stranger on London Bridge, but when the stranger heard about the dream, he mocked John: 'If I were to believe in dreams, I'd be a fool like you. Recently I dreamt that in Swaffham lived a man named Chapman, and in his garden, buried under a tree, lay a treasure.' John hurried home, did some digging, and found a jug full of gold.

It's a nice story, and it has a strong element of truth in it. There really was a man named Chapman who lived in Swaffham, and he was a successful trader and a local benefactor. He contributed a substantial amount of money to the building of Sts Peter and Paul (1454–90). On one of the stall-ends in the choir, there is a popular monument to the man and his dog. Swaffham's parish church has high Gothic arcades and a double hammerbeam roof of chestnut. On the richly decorated beams at the vertex of the roof there is a squadron of wooden angels, their wings spread wide. The effectiveness of this interior is enhanced by its harmonious proportions: the nave is 51 feet high, 51 feet wide, and 102 feet long.

An avenue of lime trees leads across the churchyard to the market-place, where there is a columned rotunda (1783); here people meet, as they have always done, beneath a dome crowned by Ceres, goddess of fertility (plate 55). During the Regency period, Norfolk's landed gentry used to meet in Swaffham to attend concerts, balls and soirées. There are still a few Georgian houses left from this time, when the little town was considered to be England's equivalent of Montpellier. It was Swaffham, incidentally, that gave to the world the man who was to discover the tomb of Tutankhamen: the archaeologist Howard Carter.

If you're interested in British village life during the Iron Age, go southwest of Swaffham to the prehistoric adventure playground of *Cockley Cley*. It's situated on Icknield Way, a Neolithic route that was probably in use seven or eight thousand years ago, and ran from Salisbury Plain in the south to the Wash in the north. It was the route taken by prehistoric settlers and later by cattle drovers. At Cockley Cley archaeologists have reconstructed an Iceni settlement from the period around AD 60 – wooden huts, with a moat, a drawbridge, palisades and a nature trail. Three miles and 1,400 years on, people still liked to live with the protection of a moat, but the protected ones preferred a feudal society. For example, in Oxburgh Hall.

Through pastureland and cornfields, the occasional wood: there is scarcely a house in sight. This is a very remote part of Norfolk, between the Brecklands and the Fens, and one can sense how totally cut off it must have been centuries ago. When eventually I saw the towers of *Oxburgh Hall*, the warm red of its Tudor bricks, and the gatehouse which rises up out of the moat like a rock from the sea, I felt quite relieved, and as I stood in the inner court, I felt completely secure, like a guest of the family. The fact that these walls and towers are welcoming and not frightening is integral to the charm of Oxburgh Hall (plate 10).

The Hall demonstrates all the typical features of medieval military architecture: gatehouse, moat and battlements. But in the hands of the Tudor master-builders, all these are transformed into ornamental quotations from the military repertoire. The walls are of domestic brick, and not deterrent stone; there are two large windows just where the gatehouse is at its most vulnerable; and the moat is shallow, a decoration rather than a defence. Nevertheless, until shortly after 1700 there was a drawbridge that could be pulled up in the event of danger. The Hundred Years War had long since ended, but there were still bands of discharged mercenaries plundering the land. It was in politically and economically unstable times, 1482, three years before the end of the Wars of the Roses, that

Sir Edmund Bedingfeld began to build his manor house. It was still fortified, but already anticipated the country house elegance of future generations. Sir Edmund was Marshal of Calais, and the gatehouse was the triumphal emblem of his nobility. Like tiaras the battlements crown the two octagonal towers that flank the central one. The towers are all seven storeys high, and covered with blind arches of brick that seem as delicate as lace. The birds whistle it from the rooftops: this is the finest gatehouse of early Tudor times that you will ever see.[1] Its main purpose was one of prestige, with defence only a marginal consideration. The spiral staircase in the northwest tower is quite ingenious, a brick masterpiece by the local craftsmen (c.1485). They also demonstrated their mastery in the rooms of these towers, with rib vaulting of brick. The Tudor-style brick decorations on the chimneys, however, are actually early 19th century. There is a magnificent view from the tower. On a clear day you can see right across the Fens as far as the towers of Ely Cathedral. At your feet, on the east side of the house, there is a French parterre garden of 1845, with balls of yew and flower beds laid out in baroque curves. Oxburgh Hall had four wings, but the south one, the Tudor hall opposite the gatehouse, was demolished by one of the Bedingfelds around 1775. His descendants closed the gap c.1835, and although what they built was not historically accurate, it retained a sense of picturesqueness. The massive southeast tower was also part of this Victorian restoration, as were most of the interiors. There are lots of heavy carvings, dark oak cabinets, brightly glazed tiles and lavish wall-coverings. History in such houses always smells of beeswax and rose leaves.

In April 1487 Henry VII stopped at Oxburgh Hall on his way to Walsingham. He stayed with his wife, Elizabeth of York, in the newly completed gatehouse. In the King's and Queen's Room, sparsely furnished, one can still feel the atmosphere of the Tudor house, and one can also see what the most famous and most unfortunate of its guests left behind: Mary Stuart's embroideries. Queen Elizabeth I did not send her rival to the Tower, but 'urgently, with an urgency that was irresistible, asked her Scottish sister to live permanently in beautiful English country houses' (Stefan Zweig). One of these golden cages was Oxburgh Hall.

The Scottish Queen lived here around 1570, at the beginning of her endless captivity, surrounded by ladies-in-waiting, confidantes, spies, and a whole mock court of servants and guards. Her truest friends were her spaniels. Here in the remote depths of Norfolk, on the edge of the Fens and of despair, Mary Stuart would spend the empty hours, days, weeks sitting with her embroidery frame, a melancholy figure in black. She sewed her royal monogram, rebuses and anagrams, birds and plants, and one of her favourite sayings: 'Virescit Vulnere Virtus' [virtue grows through wounds]. All these *petits points*, however, were simply a cover for her other, even more pointed activity: conspiracy. While she sewed her fine needlework, she also went on spinning the threads of her own hoped-for liberty. And sewing and spinning alongside her was Elizabeth, Countess of Shrewsbury, known as

1 There are similar Tudor gatehouses of brick at Queens' College (1488) and St John's (1511) in Cambridge; Layer Marney Tower in Essex (1520; colour plate 19); and the Deanery in Hadleigh, Suffolk (1495; plate 18).

Bess of Hardwick, the wife of her senior guard. *The Marian Needlework*, over a hundred embroideries on faded green silk, is now one of the great tourist attractions of the house.

It was a somewhat malicious favour that Elizabeth I granted to her Catholic rival by interning her at the Bedingfelds' country home. Oxburgh Hall was one of England's Catholic strongholds,[1] and the Bedingfelds had remained true to the old faith even after the Reformation, loyal to the Pope but also to the Crown. If they had not been loyal to her, Elizabeth would certainly not have visited Oxburgh Hall in 1578. But when, two years later, the first Jesuits entered the country, she made the sheltering of Catholic priests an offence punishable by law. The Bedingfelds immediately had a priest's hole made near the King's Rooms, just as all the great recusant houses had.[2]

It was therefore not only the Jews and, later, Nonconformists who discovered that there were limits to English liberalism. The Five Mile Act of 1593 restricted the freedom of movement of Catholics to a range of five miles from their homes. Catholics also had to pay much higher taxes, were denied entry to schools and universities and all public offices, which included the army and the navy. Many families pretended to conform, but many others lived in abject poverty. The Bedingfelds also lost their power and their status, and it was not until the Catholic Emancipation Act of 1829 that discrimination was finally ended officially. Ten years later, Oxburgh Hall had a Neo-Gothic Catholic chapel.

For almost 500 years Oxburgh Hall remained the family home of the Bedingfelds. The present generation, however, lives there rent-free as tenants of the National Trust, to whom the house was given in 1952. In their chapel, the one surviving part of the parish church, the founders of the house have their own monument, which is something quite special: two terracotta tombs, covered with ornamental pilasters and arches, dating from 1525 when terracotta became fashionable through the first artists to bring the style of the early Italian Renaissance to England.[3]

Thomas Paine of the Brecklands:
The Light of Freedom and of Flint

One Sunday in November 1979, Arthur Brooks' metal detector went wild. On Gallows Hill, an industrial site on the northern outskirts of *Thetford*, this amateur archaeologist had stumbled on one of the greatest Roman treasures found in England this century: brooches, bangles and rings of gold, many of them with inlaid jewels, a gold buckle with a satyr relief, cameos, ornate silver spoons – altogether more than eighty objects dating from the end of the 4th century, probably buried by a jeweller, together with a temple treasure,

---

1 Other traditionally Catholic strongholds in East Anglia were Broad Oaks and Ingatestone Hall (both in Essex).
2 The most ingenious builder of these priest's holes, Nicholas Owen, was starved out of one of his own hiding-places, tortured to death in the Tower in 1606, and canonized in 1970.
3 Dating from the same period, and possibly by the same artists, are the terracotta monuments in Wymondham (Norfolk) and architectural features at Layer Marney (Essex).

during the confusion of the Roman withdrawal from Britain. Today the Thetford Treasure is in the British Museum. On the site where it was found, archaeologists discovered the remains of three large round houses from the Iron Age, probably part of the palace of Boadicea, the rebel Queen of the Iceni (see page 68).

Where the River Thet and the Little Ouse join together, there was from very early days a castle to guard the crossing of the Icknield Way. Whoever controlled Thetford had the key to Norfolk. Under the Danish Kings Sweyn and Canute, Thetford was the capital of East Anglia, and when the Normans came it was a diocesan town until 1095. Then Norwich took over the leading role in the province's church affairs and politics. In Thetford's heyday, during the 14th century, it had twenty parish churches and four monasteries, the most important of which was St Mary's Abbey, a Cluniac foundation of around 1103. The ruins on the northern outskirts of the town reveal the typical ground plan of the Abbey Church in Cluny. The Dissolution of the Monasteries after the Reformation meant the decline of Thetford, whose cloth industry could not compete with those of Norwich and East Suffolk.

It was from this provincial town that there came a man who could truly claim to be a citizen of the world. His name was Thomas Paine. He wrote *The Rights of Man*, campaigned on behalf of American independence, was active in the French Revolution, was friends with Danton and George Washington, was hated by the English Establishment, died alone in New York, and even in death was spurned by the country of his birth.

Thomas Paine was born in Thetford in 1737, the son of a Quaker and stays-maker. He left school at thirteen in order to work in his parents' shop, taught himself, preferred newspapers to books, and pubs to libraries. He became a preacher, a private teacher, a tax-collector, and a tobacconist, was disappointed with all his jobs and his two marriages, and so emigrated to America in 1774. At the climax of the conflict between England and her American colonies, in January 1776, there appeared in Philadelphia an anonymous pamphlet entitled *Common Sense* – Paine's plea for American independence. 'A government of our own is our natural right,' he argued, and called for a democratic constitution of basic civil rights. Paine himself helped to formulate these for the first time in the American Bill of Rights, 1776. It was accompanied by hopes that were almost euphoric: 'the Birthday of a new world is at hand.' Liberty raised her torch, and Paine fanned the flame – first in America, then in France and England. The man from Thetford had at last found his true vocation: he was a revolutionary.

After the Republicans' victory in the American War of Independence, Tom Paine went to Paris and sided with the Girondists. 'A share in two revolutions is living to some purpose.' Back in England he published *The Rights of Man* (1791), the book of a radical democrat who proclaimed that the people and their chosen representatives were the only legitimate rulers. The second part of the book, which was published in an edition costing sixpence, was issued just two years later in a print of 200,000 copies that were distributed nationwide, from the tin-miners in Cornwall to the cutlers in Sheffield. Paine was accused of high treason, and fled to Paris, where he was made an honorary citizen and a member of the National Assembly. He rejoiced at the fall of the King, but was opposed to the death sentence passed upon him. As a result, Robespierre's Jacobins arrested him for treason, and he was thrown into prison. Here, faced with the prospect of the guillotine, he wrote *The Age of Reason*, against kingship by divine grace, against a state-run church, and against all institutionalized religion. This lost him the last vestiges of sympathy in the old world as well as in the new Puritan one. (Even Theodore Roosevelt was to call him a 'filthy little atheist.') When he was released, he went back to America, a Nonconformist who wanted total freedom, even for slaves. Politically isolated, and abandoned by his friends, Citizen Paine died in 1809 in a miserable New York boarding house, and when ten years later his admirer William Cobbett took his remains to England, the police prevented the burial. To this day, no-one knows where Paine is buried.

'From what we can foresee, all Europe may form but one great Republic and man be free of the whole.' Two hundred years later, it would seem as if Paine's ideas are on the verge of becoming a reality. In his 1988 biography, the Oxford philosopher Sir Alfred Ayer discusses the actuality of Paine's political thinking, with the emphasis on representative democracy, self-determination, and the avoidance of dominance by charismatic leaders or faceless technocrats. In Thetford there is a statue to the republican Paine, ironically situated opposite King's House in King Street (named after James I, who frequently held court here between 1608 and 1618). In White Hart Street, the Thomas Paine Hotel proudly presents what is believed to be the room where he was born as its Honeymoon Suite, with a garishly gilded four-poster bed as its centrepiece.

Thetford, once called 'Queen of the East' is now an expanding small town, the economic centre of a strange and desolate region: the *Brecklands*. The uniform conifer plantations of Thetford Forest stretch for miles and miles across southwest Norfolk, but what we see now has nothing to do with the original meaning of Brecklands. The brecks were fields planted in the barren land and later left to run wild again. For the early Stone Age settlers, the barren land of sand and stone was relatively easy to till, as there were none of the marshes or thick forests that covered large areas of the country elsewhere. When they then began to use their iron ploughs to cultivate the richer, more fertile soil of East Anglia, they left the Breckland fields for pasture. Even in prehistoric times, sheep used to graze there, and from the 13th century onwards, rabbits were also bred, as their meat and fur were important features of the medieval economy. The name 'warren' given to these fields is a leftover from the days of this huge rabbit industry.[1] Much later, Victorian landowners were to make the Brecklands fine pheasant-shooting land. But back in the Middle Ages, the great sheep boom had disastrous consequences.

Overfeeding led to erosion of the soil, and the land was devastated by sand storms. 'The great East Anglian Desert' was the name now given to it. When John Evelyn travelled

---

1 Because of the poachers, the gamekeepers' houses were fortified. The best preserved of these, Thetford Warren Lodge (*c.*1400) guarded the Prior of Thetford's rabbit reserve – then open land, but now thick forest.

through it in 1677, he described such sandstorms in his diary – giant dunes 'rolling from place to place and like the Sands in the Desert of Lybia, quite overwhelming some gentlemen's whole estates.' If you ask a Breckland farmer whether his land is in Norfolk or Suffolk, he'll tell you, 'That depends which way the wind's blowing.' It was the sand as much as the plague that depopulated the Breckland villages, which were far more densely populated in the early Middle Ages than they are now.

In order to make the sandy soil firmer and to break up the effects of the storms, the people planted those toughest of all pines which the Duke of Cumberland had admired during his inglorious campaign at Culloden and had then made fashionable in England: the Scots pine. The long rows of dark and agitated silhouettes typify the Breckland horizon, simultaneously protecting and decorating the landscape. The Forestry Commission began this large-scale afforestation in 1922, and commercially it was a success. Otherwise, it was a disaster. Initially they planted a mixture of trees, but then they confined themselves to conifers: Scots pine, Corsican pine, Douglas fir – plain and simple, fast-growing, useful trees that cover some 90 square miles in a seemingly endless monoculture. Thetford Forest is now England's largest, and where there was once heath, now there is timber, over 150,000 tonnes of it a year. The countryside lost its face and its rich ecological variety. Beneath the Forestry Commission's trees the Brecklands lie buried in a gigantic pine coffin.

England produces only ten per cent of its own timber requirements, and only ten per cent of the country's land is devoted to forest. For this reason, and in order to reduce the agricultural surpluses frowned on by the EC, the national afforestation policy is being implemented all the more intensively in the Brecklands. Under such circumstances, the military are to be welcomed almost as saviours. What has not been planted has at least been preserved, if only for training grounds: the Battle Area lies west of East Wretham, a no-go area of abandoned houses, shot to pieces, with no tourists, no litter, no trampled plants. There's no doubt about it, the military are the biggest conservationists in the country. The Ministry of Defence actually has a department (Defence Lands 3) devoted to protecting plant life and threatened animal species – an ingenious manoeuvre that enhances nature conservation and the Ministry's own image at the same time. It is, however, possible to create nature reserves for plants and animals without resorting to weapons, and this is what the Norfolk Naturalists Trust has done north of Thetford, on East Wretham Heath. It's a gently undulating area with small, shallow meres, which shelter birch, ash, blackthorn and whitethorn bushes, gorse, ferns, and tall grass where harriers, shrike and stone curlew still nest. This is how the Brecklands used to look before the forests were planted. 'A glorious landscape packed with threatened species of plants and animals and full of conservational and recreational potential has been systematically dismantled by sectional interests.' This is the bitter conclusion drawn by the landscape historian Richard Muir.

The Brecks are the site of the first known settlements in East Anglia, but this was not just because of the lightness of the soil. Northwest of Thetford, deep in the pine forests, there is a large clearing full of overgrown mounds and hollows, almost like a field of bomb craters. This strange place is known as *Grime's Graves*. It has nothing to do, though, with Wotan or any cult of the dead. In 1870, a Victorian canon named Greenwell excavated one of the hollows and revealed the true nature of the area. Grime's Graves were a prehistoric industrial zone containing over 360 flint mines, one of which is open to visitors.

Someone from English Heritage gave me a protective helmet, but otherwise everything is much as it was during the Neolithic Era, 5,000 years ago. You go some thirty feet down a steep ladder, and find yourself at the bottom of the shaft. From here the narrow tunnels radiate outwards, leading to broad, low chambers where the flint was mined. It was embedded in layers of chalk which were relatively easy to remove. For pickaxes the prehistoric miners used deer antlers, and for shovels the shoulderblades of oxen. It has been calculated that it took twenty men between 80 and 100 days to dig a shaft 40 feet deep, and another 42 days for four tunnels which would yield 36 tons of flint. This would result in some 800 tons of spoil, which would be used to fill up the old mines. Grime's Graves, with their ladders, ropes and primitive tools show how the Neolithic flint mines provided the basic experience and technology for the mines of the Bronze and Iron Ages.

Grime's Graves were an export industry. Over this area of about 90 acres, flint was not only mined but also processed. It was fashioned into axes, chisels, knife blades, spear and arrow-heads, and all the tools and weapons that the Stone Age settlers needed.[1] Flint is a very hard stone, but easy to split, and the slabs would have been rubbed and polished with wet sand until they were razor sharp and shone like black silk. The flint from Grime's Graves was top quality, and the best – known as floorstone – was to be found in the lower seams, 30 to 40 feet down. Freshly broken flint is mostly black, whereas flint in the fields tends to be brownish and often encased in a thick layer of chalk – hence the expression 'skinflint'. Its soft curves and varied shapes are fascinating, like miniature Henry Moore sculptures. It's a silicate, probably formed from the bones of dead sea creatures deposited at the bottom of the sea in layers of chalk some 65 to 100 million years ago during the Cretaceous period. From the Dorset Downs to the north coast of Norfolk there is a belt of flint running right through the country, several miles broad and between 6 and 45 feet deep. All the way along this huge seam there were flint mines from which the stone was taken for local use, but very few of them were on the scale we see in Grime's Graves. Radiocarbon dating shows that the main period of mining was between 2100 and 1800 BC. But East Anglia's Stone Age industry survived right up to the 20th century, and its centre was Brandon, just a few miles away on the Suffolk side of the Little Ouse.[2]

Brandon is a little town made of flint. The walls, the houses, the pubs, and the churches are all made of flint. Grey, blue-grey, blue-black, grey-black, black flint. In 1804 the British

---

1   In 1988, British archaeologists found flint knives and scraping tools at least 450,000 and possibly 550,000 years old in High Lodge, between Thetford and Mildenhall. This prehistoric settlement was already known, but the new dates were sensational. The settlement may have been inhabited by Proto-Neanderthal hunters.
2   From 1720 onwards, the flint was mined mainly in Lingheath, two miles southeast of Brandon.

Army drew up a contract with the workers of Brandon for 356,000 flints a month to use in their flintlocks in the war against Napoleon. At the climax of Wellington's Peninsular War, production rose to about one and a quarter million flints a month. 'The Battle of Waterloo was won in the flint knapperies of Brandon rather than on the playing fields of Eton,' says John Seymour. At the time there were some 200 flint-knappers at work in this ancient department of the British arms industry. By 1837, the number had shrunk to about 70. The flintlock had had its day, and the new percussion guns did not need flints. During the Crimean War another contract came from the Turkish army, and for a while flintlocks were still used in Africa, but after that nothing remained except a few weapons collectors in America and whatever was needed for building.

When Brandon's flint industry came to an end in the thirties, the Snares, Carters and Fields found work in the new Breckland industry of forestry. Today the old processes are only to be seen on the sign of the 'Flint Knappers Arms': quartering, flaking and knapping – the slabs are quartered, then split into long, flat flakes, and finally knapped into little flints. An efficient knapper would produce about 300 flints an hour. It was unhealthy work, though, because the workshops were badly ventilated, and the fine dust would constantly be absorbed into the workers' lungs. Death came early in Brandon, and mostly it came in the form of 'knappers' rot', or silicosis.

Like a host of little polished skulls, the flints lie buried in the walls of the houses. Flint walls have a thousand eyes, and when it rains they sparkle like black crystal. More than any other county in England, Norfolk can call itself Flint County. It's a stone that's as cold and hard and beautiful as the coast of Norfolk itself. Suffolk and, to a lesser degree, Essex also have their share of East Anglia's superabundance, and you'll find it everywhere, no doubt largely because there is no other usable local material for building. Flint was always close at hand, on the shores, in the fields, and in vast quantities underground. It could be used unhewn or split or cut, on its own or in combination with other forms of stone. As James Lees-Milne put it, when describing the flints of Norfolk cottages: 'They give a cream to the strawberry brick walls.'

Until late in the 19th century, with one last flourish in Victorian times,[1] flint (together with brick) was the most common building material for Norfolk's houses. All the way along the north coast, from Cromer to Blakeney, the sea has ground the stones until they are round, and so the houses were built from these beach pebbles, often decorated with bands of brick, at their most striking when there are many such houses grouped together, as in Upper Sheringham or on the main street in Blakeney. They are pepper and salt villages. East Anglia's flint architecture is as much a part of the landscape and its history as the flint itself. With flint (and flat bricks) the Romans built the walls of Burgh Castle, the Anglo-Saxons built their round towers, the Norman knights built their castles, the monks built their monasteries, the landowners built their manor houses, and the peasants built

---

1 More of a stylistic flourish were the prefabricated flint building blocks with which house fronts were clad in the seventies, e.g. in Thorpe Hamlet, Norwich.

their barns and cottages. The citizens of Norwich used it in the Middle Ages to build their city walls, their many churches and their Guildhall, pride of the city – 'buildings of flint so exquisitely headed and squared', as John Evelyn noted admiringly in 1671. Knapped flint rarely occurs before the 14th century, and always remained a speciality of Norfolk and Suffolk. This was a material that everyone could use for every kind of building, and only the sophistication of the work determined its place in the flint hierarchy. At the decorative head stood the technique known as flushwork.

Flushwork is ornamental masonry in which flint and dressed stone are combined to form lozenges, initials, crosses, stars, crowns, or whole sections of tracery. It is the make-up on the façade, the stonemason's free-play, flint cappricio. It expressed the taste of the Tudor period, with its love of ornament and luxury. The earliest known flushwork is that of St Ethelbert's Gate in Norwich Cathedral Close (1316; plate 64). Another early and particularly beautiful example is the gatehouse of the former Augustinian priory at Butley, near Orford (1320–5). Also in Suffolk there is a complete alphabet on a church wall – the flint and limestone intarsia of Stratford St Mary (c.1500). In the late Perpendicular style, on the gatehouse of St Osyth's Priory in Essex (colour plate 20), flushwork makes a truly grand exit.[1] The chequerboard pattern on the battlements was a popular form special to flint decoration, and indeed sometimes the builders got so carried away that they covered whole façades with it. The finest example is the Guildhall in King's Lynn (plate 34).

George Borrow: 'the Roving Life'

If you go to *Wymondham*, southwest of Norwich, you will see from a distance two church towers standing out in the water meadows on the outskirts of the little town. They glare across at each other like two quarrelsome brothers, and the fact is that they do not exactly testify to man's desire to praise God. Wymondham Abbey was founded in 1107 as a daughter house to St Albans, a monastery of the Black Friars, as the Benedictines were known on account of their black habits. They were the richest and most aristocratic order in England during the Middle Ages. The problem was that the monks and the people of Wymondham were always at loggerheads, so much so that in 1249 the Pope himself, Innocent IV, attempted to arbitrate between them. This, however, was to no avail. In the end, the church had to be split by a wall all the way across – where the choir screen is now – and then the two towers were built. For each side wanted to ring its own bells – the ordinary folk from the west tower, and the monks from the octagon over the crossing.

---

1   Other outstanding examples of flushwork in East Anglia are the tower and south portal of St Edmund's in Southwold (c.1430); St Michael Coslany (15th century) and the Guildhall in Norwich (1407–12); the Chapel of St Nicholas in Gipping, Suffolk (c.1483); and the west tower of St Mary's in Redenhall, Norfolk (begun in 1460).

Noise pollution in the little town on the Tiffey must have been pretty high in those days. After the Reformation, the whole of the eastern end was torn down, as were the cloister, chapterhouse and abbey buildings. Of the abbey church, which was completed c.1130 and was once twice its present length, all that remained was the nave with its Norman arcades and galleries, crowned by an unusually high Gothic hammerbeam roof with angels and flowery bosses. The west tower was where William Kett, one of the leaders of the Peasants' Revolt of 1549, was hung up and starved to death, as his brother Robert was from the tower of Norwich Castle. Wymondham has about 10,000 inhabitants now, and in the Market Place there is a picturesque Market Cross of 1618, an octagonal, timber-framed construction on wooden columns (plate 54).

'I love to think on thee, pretty, quiet D –, thou pattern of an English market town, with thy clean but narrow streets branching out from thy modest market place, with thine old-fashioned houses, with here and there a roof of venerable thatch.' With this eulogy to a small town, George Borrow begins his autobiographical novel *Lavengro*, a piece of Victorian sub-culture, written in 1851. 'Pretty, quiet D –' is *East Dereham*. There, or to be more precise in the neighbouring village of *Dumpling Green*, George Borrow was born in 1803: author, tinker, bible salesman, and genius of language, a tramp just like his friends the gypsies, who in *Lavengro* call him 'Wordmaster'. His first book was a translation of Klinger's novel *Faust*, and his last a dictionary of Gypsy language. His books, consisting of little 'anecdotic portions' which are 'good and useful to read' (Arno Schmidt) are the first account to depict without hostility and without – excessive – romanticism the everyday life of the gypsies.

Borrow was more interested in languages than in literature, and in people rather than in books. He was himself half gypsy, and sometimes he would say to his wife after breakfast: 'Beloved, today is a day to go walking.' And often he would not come home until months later, from Cornwall, Scotland, or Ireland, with the remark: 'Beloved, a fine walk.' After his wife's death, he lived alone in their cottage in Oulton Broad near Lowestoft, still going for his walks even in old age, wearing a Spanish cloak, a broad-brimmed hat, and singing as he went. The house and garden pavilion in which he wrote many of his books have since been demolished. In Oulton Broad there is still a pub called 'George Borrow', and his parents' house in Norwich, Borrow's Court in Willow Lane, is still standing. He is buried in Brompton Cemetery, London.

In 1803, the very year when George Borrow was born in 'pretty, quiet D-', a few miles further east the Rector of Weston Longville died. James Woodforde was a country parson, like thousands of others in the Church of England, and *Weston Longville* was as non-descript a place as you can find. He lived there for nearly thirty years, and the fact that we still take note of him and his village is due entirely to his having kept a diary. *The Diary of a Country Parson*, which was not published until 1924, describes in minute detail his daily life in this remote Norfolk village – a life that was typical for most of his 18th-century colleagues. It was a life equally divided between the harvest and the church, with the continual round of baptisms, visits to the sick, and burials. On 4 June 1776, he had to have

a tooth taken out – 'shockingly bad indeed', and on 22 November his cow had a calf. Parson Woodforde recorded all the minor and the major events that took place in Weston Longville: when in winter 1785 the frost was so fierce that it even froze the chamberpots under the beds, or when Hannah Snell made her entry into the 'White Hart', the famous woman who wore men's clothes. News of the storming of the Bastille took ten days to reach Weston Longville, but before recording this 'very great Rebellion in France', he noted his purchase of a particularly large crab. Good food was all-important to Parson Woodforde.

'We had for dinner a Calf's head, boiled Fowl and Tongue, a saddle of Mutton rosted on the Side Table, and a fine Swan rosted with Currant Jelly Sauce for the first Course. The Second Course a couple of Wild Fowl, Larks, Blamange, Tarts etc. etc. and a good Desert of Fruit after amongst which was a Damson Cheese.' Endless menus, and endless pleasure. 'What with laughing and eating hot gooseberry Pye brought on me the Hickupps with a violent pain in my stomach which lasted till I went to bed.' On 3 December 1782 Parson Woodforde sat at table in his living-room with a couple of farmers. 'Wine drank 6 bottles. Rum drank 5 bottles besides quantities of strong Beer and Ale. The pigs also enjoyed the home-brewed beer: 'My two large Piggs ... got so amazingly drunk by it, that they were not able to stand ... I never saw Piggs so drunk in my life.' It was not till the next day that they began to recover: 'In the afternoon my 2 Piggs were tolerably sober.' Like almost everybody else in those days, the parson regarded smuggling as quite normal: 'Andrews the smuggler brought me this night about 11 o'clock a bagg of Hyson Tea 6 pound weight.' The Parson also received a large quantity of gin and cognac (which at the first sign of danger he buried in the garden) from Moonshine Buck, who by day was the very respectable village blacksmith.

Parson Woodforde was a bachelor, and lived with his niece Nancy in the Rectory of this community of 360 souls. He had two manservants, two maids, and an errand boy. The really well-off people used to have a much larger staff. In those days, the slave trade was still going strong, and there was the death penalty for 160 different crimes. Smallpox was widespread, and public health and education were as non-existent as the railways. On horseback, the parson could get to Norwich in two hours, and the coach could get to London in one and a half days. But why should one travel when there was already so much variety in Weston Longville? He would, for instance, stay up all night and play cards until six in the morning. Or he would go fishing, or coursing hares with his three greyhounds Hector, Duchess and Reach'em. 'Ran 3 hares and killed 2 of them – the hare that got off shewed the best sport.' Hare-hunting, duck-roasting, whist and gin ... but Parson Wood-forde, godly pleasure-seeker, while revelling in the joys of country life, never forgot the hardships: 'Bitter cold day again with high wind, it froze in all parts of the House', he noted on 6 January 1789. 'Sent Ben round my Parish with some money to the Poor People

◁ *The only known photograph of George Borrow, 1848*

this severe Weather, chiefly those that cannot work at this time, some 1 Shilling apiece – some at 1s/6d apiece.' At Christmas he gave the poor a shilling and a meal in the Rectory: 'Beef rosted and plenty of plumb-Pudding.' And every year on St Valentine's Day he gave the children in the village a penny.

This *Diary of a Country Parson* is as far removed from the literary power and worldly wisdom of a Pepys or an Evelyn, the great English diarists, as Weston Longville is from London. But the wealth of detail, the humour, and the totally natural and unaffected presentation make Parson Woodforde's diary into a valuable personal and social document. Beside the unique Laurence Sterne, the realist George Crabbe, the natural scientist Gilbert White in Selborne, the eccentric R. S. Hawker in Cornwall, the Welsh patriot R. S. Thomas, and all the other literary parsons of the Church of England, James Woodforde of Norfolk deserves to take his distinguished place. Indeed there is a Parson Woodforde Society, which has been in existence since 1968, and in the simple village church of Weston Longville hangs his portrait, painted by his nephew Bill – a naive picture of a naive man. Opposite the church is a pub called 'The Parson Woodforde', and there I raised my beer glass to the happy parson. He died on New Year's Day 1803, and the last words that he wrote in his diary were: 'Dinner today, Rost Beef & c.'

Further Reading

Aubrey, John: *Brief Lives*, Harmondsworth 1972

Beckett, R. B. (ed.): *John Constable's Correspondence*, 6 vols, London 1962–8

Blythe, Ronald: *Akenfield. Portrait of an English Village*, Harmondsworth 1972

Blythe, Ronald & Smith, Edwin: *Divine Landscapes*, Harmondsworth 1986

Borrow, George: *Lavengro*, London 1851

Burke and Savill Guide to Country Houses, Volume III: East Anglia, London 1981

Clifton-Taylor, Alec: *The Cathedrals of England*, London 1967

―――― *The Pattern of English Building*, London 1987

Collins, Ian: *A Broad Canvas. Art in East Anglia since 1880*, Norwich 1990

Constable, Freda: *John Constable. A biography*, Lavenham 1975

Davis, Norman (ed.): *The Paston Letters*, Oxford 1983

Defoe, Daniel: *A Tour through the Whole Island of Great Britain (1724–6)*, Harmondsworth 1971

Eagle, Dorothy & Carnell, Hilary: *The Oxford Literary Guide to the British Isles*, Oxford 1977

Fincham, Paul: *The Suffolk we live in*, Woodbridge 1983

Gaye, Phoebe Fenwick: *Essex*, London 1949

Girouard, Mark: *Life in the English Country House. A Social and Architectural History*, London 1978

Green, Barbara & Young, Rachel M. R.: *Norwich: the growth of a city*, Norwich 1981

Hadfield, John (ed.): *The Shell Book of English Villages*, London 1980

Hayes, John: *Gainsborough*, London 1975

Hemingway, Andrew: *The Norwich School of Painters, 1803–33*, Oxford 1979

Hewison, Robert: *The Heritage Industry*, London 1987

Hutton, Graham & Smith, Edwin: (photos) *English Parish Churches*, London 1987

Innes, Hammond & Fox-Davies, Neville: *Hammond Innes' East Anglia*, London 1986

Lamont-Brown, Raymond: *East Anglian Epitaphs*, Fakenham 1980

Lees-Milne, James: *Ancestral Voices*, London 1975

―――― *Prophesying Peace*, London 1977

―――― *Caves of Ice*, London 1981

―――― *Midway on the Waves*, London 1985

Moore, Andrew W.: *John Sell Cotman*, Norwich 1982

―――― *The Norwich School of Artists*, Norwich 1985

―――― *Norfolk & The Grand Tour*, Norwich 1985

―――― *Dutch and Flemish Painting in Norfolk*, London 1988

Newby, Howard: *Country Life: A Social History of Rural England*, London 1987

Nicolson, Nigel: *Great Houses of Britain*, London 1965

Onslow, Richard: *Headquarters. A History of Newmarket and its Racing*, Cambridge 1983

Palmer, Alan & Veronica: *Royal England*, London 1983

Pevsner, Nikolaus: *The Buildings of England: Essex*, Harmondsworth 1954

―――― *The Buildings of England: Suffolk*, Harmondsworth 1961 and later

―――― *The Buildings of England: North-East Norfolk and Norwich*, Harmondsworth 1962

Pevsner, Nikolaus: *The Buildings of England: North-West and South Norfolk*, Harmondsworth 1962

Rackham, Oliver: *The History of the Countryside*, London 1986

Ravensdale, Jack & Muir, Richard: *East Anglian Landscapes: Past and Present*, London 1989

Rendell, Ruth & Bowden, Paul: *Ruth Rendell's Suffolk*, London 1989

Reynolds, Graham: *Constable's England*, The Metropolitan Museum of Art, New York 1983

Robinson, John Martin: *The Latest Country Houses*, London 1984

Rossiter, Stuart (ed.): *The Blue Guide to England*, London 1972

Sandon, Eric: *Suffolk Houses. A Study of Domestic Architecture*, Woodbridge 1977

Scarfe, Norman: *Essex*, London 1968

—— *The Suffolk Guide*, London 1988

Seymour, John: *East Anglia*, London 1970

Shoard, Marion: *This Land is Our Land. The Struggle for Britain's countryside*, London 1987

Simpson, Roger: *Literary Walks in Norwich*, Norwich 1983

Tate Gallery: *Constable*, London 1976

—— *Thomas Gainsborough*, London 1980

—— *George Stubbs*, London 1984

Tennyson, Julian: *Suffolk Scene*, Glasgow 1939

Thompson, Edward P.: *The Making of the English Working Class*, London 1963

Trevelyan, George Macaulay: *English Social History (1942)*, Harmondsworth 1984

Turner, Peter & Wood, Richard: *P. H. Emerson. Photographer of Norfolk*, London 1974

Wilson, Angus (ed.): *East Anglia in Verse and Prose*, Harmondsworth 1984

Wolfenden, Stephen: *To the Town. Portraits of Southwold*, Kirstead 1988

Woodforde, James: *The Diary of a Country Parson 1758–1802*, Oxford 1978

Ranworth Church, Jonah and the Whale,
Sarum antiphon, c.1400

Ron Fuller: Steam Dancing Man, 1980

SOME PRACTICAL HINTS

East Anglia from A to Z

Accommodation This ranges from camp sites to country house hotels. *Bed & Breakfast* (B&B) is the most homely and the best value, especially for travellers who prefer not to arrange things in advance. It also offers you a glimpse of other people's private lives. Over 700 good quality B&B addresses, between £9 and £20 per person, are listed in the *Good Bed and Breakfast Guide* (Consumers' Association, PO Box 44, Hertford SG14 1SH). *Hotels:* Have a look at the room, and don't always take the first one they offer you – it might be the first, but it won't necessarily be the best. The most informative guide is *Egon Ronay's Cellnet Guide to Hotels & Restaurants*, updated yearly. In addition to *Guest Houses*, East Anglia is particularly well endowed with *farmhouse Accommodation*. Another popular and good value form of accommodation, especially for families, is *self-catering*, and one of the biggest agencies in Britain is English Country Cottages, Claypit Lane, Fakenham, Norfolk NR21 8AS, ∅ 0328/4041. Interesting accommodation in restored historic houses can be obtained through The National Trust (Holiday Cottages, PO Box 101, Melksham, Wiltshire SN12 8EA, ∅ 0225/705676), and unusual holiday homes – e.g. the Martello Tower in Aldeburgh, and the Victorian Water Tower in Norfolk – can be rented from *The Landmark Trust* (Shottesbrooke, Maiden-head, Berkshire SL6 3SW, ∅ 062882/5925). If you're looking for peace and quiet, e.g. a hermitage, monastery or place of meditation, you'll find a wide choice in George Target's original guidebook *Out of This World* (Bishopgate Press Ltd). *Camping and caravan sites* are listed in the BTA's brochure *Where to Stay*. In the peak holiday season, July–August, it's advisable to book well in advance. A reasonably priced alternative to hotels, especially for group travel and conferences, is university accommodation in student halls of residence during the vacations, i.e. mid-March to mid-April and mid-June to the end of September. Information: British Universities Accommodation Consortium, PO Box 161, University Park, Nottingham NG7 2RD, ∅ 0602/504571. Also: Higher Education Accommodation Consortium (HEAC), 36 Collegiate Crescent, Sheffield S10 2BP, ∅ 0742/665274. See also under *Youth Hostels*.

Angling Plenty of river and sea fishing. Information about angling hotels, the fishing season and licences is available from the BTA (see **Information**), and a handbook *Where to Fish* (Harmsworth Publishing), which is updated every year, lists all the fishing grounds in Britain. Best time for pike on Norfolk Broads: October. Permits from local tourist offices.

Antiques You will find these in most villages and towns. Especially noteworthy are Long Melford, Coggeshall, Woodbridge and Norwich. A yearly *Guide to the Antique Shops of Britain* is published by the Antique Collectors' Club, 5 Church Street, Woodbridge, Suffolk, ∅ 0394/385501.

Arts & Crafts East Anglia is full of craft workshops: potters, weavers, cabinetmakers, woodcarvers, gold and silversmiths, etc. Addresses available from The Suffolk Craft Society, Fairfield House, Saxmundham, Suffolk IP17 1AX, ∅ 0728/602060. Workshops and holiday courses are held by Alby Crafts in Norfolk (see page 536) and others. The whole spectrum is covered by the Eastern Arts Board (see page 500). The Rural Development Commission publishes a detailed list of addresses: *Craft Workshops in the Countryside*.

Boating holidays There is no finer way of exploring the Norfolk Broads. One should not, however, overlook the ecological consequences of this pleasure (see page 409 ff.). Boating holiday season: April - early October. Houseboats and excursions organized by Blakes, the oldest boat-hire agency in the Broads, founded 1908, a co-operative of some 50 boatyards and companies with a fleet of about 700 motor and sailing boats: Blakes Holidays, Wroxham, Norwich NR12 8DH, ∅ 0603/982141.

Brass Rubbing One must generally obtain permission from the parish priest and pay a small fee. East Anglia is particularly rich in monumental brasses; the peak period was around the middle of the 15th century. The brass, an alloy of copper and zinc, was mostly imported from Flanders during the Middle Ages. In Norfolk alone there are 215 noteworthy brasses, in Suffolk a similar number, and in Essex 237. On the history, iconography and technique, see Henry Trivick's *The Craft and Design of Monumental Brasses* (1969). Another good survey is offered by the catalogue of *Brass Rubbings* published by the Victoria and Albert Museum in London (now out of print). One can also join The Monumental Brass Society (founded 1887), c/o Society of Antiquaries, Burlington House, Piccadilly, London W1.

Buses In the more remote areas, there is often no local public transport. There is, however, a broad network of country buses. All routes, timetables and prices are contained in the *Express Coach Guide* issued by the National Bus Company, 1 Vernon Road, Edgbaston, Birmingham B16 9SJ. National Express buses are much cheaper than trains. Tourists from abroad can buy a 30-day 'BritExpress Card' which will entitle them to a 30 per cent discount on all journeys (available from travel agencies).

Climate 'You can't have nice people *and* nice weather,' I was told by a waiter in Cromer one exceptionally rainy June morning. The East Anglian coast enjoys more sun and less rain than most other regions in England. The North Sea softens the winds from the North East, warming them in winter and cooling them in summer. The often biting coastal winds are described by locals as 'bracing', and certainly Adelheid, sister of the eponymous hero of Fontane's novel *Stechlin*, was exaggerating somewhat with her claim that 'When it is foggy, they get what they call the spleen, and fall into the water in their hundreds, and nobody knows what has happened to them.' The best times for travel are May and June, September and October. Autumn in East Anglia often turns out to be an Indian Summer, though it's as well to keep a sweater and umbrella handy. If it does rain, comfort yourself with Vita Sackville-West's most English of poems, which begins:

Now be you thankful, who in England dwell,
That to the starving trees and thirsty grass
Even at summer's height come cloudy fleets
Moist from the wastes of the Atlantic swell,
To spill their rain, and pass,
While fields renew their sweets.

Council for the Protection of Rural England (CPRE) A politically independent organisation, founded in 1926, which has some 45,000 members. It has mounted several very successful campaigns, and has contributed to the creation of green belts and national parks, and to the introduction of measures to prevent overdevelopment. Current campaigns include those against further nuclear power stations and the reafforestation of the fells in the Lake District.

President of the CPRE since 1991 is the broadcaster Jonathan Dimbleby. It has branches in all the counties, one of the most active being the Suffolk Preservation Society in Lavenham (see under entry). Central office: 25 Buckingham Palace Road, London SW1W 0PP.

Countryside Commission (CC) State-run organization founded in 1968 as 'the nation's landscape watchdog', whose job is 'to conserve and enhance the natural beauty of England's countryside and to give people better opportunities to enjoy and appreciate it.' In conjunction with local councils, the National Trust etc., the CC promotes such projects as national parks, long-distance paths (National Trails) and reafforestation, although it does not take direct responsibility for them. In every county it provides a 'countryside adviser' to help keep a balance between landscape conservation and agriculture. The CC is particularly concerned with Areas of Outstanding Natural Beauty (AONB), of which there are almost 40 in England and Wales, East Anglian examples being Dedham Vale, the Suffolk heaths, and the Norfolk coast. Headquarters of the CC: John Dower House, Crescent Place, Cheltenham, Gloucestershire, ℘ 0242/521381. East Anglian Regional Office: Ortona House, 110 Hills Road, Cambridge CB2 1LQ, ℘ 0223/354462.

Cycling The flat coastal regions are ideal for a cycling holiday. Useful addresses: Anglia Cycling Holidays, Ballintuim Post Office, N. Blairgowrie, Perthshire, Scotland PH10 7NJ, ℘ 0250886/201 and Norfolk Cycling Holidays, Sandy Way, King's Lynn, Norfolk PE31 6NJ, ℘ 0485/540642. Information, including bicycle hire, from: Cyclists' Touring Club (CTC), Cotterell House, 69 Meadow, Godalming, Surrey GU7 3HS, ℘ 048341/7217.

Disabled Generally the facilities are excellent. In many of the historic houses, e.g. Blickling Hall, wheelchairs are provided. For useful information and addresses, the English Tourist Board publishes a brochure, *Disabled Visitors Guide*, and one can also contact Holiday Care Service, 2 Old Bank Chambers, Station Road, Horley, Surrey RH6 9HW, ∅ 0293 774535.

Eastern Arts Board One of 12 regional arts associations in England, founded in 1972 as the Eastern Art Association. It was reformed in October 1991 and is mainly financed by the Arts Council. With a yearly budget of £4.5m. for seven counties, Eastern Arts is 'a neglected region', according to director Jeremy Newton. It is therefore all the more remarkable that the 35 employees are able to generate and promote so many cultural events: exhibitions, concerts, theatre, film, photography, dance, literature, arts and crafts, youth and community projects. Their monthly magazine *ArtEast*, gives details of all the cultural activities in the region. Central Office: Cherry Hinton Hall, Cambridge CB1 4DW, ∅ 0223/215355.

Eating and Drinking 'I could never forgo the kippers, so delicious, so digestible, but above all, so full of proteins,' raves Davey in Nancy Mitford's *Pursuit of Love*. The English breakfast remains well in evidence throughout East Anglia, but the villages and towns also boast many a gourmet restaurant well worth going out of your way for (addresses, pages 534–41). The best of these are distinguished by fresh produce from the garden or market, and by international sophistication. For an informative as well as amusing description, see the yearly *Good Food Guide*, which since its first publication in 1951 has become a national institution among food lovers everywhere (published by The Consumers Association, 359 Euston Road, London NW1, ∅ 071/4865544). The pleasures of touring East Anglia are greatly enhanced by the profusion of village pubs. More and more of these are offering a richly varied menu, though on the coast especially one should not overlook the traditional fish and chips. Two of the best fish and chip shops, incidentally, are to be found in Aldeburgh and Dunwich (see entries). Other coastal specialities: Cromer crabs (not only in Cromer), and the oysters of Colchester and Brancaster. The best local cider is to be found in Aspall, Suffolk, and the best local beer is Adnams in Southwold and Greene King in Bury St Edmunds. As for wine, since this is the sunniest and least rainy region in England, the Normans followed the example of the Romans and reintroduced winegrowing here. Several vineyards are open for viewing and tasting, e.g. Bruisyard Wines Ltd, Church Road, Bruisyard near Framlingham, ∅ 0728/75281, April–Nov. daily 10.30–5. 'England is a wine-lover's paradise, offering unparalleled choice,' writes Simon Loftus, one of England's best-known connoisseurs, although unfortunately – as landlord of The Crown in Southwold – he is actually talking of continental wines.

English Heritage (EH) A Government-funded but independent conservation body set up in 1984 to look after monuments belonging to the nation, EH administers over 400 historic sites and buildings in Britain, including Stonehenge, Hadrian's Wall, Dover Castle, and Audley End. It recommends the listing (or otherwise) of buildings and gardens, looks after prehistoric monuments, castles, monasteries, industrial sites and municipal projects. Its budget of around £91.1m is also used to give grants-in-aid to other owners of monuments. The regional headquarters in East Anglia: English Heritage, Block D, Government Buildings, Brooklands Avenue, Cambridge CB2 2DZ, ∅ 0223 462608, ext. 2285. London Head Office: Fortress House, 23 Savile Row, London W1X 2HE, ∅ 071/973 3000. In recent years people have become increasingly aware of English Heritage. The growing popularity and practicality of the link between preservation and tourism – which is not without its problems – is analyzed by Robert Hewison in his book *The Heritage Industry* (London 1987) – a polemic against the total exploitation of the past: heritage as the enemy of history.

English Nature England's main conservation body, set up in 1990 to replace the Nature Conservancy Council, English Nature manages England's 140 National Nature Reserves (NNR), with a total of some 57,424 acres, though it only owns about a quarter of the total. It is also responsible, among other things, for more than 3,700 Sites of Special Scientific Interest (SSSI). Landowners are now paid to manage environmentally sensitive areas with due care, rather than compensated for profits nominally foregone. One of the NCC's 15 regional bureaux is in Norwich, at 60 Bracondale. The Head Office is at Northminster House, Peterborough PE1 1UA, ∅ 0733/340345.

Friends of the Earth (FOE) Along with Greenpeace, Britain's internationally most active ecological movement, founded in 1971. There are about 300 local branches in Britain, with affiliated groups in over fifty countries and a membership of around 250,000. Its message is simple: only if we protect the Earth can we protect ourselves. In East Anglia FOE has organized campaigns against the destruction of nature reserves, against Sizewell B, the dumping of nuclear waste in the North Sea, and the use of pesticides in agriculture, and in favour of conserving hedgerows and wetlands. There are eight local FOE groups in East Anglia; apart from Norwich the most active of these is the Cambridge group (The Bath House, Gwydir Street, Cambridge CB1 2LW, ∅ 0223/312800 or 351227). Central Office: Friends of the Earth Trust Ltd, 26–28 Underwood Street, London N1 7JQ, ∅ 071/490 1555.

Gardens Garden-lovers will have a field day in East Anglia (see index). Of the 2,300 private gardens that are open for public viewing at least once a year, more than 600 are presented in the book *Garden Open Today*, ed. Martyn and Alison Rix (London 1987). The 1,000 best British and Irish gardens open to the public are described in *The Good Gardens Guide*, ed. Graham Rose and Peter King (Barrie and Jenkins). Yearly brochure with addresses and opening times: *Gardens of England and Wales*, issued by The National Gardens Scheme, 57 Lower Belgrave Street, London SW1W 0LR. The history of some traditional and some eccentric English gardens is traced by Penelope Hobhouse, *The Private Gardens of England* (London 1986). Lovers of old

English roses will find a selection of about 1,100 varieties at Peter Beales Roses, London Road, Attleborough, Norfolk NR17 1AY, ∅ 0953/454707.

Information East Anglia Tourist Board, Topplesfield Hall, Hadleigh, Suffolk IP7 5DN, ∅ 0473/822922. Information and reservations also from: The British Travel Centre, 4–12 Lower Regent Street, London W1 (no telephone calls) where there is also a bookshop.

Markets In the rural regions of East Anglia there are many weekly markets. Each has its own speciality and atmosphere, though not all can trace their roots back to the 11th century, like that of Norwich which, with over 200 stalls, can claim to be the biggest and oldest in England.

National Trust (NT) In 1895 three English philanthropists – a social reformer, a parish priest and a lawyer – founded The National Trust for Places of Historic Interest or Natural Beauty, with the intention of preserving for the good of the nation land and buildings of particular beauty or historical interest. This national institution, an early and momentous example of private enterprise, has no regular government subsidy but is financed by membership fees, entrance money, donations, and a chain of flourishing souvenir shops and tearooms. Next to the Crown and the State, the NT is the third biggest landowner in Britain. It owns, manages and restores country houses, castles, farmhouses, gardens, forests, battlefields, bird sanctuaries, pubs, dovecotes, industrial monuments, barns, watermills, cider presses, villages and whole islands. With over 2 million members, 10 million visitors to its historic houses, and an annual turnover of around £100m, the NT is Britain's most powerful organization for conservation and preservation. The NT's acquisitions substantially affect the tastes and values of the whole nation.

Even this most admirable and most enviable of British institutions, however, has its critics: derided by some as 'The National Dust', it has been accused of one-sidedly preserving the traditions of the aristocracy and a pastoral past, a 'fossilization of taste' (*Observer*). The Labour MP David Clark, a member of NT's governing council, accused it of being too elitist, tied to the values of the prosperous middle class of the South, and 'obsessed with buying grand houses at the expense of protecting the countryside'. If the preservation of historic houses was indeed a major preoccupation of the NT up until the 1970's, it has since the middle of the 1980's been increasingly concerned with conservation of nature and landscapes. It is thanks to the green policy of the NT that some of Britain's most beautiful landscapes have been rescued, and indeed more than 535 miles of England's coastline – about a sixth of the total – is now owned by the NT, as a result of 'Enterprise Neptune', a conservation programme begun in 1965.

The history of the NT has been told by John Gaze in *Figures in a Landscape* (1988). For a yearly subscription, members can visit all the houses, gardens and other properties of the Trust free of charge. Head Office: The National Trust, 36 Queen Anne's Gate, London SW1H 9AS, ∅ 071/

222 9251. East Anglia Regional Office: Blickling Hall, Norfolk NR11 6NF, ∅ 0263/733471.

Nature Conservation Since the late 1980's, Britain has been making increasing efforts to embrace green policies and to shed its reputation as the 'dirty man of Europe'. Particularly in rural regions like East Anglia, many private organizations as well as some state-run institutions have devoted themselves to cleaning up the environment. See entries for Council for the Protection of Rural England, Countryside Commission, Friends of the Earth, National Trust, English Nature, Norfolk Naturalists Trust, and Royal Society for the Protection of Birds. For information about National Parks, contact the Council for National Parks, 45 Shelton Street, London WC2H 9HS, ∅ 071/240 3603. For information about woodlands, contact the Forestry Commission (Information Branch), 231 Corstorphine Road, Edinburgh EH12 7AT, ∅ 031/1334 0303.

Newspapers In addition to the nationals, East Anglia has three independent regional newspapers: in Norwich, *The Eastern Daily Press* (founded 1870, circulation 91,000) and *Eastern Evening News* (founded 1882, circulation 52,000), and in Ipswich, *The East Anglian Daily Times* (founded 1874, circulation 49,000). Visitors wishing to know about cattle markets, church concerts or antique sales would do well to buy one of these.

Norfolk Naturalists Trust (NNT) The oldest private organization at county level for nature conservation, founded in 1926.

The Queen is patron. The NNT owns or manages forty nature reserves in Norfolk, five of them being of national importance. Information centres in Ranworth on the Broads, Hickling, Holme Dunes and Cley-next-the-Sea. Main Office: 72 Cathedral Close, Norwich NR1 4DF, ∅ 0603/625540.

Norfolk Mills and Pumps Trust Set up in 1963 for the preservation and restoration of historic corn mills and wind pumps, supported by Norfolk County Council. Members renovate machinery, caps and sails, and are responsible for maintenance and public relations. An exemplary programme for the preservation of 34 drainage mills on the Broads. Information: Norfolk Mills and Pumps Trust, County Council, County Hall, Martineau Lane, Norwich NR1 2DH, ∅ 0603/222705.

Preservation of Historic Buildings Britain probably has more organizations for the preservation of its heritage than any other country. A pioneer of this movement was William Morris, who in 1877 founded the still flourishing Society for the Protection of Ancient Buildings, 37 Spital Square, London E1 6DY, ∅ 071/377 1644. At the same address, ∅ 071/377 1722, is the Georgian Group, founded in 1937, which is particularly concerned with buildings from 1714–1837. The Victorian Society, 1 Priory Gardens, Bedford Park, London W4 1TT, ∅ 081/994 1019, looks after buildings from the period 1837–1918, and later buildings are the concern of the Twentieth Century Society, 58 Crescent Lane, London SW4 9PU. Prehistoric monuments are the concern of The Prehistoric Society, Institute of Archaeology, Gordon Square, London WC1, ∅ 071/580 4086. There are two main organizations that look after historic parish churches: The Redundant Churches Fund (founded 1969), 89 Fleet Street, London EC4Y 1DH, ∅ 071/936 2285; and The Historic Churches Preservation Trust, Fulham Palace, London SW6 6EA, ∅ 071/736 3054. Nonconformist buildings are looked after by the Historic Chapels Trust, 4 Cromwell Place, London SW7 2JJ, ∅ 071/589 0228. Apart from the two major institutions English Heritage and National Trust (see both entries), the most active organization is SAVE Britain's Heritage, 68 Battersea High Street, London SW11 3HX, ∅ 071/228 3336. SAVE was set up in 1975, the year of European conservation, by a group of British journalists, historians, architects and town-planners, and since then it has waged many successful campaigns to rescue countless manor houses, cottages, churches, cinemas, stations, warehouses etc. from demolition.

Fox hunt, weather vane near Harwich

Standard work by SAVE's President Marcus Binney and the architect Kit Martin: *The Country House: to be or not to be* (London, 1982). The owners of private country houses have their own organization as well: Historic Houses Association, 2 Chester Street, London SW1X 7BB, ∅ 071/259 5688. The Landmark Trust (founded 1965), Shottesbrooke, Maidenhead, Berkshire, ∅ 0628/825925, acquires and restores historic buildings threatened by decay or demolition, and rents them out as holiday homes.

Railways Two of the most scenic lines: from Ipswich through rural Suffolk to Lowestoft and Norwich (72 miles), and from Norwich through the marshlands to Great Yarmouth (20.5 miles), with Britain's only gaslit station en route, Berney Arms. For tourists without cars, it is well worth getting a Local Rover Ticket or a Flexicard for unlimited travel within East Anglia. Usual discounts apply. Further information: British Rail, 112 Prince of Wales Road, Norwich, ∅ 0603/632055, or any British Rail Travel Centre.

Riding Good facilities for 'holidays on horseback', with riding lessons and pony trekking from established riding schools. Information: The British Horse Society, National Equestrian Centre, Stoneleigh, Kenilworth, Warwickshire, ∅ 0203/696697.

Royal Society for the Protection of Birds (RSPB) With almost 830,000 members, this is the biggest animal protection society in Europe, founded in 1889 in Manchester in order to cut down on the use of tropical bird feathers in ladies' hats. Today the RSPB owns or manages 120 bird sanctuaries covering nearly 200,000 acres in Britain. Its aim is to preserve ornithologically important species and a wide variety of birds, and their habitats. East Anglian regional office: 97 Yarmouth Road, Norwich NR7 0HS, ℘ 0603/700880.

Sightseeing One needs a pair of binoculars to view the angels up in the roofs of the churches and cathedrals. For the more profane pleasures of sightseeing, all that is required is a Great British Heritage Pass, which for a single, very reasonable payment will gain you entry to over 600 castles, country houses and gardens owned by the National Trust and English Heritage. This pass – the size of a credit card – is valid for two weeks or a month,

Inn sign at Butley Orford Oysterage, Suffolk

and is available from the British Travel Centre, 12 Lower Regent Street, London. N.B. Many sights, especially country houses, have restricted visiting times in winter.

Sport Sailors, golfers, riders, cricketers, footballers, etc. will find plenty to occupy them in East Anglia. Norwich City (League Cup Winners 1962 and 1985) and Ipswich Town (League Champions 1961–2, F.A. Cup Winners 1977–8, UEFA Cup Winners 1981) are two of the top football clubs in England. Of Britain's 1,800 golf courses, some of the finest are to be found on East Anglia's coasts (to the fury of the conservationists): Caister-on-Sea, Cromer, Hunstanton, Sheringham, Thorpeness, Aldeburgh. The most exclusive club from the golfing and social point of view is the Royal West Norfolk Golf Club in Brancaster, ℘ 0485/210223. Course fee: £30 per day in the week, £40 per day at weekends and Bank Holidays. It is best to book well in advance. For sailors, the fjord-like estuaries along the East Anglian coast provide a beautiful if somewhat dangerous setting (sandbanks, currents, tides). Yachting centres include Burnham-on-Crouch,

Inn sign at Mischief Tavern, Fye Bridge, Norwich

ALE & WINE VAULTS

505

Maldon and West Mersea in Essex; Woodbridge, Aldeburgh and Lowestoft in Suffolk; Great Yarmouth, Cromer, Cley-next-the-Sea, Blakeney and King's Lynn in Norfolk. Further information: East Anglian School of Sailing, PO Box 64, Ipswich IP2 8NN, ⌀ 0473/780246. Quoits: this variant of 'boules' – particularly popular in Wales – is still played in quite a few villages in Suffolk, e.g. Butley. Cricket: Essex, five times County Champions, and winners of innumerable one-day competitions, may justifiably lay claim to having been the team of the 1980's, and perhaps of the 1990's as well. Most villages have their own team, and some boast a pub to match: e.g. The Cricketers in Danbury (4 miles east of Chelmsford), The Cricketers Arms in Rickling (5 miles south of Saffron Walden). The Cricketers at Mill Green in Ingatestone has an original collection of cricketing memorabilia. See also under Angling and Riding.

Walking When asked why he didn't use the railway, the Norfolk writer George Borrow replied: 'I am fond of the beauties of nature; now it is impossible to see much

Golfing weather vane in Dereham

of the beauties of nature unless you walk.' East Anglia should not be viewed through a windscreen either. In 1986 Prince Charles opened the long-distance Norfolk Coast Path from Holme to Cromer (about 41 miles). Enthusiastic hikers can also walk from Cromer to Great Yarmouth along Weavers Way (about 57 miles). One of the oldest paths in England, Peddars Way, is probably pre-Roman. It may have run from Colchester to Lincolnshire with a ferry or ford over the Wash. A section survives between Knettishall Heath (near Thetford) to Holme. A particularly beautiful stretch runs west of Great Massingham from Castle Acre through Anmer and Fring to Ringstead. Maps and details of overnight accommodation can be obtained from Peddars Way Association, 150 Ames Street, Norwich, Norfolk NR2 4EG,

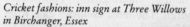

Cricket fashions: inn sign at Three Willows in Birchanger, Essex

Weather vane wanderer in Otley, Suffolk

℘ 0603/623070. If you want to follow Constable's tracks, take Painter's Way through the Stour valley, from Manningtree to Sudbury (24 miles). Further information from The Ramblers' Association (which covers some 400 clubs), 1–5 Wandsworth Road, London SW8 2LJ, ℘ 071/582 6878; and from The Long Distance Walker's Association, Lodgefield Cottage, High Street, Flimwell, Wadhurst, East Sussex TN5 7PH, ℘ 058/087341. There is a detailed description of more than 240 walks in *Walker's Britain*, Pan Books (London 1982).

Working Holidays If you are not interested in the classic holiday formula of sightseeing, bathing and walking, East Anglia can also offer you a wide range of alternatives, from restoring old churches to learning how to paint like Constable. If your interest is flora and fauna, geology and ecology, the courses given by The Field Studies Council are particularly recommended: Flatford Mill Field Centre, East Bergholt, Essex CO7 6UL, ℘ 0206/298283 and 298271. Most Working Holidays offer simple, reasonably priced accommodation, and participants should be at least 16 years old. A few addresses: National Trust Acorn Projects, PO Box 12, Westbury, Wiltshire BA13 4NA, ℘ 0373/826826; British Trust Conservation Volunteers (BTCV), 80 York Way, London N1 9AG, ℘ 071/278 4293; Cathedral Camps, Manor House, High Birtswith, Harrogate, North Yorkshire HG3 2LG, ℘ 0423/770385. 'Turn rainy days into brainy days' is the motto of the flourishing Summer Schools, whose programmes and addresses can be obtained from: Independent Schools Information Service, 56 Buckingham Gate, London SW1, ℘ 071/630 8793; also from Central Bureau for Educational Visits and Exchanges, Seymour Mews House, Seymour Mews, London W1H 9PE, ℘ 071/486 5101.

Youth Hostels There are some 300 youth hostels in the region, some in historic buildings. Addresses and information from: Youth Hostels Association (YHA), 8 St Stephen's Hill, St Albans, Herts AL1 2DY, ℘ 0727/55215.

Diary of Events

E = Essex, N = Norfolk, S = Suffolk

January
Norwich Annual Antiques Fair, Blackfriars Hall, Norwich (N).
April
Wingfield Art & Music, Wingfield (S): rural festival of concerts, exhibitions, and readings (till September).
May
1,000 Guineas and 2,000 Guineas Stakes, Newmarket (S): two of the five Classic races.
June
Barge Match: traditional regatta on the Blackwater near Maldon (E).
Suffolk Show, Suffolk Showground, Ipswich (S): county agricultural show.
Aldeburgh Festival of Music and the Arts (S): started in 1948 by Benjamin Britten; concerts, opera, exhibitions, readings, walks, chamber music in country houses and churches.
Morris Ring Meeting, Town Street, Thaxted (E): folk dancing in the streets.
Royal Norfolk Show, Dereham Road, New Costessey, Norwich (N): biggest agricultural show in East Anglia.
Dunmow Flitch Ceremony, Talberds Ley, Great Dunmow (E): a side of bacon is awarded to a married couple who have not quarrelled for a year and a day.
Trinity Fair, Southwold (S): announced by the town crier on 15 June.
Thaxted Festival (E): classical and contemporary music, begun in 1980.

July
Pin Mill Sailing Club Barge Match (S): regatta at the mouth of the Orwell, near Pin Mill, Ipswich.
King's Lynn Festival (N): classical and contemporary music, theatre, exhibitions.
Southwold Summer Theatre (S) till mid-September.
Sandringham Flower Show, Sandringham House (N).
Snape Antiques Fair(s) started in 1967, in the concert hall used for the Aldeburgh Festival.
Summer Music, The Old School, Hadleigh (S): festival of classical music started in 1978.
Wangford Festival (S): classical and contemporary music, started in 1966, with concerts in village churches at Wangford and Blythburgh.
Bruisyard Driving & Dog Show (S), including sulky and greyhound racing.
August
Wroxham Week (N): sailing regatta on the Broads.
British Crabbing Federation Open Championship, Walberswick (S).
St Benet's Open Air Service (N): held by the Bishop of Norwich in the ruins of St Benet's Abbey on the Broads (1st Sunday in August).
September
Highflyer Sales, Tattersalls, Newmarket (S): auction of thoroughbreds, named after

the founder's most successful stallion.

East Anglia Antiques Fair, Athenaeum, Bury St Edmunds (S).

October

Norfolk and Norwich Festival, Norwich (N): art and music festival begun in 1824, with concerts in churches and country houses such as Blickling and Felbrigg Hall.

Colchester Oyster Feast (E), held in the Town Hall.

Cambridgeshire and Cesarewitch, Newmarket (S): horseracing at the end of the flat season.

Essex Festival, Colchester (E): festival of literature and theatre, begun in 1981, also with concerts and exhibitions.

December

December Sales, Tattersalls, Newmarket (S): Europe's most important auction of thoroughbreds.

Mr Weller attacks the executive of Ipswich

Places to See, with Opening Times

NT = National Trust, EH = English Heritage, P = Private,

Of sea or river, or a quay or street,
The best description must be incomplete.
(George Crabbe)

Essex

Audley End (west of Saffron Walden, B1383, 15 miles south of Cambridge, A11): Jacobean mansion, 1603–16, 'one of the stateliest palaces in the Kingdom' (John Evelyn). Interiors by Robert Adam, 1762 and later. Park by Capability Brown, 1762–97. In former stables (*c.*1605–15) museum of Victorian agriculture. Narrow gauge railway with historic miniature steam engines. April–Sept. Tue.–Sun. and Bank Hol. 1–6. EH. In the village is a former almshouse, St Mark's College (*c.*1600), now a home for retired clergy.

Beeleigh Abbey (1.2 miles west of Maldon): Former Premonstratensian monastery overlooking River Chelmer, founded in 1180. Still preserved: chapterhouse and cellar of dormitory (early 13th century), incorporated into 16th-century country house of famous London bookseller William Foyle. P. Second-hand books, ∅ 0621/856308, Mon.–Thur. 9–6.

Belchamp Walter (4 miles west of Sudbury): Belchamp Hall, ∅ 0787/72744; country home of the Raymonds, George I brick building, 1720; three rooms open, with furniture, porcelain, and Gains-

borough portrait. Family atmosphere, especially when owner acts as guide. May–Sept. Tues. and Thurs. afternoon, only by appointment. 14th-century parish church with medieval frescoes.

Bourne Mill: see Colchester.

Braintree (west of Colchester, A120): Heritage Centre, Market Square: local history museum, with family history of the Courtaulds, silk and textile manufacturers. Mon.–Fri. 9–5, Sat. 10–4, closed Bank Hol. Workshops of teak specialists Barlow-Tyrie, makers of classic English garden furniture.

Brentwood: (northeast of London, A12): Catholic Cathedral of St Mary and St Helen: small, late Victorian church, extended in 1991 by Quinlan Terry in a pastiche of Wren.

Brightlingsea (southeast of Colchester, B1027): yachting centre on east bank of Colne estuary. Only Cinque Port north of the Thames. 15th-century parish church.

Bulmer (west of Sudbury, A131/B1058): brickworks probably going back to Roman times. The Bulmer Brick & Tile Company produces handmade bricks, especially for the restoration of historic buildings (Hampton Court, Windsor Castle, Blickling Hall, Oxburgh Hall, etc.).

Castle Hedingham (4 miles northwest of Halstead, A604/B1058): Norman keep, home of the Earls of Oxford. April–Oct. daily 10–5, ∅ 0473/822922.
Colne Valley Railway, Yeldham Road, ∅ 0787/61174: collection of old steam engines ('with regular steamings'). Feb.–Dec. daily 10–5.

Chappel (northwest of Colchester, A604): East Anglian Railway Museum, ∅ 07875/2571: Victorian station with collection of steam engines and other railwayana; 32-arch viaduct, 1849. 'Restoration in progress' and also 'Steamdays'. Mon.–Fri. 10–5, Sat. & Sun. 10–5.30.

Chelmsford: Chelmsford and Essex Museum, Oaklands Park, Moulsham Street, ∅ 0245/353066: town and county museum as uninspiring as the town itself. Mon.–Sat. 10–5, Sun. 2–5.
Shire Hall, High Street: neoclassical building by John Johnson, 1790–92, with Coade stone reliefs on the gables.

Chickney (southwest of Thaxted, B1051): St Mary's: small Anglo-Saxon church, full of atmosphere. 14th-century font and tower. Maintained by Redundant Churches Fund.

Chingford (northeast of London, A1069): Queen Elizabeth's Hunting Lodge, early 16th century, now Epping Forest Museum. Fri.–Mon. 2–5, Tue. 12–5.

Coggeshall (west of Colchester, A120): Paycocke's, West Street: medieval half-timbered house. April–early Oct. Tues., Thurs., Sun. and Bank Hol. Mon. 2–5.30. NT.
Grange Barn: oldest surviving barn in England, c.1140. NT.

Colchester: Bourne Mill (1.2 miles south): watermill, 1591. All Bank Hol. Sun. and Mon., July–Aug. Sun. and Tue. 2–5.30. NT.
Castle Museum, ∅ 0206/712939: Norman castle with archaeological collection, especially Roman. All year Mon.–Sat. 10–5, Mar.–Nov. also Sun. 2–5.
Colchester Arts Centre, St Mary-at-the-Walls, Church Street, ∅ 0206/577301: exhibitions, jazz, rock, folk, workshops; bookshop and café: Mon.–Fri. 10–5, telephone for details of weekend events.
Hollytree Museum, High Street (next to castle), ∅ 0206/712940: early Georgian house, 1718, with collection of costumes and dolls, Mon.–Sat. 10–5.
Mercury Theatre, Balkerne Gate, ∅ 0206/573948; municipal theatre with art gallery and restaurant.
Natural History Museum, All Saints Church, High Street (opposite castle): flora and fauna in Essex. Mon.–Sat. 10–5.
Social History Museum, Holy Trinity Church, Trinity Street, ∅ 0206/712942: situated in 14th-century church with Anglo-Saxon tower. Mon.–Sat. 10–5.
Tymperley's Clock Museum, Trinity Street, ∅ 0206/712943, situated in birthplace of William Gilberd, Elizabeth I's physician. April–Oct. Mon.–Sat. 10–5.
University of Essex, see separate entry.

Cressing Temple Barns (southeast of

Braintree, off B1018): two barns, 13th century, used by Knights Templar.

Dedham (7 miles northeast of Colchester, off A12): Castle House, ℘ 0206/322127: former home and studio of painter Sir Alfred Munnings, with large collection of his works. May–Sept. Wed., Sun. and Bank Hol. Mon., Aug. also Thurs. & Sat. 2–5.
Dedham Centre, High Street: converted church with handicrafts, antiques, snacks and teas. Daily 10–5.
Duchy Barn, ℘ 0206/323447: information centre for Council for the Protection of Rural England and also tourist office, April–Oct.
Shire Horse Centre, Barretts Farm, East Lane: farm with show horses ('Gentle Giants'), ponies, Syrian goats, carriages, gardens and teas. April–Sept. Wed. & Sun., July–Aug. daily.

Elmstead Market (4 miles east of Colchester, A133): Beth Chatto Gardens, laid out by the well-known gardener. March–Oct. Mon.–Sat. 9–5, Nov.–Feb. Mon.–Fri. 9–4, closed Bank Hol.

Finchingfield (northeast of Thaxted, B1053/B1057): St John the Baptist: Norman west portal in tower, roodscreen with elaborate Gothic tracery.
Spains Hall: Elizabethan brick-built manor house north of Finchingfield, 1585, seat of Ruggles-Brise family. Sir Evelyn established the first school for young offenders (1902), named after the town of Borstal in Kent. Gardens May–July Sun. and May Bank Hol. Mon. 2–5. Tour of house (with butler) by appointment, ℘ 0371/810266.

Foulness Island: in Thames estuary, two villages, one pub, one shop. Important breeding-grounds for seabirds. No visitors allowed, as it is a testing area for the Ministry of Defence, to whom the island belongs. It was here that Henry Shrapnel tested the projectile named after him (first used 1804).

Gosfield Hall (north of Braintree, A1017): Tudor country house with later renovations. May–Sept. Wed. & Thurs. 2–5.

Great Dunmow (west of Braintree, A120): small town famous for the Flitch Trials, held every second year: any married couple that can prove they have lived for a year and a day without quarrelling will win a flitch – a side of bacon. The custom is said to go back to 1120, introduced by an Augustinian prior in order to encourage Christian marriage; other sources attribute it to Baron Robert Fitzwalter in the 13th century. It is mentioned in *Piers Plowman* (14th century) and Chaucer's *Canterbury Tales*, and was revived through Harrison Ainsworth's novel *The Flitch of Bacon* (1854).

Great Warley Art nouveau church interior. Kept locked – contact Rectory Lodge for keys, ℘ 0277/219816 or 213660.

Harlow (north of London, M11): designed by Frederick Gibberd in 1947 to relieve London (20 years before the classic new town of Milton Keynes was built in Buckinghamshire). Originally intended for 60,000 inhabitants, it now has over 80,000. Different estates have sculptures by Barbara Hepworth, Elisabeth Frink, Henry

Moore (Family Group, 1954–5) etc. There are controversial plans for further extensions which might lead to a giant conglomerate of suburbs in London's green belt area.

Mark Hall Cycle Museum & Gardens, Muskham Road, off First Avenue, ∅ 0279/39680, housed in converted 19th-century stables. Sun.–Thur. 10–1, 2–5.

Harwich: founded *c.*1200 by Roger Bigod, Earl of Norfolk. Christopher Jones, captain of the 'Mayflower', came from here (21 King's Head Street). High & Low Lighthouses, 1818.

The Redoubt: Martello Tower, 1808, now a museum of local history. Easter–Oct. daily 2–5, Sun. 10–12.

Hempstead (east of Saffron Walden, B1054): St Andrew's, Perpendicular church with monument to William Harvey, physician to James I and Charles I, who discovered the circulation of the blood (*Circuitis Sanguinis,* 1628). Outstanding bust by London sculptor Edward Marshall (after 1657), and tomb-chest of single block of Carrara marble. The famous 18th-century highwayman Dick Turpin came from here. His father was landlord of the Bell Inn.

Horham Hall (2 miles southwest of Thaxted, B1051). Country home of Sir John Cutte, King Henry VIII's lord treasurer; begun in 1502, tower *c.*1580, one of the finest pre-Reformation brick houses in Essex. P.

Ingatestone Hall (between Chelmsford and Brentwood, off A12), ∅ 0277/353010:

Tudor country house, built 1540–65 for Sir William Petre, minister under Henry VIII and Edward VI, who organized the Dissolution of the Monasteries after the Reformation. Gatehouse with clocktower and motto 'Sans Dieu Rien'. Still owned by Petre family. April–July Fri.–Sun., July–Sep. Wed.–Sun. and Bank Hol. 1–6.

The Cricketers, Mill Green (northwest of Ingatestone): pub with collection of cricket memorabilia.

Layer Marney Tower (6 miles southwest of Colchester, B1022): Tudor gatehouse, *c.*1520. April–Sept. Thurs. & Sun. 2–6, July & Aug. also Tues., Wed., Fri. and Bank Hol. 2–6.

Saffron Walden (southeast of Cambridge, A130): The Fry Art Gallery, Bridge End Gardens, Castle Street: charming provincial gallery with works from the 1930's–80's by members of the artists' circle at Great Bardfield. Easter–Oct. Sat. & Sun. 2.45–5.30.

Museum, next to castle ruins, Museum Street, April–Oct. 10–5, Nov.–March Mon.–Sat. 11–4, Sun. & Bank Hol. 2.30–5.

Southend-on-Sea: Prittlewell Priory Museum, Priory Park, ∅ 0702/342878: former Cluniac monastery, now museum of local and natural history. Tues.–Sat. 10–1, 2–5.

Southchurch Hall: half-timbered manor house, 14th century, now municipal museum. Tues.–Sat. 10–1, 2–5.

Stondon Massey (southwest of Chelmsford): The Elizabethan composer William Byrd lived for some 30 years in Stondon Place until his death in 1623.

Tilbury Fort (22 miles east of London): 17th-century fort on north bank of Thames. April–Sep. daily 10–6, Oct.-March Tue.–Sun. 10–4. EH.

University of Essex, Wivenhoe Park (2 miles southeast of Colchester): founded 1962. Main study areas: electronics and communications, social sciences, comparative literature, philosophy, Japanese studies. Information: ∅ 0206/873333 or 873666. Own university theatre and exhibitions, ∅ 0206/861946.
The house at Wivenhoe Park is now used as a conference centre and hotel, ∅ 0206/864609.

Waltham Abbey (northeast of London, M25/A112): Epping Forest District Museum, 39/41 Sun Street, ∅ 0992/716882: local history museum in two half-timbered houses, 16th and 18th century. Fri.–Mon. 2–5, Tues. 12–5.

Walthamstow (northeast London, south of Epping Forest): William Morris Gallery, Lloyd Park, Forest Road (A503), ∅ 081/527 5544 ext. 4390: formerly home of Morris' parents; exhibition of his works and those of his friends in the Arts & Crafts Movement. Tues.–Sat. 10–1, 2–5, first Sun. of every month 10–12, 2–5. William Morris Society, Kelmscott House, 26 Upper Mall, Hammersmith, London W6.

Wickham Bishops (between Colchester and Chelmsford, B1022): Great Ruffins, house built by the architect and designer Arthur M. Mackmurdo, 1904. Opposite is another house he designed, also with a central lantern. He himself lived in a bungalow now named Mackmurdo's, Great Lodge Road, on the corner of Beacon Hill. Mackmurdo was one of the early British art nouveau designers, and a pioneer of the Arts & Crafts Movement. He died here in 1942.

Widdington (4 miles south of Saffron Walden): Prior's Hall Barn, early 14th century, 1379–1920 owned by New College, Oxford, now by English Heritage. April–Sept. Any reasonable time at weekends.

Wivenhoe Park: see University of Essex.

Suffolk

Acton (northeast of Sudbury): In the village church, All Saints, one of the oldest and finest brasses in England, a memorial to Sir Robert de Bures, c.1320. Lifesize Georgian monument to Robert Jennens (d.1725), adjutant to the Duke of Marlborough.

Aldeburgh (A1094, east of A12): Moot Hall: Tudor town hall, local history museum (fishing, coast conservation, etc.). April–May only Sun. 2.30–5, June and Sept. daily 2.30–5, July and Aug. daily 10.30–12.30, 2.30–5.
St Peter and St Paul, 16th-century parish church with 14th-century tower and octagonal Jacobean pulpit from which Crabbe preached; memorial window to Benjamin Britten by John Piper, 1980.
Aldeburgh Foundation, Box Office, High Street, Suffolk IP15 5AX, ∅ 0728/453543

or 452935: programmes and tickets for Aldeburgh Festival; also information about the Britten-Pears School for Advanced Musical Studies.
The Britten-Pears Library, The Red House, Golf Lane, ✆ 0728/852615: access only by appointment, and only for the purpose of study.

Aldringham Craft Market (northwest of Aldeburgh, B1122/B1353): ceramics and other handicrafts. Mon.–Sat. 10–5.30, Sun. 10–12, 2–5.30.

Aspall Hall (north of Ipswich, B1077): Jacobean manor house with Queen Anne façade, early 18th century. Has produced Aspall Cider since 1728. Exhibition of old stone and wooden presses, etc. Mon.–Fri. 9–12.30, 1.30–3.30. ✆ 0728/860510.

Badley (northwest of Ipswich, southwest of Stowmarket, off B1113): St Mary's, one of many fine village churches, mainly 13th century, untouched by Victorian restorers; faded, silver-grey oak seating.

Barham (northwest of Ipswich, off A140): Village church, St Mary's, with stone sculpture by Henry Moore, Madonna and Child, 1948–9, originally designed as war memorial.

Boxford (between Sudbury and Hadleigh, A1071): beautiful village from time of medieval cloth industry. Large 15th-century Perpendicular church, with 14th-century oak roof in north porch.
Laurimore Gallery, 29 Swan Street, ✆ 0787/210138: art and handicrafts, established by Jon Laurimore, actor and former son-in-law of Augustus John. Telephone for details of changing exhibitions.

Bramfield (southeast of Halesworth, A144): St Andrew's: free-standing Norman round tower, Gothic rood screens with painted dado and traceried coving (c.1500). Baroque monument by Jacobean court sculptor Nicholas Stone: Arthur Coke (d.1629) kneeling in knight's armour, next to his wife Elizabeth, lying with a baby in her arm; her alabaster figure is the more exquisitely carved, so perhaps only this is by Stone.
Crinkle-crankle wall opposite church.

Brantham (southwest of Ipswich, A137): Village church, St Michael's, with altarpiece by John Constable, *Christ and the Children*, 1804.

Brent Eleigh Hall (southeast of Lavenham, A1141): country house renovated in Neo-Georgian style by Edwin Lutyens 1933–4. Tuscan portico. P.

Bury St Edmunds: Gershom Parkington Collection of Clocks and Watches, 8 Angel Hill, ✆ 0284/60255, situated in Queen Anne house, established by local cellist Frederic Gershom Parkington; pieces by famous 17th-century English clockmakers; early German table, tabernacle and crucifix clocks; curiosities and rare items, including a Time-Stick – a sun-dial on a shepherd's crook from Tiverton, and the so-called Atmos clock, which never needs winding because it draws its energy from continual changes in temperature. Mon.–Sat. 10–5, Sun. 2–5.
Market Cross Art Gallery, Cornhill:

designed as a theatre by Robert Adam, 1774. Changing exhibitions, Tues.–Sat. 10.30–4.30.

Moyse's Hall Museum, Cornhill, ∅ 02847/69834: local history, with items from Roman times, from the Anglo-Saxon village of West Stow, the treasure of Isleham, curiosities and obscurities. Mon. –Sat. 10–5, Sun. 2–5.

Cathedral; Evensong Thurs. 5, Sun. 3.30.

Theatre Royal, Westgate Street: Regency theatre, 1819, by William Wilkins. NT. Box Office 10–6, ∅ 02847/69505.

Weekly market at Cornhill and Butter-market: Wed. & Sat.

Cattle market between King's Road and Risbygate Street: Wed.

Cavendish (7.5 miles northwest of Sud-bury, A1092): headquarters and museum of Sue Ryder Foundation, ∅ 0787/280252. Daily 10–5.30. Light meals.

Nether Hall: half-timbered house, 16th century, wine-growing (Cavendish Manor Mueller Thurgau). Wine tasting daily 11–4.

Hodder Brown Ltd: delicatessen owned by former *New York Times* correspondent Erica Brown.

Clare (7.5 miles northwest of Sudbury, A1092): beautiful little town on the Stour. Perpendicular church opposite former vicarage, 1473, now local history museum called The Ancient House: May–Sept. Wed., Fri., Sat. & Bank Hols. 2.30–4.30, Sun. 11–12.30, 2.30–4.30.

Cratfield (west of Halesworth, between B1117 and B1123): Gothic village church, St Mary's, with magnificent 15th-century Seven Sacraments font.

Crows Hall (near Debenham, north of Ipswich, B1077): early 16th-century coun-try house, brick built, surrounded by romantic moat. P.

Debenham (north of Ipswich, B1077): small town near source of Deben. Half-timbered former Town Hall, c.1500. St Mary's: pre-Norman church tower, bells 1761.

Dunwich (north of Aldeburgh, east of A12): Local history museum, tracing story of sunken town. April–Oct. daily 11.30–4.30.

East Anglia Transport Museum, Carlton Colville (southwest of Lowestoft, B1384): June–Sept. Sat. & Sun. 2–4, Aug. Mon.–Fri. 2–4.

East Bergholt (southwest of Ipswich, A12/B1070): John Constable's birthplace. St Mary's (1350–1550), church with separ-ate bell-house, 1531. Handbell-ringing. Sun. 10.30–11, and in summer 6–6.30 p.m. as well.

Easton Farm Park (2 miles northwest of Wickham Market, off A12/B1116): Vic-torian farm with old machines and implements, smithy, nature trail, adventure playground, etc. Easter–Oct. daily 10.30–6.

Erwarton Hall (near Shotley, southeast of Ipswich, A138): Elizabethan manor house, 1575. P. Spectacular gatehouse, c.1549, with gables and chimney-like turrets, more an abstract sculpture than a gatehouse. Anne Boleyn spent part of her childhood here, and her heart is said to be buried in the village church.

Euston Hall (3 miles south of Thetford, A1088): 'A place capable of all that is pleasant and delightful in Nature, and improved by Art to every extreme that Nature is able to produce' (Defoe, 1722). Country seat of Duke of Grafton. Paintings by Van Dyck, Stubbs, Lely, Reynolds, Hoppner, etc. Park by John Evelyn and William Kent, garden temple (1746), church in style of Wren. June–Sept. Thurs. 2.30–5.

Felixstowe: Britain's largest container port. Martello Tower, South Hill, 1510–12. Landguard Fort: 1540–5, erected to defend port of Harwich, renovated several times, with Victorian interior and museum. May–Sept. Wed. & Sun. 2.30–5.

Flatford Mill (½ mile southeast of East Bergholt on northern bank of Stour): watermill that belonged to Constable's father, NT. Not open to public. In 1946 The Field Studies Council converted it to a centre for studies – now one of nine such centres. Courses on plant and animal life in the region, ornithology, ecology, photography, portrait and landscape painting, etc. Accommodation in nearby Willy Lott's Cottage. Programme and registration: Flatford Mill Field Centre, East Bergholt, Essex CO7 6UL, ∅ 0206/298283 or 298271.
Bridge Cottage: NT information shop, tea garden and boat hire. Easter–Oct. Wed. –Sun. & Bank Hol. Mon., July & Aug. daily 11–5.30.

Framlingham (19 miles northeast of Ipswich, B1119/B1116): Norman castle of the Earls and Dukes of Norfolk. April–Sep. daily 10–6, Oct.–Mar. daily (except Mon.) 10–4. EH.

Gifford's Hall (south of Hadleigh, between B1070 and B1068): early 16th-century country house, begun c.1430. Brick gatehouse, inner court and half-timbered wing, hall with elaborate dragon-beam ceiling. April–Oct., daily 12–6. P.

Glevering Hall (north of Wickham Market, off A12): late 18th-century country mansion, extended 1834–5 by Decimus Burton, orangery with glass dome on wrought-iron columns, gardens by Humphry Repton. P.

Hadleigh (west of Ipswich, A1071): small town with fine 15th–18th-century houses. Birthplace of Victorian sculptor Thomas Woolner, a founder of the Pre-Raphaelite Brotherhood.
Headquarters of East Anglian Tourist Board: Toppesfield Hall, ∅ 0473/822922.

Hawstead (4 miles south of Bury St Edmunds, off A134): village church of All Saints, with alabaster monument to 12-year-old Dorothy, daughter of Sir Robert Drury, who in 1611 commissioned John Donne to write his wife's elegy *An Anatomie of the World*. Marble monument to Sir Robert by the London court sculptor Nicholas Stone (after 1615).

Helmingham Hall (between Ipswich and Debenham, B1077): Tudor country home of the Tollemaches. Only the park and

Elizabethan garden are open to the public. Cream teas. May–Sept. Sun. 2–6.

Hengrave Hall (3 miles northwest of Bury St Edmunds, A1101): Tudor country house, now centre for ecumenical meetings and other religious events, as well as seminars, concerts, summer music school, etc.: Hengrave Hall Centre, Bury St Edmunds, Suffolk, IP28 6LZ, ∅ 0284/701561. In the park a small church with early Norman round tower and monuments to the Kytsons and Gages of Hengrave Hall.

Heveningham Hall (5 miles southwest of Halesworth, B1117): Georgian country mansion, late 18th century. Interiors by James Wyatt. Park by Capability Brown. Orangery by Wyatt, 1791. P.

Hollesley (11 miles east of Ipswich, A12/B1083): Borstal overlooking Ore estuary. Brendan Behan was detained here in 1939 for IRA activities; he writes about it in *Borstal Boy*, 1958.

Hoxne (3 miles east of Diss, B1118): Pronounced Hoxen. St Edmund was found here and killed by the Danes, betrayed by the golden glint of his spurs as he hid below the bridge. St Aethelbert's: fine murals of the Seven Deadly Sins.

Ickworth (Horringer, 3 miles southwest of Bury St Edmunds, A143): country mansion of the Earls of Bristol. Paintings, furniture and silverware. Park, cafeteria. April & Oct. only Sat. & Sun., May–Sept. Tues., Wed., Fri., Sat., Sun. & Bank Holiday Mon. 1.30–5.30. NT.

Iken (west of Aldeburgh): St Botolph's, c.1300, remote thatched church on south bank of Alde estuary.

Ipswich: Christchurch Mansion, Christchurch Park, ∅ 0473/53246: built in 1548, a museum since 1896: styles of furniture, chinaware, etc. from Tudor times to 19th century; paintings by Gainsborough, Constable, Munnings, Steer, etc. Tues.–Sat. 10–5, Sun. 2.30–4.30.

Ipswich Museum, High Street, ∅ 0473/213761: local and natural history, folklore, geology, archaeology, copies of treasures from Sutton Hoo and Mildenhall, fossil collection. Tues.–Sat. 10–5.

St Peter's, St Peter Street: Norman font of black Tournai marble, one of ten in England, with lion frieze.

Ixworth (8 miles north of Bury St Edmunds, A143/A1088): Ixworth Abbey: Augustinian monastery founded c.1170; after Reformation, given to Coddington family (in exchange for site of Nonsuch Palace). Cellar with 13th-century ribbed vault. Former dormitory in east wing almost completely preserved. Georgian façade, c.1800. Now country home of a London lawyer.

Waterfowl Farm: on River Black Bourn, more than 120 species.

Kentwell Hall: see Long Melford.

Lavenham (between Ipswich and Bury St Edmunds, A1141): The Guildhall, Market Place: c.1528, exhibition of medieval textiles, chamber concerts. NT. April–Oct. daily 11–5.

The Priory, Water Street: beautifully

restored half-timbered medieval house. Pictures by Hungarian painter Ervin Bossanyi. Herb garden. April–Oct. 10.30–5.30.

Little Hall, Market Place: half-timbered house, 14–15th century, its centre consisting of what was originally a hall with open roof trusses. Headquarters of the Suffolk Preservation Society (see page 153ff.). April–Oct. Sat. & Sun. 2.30–6.

Laxfield (southwest of Halesworth, B1117): 15th-century Perpendicular church, with Seven Sacraments font. Opposite, half-timbered guild house, early 16th century, now local history museum. Behind church, King's Head, a thatched village pub with old interior: instead of a bar, there are highbacked benches round the fireplace.

Workshop of toymaker Ron Fuller and his wife, the painter Moss Fuller, who gives courses in screen printing. Willow Cottage, ∅ 098683/317.

Jacob's Farm Museum of Childhood, St Jacob's Hall (east of Laxfield, B1117): farm with toy collection 1800–1960, animals and garden. Easter–Oct. Tues.–Thurs. 10–5, Sun. all year 12–5.

Leiston (north of Aldeburgh, B1122): Summerhill School, Westward Ho! ∅ 0728/830540 & 830619: boarding school founded 1924 by A. S. Neill.

The Long Shop Museum, Main Street, ∅ 0728/832189: industrial museum in 19th-century factory for agricultural machinery, with old tractors, steamrollers, diesel engines, etc. April–Oct. Mon.–Sat. 10–5, Sun. 11–5.

Little Glemham Hall (Little Glemham, 17 miles northeast of Ipswich, A12): Elizabethan country mansion, red brick, altered 1712–22. Early Georgian interior. Apart from one Gainsborough, no paintings or furniture of note. A lot of bric-a-brac. Everyday life of the servants well documented in their attic rooms. Fine rose garden. Owned by Cobbold family since 1923. P.

Little Haugh Hall (near Norton, A1088, east of Bury St Edmunds): country home of Reverend Cox Macro, archaeologist and court chaplain to George II and patron of the Flemish painter Peter Tillemans, who died here in 1734. Some of his paintings are still here. P.

Little Wenham Hall (near Chapel St Mary, southwest of Ipswich, off A12): small, late 13th-century fortified manor house, with linked tower and two-storeyed house, one of the first brick buildings in post-Roman times, and 'one of the incunabula of English domestic architecture' (Pevsner). P.

Long Melford (13 miles south of Bury St Edmunds, A134/A1092): Melford Hall: Elizabethan country mansion and garden. Beatrix Potter Room. NT. May–Sept. Wed., Thurs., Sat., Sun. & Bank Holiday Mon. 2–6, April & Oct. Sat. & Sun. 2–5.30.

Kentwell Hall: Elizabethan mansion with moat, park and garden, restored by exemplary private initiative. Can be hired for weddings, parties, conferences and advertising. Collection of Tudor costumes. April–June, Sun. only, July–Sept. daily 2–5. Tudor Festival in summer: has its own hours at weekends, ∅ 0787/310207.

Lower Ufford (northeast of Ipswich, A12/B1438): village church with spectacularly ornate wooden Gothic font canopy, over 16 feet high, c.1450. Poppyhead and animal benches, 15th century.

Lowestoft: Maritime Museum, Whapload Road, Sparrow's Nest Park: history of local fishing industry and seafaring. May–Sept. daily 10–5.
Marina Theatre: built in 1878 as skating rink, later became a cinema, and has been a theatre since 1988. Partly Edwardian Neoclassical, partly Art Deco.

Mildenhall (northwest of Bury St Edmunds, A1101/A11): Museum, King Street: local history and archaeology. Wed., Thurs., Sat. & Sun. 2.30–4.30, Fri. 11–4.30.

Minsmere (north of Aldeburgh, east of A12): some 1,500 acres of marshland, forest and moor, where since 1948 the Royal Society for the Protection of Birds has been safeguarding some 200 species.

Moulton (east of Newmarket, B1085): packhorse bridge over River Kennet, 15th century.

Nayland (southeast of Sudbury, A134): beautiful village on the Stour, 15th- and 16th-century half-timbered houses. Perpendicular church with tower porch of 1525, painted panels from a 15th-century choir screen, altarpiece by Constable, 1810. The former village school behind the church is now the studio of the weaver Peter Collingwood, ℘ 0206/262401.

Newmarket: Jockey Club, High Street,

℘ 0638/664151: the Clerk of the Course provides information about racing and training. The National Horseracing Museum, 99 High Street, ℘ 0638/667333: opened by the Queen in 1983, with exhibits on loan from the Royal Collection. April–Nov. Tues.–Sat. & Bank Hol. Mon. 10–5, Sun. 2–5, in July & Aug. also on Mon. & Sun. 12–5.
The National Stud, ℘ 0638/663464. Visits by appointment. Guided tours April–Sept. Mon.–Fri. 11.15 & 2.30.
Tattersalls, Terrace House, ℘ 0638/665931: Europe's oldest and biggest auctioneers for thoroughbreds.

Otley Hall (10 miles northeast of Ipswich, B1077/B1079): 15th-century country house, timber and brick, with moat. Former family house of Bartholomew Gosnold, who initiated the first voyage by East Anglian settlers to America in 1606. East-Anglian-American Heritage Museum now being planned. P. Only by appointment. ℘ 047339/264.

Pakenham (6 miles northeast of Bury St Edmunds, A143): Watermill, Grimstone End, Georgian façade, Tudor foundations. April–Sept. Wed., Sat., Sun. & Bank Hol. Mon. 2–5.30.

Polstead (between Sudbury and Hadleigh): St Mary's: Norman piers with brick arches, the earliest English brickwork after Roman times.
Site of the Murder in the Red Barn (1827). The thriller-writer Ruth Rendell lives on the outskirts in a 16th-century farmhouse.

Redgrave (northeast of Bury St Edmunds,

A143/B1113): St Mary the Virgin: decorative parish church with some outstanding monuments by Nicholas Stone (1616) and others .

Redgrave Hall: country house, 18th century, demolished in 1960. Octagonal gatehouse with dome survives, 1767, by Capability Brown.

Saxtead Green Post-Mill (2 miles west of Framlingham, A1120): built 1796. April–Sept. Mon.–Sat. 10–6. EH.

Shrubland Hall (6 miles north of Ipswich, A140): manor house, c.1770, with Victorian terrace garden by Sir Charles Barry, 1848. Now Shrubland Hall Health Clinic, Coddenham, Ipswich IP6 9QH, ∅ 0473/ 830404.

Sizewell (near Leiston, east of A12): England's largest nuclear power station, 1961–6, with second station under construction, due to open 1994. Information centre daily 10–4.

Snape (6 miles west of Aldeburgh, A1094): Snape Maltings Riverside Centre: concert hall for the Aldeburgh Festivals, teashop, pub and river bar, art and handicraft galleries, daily 10–6. Malthouse museum and hotel planned.

Somerleyton Hall (5 miles northwest of Lowestoft, off B1074): early Victorian country mansion. Park with maze and miniature railway. April & May Thurs., Fri. & Bank Hol., June–Sept. Tues.–Fri. & Sun. 2–5.

Southwold: St Edmund's: one of the finest

Perpendicular churches in Suffolk, c.1430–60; south portal and west side of tower with flushwork chequered pattern; hammer-beam roof with angels and saints, c.1500; early 16th-century rood screen across nave and aisles, with Gothic tracery and painted dado with angels, prophets and 12 Apostles; 15th-century pulpit on single slender column, original colours restored (too garishly) in 1930; Gothic-style font canopy, 1935; Jack-of-the-Clock, c.1480, in authentic armour from Wars of the Roses; in the roof of the Lady Chapel two portraits on bosses: Mary Tudor and her second husband, Charles Brandon, Duke of Suffolk, who both lived for a time in the nearby Henham House.

Museum, 1 Bartholomew Green: local history, situated in so-called Dutch Cottage, 17th century. May–Sept. daily 2.30–4.30.

Stoke-by-Nayland (southwest of Ipswich, A12/B1068): former cloth trade village overlooking Stour Valley. Perpendicular church, tower 1439–62, Howard family brass with ancestors of two of Henry VIII's wives (Catherine Howard and Anne Boleyn). Maltings and Guild Hall, half-timbered, 16th century, NT.

Stowmarket (13 miles northwest of Ipswich, A45): Museum of East Anglian Life, ∅ 0449/612229: open-air, covering everyday life from 3000 BC to 1910, with collection of agricultural implements, carts, steam engines, reconstructed workshops, watermill, wind pump, smithy etc. April–Oct. daily 10–5.

Sudbury (west of Ipswich, A134): Gainsborough's house, 46 Gainsborough Street, Ø 0787/72958: painter's birthplace, with paintings, drawings, documents about his life and work, changing exhibitions by contemporary craftsmen. Tues.–Sat. 10–5, Sun. & Bank Hol. 2–5, Nov.–March Tue.–Sat. 10–4, Sun. 2–4.

The Quay, Ø 0787/74745: 18th-century silo and warehouse on the Stour, restored as arts centre with theatre, films and music, bistro and bar.

Weekly market: Thurs. & Sat.

Suffolk Wildlife & Rare Breeds Park, Kessingland (A12 south of Lowestoft): also has miniature railway, etc. April–Oct. daily 10–6.30.

Sutton Hoo (southeast of Woodbridge, B1083): Anglo-Saxon graveyard, where the famous burial ship and its treasure were found (now in British Museum). Excavations still in progress. Visits by appointment, Ø 0394/460309. Guided tours April–Oct. Sat. & Sun. 2 & 3 p.m.

Tattingstone (5 miles south of Ipswich, A137): three cottages disguised as church ruins, a folly known as the 'Tattingstone Wonder', built in 1790 as an eyecatcher for Mr White's country house: he thought that people tended to marvel so often at nothing that he should actually give them something to marvel at.

Village church, St Mary's: monumental marble sculpture by John Flaxman, 1814.

Thorington Hall (2 miles southeast of Stoke-by-Nayland, B1068, west of A12), described by the National Trust as one of the biggest and finest half-timbered houses

in Suffolk, built in the 16th century, extended 1620–30. NT. Open on written application to Thorington Hall, Stoke-by-Nayland, Colchester CO6 4SS.

Walpole (southwest of Halesworth, B1117): Congregational Chapel, 5 Salters Lane: former farmhouse (c.1600), converted to a chapel in mid-17th century. Original seating and gallery. Used since 1988 for chamber concerts: 'Summer Music at Walpole Old Chapel', Ø 098684/412.

Wenhaston (southeast of Halesworth, between A12 and B1123): parish church of St Peter, depiction of Domesday painted on wooden boards, c.1480, probably by a monk from Blythburgh: Christ as judge on the rainbow, while St Michael weighs souls; the jaws of hell are depicted as the mouth of a giant fish.

West Stow Anglo-Saxon Village (8 miles northwest of Bury St Edmunds, off A1101): April–Oct. Tues.–Sat. 2–5, Sun. 11–1, 2–5.

Wingfield College (7 miles southeast of Diss, B1118): cathedral school of 1362, restored as arts centre, and since 1981 site of one of East Anglia's most lively rural festivals, with concerts, exhibitions, readings, etc. Garden, home-made teas. April–Sept. Sat., Sun. & Bank Hol. Mon. 2–6, Ø 037984/505.

Woodbridge (northeast of Ipswich, A12): small market town and yachting port on the Deben.

Museum, Market Hill: local history, excavations from Sutton Hoo, April–Oct.

Thurs.–Sat. & Bank Hol. 11–4, Sun. 2.30–4.30.

St Mary: Perpendicular church, west tower c.1480, north porch with geometrical and emblematic flushwork.

Seckford Hospital, Seckford Street: fine Victorian almshouse, 1838–40.

Shire Hall, Market Hill: 1575/late 17th century.

Tide Mill, 1793: July–Sept. daily 11–1, 2.30–5, June & Oct. only Sat. & Sun.

Woolpit (east of Bury St Edmunds, A45): according to local etymology, Woolpit = wolf-pit, the place where the last wolf in Suffolk was killed. Large brickworks from 17th century to Second World War, famous for bright-coloured, durable limestone bricks exported worldwide, including to Washington, where they were used in the construction of The White House.

St Mary: Perpendicular church with elaborate south portal, c.1430–55, double hammer-beam with angels (mainly replicas, 1875).

Norfolk

Alby Crafts (near Erpingham, A140 Norwich–Cromer): situated in 19th-century farmhouse with workshops for potters, silversmiths, cabinet-makers, weavers, etc. Courses for beginners and advanced students. ℘ 0263/761590. Open for business and teas March–Dec. daily except Mon. 10–5.

Attleborough (southwest of Wymond-ham, A11): St Mary's, 14th-century church with Norman tower, perfectly preserved late-15th-century rood screen.

Peter Beales Roses, see under Gardens, page 501.

Beeston Hall (Beeston St Lawrence, 11 miles northeast of Norwich, A1151): country home of Preston family, built 1786 in style of Gothic Revival, with flint façade, Georgian interior. Teas in the orangery. Parish church with Anglo-Saxon round tower and monuments to the Prestons. April–mid Sept. Fri., Sun. & Bank Hol., Aug. also Wed. 2–5.30. Guided tour with owner, by appointment, ℘ 0692/630771.

Berney Arms Mill (west of Great Yarmouth, off A47): drainage mill, over 65 feet high, in Halvergate marsh, the tallest marsh mill in Norfolk, built 1870. Complete with machinery and exhibition, April–Sept. daily 10–6. EH.

Binham Priory (west of Cromer, B1388): Benedictine ruins in field on edge of village with 200 inhabitants. Founded in 1091 by nephew of William the Conqueror. The early Gothic west front with monumental traceried windows and blind arcading exhibits what is believed to be the first example of bar tracery in Britain, earlier even than that of Westminster Abbey. The Norman nave with gallery and triforium of Barnack stone, begun in 1130, became the parish church after the Reformation; the choir and eastern sections were destroyed. Magnificent Perpendicular Seven Sacrament font. Beautifully carved 16th-century benches. Of the priory buildings themselves, only the foundations remain.

Blickling Hall (2 miles northwest of Aylsham, B1354): Jacobean mansion, garden and park. Cafeteria in former servants' wing. Headquarters of National Trust in East Anglia, with workshops for restoration. April–Oct. daily exc. Mon. & Thurs. (open Bank Hol. Mon.) 1–5. NT.

Bressingham Live Steam Museum and Gardens (2.5 miles west of Diss, A1066): collection of steam engines, narrow gauge railway running through park with over 5,000 Alpine and other types of plant. April–Oct. daily 10–5.30.

Broads, The: For information, contact the Broads Authority Information Centres at Hoveton/Wroxham ⌀ 0603/782281, Ranworth ⌀ 060/549453, Beccles ⌀ 0502/713196. The Broads Authority headquarters is at 18 Colegate, Norwich NR3 1BQ, ⌀ 0603/610734.

Broadland Conservation Centre: see Ranworth.

Burnham Deepdale (north coast, A149): village church with Anglo-Saxon round tower, Norman font with magnificent allegory 'Labours of the Months': digging, sowing, weeding, etc. – an early gardening manual in stone.
The parish church in the neighbouring village of Burnham Norton has a late Gothic pulpit of 1450.

Burnham Market (north coast, B1155/ B1355): medieval centre of the seven Burnhams. Fine Georgian houses. Westgate Hall, designed by Sir John Soane in 1783. In neighbouring Burnham Overy, windmill

(1814) and Georgian complex of watermill (1737), maltings and cottages.

Caister-on-Sea (4 miles north of Great Yarmouth): Caister Castle, early 15th century, Caister Hall with Georgian façade. Large collection of vintage cars. May–Oct. daily exc. Sat. 10.30–5.

Caister St Edmund (3 miles southeast of Norwich, between A140 and B1332): The ruins of a Roman town Venta Icenorum, built after Boadicea's defeat in AD 61, inhabited till 5th century and now meadows. The town walls, built of flint at the end of the 2nd century with brick cladding, were 20 feet high and covered an area of 1,080 × 1,380 feet. After the departure of the Romans, another town profited from the decline and fall of Caister, as witnessed by an old rhyme: 'Caister was a town when Norwich was none. / Norwich was built of Caister stone.'

Castle Acre (4 miles north of Swaffham, A1065): ruins of Norman monastery, Easter–Sept. daily 10–6, Oct.–Easter daily (except Mon.) 10–4. EH.
St James: Perpendicular parish church. Painted Gothic rood screen with 12 Apostles, pulpit with pictures of the four Church Fathers – both c.1400.

Castle Rising (5 miles northeast of King's Lynn): Norman keep, Easter–Sept. daily 10–6, Oct.–Easter daily (except Mon.) 10–4. EH.
St Lawrence's: 12th-century parish church, west front with Norman blind arcades; Norman font, 13th-century choir, ribbed vault.

Trinity Hospital: almshouse 1609–15, established by the Howards. Jacobean furniture. Tues., Thurs., Sat. 10–12, 2–6.

Cawston (northwest of Norwich, B1149/B1145): Perpendicular village church of St Agnes: grand hammer-beam roof, 15th century, with tracery and angels; Gothic rood screen, 20 Apostles and saints in dado panels; Plough Gallery.

Cockley Cley (3 miles southwest of Swaffham): Iceni Village and Museum – reconstructed Iceni village. Local history museum with agricultural implements, coaches, etc. April–Oct. daily 12.30–5.30, mid-July to mid-Sept. daily 11.30–5.30.

Cromer: Perpendicular church of St Peter and St Paul, eastern window in southern aisle by Morris & Co., c.1874.
The Cromer Museum, Tucker Street: local history in former fisherman's cottage. Mon.–Sat. 10–5, Sun. 2–5.

Denver (south of King's Lynn, A10): The Old Denver Sluices, by John Rennie, extended with steel gates 1923; new sluices 1959. They drain about 860,000 acres of fenland.

Diss (southwest of Norwich, A140/A143): small town on Waveney, built round 6-acre lake. (Diss derives from Anglo-Saxon *dice* = standing waters.) Late Gothic parish church, St Mary's, west tower c.1300. Unitarian Chapel, 1822 (Denmark Street): simple Regency. Victorian Corn Hall, 1854. Some fine half-timbered pubs: Dolphin Inn, Saracen's Head, Greyhound Inn. Area in danger of overdevelopment.

Ditchingham Hall (north of Bungay, B1332): Queen Anne house, c.1711. Park by Capability Brown. Visits only by appointment, ✆ 050844/250.

Earsham (1.3 miles west of Bungay, A143): Otter Trust, on north bank of Waveney, founded by Philip Wayre, who was the first person in England since the late 19th century to breed European and Asian otters in captivity. The European otters bred here are released to settle in East Anglian rivers. There are now over 250 breeding-grounds in East Anglia. April–Oct. daily 10.30–6.

East Dereham (16 miles west of Norwich, A47): Bishop Bonner's Cottage: 16th century, with pargeting, local history. May–Sept. Tue.–Sat. 2.30–5.
William Cowper, 'England's sweetest and most pious bard' (G. Borrow), died in a house in the market-place (1800). His grave and a memorial window are in the transept of St Nicholas's.

Elsing Hall (northwest of Norwich, between A47 and A1067): flint and brick manor house, surrounded by romantic garden and moat. Hall with open roof trusses and gallery, c.1460–70. For centuries family home of the Hastings (village church contains one of the finest medieval English brasses, in memory of Sir Hugh Hastings, 1347). Since 1983 Elsing Hall has been owned by farm manager, banker and art-collector David Cargill, co-founder of the Eastern Arts Association and committee member of the Arts Council – one of the most active promoters and patrons of cultural life in East Anglia (plate 11). His wife Shirley has laid out one of the finest rose gardens in East Anglia, open on one day in July. $\emptyset$ 036283/224.

Felbrigg Hall (2 miles southwest of Cromer, A148): 17th century, garden and park. April–Oct. daily except Tues. & Fri. 1–5, park 11–5, Bank Hol. Sun. & Mon. 11–5. NT.

Fritton Lake (6 miles southwest of Great Yarmouth, A143): leisure park with garden, wood, reserve for wild duck, pony rides, windsurfing, putting, café, etc. April–Sept. 10–6.

Great Walsingham (6 miles north of Fakenham, B1105): paradoxically smaller than neighbouring, more famous Little Walsingham (see separate entry). Late Gothic parish church, St Peter's, with completely preserved benches; fine font.

Great Witchingham Hall (northwest of Norwich, A1067): Jacobean country house, extended and altered in 19th century. Since 1955 headquarters of Bernard Matthews, Europe's biggest turkey dealer.

Great Yarmouth: Maritime Museum for East Anglia, Marine Parade, $\emptyset$ 0493/ 855746: housed since 1967 in Victorian home for shipwrecked sailors (1861). June–Sept. daily (except Sat.) 10–5. Telephone for winter opening hours.
Norfolk Pillar, South Beach Parade/Fenner Road: 1817–19, by William Wilkins, 144 feet high, 217 steps, figure of Britannia on top. Panoramic view.
St George's, St George's Plain: Queen Anne brick church, 1714–16, by John Price.

The Tolhouse, Tolhouse Street, $\emptyset$ 0493/ 855746: flint building with Great Hall, c.1235, formerly court and prison (1261–1875), now museum of local history. Brass rubbing permitted. Summer Mon.- Fri. 10–1, 2–5, June–Sept. also Sun. Telephone for winter opening hours.
'Lydia Eva', South Quay: fishing boat, 1930, museum of herring fishing. June– Sept. Mon.–Fri. & Sun. 10–1, 2–6.
Elizabethan House Museum, 4 South Quay: merchant's house, 1596, with Elizabethan rooms, furniture and utensils from Tudor times. Mon.–Fri. 10–1, 2–5.30, June–Sept. also Sun.
The Old Merchant's House, Row 117 (near South Quay): together with Nos. 6–8 in Row 111, beautifully restored 17th-century houses. Collection of wrought iron from 17th–19th centuries. April–Sept. daily 10–1, 2–6. EH.
Fishermen's Hospital, 1702, with Dutch gables and tiles.
Winter Gardens, Marine Parade: built of iron and glass, designed by Watson and Harvey, 1878–81, originally in Torquay but moved and reconstructed in Great Yarmouth in 1903. Used today as Swiss Biergarten.

Gressenhall (2.5 miles northwest of East Dereham, B1146): Norfolk Rural Life Museum, Beech House, $\emptyset$ Dereham 860528: fascinating insights into country life during 18th and 19th centuries. April–Oct. Tues.–Sat. 10–5, Sun. 2–5.30.

Grimes Graves (near Weeting, 6 miles northwest of Thetford, B1108): more than 360 Neolithic flint quarries open to the public. April–Sept. daily 10–6, Oct.–March Tues.–Sun. 10–4. EH.

Gunton Park (south of Cromer, between A140 & A149): Neoclassical country house, designed after 1742 by Matthew Brettingham, extended in 1781 by Samuel Wyatt with a colonnaded southern front, which burnt down in 1882. Was home of Suffield family, and a popular centre for the sporting fraternity, especially in the reign of Edward VII. Since 1986 owned by the architect and restorer Kit Martin. In the park is a Neoclassical church designed by Robert Adam, 1769.

Hales (southeast of Norwich, A146, south of Loddon): outstanding Norman village church with round tower. Fine barn.

Happisburgh (B1159, northeast coast): lighthouse, 1791. St Mary's: 15th-century tower, octagonal Perpendicular font with lions, wild men and angels.

Heacham (12 miles north of King's Lynn, A149): Norfolk Lavender Ltd, Caley Mill, ∅ 0485/70384: largest lavender plantation in England, established 1932. Harvest July/Aug. Visits, sales and cream teas end May–mid Sept. daily 10–5.

Heydon Hall (northwest of Norwich, B1149): Elizabethan country mansion, 1581–4. Gardens open on special days, house only by appointment.

Holkham Hall (west of Cromer, A149): Palladian country mansion, early 18th century. Interiors by William Kent. Important art and furniture collection. Still

home of Coke family. Park also by William Kent. St Withburga's, church restored in 1870, with Baroque monuments by Nicholas Stone. Cafeteria. May–Sept. Sun.–Thur. & Bank Hol. Mon. 11.30–5. Aug. also Wed. 1.30–5.

Holt 9 miles southwest of Cromer, A148): Gresham's School, ∅ 026371/327, famous independent school founded in 1555 by Sir John Gresham, Lord Mayor of London. Approximately 500 pupils (mixed). Famous former pupils: Benjamin Britten, W. H. Auden. Auden ('typical little highbrow and difficult child') describes his schooldays there in an essay entitled *The Old School*, 1934.

Horsham St Faith (5 miles northwest of Norwich, A140): Priory of St Faith, founded in 1105 as Benedictine priory. Important 19th-century cycle of frescoes: Crucifixion, St Faith, history of the priory. Since 1990 it has been taken over by Belgian Carmelite nuns.

Horstead (north of Norwich, B1150/ B1354): All Saints, Victorian parish church, with Morris window in south aisle: Courage and Humility, designed by Burne-Jones in 1893.

Houghton Hall (9 miles west of Fakenham, north of A148): country mansion of first English Prime Minister, Sir Robert Walpole, designed by Colen Campbell, 1722–35, interiors by William Kent. Park, collection of model soldiers. Easter–Sept. Thurs., Sun. & Bank Hol. Mon. 12–5.

King's Lynn: Custom House, King Street,

1683. Visits by appointment, ℘ 0553/761063.

Guildhall of the Holy Trinity (Town Hall), Saturday Market Place, 1421, with Tourist Information Office.

Regalia Rooms: April–Oct. Daily 10–5.

King's Lynn Centre for the Arts, Guildhall of St George, 27 King Street, ℘ 0553/773578, medieval building, now theatre, music and exhibition centre with workshops, Mon.–Sat. 10–5.

King's Lynn Festival of Music and the Arts, held in July. Programme and tickets from Festival Box Office, King's Lynn Arts Centre (see above).

King's Lynn Preservation Trust, Thoresby College, ℘ 0553/763871, looks after and restores historic buildings.

Lynn Museum, Old Market Street, ℘ 0553/775001: town and local history, Mon.–Sat. 10–5. Closed Bank Hol.

Town House Museum of Lynn Life, Queen Street: 16th-century merchant's house, with façade and other early 18th-century alterations. Exhibition of town's history, handicrafts, and drinking glasses from 18th and 19th centuries. Tues.–Sat. 10–5. Open Sun. during the summer.

Southgate: only remaining town gate, 1520.

Toby Winteringham Furniture, Whitehouse Bawsey, ℘ 0553/841829: graduate of Royal College of Art in London, has had workshop here since 1981. Combines traditional and Shaker style with new design.

Langley Park (between Norwich and Beccles, east of A146): country mansion designed by Matthew Brettingham, c.1740. Brick-built, with four corner towers. Outstanding rococo stucco ornaments, especially in drawing-room and library. Now a school.

Little Snoring (northeast of Fakenham, off A148): St Andrew's, charming church on outskirts of village, Anglo-Saxon round tower, Norman south portal with early Gothic capitals.

Little Walsingham (5 miles north of Fakenham, B1105): place of pilgrimage since Middle Ages. Shirehall Museum, Common Place: local and pilgrimage history. Easter–Sept. Mon. 10–1, 2–5; Tue.–Sat. 10–5; Sun. 2–5.

The Friary, Fakenham Road: ruins of Franciscan friary, c.1348, P. but occasionally open to visitors.

St Mary's: 14th-century parish church, Gothic Seven Sacraments font, one of the finest examples. Epstein statue in north chapel.

Anglican Pilgrims' Office, Common Place, ℘ 030872/255. Roman Catholic Pilgrim's Office, High Street, ℘ 030872/217.

Mannington Hall (19 miles north of Norwich, east of B1149): country mansion c.1460, extended mid-19th century. Historic rose garden. April–Oct. Sun. 12–5. May–Aug. also Wed., Thur. & Fri. 11–5. Tea room with paintings by graduates of Norwich School of Art. House by appointment only, ℘ 026387/4175.

Middleton Tower (southeast of King's Lynn, off A47): mid-15th century, brick, west wing 1876, with moat. Etched by J. S. Cotman 1812 and 1817. P.

Narford Hall (northwest of Swaffham, off

A47): country seat of Fountaine family, c.1700, with Victorian extensions c.1860. Entrance hall contains 10 mythological paintings by the Venetian artist Antonio Pellegrini, 1708–13. Sir Andrew Fountaine was an important art collector in the early 18th century, as was his Victorian descendant of the same name. A large part of the collection was auctioned by Christie's in 1885. The present owner, Andrew Fountaine, is a founding member of the National Front.

New Buckenham (southwest of Norwich, B1113): founded mid-12th century by William de Albini II as a borough. Earliest known example in England of round keep, c.1145. The market is between the ruined castle and the Perpendicular parish church. Polygonal indoor market, 17th century, timber frame on wooden columns.

Norfolk Rural Life Museum: see Gressenhall.

Norfolk Shire Horse Centre: see West Runton.

North Elmham (northwest of Norwich, A1067/B1145): ruined Anglo-Saxon cathedral, early 11th century: T-shaped ground plan, with narrow apse right next to transept, rectangular west tower. From late 7th till mid-8th century, and from c.955 till c.1075, this was the residence of the Bishops of Norfolk. At the end of the 14th century, Henry le Despenser, Bishop of Norwich, incorporated the remains of the Anglo-Saxon cathedral into his manor house (ruin).

North Walsham (A149, north of the Broads): small Georgian town. St Nicholas', Decorated and Perpendicular, richly ornamental south portal (late 14th century) painted rood screen. Alabaster monument to Sir William Paston, 1608. Paston School: founded 1606, new building 1765, famous old boy: Nelson, 1768–71. Market Cross, 1602.

Norwich: Bridewell Museum of Local Industries, Bridewell Alley, off Bedford Street, ∅ 0603/667228: merchant's house, late 14th century, became museum in 1925. Includes collection of shoes from Tudor times to present. Mon.–Sat. 10–5.
Broads Authority, 18 Colegate, ∅ 0603/610734.
City Hall, St Peters Street, ∅ 0603/22233, contains medieval regalia. Mon.–Fri. 10–12, 2.30–4.30.
Craftsmen's Pottery Shop, 15 Elm Hill, ∅ 0603/629442.
Dragon Hall, 115–123 King Street: merchant's house, 15th century, hall with dragon beam ceiling. April–Nov. Mon.–Sat.
Guildhall, Gaol Hill, ∅ 0603/666071: former city hall and prison, now tourist office. Dec.–March Mon.–Fri. 10–4. April–Nov. Mon.–Sat. 9.30–5.30.
Maddermarket Theatre, St John's Alley: home of Norwich Players, established 1911, amateur company with professional management. Replica of an Elizabethan stage. Programme and tickets, ∅ 0603/620917.
Norfolk and Norwich Festival of Music and the Arts: oldest festival of its kind in East Anglia. Programme and tickets, St Andrew's Hall, ∅ 0603/614921.
Norwich Arts Centre, Reeves Yard, St

Benedict's Street, ∅ 0603/660352: art exhibitions, jazz, theatre, etc. Lunches and café. Mon.–Sat. 10.30–23.30.

Norwich Castle Museum, ∅ 0603/222222, ext. 71224: Norman keep, was a prison till end of 19th century, has been a many-sided and attractive museum since 1894; sections for archaeology, botany, geology, zoology, art, handicrafts, city history. Special collections: Lowestoft chinaware (1757–1802), British teapots, European mustard pots, model cats from all over the world. Contemporary English crafts. Ashwellthorpe triptych, c.1520: altarpiece by Flemish master depicting legend of the Magdalen. 17th-century Dutch paintings, Hobbema, Rubens. British painters include Richard Wilson, Gainsborough, Burne-Jones, Sickert. Excellent collection of work by Norwich School of Artists, especially J. S. Cotman and John Crome (see page 386 ff.). Contemporary artists include Alan Davie, Allen Jones, Michael Andrews. Changing exhibitions and café. Mon.–Sat. 10–5, Sun. 2–5.

Norwich Cathedral: Evensong daily except Sat. 5.15, Sun. 3.30.

Norwich Playhouse Theatre, St George's Street, in restored malthouse, 17th century. Opened in 1992.

Norwich Puppet Theatre, St James, Whitefriars, in medieval church, founded in 1980. Also puppet exhibition. Programme and tickets, ∅ 0603/629921 or 615564.

Norwich School of Art, St George Street, ∅ 0603/610561. Mon.–Sat. 10–5.

Royal Norfolk Regiment Museum, Britannia Barracks, Britannia Road, Mousehold Heath, ∅ 0603/28455: history of the regiment since 1685. Mon.–Fri. 9–12, 2–4.

Sainsbury Centre for Visual Arts, University of East Anglia, ∅ 0603/56060: study centre opened in 1978, with important collection of primitive and modern art, donated by Sir Robert and Lady Sainsbury. Café and restaurant. Tues.–Sun. 12–5.

Sewell Barn Theatre, Constitution Hill, small theatre in converted 19th-century barn, opened in 1979. Programme and tickets, ∅ 0603/411721.

St John's Roman Catholic Cathedral, Earlham Road: designed by George Gilbert Scott the younger in Early English style, 1894–1910, one of the few Gothic Revival buildings in Norwich.

St Michael at Plea, Redwell Street/Queen Street: antiques.

St Peter Hungate Church Museum, Princes Street: 15th-century church, which has been a museum for religious art since 1936: early bibles, books of hours, silverware, glass painting, musical instruments, etc. Brass rubbing. Mon.–Sat. 10–5.

St Peter Mancroft, Market Place, magnificent parish church, 15th century. Evensong Sun. 6.45 p.m.

Strangers' Hall Museum of Domestic Life, Charing Cross: late medieval town house, a museum since 1922, tracing domestic life between 16th & 19th centuries. Mon.–Sat. 10–5.

The Mustard Shop, 3 Bridewell Alley, ∅ 0603/627889: England's only mustard museum and specialist shop. Mon.–Sat. 9.30–5.

Theatre Royal, Theatre Street, opened 1758. Programme and tickets, ∅ 0603/628205–7.

University of East Anglia, Earlham Road, on western outskirts of city, ∅ 0603/56161: founded 1962, main areas of study: the Arts, social and natural sciences. Excellent

European Studies programme. School of Fine Arts in Sainsbury Centre (see above).

Oxburgh Hall (7 miles southwest of Swaffham): late 15th-century moated house, with French parterre. Teas in Victorian kitchen. April–Oct. Bank Hol. Mon. 11–5.30. May–Sept. daily (except Thurs. & Fri.) 1.30–5.30. NT.

Ranworth (northeast of Norwich, off B1140): Broadland Conservation Centre, ∅ 060 549 479: nature trail and exhibition of plant and animal life on Norfolk Broads, bird-watching observatory. April–Oct. Sun.–Thurs. 10.30–5.30, Sat. 2–5.30.

Raynham Hall (near East Raynham, off A1065): country seat of Townshend family, begun in 1622. Interiors by William Kent, 1720–30. Visits only by written appointment: Raynham Hall, Fakenham, Norfolk NR21 7EP. Arabian stud farm owned by Lady Townshend.

Ryston Hall (near Denver, south of King's Lynn, A10): country home of amateur architect Sir Roger Pratt, designed by him 1669–72, with alterations by Sir John Soane, c.1788. P.

Salle (northwest of Norwich, B1149/ B1145): Perpendicular church on outskirts of village, c.1405–40. Two two-storeyed portals; on first floor (former schoolroom) lierne vault with bosses. Gothic Seven Sacraments font with wooden canopy on pulley, 15th-century choir stalls with carved misericords, and many brasses.

Sandringham House (8 miles northeast of King's Lynn, A149): Queen's country estate. Motor car and doll museum, park, restaurant. April-Sept. Mon.–Thurs. 11–5, Sun. 12–5. Closed mid-July till beginning Aug.

Saxlingham Nethergate (7 miles south of Norwich, off A140): Old Rectory, 1784. Grey brick building designed by Sir John Soane before he became famous as architect of Bank of England in London. One of the few country houses by Soane still in its original form. P.

Sculthorpe (west of Fakenham, off A148): village church of All Saints: Norman font with relief of the Magi; east window in southern aisle contains stained glass by Morris, 1859, designed by Burne-Jones: allegories of Faith, Hope and Charity, triumph of the femme fatale in the guise of religion.

Sennowe Hall (near Guist, A1067/B1110, between Norwich & Fakenham): country home of pioneer travel agent Thomas Cook – originally Georgian house, altered and extended in 1908 by G. J. Skipper in opulent, Edwardian neo-Baroque. P.

Shadewell Park (east of Thetford, A1066): neo-Gothic country house, extended 1857–60 by S. S. Teulon in High Victorian style. Estate owned by horse breeder Sheikh Mohammed bin Rashid al-Maktoum. P.

Sheringham (4 miles west of Cromer): North Norfolk Railway, restored steam service to Weybourne, small railway museum. Departure times ∅ 0623/822045.

Sheringham Little Theatre: England's last weekly repertory company.

Sheringham Hall (Upper Sheringham): house and park by Humphry Repton, orginally meant as a gift from the nation to Nelson. NT. Park open to public, house only by appointment.

Shotesham Park (south of Norwich, A140): country house designed by Sir John Soane in 1785, façade with Ionic pilasters and Venetian windows. P.

Snettisham (northeast of King's Lynn, A149, north of Sandringham) in 1991, gold and silver ornaments from 1st century BC, the largest ever British treasure (now in the British Museum). Park Farm, typical of Norfolk, guided tours of fields and pastures. March–Oct. 10.30–5.

St Olave's Priory (5 miles southwest of Great Yarmouth, A143): ruins of Augustinian priory, early 13th century, on the Waveney; crypt with Gothic ribbed vault, unusually early use of brick.

Stow Bardolph (south of King's Lynn, A10): the Hare Chapel in Holy Trinity contains a marble monument by Peter Scheemakers (c.1741) and a waxwork bust of Sarah Hare (died 1744): this is a frighteningly realistic representation of a young girl in her Sunday best of linen and silk. Sarah died at 18 from blood poisoning after being pricked by a needle – presumably while sewing one Sunday, which would have been a sacrilege for Puritan families at that time (text ill., page 25).

Sutton Mill (near Stalham, northwest of Great Yarmouth, A149): the tallest windmill in England, 1789, complete with machinery and museum of local Broads history: tools and household utensils from East Anglia. April–mid May daily 1.30–6, mid May–Sept. daily 10–5.30.

Terrington St Clement (west of King's Lynn, off A17): Perpendicular parish church, known as 'The Cathedral of the Marshland', built 1342–c.1400. Jacobean font canopy, 16th century. The massive church tower was a refuge for the locals when dams broke during the floods of 1613 and 1670.

Thetford Forest: for information contact Thetford Forest District Office, Santon Downham, Brandon, Suffolk IP27 0TJ, ℘ 0842/810271.

Thursford (5 miles northeast of Fakenham, off A148): The Thursford Collection, ℘ 0328/878477: spectacular collection of steam machines, old tractors, fair and theatre organs. Easter-Oct. daily 1–5, June–Aug. 11–5. Every Tues. in summer there is a live concert on the Wurlitzer organ at 8 p.m.

University of East Anglia: see Norwich.

Walpole St Peter (southwest of King's Lynn, between A17 & A47): one of the finest Gothic village churches in the Marshlands, c.1350–1400. South portal with elaborate bosses, c.1450. Original 15th-century benches.

Walsoken (east of Wisbech, southwest of

King's Lynn, A47): All Saints: most important late Norman village church in Norfolk, c.1150. Early English west tower, side aisles, 14th century. Arcades with pillars and loft, 15th century. Seven Sacraments font, 1544. Gothic dragon beam ceiling with angels and saints. Cemetery with 17th- and 18th-century gravestones.

Wells-next-the-Sea (north coast, A149/B1105): The Wells Centre, Staithe Street, Ø 0328/710130: Cultural centre in former malthouse, with theatre, films, concerts, exhibitions.

West Runton (2.5 miles west of Cromer, A149): The Norfolk Shire Horse Centre, West Runton Stables, Ø 026 375/339: horse-breeding, with demonstrations and riding, especially for children. April–Sep. daily except Sat. 11–5.

West Tofts (north of Thetford, A134/B1108): St Mary's, isolated church in the Brecklands: chapel and choir by A. W. N. Pugin, c.1850, with glass and roof paintings designed by Pugin, who made his name as a convert to and innovator in the Gothic style.

West Walton (southwest of King's Lynn, A47): St Mary's: splendid, Early English village church, c.1240. Free-standing church tower. Round piers with detached shafts of Purbeck marble. 15th-century wooden roof with angels.

Wiggenhall St Germans (south of King's Lynn): marshland village on the Ouse, one of the four Wiggenhalls. St Germanus: church behind the dyke, 15th-century benches full of figures and stories (seven deadly sins, beasts and sinners, etc.).

Wiggenhall St Mary (south of King's Lynn): former parish church of St Mary the Virgin, c.1400, almost complete example of Perpendicular. Carved benches and painted rood screen. Font with Jacobean wooden canopy, 1625.

Wolferton Station Museum (northeast of King's Lynn, off A149): formerly royal station of Sandringham, with their Majesties' waiting rooms. Very unusual railway museum. April–Sept. daily except Sat. 11–1, 2–6, Sun. 1–5.

Wolterton Hall (southwest of Cromer, off A140, 16 miles west of Erpingham): Georgian country home of 7th Lord Walpole. Only park and garden (Humphry Repton) open to public. Home-made teas. June–Aug. Wed. 2–5.

Worstead (3 miles southeast of North Walsham, off A149): formerly weaving village, famous in Middle Ages for its worsted. Several old looms in parish church of St Mary, begun in 1379 – painted Gothic rood screen.

Food and Drink

H = Hotel, R = Restaurant, B&B = Bed and Breakfast, GF = Good Food (table reservation advisable)

'Now Sam,' said Mr Pickwick, 'the first thing to be done is to ...'
'...order dinner, Sir,' interposed Mr Weller.
(Charles Dickens: *The Pickwick Papers*, Chap. 16)

Essex

Broxted (northwest of Great Dunmow, B1051): Whitehall Hotel, Church End, ⌀ 0279/850603: 15th-century manor house. Little luxury hotel with helicopter pad. *Menu Surprise* with six courses, a touch pretentious. H + GF.

Burnham-on-Crouch (northeast of Southend, B1010): The Contented Sole, 80 High Street, ⌀ 0621/782139: best restaurant on whole Essex coast. Excellent fish dishes. GF.

Castle Hedingham (6 miles northwest of Halstead, A604/B1058): The Old School House, St James Street, ⌀ 0787/61370: Georgian house with garden, B&B of superior kind.

Chappel (west of Colchester, A604): Swan Inn, ⌀ 0787/222353: pub on river. R.

Chigwell (northeast of London, M11/A113): King's Head, High Street, ⌀ 081/5002021: 17th-century inn, immortalized in Dicken's *Barnaby Rudge* as The Maypole Inn, famous in those days for its pigeon pie; famous today only for its Dickens. R.

Coggeshall (west of Colchester, A120): Langan's, 4 Stoneham Street, ⌀ 0376/561453: offshoot of 'Langan's Brasserie', Mayfair's fashionable restaurant, started by the well-known London restaurateur, the late Peter Langan.
White Hart, Market End, ⌀ 0376/54654: former Guildhall, inn since 1489. H + GF.

Colchester: Lay and Wheeler, 6 Culver Street West, ⌀ 0206/764446: England's largest family wine business, with choice of 1,200 wines from 16 countries.
Tilly's, 33 Crouch Street: Teashop with home-made cakes and scones.
Colchester Oyster Fishery, North Farm, East Mersea, ⌀ 0206/384141: fishing co-operative, handles the region's speciality – oysters from the Colne Estuary. Oyster-eating by appointment!

Dedham (7 miles northeast of Colchester, off A12): Dedham Hall, ⌀ 0206/323027: accommodation in Constable Country, with painting courses, studios in converted barn. H + R.
Dedham Vale Hotel, Stratford Road, ⌀ 0206/322273: quiet situation, dining-room with hothouse paraphernalia and pseudo-Edwardian decor. H + R.
Maison Talbooth, ⌀ 0206/322367: small

luxury hotel outside village, overlooking Stour Valley. Rooms named after poets, including Shakespeare Suite with circular bath. Separate riverside restaurant Le Talbooth, 16th-century house on the Stour, former customs house for towboats. H + GF.

Marlborough Head Hotel, Mill Lane, ∅ 0206/323124: weaver's house, c.1500, inn since 1704. H + R.

Epping (north of London, M11/M25): Post House Hotel, High Road, ∅ 0378/73137: well-situated Trusthouse Forte hotel. H + R.

Felsted (southwest of Braintree, A120/B1417): Rumbles Cottage Restaurant, Braintree Road, ∅ 0371/820996: 16th-century house. GF.

Great Yeldham (6 miles northwest of Halstead, A604): White Hart, ∅ 0787/ 237250: Tudor half-timbered house on River Colne, classic English country pub. GF.

Harwich: The Pier at Harwich, The Quay, ∅ 0255/241212: first or last meal in England on former ferry quay. Fish specialities. R.

Maldon (east of Chelmsford, A414): The Blue Boar, Silver Street, ∅ 0621/852681: pleasant, small town hotel. H + R.

Francine's, 1A High Street, ∅ 0621/856605. R.

Wheeler's, 13 High Street, ∅ 0621/853647: Fish & chip restaurant of superior quality – 'the real thing' (*Good Food Guide*). Family business since 1895. R.

Rochford (north of Southend, B1013): Renoufs, 1 South Street, ∅ 0702/544393: smokes its own fish. Speciality: duck. GF.

Roxwell (4 miles west of Chelmsford, off A1060): Farmhouse Feast, The Street, ∅ 0245248/583: 16th-century farmhouse. GF.

Saffron Walden (southeast of Cambridge, A130): Eight Bells, 18 Bridge Street: 16th-century pub. R.

Saffron Hotel, 10–18 High Street, ∅ 0799/522676: half-timbered house. H + R.

The Staircase, 21 High Street, ∅ 0799/522226. R.

Thaxted (north of Great Dunmow, B184/B1051): Recorder's House, 17 Town Street, ∅ 0371/830438. GF.

Suffolk

Aldeburgh (A1094, east of A12): Martello Tower, Slaughden: coastal fort of 1815, restored by Landmark Trust and rented out as holiday home.

Uplands Hotel, Victoria Road, ∅ 072845/2420: Georgian house with garden, H + R.

Regatta, 171 High Street, ∅ 072845/2011. R.

Wentworth Hotel, ∅ 072845/2312: hotel by the sea. H + R.

Cross Keys Inn, ∅ 072845/2637, Crabbe Street: 16th-century pub.

Blythburgh (southwest of Lowestoft, A12): White Hart Inn, ∅ 0502/70217: 17th-century village pub, beer garden with view over marshes.

Capuccino's Red House Farm Market (2 miles south of Blythburgh, A12), ∅ 0502/70736: cream teas, lunch with home-made pasta.

Bradfield Combust (5 miles southeast of Bury St Edmunds, A134): Bradfield House, Sudbury Road, ∅ Sickelsmere 028486/301: 17th-century half-timbered house, best English cuisine. GF.

Brome (between Eye and Diss, A140/B1077): Oaksmere Country House, ∅ 0379/870326: small hotel with garden and topiary. H + R.

Bungay (west of Lowestoft, A144/A143): Brownes, 20 Earsham Street, ∅ 0986/ 892545. GF.

Bury St Edmunds: The Angel, Angel Hill, ∅ 0284/753926: stately hotel going back to 1452, present building dating from 1779. Dickens was here (see page 286). Only hotel in England that gives annual literary prize. Literary dinners and concerts. Wed. afternoon tea accompanied by live harp music from 16th to 20th century. Memorial dinners, e.g. 1985 on 500th anniversary of Battle of Bosworth: beef, yorkshire pudding, melons in Malmsey wine ('in memory of the poor Duke of Clarence who drowned in that same brew'). H + GF.
Mortimer's, 31 Churchgate Street, ∅ 0284/760623: fish restaurant, Scottish crayfish, Cromer crabs, eel from the Fens. R.
The Nutshell, Abbeygate Street, ∅ 0284/ 764867: England's smallest pub, measuring 10 × 16 feet, with the bar just 4 feet from the entrance. Local beer: Greene King.

Butley (B1084, east of Woodbridge and A12): The Oyster, ∅ 0394/450790: simple, straightforward village pub.

Campsea Ashe (B1078, east of A12): The Old Rectory, ∅ 0728/746524: 17th century, family B&B + GF.

Cattawade (8 miles southwest of Ipswich, A137): Bucks, The Street, ∅ 0206/392571; GF.

Cavendish (south of Bury St Edmunds, A1092): Alfonso, ∅ 0787/280372: Italian restaurant. R.

Chelsworth (between Hadleigh and Lavenham, A1141): The Peacock Inn, The Street, ∅ 0449/740758: 14th-century village pub. H + R.

Dunwich (east of A12, north of Alde-burgh): Flora Tea Rooms, ∅ 072873/433 & 687: seaside cafe with plaice, sole, etc. fresh from the sea – the best fish and chips on the East coast.

East Bergholt (southwest of Ipswich, A12/B1070): Fountain House, The Street, ∅ 0206/298970, family business. R.

Fressingfield (between Halesworth and Diss, B1116): Fox and Goose, near church, ∅ 037986/247: former Guildhall 1509. Village restaurant with family atmosphere and high aspirations: 'honest cooking of classic dishes.' GF.

Glemsford (south of Bury St Edmunds, B1066/A1092): Barrett's, 31 Egremont Street, ∅ 0787/281573. GF.

Village sign, Fressingfield, Suffolk

Hadleigh (west of Ipswich, A1071): Edgehill, 2 High Street, ∅ 0473/822458. Georgian town house, family guest house. H.
Weaver's, 25 High Street, ∅ 0473/827247: three converted weaver's cottages. GF.

Higham (southwest of Ipswich, A12/B1068): Old Vicarage, ∅ 047387/334: Stour Valley, family B&B.

Hintlesham Hall (5 miles west of Ipswich, A1071): early Georgian country house built round Tudor core – most famous country house hotel in East Anglia. Own golf course. ∅ 047387/268. H + GF.

Ipswich: Belstead Brook Hotel, Belstead Road, ∅ 0473/684241: country house hotel 1.2 miles southwest of town centre. H + R.
Mortimer's, Wherry Quay, ∅ 0473/230225: popular fish restaurant in old warehouse in the docks. R.
The Marlborough, 73 Henley Road, ∅ 0473/57677: Victorian luxury hotel opposite Christchurch Park. H + GF.
The Singing Chef, 200 St Helen's Street, ∅ 0473/255236: French cuisine. The francophile chef Ken Toye sometimes seasons the meal with a few 'chansons'.

Ixworth (northeast of Bury St Edmunds, A143/A1088): Theobalds, 68 High Street, ∅ Pakenham 0359/31707: French cuisine with fresh English ingredients. GF.

Lavenham (south of Bury St Edmunds, A1141): The Swan, High Street, ∅ 0787/247477: late 14th-century inn linked to neighbouring half-timbered houses as a hotel. H + R.
The Great House, Market Place, ∅ 0787/247431: restaurant with limited accommodation. The writer Stephen Spender lived here in the thirties. H + R.

Long Melford (south of Bury St Edmunds, A134): Black Lion, The Green, ∅ 0787/312356: 19th-century inn on village green. H + R.
The Bull, High Street, ∅ 0787/78494: half-timbered home of cloth merchant, c.1450, has been an inn since 1580. The perfect country inn. H + R.

Newmarket: accommodation during racing weekends, and contact with trainers and breeders arranged through Newmarket Thoroughbred Tours, Allied House, Crown Walk, ∅ 0638/666033.

Orford (B1078, east of A12): Butley-Orford Oysterage, Market Hill, ∅ 0394/450277: fish restaurant, does its own smoking and oyster-breeding. GF.

The seal designed by Lord Byron for his half-sister Augusta Leigh at Swynford Paddocks, now hotel logo. Swynford Paddocks, Six Mile Bottom, Newmarket

The Old Warehouse, Quay Street, Ø 0394450/210: cream teas, fine cakes, view over Orford Ness.

Otley (7 miles north of Ipswich, B1079): Otley House, Helmingham Road, Ø 0473890/253: Georgian country guesthouse. H + R.

Pin Mill (near Chelmondiston, north of Ipswich, A138): flounder and oysters, Ø 0473/780764: popular pub on River Orwell. R.

Purton Green Farm (just north of Stansfield, southwest of Bury St Edmunds, off A143): half-timbered farmhouse in middle of fields, last relic of a lost medieval village, built 1250, renovated in 16th century; restored by Landmark Trust and rented out as holiday accommodation.

Seckford Hall (near Great Bealings, northeast of Ipswich, off A12): Elizabethan

country house, 1553–85. Luxury hotel, Ø 039438/5678. H + R.

Six Mile Bottom (5 miles south of Newmarket, A1304): Swynford Paddocks, Ø 063870/234: country home of Lord Byron's half-sister Augusta Leigh; their romance in the summer of 1813 was the talk of London Society, and provides the juicier material of the brochure. Luxury hotel with its own stud and pheasant shooting. Prominent guns have included the Duke of Edinburgh, Prince Charles, and Prince Bernhard of the Netherlands. H + R.

Southwold: The Crown, 90 High Street, Ø 0502/722275: 18th-century inn, good fish dishes, excellent wines, selected by the host, Simon Loftus; naturally the locally brewed Adnams Bitter is also available. H + GF.
The Swan, Market Place, Ø 0502/722186: stylish Georgian hotel. H + R.

St James South Elmham (northwest of Halesworth): The Grange, Ø 098682/246: farmhouse B&B.

Stonham Aspal (near Stowmarket, A140/A1120): Mr Underhill's Restaurant, Ø 0449/711206: B&B + GF.

Sudbury: Mabey's Brasserie, 47 Gainsborough Street, Ø 0787/74298: gourmet restaurant owned by Robert Mabey, formerly chef at the London Connaught, etc. GF.
The Mill Hotel, Walnut Tree Lane, Ø 0787/75544: converted watermill on the Stour, recommended for its setting. H + R.

Theberton (B1122, east of A12): Theberton Grange, ℘ 0728/830625: small country house hotel, family run. H + R.

Walberswick (B1387, east of A12): The Bell, ℘ 0502/723109: pub with B&B + R. Mary's, Manor House, ℘ 0502/723243: family-run village restaurant, teas in garden. R + B&B.
Potter's Wheel Restaurant, Village Green, ℘ 0502/724468. R.

Westleton (B1125, east of A120): The Crown, ℘ 072873/273; village guesthouse. H + R.

Woodbridge (northeast of Ipswich, A12): Royal Bengal, 6 Quay Street, ℘ 039438/7983: Indian food. R.
The Wine Bar, 17 Thoroughfare, ℘ 039438/2557: restaurant with delicatessen shop. GF.

Norfolk

Aldborough (southwest of Cromer, off A140): Old Red Lion, The Village Green, ℘ 0263/761451: Georgian village restaurant. R.

Appleton Water Tower (northeast of King's Lynn, south of Sandringham): Victorian brick construction, fine monument to technology, restored by Landmark Trust, ℘ 0628/825925 (see page 449) and rented out as holiday home.

Blakeney (west of Cromer, A149): The Blakeney Hotel, The Quay, ℘ 0263/740797, ideal quayside situation, not just for sailors. H + R.

Blickling (north of Norwich, A140/B1354): The Buckinghamshire Arms, ℘ 0263/732133: 17th-century country pub. H + R.

Burnham Market (south of A149, B1155/B1355): Fishes', Market Place, ℘ 0328/738588: fish restaurant, speciality Brancaster oysters. GF.

Cley-next-the-Sea (west of Cromer, A149): Cley Mill, ℘ 0263/740209: early 18th-century windmill, now holiday home. B&B.

Cromer: Hotel de Paris, Jetty Cliff, ℘ 0263/513141; grand Victorian hotel, seaside meeting-place for Edwardian high society. H + R.

Crostwick (3 miles north of Norwich, B1150): The Old Rectory Hotel, North Walsham Road, ℘ 0603/738513: early 19th-century Georgian house with garden. B&B.

Felmingham (3 miles west of North Walsham, A1145): Felmingham Hall, ℘ 069269/631: comfortable country house hotel, H + R.

Great Snoring (3 miles northeast of Fakenham): The Old Rectory, Barsham Road, ℘ 032882/597: 16th-century manor house with terracotta frieze, later turned into rectory. Charming family guesthouse. Set menu, but first-class. H & GF.

Grimston (6 miles northeast of King's Lynn, off A148): Congham Hall, Lynn Road, ∅ Hillington 0485/600250. Georgian country house with large park and herb garden, luxury hotel with own helicopter pad. The chef gets his game from the Queen's suppliers in Sandringham. 8-course dinner, somewhat showy, but 'the write stuff' for Harold Pinter's wife, the writer Lady Antonia Fraser, who calls it 'an ideal writer's retreat'. H + GF.

Guist (northwest of Norwich, A1067/B1110): Tollbridge, Dereham Road, ∅ 036284/359: former customs house on River Wensum. Fish dishes. GF.

Holt (west of Cromer, A148): The Flask, 7–8 Chapel Yard, ∅ 026371/3968: Bistro. R.
Yetman's, 37 Norwich Road, ∅ 0263/713320: small country restaurant. R.

Horning (northeast of Norwich, A1151/A1062): Petersfield House Hotel: small hotel on the Broads. H + R.

King's Lynn: Ro Co Co Restaurant, 11 Saturday Market Place, ∅ 0553/771483: R. (also vegetarian).
The Duke's Head, Tuesday Market Place, ∅ 0553/774996: historic hotel dating back to 1684, with tastelessly modernized dining-room. H & R.
Riverside Rooms, 27 King Street, ∅ 0553/773134: restaurant on the Ouse, 15th-century storehouse, part of King's Lynn Arts Centre, restored by NT. R.

Morston (west of Cromer, west of Blakeney, A149): Morston Hall, ∅ 0263/

741041: small country cottage hotel on north coast. H & G.

Norwich: Adam & Eve, 17 Bishopgate, ∅ 0603/667423: rivermen's pub on the Wensum, Norwich's oldest pub, dating back to 1249.
Adlard's, 79 Upper St Giles, ∅ 0603/633522: first-rate Anglo-French cuisine. David Adlard is a former chef at the London Connaught, and elsewhere, while his wife Mary runs the place 'with the kind of *brio* you would expect in a top-class New York or French restaurant' *(Good Food Guide)*. GF.
Assembly House, Theatre Street, ∅ 0603/627526: Georgian sitting-rooms, cafeteria-restaurant with best food and best value in town. Mon.–Sat. morning coffee 10–11.45, lunch 12–2, tea 3–5, supper 5–7.30.
Green's Seafood Restaurant, 82 Upper St Giles Street, ∅ 0603/623733: fresh fish with live piano accompaniment. GF
Marco's, 17 Pottergate, ∅ 0603/624044: Italian food. GF.
Maid's Head Hotel, Tombland, ∅ 0603/761111: old posthouse inn opposite Cathedral. H + R.
Sam's, 58 Dethel Street, ∅ 0603/612139: GF.
St Benedict's Grill, 9 St Benedicts, ∅ 0603/765377: Anglo-French cuisine: GF.
The Britons Arms, 9 Elm Hill, ∅ 0603/623367: café and lunch, daily 10–5.
The Cock, Old Lakenham, ∅ 0603/626486: riverside pub on the Yare, on southern outskirts of city.
The Moorings, 6 Freeman Street: pub.
The Mousetrap, 2 St Gregory's Alley, ∅ 0603/614083: English cheese specialities.

The Tree House, 16 Dove Street: vegetarian restaurant.

Reedham (west of Great Yarmouth, B1140): Blanche's Country Restaurant, 26 The Hills, ∅ 0493/701262: guesthouse on edge of the Broads. R + B&B.

Sculthorpe Mill Country Club (west of Fakenham, off A148): on River Wensum, ∅ 0328/856161. B&B + R.

Shipdam (3 miles south of East Dereham, A1075): Shipdam Place, Church Close, ∅ 0362/820303: Regency house, former rectory. Small, exclusive country hotel with fish specialities. H + GF.

South Walsham (between Norwich & Great Yarmouth, B1140): South Walsham Hall, ∅ 060/549378: former home of Lord Fairhaven, on edge of Norfolk Broads. Country Club. H + R.

Sprowston Hall (northeast of Norwich, A1151): Wroxham Road, ∅ 0603/410871: country house hotel. H + R.

Thornage (southwest of Cromer and Holt, A148/B1110): The Black Boys, ∅ 0328/732122: small village restaurant with B&B + GF.

Tunstall (near Halvergate, west of Great Yarmouth, A47): Tunstall Camping Barn, Robert & Sally More, Manor Farm, Tunstall, Norwich NR13 3PS, ∅ 0493/700279: converted barn on the Broads, on the edge of Halvergate Marshes. Overnight accommodation for about 20 people.

Weybourne (west of Cromer, A149): Gasché's, The Street, ∅ 026370/220: Swiss restaurant, run by Edgar from Berne: he was on holiday in Cromer, married an Englishwoman, and since then has been serving Norfolk Duckling at Swiss prices. GF.

East Anglia in Brief

Area: 4,960 square miles (UK 94,248 square miles). Greatest length: approx. 110 miles. Greatest width: approx. 70 miles.
Population: 2,053,000 (UK 57,649,000)
Population density: 414 inhabitants per square mile (UK 612)

Population and Economy

The population density of East Anglia is one of the lowest in the UK but it has the greatest growth rate (1% per annum compared with UK 0.2%). Although 16.5% of the population is over pensionable age (UK 15.7%), the death rate is the lowest and it is the only region where the marriage rate in 1991 was greater than in 1981. The unemployment rate (8.6%) and the crime rate are the lowest in the country.

There is some industry in Essex (Courtaulds, Crittals, Fords) but the wealth of Norfolk and Suffolk comes from farm agriculture, fishing, tourism and associated light industry like boat building, agricultural machinery and fertilizers, and food processing. In the Middle Ages, sheep farming and the wool industry were the source of great wealth but Coke's marling transformed the acidic 'sandlands' into rich cornfields and now the main crops are grain, sugar beet (introduced in 1924), soft fruit and vegetables. The livestock is now mostly pigs and poultry in the place of sheep and rabbits. The proportion of officially designated grade I and grade II land (11% and 33% respectively) is the highest in the country.

Geography

East Anglia is low-lying with altitudes varying from 3 foot below sea level (Stow Bardolph Fen) to 320 foot above (along the Cromer Ridge). The substratum of chalk which lies under the whole region is rich in fossils (including the bones of hippopotamus, rhinoceros and mammoth) and, most importantly, flint (fossilized sponges). This works its way to the surface in many places and was mined in the Brecklands from c.2000 BC. On top of the chalk, clay deposits extend over Essex and up through the centre of Suffolk and Norfolk. The thick forests which once covered this area provided timber, and bricks were made from the clay (Tudor red buvks, later Suffolk White and grey Norfolk Gault). So flint, brick and timber were the building materials available locally and roofs were traditionally thatched using reed from the rivers (even churches often had thatched roofs). The only local stone, carrstone (or gingerbread stone), seen in the dramatically coloured cliffs at Hunstanton, was quarried at Snettisham.

The rivers meander slowly because there are few hills and because of the reeds, so wind – rather than water-powered mills were used for grinding corn, weaving cloth and draining the fens. The lighter soil deposited along the coastal region supported heaths (the

Brecklands and Sandlings); because these were easier to clear than the dense forests they were the earliest inhabited area (flint mines at Grimes Graves and Iron Age forts at Narborough and Warham St Mary). In the Fens which link Norfolk to Cambridge and Lincolnshire the rich dark soil is the result of centuries of peat cutting and artificial drainage. Here the rivers often have to be banked up above the level of the surrounding land and there is constant danger of flooding.

All around East Anglia, the coastline is changing. In some places the sea is encroaching (at two to three yards a year between Happisburgh and Yarmouth and one yard a year near Dunwich) and in others it is retreating so that old ports like Orford and Bradwell on Sea are now miles inland. Man too had long been pushing the sea back; Domesday Book and other early records show that the coastline used to run south of Whaplode Marsh through Gidney Dyke, so a strip up to six miles wide has been reclaimed. In Essex, creeks are sitting up and more land may be drained. Minsmere is one of the most important wetlands in Europe, with unusual flora and over a hundred species of birds.

Climate

East Anglia is the driest area of the UK with an average of only 20 inches of rain in the Fens. Although the rain is very acid it does less damage than elsewhere because so little falls. May, June, August and September are the best months with a daily average of six hours of sunshine, the second highest in the UK. July is warm but thundery. The winter months can be bleak with some of the lowest temperatures in the UK and little shelter from the prevailing east wind.

Kings and Queens of England

Anglo-Saxon and Danish Kings

802–839	Egbert
839–855	Ethelwulf
855–860	Ethelbald
860–865	Ethelbert
865–871	Ethelred I
871–899	Alfred the Great
899–924	Edward the Elder
924–939	Athelstan
939–946	Edmund
946–955	Edred
955–959	Edwy
959–975	Edgar
975–978	Edward the Martyr
979–1016	Ethelred II the Unready
1016	Edmund II Ironside
1016–1035	Canute
1035–1040	Harold I
1040–1042	Hardicanute
1042–1066	Edward the Confessor
1066	Harold II

Norman Kings

1066–1087	William I the Conqueror
1087–1100	William II Rufus
1100–1135	Henry I
1135–1154	Stephen

House of Plantagenet

1154–1189	Henry II
1189–1199	Richard I Lionheart
1199–1216	John Lackland
1216–1272	Henry III
1272–1307	Edward I
1307–1327	Edward II
1327–1377	Edward III
1377–1399	Richard II

House of Lancaster

1399–1413	Henry IV
1413–1422	Henry V
1422–1461	Henry VI

House of York

1461–1483	Edward IV
1483	Edward V
1483–1485	Richard III

House of Tudor

1485–1509	Henry VII
1509–1547	Henry VIII
1547–1553	Edward VI
1553–1558	Mary I
1558–1603	Elizabeth I

House of Stuart

1603–1625	James I
1625–1649	Charles I
1649–1653	Commonwealth
1653–1658	Oliver Cromwell Lord Protector
1658–1659	Protectorate
1660–1685	Charles II
1685–1688	James II
1689–1702	William III and Mary II
1702–1714	Anne

House of Hanover

1714–1727	George I
1727–1760	George II
1760–1820	George III
1820–1830	George IV
1830–1837	William IV

House of Windsor

1837–1901	Victoria
1901–1910	Edward VII
1910–1936	George V
1936	Edward VIII
1936–1952	George VI
1952–	Elizabeth II

List of Illustrations

All photographs by Peter Sager unless otherwise indicated

Colour Plates

Black and white Plates

LIST OF ILLUSTRATIONS

Illustrations in the text

CMN = Castle Museum, Norwich, Norfolk Museums Service

Frontispiece Thomas Gainsborough: Thomas William Coke, 1st Earl of Leicester, c.1782, oil on canvas (Viscount Coke and the Trustees of the Holkham Estate)

p. 15 Henry Moore: Suffolk woolly, 1972, pen-and-ink drawing. From *Sheep Sketchbook*, London 1980 (Henry Moore Foundation, Much Hadham)

LIST OF ILLUSTRATIONS

Index

Heckingham (N) 275

Hedingham Castle (E) **115ff.,**
  115, 119, 162

Helmingham Hall (S) 146, 156,
  228ff., 517 *(colour plate 13,*
  B&W plate 4)

Hempstead (E) 76, 513

Hemsby (N) 12n.

Hengrave Hall (S) 168n., **309f.,**
  518 *(colour plate 31, B&W plate*
  15)

Henham House (S) 266, 521

Herringfleet (S) **274**

Herringfleet Mill (S) 399

Herstmonceaux Castle (E. Sussex)
  83

Hertfordshire 11

Hethel (N) 13, 340

Heveningham Hall (S) 40, **232ff.,**
  236, 266n., 518 *(colour plate 18)*

Hever Castle (Kent) 421

Heydon (N) 426

Heydon Hall (N) 37, 340, **426,**
  527 *(B&W plate 12)*

Hickling Broad (N) 403, 503

High Beech (E) 103

High Laver (E) 44, **110ff.**

High Lodge (S) 486n.

Higham (S) 155, 537

Hill Hall (E) **104f.**

Hingham (N) 14

Hintlesham Hall (S) 231f, 235n.,
  249, 427, 537

Holbrook (S) **188f.**

Holkham Hall (N) 14, 35, 36, 40,
  339, 340, 412, 424, 430, **436ff.,**
  437, 443, 467, 475, 476, 527
  (B&W plates 7 and 8)

Holland *see* Netherlands

Holland–on–Sea (E) 85

Hollesley (S) 518

Holme Bird Observatory (N)
  341n.

Holme–next–the–Sea (N) 429,
  430, **446, 503, 506**

Holt (N) 272, 414, 527, 540

Holton (S) 243n., 276n.

Homersfield (S) 30, **276**

Horham Hall (E) 513

Hornchurch (E) 76

Horning (N) 396, 402, 403, 540

Horsey (N) 404

Horsey Mere (N) **404**

Horsham St Faith (N) 527

Horstead (N) 527

Houghton Hall (N) 36, 40, 339,

340, 424, 439, **465ff.,** *467, 469,*
  476, 527 *(B&W plates 1, 3,*
  and 6)

Hoveton Little Broad (N) 403,
  524

Hoxne (S) 518

Hunstanton (N) 11, 339, **446,** 505

Iceland 97, 269, 457

Icklingham (S) 28, 236, **317**
  (B&W plate 84)

Icknield Way (N) 480, 483

Ickworth (S) 232, 233, **288ff.,** 518
  (B&W plate 5)

Iken (S) 518

Ilford (GL) 97, 102

Ilketshalls, the (S) 279

India 311, 312, 344, 350, 386, 409

Ingatestone Hall (E) 482n., 506,
  513

Iona (Hebrides) 88

Ipswich (S) 10, 12, 20, 37, 42, 122,
  145, 146, 147, 153, 161, 178,
  182ff., *188–9,* 192, 228, 231, 234,
  235, 249, 254, 259, 261, 278, 287,
  504, 508, 509, 518, 537 *(B&W*
  plate 35)

Ireland 107, 198, 117, 190, 275,
  288, 305f., 307, 308, 312, 325,
  411, 412, 476, 489

Isle of Grain (Kent) 92

Isle of White 451

Italy 14, 35, 69, 75, 83, 104, 122,
  126, 149, 168, 174, 231, 233, 269,
  275, 282, 305, 307, 309, 311, 328,
  410, 418, 432, 437f., 441, 457,
  464, 470, 482

Ixworth (S) 518, 537

Japan 253

Jaywick (E) **65f.,** 93

Jerusalem 68, 260

Kennet, River (S/N) 520

Kent 44, 96

Kentwell Hall (S) 146, 166, 167,
  168f., 519 *(B&W plates 9 and 14)*

Kersey (S) 20, 145, 146, **169**
  (B&W plate 71)

Kessingland (S) 146, 278, 522

King's Lynn 11, 22, 285, 287, 338,
  339, 340, 340n., 355, 360, 432,
  433, **456ff.,** 477, 478, 488, 506,
  508, 527, 540 *(colour plate 39,*
  B&W plates 34, 94)

Kirby Bedon (N) 40

Knapton (N) 2, **412**

Knettishall Heath (N) 506

Lake District 11

Lakenheath (S) **317**

Lamas (N) **359**

Lancashire 90

Langham (E) 156n.

Langley Abbey (N) 405

Langley Park (N) 528

Lark, River (S) 226, 281, 286n.,
  309, 310, 317

Lastingham (Yorks) 88

Lavenham (S) 20, 33, 116, 146,
  161ff., 262, 284n., 518, 537
  (colour plates 25, 29, 30, B&W
  plates 37, 38)

Laxfield (S) **237f.,** 519

Layer–de–la–Haye (E) 45

Layer Marney (E) 45, 513

Layer Marney Tower (E) **83ff.,**
  168n., 481n., 482n. *(colour plate*
  19)

Lea, River (E) 44, 97

Lea Valley (E/Herts) 107

Leeds (Yorks) 387n.

Leigh–on–Sea (E) **91**

Leiston (S) 252, **254,** 256, 519

Leyton (E) 76

Libya 237, 317, 485

Lincoln 68, 282

Lincolnshire 11, 14, 83, 124, 306,
  334, 343, 357, 506

Lindisfarne (Northumberland) 88

Lingheath (S) 486

Little Bardfield (E) 112

Little Barningham (N) *25*

Little Easton (E) 20, *31,* **78ff.**

Little Glemham Hall (S) 519

Little Haugh Hall (S) 41, 519

Little Maplestead (E) **109f.**

Little Ouse, River (S/N) 145, 279,
  313, 483, 486

Little Saxham (S) 276n.

Little Snoring (N) **431, 432,** 528

Little Walsingham (N) 25, **432ff.,**
  433, 464, 478, 481, 528

Little Wenham (S) 146, 519

Liverpool 42, 85, 189, 333, 390–1

Llandaff (Glam) 99

Loddon (N) 23

London 10, 12, 14, 20, 42, 44, 66,
  68, 70, 72, 74, 75, 76, 80, 82, 84,
  86, 88, 91, 93, 94, 96f., 99, 100,
  102, 107, 108, 109, 110, 114, 117,
  124, 125, 149, 150, 153, 155, 156,

571

Subjects

577

Three landmarks in the history of East Anglia.

In East Anglia, you're never far from a chance to savour these traditional ales from Greene King, the region's finest independent brewery.

TRADITIONAL ALES FROM THE HEART OF SUFFOLK.

Greene King plc., Westgate Brewery, Bury St Edmunds, Suffolk. IP33 1QT. Tel: (0284) 763222.